PARALLEL LIVES
13 SELECTED BIOGRAPHIES

PLUTARCH

Translated by
JOHN DRYDEN

To be ignorant of the lives of the most celebrated men of antiquity is to continue in a state of childhood all our days.

— PLUTARCH

CONTENTS

1. Theseus — 7
2. Romulus — 31
3. Comparison of Romulus with Theseus — 55
4. Pericles — 59
5. Fabius — 92
6. Comparison of Pericles with Fabius — 113
7. Nicias — 116
8. Crassus — 142
9. Comparison of Crassus with Nicias — 169
10. Agesilaus — 173
11. Pompey — 203
12. Comparison of Pompey and Agesilaus — 266
13. Alexander — 270
14. Caesar — 328
15. Cato the Younger — 372
16. Demosthenes — 418
17. Cicero — 439
18. Comparison of Demosthenes and Cicero — 471

1
THESEUS

*A*s geographers, Sosius, crowd into the edges of their maps parts of the world which they do not know about, adding notes in the margin to the effect, that beyond this lies nothing but sandy deserts full of wild beasts, unapproachable bogs, Scythian ice, or a frozen sea, so, in this work of mine, in which I have compared the lives of the greatest men with one another, after passing through those periods which probable reasoning can reach to and real history find a footing in, I might very well say of those that are farther off, Beyond this there is nothing but prodigies and fictions, the only inhabitants are the poets and inventors of fables; there is no credit, or certainty any farther. Yet, after publishing an account of Lycurgus the lawgiver and Numa the king, I thought I might, not without reason, ascend as high as to Romulus, being brought by my history so near to his time.

Considering therefore with myself

Whom shall I set so great a man to face?
Or whom oppose? who's equal to the place?

(as Aeschylus expresses it), I found none so fit as him that peopled the beautiful and far-famed city of Athens, to be set in opposition with the father of the invincible and renowned city of Rome. Let us hope that Fable may, in what shall follow, so submit to the purifying processes of Reason as to take the character of exact history. In any case, however, where it shall be found contumaciously slighting credibility, and refusing to be reduced to anything like probable fact, we shall beg that we may meet with candid readers, and such as will receive with indulgence the stories of antiquity.

Theseus seemed to me to resemble Romulus in many particulars. Both of them, born out of wedlock and of uncertain parentage, had the repute of being sprung from the gods.

Both warriors; that by all the world's allowed.

Both of them united with strength of body an equal vigor mind; and of the two most famous cities of the world the one built Rome, and the other made Athens be inhabited. Both stand charged with the rape of women; neither of them could avoid domestic misfortunes nor jealousy at home; but towards the close of their lives are both of them said to have incurred great odium with their countrymen, if, that is, we may take the stories least like poetry as our guide to the truth.

The lineage of Theseus, by his father's side, ascends as high as to Erechtheus and the first inhabitants of Attica. By his mother's side he was descended of Pelops. For Pelops was the most powerful of all the kings of Peloponnesus, not so much by the greatness of his riches as the multitude of his children, having married many daughters to chief men, and put many sons in places of command in the towns round about him. One of whom named Pittheus, grandfather to Theseus, was governor of the small city of the Troezenians, and had the repute of a man of the greatest knowledge and wisdom of his time; which then, it seems, consisted chiefly in grave maxims, such as the poet Hesiod got his great fame by, in his book of Works and Days. And, indeed, among these is one that they ascribe to Pittheus —

Unto a friend suffice
A stipulated price;

which, also, Aristotle mentions. And Euripides, by calling Hippolytus " scholar of the holy Pittheus," shows the opinion that the world had of him.

Aegeus, being desirous of children, and consulting the oracle of Delphi, received the celebrated answer which forbade him the company of any woman before his return to Athens. But the oracle being so obscure as not to satisfy him that he was clearly forbid this, he went to Troezen, and communicated to Pittheus the voice of the god, which was in this manner —

Loose not the wine-skin foot, thou chief of men,
Until to Athens thou art come again.

Pittheus, therefore, taking advantage from the obscurity of the oracle, prevailed upon him, it is uncertain whether by persuasion or deceit, to lie with his daughter Aethra. Aegeus afterwards, knowing her whom he had lain with to be Pittheus's daughter, and suspecting her to be with child by him, left a sword and a pair of shoes, hiding them under a great stone that had a hollow in it exactly fitting them; and went away making her only privy to it, and commanding her, if she brought forth a son who, when he came to man's estate, should be able to lift up the stone and take away what he had left there, she should send him away to him with those things with all secrecy, and with injunctions to him as much as possible to conceal his journey from every one; for he greatly feared the Pallantidae, who were continually mutinying against him, and despised him for his want of children, they themselves being fifty brothers, all sons of Pallas.

When Aethra was delivered of a son, some say that he was immediately named Theseus, from the tokens which his father had put under the stone; others that he received his name afterwards at Athens, when Aegeus acknowledged him for his son. He was brought up under his grandfather Pittheus, and had a tutor and attendant set over him named Connidas, to whom the Athenians, even to this time, the day before the feast that is dedicated to Theseus, sacrifice a ram, giving this honor to his memory upon much juster grounds than to Silanio and Parrhasius, for making pictures and statues of Theseus. There being then a custom for the Grecian youth, upon their first coming to man's estate, to go to Delphi and offer first-fruits of their hair to the god, Theseus also went thither, and a place there to this day is yet named Thesea, as it is said, from him. He clipped only the fore part of his head, as Homer says the Abantes did. And this sort of tonsure was from him named Theseis. The Abantes first used it, not in imitation of the Arabians, as some imagine, nor of the Mysians, but because they were a warlike people, and used to close fighting, and above all other nations accustomed to engage hand to hand; as Archilochus testifies in these verses:

> *Slings shall not whirl, nor many arrows fly,*
> *When on the plain the battle joins; but swords,*
> *Man against man, the deadly conflict try,*
> *As is the practice of Euboea's lords*
> *Skilled with the spear.*

Therefore that they might not give their enemies a hold by their hair, they cut it in this manner. They write also that this was the reason why Alexander gave command to his captains that all the beards of the Macedonians should be shaved, as being the readiest hold for an enemy.

Aethra for some time concealed the true parentage of Theseus, and a report was given out by Pittheus that he was begotten by Neptune; for the Troezenians pay Neptune the highest veneration. He is their tutelar god, to him they offer all their first-fruits, and in his honor stamp their money with a trident.

Theseus displaying not only great strength of body, but equal bravery, and a quickness alike and force of understanding, his mother Aethra, conducting him to the stone, and informing him who was his true father, commanded him to take from thence the tokens that Aegeus had left, and to sail to Athens. He without any difficulty set himself to the stone and lifted it up; but refused to take his journey by sea, though it was much the safer way, and though his mother and grandfather begged him to do so. For it was at that time very dangerous to go by land on the road to Athens, no part of it being free from robbers and murderers. That age produced a sort of men, in force of hand, and swiftness of foot, and strength of body, excelling the ordinary rate, and wholly incapable of fatigue; making use, however, of these gifts of nature to no good or profitable purpose for mankind, but rejoicing and priding themselves in insolence, and taking the benefit of their superior strength in the exercise of inhumanity and cruelty, and in seizing, forcing, and committing all manner of outrages upon every thing that fell into their hands; all respect for others, all justice, they thought, all equity and humanity, though naturally lauded by common people, either out of want of courage to commit injuries or fear to receive them, yet no way concerned those who were strong enough to win for themselves. Some of these, Hercules destroyed and cut off in his passage through these countries, but some, escaping his notice while he was passing by, fled and hid themselves, or else were spared by him in contempt of their abject submission; and after that Hercules fell into misfortune, and, having slain Iphitus, retired to Lydia, and for a long time was there slave to Omphale, a punishment which he had imposed upon himself for the murder, then, indeed, Lydia enjoyed high peace and security, but in Greece and the countries about it the like villanies again revived and broke out, there being none to repress or chastise them. It was therefore a very hazardous journey to travel by land from Athens to Peloponnesus; and Pittheus, giving him an exact account of each of these robbers and villains, their strength, and the cruelty they used to all strangers, tried to persuade Theseus to go by sea. But he, it seems, had long since been secretly fired by the glory of Hercules, held him in the highest estimation, and was never more satisfied than in listening to any that gave an account of him; especially those that had seen him, or had been present at any action or saying of his. So that he was altogether in the same state of feeling as, in after ages, Themistocles was, when he said that he could not sleep for the trophy of Miltiades; entertaining such admiration for the virtue of Hercules, that in the night his dreams were all of that hero's actions. and in the day a continual emulation stirred him up to perform the like. Besides, they were related, being born of cousins-german. For Aethra was daughter of Pittheus, and Alcmena of Lysidice; and Lysidice and Pittheus were brother

PARALLEL LIVES

and sister, children of Hippodamia and Pelops. He thought it therefore a dishonorable thing, and not to be endured, that Hercules should go out everywhere, and purge both land and sea from wicked men, and he himself should fly from the like adventures that actually came in his way; disgracing his reputed father by a mean flight by sea, and not showing his true one as good evidence of the greatness of his birth by noble and worthy actions, as by the tokens that he brought with him, the shoes and the sword.

With this mind and these thoughts, he set forward with a design to do injury to nobody, but to repel and revenge himself of all those that should offer any. And first of all, in a set combat, he slew Periphetes, in the neighborhood of Epidaurus, who used a club for his arms, and from thence had the name of Corynetes, or the club-bearer; who seized upon him, and forbade him to go forward in his journey. Being pleased with the club, he took it, and made it his weapon, continuing to use it as Hercules did the lion's skin, on whose shoulders that served to prove how huge a beast he had killed; and to the same end Theseus carried about him this club; overcome indeed by him, but now, in his hands, invincible.

Passing on further towards the Isthmus of Peloponnesus, he slew Sinnis, often surnamed the Bender of Pines, after the same manner in which he himself had destroyed many others before. And this he did without having either practiced or ever learnt the art of bending these trees, to show that natural strength is above all art. This Sinnis had a daughter of remarkable beauty and stature, called Perigune, who, when her father was killed, fled, and was sought after everywhere by Theseus; and coming into a place overgrown with brushwood shrubs, and asparagus-thorn, there, in a childlike, innocent manner, prayed and begged them, as if they understood her, to give her shelter, with vows that if she escaped she would never cut them down nor burn them. But Theseus calling upon her, and giving her his promise that he would use her with respect, and offer her no injury, she came forth, and in due time bore him a son, named Melanippus; but afterwards was married to Deioneus, the son of Eurytus, the Oechalian, Theseus himself giving her to him. Ioxus, the son of this Melanippus who was born to Theseus, accompanied Ornytus in the colony that he carried with him into Caria, whence it is a family usage amongst the people called Ioxids, both male and female, never to burn either shrubs or asparagus-thorn, but to respect and honor them.

The Crommyonian sow, which they called Phaea, was a savage and formidable wild beast, by no means an enemy to be despised. Theseus killed her, going out of his way on purpose to meet and engage her, so that he might not seem to perform all his great exploits out of mere necessity; being also of opinion that it was the part of a brave man to chastise villainous and wicked men when attacked by them, but to seek out and overcome the more noble wild beasts. Others relate that Phaea was a woman, a robber full of cruelty and lust, that lived in Crommyon, and had the name of Sow given her from the foulness of her life and manners, and afterwards was killed by Theseus. He slew also Sciron, upon the borders of Megara, casting him down from the rocks, being, as most report, a notorious robber of all passengers, and, as others add, accustomed, out of insolence and wantonness, to stretch forth his feet to strangers, commanding them to wash them, and then while they did it, with a kick to send them down the rock into the sea. The writers of Megara, however, in contradiction to the received report, and, as Simonides expresses it, "fighting with all antiquity," contend that Sciron was neither a robber nor doer of violence, but a punisher of all such, and the relative and friend of good and just men; for Aeacus, they say, was ever esteemed a man of the greatest sanctity of all the Greeks; and Cychreus, the Salaminian, was honored at Athens with divine worship; and the virtues of Peleus and Telamon were not unknown to any one. Now Sciron was son-in-law to Cychreus, father-in-law to Aeacus, and grandfather to Peleus and Telamon, who were both of them sons of Endeis, the daughter of Sciron and Chariclo; it was not probable, therefore, that the best of men should make these alliances with one who was worst, giving and receiving mutually what was of greatest value and most dear to them. Theseus, by their account, did not slay Sciron in his first journey to Athens, but afterwards, when he took Eleusis, a city of the Megarians, having circumvented Diocles, the governor. Such are the contradictions in this story. In Eleusis he killed Cercyon, the Arcadian, in a wrestling match. And going on a little farther, in Erineus, he slew Damastes, otherwise called Procrustes, forcing his body to the size of his own bed, as he himself was used to do with all strangers; this he did in imitation of Hercules, who always returned upon his assailants the same sort of violence that they offered to him; sacrificed Busiris, killed Antaeus in wrestling, and Cycnus in single combat, and Termerus by breaking his skull in pieces (whence, they say, comes the proverb of "a Termerian mischief"), for it seems Termerus killed passengers that he met, by running with his head against them. And so also Theseus proceeded in the punishment of evil men, who underwent the same violence from him which they had inflicted upon others, justly suffering after the manner of their own injustice.

As he went forward on his journey, and was come as far as the river Cephisus, some of the race of the Phytalidae met him and saluted him, and, upon his desire to use the purifications, then in custom, they performed them with all the usual ceremonies, and, having offered propitiatory sacrifices to the gods, invited him and entertained him at their house, a kindness which, in all his journey hitherto, he had not met.

On the eighth day of Cronius, now called Hecatombaeon, he arrived at Athens, where he found the public affairs full of all confusion, and divided into parties and factions, Aegeus also, and his whole private family, laboring under the same distemper; for Medea, having fled from Corinth, and promised Aegeus to make him, by her art, capable of having children, was living with him. She first was aware of Theseus, whom as yet Aegeus did not know, and he being in years, full of jealousies and suspicions, and fearing every thing by reason of the faction that was then in the city, she easily persuaded him to kill him by poison at a banquet, to which he was to be invited as a stranger. He, coming to the entertainment, thought it not fit to discover himself at once, but, willing to give his father the occasion of first finding him out, the meat being on the table, he drew his sword as if he designed to cut with it; Aegeus, at once recognizing the token, threw down the cup of poison, and, questioning his son, embraced him, and, having gathered together all his citizens, owned him publicly before them, who, on their part, received him gladly for the fame of his greatness and bravery; and it is said, that when the cup fell, the poison was spilt there where now is the enclosed space in the Delphinium; for in that place stood Aegeus's house, and the figure of Mercury on the east side of the temple is called the Mercury of Acgcus's gate.

The sons of Pallas, who before were quiet, upon expectation of recovering the kingdom after Aegeus's death, who was without issue, as soon as Theseus appeared and was acknowledged the successor, highly resenting that Aegeus first, an adopted son only of Pandion, and not at all related to the family of Erechtheus, should be holding the kingdom, and that after him, Theseus, a visitor and stranger, should be destined to succeed to it, broke out into open war. And, dividing themselves into two companies, one part of them marched openly from Sphettus, with their father, against the city, the other, hiding themselves in the village of Gargettus, lay in ambush, with a design to set upon the enemy on both sides. They had with them a crier of the township of Agnus, named Leos, who discovered to Theseus all the designs of the Pallantidae He immediately fell upon those that lay in ambuscade, and cut them all off; upon tidings of which Pallas and his company fled and were dispersed.

From hence they say is derived the custom among the people of the township of Pallene to have no marriages or any alliance with the people of Agnus, nor to suffer the criers to pronounce in their proclamations the words used in all other parts of the country, Acouete Leoi (Hear ye people), hating the very sound of Leo, because of the treason of Leos.

Theseus, longing to be in action, and desirous also to make himself popular, left Athens to fight with the bull of Marathon, which did no small mischief to the inhabitants of Tetrapolis. And having overcome it, he brought it alive in triumph through the city, and afterwards sacrificed it to the Delphinian Apollo. The story of Hecale, also, of her receiving and entertaining Theseus in this expedition, seems to be not altogether void of truth; for the townships round about, meeting upon a certain day, used to offer a sacrifice, which they called Hecalesia, to Jupiter Hecaleius, and to pay honor to Hecale, whom, by a diminutive name, they called Hecalene, because she, while entertaining Theseus, who was quite a youth, addressed him, as old people do, with similar endearing diminutives; and having made a vow to Jupiter for him as he was going to the fight, that, if he returned in safety, she would offer sacrifices in thanks of it, and dying before he came back, she had these honors given her by way of return for her hospitality, by the command of Theseus, as Philochorus tells us.

Not long after arrived the third time from Crete the collectors of the tribute which the Athenians paid them upon the following occasion. Androgeus having been treacherously murdered in the confines of Attica, not only Minos, his father, put the Athenians to extreme distress by a perpetual war, but the gods also laid waste their country both famine and pestilence lay heavy upon them, and even their rivers were dried up. Being told by the oracle that, if they appeased and reconciled Minos, the anger of the gods would cease and they should enjoy rest from the miseries they labored under, they sent heralds, and with much supplication were at last reconciled, entering into an agreement to send to Crete every nine years a tribute of seven young men and as many virgins, as most writers agree in stating; and the most poetical story adds, that the Minotaur destroyed them, or that, wandering in the labyrinth, and finding no possible means of getting out, they miserably ended their lives there; and that this Minotaur was (as Euripides hath it)

> *A mingled form, where two strange shapes combined,*
> *And different natures, bull and man, were joined.*

But Philochorus says that the Cretans will by no means allow the truth of this, but say that the labyrinth was only an ordinary prison, having no other bad quality but that it secured the prisoners from escaping, and that Minos, having instituted games in honor of Androgeus, gave, as a reward to the victors, these youths, who in the mean time were kept in the labyrinth; and that the first that overcame in those games was one of the greatest power and command among them, named Taurus, a man of no merciful or gentle disposition, who treated the Athenians that were made his prize in a proud and cruel manner. Also Aristotle himself, in the account that he gives of the form of government of the Bottiaeans, is manifestly of opinion that the youths were not slain by Minos, but spent the remainder of their days in slavery in Crete; that the Cretans, in former times, to acquit themselves of an ancient vow which they had made, were used to send an offering of the first-fruits of their men to Delphi, and that some descendants of these Athenian slaves were mingled with them and sent amongst them, and, unable to get their living there, removed from thence, first into Italy, and settled about Japygia; from thence again, that they removed to Thrace, and were named Bottiaeans and that this is the reason why, in a certain sacrifice, the Bottiaean girls sing a hymn beginning Let us go to Athens. This may show us how dangerous a thing it is to incur the hostility of a city that is mistress of eloquence and song. For Minos was always ill spoken of, and represented ever as a very wicked man, in the Athenian theaters; neither did Hesiod avail him by calling him "the most royal Minos," nor Homer, who styles him "Jupiter's familiar friend;" the tragedians got the better, and from the vantage ground of the stage showered down obloquy upon him, as a man of cruelty and violence; whereas, in fact, he appears to have been a king and a lawgiver, and Rhadamanthus a judge under him, administering the statutes that he ordained.

Now when the time of the third tribute was come, and the fathers who had any young men for their sons were to proceed by lot to the choice of those that were to be sent, there arose fresh discontents and accusations against Aegeus among the people, who were full of grief and indignation that he, who was the cause of all their miseries, was the only person exempt from the punishment; adopting and settling his kingdom upon a bastard and foreign son, he took no thought, they said, of their destitution and loss, not of bastards, but lawful children. These things sensibly affected Theseus, who, thinking it but just not to disregard, but rather partake of, the sufferings of his fellow citizens, offered himself for one without any lot. All else were struck with admiration for the nobleness and with love for the goodness of the act; and Aegeus, after prayers and entreaties, finding him inflexible and not to be persuaded, proceeded to the choosing of the rest by lot. Hellanicus, however, tells us that the Athenians did not send the young men and virgins by lot, but that Minos himself used to come and make his own choice, and pitched upon Theseus before all others; according to the conditions agreed upon between them, namely, that the Athenians should furnish them with a ship, and that the young men that were to sail with him should carry no weapon of war; but that if the Minotaur was destroyed, the tribute should cease.

On the two former occasions of the payment of the tribute, entertaining no hopes of safety or return, they sent out the ship with a black sail, as to unavoidable destruction; but now, Theseus encouraging his father and speaking greatly of himself, as confident that he should kill the Minotaur, he gave the pilot another sail, which was white, commanding him, as he returned, if Theseus were safe, to make use of that; but if not, to sail with the black one, and to hang out that sign of his misfortune. Simonides says that the sail which Aegeus delivered to the pilot was not white, but

Scarlet, in the juicy bloom
Of the living oak-tree steeped,

and that this was to be the sign of their escape. Phereclus, son of

Amarsyas, according to Simonides, was pilot of the ship. But Philochorus says Theseus had sent him by Scirus, from Salamis, Nausithous to be his steersman, and Phaeax his look-out-man in the prow, the Athenians having as yet not applied themselves to navigation; and that Scirus did this because one of the young men, Menesthes, was his daughter's son; and this the chapels of Nausithous and Phaeax, built by Theseus near the temple of Scirus, confirm. He adds, also, that the feast named Cybernesia was in honor of them. The lot being cast, and Theseus having received out of the Prytaneum those upon whom it fell, he went to the Delphinium, and made an offering for them to Apollo of his suppliant's badge, which was a bough of a consecrated olive tree, with white wool tied about it.

Having thus performed his devotion, he went to sea, the sixth day of Munychion, on which day even to this time the Athenians send their virgins to the same temple to make supplication to the gods. It is farther reported that he was commanded by the oracle at Delphi to make Venus his guide, and to invoke her as the companion and conductress of his voyage, and that, as he was sacrificing a she goat to her by the seaside, it was suddenly changed into a he, and for this cause that goddess had the name of Epitrapia.

When he arrived at Crete, as most of the ancient historians as well as poets tell us, having a clue of thread given him by Ariadne, who had fallen in love with him, and being instructed by her how to use it so as to conduct him through the windings of the labyrinth, he escaped out of it and slew the Minotaur, and sailed back, taking along with him Ariadne and the young Athenian captives. Pherecydes adds that he bored holes in the bottoms of the Cretan ships to hinder their pursuit. Demon writes that Taurus, the chief captain of Minos, was slain by Theseus at the mouth of the port, in a naval combat, as he was sailing out for Athens. But Philochorus gives us the story thus: That at the setting forth of the yearly games by king Minos, Taurus was expected to carry away the prize, as he had done before; and was much grudged the honor. His character and manners made his power hateful, and he was accused moreover of too near familiarity with Pasiphae, for which reason, when Theseus desired the combat, Minos readily complied. And as it was a custom in Crete that the women also should be admitted to the sight of these games, Ariadne, being present, was struck with admiration of the manly beauty of Theseus, and the vigor and address which he showed in the combat, overcoming all that encountered with him. Minos, too, being extremely pleased with him, especially because he had overthrown and disgraced Taurus, voluntarily gave up the young captives to Theseus, and remitted the tribute to the Athenians. Clidemus gives an account peculiar to himself, very ambitiously, and beginning a great way back: That it was a decree consented to by all Greece, that no vessel from any place, containing above five persons, should be permitted to sail, Jason only excepted, who was made captain of the great ship Argo, to sail about and scour the sea of pirates. But Daedalus having escaped from Crete, and flying by sea to Athens, Minos, contrary to this decree, pursued him with his ships of war, was forced by a storm upon Sicily, and there ended his life. After his decease, Deucalion, his son, desiring a quarrel with the Athenians, sent to them, demanding that they should deliver up Daedalus to him, threatening, upon their refusal, to put to death all the young Athenians whom his father had received as hostages from the city. To this angry message Theseus returned a very gentle answer, excusing himself that he could not deliver up Daedalus, who was nearly related to him, being his cousin-german, his mother being Merope, the daughter of Erechtheus. In the meanwhile he secretly prepared a navy, part of it at home near the village of the Thymoetadae, a place of no resort, and far from any common roads, the other part by his grandfather Pittheus's means at Troezen, that so his design might be carried on with the greatest secrecy. As soon as ever his fleet was in readiness, he set sail, having with him Daedalus and other exiles from Crete for his guides; and none of the Cretans having any knowledge of his coming, but imagining, when they saw his fleet, that they were friends and vessels of their own, he soon made himself master of the port, and, immediately making a descent, reached Gnossus before any notice of his coming, and, in a battle before the gates of the labyrinth, put Deucalion and all his guards to the sword. The government by this means falling to Ariadne, he made a league with her, and received the captives of her, and ratified a perpetual friendship between the Athenians and the Cretans, whom he engaged under an oath never again to commence any war with Athens.

There are yet many other traditions about these things, and as many concerning Ariadne, all inconsistent with each other. Some relate that she hung herself, being deserted by Theseus. Others that she was carried away by his sailors to the isle of Naxos, and married to Oenarus, priest of Bacchus; and that Theseus left her because he fell in love with another,

For Aegle's love was burning in his breast;

a verse which Hereas, the Megarian, says, was formerly in the poet Hesiod's works, but put out by Pisistratus, in like manner as he added in Homer's Raising of the Dead, to gratify the Athenians, the line

Theseus, Pirithous, mighty sons of gods.

Others say Ariadne had sons also by Theseus, Oenopion and Staphylus; and among these is the poet Ion of Chios, who writes of his own native city

Which once Oenopion, son of Theseus, built.

But the more famous of the legendary stories everybody (as I may say) has in his mouth. In Paeon, however, the Amathusian, there is a story given, differing from the rest. For he writes that Theseus, being driven by a storm upon the isle of Cyprus, and having aboard with him Ariadne, big with child, and extremely discomposed with the rolling of the sea, set her on shore, and left her there alone, to return himself and help the ship, when, on a sudden, a violent wind carried him again out to sea. That the women of the island received Ariadne very kindly, and did all they could to console and alleviate her distress at being left behind. That they counterfeited kind letters, and delivered them to her, as sent from Theseus, and, when she fell in labor, were diligent in performing to her every needful service; but that she died before she could be delivered, and was honorably interred. That soon after Theseus returned, and was greatly afflicted for her loss, and at his departure left a sum of money among the people of the island, ordering them to do sacrifice to Ariadne; and caused two little images to be made and dedicated to her, one of silver and the other of brass. Moreover, that on the second day of Gorpiaeus, which is sacred to Ariadne, they have this ceremony among their sacrifices, to have a youth lie down and with his voice and gesture represent the pains of a woman in travail; and that the Amathusians call the grove in which they show her tomb, the grove of Venus Ariadne.

Differing yet from this account, some of the Naxians write that there were two Minoses and two Ariadnes, one of whom, they say, was married to Bacchus, in the isle of Naxos, and bore the children Staphylus and his brother; but that the other, of a later age, was carried off by Theseus, and, being afterwards deserted by him, retired to Naxos with her nurse Corcyna, whose grave they yet show. That this Ariadne also died there, and was worshiped by the island, but in a different manner from the former; for her day is celebrated with general joy and revelling, but all the sacrifices performed to the latter are attended with mourning and gloom.

Now Theseus, in his return from Crete, put in at Delos, and, having sacrificed to the god of the island, dedicated to the temple the image of Venus which Ariadne had given him, and danced with the young Athenians a dance that, in memory of him, they say is still preserved among the inhabitants of Delos, consisting in certain measured turnings and returnings, imitative of the windings and twistings of the labyrinth. And this dance, as Dicaearchus writes, is called among the Delians, the Crane. This he danced round the Ceratonian Altar, so called from its consisting of horns taken from the left side of the head. They say also that he instituted games in Delos where he was the first that began the custom of giving a palm to the victors.

When they were come near the coast of Attica, so great was the joy for the happy success of their voyage, that neither Theseus himself nor the pilot remembered to hang out the sail which should have been the token of their safety to Aegeus, who, in despair at the sight, threw himself headlong from a rock, and perished in the sea. But Theseus, being arrived at the port of Phalerum, paid there the sacrifices which he had vowed to the gods at his setting out to sea, and sent a herald to the city to carry the news of his safe return. At his entrance, the herald found the people for the most part full of grief for the loss of their king, others, as may well be believed, as full of joy for the tidings that he brought, and eager to welcome him and crown him with garlands for his good news, which he indeed accepted of, but hung them upon his herald's staff; and thus returning to the seaside before Theseus had finished his libation to the gods, he stayed apart for fear of disturbing the holy rites, but, as soon as the libation was ended, went up and related the king's death, upon the hearing of which, with great lamentations and a confused tumult of grief, they ran with all haste to the city. And from hence, they say, it comes that at this day, in the feast of Oschophoria, the herald is not crowned, but his staff, and all who are present at the libation cry out eleleu iou iou, the first of which confused sounds is commonly used by men in haste, or at a triumph, the other is proper to people in consternation or disorder of mind.

Theseus, after the funeral of his father, paid his vows to Apollo the seventh day of Pyanepsion; for on that day the youth that returned with him safe from Crete made their entry into the city. They say, also, that the custom of boiling pulse at this feast is derived from hence; because the young men that escaped put all that was left of their provision together, and, boiling it in one common pot, feasted themselves with it, and ate it all up together. Hence, also, they carry in procession an olive branch bound about with wool (such as they then made use of in their supplications), which they call Eiresione, crowned with all sorts of fruits, to signify that scarcity and barrenness was ceased, singing in their procession this song:

Eiresione bring figs, and Eiresione bring loaves; Bring us honey in pints, and oil to rub on our bodies, And a strong flagon of wine, for all to go mellow to bed on.

Although some hold opinion that this ceremony is retained in memory of the Heraclidae, who were thus entertained and brought up by the Athenians. But most are of the opinion which we have given above.

The ship wherein Theseus and the youth of Athens returned had thirty oars, and was preserved by the Athenians down even to the time of Demetrius Phalereus, for they took away the old planks as they decayed, putting in new and stronger timber in their place, insomuch that this ship became a standing example among the philosophers, for the logical question as to things that grow; one side holding that the ship remained the same, and the other contending that it was not the same.

The feast called Oschophoria, or the feast of boughs, which to this day the Athenians celebrate, was then first instituted by Theseus. For he took not with him the full number of virgins which by lot were to be carried away, but selected two youths of his acquaintance, of fair and womanish faces, but of a manly and forward spirit, and having, by frequent baths, and avoiding the heat and scorching of the sun, with a constant use of all the ointments and washes and dresses that serve to the adorning of the head or smoothing the skin or improving the complexion, in a manner changed them from what they were before, and having taught them farther to counterfeit the very voice and carriage and gait of virgins, so that there could not be the least difference perceived; he, undiscovered by any, put them into the number of the Athenian maids designed for Crete. At his return, he and these two youths led up a solemn procession, in the same habit that is now worn by those who carry the vine-branches. These branches they carry in honor of Bacchus and Ariadne, for the sake of their story before related; or rather because they happened to return in autumn, the time of gathering the grapes. The women whom they call Deipnopherae, or supper-carriers, are taken into these ceremonies, and assist at the sacrifice, in remembrance and imitation of the mothers of the young men and virgins upon whom the lot fell, for thus they ran about bringing bread and meat to their children; and because the women then told their sons and daughters many tales and stories, to comfort and encourage them under the danger they were going upon, it has still continued a custom that at this feast old fables and tales should be told. For these particularities we are indebted to the history of Demon. There was then a place chosen out, and a temple erected in it to Theseus, and those families out of whom the tribute of the youth was gathered were appointed to pay a tax to the temple for sacrifices to him. And the house of the Phytalidae had the overseeing of these sacrifices, Theseus doing them that honor in recompense of their former hospitality.

    Now, after the death of his father Aegeus, forming in his mind a great and wonderful design, he gathered together all the inhabitants of Attica into one town, and made them one people of one city, whereas before they lived dispersed, and were not easy to assemble upon any affair for the common interest. Nay, differences and even wars often occurred between them, which he by his persuasions appeased, going from township to township, and from tribe to tribe. And those of a more private and mean condition readily embracing such good advice, to those of greater power he promised a commonwealth without monarchy, a democracy, or people's government in which he should only be continued as their commander in war and the protector of their laws, all things else being equally distributed among them; and by this means brought a part of them over to his proposal. The rest, fearing his power, which was already grown very formidable, and knowing his courage and resolution, chose rather to be persuaded than forced into a compliance. He then dissolved all the distinct state-houses, council halls, and magistracies, and built one common state-house and council hall on the site of the present upper town, and gave the name of Athens to the whole state, ordaining a common feast and sacrifice, which he called Panathenaea, or the sacrifice of all the united Athenians. He instituted also another sacrifice, called Metoecia, or Feast of Migration, which is yet celebrated on the sixteenth day of Hecatombaeon. Then, as he had promised, he laid down his regal power and proceeded to order a commonwealth, entering upon this great work not without advice from the gods. For having sent to consult the oracle of Delphi concerning the fortune of his new government and city, he received this answer:

> *Son of the Pitthean maid,*
> *To your town the terms and fates,*
> *My father gives of many states.*
> *Be not anxious nor afraid;*
> *The bladder will not fail so swim*
> *On the waves that compass him.*

Which oracle, they say, one of the sibyls long after did in a manner repeat to the Athenians, in this verse,

> *The bladder may be dipt, but not be drowned.*

Farther yet designing to enlarge his city, he invited all strangers to come and enjoy equal privileges with the natives, and it is said that the common form, Come hither all ye people, was the words that Theseus proclaimed when he thus set up a commonwealth, in a manner, for all nations. Yet he did not suffer his state, by the promiscuous multitude that flowed in, to be turned into confusion and be left without any order or degree, but was the first that divided the Commonwealth into three distinct ranks, the noblemen, the husbandmen, and artificers.

To the nobility he committed the care of religion, the choice of magistrates, the teaching and dispensing of the laws, and interpretation and direction in all sacred matters; the whole city being, as it were, reduced to an exact equality, the nobles excelling the rest in honor, the husbandmen in profit, and the artificers in number. And that Theseus was the first, who, as Aristotle says, out of an inclination to popular government, parted with the regal power, Homer also seems to testify, in his catalogue of the ships, where he gives the name of People to the Athenians only.

He also coined money, and stamped it with the image of an ox, either in memory of the Marathonian bull, or of Taurus, whom he vanquished, or else to put his people in mind to follow husbandry; and from this coin came the expression so frequent among the Greeks, of a thing being worth ten or a hundred oxen. After this he joined Megara to Attica, and erected that famous pillar on the Isthmus, which bears an inscription of two lines, showing the bounds of the two countries that meet there. On the east side the inscription is —

Peloponnesus there, Ionia here,

and on the west side —

Peloponnesus here, Ionia there.

He also instituted the games, in emulation of Hercules, being ambitious that as the Greeks, by that hero's appointment, celebrated the Olympian games to the honor of Jupiter, so, by his institution, they should celebrate the Isthmian to the honor of Neptune. For those that were there before observed, dedicated to Melicerta, were performed privately in the night, and had the form rather of a religious rite than of an open spectacle or public feast. There are some who say that the Isthmian games were first instituted in memory of Sciron, Theseus thus making expiation for his death, upon account of the nearness of kindred between them, Sciron being the son of Canethus and Heniocha, the daughter of Pittheus; though others write that Sinnis, not Sciron, was their son, and that to his honor, and not to the other's, these games were ordained by Theseus. At the same time he made an agreement with the Corinthians, that they should allow those that came from Athens to the celebration of the Isthmian games as much space of honor before the rest to behold the spectacle in, as the sail of the ship that brought them thither, stretched to its full extent, could cover; so Hellanicus and Andro of Halicarnassus have established.

Concerning his voyage into the Euxine Sea, Philochorus and some others write that he made it with Hercules, offering him his service in the war against the Amazons, and had Antiope given him for the reward of his valor; but the greater number, of whom are Pherecydes, Hellanicus, and Herodorus, write that he made this voyage many years after Hercules, with a navy under his own command, and took the Amazon prisoner, the more probable story, for we do not read that any other, of all those that accompanied him in this action, took any Amazon prisoner. Bion adds, that, to take her, he had to use deceit and fly away; for the Amazons, he says, being naturally lovers of men, were so far from avoiding Theseus when he touched upon their coasts, that they sent him presents to his ship; but he, having invited Antiope, who brought them, to come aboard, immediately set sail and carried her away. An author named Menecrates, that wrote the History of Nicaea in Bithynia, adds, that

Theseus, having Antiope aboard his vessel, cruised for some time about those coasts, and that there were in the same ship three young men of Athens, that accompanied him in this voyage, all brothers, whose names were Euneos, Thoas, and Soloon. The last of these fell desperately in love with Antiope; and, escaping the notice of the rest, revealed the secret only to one of his most intimate acquaintance, and employed him to disclose his passion to Antiope, she rejected his pretenses with a very positive denial, yet treated the matter with much gentleness and discretion, and made no complaint to Theseus of any thing that had happened; but Soloon, the thing being desperate, leaped into a river near the seaside and drowned himself. As soon as Theseus was acquainted with his death, and his unhappy love that was the cause of it, he was extremely distressed, and, in the height of his grief, an oracle which he had formerly received at Delphi came into his mind, for he had been commanded by the priestess of Apollo Pythius, that, wherever in a strange land he was most sorrowful and under the greatest affliction, he should build a city there, and leave some of his followers to be governors of the place. For this cause he there founded a city, which he called, from the name of Apollo, Pythopolis, and, in honor of the unfortunate youth, he named the river that runs by it Soloon, and left the two surviving brothers entrusted with the care of the government and laws, joining with them Hermus, one of the nobility of Athens, from whom a place in the city is called the House of Hermus; though by an error in the accent it has been taken for the House of Hermes, or Mercury, and the honor that was designed to the hero transferred to the god.

This was the origin and cause of the Amazonian invasion of Attica, which would seem to have been no slight or womanish enterprise. For it is impossible that they should have placed their camp in the very city, and joined battle close by the Pnyx and the hill called Museum, unless, having first conquered the country round about, they had thus with impunity advanced to the city. That they made so long a journey by land, and passed the Cimmerian Bosphorus when frozen, as Hellanicus writes, is difficult to be believed. That they encamped all but in the city is certain, and may be sufficiently confirmed by the names that the places thereabout yet retain, and the graves and monuments of those that fell in the battle. Both armies being in sight, there was a long pause and doubt on each side which should give the first onset; at last Theseus, having sacrificed to Fear, in obedience to the command of an oracle he had received, gave them battle; and this happened in the month of Boedromion, in which to this very day the Athenians celebrate the Feast Boedromia. Clidemus, desirous to be very circumstantial, writes that the left wing of the Amazons moved towards the place which is yet called Amazonium and the right towards the Pnyx, near Chrysa, that with this wing the Athenians, issuing from behind the Museum, engaged, and that the graves of those that were slain are to be seen in the street that leads to the gate called the

Piraic, by the chapel of the hero Chalcodon; and that here the Athenians were routed, and gave way before the women, as far as to the temple of the Furies, but, fresh supplies coming in from the Palladium, Ardettus, and the Lyceum, they charged their right wing, and beat them back into their tents, in which action a great number of the Amazons were slain. At length, after four months, a peace was concluded between them by the mediation of Hippolyta (for so this historian calls the Amazon whom Theseus married, and not Antiope), though others write that she was slain with a dart by Molpadia, while fighting by Theseus's side, and that the pillar which stands by the temple of Olympian Earth was erected to her honor. Nor is it to be wondered at, that in events of such antiquity, history should be in disorder. For indeed we are also told that those of the Amazons that were wounded were privately sent away by Antiope to Chalcis, where many by her care recovered, but some that died were buried there in the place that is to this time called Amazonium. That this war, however, was ended by a treaty is evident, both from the name of the place adjoining to the temple of Theseus, called, from the solemn oath there taken, Horcomosium; and also from the ancient sacrifice which used to be celebrated to the Amazons the day before the Feast of Theseus. The Megarians also show a spot in their city where some Amazons were buried, on the way from the market to a place called Rhus, where the building in the shape of a lozenge stands. It is said, likewise, that others of them were slain near Chaeronea, and buried near the little rivulet, formerly called Thermodon, but now Haemon, of which an account is given in the life of Demosthenes. It appears further that the passage of the Amazons through Thessaly was not without opposition, for there are yet shown many tombs of them near Scotussa and Cynoscephalae.

This is as much as is worth telling concerning the Amazons. For the account which the author of the poem called the Theseid gives of this rising of the Amazons, how Antiope, to revenge herself upon Theseus for refusing her and marrying Phaedra, came down upon the city with her train of Amazons, whom Hercules slew, is manifestly nothing else but fable and invention. It is true, indeed, that Theseus married Phaedra, but that was after the death of Antiope, by whom he had a son called Hippolytus, or, as Pindar writes, Demophon. The calamities which befell Phaedra and this son, since none of the historians have contradicted the tragic poets that have written of them, we must suppose happened as represented uniformly by them.

There are also other traditions of the marriages of Theseus, neither honorable in their occasions nor fortunate in their events, which yet were never represented in the Greek plays. For he is said to have carried off Anaxo, a Troezenian, and, having slain Sinnis and Cercyon, to have ravished their daughters; to have married Periboea, the mother of Ajax, and then Phereboea, and then Iope, the daughter of Iphicles. And further, he is accused of deserting

Ariadne (as is before related), being in love with Aegle the daughter of Panopeus, neither justly nor honorably; and lastly, of the rape of Helen, which filled all Attica with war and blood, and was in the end the occasion of his banishment and death, as will presently be related.

Herodorus is of opinion, that though there were many famous expeditions undertaken by the bravest men of his time, yet Theseus never joined in any of them, once only excepted, with the Lapithae, in their war against the Centaurs; but others say that he accompanied Jason to Colchis and Meleager to the slaying of the Calydonian boar, and that hence it came to be a proverb, Not without Theseus; that he himself, however, without aid of any one, performed many glorious exploits, and that from him began the saying, He is a second Hercules. He also joined Adrastus in recovering the bodies of those that were slain before Thebes, but not as Euripides in his tragedy says, by force of arms, but by persuasion and mutual agreement and composition, for so the greater part of the historians write; Philochorus adds further that this was the first treaty that ever was made for the recovering the bodies of the dead, but in the history of Hercules it is shown that it was he who first gave leave to his enemies to carry off their slain. The burying-places of the most part are yet to be seen in the village called Eleutherae; those of the commanders, at Eleusis, where Theseus allotted them a place, to oblige Adrastus. The story of Euripides in his Suppliants is disproved by Aeschylus in his Eleusinians, where Theseus himself relates the facts as here told.

The celebrated friendship between Theseus and Pirithous is said to have been thus begun: the fame of the strength and valor of Theseus being spread through Greece, Pirithous was desirous to make a trial and proof of it himself, and to this end seized a herd of oxen which belonged to Theseus, and was driving them away from Marathon, and, when news was brought that Theseus pursued him in arms, he did not fly, but turned back and went to meet him. But as soon as they had viewed one another, each so admired the gracefulness and beauty, and was seized with such a respect for the courage, of the other, that they forgot all thoughts of fighting; and Pirithous, first stretching out his hand to Theseus, bade him be judge in this case himself, and promised to submit willingly to any penalty he should impose. But Theseus not only forgave him all, but entreated him to be his friend and brother in arms; and they ratified their friendship by oaths. After this Pirithous married Deidamia, and invited Theseus to the wedding, entreating him to come and see his country, and make acquaintance with the Lapithae; he had at the same time invited the Centaurs to the feast, who growing hot with wine and beginning to be insolent and wild, and offering violence to the women, the Lapithae took immediate revenge upon them, slaying many of them upon the place, and afterwards, having overcome them in battle, drove the whole race of them out of their country, Theseus all along taking their part and fighting on their side.

But Herodorus gives a different relation of these things: that Theseus came not to the assistance of the Lapithae till the war was already begun; and that it was in this journey that he had the first sight of Hercules, having made it his business to find him out at Trachis, where he had chosen to rest himself after all his wanderings and his labors; and that this interview was honorably performed on each part, with extreme respect, good-will, and admiration of each other. Yet it is more credible, as others write, that there were, before, frequent interviews between them, and that it was by the means of Theseus that Hercules was initiated at Eleusis, and purified before initiation, upon account of several rash actions of his former life.

Theseus was now fifty years old, as Hellanicus states, when he carried off Helen, who was yet too young to be married. Some writers, to take away this accusation of one of the greatest crimes laid to his charge, say, that he did not steal away Helen himself, but that Idas and Lynceus were the ravishers, who brought her to him, and committed her to his charge, and that, therefore, he refused to restore her at the demand of Castor and Pollux; or, indeed, they say her own father, Tyndarus, had sent her to be kept by him, for fear of Enarophorus, the son of Hippocoon, who would have carried her away by force when she was yet a child. But the most probable account, and that which has most witnesses on its side, is this: Theseus and Pirithous went both together to Sparta, and, having seized the young lady as she was dancing in the temple of Diana Orthia, fled away with her. There were presently men in arms sent to pursue, but they followed no further than to Tegea; and Theseus and Pirithous, being now out of danger, having passed through Peloponnesus, made an agreement between themselves, that he to whom the lot should fall should have Helen to his wife, but should be obliged to assist in procuring another for his friend. The lot fell upon Theseus, who conveyed her to Aphidnae, not being yet marriageable, and delivered her to one of his allies, called Aphidnus, and, having sent his mother Aethra after to take care of her, desired him to keep them so secretly, that none might know where they were; which done, to return the same service to his friend Pirithous, he accompanied him in his journey to Epirus, in order to steal away the king of the Molossians' daughter. The king, his own name being Aidoneus, or Pluto, called his wife Proserpina, and his daughter Cora, and a great dog which he kept Cerberus, with whom he ordered all that came as suitors to his daughter to fight, and promised her to him that should overcome the beast. But having been informed that the design of Pirithous and his companion was not to court his daughter, but to force her away, he caused them both to be seized, and threw Pirithous to be torn in pieces by his dog, and put Theseus into prison, and kept him.

About this time, Menestheus, the son of Peteus, grandson of Orneus, and great-grandson to Erechtheus, the first man that is recorded to have affected popularity and ingratiated himself with the multitude, stirred up and exasperated the most eminent men of the city, who had long borne a secret grudge to Theseus, conceiving that he had robbed them of their several little kingdoms and lordships, and, having pent them all up in one city, was using them as his subjects and slaves. He put also the meaner people into commotion, telling them, that, deluded with a mere dream of liberty, though indeed they were deprived both of that and of their proper homes and religious usages, instead of many good and gracious kings of their own, they had given themselves up to be lorded over by a new-comer and a stranger. Whilst he was thus busied in infecting the minds of the citizens, the war that Castor and Pollux brought against Athens came very opportunely to further the sedition he had been promoting, and some say that he by his persuasions was wholly the cause of their invading the city. At their first approach, they committed no acts of hostility, but peaceably demanded their sister Helen; but the Athenians returning answer that they neither had her there nor knew where she was disposed of, they prepared to assault the city, when Academus, having, by whatever means, found it out, disclosed to them that she was secretly kept at Aphidnae. For which reason he was both highly honored during his life by Castor and Pollux, and the Lacedaemonians, when often in aftertimes they made incursions into Attica, and destroyed all the country round about, spared the Academy for the sake of Academus. But Dicaearchus writes that there were two Arcadians in the army of Castor and Pollux, the one called Echedemus and the other Marathus; from the first that which is now called Academia was then named Echedemia, and the village Marathon had its name from the other, who, to fulfill some oracle, voluntarily offered himself to be made a sacrifice before battle. As soon as they were arrived at Aphidnae, they overcame their enemies in a set battle, and then assaulted and took the town. And here, they say, Alycus, the son of Sciron, was slain, of the party of the Dioscuri (Castor and Pollux), from whom a place in Megara, where he was buried, is called Alycus to this day. And Hereas writes that it was Theseus himself that killed him, in witness of which he cites these verses concerning Alycus

> *And Alycus, upon Aphidna's plain*
> *By Theseus in the cause of Helen slain.*

Though it is not at all probable that Theseus himself was there when both the city and his mother were taken.

Aphidnae being won by Castor and Pollux, and the city of Athens being in consternation, Menestheus persuaded the people to open their gates, and receive them with all manner of friendship, for they were, he told them, at enmity with none but Theseus, who had first injured them, and were benefactors and saviors to all mankind beside. And their behavior gave credit to those promises; for, having made themselves absolute masters of the place, they demanded no more than to be initiated, since they were as nearly related to the city as Hercules was, who had received the same honor. This their desire they easily obtained, and were adopted by Aphidnus, as Hercules had been by Pylius. They were honored also like gods, and were called by a new name, Anaces, either from the cessation (Anokhe) of the war, or from the care they took that none should suffer any injury, though there was so great an army within the walls; for the phrase anakos ekhein is used of those who look to or care for any thing; kings for this reason, perhaps, are called anactes. Others say, that from the appearance of their star in the heavens, they were thus called, for in the Attic dialect this name comes very near the words that signify above.

Some say that Aethra, Theseus's mother, was here taken prisoner, and carried to Lacedaemon, and from thence went away with Helen to Troy, alleging this verse of Homer, to prove that she waited upon Helen,

Aethra of Pittheus born, and large-eyed Clymene.

Others reject this verse as none of Homer's, as they do likewise the whole fable of Munychus, who, the story says, was the son of Demophon and Laodice, born secretly, and brought up by Aethra at Troy. But Ister, in the thirteenth book of his Attic History, gives us an account of Aethra, different yet from all the rest: that Achilles and Patroclus overcame Paris in Thessaly, near the river Sperchius, but that Hector took and plundered the city of the Troezenians, and made Aethra prisoner there. But this seems a groundless tale.

Now Hercules, passing by the Molossians, was entertained in his way by Aidoneus the king, who, in conversation, accidentally spoke of the journey of Theseus and Pirithous into his country, of what they had designed to do, and what they were forced to suffer. Hercules was much grieved for the inglorious death of the one and the miserable condition of the other. As for Pirithous, he thought it useless to complain; but begged to have Theseus released for his sake, and obtained that favor from the king. Theseus, being thus set at liberty, returned to Athens, where his friends were not yet wholly suppressed, and dedicated to Hercules all the sacred places which the city had set apart for himself, changing their names from Thesea to Heraclea, four only excepted, as Philochorus writes. And wishing immediately to resume the first place in the commonwealth, and manage the state as before, he soon found himself involved in factions and troubles; those who long had hated him had now added to their hatred contempt; and the minds of the people were so generally corrupted, that, instead of obeying commands with silence, they expected to be flattered into their duty. He had some thoughts to have reduced them by force, but was overpowered by demagogues and factions. And at last, despairing of any good success of his affairs in Athens, he sent away his children privately to Euboea, commending them to the care of Elephenor, the son of Chalcodon; and he himself, having solemnly cursed the people of Athens in the village of Gargettus, in which there yet remains the place called Araterion, or the place of cursing, sailed to Scyros, where he had lands left him by his father, and friendship, as he thought, with those of the island. Lycomedes was then king of Scyros. Theseus, therefore, addressed himself to him, and desired to have his lands put into his possession, as designing to settle and to dwell there, though others say that he came to beg his assistance against the Athenians. But Lycomedes, either jealous of the glory of so great a man, or to gratify Menestheus, having led him up to the highest cliff of the island, on pretense of showing him from thence the lands that he desired, threw him headlong down from the rock, and killed him. Others say he fell down of himself by a slip of his foot, as he was walking there, according to his custom, after supper. At that time there was no notice taken, nor were any concerned for his death, but Menestheus quietly possessed the kingdom of Athens. His sons were brought up in a private condition, and accompanied Elephenor to the Trojan war, but, after the decease of Menestheus in that expedition, returned to Athens, and recovered the government. But in succeeding ages, beside several other circumstances that moved the Athenians to honor Theseus as a demigod, in the battle which was fought at Marathon against the Medes, many of the soldiers believed they saw an apparition of Theseus in arms, rushing on at the head of them against the barbarians. And after the Median war, Phaedo being archon of Athens, the Athenians, consulting the oracle at Delphi, were commanded to gather together the bones of Theseus, and, laying them in some honorable place, keep them as sacred in the city. But it was very difficult to recover these relics, or so much as to find out the place where they lay, on account of the inhospitable and savage temper of the barbarous people that inhabited the island. Nevertheless, afterwards, when Cimon took the island (as is related in his life), and had a great ambition to find out the place where Theseus was buried, he, by chance, spied an eagle upon a rising ground pecking with her beak and tearing up the earth with her talons, when on the sudden it came into his mind, as it were by some divine inspiration, to dig there, and search for the bones of Theseus. There were found in that place a coffin of a man of more than ordinary size, and a brazen spear-head, and a sword lying by it, all which he took aboard his galley and brought with him to Athens. Upon which the Athenians, greatly delighted, went out to meet and receive the relics with splendid processions and with sacrifices, as if it were Theseus himself returning alive to the city. He lies interred in the middle of the city, near the present gymnasium. His tomb is a sanctuary and refuge for slaves, and all those of mean condition that fly from the persecution of men in power, in memory that Theseus while he lived was an assister and protector of the distressed, and never refused the petitions of the afflicted that fled to him. The chief and most solemn sacrifice which they celebrate to him is kept on the eighth day of Pyanepsion, on which he returned with the Athenian young men from Crete. Besides which, they sacrifice to him on the eighth day of every month, either because he returned from Troezen the eighth day of Hecatombaeon, as Diodorus the geographer writes, or else thinking that number to be proper to him, because he was reputed to be born of Neptune, because they sacrifice to Neptune on the eighth day of every month. The number eight being the first cube of an even number, and the double of the first square, seemed to be an emblem of the steadfast and immovable power of this god, who from thence has the names of Asphalius and Gaeiochus, that is, the establisher and stayer of the earth.

2
ROMULUS

From whom, and for what reason, the city of Rome, a name so great in glory, and famous in the mouths of all men, was so first called, authors do not agree. Some are of opinion that the Pelasgians, wandering over the greater part of the habitable world, and subduing numerous nations, fixed themselves here, and, from their own great strength in war, called the city Rome. Others, that at the taking of Troy, some few that escaped and met with shipping, put to sea, and, driven by winds, were carried upon the coasts of Tuscany, and came to anchor off the mouth of the river Tiber, where their women, out of heart and weary with the sea, on its being proposed by one of the highest birth and best understanding amongst them, whose name was Roma, burnt the ships. With which act the men at first were angry, but afterwards, of necessity, seating themselves near Palatium, where things in a short while succeeded far better than they could hope, in that they found the country very good, and the people courteous, they not only did the lady Roma other honors, but added also this, of calling after her name the city which she had been the occasion of their founding. From this, they say, has come down that custom at Rome for women to salute their kinsmen and husbands with kisses; because these women, after they had burnt the ships, made use of such endearments when entreating and pacifying their husbands.

Some again say that Roma, from whom this city was so called, was daughter of Italus and Leucaria; or, by another account, of Telephus, Hercules's son, and that she was married to Aeneas, or, according to others again, to Ascanius, Aeneas's son. Some tell us that Romanus, the son of Ulysses and Circe, built it; some, Romus the son of Emathion, Diomede having sent him from Troy; and others, Romus, king of the Latins, after driving out the Tyrrhenians, who had come from Thessaly into Lydia, and from thence into Italy. Those very authors, too, who, in accordance with the safest account, make Romulus give the name to the city, yet differ concerning his birth and family. For some say, he was son to Aeneas and Dexithea, daughter of Phorbas, and was, with his brother Remus, in their infancy, carried into Italy, and being on the river when the waters came down in a flood, all the vessels were cast away except only that where the young children were, which being gently landed on a level bank of the river, they were both unexpectedly saved, and from them the place was called Rome. Some say, Roma, daughter of the Trojan lady above mentioned, was married to Latinus, Telemachus's son, and became mother to Romulus; others, that Aemilia, daughter of Aeneas and Lavinia, had him by the god Mars; and others give you mere fables of his origin. For to Tarchetius, they say, king of Alba, who was a most wicked and cruel man, there appeared in his own house a strange vision, a male figure that rose out of a hearth, and stayed there for many days. There was an oracle of Tethys in Tuscany which Tarchetius consulted, and received an answer that a virgin should give herself to the apparition, and that a son should be born of her, highly renowned, eminent for valor, good fortune, and strength of body. Tarchetius told the prophecy to one of his own daughters, and commanded her to do this thing; which she avoiding as an indignity, sent her handmaid. Tarchetius, hearing this, in great anger imprisoned them both, purposing to put them to death; but being deterred from murder by the goddess Vesta in a dream, enjoined them for their punishment the working a web of cloth, in their chains as they were, which when they finished, they should be suffered to marry; but whatever they worked by day, Tarchetius commanded others to unravel in the night. In the meantime, the waiting-woman was delivered of two boys, whom Tarchetius gave into the hands of one Teratius, with command to destroy them; he, however, carried and laid them by the river side, where a wolf came and continued to suckle them, while birds of various sorts brought little morsels of food, which they put into their mouths; till a cow-herd, spying them, was first strangely surprised, but, venturing to draw nearer, took the children up in his arms. Thus they were saved, and, when they grew up, set upon Tarchetius and overcame him. This one Promathion says, who compiled a history of Italy.

But the story which is most believed and has the greatest number of vouchers was first published, in its chief particulars, amongst the Greeks by Diocles of Peparethus, whom Fabius Pictor also follows in most points. Here again there are variations, but in general outline it runs thus: the kings of Alba reigned in lineal descent from Aeneas and the succession devolved at length upon two brothers, Numitor and Amulius. Amulius proposed to divide things into two equal shares, and set as equivalent to the kingdom the treasure and gold that were brought from Troy. Numitor chose the kingdom; but Amulius, having the money, and being able to do more with that than Numitor, took his kingdom from him with great ease, and, fearing lest his daughter might have children, made her a Vestal, bound in that condition forever to live a single and maiden life. This lady some call Ilia, others Rhea, and others Silvia; however, not long after, she was, contrary to the established laws of the Vestals, discovered to be with child, and should have suffered the most cruel punishment, had not Antho, the king's daughter, mediated with her father for her; nevertheless, she was confined, and debarred all company, that she might not be delivered without the king's knowledge. In time she brought forth two boys, of more than human size and beauty, whom Amulius, becoming yet more alarmed, commanded a servant to take and cast away; this man some call Faustulus, others say Faustulus was the man who brought them up. He put the children, however, in a small trough, and went towards the river with a design to cast them in; but, seeing the waters much swollen and coming violently down, was afraid to go nearer, and, dropping the children near the bank, went away. The river overflowing, the flood at last bore up the trough, and, gently wafting it, landed them on a smooth piece of ground, which they now call Cermanes, formerly Germanus, perhaps from Germani, which signifies brothers.

Near this place grew a wild fig-tree, which they called Ruminalis, either from Romulus (as it is vulgarly thought), or from ruminating, because cattle did usually in the heat of the day seek cover under it, and there chew the cud; or, better, from the suckling of these children there, for the ancients called the dug or teat of any creature ruma, and there is a tutelar goddess of the rearing of children whom they still call Rumilia, in sacrificing to whom they use no wine, but make libations of milk. While the infants lay here, history tells us, a she-wolf nursed them, and a woodpecker constantly fed and watched them; these creatures are esteemed holy to the god Mars, the woodpecker the Latins still especially worship and honor. Which things, as much as any, gave credit to what the mother of the children said, that their father was the god Mars: though some say that it was a mistake put upon her by Amulius, who himself had come to her dressed up in armor.

Others think that the first rise of this fable came from the children's nurse, through the ambiguity of her name; for the Latins not only called wolves lupae, but also women of loose life; and such an one was the wife of Faustulus, who nurtured these children, Acca Larentia by name. To her the Romans offer sacrifices, and in the month of April the priest of Mars makes libations there; it is called the Larentian Feast. They honor also another Larentia, for the following reason: the keeper of Hercules's temple having, it seems, little else to do, proposed to his deity a game at dice, laying down that, if he himself won, he would have something valuable of the god; but if he were beaten, he would spread him a noble table, and procure him a fair lady's company. Upon these terms, throwing first for the god and then for himself, he found himself beaten. Wishing to pay his stakes honorably, and holding himself bound by what he had said, he both provided the deity a good supper, and, giving money to Larentia, then in her beauty, though not publicly known, gave her a feast in the temple, where he had also laid a bed, and after supper locked her in, as if the god were really to come to her. And indeed, it is said, the deity did truly visit her, and commanded her in the morning to walk to the market-place, and, whatever man see met first, to salute him, and make him her friend. She met one named Tarrutius, who was a man advanced in years, fairly rich without children, and had always lived a single life. He received Larentia, and loved her well, and at his death left her sole heir of all his large and fair possessions, most of which she, in her last will and testament, bequeathed to the people. It was reported of her, being now celebrated and esteemed the mistress of a god, that she suddenly disappeared near the place where the first Larentia lay buried; the spot is at this day called Velabrum, because, the river frequently overflowing, they went over in ferry-boats somewhere hereabouts to the forum, the Latin word for ferrying being velatura. Others derive the name from velum, a sail; because the exhibitors of public shows used to hang the road that leads from the forum to the Circus Maximus with sails, beginning at this spot. Upon these accounts the second Larentia is honored at Rome.

Meantime Faustulus, Amulius's swineherd, brought up the children without any man's knowledge; or, as those say who wish to keep closer to probabilities, with the knowledge and secret assistance of Numitor; for it is said, they went to school at Gabii, and were well instructed in letters, and other accomplishments befitting their birth. And they were called Romulus and Remus, (from ruma, the dug,) as we had before, because they were found sucking the wolf. In their very infancy, the size and beauty of their bodies intimated their natural superiority; and when they grew up, they both proved brave and manly, attempting all enterprises that seemed hazardous, and showing in them a courage altogether undaunted. But Romulus seemed rather to act by counsel, and to show the sagacity of a statesman, and in all his dealings with their neighbors, whether relating to feeding of flocks or to hunting, gave the idea of being born rather to rule than to obey. To their comrades and inferiors they were therefore dear; but the king's servants, his bailiffs and overseers, as being in nothing better men than themselves, they despised and slighted, nor were the least concerned at their commands and menaces. They used honest pastimes and liberal studies, not esteeming sloth and idleness honest and liberal, but rather such exercises as hunting and running, repelling robbers, taking of thieves, and delivering the wronged and oppressed from injury. For doing such things they became famous.

A quarrel occurring between Numitor's and Amulius's cowherds, the latter, not enduring the driving away of their cattle by the others, fell upon them and put them to flight, and rescued the greatest part of the prey. At which Numitor being highly incensed, they little regarded it, but collected and took into their company a number of needy men and runaway slaves — acts which looked like the first stages of rebellion. It so happened, that when Romulus was attending a sacrifice, being fond of sacred rites and divination, Numitor's herdsmen, meeting with Remus on a journey with few companions, fell upon him, and, after some fighting, took him prisoner, carried him before Numitor, and there accused him. Numitor would not punish him himself, fearing his brother's anger, but went to Amulius, and desired justice, as he was Amulius's brother and was affronted by Amulius's servants. The men of Alba likewise resenting the thing, and thinking he had been dishonorably used, Amulius was induced to deliver Remus up into Numitor's hands, to use him as he thought fit. He therefore took and carried him home, and, being struck with admiration of the youth's person, in stature and strength of body exceeding all men, and perceiving in his very countenance the courage and force of his mind, which stood unsubdued and unmoved by his present circumstances, and hearing further that all the enterprises and actions of his life were answerable to what he saw of him, but chiefly, as it seemed, a divine influence aiding and directing the first steps that were to lead to great results, out of the mere thought of his mind, and casually, as it were, he put his hand upon the fact, and, in gentle terms and with a kind aspect, to inspire him with confidence and hope, asked him who he was, and whence he was derived. He, taking heart, spoke thus: " I will hide nothing from you, for you seem to be of a more princely temper than Amulius, in that you give a hearing and examine before you punish, while he condemns before the cause is heard. Formerly, then, we (for we are twins) thought ourselves the sons of Faustulus and Larentia, the king's servants; but since we have been accused and aspersed with calumnies, and brought in peril of our lives here before you, we hear great things of ourselves, the truth of which my present danger is likely to bring to the test. Our birth is said to have been secret, our fostering and nurture in our infancy still more strange; by birds and beasts, to whom we were cast out, we were fed, by the milk of a wolf, and the morsels of a woodpecker, as we lay in a little trough by the side of the river. The trough is still in being, and is preserved, with brass plates round it, and an inscription in letters almost effaced; which may prove hereafter unavailing tokens to our parents when we are dead and gone." Numitor, upon these words, and computing the dates by the young man's looks, slighted not the hope that flattered him, but considered how to come at his daughter privately (for she was still kept under restraint), to talk with her concerning these matters.

Faustulus, hearing Remus was taken and delivered up, called on Romulus to assist in his rescue, informing him then plainly of the particulars of his birth, not but he had before given hints of it, and told as much as an attentive man might make no small conclusions from; he himself, full of concern and fear of not coming in time, took the trough, and ran instantly to Numitor; but giving a suspicion to some of the king's sentry at his gate, and being gazed upon by them and perplexed with their questions, he let it be seen that he was hiding the trough under his cloak. By chance there was one among them who was at the exposing of the children, and was one employed in the office; he, seeing the trough and knowing it by its make and inscription, guessed at the business, and, without further delay, telling the king of it, brought in the man to be examined. Faustulus, hard beset, did not show himself altogether proof against terror; nor yet was he wholly forced out of all; confessed indeed the children were alive, but lived, he said, as shepherds, a great way from Alba; he himself was going to carry the trough to Ilia, who had often greatly desired to see and handle it, for a confirmation of her hopes of her children. As men generally do who are troubled in mind and act either in fear or passion, it so fell out Amulius now did; for he sent in haste as a messenger, a man, otherwise honest, and friendly to Numitor, with commands to learn from Numitor whether any tidings were come to him of the children's being alive. He, coming and seeing how little Remus wanted of being received into the arms and embraces of Numitor, both gave him surer confidence in his hope, and advised them, with all expedition, to proceed to action; himself too joining and assisting them, and indeed, had they wished it, the time would not have let them demur. For Romulus was now come very near, and many of the citizens, out of fear and hatred of Amulius, were running out to join him; besides, he brought great forces with him, divided into companies, each of an hundred men, every captain carrying a small bundle of grass and shrubs tied to a pole. The Latins call such bundles manipuli and from hence it is that in their armies still they call their captains manipulares. Remus rousing the citizens within to revolt, and Romulus making attacks from without, the tyrant, not knowing either what to do, or what expedient to think of for his security, in this perplexity and confusion was taken and put to death. This narrative, for the most part given by Fabius and Diocles of Peparethus, who seem to be the earliest historians of the foundation of Rome, is suspected by some, because of its dramatic and fictitious appearance; but it would not wholly be disbelieved, if men would remember what a poet fortune sometimes shows herself, and consider that the Roman power would hardly have reached so high a pitch without a divinely ordered origin, attended with great and extraordinary circumstances.

Amulius now being dead and matters quietly disposed, the two brothers would neither dwell in Alba without governing there, nor take the government into their own hands during the life of their grandfather. Having therefore delivered the dominion up into his hands, and paid their mother befitting honor, they resolved to live by themselves, and build a city in the same place where they were in their infancy brought up. This seems the most honorable reason for their departure; though perhaps it was necessary, having such a body of slaves and fugitives collected about them, either to come to nothing by dispersing them, or if not so, then to live with them elsewhere. For that the inhabitants of Alba did not think fugitives worthy of being received and incorporated as citizens among them plainly appears from the matter of the women, an attempt made not wantonly but of necessity, because they could not get wives by good-will. For they certainly paid unusual respect and honor to those whom they thus forcibly seized.

Not long after the first foundation of the city, they opened a sanctuary of refuge for all fugitives, which they called the temple of the god Asylaeus, where they received and protected all, delivering none back, neither the servant to his master, the debtor to his creditor, nor the murderer into the hands of the magistrate, saying it was a privileged place, and they could so maintain it by an order of the holy oracle, insomuch that the city grew presently very populous, for, they say, it consisted at first of no more than a thousand houses.

But of that hereafter.

Their minds being fully bent upon building, there arose presently a difference about the place where. Romulus chose what was called Roma Quadrata, or the Square Rome, and would have the city there. Remus laid out a piece of ground on the Aventine Mount, well fortified by nature, which was from him called Remonium, but now Rignarium. Concluding at last to decide the contest by a divination from a flight of birds, and placing themselves apart at some distance, Remus, they say, saw six vultures, and Romulus double the number; others say Remus did truly see his number, and that Romulus feigned his, but, when Remus came to him, that then he did, indeed, see twelve. Hence it is that the Romans, in their divinations from birds, chiefly regard the vulture, though Herodorus Ponticus relates that Hercules was always very joyful when a vulture appeared to him upon any action. For it is a creature the least hurtful of any, pernicious neither to corn, fruit-tree, nor cattle; it preys only upon carrion, and never kills or hurts any living thing; and as for birds, it touches not them, though they are dead, as being of its own species, whereas eagles, owls, and hawks mangle and kill their own fellow-creatures; yet, as Aeschylus says —

What bird is clean that preys on fellow bird?

Besides all other birds are, so to say, never out of our eyes; they let themselves be seen of us continually; but a vulture is a very rare sight, and you can seldom meet with a man that has seen their young; their rarity and infrequency has raised a strange opinion in some, that they come to us from some other world; as soothsayers ascribe a divine origination to all things not produced either of nature or of themselves.

When Remus knew the cheat, he was much displeased; and as Romulus was casting up a ditch, where he designed the foundation of the citywall, he turned some pieces of the work to ridicule, and obstructed others: at last, as he was in contempt leaping over it, some say Romulus himself struck him, others Celer, one of his companions; he fell, however, and in the scuffle Faustulus also was slain, and Plistinus, who, being Faustulus's brother, story tells us, helped to bring up Romulus. Celer upon this fled instantly into Tuscany, and from him the Romans call all men that are swift of foot Celeres; and because Quintus Metellus, at his father's funeral, in a few days' time gave the people a show of gladiators, admiring his expedition in getting it ready, they gave him the name of Celer.

Romulus, having buried his brother Remus, together with his two fosterfathers, on the mount Remonia, set to building his city; and sent for men out of Tuscany, who directed him by sacred usages and written rules in all the ceremonies to be observed, as in a religious rite. First, they dug a round trench about that which is now the Comitium, or Court of Assembly, and into it solemnly threw the first-fruits of all things either good by custom or necessary by nature; lastly, every man taking a small piece of earth of the country from whence he came, they all threw them in promiscuously together. This trench they call, as they do the heavens, Mundus; making which their center, they described the city in a circle round it. Then the founder fitted to a plow a brazen plowshare, and, yoking together a bull and a cow, drove himself a deep line or furrow round the bounds; while the business of those that followed after was to see that whatever earth was thrown up should be turned all inwards towards the city, and not to let any clod lie outside. With this line they described the wall, and called it, by a contraction, Pomoerium, that is, post murum, after or beside the wall; and where they designed to make a gate, there they took out the share, carried the plow over, and left a space; for which reason they consider the whole wall as holy, except where the gates are; for had they adjudged them also sacred, they could not, without offense to religion, have given free ingress and egress for the necessaries of human life, some of which are in themselves unclean.

As for the day they began to build the city, it is universally agreed to have been the twenty-first of April, and that day the Romans annually keep holy, calling it their country's birthday. At first, they say, they sacrificed no living creature on this day, thinking it fit to preserve the feast of their country's birthday pure and without stain of blood. Yet before ever the city was built, there was a feast of herdsmen and shepherds kept on this day, which went by the name of Palilia. The Roman and Greek months have now little or no agreement; they say, however, the day on which Romulus began to build was quite certainly the thirtieth of the month, at which time there was an eclipse of the sun which they conceive to be that seen by Antimachus, the Teian poet, in the third year of the sixth Olympiad. In the times of Varro the philosopher, a man deeply read in Roman history, lived one Tarrutius, his familiar acquaintance, a good philosopher and mathematician, and one, too, that out of curiosity had studied the way of drawing schemes and tables, and was thought to be a proficient in the art; to him Varro propounded to cast Romulus's nativity, even to the first day and hour, making his deductions from the several events of the man's life which he should be informed of, exactly as in working back a geometrical problem; for it belonged, he said, to the same science both to foretell a man's life by knowing the time of his birth, and also to find out his birth by the knowledge of his life. This task Tarrutius undertook, and first looking into the actions and casualties of the man, together with the time of his life and manner of his death, and then comparing all these remarks together, he very confidently and positively pronounced that Romulus was conceived in his mother's womb the first year of the second Olympiad, the twenty-third day of the month the Egyptians call Choeac, and the third hour after sunset, at which time there was a total eclipse of the sun; that he was born the twenty-first day of the month Thoth, about sun-rising; and that the first stone of Rome was laid by him the ninth day of the month Pharmuthi, between the second and third hour. For the fortunes of cities as well as of men, they think, have their certain periods of time prefixed, which may be collected and foreknown from the position of the stars at their first foundation. But these and the like relations may perhaps not so much take and delight the reader with their novelty and curiosity, as offend him by their extravagance.

The city now being built, Romulus enlisted all that were of age to bear arms into military companies, each company consisting of three thousand footmen and three hundred horse. These companies were called legions, because they were the choicest and most select of the people for fighting men. The rest of the multitude he called the people; one hundred of the most eminent he chose for counselors; these he styled patricians, and their assembly the senate, which signifies a council of elders. The patricians, some say, were so called because they were the fathers of lawful children; others, because they could give a good account who their own fathers were, which not every one of the rabble that poured into the city at first could do; others, from patronage, their word for protection of inferiors, the origin of which they attribute to Patron, one of those that came over with Evander, who was a great protector and defender of the weak and needy. But perhaps the most probable judgment might be, that Romulus, esteeming it the duty of the chiefest and wealthiest men, with a fatherly care and concern to look after the meaner, and also encouraging the commonalty not to dread or be aggrieved at the honors of their superiors, but to love and respect them, and to think and call them their fathers, might from hence give them the name of patricians. For at this very time all foreigners give senators the style of lords; but the Romans, making use of a more honorable and less invidious name, call them Patres Conscripti; at first indeed simply Patres, but afterwards, more being added, Patres Conscripti. By this more imposing title he distinguished the senate from the populace; and in other ways also separated the nobles and the commons — calling them patrons, and these their clients — by which means he created wonderful love and amity between them, productive of great justice in their dealings. For they were always their clients' counselors in law cases, their advocates in courts of justice, in fine their advisers and supporters in all affairs whatever. These again faithfully served their patrons, not only paying them all respect and deference, but also, in case of poverty, helping them to portion their daughters and pay off their debts; and for a patron to witness against his client, or a client against his patron, was what no law nor magistrate could enforce. In after times all other duties subsisting still between them, it was thought mean and dishonorable for the better sort to take money from their inferiors. And so much of these matters.

In the fourth month, after the city was built, as Fabius writes, the adventure of stealing the women was attempted; and some say Romulus himself, being naturally a martial man, and predisposed too, perhaps, by certain oracles, to believe the fates had ordained the future growth and greatness of Rome should depend upon the benefit of war, upon these accounts first offered violence to the Sabines, since he took away only thirty virgins, more to give an occasion of war than out of any want of women. But this is not very probable; it would seem rather that, observing his city to be filled by a confluence of foreigners, few of whom had wives, and that the multitude in general, consisting of a mixture of mean and obscure men, fell under contempt, and seemed to be of no long continuance together, and hoping farther, after the women were appeased, to make this injury in some measure an occasion of confederacy and mutual commerce with the Sabines, he took in hand this exploit after this manner. First, he gave it out as if he had found an altar of a certain god hid under ground; the god they called Consus, either the god of counsel (for they still call a consultation consilium and their chief magistrates consules, namely, counselors), or else the equestrian Neptune, for the altar is kept covered in the circus maximus at all other times, and only at horse-races is exposed to public view; others merely say that this god had his altar hid under ground because counsel ought to be secret and concealed. Upon discovery of this altar, Romulus, by proclamation, appointed a day for a splendid sacrifice, and for public games and shows, to entertain all sorts of people; many flocked thither, and he himself sat in front, amidst his nobles, clad in purple. Now the signal for their falling on was to be whenever he rose and gathered up his robe and threw it over his body; his men stood all ready armed, with their eyes intent upon him, and when the sign was given, drawing their swords and falling on with a great shout, they ravished away the daughters of the Sabines, they themselves flying without any let or hindrance. They say there were but thirty taken, and from them the Curiae or Fraternities were named; but Valerius Antias says five hundred and twenty-seven, Juba, six hundred and eighty-three virgins; which was indeed the greatest excuse Romulus could allege, namely, that they had taken no married woman, save one only, Hersilia by name, and her too unknowingly; which showed they did not commit this rape wantonly, but with a design purely of forming alliance with their neighbors by the greatest and surest bonds. This Hersilia some say Hostilius married, a most eminent man among the Romans; others, Romulus himself, and that she bore two children to him, a daughter, by reason of primogeniture called Prima, and one only son, whom, from the great concourse of citizens to him at that time, he called Aollius, but after ages Abillius. But Zenodotus the Troezenian, in giving this account, is contradicted by many.

Among those who committed this rape upon the virgins, there were, they say, as it so then happened, some of the meaner sort of men, who were carrying off a damsel, excelling all in beauty and comeliness of stature, whom when some of superior rank that met them attempted to take away, they cried out they were carrying her to Talasius, a young man, indeed, but brave and worthy; hearing that, they commended and applauded them loudly, and also some, turning back, accompanied them with good-will and pleasure, shouting out the name of Talasius. Hence the Romans to this very time, at their weddings, sing Talasius for their nuptial word, as the Greeks do Hymenaeus, because, they say, Talasius was very happy in his marriage. But Sextius Sylla the Carthaginian, a man wanting neither learning nor ingenuity, told me Romulus gave this word as a sign when to begin the onset; everybody, therefore, who made prize of a maiden, cried out, Talasius; and for that reason the custom continues so now at marriages. But most are of opinion (of whom Juba particularly is one) that this word was used to new-married women by way of incitement to good housewifery and talasia (spinning), as we say in Greek, Greek words at that time not being as yet overpowered by Italian. But if this be the case, and if the Romans did at that time use the word talasia as we do, a man might fancy a more probable reason of the custom. For when the Sabines, after the war against the Romans, were reconciled, conditions were made concerning their women, that they should be obliged to do no other servile offices to their husbands but what concerned spinning; it was customary, therefore, ever after, at weddings, for those that gave the bride or escorted her or otherwise were present, sportingly to say Talasius, intimating that she was henceforth to serve in spinning and no more. It continues also a custom at this very day for the bride not of herself to pass her husband's threshold, but to be lifted over, in memory that the Sabine virgins were carried in by violence, and did not go in of their own will. Some say, too, the custom of parting the bride's hair with the head of a spear was in token their marriages began at first by war and acts of hostility, of which I have spoken more fully in my book of Questions.

This rape was committed on the eighteenth day of the month Sextilis, now called August, on which the solemnities of the Consualia are kept.

The Sabines were a numerous and martial people, but lived in small, unfortified villages, as it befitted, they thought, a colony of the Lacedaemonians to be bold and fearless; nevertheless, seeing themselves bound by such hostages to their good behavior, and being solicitous for their daughters, they sent ambassadors to Romulus with fair and equitable requests, that he would return their young women and recall that act of violence, and afterwards, by persuasion and lawful means, seek friendly correspondence between both nations. Romulus would not part with the young women, yet proposed to the Sabines to enter into an alliance with them; upon which point some consulted and demurred long, but Acron, king of the Ceninenses, a man of high spirit and a good warrior, who had all along a jealousy of Romulus's bold attempts, and considering particularly from this exploit upon the women that he was growing formidable to all people, and indeed insufferable, were he not chastised, first rose up in arms, and with a powerful army advanced against him. Romulus likewise prepared to receive him; but when they came within sight and viewed each other, they made a challenge to fight a single duel, the armies standing by under arms, without participation. And Romulus, making a vow to Jupiter, if he should conquer, to carry, himself, and dedicate his adversary's armor to his honor, overcame him in combat, and, a battle ensuing, routed his army also, and then took his city; but did those he found in it no injury, only commanded them to demolish the place and attend him to Rome, there to be admitted to all the privileges of citizens. And indeed there was nothing did more advance the greatness of Rome, than that she did always unite and incorporate those whom she conquered into herself. Romulus, that he might perform his vow in the most acceptable manner to Jupiter, and withal make the pomp of it delightful to the eye of the city, cut down a tall oak which he saw growing in the camp, which he trimmed to the shape of a trophy, and fastened on it Acron's whole suit of armor disposed in proper form; then he himself, girding his clothes about him, and crowning his head with a laurel-garland, his hair gracefully flowing, carried the trophy resting erect upon his right shoulder, and so marched on, singing songs of triumph, and his whole army following after, the citizens all receiving him with acclamations of joy and wonder. The procession of this day was the origin and model of all after triumphs. This trophy was styled an offering to Jupiter Feretrius, from ferire, which in Latin is to smite; for Romulus prayed he might smite and overthrow his enemy; and the spoils were called opima, or royal spoils, says Varro, from their richness, which the word opes signifies; though one would more probably conjecture from opus, an act; for it is only to the general of an army who with his own hand kills his enemies' general that this honor is granted of offering the opima spolia. And three only of the Roman captains have had it conferred on them: first, Romulus, upon killing Acron the Ceninensian; next, Cornelius Cossus, for slaying Tolumnius the Tuscan; and lastly, Claudius Marcellus, upon his conquering Viridomarus, king of the Gauls. The two latter, Cossus and Marcellus, made their entries in triumphant chariots, bearing their trophies themselves; but that Romulus made use of a chariot, Dionysius is wrong in asserting. History says, Tarquinius, Damaratus's son, was the first that brought triumphs to this great pomp and grandeur; others, that Publicola was the first that rode in triumph. The statues of Romulus in triumph are, as may be seen in Rome, all on foot.

    After the overthrow of the Ceninensians, the other Sabines still protracting the time in preparations, the people of Fidenae, Crustumerium, and Antemna, joined their forces against the Romans; they in like manner were defeated in battle, and surrendered up to Romulus their cities to be seized, their lands and territories to be divided, and themselves to be transplanted to Rome. All the lands which Romulus acquired, he distributed among the citizens, except only what the parents of the stolen virgins had; these he suffered to possess their own. The rest of the Sabines, enraged hereat, choosing Tatius their captain, marched straight against Rome. The city was almost inaccessible, having for its fortress that which is now the Capitol, where a strong guard was placed, and Tarpeius their captain; not Tarpeia the virgin, as some say who would make Romulus a fool. But Tarpeia, daughter to the captain, coveting the golden bracelets she saw them wear, betrayed the fort into the Sabines' hands, and asked, in reward of her treachery, the things they wore on their left arms. Tatius conditioning thus with her, in the night she opened one of the gates, and received the Sabines in. And truly Antigonus, it would seem, was not solitary in saying, he loved betrayers, but hated those who had betrayed; nor Caesar, who told Rhymitalces the Thracian, that he loved the treason, but hated the traitor; but it is the general feeling of all who have occasion for wicked men's service, as people have for the poison of venomous beasts; they are glad of them while they are of use, and abhor their baseness when it is over. And so then did Tatius behave towards Tarpeia, for he commanded the Sabines, in regard to their contract, not to refuse her the least part of what they wore on their left arms; and he himself first took his bracelet of his arm, and threw that, together with his buckler, at her; and all the rest following, she, being borne down and quite buried with the multitude of gold and their shields, died under the weight and pressure of them; Tarpeius also himself, being prosecuted by Romulus, was found guilty of treason, as Juba says Sulpicius Galba relates. Those who write otherwise concerning Tarpeia, as that she was the daughter of Tatius, the Sabine captain, and, being forcibly detained by Romulus, acted and suffered thus by her father's contrivance, speak very absurdly, of whom Antigonus is one. And Simylus, the poet, who thinks Tarpeia betrayed the Capitol, not to the Sabines, but the Gauls, having fallen in love with their king, talks mere folly, saying thus:

> *Tarpeia 'twas, who, dwelling close thereby,*
> *Laid open Rome unto the enemy.*
> *She, for the love of the besieging Gaul,*
> *Betrayed the city's strength, the Capitol.*

And a little after, speaking of her death:

> *The numerous nations of the Celtic foe*
> *Bore her not living to the banks of Po;*
> *Their heavy shields upon the maid they threw,*
> *And with their splendid gifts entombed at once and slew.*

Tarpeia afterwards was buried there, and the hill from her was called Tarpeius, until the reign of king Tarquin, who dedicated the place to Jupiter, at which time her bones were removed, and so it lost her name, except only that part of the Capitol which they still call the Tarpeian Rock, from which they used to cast down malefactors.

The Sabines being possessed of the hill, Romulus, in great fury, bade them battle, and Tatius was confident to accept it, perceiving, if they were overpowered, that they had behind them a secure retreat. The level in the middle, where they were to join battle, being surrounded with many little hills, seemed to enforce both parties to a sharp and desperate conflict, by reason of the difficulties of the place, which had but a few outlets, inconvenient either for refuge or pursuit. It happened, too, the river having overflowed not many days before, there was left behind in the plain, where now the forum stands, a deep blind mud and slime, which, though it did not appear much to the eye, and was not easily avoided, at bottom was deceitful and dangerous; upon which the Sabines being unwarily about to enter, met with a piece of good fortune; for Curtius, a gallant man, eager of honor, and of aspiring thoughts, being mounted on horseback, was galloping on before the rest, and mired his horse here, and, endeavoring for awhile by whip and spur and voice to disentangle him, but finding it impossible, quitted him and saved himself; the place from him to this very time is called the Curtian Lake. The Sabines, having avoided this danger, began the fight very smartly, the fortune of the day being very dubious, though many were slain; amongst whom was Hostilius, who, they say, was husband to Hersilia, and grandfather to that Hostilius who reigned after Numa. There were many other brief conflicts, we may suppose, but the most memorable was the last, in which Romulus having received a wound on his head by a stone, and being almost felled to the ground by it, and disabled, the Romans gave way, and, being driven out of the level ground, fled towards the Palatium. Romulus, by this time recovering from his wound a little, turned about to renew the battle, and, facing the fliers, with a loud voice encouraged them to stand and fight. But being overborne with numbers, and nobody daring to face about, stretching out his hands to heaven, he prayed to Jupiter to stop the army, and not to neglect but maintain the Roman cause, now in extreme danger. The prayer was no sooner made, than shame and respect for their king checked many; the fears of the fugitives changed suddenly into confidence. The place they first stood at was where now is the temple of Jupiter Stator (which may be translated the Stayer); there they rallied again into ranks, and repulsed the Sabines to the place called now Regia, and to the temple of Vesta; where both parties, preparing to begin a second battle, were prevented by a spectacle, strange to behold, and defying description. For the daughters of the Sabines, who had been carried off, came running, in great confusion, some on this side, some on that, with miserable cries and lamentations, like creatures possessed, in the midst of the army, and among the dead bodies, to come at their husbands and their fathers, some with their young babes in their arms, others their hair loose about their ears, but all calling, now upon the Sabines, now upon the Romans, in the most tender and endearing words. Hereupon both melted into compassion, and fell back, to make room for them between the armies. The sight of the women carried sorrow and commiseration upon both sides into the hearts of all, but still more their words, which began with expostulation and upbraiding, and ended with entreaty and supplication.

"Wherein," say they, "have we injured or offended you, as to deserve such sufferings, past and present? We were ravished away unjustly and violently by those whose now we are; that being done, we were so long neglected by our fathers, our brothers, and countrymen, that time, having now by the strictest bonds united us to those we once mortally hated, has made it impossible for us not to tremble at the danger and weep at the death of the very men who once used violence to us. You did not come to vindicate our honor, while we were virgins, against our assailants; but do come now to force away wives from their husbands and mothers from their children, a succor more grievous to its wretched objects than the former betrayal and neglect of them. Which shall we call the worst, their love-making or your compassion? If you were making war upon any other occasion, for our sakes you ought to withhold your hands from those to whom we have made you fathers-in-law and grandsires. If it be for our own cause, then take us, and with us your sons-in-law and grandchildren. Restore to us our parents and kindred, but do not rob us of our children and husbands. Make us not, we entreat you, twice captives." Hersilia having spoken many such words as these, and the others earnestly praying, a truce was made, and the chief officers came to a parley; the women, in the mean time, brought and presented their husbands and children to their fathers and brothers; gave those that wanted, meat and drink, and carried the wounded home to be cured, and showed also how much they governed within doors, and how indulgent their husbands were to them, in demeaning themselves towards them with all kindness and respect imaginable. Upon this, conditions were agreed upon, that what women pleased might stay where they were, exempt, as aforesaid, from all drudgery and labor but spinning; that the Romans and Sabines should inhabit the city together; that the city should be called Rome, from Romulus; but the Romans, Quirites, from the country of Tatius; and that they both should govern and command in common. The place of the ratification is still called Comitium, from coire, to meet.

The city being thus doubled in number, one hundred of the Sabines were elected senators, and the legions were increased to six thousand foot and six hundred horse; then they divided the people into three tribes; the first, from Romulus, named Ramnenses; the second, from Tatius, Tatienses; the third, Luceres, from the lucus, or grove, where the Asylum stood, whither many fled for sanctuary, and were received into the city. And that they were just three, the very name of tribe and tribune seems to show; each tribe contained ten curiae, or brotherhoods, which, some say, took their names from the Sabine women; but that seems to be false, because many had their names from various places. Though it is true, they then constituted many things in honor to the women; as to give them the way wherever they met them; to speak no ill word in their presence; not to appear naked before them, or else be liable to prosecution before the judges of homicide; that their children should wear an ornament about their necks called the bulla (because it was like a bubble), and the praetexta, a gown edged with purple.

The princes did not immediately join in council together, but at first each met with his own hundred; afterwards all assembled together. Tatius dwelt where now the temple of Moneta stands, and Romulus, close by the steps, as they call them, of the Fair Shore, near the descent from the Mount Palatine to the Circus Maximus. There, they say, grew the holy cornel tree, of which they report, that Romulus once, to try his strength, threw a dart from the Aventine Mount, the staff of which was made of cornel, which struck so deep into the ground, that no one of many that tried could pluck it up; and the soil, being fertile, gave nourishment to the wood, which sent forth branches, and produced a cornel-stock of considerable bigness. This did posterity preserve and worship as one of the most sacred things; and, therefore, walled it about; and if to any one it appeared not green nor flourishing, but inclining to pine and wither, he immediately made outcry to all he met, and they, like people hearing of a house on fire, with one accord would cry for water, and run from all parts with buckets full to the place. But when Caius Caesar, they say, was repairing the steps about it, some of the laborers digging too close, the roots were destroyed, and the tree withered.

The Sabines adopted the Roman months, of which whatever is remarkable is mentioned in the Life of Numa. Romulus, on the other hand, adopted their long shields, and changed his own armor and that of all the Romans, who before wore round targets of the Argive pattern. Feasts and sacrifices they partook of in common, not abolishing any which either nation observed before, and instituting several new ones; of which one was the Matronalia, instituted in honor of the women. for their extinction of the war; likewise the Carmentalia. This Carmenta some think a deity presiding over human birth; for which reason she is much honored by mothers. Others say she was the wife of Evander, the Arcadian, being a prophetess, and wont to deliver her oracles in verse, and from carmen, a verse, was called Carmenta; her proper name being Nicostrata. Others more probably derive Carmenta from carens mente, or insane, in allusion to her prophetic frenzies. Of the Feast of Palilia we have spoken before. The Lupercalia, by the time of its celebration, may seem to be a feast of purification, for it is solemnized on the dies nefasti, or non-court days, of the month February, which name signifies purification, and the very day of the feast was anciently called Februata; but its name is equivalent to the Greek Lycaea; and it seems thus to be of great antiquity, and brought in by the Arcadians who came with Evander. Yet this is but dubious, for it may come as well from the wolf that nursed Romulus; and we see the Luperci, the priests, begin their course from the place where they say Romulus was exposed. But the ceremonies performed in it render the origin of the thing more difficult to be guessed at; for there are goats killed, then, two young noblemen's sons being brought, some are to stain their foreheads with the bloody knife, others presently to wipe it off with wool dipped in milk; then the young boys must laugh after their foreheads are wiped; that done, having cut the goats' skins into thongs, they run about naked, only with something about their middle, lashing all they meet; and the young wives do not avoid their strokes, fancying they will help conception and child-birth. Another thing peculiar to this feast is for the Luperci to sacrifice a dog. But as, a certain poet who wrote fabulous explanations of Roman customs in elegiac verses, says, that Romulus and Remus, after the conquest of Amulius, ran joyfully to the place where the wolf gave them suck; and that in imitation of that, this feast was held, and two young noblemen ran —

> *Striking at all, as when from Alba town,*
> *With sword in hand, the twins came hurrying down;*

and that the bloody knife applied to their foreheads was a sign of the danger and bloodshed of that day; the cleansing of them in milk, a remembrance of their food and nourishment. Caius Acilius writes, that, before the city was built, the cattle of Romulus and Remus one day going astray, they, praying to the god Faunus, ran out to seek them naked, wishing not to be troubled with sweat, and that this is why the Luperci run naked. If the sacrifice be by way of purification, a dog might very well be sacrificed; for the Greeks, in their lustrations, carry out young dogs, and frequently use this ceremony of periscylacismus as they call it. Or if again it is a sacrifice of gratitude to the wolf that nourished and preserved Romulus, there is good reason in killing a dog, as being an enemy to wolves. Unless indeed, after all, the creature is punished for hindering the Luperci in their running.

They say, too, Romulus was the first that consecrated holy fire, and instituted holy virgins to keep it, called vestals; others ascribe it to Numa Pompilius; agreeing, however, that Romulus was otherwise eminently religious, and skilled in divination, and for that reason carried the lituus, a crooked rod with which soothsayers describe the quarters of the heavens, when they sit to observe the flights of birds. This of his, being kept in the Palatium, was lost when the city was taken by the Gauls; and afterwards, that barbarous people being driven out, was found in the ruins, under a great heap of ashes, untouched by the fire, all things about it being consumed and burnt. He instituted also certain laws, one of which is somewhat severe, which suffers not a wife to leave her husband, but grants a husband power to turn off his wife, either upon poisoning her children; or counterfeiting his keys, or for adultery; but if the husband upon any other occasion put her away, he ordered one moiety of his estate to be given to the wife, the other to fall to the goddess Ceres; and whoever cast off his wife, to make an atonement by sacrifice to the gods of the dead. This, too, is observable as a singular thing in Romulus, that he appointed no punishment for real parricide, but called all murder so, thinking the one an accursed thing, but the other a thing impossible; and, for a long time, his judgment seemed to have been right; for in almost six hundred years together, nobody committed the like in Rome; and Lucius Hostius, after the wars of Hanibal, is recorded to have been the first parricide.

Let thus much suffice concerning these matters.

In the fifth year of the reign of Tatius, some of his friends and kinsmen, meeting ambassadors coming from Laurentum to Rome, attempted on the road to take away their money by force, and, upon their resistance, killed them. So great a villainy having been committed, Romulus thought the malefactors ought at once to be punished, but Tatius shuffled off and deferred the execution of it; and this one thing was the beginning of open quarrel between them; in all other respects they were very careful of their conduct, and administered affairs together with great unanimity. The relations of the slain, being debarred of lawful satisfaction by reason of Tatius, fell upon him as he was sacrificing with Romulus at Lavinium, and slew him; but escorted Romulus home, commending and extolling him for a just prince. Romulus took the body of Tatius, and buried it very splendidly in the Aventine Mount, near the place called Armilustrium, but altogether neglected revenging his murder. Some authors write, the city of Laurentum, fearing the consequence, delivered up the murderers of Tatius; but Romulus dismissed them, saying, one murder was requited with another. This gave occasion of talk and jealousy, as if he were well pleased at the removal of his copartner in the government. Nothing of these things, however, raised any sort of feud or disturbance among the Sabines; but some out of love to him, others out of fear of his power, some again reverencing him as a god, they all continued living peacefully in admiration and awe of him; many foreign nations, too, showed respect to Romulus; the Ancient Latins sent, and entered into league and confederacy with him. Fidenae he took, a neighboring city to Rome, by a party of horse, as some say, whom he sent before with commands to cut down the hinges of the gates, himself afterwards unexpectedly coming up. Others say, they having first made the invasion, plundering and ravaging the country and suburbs, Romulus lay in ambush for them, and, having killed many of their men, took the city; but, nevertheless, did not raze or demolish it, but made it a Roman colony, and sent thither, on the Ides of April, two thousand five hundred inhabitants.

Soon after a plague broke out, causing sudden death without any previous sickness; it infected also the corn with unfruitfulness, and cattle with barrenness; there rained blood, too, in the city; so that, to their actual sufferings, fear of the wrath of the gods was added. But when the same mischiefs fell upon Laurentum, then everybody judged it was divine vengeance that fell upon both cities, for the neglect of executing justice upon the murder of Tatius and the ambassadors. But the murderers on both sides being delivered up and punished, the pestilence visibly abated; and Romulus purified the cities with lustrations, which, they say, even now are performed at the wood called Ferentina. But before the plague ceased, the Camertines invaded the Romans and overran the country, thinking them, by reason of the distemper, unable to resist; but Romulus at once made head against them, and gained the victory, with the slaughter of six thousand men; then took their city, and brought half of those he found there to Rome; sending from Rome to Camerium double the number he left there. This was done the first of August. So many citizens had he to spare, in sixteen years' time from his first founding Rome. Among other spoils, he took a brazen four-horse chariot from Camerium, which he placed in the temple of Vulcan, setting on it his own statue, with a figure of Victory crowning him.

The Roman cause thus daily gathering strength, their weaker neighbors shrunk away, and were thankful to be left untouched; but the stronger, out of fear or envy, thought they ought not to give way to Romulus, but to curb and put a stop to his growing greatness. The first were the Veientes, a people of Tuscany, who had large possessions, and dwelt in a spacious city; they took occasion to commence a war, by claiming Fidenae as belonging to them; a thing not only very unreasonable, but very ridiculous, that they, who did not assist them in the greatest extremities, but permitted them to be slain, should challenge their lands and houses when in the hands of others. But being scornfully retorted upon by Romulus in his answers, they divided themselves into two bodies; with one they attacked the garrison of Fidenae, the other marched against Romulus; that which went against Fidenae got the victory, and slew two thousand Romans; the other was worsted by Romulus, with the loss of eight thousand men. A fresh battle was fought near Fidenae, and here all men acknowledge the day's success to have been chiefly the work of Romulus himself, who showed the highest skill as well as courage, and seemed to manifest a strength and swiftness more than human. But what some write, that, of fourteen thousand that fell that day, above half were slain by Romulus's own hand, verges too near to fable, and is, indeed, simply incredible; since even the Messenians are thought to go too far in saying that Aristomenes three times offered sacrifice for the death of a hundred enemies, Lacedaemonians, slain by himself. The army being thus routed, Romulus, suffering those that were left to make their escape, led his forces against the city; they, having suffered such great losses, did not venture to oppose, but, humbly suing to him, made a league and friendship for an hundred years; surrendering also a large district of land called Septempagium, that is, the seven parts, as also their salt-works upon the river, and fifty noblemen for hostages. He made his triumph for this on the Ides of October, leading, among the rest of his many captives, the general of the Veientes, an elderly man, but who had not, it seemed, acted with the prudence of age; whence even now, in sacrifices for victories, they lead an old man through the market place to the Capitol, appareled in purple, with a bulla, or child's toy, tied to it, and the crier cries, Sardians to be sold; for the Tuscans are said to be a colony of the Sardians, and the Veientes are a city of Tuscany.

This was the last battle Romulus ever fought; afterwards he, as most, nay all men, very few excepted, do, who are raised by great and miraculous goodhaps of fortune to power and greatness, so, I say, did he; relying upon his own great actions, and growing of an haughtier mind, he forsook his popular behavior for kingly arrogance, odious to the people; to whom in particular the state which he assumed was hateful. For he dressed in scarlet, with the purple-bordered robe over it; he gave audience on a couch of state, having always about him some young men called Celeres, from their swiftness in doing commissions; there went before him others with staves, to make room, with leather thongs tied on their bodies, to bind on the moment whomever he commanded. The Latins formerly used ligare in the same sense as now alligare, to bind, whence the name lictors, for these officers, and bacula, or staves, for their rods, because staves were then used. It is probable, however, they were first called litores, afterwards, by putting in a c, lictores, or, in Greek, liturgi, or people's officers, for leitos is still Greek for the commons, and laos for the people in general.

But when, after the death of his grandfather Numitor in Alba, the throne devolving upon Romulus, he, to court the people, put the government into their own hands, and appointed an annual magistrate over the Albans, this taught the great men of Rome to seek after a free and anti-monarchical state, wherein all might in turn be subjects and rulers. For neither were the patricians any longer admitted to state affairs, only had the name and title left them, convening in council rather for fashion's sake than advice, where they heard in silence the king's commands, and so departed, exceeding the commonalty only in hearing first what was done. These and the like were matters of small moment; but when he of his own accord parted among his soldiers what lands were acquired by war, and restored the Veientes their hostages, the senate neither consenting nor approving of it, then, indeed, he seemed to put a great affront upon them; so that, on his sudden and strange disappearance a short while after, the senate fell under suspicion and calumny. He disappeared on the Nones of July, as they now call the month which was then Quintilis, leaving nothing of certainty to be related of his death; only the time, as just mentioned, for on that day many ceremonies are still performed in representation of what happened. Neither is this uncertainty to be thought strange, seeing the manner of the death of Scipio Africanus, who died at his own home after supper, has been found capable neither of proof or disproof; for some say he died a natural death, being of a sickly habit; others, that he poisoned himself; others again, that his enemies, breaking in upon him in the night, stifled him. Yet Scipio's dead body lay open to be seen of all, and any one, from his own observation, might form his suspicions and conjectures; whereas Romulus, when he vanished, left neither the least part of his body, nor any remnant of his clothes to be seen. So that some fancied, the senators, having fallen upon him in the temple of Vulcan, cut his body into pieces, and took each a part away in his bosom; others think his disappearance was neither in the temple of Vulcan, nor with the senators only by, but that, it came to pass that, as he was haranguing the people without the city, near a place called the Goat's Marsh, on a sudden strange and unaccountable disorders and alterations took place in the air; the face of the sun was darkened, and the day turned into night, and that, too, no quiet, peaceable night, but with terrible thunderings, and boisterous winds from all quarters; during which the common people dispersed and fled, but the senators kept close together. The tempest being over and the light breaking out, when the people gathered again, they missed and inquired for their king; the senators suffered them not to search, or busy themselves about the matter, but commanded them to honor and worship Romulus as one taken up to the gods, and about to be to them, in the place of a good prince, now a propitious god. The multitude, hearing this, went away believing and rejoicing in hopes of good things from him; but there were some, who, canvassing the matter in a hostile temper, accused and aspersed the patricians, as men that persuaded the people to believe ridiculous tales, when they themselves were the murderers of the king.

Things being in this disorder, one, they say, of the patricians, of noble family and approved good character, and a faithful and familiar friend of Romulus himself, having come with him from Alba, Julius Proculus by name, presented himself in the forum; and, taking a most sacred oath, protested before them all, that, as he was traveling on the road, he had seen Romulus coming to meet him, looking taller and comelier than ever, dressed in shining and faming armor; and he, being affrighted at the apparition, said, "Why, O king, or for what purpose have you abandoned us to unjust and wicked surmises, and the whole city to bereavement and endless sorrow?" and that he made answer, "It pleased the gods, O Proculus, that we, who came from them, should remain so long a time amongst men as we did; and, having built a city to be the greatest in the world for empire and glory, should again return to heaven. But farewell; and tell the Romans, that, by the exercise of temperance and fortitude, they shall attain the height of human power; we will be to you the propitious god Quirinus." This seemed credible to the Romans, upon the honesty and oath of the relater, and indeed, too, there mingled with it a certain divine passion, some preternatural influence similar to possession by a divinity; nobody contradicted it, but, laying aside all jealousies and detractions, they prayed to Quirinus and saluted him as a god.

This is like some of the Greek fables of Aristeas the Proconnesian, and Cleomedes the Astypalaean; for they say Aristeas died in a fuller's work-shop, and his friends, coming to look for him, found his body vanished; and that some presently after, coming from abroad, said they met him traveling towards Croton. And that Cleomedes, being an extraordinarily strong and gigantic man, but also wild and mad, committed many desperate freaks; and at last, in a school-house, striking a pillar that sustained the roof with his fist, broke it in the middle, so that the house fell and destroyed the children in it; and being pursued, he fled into a great chest, and, shutting to the lid, held it so fast, that many men, with their united strength, could not force it open; afterwards, breaking the chest to pieces, they found no man in it alive or dead; in astonishment at which, they sent to consult the oracle at Delphi; to whom the prophetess made this answer,

Of all the heroes, Cleomede is last.

They say, too, the body of Alcmena, as they were carrying her to her grave, vanished, and a stone was found lying on the bier. And many such improbabilities do your fabulous writers relate, deifying creatures naturally mortal; for though altogether to disown a divine nature in human virtue were impious and base, so again to mix heaven with earth is ridiculous. Let us believe with Pindar, that

All human bodies yield to Death's decree,
The soul survives to all eternity.

For that alone is derived from the gods, thence comes, and thither returns; not with the body, but when most disengaged and separated from it, and when most entirely pure and clean and free from the flesh; for the most perfect soul, says Heraclitus, is a dry light, which flies out of the body as lightning breaks from a cloud; but that which is clogged and surfeited with body is like gross and humid incense, slow to kindle and ascend. We must not, therefore, contrary to nature, send the bodies, too, of good men to heaven; but we must really believe that, according to their divine nature and law, their virtue and their souls are translated out of men into heroes, out of heroes into demi-gods, out of demi-gods, after passing, as in the rite of initiation, through a final cleansing and sanctification, and so freeing themselves from all that pertains to mortality and sense, are thus, not by human decree, but really and according to right reason, elevated into gods, admitted thus to the greatest and most blessed perfection.

Romulus's surname Quirinus, some say, is equivalent to Mars; others, that he was so called because the citizens were called Quirites; others, because the ancients called a dart or spear Quiris; thus, the statue of Juno resting on a spear is called Quiritis, and the dart in the Regia is addressed as Mars, and those that were distinguished in war were usually presented with a dart; that, therefore, Romulus, being a martial god, or a god of darts, was called Quirinus. A temple is certainly built to his honor on the mount called from him Quirinalis.

The day he vanished on is called the Flight of the People, and the Nones of the Goats, because they go then out of the city, and sacrifice at the Goat's Marsh, and, as they go, they shout out some of the Roman names, as Marcus, Lucius, Caius, imitating the way in which they then fled and called upon one another in that fright and hurry. Some, however, say, this was not in imitation of a flight, but of a quick and hasty onset, referring it to the following occasion: after the Gauls who had taken Rome were driven out by Camillus, and the city was scarcely as yet recovering her strength, many of the Latins, under the command of Livius Postumius, took this time to march against her. Postumius, halting not far from Rome, sent a herald, signifying that the Latins were desirous to renew their former alliance and affinity (that was now almost decayed) by contracting new marriages between both nations; if, therefore, they would send forth a good number of their virgins and widows, they should have peace and friendship, such as the Sabines had formerly had on the like conditions. The Romans, hearing this, dreaded a war, yet thought a surrender of their women little better than mere captivity. Being in this doubt, a servant-maid called Philotis (or, as some say, Tutola), advised them to do neither, but, by a stratagem, avoid both fighting and the giving up of such pledges. The stratagem was this, that they should send herself, with other well-looking servant-maids, to the enemy, in the dress of free-born virgins, and she should in the night light up a fire-signal, at which the Romans should come armed and surprise them asleep. The Latins were thus deceived, and accordingly Philotis set up a torch in a wild fig-tree, screening it behind with curtains and coverlets from the sight of the enemy, while visible to the Romans. They, when they saw it, eagerly ran out of the gates, calling in their haste to each other as they went out, and so, falling in unexpectedly upon the enemy, they defeated them, and upon that made a feast of triumph, called the Nones of the Goats, because of the wild fig-tree, called by the Romans Caprificus, or the goat-fig. They feast the women without the city in arbors made of fig-tree boughs and the maid-servants gather together and run about playing; afterwards they fight in sport, and throw stones one at another, in memory that they then aided and assisted the Roman men in fight. This only a few authors admit for true; For the calling upon one another's names by day and the going out to the Goat's Marsh to do sacrifice seem to agree more with the former story, unless, indeed, we shall say that both the actions might have happened on the same day in different years. It was in the fifty-fourth year of his age and the thirty-eighth of his reign that Romulus, they tell us, left the world.

3
COMPARISON OF ROMULUS WITH THESEUS

This is what I have learnt of Romulus and Theseus, worthy of memory. It seems, first of all, that Theseus, out of his own free-will, without any compulsion, when he might have reigned in security at Troezen in the enjoyment of no inglorious empire, of his own motion affected great actions, whereas the other, to escape present servitude and a punishment that threatened him, (according to Plato's phrase) grew valiant purely out of fear, and dreading the extremest inflictions, attempted great enterprises out of mere necessity. Again, his greatest action was only the killing of one king of Alba; while, as mere by-adventures and preludes, the other can name Sciron, Sinnis, Procrustes, and Corynetes; by reducing and killing of whom, he rid Greece of terrible oppressors, before any of them that were relieved knew who did it; moreover, he might without any trouble as well have gone to Athens by sea, considering he himself never was in the least injured by those robbers; where as Romulus could not but be in trouble whilst Amulius lived. Add to this the fact that Theseus, for no wrong done to himself, but for the sake of others, fell upon these villains; but Romulus and Remus, as long as they themselves suffered no ill by the tyrant, permitted him to oppress all others. And if it be a great thing to have been wounded in battle by the Sabines, to have killed king Acron, and to have conquered many enemies, we may oppose to these actions the battle with the Centaurs and the feats done against the Amazons. But what Theseus adventured, in offering himself voluntarily with young boys and virgins, as part of the tribute unto Crete, either to be a prey to a monster or a victim upon the tomb of Androgeus, or, according to the mildest form of the story, to live vilely and dishonorably in slavery to insulting and cruel men; it is not to be expressed what an act of courage, magnanimity, or justice to the public, or of love for honor and bravery, that was. So that methinks the philosophers did not ill define love to be the provision of the gods for the care and preservation of the young; for the love of Ariadne, above all, seems to have been the proper work and design of some god in order to preserve Theseus; and, indeed, we ought not to blame her for loving him, but rather wonder all men and women were not alike affected towards him; and if she alone were so. truly I dare pronounce her worthy of the love of a god, who was herself so great a lover of virtue and goodness, and the bravest man.

Both Theseus and Romulus were by nature meant for governors; yet neither lived up to the true character of a king, but fell off, and ran, the one into popularity, the other into tyranny, falling both into the same fault out of different passions. For a ruler's first end is to maintain his office, which is done no less by avoiding what is unfit than by observing what is suitable. Whoever is either too remiss or too strict is no more a king or a governor, but either a demagogue or a despot, and so becomes either odious or contemptible to his subjects. Though certainly the one seems to be the fault of easiness and good-nature, the other of pride and severity.

If men's calamities, again, are not to be wholly imputed to fortune, but refer themselves to differences of character, who will acquit either Theseus of rash and unreasonable anger against his son, or Romulus against his brother? Looking at motives, we more easily excuse the anger which a stronger cause, like a severer blow, provoked. Romulus, having disagreed with his brother advisedly and deliberately on public matters, one would think could not on a sudden have been put into so great a passion; but love and jealousy and the complaints of his wife, which few men can avoid being moved by, seduced Theseus to commit that outrage upon his son. And what is more, Romulus, in his anger, committed an action of unfortunate consequence; but that of Theseus ended only in words, some evil speaking, and an old man's curse; the rest of the youth's disasters seem to have proceeded from fortune; so that, so far, a man would give his vote on Theseus's part.

But Romulus has, first of all, one great plea, that his performances proceeded from very small beginnings; for both the brothers being thought servants and the sons of swineherds, before becoming freemen themselves, gave liberty to almost all the Latins, obtaining at once all the most honorable titles, as destroyers of their country's enemies, preservers of their friends and kindred, princes of the people, founders of cities, not removers, like Theseus, who raised and compiled only one house out of many, demolishing many cities bearing the names of ancient kings and heroes. Romulus, indeed, did the same afterwards, forcing his enemies to deface and ruin their own dwellings, and to sojourn with their conquerors; but at first, not by removal, or increase of an existing city, but by foundation of a new one, he obtained himself lands, a country, a kingdom, wives, children, and relations. And, in so doing, he killed or destroyed nobody, but benefited those that wanted houses and homes and were willing to be of a society and become citizens. Robbers and malefactors he slew not; but he subdued nations, he overthrew cities, he triumphed over kings and commanders. As to Remus, it is doubtful by whose hand he fell; it is generally imputed to others. His mother he clearly retrieved from death, and placed his grandfather who was brought under base and dishonorable vassalage, on the ancient throne of Aeneas, to whom he did voluntarily many good offices, but never did him harm even inadvertently. But Theseus, in his forgetfulness and neglect of the command concerning the flag, can scarcely, methinks, by any excuses, or before the most indulgent judges, avoid the imputation of parricide. And, indeed, one of the Attic writers, perceiving it to be very hard to make an excuse for this, feigns that Aegeus, at the approach of the ship, running hastily to the Acropolis to see what news, slipped and fell down, as if he had no servants, or none would attend him on his way to the shore.

And, indeed, the faults committed in the rapes of women admit of no plausible excuse in Theseus. First, because of the often repetition of the crime; for he stole Ariadne, Antiope, Anaxo the Troezenian, at last Helen, when he was an old man, and she not marriageable; she a child, and he at an age past even lawful wedlock. Then, on account of the cause; for the Troezenian, Lacedaemonian, and Amazonian virgins, beside that they were not betrothed to him, were not worthier to raise children by than the Athenian women, derived from Erechtheus and Cecrops; but it is to be suspected these things were done out of wantonness and lust. Romulus, when he had taken near eight hundred women, chose not all, but only Hersilia, as they say, for himself; the rest he divided among the chief of the city; and afterwards, by the respect and tenderness and justice shown towards them, he made it clear that this violence and injury was a commendable and politic exploit to establish a society; by which he intermixed and united both nations, and made it the fountain of after friendship and public stability. And to the reverence and love and constancy he established in matrimony, time can witness; for in two hundred and thirty years, neither any husband deserted his wife, nor any wife her husband; but, as the curious among the Greeks can name the first case of parricide or matricide, so the Romans all well know that Spurius Carvilius was the first who put away his wife, accusing her of barrenness. The immediate results were similar; for upon those marriages the two princes shared in the dominion, and both nations fell under the same government. But from the marriages of Theseus proceeded nothing of friendship or correspondence for the advantage of commerce, but enmities and wars and the slaughter of citizens, and, at last, the loss of the city Aphidnae, when only out of the compassion of the enemy, whom they entreated and caressed like gods, they escaped suffering what Troy did by Paris. Theseus's mother, however, was not only in danger, but suffered actually what Hecuba did, deserted and neglected by her son, unless her captivity be not a fiction, as I could wish both that and other things were. The circumstances of the divine intervention, said to have preceded or accompanied their births, are also in contrast; for Romulus was preserved by the special favor of the gods; but the oracle given to Aegeus, commanding him to abstain, seems to demonstrate that the birth of Theseus was not agreeable to the will of the gods.

4
PERICLES

Caesar once, seeing some wealthy strangers at Rome, carrying up and down with them in their arms and bosoms young puppy-dogs and monkeys, embracing and making much of them, took occasion not unnaturally to ask whether the women in their country were not used to bear children; by that prince-like reprimand gravely reflecting upon persons who spend and lavish upon brute beasts that affection and kindness which nature has implanted in us to be bestowed on those of our own kind. With like reason may we blame those who misuse that love of inquiry and observation which nature has implanted in our souls, by expending it on objects unworthy of the attention either of their eyes or their ears, while they disregard such as are excellent in themselves, and would do them good.

The mere outward sense, being passive in responding to the impression of the objects that come in its way and strike upon it, perhaps cannot help entertaining and taking notice of everything that addresses it, be it what it will, useful or unuseful; but, in the exercise of his mental perception, every man, if he chooses, has a natural power to turn himself upon all occasions, and to change and shift with the greatest ease to what he shall himself judge desirable. So that it becomes a man's duty to pursue and make after the best and choicest of everything, that he may not only employ his contemplation, but may also be improved by it. For as that color is most suitable to the eye whose freshness and pleasantness stimulates and strengthens the sight, so a man ought to apply his intellectual perception to such objects as, with the sense of delight, are apt to call it forth, and allure it to its own proper good and advantage.

Such objects we find in the acts of virtue, which also produce in the minds of mere readers about them, an emulation and eagerness that may lead them on to imitation. In other things there does not immediately follow upon the admiration and liking of the thing done, any strong desire of doing the like. Nay, many times, on the very contrary, when we are pleased with the work, we slight and set little by the workman or artist himself, as, for instance, in perfumes and purple dyes, we are taken with the things themselves well enough, but do not think dyers and perfumers otherwise than low and sordid people. It was not said amiss by Antisthenes, when people told him that one Ismenias was an excellent piper, "It may be so," said he, "but he is but a wretched human being, otherwise he would not have been an excellent piper." And king Philip, to the same purpose, told his son Alexander, who once at a merry-meeting played a piece of music charmingly and skillfully, "Are you not ashamed, son, to play so well?" For it is enough for a king, or prince to find leisure sometimes to hear others sing, and he does the muses quite honor enough when he pleases to be but present, while others engage in such exercises and trials of skill.

He who busies himself in mean occupations produces, in the very pains he takes about things of little or no use, an evidence against himself of his negligence and indisposition to what is really good. Nor did any generous and ingenuous young man, at the sight of the statue of Jupiter at Pisa, ever desire to be a Phidias, or, on seeing that of Juno at Argos, long to be a Polycletus, or feel induced by his pleasure in their poems to wish to be an Anacreon or Philetas or Archilochus. For it does not necessarily follow, that, if a piece of work please for its gracefulness, therefore he that wrought it deserves our admiration. Whence it is that neither do such things really profit or advantage the beholders, upon the sight of which no zeal arises for the imitation of them, nor any impulse or inclination, which may prompt any desire or endeavor of doing the like. But virtue, by the bare statement of its actions, can so affect men's minds as to create at once both admiration of the things done and desire to imitate the doers of them. The goods of fortune we would possess and would enjoy; those of virtue we long to practice and exercise; we are content to receive the former from others, the latter we wish others to experience from us. Moral good is a practical stimulus; it is no sooner seen, than it inspires an impulse to practice; and influences the mind and character not by a mere imitation which we look at, but, by the statement of the fact, creates a moral purpose which we form.

And so we have thought fit to spend our time and pains in writing of the lives of famous persons; and have composed this tenth book upon that subject, containing the life of Pericles, and that of Fabius Maximus, who carried on the war against Hannibal, men alike, as in their other virtues and good parts, so especially in their mild and upright temper and demeanor, and in that capacity to bear the cross-grained humors of their fellow-citizens and colleagues in office which made them both most useful and serviceable to the interests of their countries. Whether we take a right aim at our intended purpose, it is left to the reader to judge by what he shall here find.

Pericles was of the tribe Acamantis, and the township Cholargus, of the noblest birth both on his father's and mother's side. Xanthippus, his father, who defeated the king of Persia's generals in the battle at Mycale, took to wife Agariste, the grandchild of Clisthenes, who drove out the sons of Pisistratus, and nobly put an end to their tyrannical usurpation, and moreover made a body of laws, and settled a model of government admirably tempered and suited for the harmony and safety of the people.

His mother, being near her time, fancied in a dream that she was brought to bed of a lion, and a few days after was delivered of Pericles, in other respects perfectly formed, only his head was somewhat longish and out of proportion. For which reason almost all the images and statues that were made of him have the head covered with a helmet, the workmen apparently being willing not to expose him. The poets of Athens called him Schinocephalos, or squill-head, from schinos, a squill, or sea-onion. One of the comic poets, Cratinus, in the Chirons, tells us that —

> *Old Chronos once took queen Sedition to wife;*
> *Which two brought to life*
> *That tyrant far-famed,*
> *Whom the gods the supreme skull-compeller have named.*

And, in the Nemesis, addresses him —

> *Come, Jove, thou head of gods.*

And a second, Teleclides, says, that now, in embarrassment with political difficulties, he sits in the city —

> *Fainting underneath the load*
> *Of his own head; and now abroad,*
> *From his huge gallery of a pate,*
> *Sends forth trouble to the state.*

And a third, Eupolis, in the comedy called the Demi, in a series of questions about each of the demagogues, whom he makes in the play to come up from hell, upon Pericles being named last, exclaims —

> *And here by way of summary, now we've done,*

Behold, in brief, the heads of all in one.

The master that taught him music, most authors are agreed, was Damon (whose name, they say, ought to be pronounced with the first syllable short). Though Aristotle tells us that he was thoroughly practiced in all accomplishments of this kind by Pythoclides. Damon, it is not unlikely, being a sophist, out of policy, sheltered himself under the profession of music to conceal from people in general his skill in other things, and under this pretense attended Pericles, the young athlete of politics, so to say, as his training-master in these exercises. Damon's lyre, however, did not prove altogether a successful blind; he was banished the country by ostracism for ten years, as a dangerous intermeddler and a favorer of arbitrary power, and, by this means, gave the stage occasion to play upon him. As, for instance, Plato, the comic poet, introduces a character, who questions him —

Tell me, if you please,
Since you're the Chiron who taught Pericles.

Pericles, also, was a hearer of Zeno, the Eleatic, who treated of natural philosophy in the same manner as Parmenides did, but had also perfected himself in an art of his own for refuting and silencing opponents in argument; as Timon of Phlius describes it, —

Also the two-edged tongue of mighty Zeno, who,
Say what one would, could argue it untrue.

But he that saw most of Pericles, and furnished him most especially with a weight and grandeur of sense, superior to all arts of popularity, and in general gave him his elevation and sublimity of purpose and of character, was Anaxagoras of Clazomenae; whom the men of those times called by the name of Nous, that is, mind, or intelligence, whether in admiration of the great and extraordinary gift he displayed for the science of nature, or because that he was the first of the philosophers who did not refer the first ordering of the world to fortune or chance, nor to necessity or compulsion, but to a pure, unadulterated intelligence, which in all other existing mixed and compound things acts as a principle of discrimination, and of combination of like with like.

For this man, Pericles entertained an extraordinary esteem and admiration, and, filling himself with this lofty, and, as they call it, up-in-the-air sort of thought, derived hence not merely, as was natural, elevation of purpose and dignity of language, raised far above the base and dishonest buffooneries of mob-eloquence, but, besides this, a composure of countenance, and a serenity and calmness in all his movements, which no occurrence whilst he was speaking could disturb, a sustained and even tone of voice, and various other advantages of a similar kind, which produced the greatest effect on his hearers. Once, after being reviled and ill-spoken of all day long in his own hearing by some vile and abandoned fellow in the open marketplace, where he was engaged in the dispatch of some urgent affair, he continued his business in perfect silence, and in the evening returned home composedly, the man still dogging him at the heels, and pelting him all the way with abuse and foul language; and stepping into his house, it being by this time dark, he ordered one of his servants to take a light, and to go along with the man and see him safe home. Ion, it is true, the dramatic poet, says that Pericles's manner in company was somewhat over-assuming and pompous; and that into his high bearing there entered a good deal of slightingness and scorn of others; he reserves his commendation for Cimon's ease and pliancy and natural grace in society. Ion, however, who must needs make virtue, like a show of tragedies, include some comic scenes, we shall not altogether rely upon; Zeno used to bid those who called Pericles's gravity the affectation of a charlatan, to go and affect the like themselves; inasmuch as this mere counterfeiting might in time insensibly instill into them a real love and knowledge of those noble qualities.

Nor were these the only advantages which Pericles derived from Anaxagoras's acquaintance; he seems also to have become, by his instructions, superior to that superstition with which an ignorant wonder at appearances, for example, in the heavens possesses the minds of people unacquainted with their causes, eager for the supernatural, and excitable through an inexperience which the knowledge of natural causes removes, replacing wild and timid superstition by the good hope and assurance of an intelligent piety.

There is a story, that once Pericles had brought to him from a country farm of his, a ram's head with one horn, and that Lampon, the diviner, upon seeing the horn grow strong and solid out of the midst of the forehead, gave it as his judgment, that, there being at that time two potent factions, parties, or interests in the city, the one of Thucydides and the other of Pericles, the government would come about to that one of them in whose ground or estate this token or indication of fate had shown itself. But that Anaxagoras, cleaving the skull in sunder, showed to the bystanders that the brain had not filled up its natural place, but being oblong, like an egg, had collected from all parts of the vessel which contained it, in a point to that place from whence the root of the horn took its rise. And that, for that time, Anaxagoras was much admired for his explanation by those that were present; and Lampon no less a little while after, when Thucydides was overpowered, and the whole affairs of the state and government came into the hands of Pericles.

And yet, in my opinion, it is no absurdity to say that they were both in the right, both natural philosopher and diviner, one justly detecting the cause of this event, by which it was produced, the other the end for which it was designed. For it was the business of the one to find out and give an account of what it was made, and in what manner and by what means it grew as it did; and of the other to foretell to what end and purpose it was so made, and what it might mean or portend. Those who say that to find out the cause of a prodigy is in effect to destroy its supposed signification as such, do not take notice that, at the same time, together with divine prodigies, they also do away with signs and signals of human art and concert, as, for instance, the clashings of quoits, fire-beacons, and the shadows on sun-dials, every one of which things has its cause, and by that cause and contrivance is a sign of something else. But these are subjects, perhaps, that would better befit another place.

Pericles, while yet but a young man, stood in considerable apprehension of the people, as he was thought in face and figure to be very like the tyrant Pisistratus, and those of great age remarked upon the sweetness of his voice, and his volubility and rapidity in speaking, and were struck with amazement at the resemblance. Reflecting, too, that he had a considerable estate, and was descended of a noble family, and had friends of great influence, he was fearful all this might bring him to be banished as a dangerous person; and for this reason meddled not at all with state affairs, but in military service showed himself of a brave and intrepid nature. But when Aristides was now dead, and Themistocles driven out, and Cimon was for the most part kept abroad by the expeditions he made in parts out of Greece, Pericles, seeing things in this posture, now advanced and took his side, not with the rich and few, but with the many and poor, contrary to his natural bent, which was far from democratical; but, most likely, fearing he might fall under suspicion of aiming at arbitrary power, and seeing Cimon on the side of the aristocracy, and much beloved by the better and more distinguished people, he joined the party of the people, with a view at once both to secure himself and procure means against Cimon.

He immediately entered, also, on quite a new course of life and management of his time. For he was never seen to walk in any street but that which led to the marketplace and the council-hall, and he avoided invitations of friends to supper, and all friendly visiting and intercourse whatever; in all the time he had to do with the public, which was not a little, he was never known to have gone to any of his friends to a supper, except that once when his near kinsman Euryptolemus married, he remained present till the ceremony of the drink-offering, and then immediately rose from table and went his way. For these friendly meetings are very quick to defeat any assumed superiority, and in intimate familiarity an exterior of gravity is hard to maintain. Real excellence, indeed, is most recognized when most openly looked into; and in really good men, nothing which meets the eyes of external observers so truly deserves their admiration, as their daily common life does that of their nearer friends. Pericles, however, to avoid any feeling of commonness, or any satiety on the part of the people, presented himself at intervals only, not speaking to every business, nor at all times coming into the assembly, but, as Critolaus says, reserving himself, like the Salaminian galley, for great occasions, while matters of lesser importance were dispatched by friends or other speakers under his direction. And of this number we are told Ephialtes made one, who broke the power of the council of Areopagus, giving the people, according to Plato's expression, so copious and so strong a draught of liberty, that, growing wild and unruly, like an unmanageable horse, it, as the comic poets say, —

" — *got beyond all keeping in, Champing at Euboea, and among the islands leaping in.*"

The style of speaking most consonant to his form of life and the dignity of his views he found, so to say, in the tones of that instrument with which Anaxagoras had furnished him; of his teaching he continually availed himself, and deepened the colors of rhetoric with the dye of natural science. For having, in addition to his great natural genius, attained, by the study of nature, to use the words of the divine Plato, this height of intelligence, and this universal consummating power, and drawing hence whatever might be of advantage to him in the art of speaking, he showed himself far superior to all others. Upon which account, they say, he had his nickname given him, though some are of opinion he was named the Olympian from the public buildings with which he adorned the city; and others again, from his great power in public affairs, whether of war or peace. Nor is it unlikely that the confluence of many attributes may have conferred it on him. However, the comedies represented at the time, which, both in good earnest and in merriment, let fly many hard words at him, plainly show that he got that appellation especially from his speaking; they speak of his "thundering and lightning" when he harangued the people, and of his wielding a dreadful thunderbolt in his tongue.

A saying also of Thucydides, the son of Melesias, stands on record, spoken by him by way of pleasantry upon Pericles's dexterity. Thucydides was one of the noble and distinguished citizens, and had been his greatest opponent; and, when Archidamus, the king of the Lacedaemonians, asked him whether he or Pericles were the better wrestler, he made this answer: "When I," said he, "have thrown him and given him a fair fall, by persisting that he had no fall, he gets the better of me, and makes the bystanders, in spite of their own eyes, believe him." The truth, however, is, that Pericles himself was very careful what and how he was to speak, insomuch that, whenever he went up to the hustings, he prayed the gods that no one word might unawares slip from him unsuitable to the matter and the occasion.

He has left nothing in writing behind him, except some decrees; and there are but very few of his sayings recorded; one, for example, is, that he said Aegina must, like a gathering in a man's eye, be removed from Piraeus; and another, that he said he saw already war moving on its way towards them out of Peloponnesus. Again, when on a time Sophocles, who was his fellow-commissioner in the generalship, was going on board with him, and praised the beauty of a youth they met with in the way to the ship, "Sophocles," said he, "a general ought not only to have clean hands, but also clean eyes." And Stesimbrotus tells us, that, in his encomium on those who fell in battle at Samos, he said they were become immortal, as the gods were. "For," said he, "we do not see them themselves, but only by the honors we pay them, and by the benefits they do us, attribute to them immortality; and the like attributes belong also to those that die in the service of their country."

Since Thucydides describes the rule of Pericles as an aristocratical government, that went by the name of a democracy, but was, indeed, the supremacy of a single great man, while many others say, on the contrary, that by him the common people were first encouraged and led on to such evils as appropriations of subject territory; allowances for attending theaters, payments for performing public duties, and by these bad habits were, under the influence of his public measures, changed from a sober, thrifty people, that maintained themselves by their own labors, to lovers of expense, intemperance, and license, let us examine the cause of this change by the actual matters of fact.

At the first, as has been said, when he set himself against Cimon's great authority, he did caress the people. Finding himself come short of his competitor in wealth and money, by which advantages the other was enabled to take care of the poor, inviting every day some one or other of the citizens that was in want to supper, and bestowing clothes on the aged people, and breaking down the hedges and enclosures of his grounds, that all that would might freely gather what fruit they pleased, Pericles, thus outdone in popular arts, by the advice of one Damonides of Oea, as Aristotle states, turned to the distribution of the public moneys; and in a short time having bought the people over, what with moneys allowed for shows and for service on juries, and what with other forms of pay and largess, he made use of them against the council of Areopagus, of which he himself was no member, as having never been appointed by lot either chief archon, or lawgiver, or king, or captain. For from of old these offices were conferred on persons by lot, and they who had acquitted themselves duly in the discharge of them were advanced to the court of Areopagus. And so Pericles, having secured his power and interest with the populace, directed the exertions of his party against this council with such success, that most of those causes and matters which had been used to be tried there, were, by the agency of Ephialtes, removed from its cognizance, Cimon, also, was banished by ostracism as a favorer of the Lacedaemonians and a hater of the people, though in wealth and noble birth he was among the first, and had won several most glorious victories over the barbarians, and had filled the city with money and spoils of war; as is recorded in the history of his life. So vast an authority had Pericles obtained among the people.

The ostracism was limited by law to ten years; but the Lacedaemonians, in the mean time, entering with a great army into the territory of Tanagra, and the Athenians going out against them, Cimon, coming from his banishment before his time was out, put himself in arms and array with those of his fellow-citizens that were of his own tribe, and desired by his deeds to wipe off the suspicion of his favoring the Lacedaemonians, by venturing his own person along with his country-men. But Pericles's friends, gathering in a body, forced him to retire as a banished man. For which cause also Pericles seems to have exerted himself more in that than in any battle, and to have been conspicuous above all for his exposure of himself to danger. All Cimon's friends, also, to a man, fell together side by side, whom Pericles had accused with him of taking part with the Lacedaemonians. Defeated in this battle on their own frontiers, and expecting a new and perilous attack with return of spring, the Athenians now felt regret and sorrow for the loss of Cimon, and repentance for their expulsion of him. Pericles, being sensible of their feelings, did not hesitate or delay to gratify it, and himself made the motion for recalling him home. He, upon his return, concluded a peace betwixt the two cities; for the Lacedaemonians entertained as kindly feelings towards him as they did the reverse towards Pericles and the other popular leaders.

Yet some there are who say that Pericles did not propose the order for Cimon's return till some private articles of agreement had been made between them, and this by means of Elpinice, Cimon's sister; that Cimon, namely, should go out to sea with a fleet of two hundred ships, and be commander-in-chief abroad, with a design to reduce the king of Persia's territories, and that Pericles should have the power at home.

This Elpinice, it was thought, had before this time procured some favor for her brother Cimon at Pericles's hands, and induced him to be more remiss and gentle in urging the charge when Cimon was tried for his life; for Pericles was one of the committee appointed by the commons to plead against him. And when Elpinice came and besought him in her brother's behalf, he answered, with a smile, "O Elpinice, you are too old a woman to undertake such business as this." But, when he appeared to impeach him, he stood up but once to speak, merely to acquit himself of his commission, and went out of court, having done Cimon the least prejudice of any of his accusers.

How, then, can one believe Idomeneus, who charges Pericles as if he had by treachery procured the murder of Ephialtes, the popular statesman, one who was his friend, and of his own party in all his political course, out of jealousy, forsooth, and envy of his great reputation? This historian, it seems, having raked up these stories, I know not whence, has befouled with them a man who, perchance, was not altogether free from fault or blame, but yet had a noble spirit, and a soul that was bent on honor; and where such qualities are, there can no such cruel and brutal passion find harbor or gain admittance. As to Ephialtes, the truth of the story, as Aristotle has told it, is this: that having made himself formidable to the oligarchical party, by being an uncompromising asserter of the people's rights in calling to account and prosecuting those who any way wronged them, his enemies, lying in wait for him, by the means of Aristodicus the Tanagraean, privately dispatched him.

Cimon, while he was admiral, ended his days in the Isle of Cyprus. And the aristocratical party, seeing that Pericles was already before this grown to be the greatest and foremost man of all the city, but nevertheless wishing there should be somebody set up against him, to blunt and turn the edge of his power, that it might not altogether prove a monarchy, put forward Thucydides of Alopece, a discreet person, and a near kinsman of Cimon's, to conduct the opposition against him; who, indeed, though less skilled in warlike affairs than Cimon was, yet was better versed in speaking and political business, and keeping close guard in the city, and engaging with Pericles on the hustings, in a short time brought the government to an equality of parties. For he would not suffer those who were called the honest and good (persons of worth and distinction) to be scattered up and down and mix themselves and be lost among the populace, as formerly, diminishing and obscuring their superiority amongst the masses; but taking them apart by themselves and uniting them in one body, by their combined weight he was able, as it were upon the balance, to make a counter-poise to the other party.

For, indeed, there was from the beginning a sort of concealed split, or seam, as it might be in a piece of iron, marking the different popular and aristocratical tendencies; but the open rivalry and contention of these two opponents made the gash deep, and severed the city into the two parties of the people and the few. And so Pericles, at that time more than at any other, let loose the reins to the people, and made his policy subservient to their pleasure, contriving continually to have some great public show or solemnity, some banquet, or some procession or other in the town to please them, coaxing his countrymen like children, with such delights and pleasures as were not, however, unedifying. Besides that every year he sent out threescore galleys, on board of which there went numbers of the citizens, who were in pay eight months, learning at the same time and practicing the art of seamanship.

He sent, moreover, a thousand of them into the Chersonese as planters, to share the land among them by lot, and five hundred more into the isle of Naxos, and half that number to Andros, a thousand into Thrace to dwell among the Bisaltae, and others into Italy, when the city Sybaris, which now was called Thurii, was to be repeopled. And this he did to ease and discharge the city of an idle, and, by reason of their idleness, a busy, meddling crowd of people; and at the same time to meet the necessities and restore the fortunes of the poor townsmen, and to intimidate, also, and check their allies from attempting any change, by posting such garrisons, as it were, in the midst of them.

That which gave most pleasure and ornament to the city of Athens, and the greatest admiration and even astonishment to all strangers, and that which now is Greece's only evidence that the power she boasts of and her ancient wealth are no romance or idle story, was his construction of the public and sacred buildings. Yet this was that of all his actions in the government which his enemies most looked askance upon and caviled at in the popular assemblies, crying out how that the commonwealth of Athens had lost its reputation and was ill-spoken of abroad for removing the common treasure of the Greeks from the isle of Delos into their own custody; and how that their fairest excuse for so doing, namely, that they took it away for fear the barbarians should seize it, and on purpose to secure it in a safe place, this Pericles had made unavailable, and how that "Greece cannot but resent it as an insufferable affront, and consider herself to be tyrannized over openly, when she sees the treasure, which was contributed by her upon a necessity for the war, wantonly lavished out by us upon our city, to gild her all over, and to adorn and set her forth, as it were some vain woman, hung round with precious stones and figures and temples, which cost a world of money."

Pericles, on the other hand, informed the people, that they were in no way obliged to give any account of those moneys to their allies, so long as they maintained their defense, and kept off the barbarians from attacking them; while in the meantime they did not so much as supply one horse or man or ship, but only found money for the service; "which money," said he, "is not theirs that give it, but theirs that receive it, if so be they perform the conditions upon which they receive it." And that it was good reason, that, now the city was sufficiently provided and stored with all things necessary for the war, they should convert the overplus of its wealth to such undertakings, as would hereafter, when completed, give them eternal honor, and, for the present, while in process, freely supply all the inhabitants with plenty. With their variety of workmanship and of occasions for service, which summon all arts and trades and require all hands to be employed about them, they do actually put the whole city, in a manner, into state-pay; while at the same time she is both beautified and maintained by herself. For as those who are of age and strength for war are provided for and maintained in the armaments abroad by their pay out of the public stock, so, it being his desire and design that the undisciplined mechanic multitude that stayed at home should not go without their share of public salaries, and yet should not have them given them for sitting still and doing nothing, to that end he thought fit to bring in among them, with the approbation of the people, these vast projects of buildings and designs of works, that would be of some continuance before they were finished, and would give employment to numerous arts, so that the part of the people that stayed at home might, no less than those that were at sea or in garrisons or on expeditions, have a fair and just occasion of receiving the benefit and having their share of the public moneys.

The materials were stone, brass, ivory, gold, ebony cypress-wood; and the arts or trades that wrought and fashioned them were smiths and carpenters, molders, founders and braziers, stone-cutters, dyers, goldsmiths, ivory-workers, painters, embroiderers, turners; those again that conveyed them to the town for use, merchants and mariners and ship-masters by sea, and by land, cartwrights, cattle-breeders, waggoners, rope-makers, flax-workers, shoemakers and leather-dressers, roadmakers, miners. And every trade in the same nature, as a captain in an army has his particular company of soldiers under him, had its own hired company of journeymen and laborers belonging to it banded together as in array, to be as it were the instrument and body for the performance of the service. Thus, to say all in a word, the occasions and services of these public works distributed plenty through every age and condition.

As then grew the works up, no less stately in size than exquisite in form, the workmen striving to outvie the material and the design with the beauty of their workmanship, yet the most wonderful thing of all was the rapidity of their execution. Undertakings, any one of which singly might have required, they thought, for their completion, several successions and ages of men, were every one of them accomplished in the height and prime of one man's political service. Although they say, too, that Zeuxis once, having heard Agatharchus the painter boast of dispatching his work with speed and ease, replied, "I take a long time." For ease and speed in doing a thing do not give the work lasting solidity or exactness of beauty; the expenditure of time allowed to a man's pains beforehand for the production of a thing is repaid by way of interest with a vital force for its preservation when once produced. For which reason Pericles's works are especially admired, as having been made quickly, to last long. For every particular piece of his work was immediately, even at that time, for its beauty and elegance, antique; and yet in its vigor and freshness looks to this day as if it were just executed. There is a sort of bloom of newness upon those works of his, preserving them from the touch of time, as if they had some perennial spirit and undying vitality mingled in the composition of them.

Phidias had the oversight of all the works, and was surveyor-general, though upon the various portions other great masters and workmen were employed. For Callicrates and Ictinus built the Parthenon; the chapel at Eleusis, where the mysteries were celebrated, was begun by Coroebus, who erected the pillars that stand upon the floor or pavement, and joined them to the architraves; and after his death Metagenes of Xypete added the frieze and the upper line of columns; Xenocles of Cholargus roofed or arched the lantern on the top of the temple of Castor and Pollux; and the long wall, which Socrates says he himself heard Pericles propose to the people, was undertaken by Callicrates. This work

> *Cratinus ridicules, as long in finishing, —*

'Tis long since Pericles, if words would do it, Talk'd up the wall; yet adds not one mite to it.

The Odeum, or music-room, which in its interior was full of seats and ranges of pillars, and outside had its roof made to slope and descend from one single point at the top, was constructed, we are told, in imitation of the king of Persia's Pavilion; this likewise by Pericles's order; which Cratinus again, in his comedy called The Thracian Women, made an occasion of raillery, —

> *So, we see here,*
> *Jupiter Long-pate Pericles appear,*
> *Since ostracism time, he's laid aside his head,*
> *And wears the new Odeum in its stead.*

Pericles, also, eager for distinction, then first obtained the decree for a contest in musical skill to be held yearly at the Panathenaea, and he himself, being chosen judge, arranged the order and method in which the competitors should sing and play on the flute and on the harp. And both at that time, and at other times also, they sat in this music-room to see and hear all such trials of skill.

The propylaea, or entrances to the Acropolis, were finished in five years' time, Mnesicles being the principal architect. A strange accident happened in the course of building, which showed that the goddess was not averse to the work, but was aiding and cooperating to bring it to perfection. One of the artificers, the quickest and the handiest workman among them all, with a slip of his foot fell down from a great height, and lay in a miserable condition, the physicians having no hopes of his recovery. When Pericles was in distress about this, Minerva appeared to him at night in a dream, and ordered a course of treatment, which he applied, and in a short time and with great ease cured the man. And upon this occasion it was that he set up a brass statue of Minerva, surnamed Health, in the citadel near the altar, which they say was there before. But it was Phidias who wrought the goddess's image in gold, and he has his name inscribed on the pedestal as the workman of it; and indeed the whole work in a manner was under his charge, and he had, as we have said already, the oversight over all the artists and workmen, through Pericles's friendship for him; and this, indeed, made him much envied, and his patron shamefully slandered with stories, as if Phidias were in the habit of receiving, for Pericles's use, freeborn women that came to see the works. The comic writers of the town, when they had got hold of this story, made much of it, and bespattered him with all the ribaldry they could invent, charging him falsely with the wife of Menippus, one who was his friend and served as lieutenant under him in the wars; and with the birds kept by Pyrilampes, an acquaintance of Pericles, who, they pretended, used to give presents of peacocks to Pericles's female friends. And how can one wonder at any number of strange assertions from men whose whole lives were devoted to mockery, and who were ready at any time to sacrifice the reputation of their superiors to vulgar envy and spite, as to some evil genius, when even Stesimbrotus the Thasian has dared to lay to the charge of Pericles a monstrous and fabulous piece of criminality with his son's wife? So very difficult a matter is it to trace and find out the truth of anything by history, when, on the one hand, those who afterwards write it find long periods of time intercepting their view, and, on the other hand, the contemporary records of any actions and lives, partly through envy and ill-will, partly through favor and flattery, pervert and distort truth.

When the orators, who sided with Thucydides and his party, were at one time crying out, as their custom was, against Pericles, as one who squandered away the public money, and made havoc of the state revenues, he rose in the open assembly and put the question to the people, whether they thought that he had laid out much; and they saying, "Too much, a great deal." "Then," said he, "since it is so, let the cost not go to your account, but to mine; and let the inscription upon the buildings stand in my name." When they heard him say thus, whether it were out of a surprise to see the greatness of his spirit, or out of emulation of the glory of the works, they cried aloud, bidding him to spend on, and lay out what he thought fit from the public purse, and to spare no cost, till all were finished.

At length, coming to a final contest with Thucydides, which of the two should ostracize the other out of the country, and having gone through this peril, he threw his antagonist out, and broke up the confederacy that had been organized against him. So that now all schism and division being at an end, and the city brought to evenness and unity, he got all Athens and all affairs that pertained to the Athenians into his own hands, their tributes, their armies, and their galleys, the islands, the sea, and their wide-extended power, partly over other Greeks and partly over barbarians, and all that empire, which they possessed, founded and fortified upon subject nations and royal friendships and alliances.

After this he was no longer the same man he had been before, nor as tame and gentle and familiar as formerly with the populace, so as readily to yield to their pleasures and to comply with the desires of the multitude, as a steersman shifts with the winds. Quitting that loose, remiss, and, in some cases, licentious court of the popular will, he turned those soft and flowery modulations to the austerity of aristocratical and regal rule; and employing this uprightly and undeviatingly for the country's best interests, he was able generally to lead the people along, with their own wills and consents, by persuading and showing them what was to be done; and sometimes, too, urging and pressing them forward extremely against their will, he made them, whether they would or no, yield submission to what was for their advantage. In which, to say the truth, he did but like a skillful physician, who, in a complicated and chronic disease, as he sees occasion, at one while allows his patient the moderate use of such things as please him, at another while gives him keen pains and drugs to work the cure. For there arising and growing up, as was natural, all manner of distempered feelings among a people which had so vast a command and dominion, he alone, as a great master, knowing how to handle and deal fitly with each one of them, and, in an especial manner, making that use of hopes and fears, as his two chief rudders, with the one to check the career of their confidence at any time, with the other to raise them up and cheer them when under any discouragement, plainly showed by this, that rhetoric, or the art of speaking, is, in Plato's language, the government of the souls of men, and that her chief business is to address the affections and passions, which are as it were the strings and keys to the soul, and require a skillful and careful touch to be played on as they should be. The source of this predominance was not barely his power of language, but, as Thucydides assures us, the reputation of his life, and the confidence felt in his character; his manifest freedom from every kind of corruption, and superiority to all considerations of money. Notwithstanding he had made the city Athens, which was great of itself, as great and rich as can be imagined, and though he were himself in power and interest more than equal to many kings and absolute rulers, who some of them also bequeathed by will their power to their children, he, for his part, did not make the patrimony his father left him greater than it was by one drachma.

Thucydides, indeed, gives a plain statement of the greatness of his power; and the comic poets, in their spiteful manner, more than hint at it, styling his companions and friends the new Pisistratidae, and calling on him to abjure any intention of usurpation, as one whose eminence was too great to be any longer proportionable to and compatible with a democracy or popular government. And Teleclides says the

Athenians had surrendered up to him —

The tribute of the cities, and with them, the cities too, to do with them as he pleases, and undo; To build up, if he likes, stone walls around a town; and again, if so he likes, to pull them down; Their treaties and alliances, power, empire, peace, and war, their wealth and their success forevermore.

Nor was all this the luck of some happy occasion; nor was it the mere bloom and grace of a policy that flourished for a season; but having for forty years together maintained the first place among statesmen such as Ephialtes and Leocrates and Myronides and Cimon and Tolmides and Thucydides were, after the defeat and banishment of Thucydides, for no less than fifteen years longer, in the exercise of one continuous unintermitted command in the office, to which he was annually reelected, of General, he preserved his integrity unspotted; though otherwise he was not altogether idle or careless in looking after his pecuniary advantage; his paternal estate, which of right belonged to him, he so ordered that it might neither through negligence be wasted or lessened, nor yet, being so full of business as he was, cost him any great trouble or time with taking care of it; and put it into such a way of management as he thought to be the most easy for himself, and the most exact. All his yearly products and profits he sold together in a lump, and supplied his household needs afterward by buying everything that he or his family wanted out of the market. Upon which account, his children, when they grew to age, were not well pleased with his management, and the women that lived with him were treated with little cost, and complained of this way of housekeeping, where everything was ordered and set down from day to day, and reduced to the greatest exactness; since there was not there, as is usual in a great family and a plentiful estate, any thing to spare, or over and above; but all that went out or came in, all disbursements and all receipts, proceeded as it were by number and measure. His manager in all this was a single servant, Evangelus by name, a man either naturally gifted or instructed by Pericles so as to excel every one in this art of domestic economy.

All this, in truth, was very little in harmony with Anaxagoras's wisdom; if, indeed, it be true that he, by a kind of divine impulse and greatness of spirit, voluntarily quitted his house, and left his land to lie fallow and to be grazed by sheep like a common. But the life of a contemplative philosopher and that of an active statesman are, I presume, not the same thing; for the one merely employs, upon great and good objects of thought, an intelligence that requires no aid of instruments nor supply of any external materials; whereas the other, who tempers and applies his virtue to human uses, may have occasion for affluence, not as a matter of mere necessity, but as a noble thing; which was Pericles's case, who relieved numerous poor citizens.

However, there is a story, that Anaxagoras himself, while Pericles was taken up with public affairs, lay neglected, and that, now being grown old, he wrapped himself up with a resolution to die for want of food; which being by chance brought to Pericles's ear, he was horror-struck, and instantly ran thither, and used all the arguments and entreaties he could to him, lamenting not so much Anaxagoras's condition as his own, should he lose such a counselor as he had found him to be; and that, upon this, Anaxagoras unfolded his robe, and showing himself, made answer: "Pericles," said he, "even those who have occasion for a lamp supply it with oil."

The Lacedaemonians beginning to show themselves troubled at the growth of the Athenian power, Pericles, on the other hand, to elevate the people's spirit yet more, and to raise them to the thought of great actions, proposed a decree, to summon all the Greeks in what part soever, whether of Europe or Asia, every city, little as well as great, to send their deputies to Athens to a general assembly, or convention, there to consult and advise concerning the Greek temples which the barbarians had burnt down, and the sacrifices which were due from them upon vows they had made to their gods for the safety of Greece when they fought against the barbarians; and also concerning the navigation of the sea, that they might henceforward all of them pass to and fro and trade securely, and be at peace among themselves.

Upon this errand, there were twenty men, of such as were above fifty years of age, sent by commission; five to summon the Ionians and Dorians in Asia, and the islanders as far as Lesbos and Rhodes; five to visit all the places in the Hellespont and Thrace, up to Byzantium; and other five besides these to go to Boeotia and Phocis and Peloponnesus, and from hence to pass through the Locrians over to the neighboring continent, as far as Acarnania and Ambracia; and the rest to take their course through Euboea to the Oetaeans and the Malian Gulf, and to the Achaeans of Phthiotis and the Thessalians; all of them to treat with the people as they passed, and to persuade them to come and take their part in the debates for settling the peace and jointly regulating the affairs of Greece.

Nothing was effected, nor did the cities meet by their deputies, as was desired; the Lacedaemonians, as it is said, crossing the design underhand, and the attempt being disappointed and baffled first in Peloponnesus. I thought fit, however, to introduce the mention of it, to show the spirit of the man and the greatness of his thoughts.

In his military conduct, he gained a great reputation for wariness; he would not by his good-will engage in any fight which had much uncertainty or hazard; he did not envy the glory of generals whose rash adventures fortune favored with brilliant success, however they were admired by others; nor did he think them worthy his imitation, but always used to say to his citizens that, so far as lay in his power, they should continue immortal, and live forever. Seeing Tolmides, the son of Tolmaeus, upon the confidence of his former successes, and flushed with the honor his military actions had procured him, making preparation to attack the Boeotians in their own country, when there was no likely opportunity, and that he had prevailed with the bravest and most enterprising of the youth to enlist themselves as volunteers in the service, who besides his other force made up a thousand, he endeavored to withhold him and to advise him from it in the public assembly, telling him in a memorable saying of his, which still goes about, that, if he would not take Pericles's advice, yet he would not do amiss to wait and be ruled by time, the wisest counselor of all. This saying, at that time, was but slightly commended; but within a few days after, when news was brought that Tolmides himself had been defeated and slain in battle near Coronea, and that many brave citizens had fallen with him, it gained him great repute as well as good-will among the people, for wisdom and for love of his countrymen.

But of all his expeditions, that to the Chersonese gave most satisfaction and pleasure, having proved the safety of the Greeks who inhabited there. For not only by carrying along with him a thousand fresh citizens of Athens he gave new strength and vigor to the cities, but also by belting the neck of land, which joins the peninsula to the continent, with bulwarks and forts from sea to sea, he put a stop to the inroads of the Thracians, who lay all about the Chersonese, and closed the door against a continual and grievous war, with which that country had been long harassed, lying exposed to the encroachments and influx of barbarous neighbors, and groaning under the evils of a predatory population both upon and within its borders.

Nor was he less admired and talked of abroad for his sailing round the Peloponnesus, having set out from Pegae, or The Fountains, the port of Megara, with a hundred galleys. For he not only laid waste the sea-coast, as Tolmides had done before, but also, advancing far up into main land with the soldiers he had on board, by the terror of his appearance drove many within their walls; and at Nemea, with main force, routed and raised a trophy over the Sicyonians, who stood their ground and joined battle with him. And having taken on board a supply of soldiers into the galleys, out of Achaia, then in league with Athens he crossed with the fleet to the opposite continent, and, sailing along by the mouth of the river Achelous overran Acarnania, and shut up the Oeniadae within their city walls, and having ravaged and wasted their country, weighed anchor for home with the double advantage of having shown himself formidable to his enemies, and at the same time safe and energetic to his fellow-citizens; for there was not so much as any chance-miscarriage that happened, the whole voyage through, to those who were under his charge.

Entering also the Euxine Sea with a large and finely equipped fleet, he obtained for the Greek cities any new arrangements they wanted, and entered into friendly relations with them; and to the barbarous nations, and kings and chiefs round about them, displayed the greatness of the power of the Athenians, their perfect ability and confidence to sail wherever they had a mind, and to bring the whole sea under their control. He left the Sinopians thirteen ships of war, with soldiers under the command of Lamachus, to assist them against Timesileus the tyrant; and when he and his accomplices had been thrown out, obtained a decree that six hundred of the Athenians that were willing should sail to Sinope and plant themselves there with the Sinopians, sharing among them the houses and land which the tyrant and his party had previously held.

But in other things he did not comply with the giddy impulses of the citizens, nor quit his own resolutions to follow their fancies, when, carried away with the thought of their strength and great success, they were eager to interfere again in Egypt, and to disturb the king of Persia's maritime dominions. Nay, there were a good many who were, even then, possessed with that unblessed and inauspicious passion for Sicily, which afterward the orators of Alcibiades's party blew up into a flame. There were some also who dreamt of Tuscany and of Carthage, and not without plausible reason in their present large dominion and the prosperous course of their affairs.

But Pericles curbed this passion for foreign conquest, and unsparingly pruned and cut down their ever busy fancies for a multitude of undertakings; and directed their power for the most part to securing and consolidating what they had already got, supposing it would be quite enough for them to do, if they could keep the Lacedaemonians in check; to whom he entertained all along a sense of opposition; which, as upon many other occasions, so he particularly showed by what he did in the time of the holy war. The Lacedaemonians, having gone with an army to Delphi, restored Apollo's temple, which the Phocians had got into their possession, to the Delphians; immediately after their departure, Pericles, with another army, came and restored the Phocians. And the Lacedaemonians having engraven the record of their privilege of consulting the oracle before others, which the Delphians gave them, upon the forehead of the brazen wolf which stands there, he, also, having received from the Phocians the like privilege for the Athenians, had it cut upon the same wolf of brass on his right side.

That he did well and wisely in thus restraining the exertions of the Athenians within the compass of Greece, the events themselves that happened afterward bore sufficient witness. For, in the first place, the Euboeans revolted, against whom he passed over with forces; and then, immediately after, news came that the Megarians were turned their enemies, and a hostile army was upon the borders of Attica, under the conduct of Plistoanax, king of the Lacedaemonians. Wherefore Pericles came with his army back again in all haste out of Euboea, to meet the war which threatened at home; and did not venture to engage a numerous and brave army eager for battle; but perceiving that Plistoanax was a very young man, and governed himself mostly by the counsel and advice of Cleandrides, whom the ephors had sent with him, by reason of his youth, to be a kind of guardian and assistant to him, he privately made trial of this man's integrity, and, in a short time, having corrupted him with money, prevailed with him to withdraw the Peloponnesians out of Attica. When the army had retired and dispersed into their several states, the

Lacedaemonians in anger fined their king in so large a sum of money, that, unable to pay it, he quitted Lacedaemon; while Cleandrides fled, and had sentence of death passed upon him in his absence. This was the father of Gylippus, who overpowered the Athenians in Sicily. And it seems that this covetousness was an hereditary disease transmitted from father to son; for Gylippus also afterwards was caught in foul practices, and expelled from Sparta for it. But this we have told at large in the account of Lysander.

When Pericles, in giving up his accounts of this expedition, stated a disbursement of ten talents, as laid out upon fit occasion, the people, without any question, nor troubling themselves to investigate the mystery, freely allowed of it. And some historians, in which number is Theophrastus the philosopher, have given it as a truth that Pericles every year used to send privately the sum of ten talents to Sparta, with which he complimented those in office, to keep off the war; not to purchase peace neither, but time, that he might prepare at leisure, and be the better able to carry on war hereafter.

Immediately after this, turning his forces against the revolters, and passing over into the island of Euboea with fifty sail of ships and five thousand men in arms, he reduced their cities, and drove out the citizens of the Chalcidians, called Hippobotae, horse-feeders, the chief persons for wealth and reputation among them; and removing all the Histiaeans out of the country, brought in a plantation of Athenians in their room; making them his one example of severity, because they had captured an Attic ship and killed all on board.

After this, having made a truce between the Athenians and Lacedaemonians for thirty years, he ordered, by public decree, the expedition against the Isle of Samos, on the ground, that, when they were bid to leave off their war with the Milesians, they had not complied. And as these measures against the Samians are thought to have been taken to please Aspasia, this may be a fit point for inquiry about the woman, what art or charming faculty she had that enabled her to captivate, as she did, the greatest statesmen, and to give the philosophers occasion to speak so much about her, and that, too, not to her disparagement. That she was a Milesian by birth, the daughter of Axiochus, is a thing acknowledged. And they say it was in emulation of Thargelia, a courtesan of the old Ionian times, that she made her addresses to men of great power. Thargelia was a great beauty, extremely charming, and at the same time sagacious; she had numerous suitors among the Greeks, and brought all who had to do with her over to the Persian interest, and by their means, being men of the greatest power and station, sowed the seeds of the Median faction up and down in several cities. Aspasia, some say, was courted and caressed by Pericles upon account of her knowledge and skill in politics. Socrates himself would sometimes go to visit her, and some of his acquaintance with him; and those who frequented her company would carry their wives with them to listen to her. Her occupation was any thing but creditable, her house being a home for young courtesans. Aeschines tells us also, that Lysicles, a sheep-dealer, a man of low birth and character, by keeping Aspasia company after Pericles's death, came to be a chief man in Athens. And in Plato's Menexenus, though we do not take the introduction as quite serious, still thus much seems to be historical, that she had the repute of being resorted to by many of the Athenians for instruction in the art of speaking. Pericles's inclination for her seems, however, to have rather proceeded from the passion of love. He had a wife that was near of kin to him, who had been married first to Hipponicus, by whom she had Callias, surnamed the Rich; and also she brought Pericles, while she lived with him, two sons, Xanthippus and Paralus. Afterwards, when they did not well agree nor like to live together, he parted with her, with her own consent, to another man, and himself took Aspasia, and loved her with wonderful affection; every day, both as he went out and as he came in from the marketplace, he saluted and kissed her.

In the comedies she goes by the nicknames of the new Omphale and Deianira, and again is styled Juno. Cratinus, in downright terms, calls her a harlot.

> *To find him a Juno the goddess of lust*
> *Bore that harlot past shame,*
> *Aspasia by name.*

It should seem, also, that he had a son by her; Eupolis, in his Demi, introduced Pericles asking after his safety, and Myronides replying,

"My son?" "He lives; a man he had been long, But that the harlot-mother did him wrong."

Aspasia, they say, became so celebrated and renowned, that Cyrus also, who made war against Artaxerxes for the Persian monarchy, gave her whom he loved the best of all his concubines the name of Aspasia, who before that was called Milto. She was a Phocaean by birth, the daughter of one Hermotimus, and, when Cyrus fell in battle, was carried to the king, and had great influence at court. These things coming into my memory as I am writing this story, it would be unnatural for me to omit them.

Pericles, however, was particularly charged with having proposed to the assembly the war against the Samians, from favor to the Milesians, upon the entreaty of Aspasia. For the two states were at war for the possession of Priene; and the Samians, getting the better, refused to lay down their arms and to have the controversy betwixt them decided by arbitration before the Athenians. Pericles, therefore, fitting out a fleet, went and broke up the oligarchical government at Samos, and, taking fifty of the principal men of the town as hostages, and as many of their children, sent them to the isle of Lemnos, there to be kept, though he had offers, as some relate, of a talent a piece for himself from each one of the hostages, and of many other presents from those who were anxious not to have a democracy. Moreover, Pissuthnes the Persian, one of the king's lieutenants, bearing some good-will to the Samians, sent him ten thousand pieces of gold to excuse the city. Pericles, however, would receive none of all this; but after he had taken that course with the Samians which he thought fit, and set up a democracy among them, sailed back to Athens.

But they, however, immediately revolted, Pissuthnes having privily got away their hostages for them, and provided them with means for the war. Whereupon Pericles came out with a fleet a second time against them, and found them not idle nor slinking away, but manfully resolved to try for the dominion of the sea. The issue was, that, after a sharp sea-fight about the island called Tragia, Pericles obtained a decisive victory, having with forty-four ships routed seventy of the enemy's, twenty of which were carrying soldiers.

Together with his victory and pursuit, having made himself master of the port, he laid siege to the Samians, and blocked them up, who yet, one way or other, still ventured to make sallies, and fight under the city walls. But after that another greater fleet from Athens was arrived, and that the Samians were now shut up with a close leaguer on every side, Pericles, taking with him sixty galleys, sailed out into the main sea, with the intention, as most authors give the account, to meet a squadron of Phoenician ships that were coming for the Samians' relief, and to fight them at as great distance as could be from the island; but, as Stesimbrotus says, with a design of putting over to Cyprus; which does not seem to be probable. But whichever of the two was his intent, it seems to have been a miscalculation. For on his departure, Melissus, the son of Ithagenes, a philosopher, being at that time general in Samos, despising either the small number of the ships that were left or the inexperience of the commanders, prevailed with the citizens to attack the Athenians. And the Samians having won the battle, and taken several of the men prisoners, and disabled several of the ships, were masters of the sea, and brought into port all necessaries they wanted for the war, which they had not before. Aristotle says, too, that Pericles himself had been once before this worsted by this Melissus in a sea-fight.

The Samians, that they might requite an affront which had before been put upon them, branded the Athenians, whom they took prisoners, in their foreheads, with the figure of an owl. For so the Athenians had marked them before with a Samaena, which is a sort of ship, low and flat in the prow, so as to look snub-nosed, but wide and large and well-spread in the hold, by which it both carries a large cargo and sails well. And it was so called, because the first of that kind was seen at Samos, having been built by order of Polycrates the tyrant. These brands upon the Samians' foreheads, they say, are the allusion in the passage of Aristophanes, where he says, —

For, oh, the Samians are a lettered people.

Pericles, as soon as news was brought him of the disaster that had befallen his army, made all the haste he could to come in to their relief, and having defeated Melissus, who bore up against him, and put the enemy to flight, he immediately proceeded to hem them in with a wall, resolving to master them and take the town, rather with some cost and time, than with the wounds and hazards of his citizens. But as it was a hard matter to keep back the Athenians, who were vexed at the delay, and were eagerly bent to fight, he divided the whole multitude into eight parts, and arranged by lot that that part which had the white bean should have leave to feast and take their ease, while the other seven were fighting. And this is the reason, they say, that people, when at any time they have been merry, and enjoyed themselves, call it white day, in allusion to this white bean.

Ephorus the historian tells us besides, that Pericles made use of engines of battery in this siege, being much taken with the curiousness of the invention, with the aid and presence of Artemon himself, the engineer, who, being lame, used to be carried about in a litter, where the works required his attendance, and for that reason was called Periphoretus. But Heraclides Ponticus disproves this out of Anacreon's poems, where mention is made of this Artemon Periphoretus several ages before the Samian war, or any of these occurrences. And he says that Artemon, being a man who loved his ease, and had a great apprehension of danger, for the most part kept close within doors, having two of his servants to hold a brazen shield over his head, that nothing might fall upon him from above; and if he were at any time forced upon necessity to go abroad, that he was carried about in a little hanging bed, close to the very ground, and that for this reason he was called Periphoretus.

In the ninth month, the Samians surrendering themselves and delivering up the town, Pericles pulled down their walls, and seized their shipping, and set a fine of a large sum of money upon them, part of which they paid down at once, and they agreed to bring in the rest by a certain time, and gave hostages for security. Duris the Samian makes a tragical drama out of these events, charging the Athenians and Pericles with a great deal of cruelty, which neither Thucydides, nor Ephorus, nor Aristotle have given any relation of, and probably with little regard to truth; how, for example, he brought the captains and soldiers of the galleys into the market-place at Miletus, and there having bound them fast to boards for ten days, then, when they were already all but half dead, gave order to have them killed by beating out their brains with clubs, and their dead bodies to be flung out into the open streets and fields, unburied. Duris, however, who even where he has no private feeling concerned, is not wont to keep his narrative within the limits of truth, is the more likely upon this occasion to have exaggerated the calamities which befell his country, to create odium against the Athenians. Pericles, however, after the reduction of Samos, returning back to Athens, took care that those who died in the war should be honorably buried, and made a funeral harangue, as the custom is, in their commendation at their graves, for which he gained great admiration. As he came down from the stage on which he spoke, the rest of the women came and complimented him, taking him by the hand, and crownings him with garlands and ribbons, like a victorious athlete in the games; but Elpinice, coming near to him, said, "These are brave deeds, Pericles, that you have done, and such as deserve our chaplets; who have lost us many a worthy citizen, not in a war with Phoenicians or Medes, like my brother Cimon, but for the overthrow of an allied and kindred city." As Elpinice spoke these words, he, smiling quietly, as it is said, returned her answer with this verse, —

Old women should not seek to be perfumed.

Ion says of him, that, upon this exploit of his, conquering the Samians, he indulged very high and proud thoughts of himself: whereas Agamemnon was ten years taking a barbarous city, he had in nine months' time vanquished and taken the greatest and most powerful of the Ionians. And indeed it was not without reason that he assumed this glory to himself, for, in real truth, there was much uncertainty and great hazard in this war, if so be, as Thucydides tells us, the Samian state were within a very little of wresting the whole power and dominion of the sea out of the Athenians' hands.

After this was over, the Peloponnesian war beginning to break out in full tide, he advised the people to send help to the Corcyrseans, who were attacked by the Corinthians, and to secure to themselves an island possessed of great naval resources, since the Peloponnesians were already all but in actual hostilities against them. The people readily consenting to the motion, and voting an aid and succor for them, he dispatched Lacedaemonius, Cimon's son, having only ten ships with him, as it were out of a design to affront him; for there was a great kindness and friendship betwixt Cimon's family and the Lacedaemonians; so, in order that Lacedaemonius might lie the more open to a charge, or suspicion at least, of favoring the Lacedaemonians and playing false, if he performed no considerable exploit in this service, he allowed him a small number of ships, and sent him out against his will; and indeed he made it somewhat his business to hinder Cimon's sons from rising in the state, professing that by their very names they were not to be looked upon as native and true Athenians, but foreigners and strangers, one being called Lacedaemonius, another Thessalus, and the third Eleus; and they were all three of them, it was thought, born of an Arcadian woman. Being, however, ill spoken of on account of these ten galleys, as having afforded but a small supply to the people that were in need, and yet given a great advantage to those who might complain of the act of intervention, Pericles sent out a larger force afterward to Corcyra, which arrived after the fight was over. And when now the Corinthians, angry and indignant with the Athenians, accused them publicly at Lacedaemon, the Megarians joined with them, complaining that they were, contrary to common right and the articles of peace sworn to among the Greeks, kept out and driven away from every market and from all ports under the control of the Athenians. The Aeginetans, also, professing to be ill-used and treated with violence, made supplications in private to the Lacedaemonians for redress, though not daring openly to call the Athenians in question. In the meantime, also, the city Potidaea, under the dominion of the Athenians, but a colony formerly of the Corinthians, had revolted, and was beset with a formal siege, and was a further occasion of precipitating the war.

Yet notwithstanding all this, there being embassies sent to Athens, and Archidamus, the king of the Lacedaemonians, endeavoring to bring the greater part of the complaints and matters in dispute to a fair determination, and to pacify and allay the heats of the allies, it is very likely that the war would not upon any other grounds of quarrel have fallen upon the Athenians, could they have been prevailed with to repeal the ordinance against the Megarians, and to be reconciled to them. Upon which account, since Pericles was the man who mainly opposed it, and stirred up the people's passions to persist in their contention with the Megarians, he was regarded as the sole cause of the war.

They say, moreover, that ambassadors went, by order from Lacedaemon to Athens about this very business, and that when Pericles was urging a certain law which made it illegal to take down or withdraw the tablet of the decree, one of the ambassadors, Polyalces by name, said, "Well, do not take it down then, but turn it; there is no law, I suppose, which forbids that;" which, though prettily said, did not move Pericles from his resolution. There may have been, in all likelihood, something of a secret grudge and private animosity which he had against the Megarians. Yet, upon a public and open charge against them, that they had appropriated part of the sacred land on the frontier, he proposed a decree that a herald should be sent to them, and the same also to the Lacedaemonians, with an accusation of the Megarians; an order which certainly shows equitable and friendly proceeding enough. And after that the herald who was sent, by name Anthemocritus, died, and it was believed that the Megarians had contrived his death, then Charinus proposed a decree against them, that there should be an irreconcilable and implacable enmity thenceforward betwixt the two commonwealths; and that if any one of the Megarians should but set his foot in Attica, he should be put to death; and that the commanders, when they take the usual oath, should, over and above that, swear that they will twice every year make an inroad into the Megarian country; and that Anthemocritus should be buried near the Thriasian Gates, which are now called the Dipylon, or Double Gate.

On the other hand, the Megarians, utterly denying and disowning the murder of Anthemocritus, throw the whole matter upon Aspasia and Pericles, availing themselves of the famous verses in the Acharnians,

> *To Megara some of our madcaps ran,*
> *And stole Simaetha thence, their courtesan.*
> *Which exploit the Megarians to outdo,*
> *Came to Aspasia's house, and took off two.*

The true occasion of the quarrel is not so easy to find out. But of inducing the refusal to annul the decree, all alike charge Pericles. Some say he met the request with a positive refusal, out of high spirit and a view of the state's best interests, accounting that the demand made in those embassies was designed for a trial of their compliance, and that a concession would be taken for a confession of weakness, as if they durst not do otherwise; while other some there are who say that it was rather out of arrogance and a willful spirit of contention, to show his own strength, that he took occasion to slight the Lacedaemonians. The worst motive of all, which is confirmed by most witnesses, is to the following effect. Phidias the Molder had, as has before been said, undertaken to make the statue of Minerva. Now he, being admitted to friendship with Pericles, and a great favorite of his, had many enemies upon this account, who envied and maligned him; who also, to make trial in a case of his, what kind of judges the commons would prove, should there be occasion to bring Pericles himself before them, having tampered with Menon, one who had been a workman with Phidias, stationed him ill the market-place, with a petition desiring public security upon his discovery and impeachment of Phidias. The people admitting the man to tell his story, and the prosecution proceeding in the assembly, there was nothing of theft or cheat proved against him; for Phidias, from the very first beginning, by the advice of Pericles, had so wrought and wrapt the gold that was used in the work about the statue, that they might take it all off and make out the just weight of it, which Pericles at that time bade the accusers do. But the reputation of his works was what brought envy upon Phidias, especially that where he represents the fight of the Amazons upon the goddesses' shield, he had introduced a likeness of himself as a bald old man holding up a great stone with both hands, and had put in a very fine representation of Pericles fighting with an Amazon. And the position of the hand, which holds out the spear in front of the face, was ingeniously contrived to conceal in some degree the likeness, which, meantime, showed itself on either side.

Phidias then was carried away to prison, and there died of a disease; but, as some say, of poison, administered by the enemies of Pericles, to raise a slander, or a suspicion, at least, as though he had procured it. The informer Menon, upon Glycon's proposal, the people made free from payment of taxes and customs, and ordered the generals to take care that nobody should do him any hurt. About the same time, Aspasia was indicted of impiety, upon the complaint of Hermippus the comedian, who also laid further to her charge that she received into her house freeborn women for the uses of Pericles. And Diopithes proposed a decree, that public accusation should be laid against persons who neglected religion, or taught new doctrines about things above, directing suspicion, by means of Anaxagoras, against Pericles himself. The people receiving and admitting these accusations and complaints, at length, by this means, they came to enact a decree, at the motion of Dracontides, that Pericles should bring in the accounts of the moneys he had expended, and lodge them with the Prytanes; and that the judges, carrying their suffrage from the altar in the Acropolis, should examine and determine the business in the city. This last clause Hagnon took out of the decree, and moved that the causes should be tried before fifteen hundred jurors, whether they should be styled prosecutions for robbery, or bribery, or any kind of malversation. Aspasia, Pericles begged off, shedding, as Aeschines says, many tears at the trial, and personally entreating the jurors. But fearing how it might go with Anaxagoras, he sent him out of the city. And finding that in Phidias's case he had miscarried with the people, being afraid of impeachment, he kindled the war, which hitherto had lingered and smothered, and blew it up into a flame; hoping, by that means, to disperse and scatter these complaints and charges, and to allay their jealousy; the city usually throwing herself upon him alone, and trusting to his sole conduct, upon the urgency of great affairs and public dangers, by reason of his authority and the sway he bore.

These are given out to have been the reasons which induced Pericles not to suffer the people of Athens to yield to the proposals of the

Lacedaemonians; but their truth is uncertain.

The Lacedaemonians, for their part, feeling sure that if they could once remove him, they might be at what terms they pleased with the Athenians, sent them word that they should expel the "Pollution" with which Pericles on the mother's side was tainted, as Thucydides tells us. But the issue proved quite contrary to what those who sent the message expected; instead of bringing Pericles under suspicion and reproach, they raised him into yet greater credit and esteem with the citizens, as a man whom their enemies most hated and feared. In the same way, also, before Archidamus, who was at the head of the Peloponnesians, made his invasion into Attica, he told the Athenians beforehand, that if Archidamus, while he laid waste the rest of the country, should forbear and spare his estate, either on the ground of friendship or right of hospitality that was betwixt them, or on purpose to give his enemies an occasion of traducing him, that then he did freely bestow upon the state all that his land and the buildings upon it for the public use. The Lacedaemonians, therefore, and their allies, with a great army, invaded the Athenian territories, under the conduct of king Archidamus, and laying waste the country, marched on as far as Acharnae, and there pitched their camp, presuming that the Athenians would never endure that, but would come out and fight them for their country's and their honor's sake. But Pericles looked upon it as dangerous to engage in battle, to the risk of the city itself, against sixty thousand men-at-arms of Peloponnesians and Boeotians; for so many they were in number that made the inroad at first; and he endeavored to appease those who were desirous to fight, and were grieved and discontented to see how things went, and gave them good words, saying, that "trees, when they are lopped and cut, grow up again in a short time but men, being once lost, cannot easily be recovered." He did not convene the people into an assembly, for fear lest they should force him to act against his judgment; but, like a skillful steersman or pilot of a ship, who, when a sudden squall comes on, out at sea, makes all his arrangements, sees that all is tight and fast, and then follows the dictates of his skill, and minds the business of the ship, taking no notice of the tears and entreaties of the sea-sick and fearful passengers, so he, having shut up the city gates, and placed guards at all posts for security, followed his own reason and judgment, little regarding those that cried out against him and were angry at his management, although there were a great many of his friends that urged him with requests, and many of his enemies threatened and accused him for doing as he did, and many made songs and lampoons upon him, which were sung about the town to his disgrace, reproaching him with the cowardly exercise of his office of general, and the tame abandonment of everything to the enemy's hands.

Cleon, also, already was among his assailants, making use of the feeling against him as a step to the leadership of the people, as appears in the anapaestic verses of Hermippus.

> *Satyr-king, instead of swords,*
> *Will you always handle words?*
> *Very brave indeed we find them,*
> *But a Teles lurks behind them.*
>
> *Yet to gnash your teeth you're seen,*
> *When the little dagger keen,*
> *Whetted every day anew,*
> *Of sharp Cleon touches you.*

Pericles, however, was not at all moved by any attacks, but took all patiently, and submitted in silence to the disgrace they threw upon him and the ill-will they bore him; and, sending out a fleet of a hundred galleys to Peloponnesus, he did not go along with it in person, but stayed behind, that he might watch at home and keep the city under his own control, till the Peloponnesians broke up their camp and were gone. Yet to soothe the common people, jaded and distressed with the war, he relieved them with distributions of public moneys, and ordained new divisions of subject land. For having turned out all the people of Aegina, he parted the island among the Athenians, according to lot. Some comfort, also, and ease in their miseries, they might receive from what their enemies endured. For the fleet, sailing round the Peloponnese, ravaged a great deal of the country, and pillaged and plundered the towns and smaller cities; and by land he himself entered with an army the Megarian country, and made havoc of it all. Whence it is clear that the Peloponnesians, though they did the Athenians much mischief by land, yet suffering as much themselves from them by sea, would not have protracted the war to such a length, but would quickly have given it over, as Pericles at first foretold they would, had not some divine power crossed human purposes.

In the first place, the pestilential disease, or plague, seized upon the city, and ate up all the flower and prime of their youth and strength. Upon occasion of which, the people, distempered and afflicted in their souls, as well as in their bodies, were utterly enraged like madmen against Pericles, and, like patients grown delirious, sought to lay violent hands on their physician, or, as it were, their father. They had been possessed, by his enemies, with the belief that the occasion of the plague was the crowding of the country people together into the town, forced as they were now, in the heat of the summer-weather, to dwell many of them together even as they could, in small tenements and stifling hovels, and to be tied to a lazy course of life within doors, whereas before they lived in a pure, open, and free air. The cause and author of all this, said they, is he who on account of the war has poured a multitude of people from the country in upon us within the walls, and uses all these many men that he has here upon no employ or service, but keeps them pent up like cattle, to be overrun with infection from one another, affording them neither shift of quarters nor any refreshment.

With the design to remedy these evils, and do the enemy some inconvenience, Pericles got a hundred and fifty galleys ready, and having embarked many tried soldiers, both foot and horse, was about to sail out, giving great hope to his citizens, and no less alarm to his enemies, upon the sight of so great a force. And now the vessels having their complement of men, and Pericles being gone aboard his own galley, it happened that the sun was eclipsed, and it grew dark on a sudden, to the affright of all, for this was looked upon as extremely ominous. Pericles, therefore, perceiving the steersman seized with fear and at a loss what to do, took his cloak and held it up before the man's face, and, screening him with it so that he could not see, asked him whether he imagined there was any great hurt, or the sign of any great hurt in this, and he answering No, "Why," said he, "and what does that differ from this, only that what has caused that darkness there, is something greater than a cloak?" This is a story which philosophers tell their scholars. Pericles, however after putting out to sea, seems not to have done any other exploit befitting such preparations, and when he had laid siege to the holy city Epidaurus, which gave him some hope of surrender, miscarried in his design by reason of the sickness. For it not only seized upon the Athenians, but upon all others, too, that held any sort of communication with the army. Finding after this the Athenians ill affected and highly displeased with him, he tried and endeavored what he could to appease and re-encourage them. But he could not pacify or allay their anger, nor persuade or prevail with them any way, till they freely passed their votes upon him, resumed their power, took away his command from him, and fined him in a sum of money; which, by their account that say least, was fifteen talents, while they who reckon most, name fifty. The name prefixed to the accusation was Cleon, as Idomeneus tells us; Simmias, according to Theophrastus; and Heraclides Ponticus gives it as Lacratidas.

After this, public troubles were soon to leave him unmolested; the people, so to say, discharged their passion in their stroke, and lost their stings in the wound. But his domestic concerns were in an unhappy condition many of his friends and acquaintance having died in the plague time, and those of his family having long since been in disorder and in a kind of mutiny against him. For the eldest of his lawfully begotten sons, Xanthippus by name, being naturally prodigal, and marrying a young and expensive wife, the daughter of Tisander, son of Epilycus, was highly offended at his father's economy in making him but a scanty allowance, by little and little at a time. He sent, therefore, to a friend one day, and borrowed some money of him in his father Pericles's name, pretending it was by his order. The man coming afterward to demand the debt, Pericles was so far from yielding to pay it, that he entered an action against him. Upon which the young man, Xanthippus, thought himself so ill used and disobliged, that he openly reviled his father; telling first, by way of ridicule, stories about his conversations at home, and the discourses he had with the sophists and scholars that came to his house. As for instance, how one who was a practicer of the five games of skill, having with a dart or javelin unawares against his will struck and killed Epitimus the Pharsalian, his father spent a whole day with Protagoras in a serious dispute, whether the javelin, or the man that threw it, or the masters of the games who appointed these sports, were, according to the strictest and best reason, to be accounted the cause of this mischance. Besides this, Stesimbrotus tells us that it was Xanthippus who spread abroad among the people the infamous story concerning his own wife; and in general that this difference of the young man's with his father, and the breach betwixt them, continued never to be healed or made up till his death. For Xanthippus died in the plague time of the sickness. At which time Pericles also lost his sister, and the greatest part of his relations and friends, and those who had been most useful and serviceable to him in managing the affairs of state. However, he did not shrink or give in upon these occasions, nor betray or lower his high spirit and the greatness of his mind under all his misfortunes; he was not even so much as seen to weep or to mourn, or even attend the burial of any of his friends or relations, till at last he lost his only remaining legitimate son. Subdued by this blow and yet striving still, as far as he could, to maintain his principle and to preserve and keep up the greatness of his soul when he came, however, to perform the ceremony of putting a garland of flowers upon the head of the corpse, he was vanquished by his passion at the sight, so that he burst into exclamations, and shed copious tears, having never done any such thing in all his life before.

The city having made trial of other generals for the conduct of war, and orators for business of state, when they found there was no one who was of weight enough for such a charge, or of authority sufficient to be trusted with so great a command, regretted the loss of him, and invited him again to address and advise them, and to reassume the office of general. He, however, lay at home in dejection and mourning; but was persuaded by Alcibiades and others of his friends to come abroad and show himself to the people; who having, upon his appearance, made their acknowledgments, and apologized for their untowardly treatment of him, he undertook the public affairs once more; and, being chosen general, requested that the statute concerning baseborn children, which he himself had formerly caused to be made, might be suspended; that so the name and race of his family might not, for absolute want of a lawful heir to succeed, be wholly lost and extinguished. The case of the statute was thus: Pericles, when long ago at the height of his power in the state, having then, as has been said, children lawfully begotten, proposed a law that those only should be reputed true citizens of Athens who were born of such parents as were both Athenians. After this, the king of Egypt having sent to the people, by way of present, forty thousand bushels of wheat, which were to be shared out among the citizens, a great many actions and suits about legitimacy occurred, by virtue of that edict; cases which, till that time, had not been known nor taken notice of; and several persons suffered by false accusations. There were little less than five thousand who were convicted and sold for slaves; those who, enduring the test, remained in the government and passed muster for true Athenians were found upon the poll to be fourteen thousand and forty persons in number.

It looked strange, that a law, which had been carried so far against so many people, should be canceled again by the same man that made it; yet the present calamity and distress which Pericles labored under in his family broke through all objections, and prevailed with the Athenians to pity him, as one whose losses and misfortunes had sufficiently punished his former arrogance and haughtiness. His sufferings deserved, they thought, their pity, and even indignation, and his request was such as became a man to ask and men to grant; they gave him permission to enroll his son in the register of his fraternity, giving him his own name. This son afterward, after having defeated the Peloponnesians at Arginusae, was, with his fellow-generals, put to death by the people.

About the time when his son was enrolled, it should seem, the plague seized Pericles, not with sharp and violent fits, as it did others that had it, but with a dull and lingering distemper, attended with various changes and alterations, leisurely, by little and little, wasting the strength of his body, and undermining the noble faculties of his soul. So that Theophrastus, in his Morals, when discussing whether men's characters change with their circumstances, and their moral habits, disturbed by the ailings of their bodies, start aside from the rules of virtue, has left it upon record, that Pericles, when he was sick, showed one of his friends that came to visit him, an amulet or charm that the women had hung about his neck; as much as to say, that he was very sick indeed when he would admit of such a foolery as that was.

When he was now near his end, the best of the citizens and those of his friends who were left alive, sitting about him, were speaking of the greatness of his merit, and his power, and reckoning up his famous actions and the number of his victories; for there were no less than nine trophies, which, as their chief commander and conqueror of their enemies, he had set up, for the honor of the city. They talked thus together among themselves, as though he were unable to understand or mind what they said, but had now lost his consciousness. He had listened, however, all the while, and attended to all, and speaking out among them, said, that he wondered they should commend and take notice of things which were as much owing to fortune as to anything else, and had happened to many other commanders, and, at the same time, should not speak or make mention of that which was the most excellent and greatest thing of all. "For," said he, "no Athenian, through my means, ever wore mourning."

He was indeed a character deserving our high admiration, not only for his equitable and mild temper, which all along in the many affairs of his life, and the great animosities which he incurred, he constantly maintained; but also for the high spirit and feeling which made him regard it the noblest of all his honors that, in the exercise of such immense power, he never had gratified his envy or his passion, nor ever had treated any enemy as irreconcilably opposed to him. And to me it appears that this one thing gives that otherwise childish and arrogant title a fitting and becoming significance; so dispassionate a temper, a life so pure and unblemished, in the height of power and place, might well be called Olympian, in accordance with our conceptions of the divine beings, to whom, as the natural authors of all good and of nothing evil, we ascribe the rule and government of the world. Not as the poets represent, who, while confounding us with their ignorant fancies, are themselves confuted by their own poems and fictions, and call the place, indeed, where they say the gods make their abode, a secure and quiet seat, free from all hazards and commotions, untroubled with winds or with clouds, and equally through all time illumined with a soft serenity and a pure light, as though such were a home most agreeable for a blessed and immortal nature; and yet, in the meanwhile, affirm that the gods themselves are full of trouble and enmity and anger and other passions, which no way become or belong to even men that have any understanding. But this will, perhaps, seem a subject fitter for some other consideration, and that ought to be treated of in some other place.

The course of public affairs after his death produced a quick and speedy sense of the loss of Pericles. Those who, while he lived, resented his great authority, as that which eclipsed themselves, presently after his quitting the stage, making trial of other orators and demagogues, readily acknowledged that there never had been in nature such a disposition as his was, more moderate and reasonable in the height of that state he took upon him, or more grave and impressive in the mildness which he used. And that invidious arbitrary power, to which formerly they gave the name of monarchy and tyranny, did then appear to have been the chief bulwark of public safety; so great a corruption and such a flood of mischief and vice followed, which he, by keeping weak and low, had withheld from notice, and had prevented from attaining incurable height through a licentious impunity.

5
FABIUS

Having related the memorable actions of Pericles, our history now proceeds to the life of Fabius. A son of Hercules and a nymph, or some woman of that country, who brought him forth on the banks of Tiber, was, it is said, the first Fabius, the founder of the numerous and distinguished family of the name. Others will have it that they were first called Fodii, because the first of the race delighted in digging pitfalls for wild beasts, fodere being still the Latin for to dig, and fossa for a ditch, and that in process of time, by the change of the two letters they grew to be called Fabii. But be these things true or false, certain it is that this family for a long time yielded a great number of eminent persons. Our Fabius, who was fourth in descent from that Fabius Rullus who first brought the honorable surname of Maximus into his family, was also, by way of personal nickname, called Verrucosus, from a wart on his upper lip; and in his childhood they in like manner named him Ovicula, or The Lamb, on account of his extreme mildness of temper. His slowness in speaking, his long labor and pains in learning, his deliberation in entering into the sports of other children, his easy submission to everybody, as if he had no will of his own, made those who judged superficially of him, the greater number, esteem him insensible and stupid; and few only saw that this tardiness proceeded from stability, and discerned the greatness of his mind, and the lionlikeness of his temper. But as soon as he came into employments, his virtues exerted and showed themselves; his reputed want of energy then was recognized by people in general, as a freedom of passion; his slowness in words and actions, the effect of a true prudence; his want of rapidity, and his sluggishness, as constancy and firmness.

Living in a great commonwealth, surrounded by many enemies, he saw the wisdom of inuring his body (nature's own weapon) to warlike exercises, and disciplining his tongue for public oratory in a style comfortable to his life and character. His eloquence, indeed, had not much of popular ornament, nor empty artifice, but there was in it great weight of sense; it was strong and sententious, much after the way of Thucydides. We have yet extant his funeral oration upon the death of his son, who died consul, which he recited before the people.

He was five times consul, and in his first consulship had the honor of a triumph for the victory he gained over the Ligurians, whom he defeated in a set battle, and drove them to take shelter in the Alps, from whence they never after made any inroad nor depredation upon their neighbors. After this, Hannibal came into Italy, who, at his first entrance, having gained a great battle near the river Trebia, traversed all Tuscany with his victorious army, and, desolating the country round about, filled Rome itself with astonishment and terror. Besides the more common signs of thunder and lightning then happening, the report of several unheard of and utterly strange portents much increased the popular consternation. For it was said that some targets sweated blood; that at Antium, when they reaped their corn, many of the ears were filled with blood; that it had rained redhot stones; that the Falerians had seen the heavens open and several scrolls falling down, in one of which was plainly written, "Mars himself stirs his arms." But these prodigies had no effect upon the impetuous and fiery temper of the consul Flaminius, whose natural promptness had been much heightened by his late unexpected victory over the Gauls, when he fought them contrary to the order of the senate and the advice of his colleague. Fabius, on the other side, thought it not seasonable to engage with the enemy; not that he much regarded the prodigies, which he thought too strange to be easily understood, though many were alarmed by them; but in regard that the Carthaginians were but few, and in want of money and supplies, he deemed it best not to meet in the field a general whose army had been tried in many encounters, and whose object was a battle, but to send aid to their allies, control the movements of the various subject cities, and let the force and vigor of Hannibal waste away and expire, like a flame, for want of aliment.

These weighty reasons did not prevail with Flaminius, who protested he would never suffer the advance of the enemy to the city, nor be reduced, like Camillus in former time, to fight for Rome within the walls of Rome. Accordingly he ordered the tribunes to draw out the army into the field; and though he himself, leaping on horseback to go out, was no sooner mounted but the beast, without any apparent cause, fell into so violent a fit of trembling and bounding that he cast his rider headlong on the ground, he was no ways deterred; but proceeded as he had begun, and marched forward up to Hannibal, who was posted near the Lake Thrasymene in Tuscany. At the moment of this engagement, there happened so great an earthquake, that it destroyed several towns, altered the course of rivers, and carried off parts of high cliffs, yet such was the eagerness of the combatants, that they were entirely insensible of it.

In this battle Flaminius fell, after many proofs of his strength and courage, and round about him all the bravest of the army, in the whole, fifteen thousand were killed, and as many made prisoners. Hannibal, desirous to bestow funeral honors upon the body of Flaminius, made diligent search after it, but could not find it among the dead, nor was it ever known what became of it. Upon the former engagement near Trebia, neither the general who wrote, nor the express who told the news, used straightforward and direct terms, nor related it otherwise than as a drawn battle, with equal loss on either side; but on this occasion, as soon as Pomponius the praetor had the intelligence, he caused the people to assemble, and, without disguising or dissembling the matter, told them plainly, "We are beaten, O Romans, in a great battle; the consul Flaminius is killed; think, therefore, what is to be done for your safety." Letting loose his news like a gale of wind upon an open sea, he threw the city into utter confusion: in such consternation, their thoughts found no support or stay. The danger at hand at last awakened their judgments into a resolution to choose a dictator, who, by the sovereign authority of his office and by his personal wisdom and courage, might be able to manage the public affairs. Their choice unanimously fell upon Fabius, whose character seemed equal to the greatness of the office; whose age was so far advanced as to give him experience, without taking from him the vigor of action; his body could execute what his soul designed; and his temper was a happy compound of confidence and cautiousness.

Fabius, being thus installed in the office of dictator, in the first place gave the command of the horse to Lucius Minucius; and next asked leave of the senate for himself, that in time of battle he might serve on horseback, which by an ancient law amongst the Romans was forbid to their generals; whether it were, that, placing their greatest strength in their foot, they would have their commanders-in-chief posted amongst them, or else to let them know, that, how great and absolute soever their authority were, the people and senate were still their masters, of whom they must ask leave. Fabius, however, to make the authority of his charge more observable, and to render the people more submissive and obedient to him, caused himself to be accompanied with the full body of four and twenty lictors; and, when the surviving consul came to visit him, sent him word to dismiss his lictors with their fasces, the ensigns of authority, and appear before him as a private person.

The first solemn action of his dictatorship was very fitly a religious one: an admonition to the people, that their late overthrow had not befallen them through want of courage in their soldiers, but through the neglect of divine ceremonies in the general. He therefore exhorted them not to fear the enemy, but by extraordinary honor to propitiate the gods. This he did, not to fill their minds with superstition, but by religious feeling to raise their courage, and lessen their fear of the enemy by inspiring the belief that Heaven was on their side. With this view, the secret prophecies called the Sibylline Books were consulted; sundry predictions found in them were said to refer to the fortunes and events of the time; but none except the consulter was informed. Presenting himself to the people, the dictator made a vow before them to offer in sacrifice the whole product of the next season, all Italy over, of the cows, goats, swine, sheep, both in the mountains and the plains; and to celebrate musical festivities with an expenditure of the precise sum of 333 sestertia and 333 denarii, with one third of a denarius over. The sum total of which is, in our money, 83,583 drachmas and 2 obols. What the mystery might be in that exact number is not easy to determine, unless it were in honor of the perfection of the number three, as being the first of odd numbers, the first that contains in itself multiplication, with all other properties whatsoever belonging to numbers in general.

In this manner Fabius having given the people better heart for the future, by making them believe that the gods took their side, for his own part placed his whole confidence in himself, believing that the gods bestowed victory and good fortune by the instrumentality of valor and of prudence; and thus prepared he set forth to oppose Hannibal, not with intention to fight him, but with the purpose of wearing out and wasting the vigor of his arms by lapse of time, of meeting his want of resources by superior means, by large numbers the smallness of his forces. With this design, he always encamped on the highest grounds, where the enemy's horse could have no access to him. Still he kept pace with them; when they marched he followed them, when they encamped he did the same, but at such a distance as not to be compelled to an engagement, and always keeping upon the hills, free from the insults of their horse; by which means he gave them no rest, but kept them in a continual alarm.

But this his dilatory way gave occasion in his own camp for suspicion of want of courage; and this opinion prevailed yet more in Hannibal's army. Hannibal was himself the only man who was not deceived, who discerned his skill and detected his tactics, and saw, unless he could by art or force bring him to battle, that the Carthaginians, unable to use the arms in which they were superior, and suffering the continual drain of lives and treasure in which they were inferior, would in the end come to nothing. He resolved, therefore, with all the arts and subtilties of war to break his measures, and to bring Fabius to an engagement; like a cunning wrestler, watching every opportunity to get good hold and close with his adversary. He at one time attacked, and sought to distract his attention, tried to draw him off in various directions, endeavored in all ways to tempt him from his safe policy. All this artifice, though it had no effect upon the firm judgment and conviction of the dictator, yet upon the common soldier and even upon the general of the horse himself, it had too great an operation: Minucius, unseasonably eager for action, bold and confident, humored the soldiery, and himself contributed to fill them with wild eagerness and empty hopes, which they vented in reproaches upon Fabius, calling him Hannibal's pedagogue, since he did nothing else but follow him up and down and wait upon him. At the same time, they cried up Minucius for the only captain worthy to command the Romans; whose vanity and presumption rose so high in consequence, that he insolently jested at Fabius's encampments upon the mountains, saying that he seated them there as on a theater, to behold the flames and desolation of their country. And he would sometimes ask the friends of the general, whether it were not his meaning, by thus leading them from mountain to mountain, to carry them at last (having no hopes on earth) up into heaven, or to hide them in the clouds from Hannibal's army? When his friends reported these things to the dictator, persuading him that, to avoid the general obloquy, he should engage the enemy, his answer was, "I should be more fainthearted than they make me, if, through fear of idle reproaches, I should abandon my own convictions. It is no inglorious thing to have fear for the safety of our country, but to be turned from one's course by men's opinions, by blame, and by misrepresentation, shows a man unfit to hold an office such as this, which, by such conduct, he makes the slave of those whose errors it is his business to control."

An oversight of Hannibal occurred soon after. Desirous to refresh his horse in some good pasture-grounds, and to draw off his army, he ordered his guides to conduct him to the district of Casinum. They, mistaking his bad pronunciation, led him and his army to the town of Casilinum, on the frontier of Campania which the river Lothronus, called by the Romans Vulturnus, divides in two parts. The country around is enclosed by mountains, with a valley opening towards the sea, in which the river overflowing forms a quantity of marsh land with deep banks of sand, and discharges itself into the sea on a very unsafe and rough shore. While Hannibal was proceeding hither, Fabius, by his knowledge of the roads, succeeded in making his way around before him, and dispatched four thousand choice men to seize the exit from it and stop him up, and lodged the rest of his army upon the neighboring hills in the most advantageous places; at the same time detaching a party of his lightest armed men to fall upon Hannibal's rear; which they did with such success, that they cut off eight hundred of them, and put the whole army in disorder. Hannibal, finding the error and the danger he was fallen into, immediately crucified the guides; but considered the enemy to be so advantageously posted, that there was no hopes of breaking through them; while his soldiers began to be despondent and terrified, and to think themselves surrounded with embarrassments too difficult to be surmounted.

Thus reduced, Hannibal had recourse to stratagem; he caused two thousand head of oxen which he had in his camp, to have torches or dry fagots well fastened to their horns, and lighting them in the beginning of the night, ordered the beasts to be driven on towards the heights commanding the passages out of the valley and the enemy's posts; when this was done, he made his army in the dark leisurely march after them. The oxen at first kept a slow, orderly pace, and with their lighted heads resembled an army marching by night, astonishing the shepherds and herds men of the hills about. But when the fire had burnt down the horns of the beasts to the quick, they no longer observed their sober pace, but, unruly and wild with their pain, ran dispersed about, tossing their heads and scattering the fire round about them upon each other and setting light as they passed to the trees. This was a surprising spectacle to the Romans on guard upon the heights. Seeing flames which appeared to come from men advancing with torches, they were possessed with the alarm that the enemy was approaching in various quarters, and that they were being surrounded; and, quitting their post, abandoned the pass, and precipitately retired to their camp on the hills. They were no sooner gone, but the light-armed of Hannibal's men, according to his order, immediately seized the heights, and soon after the whole army, with all the baggage, came up and safely marched through the passes.

Fabius, before the night was over, quickly found out the trick; for some of the beasts fell into his hands; but for fear of an ambush in the dark, he kept his men all night to their arms in the camp. As soon as it was day, he attacked the enemy in the rear, where, after a good deal of skirmishing in the uneven ground, the disorder might have become general, but that Hannibal detached from his van a body of Spaniards, who, of themselves active and nimble, were accustomed to the climbing of mountains. These briskly attacked the Roman troops who were in heavy armor, killed a good many, and left Fabius no longer in condition to follow the enemy. This action brought the extreme of obloquy and contempt upon the dictator; they said it was now manifest that he was not only inferior to his adversary, as they had always thought, in courage, but even in that conduct, foresight, and generalship, by which he had proposed to bring the war to an end.

And Hannibal, to enhance their anger against him, marched with his army close to the lands and possessions of Fabius, and, giving orders to his soldiers to burn and destroy all the country about, forbade them to do the least damage in the estates of the Roman general, and placed guards for their security. This, when reported at Rome, had the effect with the people which Hannibal desired. Their tribunes raised a thousand stories against him, chiefly at the instigation of Metilius, who, not so much out of hatred to him as out of friendship to Minucius, whose kinsman he was, thought by depressing Fabius to raise his friend. The senate on their part were also offended with him, for the bargain he had made with Hannibal about the exchange of prisoners, the conditions of which were, that, after exchange made of man for man, if any on either side remained, they should be redeemed at the price of two hundred and fifty drachmas a head. Upon the whole account, there remained two hundred and forty Romans unexchanged, and the senate now not only refused to allow money for the ransoms, but also reproached Fabius for making a contract, contrary to the honor and interest of the commonwealth, for redeeming men whose cowardice had put them in the hands of the enemy. Fabius heard and endured all this with invincible patience; and, having no money by him, and on the other side being resolved to keep his word with Hannibal and not to abandon the captives, he dispatched his son to Rome to sell land, and to bring with him the price, sufficient to discharge the ransoms; which was punctually performed by his son, and delivery accordingly made to him of the prisoners, amongst whom many, when they were released, made proposals to repay the money; which Fabius in all cases declined.

About this time, he was called to Rome by the priests, to assist, according to the duty of his office, at certain sacrifices, and was thus forced to leave the command of the army with Minucius; but before he parted, not only charged him as his commander-in-chief, but besought and entreated him, not to come, in his absence, to a battle with Hannibal. His commands, entreaties, and advice were lost upon Minucius; for his back was no sooner turned but the new general immediately sought occasions to attack the enemy. And notice being brought him that Hannibal had sent out a great part of his army to forage, he fell upon a detachment of the remainder, doing great execution, and driving them to their very camp, with no little terror to the rest, who apprehended their breaking in upon them; and when Hannibal had recalled his scattered forces to the camp, he, nevertheless, without any loss, made his retreat, a success which aggravated his boldness and presumption, and filled the soldiers with rash confidence. The news spread to Rome, where Fabius, on being told it, said that what he most feared was Minucius's success: but the people, highly elated, hurried to the forum to listen to an address from Metilius the tribune, in which he infinitely extolled the valor of Minucius, and fell bitterly upon Fabius, accusing him for want not merely of courage, but even of loyalty; and not only him, but also many other eminent and considerable persons; saying that it was they that had brought the Carthaginians into Italy, with the design to destroy the liberty of the people; for which end they had at once put the supreme authority into the hands of a single person, who by his slowness and delays might give Hannibal leisure to establish himself in Italy, and the people of Carthage time and opportunity to supply him with fresh succors to complete his conquests

Fabius came forward with no intention to answer the tribune, but only said, that they should expedite the sacrifices, that so he might speedily return to the army to punish Minucius, who had presumed to fight contrary to his orders; words which immediately possessed the people with the belief that Minucius stood in danger of his life. For it was in the power of the dictator to imprison and to put to death, and they feared that Fabius, of a mild temper in general, would be as hard to be appeased when once irritated, as he was slow to be provoked. Nobody dared to raise his voice in opposition. Metilius alone, whose office of tribune gave him security to say what he pleased (for in the time of a dictatorship that magistrate alone preserves his authority), boldly applied himself to the people in the behalf of Minucius: that they should not suffer him to be made a sacrifice to the enmity of Fabius, nor permit him to be destroyed, like the son of Manlius Torquatus, who was beheaded by his father for a victory fought and triumphantly won against order; he exhorted them to take away from Fabius that absolute power of a dictator, and to put it into more worthy hands, better able and more inclined to use it for the public good. These impressions very much prevailed upon the people, though not so far as wholly to dispossess Fabius of the dictatorship. But they decreed that Minucius should have an equal authority with the dictator in the conduct of the war; which was a thing then without precedent, though a little later it was again practiced after the disaster at Cannae; when the dictator, Marcus Junius, being with the army, they chose at Rome Fabius Buteo dictator, that he might create new senators, to supply the numerous places of those who were killed. But as soon as, once acting in public, he had filled those vacant places with a sufficient number, he immediately dismissed his lictors, and withdrew from all his attendance, and, mingling like a common person with the rest of the people, quietly went about his own affairs in the forum.

The enemies of Fabius thought they had sufficiently humiliated and subdued him by raising Minucius to be his equal in authority; but they mistook the temper of the man, who looked upon their folly as not his loss, but like Diogenes, who, being told that some persons derided him, made answer, "But I am not derided," meaning that only those were really insulted on whom such insults made an impression, so Fabius, with great tranquillity and unconcern, submitted to what happened, and contributed a proof to the argument of the philosophers that a just and good man is not capable of being dishonored. His only vexation arose from his fear lest this ill counsel, by supplying opportunities to the diseased military ambition of his subordinate, should damage the public cause. Lest the rashness of Minucius should now at once run headlong into some disaster, he returned back with all privacy and speed to the army; where he found Minucius so elevated with his new dignity, that, a joint-authority not contenting him, he required by turns to have the command of the army every other day. This Fabius rejected, but was contented that the army should be divided; thinking each general singly would better command his part, than partially command the whole. The first and fourth legion he took for his own division, the second and third he delivered to Minucius; so also of the auxiliary forces each had an equal share.

Minucius, thus exalted, could not contain himself from boasting of his success in humiliating the high and powerful office of the dictatorship. Fabius quietly reminded him that it was, in all wisdom, Hannibal, and not Fabius, whom he had to combat; but if he must needs contend with his colleague, it had best be in diligence and care for the preservation of Rome; that it might not be said, a man so favored by the people served them worse than he who had been ill-treated and disgraced by them.

The young general, despising these admonitions as the false humility of age, immediately removed with the body of his army, and encamped by himself. Hannibal, who was not ignorant of all these passages, lay watching his advantage from them. It happened that between his army and that of Minucius there was a certain eminence, which seemed a very advantageous and not difficult post to encamp upon; the level field around it appeared, from a distance, to be all smooth and even, though it had many inconsiderable ditches and dips in it, not discernible to the eye. Hannibal, had he pleased, could easily have possessed himself of this ground; but he had reserved it for a bait, or train, in proper season, to draw the Romans to an engagement. Now that Minucius and Fabius were divided, he thought the opportunity fair for his purpose; and, therefore, having in the night time lodged a convenient number of his men in these ditches and hollow places, early in the morning he sent forth a small detachment, who, in the sight of Minucius, proceeded to possess themselves of the rising ground. According to his expectation, Minucius swallowed the bait, and first sends out his light troops, and after them some horse, to dislodge the enemy; and, at last, when he saw Hannibal in person advancing to the assistance of his men, marched down with his whole army drawn up. He engaged with the troops on the eminence, and sustained their missiles; the combat for some time was equal; but as soon as Hannibal perceived that the whole army was now sufficiently advanced within the toils he had set for them, so that their backs were open to his men whom he had posted in the hollows, he gave the signal; upon which they rushed forth from various quarters, and with loud cries furiously attacked Minucius in the rear. The surprise and the slaughter was great, and struck universal alarm and disorder through the whole army. Minucius himself lost all his confidence; he looked from officer to officer, and found all alike unprepared to face the danger, and yielding to a flight, which, however, could not end in safety. The Numidian horsemen were already in full victory riding about the plain, cutting down the fugitives.

Fabius was not ignorant of this danger of his countrymen; he foresaw what would happen from the rashness of Minucius, and the cunning of Hannibal; and, therefore, kept his men to their arms, in readiness to wait the event; nor would he trust to the reports of others, but he himself, in front of his camp, viewed all that passed. When, therefore, he saw the army of Minucius encompassed by the enemy, and that by their countenance and shifting their ground, they appeared more disposed to flight than to resistance, with a great sigh, striking his hand upon his thigh, he said to those about him, "O Hercules! how much sooner than I expected, though later than he seemed to desire, hath Minucius destroyed himself!" He then commanded the ensigns to be led forward and the army to follow, telling them, "We must make haste to rescue Minucius, who is a valiant man, and a lover of his country; and if he hath been too forward to engage the enemy, at another time we will tell him of it." Thus, at the head of his men, Fabius marched up to the enemy, and first cleared the plain of the Numidians; and next fell upon those who were charging the Romans in the rear, cutting down all that made opposition, and obliging the rest to save themselves by a hasty retreat, lest they should be environed as the Romans had been. Hannibal, seeing so sudden a change of affairs, and Fabius, beyond the force of his age, opening his way through the ranks up the hillside, that he might join Minucius, warily forbore, sounded a retreat, and drew off his men into their camp; while the Romans on their part were no less contented to retire in safety. It is reported that upon this occasion Hannibal said jestingly to his friends: "Did not I tell you, that this cloud which always hovered upon the mountains would, at some time or other, come down with a storm upon us?"

Fabius, after his men had picked up the spoils of the field, retired to his own camp, without saying any harsh or reproachful thing to his colleague; who also on his part, gathering his army together, spoke and said to them: "To conduct great matters and never commit a fault is above the force of human nature; but to learn and improve by the faults we have committed, is that which becomes a good and sensible man. Some reasons I may have to accuse fortune, but I have many more to thank her; for in a few hours she hath cured a long mistake, and taught me that I am not the man who should command others, but have need of another to command me; and that we are not to contend for victory over those to whom it is our advantage to yield. Therefore in everything else henceforth the dictator must be your commander; only in showing gratitude towards him I will still be your leader, and always be the first to obey his orders." Having said this, he commanded the Roman eagles to move forward, and all his men to follow him to the camp of Fabius. The soldiers, then, as he entered, stood amazed at the novelty of the sight, and were anxious and doubtful what the meaning might be. When he came near the dictator's tent, Fabius went forth to meet him, on which he at once laid his standards at his feet, calling him with a loud voice his father; while the soldiers with him saluted the soldiers here as their patrons, the term employed by freedmen to those who gave them their liberty. After silence was obtained, Minucius said, "You have this day, O dictator, obtained two victories; one by your valor and conduct over Hannibal, and another by your wisdom and goodness over your colleague; by one victory you preserved, and by the other instructed us; and when we were already suffering one shameful defeat from Hannibal, by another welcome one from you we were restored to honor and safety. I can address you by no nobler name than that of a kind father, though a father's beneficence falls short of that I have received from you. From a father I individually received the gift of life; to you I owe its preservation not for myself only, but for all these who are under me." After this, he threw himself into the arms of the dictator; and in the same manner the soldiers of each army embraced one another with gladness and tears of joy.

Not long after, Fabius laid down the dictatorship, and consuls were again created. Those who immediately succeeded, observed the same method in managing the war, and avoided all occasions of fighting Hannibal in a pitched battle; they only succored their allies, and preserved the towns from falling off to the enemy. but afterwards, when Terentius Varro, a man of obscure birth, but very popular and bold, had obtained the consulship, he soon made it appear that by his rashness and ignorance he would stake the whole commonwealth on the hazard. For it was his custom to declaim in all assemblies, that, as long as Rome employed generals like Fabius there never would be an end of the war; vaunting that whenever he should get sight of the enemy, he would that same day free Italy from the strangers. With these promises he so prevailed, that he raised a greater army than had ever yet been sent out of Rome. There were enlisted eighty-eight thousand fighting men; but what gave confidence to the populace, only terrified the wise and experienced, and none more than Fabius; since if so great a body, and the flower of the Roman youth, should be cut off, they could not see any new resource for the safety of Rome. They addressed themselves, therefore, to the other consul, Aemilius Paulus, a man of great experience in war, but unpopular, and fearful also of the people, who once before upon some impeachment had condemned him; so that he needed encouragement to withstand his colleague's temerity. Fabius told him, if he would profitably serve his country, he must no less oppose Varro's ignorant eagerness than Hannibal's conscious readiness, since both alike conspired to decide the fate of Rome by a battle. "It is more reasonable," he said to him, "that you should believe me than Varro, in matters relating to Hannibal, when I tell you, that if for this year you abstain from fighting with him, either his army will perish of itself, or else he will be glad to depart of his own will. This evidently appears, inasmuch as, notwithstanding his victories, none of the countries or towns of Italy come in to him, and his army is not now the third part of what it was at first." To this Paulus is said to have replied, "Did I only consider myself, I should rather choose to be exposed to the weapons of Hannibal than once more to the suffrages of my fellow-citizens, who are urgent for what you disapprove; yet since the cause of Rome is at stake, I will rather seek in my conduct to please and obey Fabius than all the world besides."

These good measures were defeated by the importunity of Varro; whom, when they were both come to the army, nothing would content but a separate command, that each consul should have his day; and when his turn came, he posted his army close to Hannibal, at a village called Cannae, by the river Aufidus. It was no sooner day, but he set up the scarlet coat flying over his tent, which was the signal of battle. This boldness of the consul, and the numerousness of his army, double theirs, startled the Carthaginians; but Hannibal commanded them to their arms, and with a small train rode out to take a full prospect of the enemy as they were now forming in their ranks, from a rising ground not far distant. One of his followers, called Gisco, a Carthaginian of equal rank with himself, told him that the numbers of the enemy were astonishing; to which Hannibal replied, with a serious countenance, "There is one thing, Gisco, yet more astonishing, which you take no notice of;" and when Gisco inquired what, answered, that "in all those great numbers before us, there is not one man called Gisco." This unexpected jest of their general made all the company laugh, and as they came down from the hill, they told it to those whom they met, which caused a general laughter amongst them all, from which they were hardly able to recover themselves. The army, seeing Hannibal's attendants come back from viewing the enemy in such a laughing condition, concluded that it must be profound contempt of the enemy, that made their general at this moment indulge in such hilarity.

According to his usual manner, Hannibal employed stratagems to advantage himself. In the first place, he so drew up his men that the wind was at their backs, which at that time blew with a perfect storm of violence, and, sweeping over the great plains of sand, carried before it a cloud of dust over the Carthaginian army into the faces of the Romans, which much disturbed them in the fight. In the next place, all his best men he put into his wings; and in the body, which was somewhat more advanced than the wings, placed the worst and the weakest of his army. He commanded those in the wings, that, when the enemy had made a thorough charge upon that middle advanced body, which he knew would recoil, as not being able to withstand their shock, and when the Romans, in their pursuit, should be far enough engaged within the two wings, they should, both on the right and the left, charge them in the flank, and endeavor to encompass them. This appears to have been the chief cause of the Roman loss. Pressing upon Hannibal's front, which gave ground, they reduced the form of his army into a perfect half-moon, and gave ample opportunity to the captains of the chosen troops to charge them right and left on their flanks, and to cut off and destroy all who did not fall back before the Carthaginian wings united in their rear. To this general calamity, it is also said, that a strange mistake among the cavalry much contributed. For the horse of Aemilius receiving a hurt and throwing his master, those about him immediately alighted to aid the consul; and the Roman troops, seeing their commanders thus quitting their horses, took it for a sign that they should all dismount and charge the enemy on foot. At the sight of this, Hannibal was heard to say, "This pleases me better than if they had been delivered to me bound hand and foot." For the particulars of this engagement, we refer our reader to those authors who have written at large upon the subject.

The consul Varro, with a thin company, fled to Venusia; Aemilius Paulus, unable any longer to oppose the flight of his men, or the pursuit of the enemy, his body all covered with wounds, and his soul no less wounded with grief, sat himself down upon a stone, expecting the kindness of a dispatching blow. His face was so disfigured, and all his person so stained with blood, that his very friends and domestics passing by knew him not. At last Cornelius Lentulus, a young man of patrician race, perceiving who he was, alighted from his horse, and, tendering it to him, desired him to get up and save a life so necessary to the safety of the commonwealth, which, at this time, would dearly want so great a captain. But nothing could prevail upon him to accept of the offer; he obliged young Lentulus, with tears in his eyes, to remount his horse; then standing up, he gave him his hand, and commanded him to tell Fabius Maximus that Aemilius Paulus had followed his directions to his very last, and had not in the least deviated from those measures which were agreed between them; but that it was his hard fate to be overpowered by Varro in the first place, and secondly by Hannibal. Having dispatched Lentulus with this commission, he marked where the slaughter was greatest, and there threw himself upon the swords of the enemy. In this battle it is reported that fifty thousand Romans were slain, four thousand prisoners taken in the field, and ten thousand in the camp of both consuls.

The friends of Hannibal earnestly persuaded him to follow up his victory, and pursue the flying Romans into the very gates of Rome, assuring him that in five days' time he might sup in the capitol; nor is it easy to imagine what consideration hindered him from it. It would seem rather that some supernatural or divine intervention caused the hesitation and timidity which he now displayed, and which made Barcas, a Carthaginian, tell him with indignation, "You know, Hannibal, how to gain a victory, but not how to use it." Yet it produced a marvelous revolution in his affairs; he, who hitherto had not one town, market, or seaport in his possession, who had nothing for the subsistence of his men but what he pillaged from day to day, who had no place of retreat or basis of operation, but was roving, as it were, with a huge troop of banditti, now became master of the best provinces and towns of Italy, and of

Capua itself, next to Rome the most flourishing and opulent city, all which came over to him, and submitted to his authority.

It is the saying of Euripides, that "a man is in ill-case when he must try a friend," and so neither, it would seem, is a state in a good one, when it needs an able general. And so it was with the Romans; the counsels and actions of Fabius, which, before the battle, they had branded as cowardice and fear, now, in the other extreme they accounted to have been more than human wisdom; as though nothing but a divine power of intellect could have seen so far, and foretold, contrary to the judgment of all others, a result which, even now it had arrived, was hardly credible. In him, therefore, they placed their whole remaining hopes; his wisdom was the sacred altar and temple to which they fled for refuge, and his counsels, more than anything, preserved them from dispersing and deserting their city, as in the time when the Gauls took possession of Rome. He, whom they esteemed fearful and pusillanimous when they were, as they thought, in a prosperous condition, was now the only man, in this general and unbounded dejection and confusion, who showed no fear, but walked the streets with an assured and serene countenance, addressed his fellow-citizens, checked the women's lamentations, and the public gatherings of those who wanted thus to vent their sorrows. He caused the senate to meet, he heartened up the magistrates, and was himself as the soul and life of every office.

He placed guards at the gates of the city to stop the frighted multitude from flying; he regulated and controlled their mournings for their slain friends, both as to time and place; ordering that each family should perform such observances within private walls, and that they should continue only the space of one month, and then the whole city should be purified. The feast of Ceres happening to fall within this time, it was decreed that the solemnity should be intermitted, lest the fewness, and the sorrowful countenance of those who should celebrate it, might too much expose to the people the greatness of their loss; besides that, the worship most acceptable to the gods is that which comes from cheerful hearts. But those rites which were proper for appeasing their anger, and procuring auspicious signs and presages, were by the direction of the augurs carefully performed. Fabius Pictor, a near kinsman to Maximus, was sent to consult the oracle of Delphi; and about the same time, two vestals having been detected to have been violated, the one killed herself, and the other, according to custom, was buried alive.

Above all, let us admire the high spirit and equanimity of this Roman commonwealth; that when the consul Varro came beaten and flying home, full of shame and humiliation, after he had so disgracefully and calamitously managed their affairs, yet the whole senate and people went forth to meet him at the gates of the city, and received him with honor and respect. And, silence being commanded, the magistrates and chief of the senate, Fabius amongst them, commended him before the people, because he did not despair of the safety of the commonwealth, after so great a loss, but was come to take the government into his hands, to execute the laws, and aid his fellow-citizens in their prospect of future deliverance.

When word was brought to Rome that Hannibal, after the fight, had marched with his army into other parts of Italy, the hearts of the Romans began to revive, and they proceeded to send out generals and armies. The most distinguished commands were held by Fabius Maximus and Claudius Marcellus, both generals of great fame, though upon opposite grounds. For Marcellus, as we have set forth in his life, was a man of action and high spirit, ready and bold with his own hand, and, as Homer describes his warriors, fierce, and delighting in fights. Boldness, enterprise, and daring, to match those of Hannibal, constituted his tactics, and marked his engagements. But Fabius adhered to his former principles, still persuaded that, by following close and not fighting him, Hannibal and his army would at last be tired out and consumed, like a wrestler in too high condition, whose very excess of strength makes him the more likely suddenly to give way and lose it. Posidonius tells us that the Romans called Marcellus their sword, and Fabius their buckler; and that the vigor of the one, mixed with the steadiness of the other, made a happy compound that proved the salvation of Rome. So that Hannibal found by experience that, encountering the one, he met with a rapid, impetuous river, which drove him back, and still made some breach upon him; and by the other, though silently and quietly passing by him, he was insensibly washed away and consumed; and, at last, was brought to this, that he dreaded Marcellus when he was in motion, and Fabius when he sat still. During the whole course of this war, he had still to do with one or both of these generals; for each of them was five times consul, and, as praetors or proconsuls or consuls, they had always a part in the government of the army, till, at last, Marcellus fell into the trap which Hannibal had laid for him, and was killed in his fifth consulship. But all his craft and subtlety were unsuccessful upon Fabius, who only once was in some danger of being caught, when counterfeit letters came to him from the principal inhabitants of Metapontum, with promises to deliver up their town if he would come before it with his army, and intimations that they should expect him, This train had almost drawn him in; he resolved to march to them with part of his army, and was diverted only by consulting the omens of the birds, which he found to be inauspicious; and not long after it was discovered that the letters had been forged by Hannibal, who, for his reception, had laid an ambush to entertain him. This, perhaps, we must rather attribute to the favor of the gods than to the prudence of Fabius.

In preserving the towns and allies from revolt by fair and gentle treatment, and in not using rigor, or showing a suspicion upon every light suggestion, his conduct was remarkable. It is told of him, that, being informed of a certain

Marsian, eminent for courage and good birth, who had been speaking underhand with some of the soldiers about deserting, Fabius was so far from using severity against him, that he called for him, and told him he was sensible of the neglect that had been shown to his merit and good service, which, he said, was a great fault in the commanders who reward more by favor than by desert; "but henceforward, whenever you are aggrieved," said Fabius, "I shall consider it your fault, if you apply yourself to any but to me;" and when he had so spoken, he bestowed an excellent horse and other presents upon him; and, from that time forwards, there was not a faithfuller and more trusty man in the whole army. With good reason he judged, that, if those who have the government of horses and dogs endeavor by gentle usage to cure their angry and untractable tempers, rather than by cruelty and beating, much more should those who have the command of men try to bring them to order and discipline by the mildest and fairest means, and not treat them worse than gardeners do those wild plants, which, with care and attention, lose gradually the savageness of their nature, and bear excellent fruit.

At another time, some of his officers informed him that one of their men was very often absent from his place, and out at nights; he asked them what kind of man he was; they all answered, that the whole army had not a better man, that he was a native of Lucania, and proceeded to speak of several actions which they had seen him perform. Fabius made strict inquiry, and discovered at last that these frequent excursions which he ventured upon were to visit a young girl, with whom he was in love. Upon which he gave private order to some of his men to find out the woman and secretly convey her into his own tent; and then sent for the Lucanian, and, calling him aside, told him, that he very well knew how often he had been out away from the camp at night, which was a capital transgression against military discipline and the Roman laws, but he knew also how brave he was, and the good services he had done; therefore, in consideration of them, he was willing to forgive him his fault; but to keep him in good order, he was resolved to place one over him to be his keeper, who should be accountable for his good behavior. Having said this, he produced the woman, and told the soldier, terrified and amazed at the adventure, "This is the person who must answer for you; and by your future behavior we shall see whether your night rambles were on account of love, or for any other worse design."

Another passage there was, something of the same kind, which gained him possession of Tarentum. There was a young Tarentine in the army that had a sister in Tarentum, then in possession of the enemy, who entirely loved her brother, and wholly depended upon him. He, being informed that a certain Bruttian, whom Hannibal had made a commander of the garrison, was deeply in love with his sister, conceived hopes that he might possibly turn it to the advantage of the Romans. And having first communicated his design to

Fabius, he left the army as a deserter in show, and went over to Tarentum. The first days passed, and the Bruttian abstained from visiting the sister; for neither of them knew that the brother had notice of the amour between them. The young Tarentine, however, took an occasion to tell his sister how he had heard that a man of station and authority had made his addresses to her; and desired her, therefore, to tell him who it was; "for," said he, "if he be a man that has bravery and reputation, it matters not what countryman he is, since at this time the sword mingles all nations, and makes them equal; compulsion makes all things honorable; and in a time when right is weak, we may be thankful if might assumes a form of gentleness." Upon this the woman sends for her friend, and makes the brother and him acquainted; and whereas she henceforth showed more countenance to her lover than formerly, in the same degrees that her kindness increased, his friendship, also, with the brother advanced. So that at last our Tarentine thought this Bruttian officer well enough prepared to receive the offers he had to make him; and that it would be easy for a mercenary man, who was in love, to accept, upon the terms proposed, the large rewards promised by Fabius. In conclusion, the bargain was struck, and the promise made of delivering the town. This is the common tradition, though some relate the story otherwise, and say, that this woman, by whom the Bruttian was inveigled, to betray the town, was not a native of Tarentum, but a Bruttian born, and was kept by Fabius as his concubine; and being a countrywoman and an acquaintance of the Bruttian governor, he privately sent her to him to corrupt him.

Whilst these matters were thus in process, to draw off Hannibal from scenting the design, Fabius sends orders to the garrison in Rhegium, that they should waste and spoil the Bruttian country, and should also lay siege to Caulonia, and storm the place with all their might. These were a body of eight thousand men, the worst of the Roman army, who had most of them been runaways, and had been brought home by Marcellus from Sicily, in dishonor, so that the loss of them would not be any great grief to the Romans. Fabius, therefore, threw out these men as a bait for Hannibal, to divert him from Tarentum; who instantly caught at it, and led his forces to Caulonia; in the meantime, Fabius sat down before Tarentum. On the sixth day of the siege, the young Tarentine slips by night out of the town, and, having carefully observed the place where the Bruttian commander, according to agreement, was to admit the Romans, gave an account of the whole matter to Fabius; who thought it not safe to rely wholly upon the plot, but, while proceeding with secrecy to the post, gave order for a general assault to be made on the other side of the town, both by land and sea. This being accordingly executed, while the Tarentines hurried to defend the town on the side attacked, Fabius received the signal from the Bruttian, scaled the walls, and entered the town unopposed.

Here, we must confess, ambition seems to have overcome him. To make it appear to the world that he had taken Tarentum by force and his own prowess, and not by treachery, he commanded his men to kill the Bruttians before all others; yet he did not succeed in establishing the impression he desired, but merely gained the character of perfidy and cruelty. Many of the Tarentines were also killed, and thirty thousand of them were sold for slaves; the army had the plunder of the town, and there was brought into the treasury three thousand talents. Whilst they were carrying off everything else as plunder, the officer who took the inventory asked what should be done with their gods, meaning the pictures and statues; Fabius answered, "Let us leave their angry gods to the Tarentines." Nevertheless, he removed the colossal statue of Hercules, and had it set up in the capitol, with one of himself on horseback, in brass, near it; proceedings very different from those of Marcellus on a like occasion, and which, indeed, very much set off in the eyes of the world his clemency and humanity, as appears in the account of his life.

Hannibal, it is said, was within five miles of Tarentum, when he was informed that the town was taken. He said openly, "Rome, then, has also got a Hannibal; as we won Tarentum, so have we lost it." And, in private with some of his confidants, he told them, for the first time, that he always thought it difficult, but now he held it impossible, with the forces he then had, to master Italy.

Upon this success, Fabius had a triumph decreed him at Rome, much more splendid than his first; they looked upon him now as a champion who had learned to cope with his antagonist, and could now easily foil his arts and prove his best skill ineffectual. And, indeed, the army of Hannibal was at this time partly worn away with continual action, and partly weakened and become dissolute with overabundance and luxury. Marcus Livius, who was governor of Tarentum when it was betrayed to Hannibal, and then retired into the citadel, which he kept till the town was retaken, was annoyed at these honors and distinctions, and, on one occasion, openly declared in the senate, that by his resistance, more than by any action of Fabius, Tarentum had been recovered; on which Fabius laughingly replied: "You say very true, for if Marcus Livius had not lost Tarentum, Fabius Maximus had never recovered it." The people, amongst other marks of gratitude, gave his son the consulship of the next year; shortly after whose entrance upon his office, there being some business on foot about provision for the war, his father, either by reason of age and infirmity, or perhaps out of design to try his son, came up to him on horseback. While he was still at a distance, the young consul observed it, and bade one of his lictors command his father to alight, and tell him that, if be had any business with the consul, he should come on foot. The standers by seemed offended at the imperiousness of the son towards a father so venerable for his age and his authority, and turned their eyes in silence towards Fabius.

He, however, instantly alighted from his horse, and with open arms came up, almost running, and embraced his son, saying, "Yes, my son, you do well, and understand well what authority you have received, and over whom you are to use it. This was the way by which we and our forefathers advanced the dignity of Rome, preferring ever her honor and service to our own fathers and children."

And, in fact, it is told that the great-grandfather of our Fabius, who was undoubtedly the greatest man of Rome in his time, both in reputation and authority, who had been five times consul, and had been honored with several triumphs for victories obtained by him, took pleasure in serving as lieutenant under his own son, when he went as consul to his command. And when afterwards his son had a triumph bestowed upon him for his good service, the old man followed, on horseback, his triumphant chariot, as one of his attendants; and made it his glory, that while he really was, and was acknowledged to be, the greatest man in Rome, and held a father's full power over his son, he yet submitted himself to the laws and the magistrate.

But the praises of our Fabius are not bounded here. He afterwards lost this son, and was remarkable for bearing the loss with the moderation becoming a pious father and a wise man, and, as it was the custom amongst the Romans, upon the death of any illustrious person, to have a funeral oration recited by some of the nearest relations, he took upon himself that office, and delivered a speech in the forum, which he committed afterwards to writing.

After Cornelius Scipio, who was sent into Spain, had driven the Carthaginians, defeated by him in many battles, out of the country, and had gained over to Rome many towns and nations with large resources, he was received at his coming home with unexampled joy and acclamation of the people; who, to show their gratitude, elected him consul for the year ensuing. Knowing what high expectation they had of him, he thought the occupation of contesting Italy with Hannibal a mere old man's employment, and proposed no less a task to himself than to make Carthage the seat of the war, fill Africa with arms and devastation, and so oblige Hannibal, instead of invading the countries of others, to draw back and defend his own. And to this end he proceeded to exert all the influence he had with the people. Fabius, on the other side, opposed the undertaking with all his might, alarming the city, and telling them that nothing but the temerity of a hot young man could inspire them with such dangerous counsels, and sparing no means, by word or deed, to prevent it. He prevailed with the senate to espouse his sentiments; but the common people thought that he envied the fame of Scipio, and that he was afraid lest this young conqueror should achieve some great and noble exploit, and have the glory, perhaps, of driving Hannibal out of Italy, or even of ending the war, which had for so many years continued and been protracted under his management.

To say the truth, when Fabius first opposed this project of Scipio, he probably did it out of caution and prudence, in consideration only of the public safety, and of the danger which the commonwealth might incur; but when he found Scipio every day increasing in the esteem of the people, rivalry and ambition led him further, and made him violent and personal in his opposition. For he even applied to Crassus, the colleague of Scipio, and urged him not to yield the command to Scipio, but that, if his inclinations were for it, he should himself in person lead the army to Carthage. He also hindered the giving money to Scipio for the war; so that he was forced to raise it upon his own credit and interest from the cities of Etruria, which were extremely attached to him. On the other side, Crassus would not stir against him, nor remove out of Italy, being, in his own nature, averse to all contention, and also having, by his office of high priest, religious duties to retain him. Fabius, therefore, tried other ways to oppose the design; he impeded the levies, and he declaimed, both in the senate and to the people, that Scipio was not only himself flying from Hannibal, but was also endeavoring to drain Italy of all its forces, and to spirit away the youth of the country to a foreign war, leaving behind them their parents, wives, and children, and the city itself, a defenseless prey to the conquering and undefeated enemy at their doors. With this he so far alarmed the people, that at last they would only allow Scipio for the war the legions which were in Sicily, and three hundred, whom he particularly trusted, of those men who had served with him in Spain. In these transactions, Fabius seems to have followed the dictates of his own wary temper.

But, after that Scipio was gone over into Africa, when news almost immediately came to Rome of wonderful exploits and victories, of which the fame was confirmed by the spoils he sent home; of a Numidian king taken prisoner; of a vast slaughter of their men; of two camps of the enemy burnt and destroyed, and in them a great quantity of arms and horses; and when, hereupon, the Carthaginians were compelled to send envoys to Hannibal to call him home, and leave his idle hopes in Italy, to defend Carthage; when, for such eminent and transcending services, the whole people of Rome cried up and extolled the actions of Scipio; even then, Fabius contended that a successor should be sent in his place, alleging for it only the old reason of the mutability of fortune, as if she would be weary of long favoring the same person. With this language many did begin to feel offended; it seemed to be morosity and ill-will, the pusillanimity of old age, or a fear, that had now become exaggerated, of the skill of Hannibal. Nay, when Hannibal had put his army on shipboard, and taken his leave of Italy, Fabius still could not forbear to oppose and disturb the universal joy of Rome, expressing his fears and apprehensions, telling them that the commonwealth was never in more danger than now, and that Hannibal was a more formidable enemy under the walls of Carthage than ever he had been in Italy; that it would be fatal to Rome, whenever Scipio should encounter his victorious army, still warm with the blood of so many Roman generals, dictators, and consuls slain. And the people were, in some degree, startled with these declamations, and were brought to believe, that the further off Hannibal was, the nearer was their danger. Scipio, however, shortly afterwards fought Hannibal, and utterly defeated him, humbled the pride of Carthage beneath his feet, gave his countrymen joy and exultation beyond all their hopes, and

> *"Long shaken on the seas restored the state."*

Fabius Maximus, however, did not live to see the prosperous end of this war, and the final overthrow of Hannibal, nor to rejoice in the reestablished happiness and security of the commonwealth; for about the time that Hannibal left Italy, he fell sick and died. At Thebes, Epaminondas died so poor that he was buried at the public charge; one small iron coin was all, it is said, that was found in his house. Fabius did not need this, but the people, as a mark of their affection, defrayed the expenses of his funeral by a private contribution from each citizen of the smallest piece of coin; thus owning him their common father, and making his end no less honorable than his life.

6
COMPARISON OF PERICLES WITH FABIUS

We have here had two lives rich in examples, both of civil and military excellence. Let us first compare the two men in their warlike capacity. Pericles presided in his commonwealth when it was in its most flourishing and opulent condition, great and growing in power; so that it may be thought it was rather the common success and fortune that kept him from any fall or disaster. But the task of Fabius, who undertook the government in the worst and most difficult times, was not to preserve and maintain the well-established felicity of a prosperous state, but to raise and uphold a sinking and ruinous commonwealth. Besides, the victories of Cimon, the trophies of Myronides and Leocrates, with the many famous exploits of Tolmides, were employed by Pericles rather to fill the city with festive entertainments and solemnities than to enlarge and secure its empire. Whereas Fabius, when he took upon him the government, had the frightful object before his eyes of Roman armies destroyed, of their generals and consuls slain, of lakes and plains and forests strewed with the dead bodies, and rivers stained with the blood of his fellow-citizens; and yet, with his mature and solid cousels, with the firmness of his resolution, he, as it were, put his shoulder to the falling commonwealth, and kept it up from foundering through the failings and weakness of others. Perhaps it may be more easy to govern a city broken and tamed with calamities and adversity, and compelled by danger and necessity to listen to wisdom, than to set a bridle on wantonness and temerity, and rule a people pampered and restive with long prosperity as were the Athenians when Pericles held the reins of government. But then again, not to be daunted nor discomposed with the vast heap of calamities under which the people of Rome at that time groaned and succumbed, argues a courage in Fabius and a strength of purpose more than ordinary.

We may set Tarentum retaken against Samos won by Pericles, and the conquest of Euboea we may well balance with the towns of Campania; though Capua itself was reduced by the consuls Fulvius and Appius. I do not find that Fabius won any set battle but that against the Ligurians, for which he had his triumph; whereas Pericles erected nine trophies for as many victories obtained by land and by sea. But no action of Pericles can be compared to that memorable rescue of Minucius, when Fabius redeemed both him and his army from utter destruction; a noble act, combining the highest valor, wisdom, and humanity. On the other side, it does not appear that Pericles was ever so overreached as Fabius was by Hannibal with his flaming oxen. His enemy there had, without his agency, put himself accidentally into his power, yet Fabius let him slip in the night, and, when day came, was worsted by him, was anticipated in the moment of success, and mastered by his prisoner. If it is the part of a good general, not only to provide for the present, but also to have a clear foresight of things to come, in this point Pericles is the superior; for he admonished the Athenians, and told them beforehand the ruin the war would bring upon them, by their grasping more than they were able to manage. But Fabius was not so good a prophet, when he denounced to the Romans that the undertaking of Scipio would be the destruction of the commonwealth. So that Pericles was a good prophet of bad success, and Fabius was a bad prophet of success that was good. And, indeed, to lose an advantage through diffidence is no less blamable in a general than to fall into danger for want of foresight; for both these faults, though of a contrary nature, spring from the same root, want of judgment and experience.

As for their civil policy, it is imputed to Pericles that he occasioned the war, since no terms of peace, offered by the Lacedaemonians, would content him. It is true, I presume, that Fabius, also, was not for yielding any point to the Carthaginians, but was ready to hazard all, rather than lessen the empire of Rome. The mildness of Fabius towards his colleague Minucius does, by way of comparison, rebuke and condemn the exertions of Pericles to banish Cimon and Thucydides, noble, aristocratic men, who by his means suffered ostracism. The authority of Pericles in Athens was much greater than that of Fabius in Rome. Hence it was more easy for him to prevent miscarriages arising from the mistakes and insufficiency of other officers; only Tolmides broke loose from him, and, contrary to his persuasions, unadvisedly fought with the Boeotians, and was slain. The greatness of his influence made all others submit and conform themselves to his judgment. Whereas Fabius, sure and unerring himself, for want of that general power, had not the means to obviate the miscarriages of others; but it had been happy for the Romans if his authority had been greater, for so, we may presume, their disasters had been fewer.

As to liberality and public spirit, Pericles was eminent in never taking any gifts, and Fabius, for giving his own money to ransom his soldiers, though the sum did not exceed six talents. Than Pericles, meantime, no man had ever greater opportunities to enrich himself, having had presents offered him from so many kings and princes and allies, yet no man was ever more free from corruption. And for the beauty and magnificence of temples and public edifices with which he adorned his country, it must be confessed, that all the ornaments and structures of Rome, to the time of the Caesars, had nothing to compare, either in greatness of design or of expense, with the luster of those which Pericles only erected at Athens.

7
NICIAS

Crassus, in my opinion, may most properly be set against Nicias, and the Parthian disaster compared with that in Sicily. But here it will be well for me to entreat the reader, in all courtesy, not to think that I contend with Thucydides in matters so pathetically, vividly, and eloquently, beyond all imitation, and even beyond himself, expressed by him; nor to believe me guilty of the like folly with Timaeus, who, hoping in his history to surpass Thucydides in art, and to make Philistus appear a trifler and a novice, pushes on in his descriptions, through all the battles, sea-fights, and public speeches, in recording which they have been most successful, without meriting so much as to be compared in Pindar's phrase, to

> *One that on his feet*
> *Would with the Lydian cars compete.*

He simply shows himself all along a half-lettered, childish writer; in the words of Diphilus,

> *— of wit obese,*
> *O'erlarded with Sicilian grease.*

Often he sinks to the very level of Xenarchus, telling us that he thinks it ominous to the Athenians that their general, who had victory in his name, was unwilling to take command in the expedition; and that the defacing of the Hermae was a divine intimation that they should suffer much in the war by

Hermocrates, the son of Hermon; and, moreover, how it was likely that Hercules should aid the Syracusans for the sake of Proserpine, by whose means he took Cerberus, and should be angry with the Athenians for protecting the Egesteans, descended from Trojan ancestors, whose city he, for an injury of their king Laomedon, had overthrown. However, all these may be merely other instances of the same happy taste that makes him correct the diction of Philistus, and abuse Plato and Aristotle. This sort of contention and rivalry with others in matter of style, to my mind, in any case, seems petty and pedantic, but when its objects are works of inimitable excellence, it is absolutely senseless. Such actions in Nicias's life as Thucydides and Philistus have related, since they cannot be passed by, illustrating as they do most especially his character and temper, under his many and great troubles, that I may not seem altogether negligent, I shall briefly run over. And such things as are not commonly known, and lie scattered here and there in other men's writings, or are found amongst the old monuments and archives, I shall endeavor to bring together; not collecting mere useless pieces of learning, but adducing what may make his disposition and habit of mind understood.

First of all, I would mention what Aristotle has said of Nicias, that there had been three good citizens, eminent above the rest for their hereditary affection and love to the people, Nicias the son of Niceratus, Thucydides the son of Melesias, and Theramenes the son of Hagnon, but the last less than the others; for he had his dubious extraction cast in his teeth, as a foreigner from Ceos, and his inconstancy, which made him side sometimes with one party, sometimes with another in public life, and which obtained him the nickname of the Buskin.

Thucydides came earlier, and, on the behalf of the nobility, was a great opponent of the measures by which Pericles courted the favor of the people.

Nicias was a younger man, yet was in some reputation even whilst Pericles lived; so much so as to have been his colleague in the office of general, and to have held command by himself more than once. But on the death of Pericles, he presently rose to the highest place, chiefly by the favor of the rich and eminent citizens, who set him up for their bulwark against the presumption and insolence of Cleon; nevertheless, he did not forfeit the good-will of the commonalty, who, likewise, contributed to his advancement. For though Cleon got great influence by his exertions

> — *to please*
> *The old men, who trusted him to find them fees.*

Yet even those, for whose interest, and to gain whose favor he acted, nevertheless observing the avarice, the arrogance, and the presumption of the man, many of them supported Nicias. For his was not that sort of gravity which is harsh and offensive, but he tempered it with a certain caution and deference, winning upon the people, by seeming afraid of them. And being naturally diffident and unhopeful in war, his good fortune supplied his want of courage, and kept it from being detected, as in all his commands he was constantly successful. And his timorousness in civil life, and his extreme dread of accusers, was thought very suitable in a citizen of a free State; and from the people's good-will towards him, got him no small power over them, they being fearful of all that despised them, but willing to promote one who seemed to be afraid of them; the greatest compliment their betters could pay them being not to contemn them.

Pericles, who by solid virtue and the pure force of argument ruled the commonwealth, had stood in need of no disguises nor persuasions with the people. Nicias, inferior in these respects, used his riches, of which he had abundance, to gain popularity. Neither had he the nimble wit of Cleon, to win the Athenians to his purposes by amusing them with bold jests; unprovided with such qualities, he courted them with dramatic exhibitions, gymnastic games, and other public shows, more sumptuous and more splendid than had been ever known in his, or in former ages. Amongst his religious offerings, there was extant, even in our days, the small figure of Minerva in the citadel, having lost the gold that covered it; and a shrine in the temple of Bacchus, under the tripods, that were presented by those who won the prize in the shows of plays. For at these he had often carried off the prize, and never once failed. We are told that on one of these occasions, a slave of his appeared in the character of Bacchus, of a beautiful person and noble stature, and with as yet no beard upon his chin; and on the Athenians being pleased with the sight, and applauding a long time, Nicias stood up, and said he could not in piety keep as a slave, one whose person had been consecrated to represent a god. And forthwith he set the young man free. His performances at Delos are, also, on record, as noble and magnificent works of devotion. For whereas the choruses which the cities sent to sing hymns to the god were wont to arrive in no order, as it might happen, and, being there met by a crowd of people crying out to them to sing, in their hurry to begin, used to disembark confusedly, putting on their garlands, and changing their dresses as they left the ships, he, when he had to convoy the sacred company, disembarked the chorus at Rhenea, together with the sacrifice, and other holy appurtenances. And having brought along with him from Athens a bridge fitted by measurement for the purpose, and magnificently adorned with gilding and coloring, and with garlands and tapestries; this he laid in the night over the channel betwixt Rhenea and Delos, being no great distance. And at break of day he marched forth with all the procession to the god, and led the chorus, sumptuously ornamented, and singing their hymns, along over the bridge. The sacrifices, the games, and the feast being over, he set up a palm-tree of brass for a present to the god, and bought a parcel of land with ten thousand drachmas which he consecrated; with the revenue the inhabitants of Delos were to sacrifice and to feast, and to pray the gods for many good things to Nicias. This he engraved on a pillar, which he left in Delos to be a record of his bequest. This same palm-tree, afterwards broken down by the wind, fell on the great statue which the men of Naxos presented, and struck it to the ground.

It is plain that much of this might be vainglory, and the mere desire of popularity and applause; yet from other qualities and carriage of the man, one might believe all this cost and public display to be the effect of devotion. For he was one of those who dreaded the divine powers extremely, and, as Thucydides tells us, was much given to arts of divination. In one of Pasiphon's dialogues, it is stated that he daily sacrificed to the gods, and keeping a diviner at his house, professed to be consulting always about the commonwealth, but for the most part, inquired about his own private affairs, more especially concerning his silver mines; for he owned many works at Laurium, of great value, but somewhat hazardous to carry on. He maintained there a multitude of slaves, and his wealth consisted chiefly in silver. Hence he had many hangers-on about him, begging and obtaining. For he gave to those who could do him mischief, no less than to those who deserved well. In short, his timidity was a revenue to rogues, and his humanity to honest men. We find testimony in the comic writers, as when Teleclides, speaking of one of the professed informers, says:—

> *Charicles gave the man a pound, the matter not to name,*
> *That from inside a money-bag into the world he came;*
> *And Nicias, also, paid him four; I know the reason well,*
> *But Nicias is a worthy man, and so I will not tell.*

So, also, the informer whom Eupolis introduces in his Maricas, attacking a good, simple, poor man:—

> *How long ago did you and Nicias meet?*
> *I did but see him just now in the street.*
> *The man has seen him and denies it not,*
> *'Tis evident that they are in a plot.*
> *See you, O citizens! 'tis fact,*
> *Nicias is taken in the act.*
> *Taken, Fools! take so good a man*
> *In aught that's wrong none will or can.*

Cleon, in Aristophanes, makes it one of his threats:—

PLUTARCH

> *I'll outscream all the speakers, and make Nicias stand aghast!*

Phrynichus also implies his want of spirit, and his easiness to be intimidated in the verses,

> *A noble man he was, I well can say,*
> *Nor walked like Nicias, cowering on his way.*

So cautious was he of informers, and so reserved, that he never would dine out with any citizen, nor allowed himself to indulge in talk and conversation with his friends, nor gave himself any leisure for such amusements; but when he was general he used to stay at the office till night, and was the first that came to the council-house, and the last that left it. And if no public business engaged him, it was very hard to have access, or to speak with him, he being retired at home and locked up. And when any came to the door, some friend of his gave them good words, and begged them to excuse him, Nicias was very busy; as if affairs of State and public duties still kept him occupied. He who principally acted this part for him, and contributed most to this state and show, was Hiero, a man educated in Nicias's family, and instructed by him in letters and music. He professed to be the son of Dionysius, surnamed Chalcus, whose poems are yet extant, and had led out the colony to Italy, and founded Thurii. This Hiero transacted all his secrets for Nicias with the dinners; and gave out to the people, what a toilsome and miserable life he led, for the sake of the commonwealth. "He," said Hiero, "can never be either at the bath, or at his meat, but some public business interferes. Careless of his own, and zealous for the public good, he scarcely ever goes to bed till after others have had their first sleep. So that his health is impaired, and his body out of order, nor is he cheerful or affable with his friends, but loses them as well as his money in the service of the State, while other men gain friends by public speaking, enrich themselves, fare delicately, and make government their amusement." And in fact this was Nicias's manner of life, so that he well might apply to himself the words of Agamemnon:—

> *Vain pomp's the ruler of the life we live,*
> *And a slave's service to the crowd we give.*

He observed that the people, in the case of men of eloquence, or of eminent parts, made use of their talents upon occasion, but were always jealous of their abilities, and held a watchful eye upon them, taking all opportunities to humble their pride and abate their reputation; as was manifest in their condemnation of Pericles, their banishment of Damon, their distrust of Antiphon the Rhamnusian, but especially in the case of Paches who took

Lesbos, who, having to give an account of his conduct, in the very court of justice unsheathed his sword and slew himself. Upon such considerations, Nicias declined all difficult and lengthy enterprises; if he took a command, he was for doing what was safe; and if, as thus was likely, he had for the most part success, he did not attribute it to any wisdom, conduct, or courage of his own, but, to avoid envy, he thanked fortune for all, and gave the glory to the divine powers. And the actions themselves bore testimony in his favor; the city met at that time with several considerable reverses, but he had not a hand in any of them. The Athenians were routed in Thrace by the Chalcidians, Calliades and Xenophon commanding in chief. Demosthenes was the general when they were unfortunate in Aetolia. At Delium, they lost a thousand citizens under the conduct of Hippocrates; the plague was principally laid to the charge of Pericles, he, to carry on the war, having shut up close together in the town the crowd of people from the country, who, by the change of place, and of their usual course of living, bred the pestilence. Nicias stood clear of all this; under his conduct was taken Cythera, an island most commodious against Laconia, and occupied by the Lacedaemonian settlers; many places, likewise, in Thrace, which had revolted, were taken or won over by him; he, shutting up the Megarians within their town, seized upon the isle of Minoa; and soon after, advancing from thence to Nisaea, made himself master there, and then making a descent upon the Corinthian territory, fought a successful battle, and slew a great number of the Corinthians with their captain Lycophron. There it happened that two of his men were left by an oversight, when they carried off the dead, which when he understood, he stopped the fleet, and sent a herald to the enemy for leave to carry off the dead; though by law and custom, he that by a truce craved leave to carry off the dead, was hereby supposed to give up all claim to the victory. Nor was it lawful for him that did this to erect a trophy, for his is the victory who is master of the field, and he is not master who asks leave, as wanting power to take. But he chose rather to renounce his victory and his glory, than to let two citizens lie unburied. He scoured the coast of Laconia all along, and beat the Lacedaemonians that made head against him. He took Thyrea, occupied by the Aeginetans, and carried the prisoners to Athens.

When Demosthenes had fortified Pylos, and the Peloponnesians brought together both their sea and land forces before it, after the fight, about the number of four hundred native Spartans were left ashore in the isle Sphacteria. The Athenians thought it a great prize, as indeed it was, to take these men prisoners. But the siege, in places that wanted water, being very difficult and untoward, and to convey necessaries about by sea in summer tedious and expensive, in winter doubtful, or plainly impossible, they began to be annoyed, and to repent their having rejected the embassy of the Lacedaemonians that had been sent to propose a treaty of peace, which had been done at the importunity of Cleon, who opposed it chiefly out of a pique to Nicias; for, being his enemy, and observing him to be extremely solicitous to support the offers of the Lacedaemonians, he persuaded the people to refuse them.

Now, therefore, that the siege was protracted, and they heard of the difficulties that pressed their army, they grew enraged against Cleon. But he turned all the blame upon Nicias, charging it on his softness and cowardice, that the besieged were not yet taken. "Were I general," said he, "they should not hold out so long." The Athenians not unnaturally asked the question, "Why then, as it is, do not you go with a squadron against them?" And Nicias standing up resigned his command at Pylos to him, and bade him take what forces he pleased along with him, and not be bold in words, out of harm's way, but go forth and perform some real service for the commonwealth. Cleon, at the first, tried to draw back, disconcerted at the proposal, which he had never expected; but the Athenians insisting, and Nicias loudly upbraiding him, he thus provoked, and fired with ambition, took upon him the charge, and said further, that within twenty days after he embarked, he would either kill the enemy upon the place, or bring them alive to Athens. This the Athenians were readier to laugh at than to believe, as on other occasions, also, his bold assertions and extravagances used to make them sport, and were pleasant enough. As, for instance, it is reported that once when the people were assembled, and had waited his coming a long time, at last he appeared with a garland on his head, and prayed them to adjourn to the next day. "For," said he, "I am not at leisure to-day; I have sacrificed to the gods, and am to entertain some strangers." Whereupon the Athenians laughing rose up, and dissolved the assembly. However, at this time he had good fortune, and in conjunction with Demosthenes, conducted the enterprise so well, that within the time he had limited, he carried captive to Athens all the Spartans that had not fallen in battle.

This brought great disgrace on Nicias; for this was not to throw away his shield, but something yet more shameful and ignominious, to quit his charge voluntarily out of cowardice, and voting himself, as it were, out of his command of his own accord, to put into his enemy's hand the opportunity of achieving so brave an action. Aristophanes has a jest against him on this occasion in the Birds:—

> *Indeed, not now the word that must be said*
> *Is, do like Nicias, or retire to bed.*

And, again, in his Husbandmen:—

> *I wish to stay at home and farm.*
> *What then?*
> *Who should prevent you?*

You, my countrymen;
Whom I would pay a thousand drachmas down,
To let me give up office and leave town

Enough; content; the sum two thousand is,
With those that Nicias paid to give up his.

Besides all this, he did great mischief to the city by suffering the accession of so much reputation and power to Cleon, who now assumed such lofty airs, and allowed himself in such intolerable audacity, as led to many unfortunate results, a sufficient part of which fell to his own share. Amongst other things, he destroyed all the decorum of public speaking; he was the first who ever broke out into exclamations, flung open his dress, smote his thigh, and ran up and down whilst he was speaking, things which soon after introduced amongst those who managed the affairs of State, such license and contempt of decency, as brought all into confusion.

Already, too, Alcibiades was beginning to show his strength at Athens, a popular leader, not, indeed, as utterly violent as Cleon, but as the land of Egypt, through the richness of its soil, is said,

— great plenty to produce,
Both wholesome herbs, and drugs of deadly juice,

so the nature of Alcibiades was strong and luxuriant in both kinds, and made way for many serious innovations. Thus it fell out that after Nicias had got his hands clear of Cleon, he had not opportunity to settle the city perfectly into quietness. For having brought matters to a pretty hopeful condition, he found everything carried away and plunged again into confusion by Alcibiades, through the wildness and vehemence of his ambition, and all embroiled again in war worse than ever. Which fell out thus. The persons who had principally hindered the peace were Cleon and Brasidas. War setting off the virtue of the one, and hiding the villainy of the other, gave to the one occasions of achieving brave actions, to the other opportunity of committing equal dishonesties. Now when these two were in one battle both slain near Amphipolis, Nicias was aware that the Spartans had long been desirous of a peace, and that the Athenians had no longer the same confidence in the war. Both being alike tired, and, as it were by consent, letting fall their hands, he, therefore, in this nick of time, employed his efforts to make a friendship betwixt the two cities, and to deliver the other States of Greece from the evils and calamities they labored under, and so establish his own good name for success as a statesman for all future time. He found the men of substance, the elder men, and the land-owners and farmers pretty generally, all inclined to peace. And when, in addition to these, by conversing and reasoning, he had cooled the wishes of a good many others for war, he now encouraged the hopes of the Lacedaemonians, and counseled them to seek peace. They confided in him, as on account of his general character for moderation and equity, so, also, because of the kindness and care he had shown to the prisoners taken at Pylos and kept in confinement, making their misfortune the more easy to them.

The Athenians and the Spartans had before this concluded a truce for a year, and during this, by associating with one another, they had tasted again the sweets of peace and security, and unimpeded intercourse with friends and connections, and thus longed for an end of that fighting and bloodshed, and heard with delight the chorus sing such verses as

> — *my lance I'll leave*
> *Laid by, for spiders to o'erweave,*

and remembered with joy the saying, In peace, they who sleep are awaked by the cock-crow, not by the trumpet. So shutting their ears, with loud reproaches, to the forebodings of those who said that the Fates decreed this to be a war of thrice nine years, the whole question having been debated, they made a peace. And most people thought, now, indeed, they had got an end of all their evils. And Nicias was in every man's mouth, as one especially beloved of the gods, who, for his piety and devotion, had been appointed to give a name to the fairest and greatest of all blessings. For in fact they considered the peace Nicias's work, as the war the work of Pericles; because he, on light occasions, seemed to have plunged the Greeks into great calamities, while Nicias had induced them to forget all the evils they had done each other and to be friends again; and so to this day it is called the Peace of Nicias.

The articles being, that the garrisons and towns taken on either side, and the prisoners should be restored, and they to restore the first to whom it should fall by lot, Nicias, as Theophrastus tells us, by a sum of money procured that the lot should fall for the Lacedaemonians to deliver the first. Afterwards, when the Corinthians and the Boeotians showed their dislike of what was done, and by their complaints and accusations were wellnigh bringing the war back again, Nicias persuaded the Athenians and the Lacedaemonians, besides the peace, to make a treaty of alliance, offensive and defensive, as a tie and confirmation of the peace, which would make them more terrible to those that held out, and the firmer to each other. Whilst these matters were on foot, Alcibiades, who was no lover of tranquillity, and who was offended with the Lacedaemonians because of their applications and attentions to Nicias, while they overlooked and despised himself, from first to last, indeed, had opposed the peace, though all in vain, but now finding that the Lacedaemonians did not altogether continue to please the Athenians, but were thought to have acted unfairly in having made a league with the Boeotians, and had not given up Panactum, as they should have done, with its fortifications unrazed, nor yet Amphipolis, he laid hold on these occasions for his purpose, and availed himself of every one of them to irritate the people. And, at length, sending for ambassadors from the Argives, he exerted himself to effect a confederacy between the Athenians and them. And now, when Lacedaemonian ambassadors were come with full powers, and at their preliminary audience by the council seemed to come in all points with just proposals, he, fearing that the general assembly, also, would be won over to their offers, overreached them with false professions and oaths of assistance, on the condition that they would not avow that they came with full powers, this, he said, being the only way for them to attain their desires. They being overpersuaded and decoyed from Nicias to follow him, he introduced them to the assembly, and asked them presently whether or no they came in all points with full powers, which when they denied, he, contrary to their expectation, changing his countenance, called the council to witness their words, and now bade the people beware how they trust, or transact anything with such manifest liars, who say at one time one thing, and at another the very opposite upon the same subject. These plenipotentiaries were, as well they might be, confounded at this, and Nicias, also, being at a loss what to say, and struck with amazement and wonder, the assembly resolved to send immediately for the Argives, to enter into a league with them. An earthquake, which interrupted the assembly, made for Nicias's advantage; and the next day the people being again assembled, after much speaking and soliciting, with great ado he brought it about, that the treaty with the Argives should be deferred, and he be sent to the Lacedaemonians, in full expectation that so all would go well.

When he arrived at Sparta, they received him there as a good man, and one well inclined towards them; yet he effected nothing, but, baffled by the party that favored the Boeotians, he returned home, not only dishonored and hardly spoken of, but likewise in fear of the Athenians, who were vexed and enraged that through his persuasions they had released so many and such considerable persons, their prisoners, for the men who had been brought from Pylos were of the chiefest families of Sparta, and had those who were highest there in place and power for their friends and kindred. Yet did they not in their heat proceed against him, otherwise than that they chose Alcibiades general, and took the Mantineans and Eleans, who had thrown up their alliance with the Lacedaemonians, into the league, together with the Argives, and sent to Pylos freebooters to infest Laconia, whereby the war began to break out afresh.

But the enmity betwixt Nicias and Alcibiades running higher and higher, and the time being at hand for decreeing the ostracism or banishment, for ten years, which the people, putting the name on a sherd, were wont to inflict at certain times on some person suspected or regarded with jealousy for his popularity or wealth, both were now in alarm and apprehension, one of them, in all likelihood, being to undergo this ostracism; as the people abominated the life of Alcibiades, and stood in fear of his boldness and resolution, as is shown particularly in the history of him; while as for Nicias, his riches made him envied, and his habits of living, in particular, his unsociable and exclusive ways, not like those of a fellow-citizen, or even a fellow-man, went against him, and having many times opposed their inclinations, forcing them against their feelings to do what was their interest, he had got himself disliked.

To speak plainly, it was a contest of the young men who were eager for war, against the men of years and lovers of peace, they turning the ostracism upon the one, these upon the other. But

In civil strife e'en villains rise to fame.

And so now it happened that the city, distracted into two factions, allowed free course to the most impudent and profligate persons, among whom was Hyperbolus of the Perithoedae, one who could not, indeed, be said to be presuming upon any power, but rather by his presumption rose into power, and by the honor he found in the city, became the scandal of it. He, at this time, thought himself far enough from the ostracism, as more properly deserving the slave's gallows, and made account, that one of these men being dispatched out of the way, he might be able to play a part against the other that should be left, and openly showed his pleasure at the dissension, and his desire to inflame the people against both of them. Nicias and Alcibiades, perceiving his malice, secretly combined together, and setting both their interests jointly at work, succeeded in fixing the ostracism not on either of them, but even on Hyperbolus. This, indeed, at the first, made sport, and raised laughter among the people; but afterwards it was felt as an affront, that the thing should be dishonored by being employed upon so unworthy a subject; punishment, also, having its proper dignity, and ostracism being one that was appropriate rather for Thucydides, Aristides, and such like persons; whereas for Hyperbolus it was a glory, and a fair ground for boasting on his part, when for his villainy he suffered the same with the best men. As Plato, the comic poet said of him,

> *The man deserved the fate, deny who can;*
> *Yes, but the fate did not deserve the man;*
> *Not for the like of him and his slave-brands,*
> *Did Athens put the sherd into our hands.*

And, in fact, none ever afterwards suffered this sort of punishment, but Hyperbolus was the last, as Hipparchus the Cholargian, who was kin to the tyrant, was the first.

There is no judgment to be made of fortune; nor can any reasoning bring us to a certainty about it. If Nicias had run the risk with Alcibiades, whether of the two should undergo the ostracism, he had either prevailed, and, his rival being expelled the city, he had remained secure; or, being overcome, he had avoided the utmost disasters, and preserved the reputation of a most excellent commander. Meantime I am not ignorant that Theophrastus says, that when Hyperbolus was banished Phaeax, not Nicias, contested it with

Alcibiades; but most authors differ from him.

It was Alcibiades, at any rate, whom when the Aegestean and Leontine ambassadors arrived and urged the Athenians to make an expedition against Sicily, Nicias opposed, and by whose persuasions and ambition he found himself overborne, who even before the people could be assembled, had preoccupied and corrupted their judgment with hopes and with speeches; insomuch that the young men at their sports, and the old men in their workshops, and sitting together on the benches, would be drawing maps of Sicily, and making charts showing the seas, the harbors, and general character of the coast of the island opposite Africa. For they made not Sicily the end of the war, but rather its starting point and head-quarters from whence they might carry it to the Carthaginians, and possess themselves of Africa, and of the seas as far as the pillars of Hercules. The bulk of the people, therefore, pressing this way, Nicias, who opposed them, found but few supporters, nor those of much influence; for the men of substance, fearing lest they should seem to shun the public charges and ship-money, were quiet against their inclination; nevertheless he did not tire nor give it up, but even after the Athenians decreed a war and chose him in the first place general, together with Alcibiades and Lamachus, when they were again assembled, he stood up, dissuaded them, and protested against the decision, and laid the blame on Alcibiades, charging him with going about to involve the city in foreign dangers and difficulties, merely with a view to his own private lucre and ambition. Yet it came to nothing. Nicias, because of his experience, was looked upon as the fitter for the employment, and his wariness with the bravery of Alcibiades, and the easy temper of Lamachus, all compounded together, promised such security, that he did but confirm the resolution. Demostratus, who, of the popular leaders, was the one who chiefly pressed the Athenians to the expedition, stood up and said he would stop the mouth of Nicias from urging any more excuses, and moved that the generals should have absolute power both at home and abroad, to order and to act as they thought best; and this vote the people passed.

The priests, however, are said to have very earnestly opposed the enterprise. But Alcibiades had his diviners of another sort, who from some old prophesies announced that "there shall be great fame of the Athenians in Sicily," and messengers came back to him from Jupiter Ammon, with oracles importing that "the Athenians shall take all the Syracusans." Those, meanwhile, who knew anything that boded ill, concealed it, lest they might seem to forespeak ill-luck. For even prodigies that were obvious and plain would not deter them; not the defacing of the Hermue, all maimed in one night except one, called the Hermes of Andocides, erected by the tribe of Aegeus, placed directly before the house then occupied by Andocides; nor what was perpetrated on the altar of the twelve gods, upon which a certain man leaped suddenly up, and then turning round, mutilated himself with a stone. Likewise at Delphi, there stood a golden image of Minerva, set on a palm-tree of brass, erected by the city of Athens from the spoils they won from the Medes; this was pecked at several days together by crows flying upon it, who, also, plucked off and knocked down the fruit, made of gold, upon the palm-tree. But the Athenians said these were all but inventions of the Delphians, corrupted by the men of Syracuse. A certain oracle bade them bring from Clazomenae the priestess of Minerva there; they sent for the woman and found her named Hesychia, Quietness, this being, it would seem, what the divine powers advised the city at this time, to be quiet. Whether, therefore, the astrologer Meton feared these presages, or that from human reason he doubted its success, (for he was appointed to a command in it,) feigning himself mad, he set his house on fire. Others say he did not counterfeit madness, but set his house on fire in the night, and he next morning came before the assembly in great distress, and besought the people, in consideration of the sad disaster, to release his son from the service, who was about to go captain of a galley for Sicily. The genius, also, of the philosopher Socrates, on this occasion, too, gave him intimation by the usual tokens, that the expedition would prove the ruin of the commonwealth; this he imparted to his friends and familiars, and by them it was mentioned to a number of people. Not a few were troubled because the days on which the fleet set sail happened to be the time when the women celebrated the death of Adonis; there being everywhere then exposed to view images of dead men, carried about with mourning and lamentation, and women beating their breasts. So that such as laid any stress on these matters were extremely troubled, and feared lest that all this warlike preparation, so splendid and so glorious, should suddenly, in a little time, be blasted in its very prime of magnificence, and come to nothing.

Nicias, in opposing the voting of this expedition, and neither being puffed up with hopes, nor transported with the honor of his high command so as to modify his judgment, showed himself a man of virtue and constancy. But when his endeavors could not divert the people from the war, nor get leave for himself to be discharged of the command, but the people, as it were, violently took him up and carried him, and against his will put him in the office of general, this was no longer now a time for his excessive caution and his delays, nor was it for him, like a child, to look back from the ship, often repeating and reconsidering over and over again how that his advice had not been overruled by fair arguments, thus blunting the courage of his fellow commanders and spoiling the season of action. Whereas, he ought speedily to have closed with the enemy and brought the matter to an issue, and put fortune immediately to the test in battle. But, on the contrary, when Lamachus counseled to sail directly to Syracuse, and fight the enemy under their city walls, and Alcibiades advised to secure the friendship of the other towns, and then to march against them, Nicias dissented from them both, and insisted that they should cruise quietly around the island and display their armament, and, having landed a small supply of men for the Egesteans, return to Athens, weakening at once the resolution and casting down the spirits of the men. And when, a little while after, the Athenians called home Alcibiades in order to his trial, he being, though joined nominally with another in commission, in effect the only general, made now no end of loitering, of cruising, and considering, till their hopes were grown stale, and all the disorder and consternation which the first approach and view of their forces had cast amongst the enemy was worn off, and had left them.

Whilst yet Alcibiades was with the fleet, they went before Syracuse with a squadron of sixty galleys, fifty of them lying in array without the harbor, while the other ten rowed in to reconnoiter, and by a herald called upon the citizens of Leontini to return to their own country. These scouts took a galley of the enemy's, in which they found certain tablets, on which was set down a list of all the Syracusans, according to their tribes. These were wont to be laid up at a distance from the city, in the temple of Jupiter Olympius, but were now brought forth for examination to furnish a muster-roll of young men for the war. These being so taken by the Athenians, and carried to the officers, and the multitude of names appearing, the diviners thought it unpropitious, and were in apprehension lest this should be the only destined fullfilment of the prophecy, that "the Athenians shall take all the Syracusans." Yet, indeed, this was said to be accomplished by the Athenians at another time, when Callippus the Athenian, having slain Dion, became master of Syracuse. But when Alcibiades shortly after sailed away from Sicily, the command fell wholly to Nicias. Lamachus was, indeed, a brave and honest man, and ready to fight fearlessly with his own hand in battle, but so poor and ill off, that whenever he was appointed general, he used always, in accounting for his outlay of public money, to bring some little reckoning or other of money for his very clothes and shoes. On the contrary, Nicias, as on other accounts, so, also, because of his wealth and station, was very much thought of. The story is told that once upon a time the commission of generals being in consultation together in their public office, he bade Sophocles the poet give his opinion first, as the senior of the board. "I," replied Sophocles, "am the older, but you are the senior." And so now, also, Lamachus, who better understood military affairs, being quite his subordinate, he himself, evermore delaying and avoiding risk, and faintly employing his forces, first by his sailing about Sicily at the greatest distance aloof from the enemy, gave them confidence, then by afterwards attacking Hybla, a petty fortress, and drawing off before he could take it, made himself utterly despised. At the last he retreated to Catana without having achieved anything, save that he demolished Hyocara, a humble town of the barbarians, out of which the story goes that Lais the courtesan, yet a mere girl, was sold amongst the other prisoners, and carried thence away to Peloponnesus.

But when the summer was spent, after reports began to reach him that the Syracusans were grown so confident that they would come first to attack him, and troopers skirmishing to the very camp twitted his soldiers, asking whether they came to settle with the Catanians, or to put the Leontines in possession of their city, at last, with much ado, Nicias resolved to sail against Syracuse. And wishing to form his camp safely and without molestation, he procured a man to carry from Catana intelligence to the Syracusans that they might seize the camp of the Athenians unprotected, and all their arms, if on such a day they should march with all their forces to Catana; and that, the Athenians living mostly in the town, the friends of the Syracusans had concerted, as soon as they should perceive them coming, to possess themselves of one of the gates, and to fire the arsenal; that many now were in the conspiracy and awaited their arrival. This was the ablest thing Nicias did in the whole of his conduct of the expedition. For having drawn out all the strength of the enemy, and made the city destitute of men, he set out from Catana, entered the harbor, and chose a fit place for his camp, where the enemy could least incommode him with the means in which they were superior to him, while with the means in which he was superior to them, he might expect to carry on the war without impediment.

When the Syracusans returned from Catana, and stood in battle array before the city gates, he rapidly led up the Athenians and fell on them and defeated them, but did not kill many, their horse hindering the pursuit. And his cutting and breaking down the bridges that lay over the river gave Hermocrates, when cheering up the Syracusans, occasion to say, that Nicias was ridiculous, whose great aim seemed to be to avoid fighting, as if fighting were not the thing he came for. However, he put the Syracusans into a very great alarm and consternation, so that instead of fifteen generals then in service, they chose three others, to whom the people engaged by oath to allow absolute authority.

There stood near them the temple of Jupiter Olympius, which the Athenians (there being in it many consecrated things of gold and silver) were eager to take, but were purposely withheld from it by Nicias, who let the opportunity slip, and allowed a garrison of the Syracusans to enter it, judging that if the soldiers should make booty of that wealth, it would be no advantage to the public, and he should bear the guilt of the impiety. Not improving in the least this success, which was everywhere famous, after a few days' stay, away he goes to Naxos, and there winters, spending largely for the maintenance of so great an army, and not doing anything except some matters of little consequence with some native Sicilians that revolted to him. Insomuch that the Syracusans took heart again, made excursions to Catana, wasted the country, and fired the camp of the Athenians. For which everybody blamed Nicias, who, with his long reflection, his deliberateness, and his caution, had let slip the time for action. None ever found fault with the man when once at work, for in the brunt he showed vigor and activity enough, but was slow and wanted assurance to engage.

When, therefore, he brought again the army to Syracuse, such was his conduct, and with such celerity, and at the same time security, he came upon them, that nobody knew of his approach, when already he had come to shore with his galleys at Thapsus, and had landed his men; and before any could help it he had surprised Epipolae, had defeated the body of picked men that came to its succor, took three hundred prisoners, and routed the cavalry of the enemy, which had been thought invincible. But what chiefly astonished the Syracusans, and seemed incredible to the Greeks, was, in so short a space of time the walling about of Syracuse, a town not less than Athens, and far more difficult, by the unevenness of the ground, and the nearness of the sea and the marshes adjacent, to have such a wall drawn in a circle round it; yet this, all within a very little, finished by a man that had not even his health for such weighty cares, but lay ill of the stone, which may justly bear the blame for what was left undone. I admire the industry of the general, and the bravery of the soldiers for what they succeeded in. Euripides, after their ruin and disaster, writing their funeral elegy, said that

> *Eight victories over Syracuse they gained,*
> *While equal yet to both the gods remained.*

And in truth one shall not find eight, but many more victories, won by these men against the Syracusans, till the gods, in real truth, or fortune intervened to check the Athenians in this advance to the height of power and greatness.

Nicias, therefore, doing violence to his body, was present in most actions. But once, when his disease was the sharpest upon him, he lay in the camp with some few servants to attend him. And Lamachus having the command fought the Syracusans, who were bringing a cross-wall from the city along to that of the Athenians, to hinder them from carrying it round; and in the victory, the Athenians hurrying in some disorder to the pursuit, Lamachus getting separated from his men, had to resist the Syracusan horse that came upon him. Before the rest advanced Callicrates, a man of good courage and skill in war. Lamachus, upon a challenge, engaged with him in single combat, and receiving the first wound, returned it so home to Callicrates, that they both fell and died together. The Syracusans took away his body and arms, and at full speed advanced to the wall of the Athenians, where Nicias lay without any troops to oppose to them, yet roused by this necessity, and seeing the danger, he bade those about him go and set on fire all the wood and materials that lay provided before the wall for the engines, and the engines themselves; this put a stop to the Syracusans, saved Nicias, saved the walls, and all the money of the Athenians. For when the Syracusans raw such a fire blazing up between them and the wall, they retired.

Nicias now remained sole general, and with great prospects; for cities began to come over to alliance with him, and ships laden with corn from every coast came to the camp, everyone favoring when matters went well. And some proposals from among the Syracusans despairing to defend the city, about a capitulation, were already conveyed to him. And in fact Gylippus, who was on his way with a squadron to their aid from Lacedaemon, hearing, on his voyage, of the wall surrounding them, and of their distress, only continued his enterprise thenceforth, that, giving Sicily up for lost, he might, if even that should be possible, secure the Italians their cities. For a strong report was everywhere spread about that the Athenians carried all before them, and had a general alike for conduct and for fortune invincible.

And Nicias himself, too, now against his nature grown bold in his present strength and success, especially from the intelligence he received under hand of the Syracusans, believing they would almost immediately surrender the town upon terms, paid no manner of regard to Gylippus coming to their assistance, nor kept any watch of his approach so that, neglected altogether and despised, Gylippus went in a longboat ashore without the knowledge of Nicias, and, having landed in the remotest parts from Syracuse, mustered up a considerable force, the Syracusans not so much as knowing of his arrival nor expecting him; so that an assembly was summoned to consider the terms to be arranged with Nicias, and some were actually on the way, thinking it essential to have all dispatched before the town should be quite walled round, for now there remained very little to be done, and the materials for the building lay all ready along the line.

In this very nick of time and danger arrived Gongylus in one galley from Corinth, and everyone, as may be imagined, flocking about him, he told them that Gylippus would be with them speedily, and that other ships were coming to relieve them. And, ere yet they could perfectly believe Gongylus, an express was brought from Gylippus, to bid them go forth to meet him. So now taking good heart, they armed themselves; and Gylippus at once led on his men from their march in battle array against the Athenians, as Nicias also embattled these. And Gylippus, piling his arms in view of the Athenians, sent a herald to tell them he would give them leave to depart from Sicily without molestation. To this Nicias would not vouchsafe any answer, but some of his soldiers laughing asked if with the sight of one coarse coat and Laconian staff the Syracusan prospects had become so brilliant that they could despise the Athenians, who had released to the Lacedaemonians three hundred, whom they held in chains, bigger men than Gylippus, and longer-haired? Timaeus, also, writes that even the Syracusans made no account of Gylippus, at the first sight mocking at his staff and long hair, as afterwards they found reason to blame his covetousness and meanness. The same author, however, adds that on Gylippus's first appearance, as it might have been at the sight of an owl abroad in the air, there was a general flocking together of men to serve in the war. And this is the truer saying of the two; for in the staff and the cloak they saw the badge and authority of Sparta, and crowded to him accordingly. And not only Thucydides affirms that the whole thing was done by him alone, but so, also, does Philistus, who was a Syracusan and an actual witness of what happened.

However, the Athenians had the better in the first encounter, and slew some few of the Syracusans, and amongst them Gongylus of Corinth. But on the next day Gylippus showed what it is to be a man of experience; for with the same arms, the same horses, and on the same spot of ground, only employing them otherwise, he overcame the Athenians; and they fleeing to their camp, he set the Syracusans to work, and with the stone and materials that had been brought together for finishing the wall of the Athenians, he built a cross wall to intercept theirs and break it off, so that even if they were successful in the field, they would not be able to do anything. And after this the Syracusans taking courage manned their galleys, and with their horse and followers ranging about took a good many prisoners; and Gylippus going himself to the cities, called upon them to join with him, and was listened to and supported vigorously by them. So that Nicias fell back again to his old views, and, seeing the face of affairs change, desponded, and wrote to Athens, bidding them either send another army, or recall this out of Sicily, and that he might, in any case, be wholly relieved of the command, because of his disease.

Before this, the Athenians had been intending to send another army to Sicily, but envy of Nicias's early achievements and high fortune had occasioned, up to this time, many delays; but now they were all eager to send off succors. Eurymedon went before, in midwinter, with money, and to announce that Euthydemus and Menander were chosen out of those that served there under Nicias to be joint commanders with him. Demosthenes was to go after in the spring with a great armament. In the meantime Nicias was briskly attacked, both by sea and land; in the beginning he had the disadvantage on the water, but in the end repulsed and sunk many galleys of the enemy. But by land he could not provide succor in time, so Gylippus surprised and captured Plemmyrium, in which the stores for the navy, and a great sum of money being there kept, all fell into his hands, and many were slain, and many taken prisoners. And what was of greatest importance, he now cut off Nicias's supplies, which had been safely and readily conveyed to him under Plemmyrium, while the Athenians still held it, but now that they were beaten out, he could only procure them with great difficulty, and with opposition from the enemy, who lay in wait with their ships under that fort. Moreover, it seemed manifest to the Syracusans that their navy had not been beaten by strength, but by their disorder in the pursuit. Now, therefore, all hands went to work to prepare for a new attempt, that should succeed better than the former. Nicias had no wish for a sea-fight, but said it was mere folly for them, when Demosthenes was coming in all haste with so great a fleet and fresh forces to their succor, to engage the enemy with a less number of ships and ill provided. But, on the other hand, Menander and Euthydemus, who were just commencing their new command, prompted by a feeling of rivalry and emulation of both the generals, were eager to gain some great success before Demosthenes came, and to prove themselves superior to Nicias. They urged the honor of the city, which, said they, would be blemished and utterly lost, if they should decline a challenge from the Syracusans. Thus they forced Nicias to a sea-fight; and by the stratagem of Ariston, the Corinthian pilot, (his trick, described by Thucydides, about the men's dinners,) they were worsted, and lost many of their men, causing the greatest dejection to Nicias, who had suffered so much from having the sole command, and now again miscarried through his colleagues.

 But now, by this time, Demosthenes with his splendid fleet came in sight outside the harbor, a terror to the enemy. He brought along, in seventy-three galleys, five thousand men at arms; of darters, archers, and slingers, not less than three thousand; with the glittering of their armor, the flags waving from the galleys, the multitude of coxswains and flute-players giving time to the rowers, setting off the whole with all possible warlike pomp and ostentation to dismay the enemy. Now, one may believe the Syracusans were again in extreme alarm, seeing no end or prospect of release before them, toiling, as it seemed, in vain, and perishing to no purpose. Nicias, however, was not long overjoyed with the reinforcement, for the first time he conferred with Demosthenes, who advised forthwith to attack the Syracusans, and to put all to the speediest hazard, to win Syracuse, or else return home, afraid, and wondering at his promptness and audacity, he besought him to do nothing rashly and desperately, since delay would be the ruin of the enemy, whose money would not hold out, nor their confederates be long kept together; that when once they came to be pinched with want, they would presently come again to him for terms, as formerly. For, indeed, many in Syracuse held secret correspondence with him, and urged him to stay, declaring that even now the people were quite worn out with the war, and weary of Gylippus. And if their necessities should the least sharpen upon them they would give up all.

Nicias glancing darkly at these matters, and unwilling to speak out plainly, made his colleagues imagine that it was cowardice which made him talk in this manner. And saying that this was the old story over again, the well known procrastinations and delays and refinements with which at first he let slip the opportunity in not immediately falling on the enemy, but suffering the armament to become a thing of yesterday, that nobody was alarmed with, they took the side of Demosthenes, and with much ado forced Nicias to comply. And so Demosthenes, taking the land-forces, by night made an assault upon Epipolae; part of the enemy he slew ere they took the alarm, the rest defending themselves he put to flight. Nor was he content with this victory there, but pushed on further, till he met the Bocotians. For these were the first that made head against the Athenians, and charged them with a shout, spear against spear, and killed many on the place. And now at once there ensued a panic and confusion throughout the whole army; the victorious portion got infected with the fears of the flying part, and those who were still disembarking and coming forward, falling foul of the retreaters, came into conflict with their own party, taking the fugitives for pursuers, and treating their friends as if they were the enemy.

Thus huddled together in disorder, distracted with fear and uncertainties, and unable to be sure of seeing anything, the night not being absolutely dark, nor yielding any steady light, the moon then towards setting, shadowed with the many weapons and bodies that moved to and fro, and glimmering so as not to show an object plain, but to make friends through fear suspected for foes, the Athenians fell into utter perplexity and desperation. For, moreover, they had the moon at their backs, and consequently their own shadows fell upon them, and both hid the number and the glittering of their arms; while the reflection of the moon from the shields of the enemy made them show more numerous and better appointed than, indeed, they were. At last, being pressed on every side, when once they had given way, they took to rout, and in their flight were destroyed, some by the enemy, some by the hand of their friends, and some tumbling down the rocks, while those that were dispersed and straggled about were picked off in the morning by the horsemen and put to the sword. The slain were two thousand; and of the rest few came off safe with their arms.

Upon this disaster, which to him was not wholly an unexpected one, Nicias accused the rashness of Demosthenes; but he, making his excuses for the past, now advised to be gone in all haste, for neither were other forces to come, nor could the enemy be beaten with the present. And, indeed, even supposing they were yet too hard for the enemy in any case, they ought to remove and quit a situation which they understood to be always accounted a sickly one, and dangerous for an army, and was more particularly unwholesome now, as they could see themselves, because of the time of year. It was the beginning of autumn, and many now lay sick, and all were out of heart.

It grieved Nicias to hear of flight and departing home, not that he did not fear the Syracusans, but he was worse afraid of the Athenians, their impeachments and sentences; he professed that he apprehended no further harm there, or if it must be, he would rather die by the hand of an enemy, than by his fellow-citizens. He was not of the opinion which Leo of Byzantium declared to his fellow-citizens: "I had rather," said he, "perish by you, than with you." As to the matter of place and quarter whither to remove their camp, that, he said, might be debated at leisure. And Demosthenes, his former counsel having succeeded so ill, ceased to press him further; others thought Nicias had reasons for expectation, and relied on some assurance from people within the city, and that this made him so strongly oppose their retreat, so they acquiesced. But fresh forces now coming to the Syracusans, and the sickness growing worse in his camp, he, also, now approved of their retreat, and commanded the soldiers to make ready to go aboard.

And when all were in readiness, and none of the enemy had observed them, not expecting such a thing, the moon was eclipsed in the night, to the great fright of Nicias and others, who, for want of experience, or out of superstition, felt alarm at such appearances. That the sun might be darkened about the close of the month, this even ordinary people now understood pretty well to be the effect of the moon; but the moon itself to be darkened, how that could come about, and how, on the sudden, a broad full moon should lose her light, and show such various colors, was not easy to be comprehended; they concluded it to be ominous, and a divine intimation of some heavy calamities. For he who the first, and the most plainly of any, and with the greatest assurance committed to writing how the moon is enlightened and overshadowed, was Anaxagoras; and he was as yet but recent, nor was his argument much known, but was rather kept secret, passing only amongst a few, under some kind of caution and confidence. People would not then tolerate natural philosophers, and theorists, as they then called them, about things above; as lessening the divine power, by explaining away its agency into the operation of irrational causes and senseless forces acting by necessity, without anything of Providence, or a free agent. Hence it was that Protagoras was banished, and Anaxagoras cast in prison, so that Pericles had much difficulty to procure his liberty; and Socrates, though he had no concern whatever with this sort of learning, yet was put to death for philosophy. It was only afterwards that the reputation of Plato, shining forth by his life, and because he subjected natural necessity to divine and more excellent principles, took away the obloquy and scandal that had attached to such contemplations, and obtained these studies currency among all people. So his friend Dion, when the moon, at the time he was to embark from Zacynthus to go against Dionysius, was eclipsed, was not in the least disturbed, but went on, and, arriving at Syracuse, expelled the tyrant. But it so fell out with Nicias, that he had not at this time a skillful diviner with him; his former habitual adviser who used to moderate much of his superstition, Stilbides, had died a little before. For in fact, this prodigy, as Philochorus observes, was not unlucky for men wishing to fly, but on the contrary very favorable; for things done in fear require to be hidden, and the light is their foe. Nor was it usual to observe signs in the sun or moon more than three days, as Autoclides states in his Commentaries. But Nicias persuaded them to wait another full course of the moon, as if he had not seen it clear again as soon as ever it had passed the region of shadow where the light was obstructed by the earth.

In a manner abandoning all other cares, he betook himself wholly to his sacrifices, till the enemy came upon them with their infantry, besieging the forts and camp, and placing their ships in a circle about the harbor. Nor did the men in the galleys only, but the little boys everywhere got into the fishing-boats and rowed up and challenged the Athenians, and insulted over them. Amongst these a youth of noble parentage, Heraclides by name, having ventured out beyond the rest, an Athenian ship pursued and wellnigh took him. His uncle Pollichus, in fear for him, put out with ten galleys which he commanded, and the rest, to relieve Pollichus, in like manner drew forth; the result of it being a very sharp engagement, in which the Syracusans had the victory, and slew Eurymedon, with many others. lifter this the Athenian soldiers had no patience to stay longer, but raised an outcry against their officers, requiring them to depart by land; for the Syracusans, upon their victory, immediately shut and blocked up the entrance of the harbor; but Nicias would not consent to this, as it was a shameful thing to leave behind so many ships of burden, and galleys little less than two hundred. Putting, therefore, on board the best of the foot, and the most serviceable darters, they filled one hundred and ten galleys; the rest wanted oars. The remainder of his army Nicias posted along by the sea-side, abandoning the great camp and the fortifications adjoining the temple of Hercules; so the Syracusans, not having for a long time performed their usual sacrifice to Hercules, went up now, both priests and captains, to sacrifice.

And their galleys being manned, the diviners predicted from their sacrifices victory and glory to the Syracusans, provided they would not be the aggressors, but fight upon the defensive; for so Hercules overcame all, by only de. fending himself when set upon. In this confidence they set out; and this proved the hottest and fiercest of all their sea-fights, raising no less concern and passion in the beholders than in the actors; as they could oversee the whole action with all the various and unexpected turns of fortune which, in a short space, occurred in it; the Athenians suffering no less from their own preparations, than from the enemy; for they fought against light and nimble ships, that could attack from any quarter, with theirs laden and heavy. And they were thrown at with stones that fly indifferently any way, for which they could only return darts and arrows, the direct aim of which the motion of the water disturbed, preventing their coming true, point foremost to their mark. This the Syracusans had learned from Ariston the Corinthian pilot, who, fighting stoutly, fell himself in this very engagement, when the victory had already declared for the Syracusans.

The Athenians, their loss and slaughter being very great, their flight by sea cut off, their safety by land so difficult, did not attempt to hinder the enemy towing away their ships, under their eves, nor demanded their dead, as, indeed, their want of burial seemed a less calamity than the leaving behind the sick and wounded which they now had before them. Yet more miserable still than those did they reckon themselves, who were to work on yet, through more such sufferings, after all to reach the same end.

They prepared to dislodge that night. And Gylippus and his friends seeing the Syracusans engaged in their sacrifices and at their cups, for their victories, and it being also a holiday, did not expect either by persuasion or by force to rouse them up and carry them against the Athenians as they decamped. But Hermocrates, of his own head, put a trick upon Nicias, and sent some of his companions to him, who pretended they came from those that were wont to hold secret intelligence with him, and advised him not to stir that night, the Syracusans having laid ambushes and beset the ways. Nicias, caught with this stratagem, remained, to encounter presently in reality, what he had feared when there was no occasion. For they, the next morning, marching before, seized the defiles, fortified the passes where the rivers were fordable, cut down the bridges, and ordered their horsemen to range the plains and ground that lay open, so as to leave no part of the country where the Athenians could move without fighting. They stayed both that day and another night, and then went along as if they were leaving their own, not an enemy's country, lamenting and bewailing for want of necessaries, and for their parting from friends and companions that were not, able to help themselves; and, nevertheless, judging the present evils lighter than those they expected to come. But among the many miserable spectacles that appeared up and down in the camp, the saddest sight of all was Nicias himself, laboring under his malady, and unworthily reduced to the scantiest supply of all the accommodations necessary for human wants, of which he in his condition required more than ordinary, because of his sickness; yet bearing; up under all this illness, and doing and undergoing more than many in perfect health. And it was plainly evident, that all this toil was not for himself, or from any regard to his own life, but that purely for the sake of those under his command he would not abandon hope. And, indeed, the rest were given over to weeping and lamentation through fear or sorrow, but he, whenever he yielded to anything of the kind, did so, it was evident, from reflection upon the shame and dishonor of the enterprise, contrasted with the greatness and glory of the success he had anticipated, and not only the sight of his person, but, also, the recollection of the arguments and the dissuasions he used to prevent this expedition, enhanced their sense of the undeservedness of his sufferings, nor had they any heart to put their trust in the gods, considering that a man so religious, who had performed to the divine powers so many and so great acts of devotion, should have no more favorable treatment than the wickedest and meanest of the army.

Nicias, however, endeavored all the while by his voice, his countenance, and his carriage, to show himself undefeated by these misfortunes. And all along the way shot at, and receiving wounds eight days continually from the enemy, he yet preserved the forces with him in a body entire, till that Demosthenes was taken prisoner with the party that he led, whilst they fought and made a resistance, and so got behind and were surrounded near the country house of Polyzelus. Demosthenes thereupon drew his sword, and wounded but did not kill himself, the enemy speedily running in and seizing upon him. So soon as the Syracusans had gone and informed Nicias of this, and he had sent some horsemen, and by them knew the certainty of the defeat of that division, he then vouchsafed to sue to Gylippus for a truce for the Athenians to depart out of Sicily, leaving hostages for payment of the money that the Syracusans had expended in the war.

But now they would not hear of these proposals, but threatening and reviling them, angrily and insultingly continued to ply their missiles at them, now destitute of every necessary. Yet Nicias still made good his retreat all that night, and the next day, through all their darts, made his way to the river Asinarus. There, however, the enemy encountering them, drove some into the stream, while others ready to die for thirst plunged in headlong, while they drank at the same time, and were cut down by their enemies. And here was the cruelest and the most immoderate slaughter. Till at last Nicias falling down to Gylippus, "Let pity, O Gylippus," said he, "move you in your victory; not for me, who was destined, it seems, to bring the glory I once had to this end, but for the other Athenians; as you well know that the chances of war are common to all, and the Athenians used them moderately and mildly towards you in their prosperity."

At these words, and at the sight of Nicias, Gylippus was somewhat troubled, for he was sensible that the Lacedaemonians had received good offices from Nicias in the late treaty; and he thought it would be a great and glorious thing for him to carry off the chief commanders of the Athenians alive. He, therefore, raised Nicias with respect, and bade him be of good cheer, and commanded his men to spare the lives of the rest. But the word of command being communicated slowly, the slain were a far greater number than the prisoners. Many, however, were privily conveyed away by particular soldiers. Those taken openly were hurried together in a mass; their arms and spoils hung up on the finest and largest trees along the river. The conquerors, with garlands on their heads, with their own horses splendidly adorned, and cropping short the manes and tails of those of their enemies, entered the city, having, in the most signal conflict ever waged by Greeks against Greeks, and with the greatest strength and the utmost effort of valor and manhood, won a most entire victory.

And a general assembly of the people of Syracuse and their confederates sitting, Eurycles, the popular leader, moved, first, that the day on which they took Nicias should from thenceforward be kept holiday by sacrificing and forbearing all manner of work, and from the river be called the Asinarian Feast. This was the twenty-sixth day of the month Carneus, the Athenian Metagitnion. And that the servants of the Athenians with the other confederates be sold for slaves, and they themselves and the Sicilian auxiliaries be kept and employed in the quarries, except the generals, who should be put to death. The Syracusans favored the proposal, and when Hermocrates said, that to use well a victory was better than to gain a victory, he was met with great clamor and outcry. When Gylippus, also, demanded the Athenian generals to be delivered to him, that he might carry them to the Lacedaemonians, the Syracusans, now insolent with their good fortune, gave him ill words. Indeed, before this, even in the war, they had been impatient at his rough behavior and Lacedaemonian haughtiness, and had, as Timaeus tells us, discovered sordidness and avarice in his character, vices which may have descended to him from his father Cleandrides, who was convicted of bribery and banished. And the very man himself, of the one thousand talents which Lysander sent to Sparta, embezzled thirty, and hid them under the tiles of his house, and was detected and shamefully fled his country. But this is related more at large in the life of Lysander. Timaeus says that Demosthenes and Nicias did not die, as Thucydides and Philistus have written, by the order of the Syracusans, but that upon a message sent them from Hermocrates, whilst yet the assembly were sitting, by the connivance of some of their guards, they were enabled to put an end to themselves. Their bodies, however, were thrown out before the gates and offered for a public spectacle. And I have heard that to this day in a temple at Syracuse is shown a shield, said to have been Nicias's, curiously wrought and embroidered with gold and purple intermixed. Most of the Athenians perished in the quarries by diseases and ill diet, being allowed only one pint of barley every day, and one half pint of water. Many of them, however, were carried off by stealth, or, from the first, were supposed to be servants, and were sold as slaves. These latter were branded on their foreheads with the figure of a horse. There were, however, Athenians, who, in addition to slavery, had to endure even this. But their discreet and orderly conduct was an advantage to them; they were either soon set free, or won the respect of their masters with whom they continued to live. Several were saved for the sake of Euripides, whose poetry, it appears, was in request among the Sicilians more than among any of the settlers out of Greece. And when any travelers arrived that could tell them some passage, or give them any specimen of his verses, they were delighted to be able to communicate them to one another. Many of the captives who got safe back to Athens are said, after they reached home, to have gone and made their acknowledgments to Euripides, relating how that some of them had been released from their slavery by teaching what they could remember of his poems, and others, when straggling after the fight, been relieved with meat and drink for repeating some of his lyrics. Nor need this be any wonder, for it is told that a ship of Caunus fleeing into one of their harbors for protection, pursued by pirates, was not received, but forced back, till one asked if they knew any of Euripides's verses, and on their saying they did, they were admitted, and their ship brought into harbor.

It is said that the Athenians would not believe their loss, in a great degree because of the person who first brought them news of it. For a certain stranger, it seems, coming to Piraeus, and there sitting in a barber's shop, began to talk of what had happened, as if the Athenians already knew all that had passed; which the barber hearing, before he acquainted anybody else, ran as fast as he could up into the city, addressed himself to the Archons, and presently spread it about in the public Place. On which, there being everywhere, as may be imagined, terror and consternation, the Archons summoned a general assembly, and there brought in the man and questioned him how he came to know. And he, giving no satisfactory account, was taken for a spreader of false intelligence and a disturber of the city, and was, therefore, fastened to the wheel and racked a long time, till other messengers arrived that related the whole disaster particularly. So hardly was Nicias believed to have suffered the calamity which he had often predicted.

8
CRASSUS

Marcus Crassus, whose father had borne the office of a censor, and received the honor of a triumph, was educated in a little house together with his two brothers, who both married in their parents' lifetime; they kept but one table amongst them; all which, perhaps, was not the least reason of his own temperance and moderation in diet. One of his brothers dying, he married his widow, by whom he had his children; neither was there in these respects any of the Romans who lived a more orderly life than he did, though later in life he was suspected to have been too familiar with one of the vestal virgins, named Licinia, who was, nevertheless, acquitted, upon an impeachment brought against her by one Plotinus. Licinia stood possessed of a beautiful property in the suburbs, which Crassus desiring to purchase at a low price, for this reason was frequent in his attentions to her, which gave occasion to the scandal, and his avarice, so to say, serving to clear him of the crime, he was acquitted. Nor did he leave the lady till he had got the estate.

People were wont to say that the many virtues of Crassus were darkened by the one vice of avarice, and indeed he seemed to have no other but that; for it being the most predominant, obscured others to which he was inclined. The arguments in proof of his avarice were the vastness of his estate, and the manner of raising it; for whereas at first he was not worth above three hundred talents, yet, though in the course of his political life he dedicated the tenth of all he had to Hercules, and feasted the people, and gave to every citizen corn enough to serve him three months, upon casting up his accounts, before he went upon his Parthian expedition, he found his possessions to amount to seven thousand one hundred talents; most of which, if we may scandal him with a truth, he got by fire and rapine, making his advantages of the public calamities. For when Sylla seized the city, and exposed to sale the goods of those that he had caused to be slain, accounting them booty and spoils, and, indeed, calling them so too, and was desirous of making as many, and as eminent men as he could, partakers in the crime, Crassus never was the man that refused to accept, or give money for them. Moreover observing how extremely subject the city was to fire, and falling down of houses, by reason of their height and their standing so near together, he bought slaves that were builders and architects, and when he had collected these to the number of more than five hundred, he made it his practice to buy houses that were on fire, and those in the neighborhood, which, in the immediate danger and uncertainty, the proprietors were willing to part with for little, or nothing; so that the greatest part of Rome, at one time or other, came into his hands. Yet for all he had so many workmen, he never built anything but his own house, and used to say that those that were addicted to building would undo themselves soon enough without the help of other enemies. And though he had many silver mines, and much valuable land, and laborers to work in it, yet all this was nothing in comparison of his slaves, such a number and variety did he possess of excellent readers, amanuenses, silversmiths, stewards, and table-waiters, whose instruction he always attended to himself, superintending in person while they learned, and teaching them himself, accounting it the main duty of a master to look over the servants, that are, indeed, the living tools of housekeeping; and in this, indeed, he was in the right, in thinking, that is, as he used to say, that servants ought to look after all other things, and the master after them. For economy, which in things inanimate is but money-making when exercised over men becomes policy. But it was surely a mistaken judgment, when he said no man was to be accounted rich that could not maintain an army at his own cost and charges, for war, as Archidamus well observed, is not fed at a fixed allowance, so that there is no saying what wealth suffices for it, and certainly it was one very far removed from that of Marius; for when he had distributed fourteen acres of land a man, and understood that some desired more, "God forbid," said he, "that any Roman should think that too little which is enough to keep him alive and well."

Crassus, however, was very eager to be hospitable to strangers; he kept open house, and to his friends he would lend money without interest, but called it in precisely at the time; so that his kindness was often thought worse than the paying the interest would have been. His entertainments were, for the most part, plain and citizenlike, the company general and popular; good taste and kindness made them pleasanter than sumptuosity would have done. As for learning, he chiefly cared for rhetoric, and what would be serviceable with large numbers; he became one of the best speakers at Rome, and by his pains and industry outdid the best natural orators. For there was no trial how mean and contemptible soever that he came to unprepared; nay, several times he undertook and concluded a cause, when Pompey and Caesar and Cicero refused to stand up, upon which account particularly he got the love of the people, who looked upon him as a diligent and careful man, ready to help and succor his fellow-citizens. Besides, the people were pleased with his courteous and unpretending salutations and greetings; for he never met any citizen however humble and low, but he returned him his salute by name. He was looked upon as a man well-read in history, and pretty well versed in Aristotle's philosophy, in which one Alexander instructed him, a man whose intercourse with Crassus gave a sufficient proof of his good-nature, and gentle disposition; for it is hard to say whether he was poorer when he entered into his service, or while he continued in it; for being his only friend that used to accompany him when traveling, he used to receive from him a cloak for the journey, and when he came home had it demanded from him again; poor patient sufferer, when even the philosophy he professed did not look upon poverty as a thing indifferent. But of this hereafter.

When Cinna and Marius got the power in their hands, it was soon perceived that they had not come back for any good they intended to their country, but to effect the ruin and utter destruction of the nobility. And as many as they could lay their hands on they slew, amongst whom were Crassus's father and brother; he himself, being very young, for the moment escaped the danger; but understanding that he was every way beset and hunted after by the tyrants, taking with him three friends and ten servants, with all possible speed he fled into Spain, having formerly been there and secured a great number of friends, while his father was Praetor of that country. But finding all people in a consternation, and trembling at the cruelty of Marius, as if he was already standing over them in person, he durst not discover himself to anybody, but hid himself in a large cave, which was by the sea-shore, and belonged to Vibius Pacianus, to whom he sent one of his servants to sound him, his provisions, also, beginning to fail. Vibius was well pleased at his escape, and inquiring the place of his abode and the number of his companions, he went not to him himself, but commanded his steward to provide every day a good meal's meat, and carry it and leave it near such a rock, and so return without taking any further notice or being inquisitive, promising him his liberty if he did as he commanded, and that he would kill him if he intermeddled. The cave is not far from the sea; a small and insignificant looking opening in the cliffs conducts you in; when you are entered, a wonderfully high roof spreads above you, and large chambers open out one beyond another, nor does it lack either water or light, for a very pleasant and wholesome spring runs at the foot of the cliffs, and natural chinks, in the most advantageous place, let in the light all day long; and the thickness of the rock makes the air within pure and clear, all the wet and moisture being carried off into the spring.

While Crassus remained here, the steward brought them what was necessary, but never saw them, nor knew anything of the matter, though they within saw, and expected him at the customary times. Neither was their entertainment such as just to keep them alive, but given them in abundance and for their enjoyment; for Pacianus resolved to treat him with all imaginable kindness, and considering he was a young man, thought it well to gratify a little his youthful inclinations; for to give just what is needful, seems rather to come from necessity than from a hearty friendship. Once taking with him two female servants, he showed them the place and bade them go in boldly, whom when Crassus and his friends saw, they were afraid of being betrayed, and demanded what they were, and what they would have. They, according as they were instructed, answered, they came to wait upon their master who was hid in that cave. And so Crassus perceiving it was a piece of pleasantry and of goodwill on the part of Vibius, took them in and kept them there with him as long as he stayed, and employed them to give information to Vibius of what they wanted, and how they were. Fenestella says he saw one of them, then very old, and often heard her speak of the time and repeat the story with pleasure.

After Crassus had lain concealed there eight months, on hearing that Cinna was dead, he appeared abroad, and a great number of people flocking to him, out of whom he selected a body of two thousand five hundred, he visited many cities, and, as some write, sacked Malaca, which he himself, however, always denied, and contradicted all who said so. Afterwards, getting together some ships, he passed into Africa, and joined with Metellus Pius, an eminent person that had raised a very considerable force; but upon some difference between him and Metellus, he stayed not long there, but went over to Sylla, by whom he was very much esteemed. When Sylla passed over into Italy, he was anxious to put all the young men that were with him in employment; and as he dispatched some one way, and some another, Crassus, on its falling to his share to raise men among the Marsians, demanded a guard, being to pass through the enemy's country, upon which Sylla replied sharply, "I give you for guard your father, your brother, your friends and kindred, whose unjust and cruel murder I am now going to revenge;" and Crassus, being nettled, went his way, broke boldly through the enemy, collected a considerable force, and in all Sylla's wars acted with great zeal and courage. And in these times and occasions, they say, began the emulation and rivalry for glory between him and Pompey; for though Pompey was the younger man, and had the disadvantage to be descended of a father that was disesteemed by the citizens, and hated as much as ever man was, yet in these actions he shone out, and was proved so great, that Sylla always used, when he came in, to stand up and uncover his head, an honor which he seldom showed to older men and his own equals, and always saluted him Imperator. This fired and stung Crassus, though, indeed, he could not with any fairness claim to be preferred; for he both wanted experience, and his two innate vices, sordidness and avarice, tarnished all the lustre of his actions. For when he had taken Tudertia, a town of the Umbrians, he converted, it was said, all the spoil to his own use, for which he was complained of to Sylla. But in the last and greatest battle before Rome itself, where Sylla was worsted, some of his battalions giving ground, and others being quite broken, Crassus got the victory on the right wing, which he commanded, and pursued the enemy till night, and then sent to Sylla to acquaint him with his success, and demand provision for his soldiers. In the time, however, of the proscriptions and sequestrations, he lost his repute again, by making great purchases for little or nothing, and asking for grants. Nay, they say he proscribed one of the Bruttians without Sylla's order, only for his own profit, and that, on discovering this, Sylla never after trusted him in any public affairs. As no man was more cunning than Crassus to ensnare others by flattery, so no man lay more open to it, or swallowed it more greedily than himself. And this particularly was observed of him, that though he was the most covetous man in the world, yet he habitually disliked and cried out against others who were so.

It troubled him to see Pompey so successful in all his undertakings; that he had had a triumph before he was capable to sit in the senate, and that the people had surnamed him Magnus, or the Great. When somebody was saying Pompey the Great was coming, he smiled, and asked him, "How big is he?" Despairing to equal him by feats of arms, he betook himself to civil life, where by doing kindnesses, pleading, lending money, by speaking and canvassing among the people for those who had objects to obtain from them, he gradually gained as great honor and power as Pompey had from his many famous expeditions. And it was a curious thing in their rivalry, that Pompey's name and interest in the city was greatest when he was absent, for his renown in war, but when present he was often less successful than Crassus, by reason of his superciliousness and haughty way of living, shunning crowds of people, and appearing rarely in the forum, and assisting only some few, and that not readily, that his interest might be the stronger when he came to use it for himself. Whereas Crassus, being a friend always at hand, ready to be had and easy of access, and always with his hands full of other people's business, with his freedom and courtesy, got the better of Pompey's formality. In point of dignity of person, eloquence of language, and attractiveness of countenance, they were pretty equally excellent. But, however, this emulation never transported Crassus so far as to make him bear enmity, or any ill-will; for though he was vexed to see Pompey and Caesar preferred to him, yet he never minded any hostility or malice with his jealousy; though Caesar when he was taken captive by the corsairs in Asia, cried out, "O Crassus, how glad you will be at the news of my captivity!" Afterwards they lived together on friendly terms, for when Caesar was going praetor into Spain, and his creditors, he being then in want of money, came upon him and seized his equipage, Crassus then stood by him and relieved him, and was his security for eight hundred and thirty talents. And, in general, Rome being divided into three great interests, those of Pompey, Caesar, and Crassus, (for as for Cato, his fame was greater than his power, and he was rather admired than followed,) the sober and quiet part were for Pompey, the restless and hotheaded followed Caesar's ambition, but Crassus trimmed between them, making advantages of both, and changed sides continually, being neither a trusty friend nor an implacable enemy, and easily abandoned both his attachments and his animosities, as he found it for his advantage, so that in short spaces of time, the same men and the same measures had him both as their supporter and as their opponent. He was much liked, but was feared as much or even more. At any rate, when Sicinius, who was the greatest troubler of the magistrates and ministers of his time, was asked how it was he let Crassus alone, "Oh," said he, "he carries hay on his horns," alluding to the custom of tying hay to the horns of a bull that used to butt, that people might keep out of his way.

The insurrection of the gladiators and the devastation of Italy, commonly called the war of Spartacus, began upon this occasion. One Lentulus Batiates trained up a great many gladiators in Capua, most of them Gauls and Thracians, who, not for any fault by them committed, but simply through the cruelty of their master, were kept in confinement for this object of fighting one with another. Two hundred of these formed a plan to escape, but their plot being discovered, those of them who became aware of it in time to anticipate their master, being seventy-eight, got out of a cook's shop chopping-knives and spits, and made their way through the city, and lighting by the way on several wagons that were carrying gladiator's arms to another city, they seized upon them and armed themselves. And seizing upon a defensible place, they chose three captains, of whom Spartacus was chief, a Thracian of one of the nomad tribes, and a man not only of high spirit and valiant, but in understanding, also, and in gentleness, superior to his condition, and more of a Grecian than the people of his country usually are. When he first came to be sold at Rome, they say a snake coiled itself upon his face as he lay asleep, and his wife, who at this latter time also accompanied him in his flight, his countrywoman, a kind of prophetess, and one of those possessed with the bacchanal frenzy, declared that it was a sign portending great and formidable power to him with no happy event.

First, then, routing those that came out of Capua against them, and thus procuring a quantity of proper soldiers' arms, they gladly threw away their own as barbarous and dishonorable. Afterwards Clodius, the praetor, took the command against them with a body of three thousand men from Rome, and besieged them within a mountain, accessible only by one narrow and difficult passage, which Clodius kept guarded, encompassed on all other sides with steep and slippery precipices. Upon the top, however, grew a great many wild vines, and cutting down as many of their boughs as they had need of, they twisted them into strong ladders long enough to reach from thence to the bottom, by which, without any danger, they got down all but one, who stayed there to throw them down their arms, and after this succeeded in saving himself. The Romans were ignorant of all this, and, therefore, coming upon them in the rear, they assaulted them unawares and took their camp. Several, also, of the shepherds and herdsman that were there, stout and nimble fellows, revolted over to them, to some of whom they gave complete arms, and made use of others as scouts and light-armed soldiers. Publius Varinus, the praetor, was now sent against them, whose lieutenant, Furius, with two thousand men, they fought and routed. Then Cossinius was sent, with considerable forces, to give his assistance and advice, and him Spartacus missed but very little of capturing in person, as he was bathing at Salinae; for he with great difficulty made his escape, while Spartacus possessed himself of his baggage, and following the chase with a great slaughter, stormed his camp and took it, where Cossinius himself was slain. After many successful skirmishes with the praetor himself, in one of which he took his lictors and his own horse, he began to be great and terrible; but wisely considering that he was not to expect to match the force of the empire, he marched his army towards the Alps, intending, when he had passed them, that every man should go to his own home, some to Thrace, some to Gaul. But they, grown confident in their numbers, and puffed up with their success, would give no obedience to him, but went about and ravaged Italy; so that now the senate was not only moved at the indignity and baseness, both of the enemy and of the insurrection, but, looking upon it as a matter of alarm and of dangerous consequence, sent out both the consuls to it, as to a great and difficult enterprise. The consul Gellius, falling suddenly upon a party of Germans, who through contempt and confidence had straggled from Spartacus, cut them all to pieces. But when Lentulus with a large army besieged Spartacus, he sallied out upon him, and, joining battle, defeated his chief officers, and captured all his baggage. As he made toward the Alps, Cassius, who was praetor of that part of Gaul that lies about the Po, met him with ten thousand men, but being overcome in battle, he had much ado to escape himself, with the loss of a great many of his men.

When the senate understood this, they were displeased at the consuls, and ordering them to meddle no further, they appointed Crassus general of the war, and a great many of the nobility went volunteers with him, partly out of friendship, and partly to get honor. He stayed himself on the borders of Picenum, expecting Spartacus would come that way, and sent his lieutenant,

Mummius, with two legions, to wheel about and observe the enemy's motions, but upon no account to engage or skirmish. But he, upon the first opportunity, joined battle, and was routed, having a great many of his men slain, and a great many only saving their lives, with the loss of their arms. Crassus rebuked Mummius severely, and arming the soldiers again, he made them find sureties for their arms, that they would part with them no more, and five hundred that were the beginners of the flight, he divided into fifty tens, and one of each was to die by lot, thus reviving the ancient Roman punishment of decimation, where ignominy is added to the penalty of death, with a variety of appalling and terrible circumstances, presented before the eyes of the whole army, assembled as spectators. When he had thus reclaimed his men, he led them against the enemy; but Spartacus retreated through Lucania toward the sea, and in the straits meeting with some Cilician pirate ships, he had thoughts of attempting Sicily, where, by landing two thousand men, he hoped to new kindle the war of the slaves, which was but lately extinguished, and seemed to need but a little fuel to set it burning again. But after the pirates had struck a bargain with him, and received his earnest, they deceived him and sailed away. He thereupon retired again from the sea, and established his army in the peninsula of Rhegium; there Crassus came upon him, and considering the nature of the place, which of itself suggested the undertaking, he set to work to build a wall across the isthmus; thus keeping his soldiers at once from idleness, and his foes from forage. This great and difficult work he perfected in a space of time short beyond all expectation, making a ditch from one sea to the other, over the neck of land, three hundred furlongs long, fifteen feet broad, and as much in depth, and above it built a wonderfully high and strong wall. All which Spartacus at first slighted and despised, but when provisions began to fail, and on his proposing to pass further, he found he was walled in, and no more was to be had in the peninsula, taking the opportunity of a snowy, stormy night, he filled up part of the ditch with earth and boughs of trees, and so passed the third part of his army over.

Crassus was afraid lest he should march directly to Rome, but was soon eased of that fear when he saw many of his men break out in a mutiny and quit him, and encamp by themselves upon the Lucanian lake. This lake they say changes at intervals of time, and is sometimes sweet, and sometimes so salt that it cannot be drunk. Crassus falling upon these beat them from the lake, but he could not pursue the slaughter, because of Spartacus suddenly coming up, and checking the flight. Now he began to repent that he had previously written to the senate to call Lucullus out of Thrace, and Pompey out of Spain; so that he did all he could to finish the war before they came, knowing that the honor of the action would redound to him that came to his assistance. Resolving, therefore, first to set upon those that had mutinied and encamped apart, whom Caius Cannicius and Castus commanded, he sent six thousand men before to secure a little eminence, and to do it as privately as possible, which that they might do, they covered their helmets, but being discovered by two women that were sacrificing for the enemy, they had been in great hazard, had not Crassus immediately appeared, and engaged in a battle which proved a most bloody one. Of twelve thousand three hundred whom he killed, two only were found wounded in their backs, the rest all having died standing in their ranks, and fighting bravely. Spartacus, after this discomfiture, retired to the mountains of Petelia, but Quintius, one of Crassus's officers, and Scrofa, the quaestor, pursued and overtook him. But when Spartacus rallied and faced them, they were utterly routed and fled, and had much ado to carry off their quaestor, who was wounded. This success, however, ruined Spartacus, because it encouraged the slaves, who now disdained any longer to avoid fighting, or to obey their officers, but as they were upon their march, they came to them with their swords in their hand, and compelled them to lead them back again through Lucania, against the Romans, the very thing which Crassus was eager for. For news was already brought that Pompey was at hand; and people began to talk openly, that the honor of this war was reserved for him, who would come and at once oblige the enemy to fight and put an end to the war. Crassus, therefore, eager to fight a decisive battle, encamped very near the enemy, and began to make lines of circumvallation; but the slaves made a sally, and attacked the pioneers. As fresh supplies came in on either side, Spartacus, seeing there was no avoiding it, set all his army in array, and when his horse was brought him, he drew out his sword and killed him, saying, if he got the day, he should have a great many better horses of the enemies, and if he lost it, he should have no need of this. And so making directly towards Crassus himself, through the midst of arms and wounds, he missed him, but slew two centurions that fell upon him together. At last being deserted by those that were about him, he himself stood his ground, and, surrounded by the enemy, bravely defending himself, was cut in pieces. But though Crassus had good fortune, and not only did the part of a good general, but gallantly exposed his person, yet Pompey had much of the credit of the action. For he met with many of the fugitives, and slew them, and wrote to the senate that Crassus indeed had vanquished the slaves in a pitched battle, but that he had put an end to the war. Pompey was honored with a magnificent triumph for his conquest over Sertorius and Spain, while Crassus could not himself so much as desire a triumph in its full form, and indeed it was thought to look but meanly in him to accept of the lesser honor, called the ovation, for a servile war, and perform a procession on foot. The difference between this and the other, and the origin of the name, are explained in the life of Marcellus.

And Pompey being immediately invited to the consulship, Crassus, who had hoped to be joined with him, did not scruple to request his assistance.

Pompey most readily seized the opportunity, as he desired by all means to lay some obligation upon Crassus, and zealously promoted his interest; and at last he declared in one of his speeches to the people, that he should be not less beholden to them for his colleague, than for the honor of his own appointment. But once entered upon the employment, this amity continued not long; but differing almost in everything, disagreeing, quarrelling, and contending, they spent the time of their consulship, without effecting any measure of consequence, except that Crassus made a great sacrifice to Hercules, and feasted the people at ten thousand tables, and measured them out corn for three months. When their command was now ready to expire, and they were, as it happened addressing the people, a Roman knight, one Onatius Aurelius, an ordinary private person, living in the country, mounted the hustings, and declared a vision he had in his sleep: "Jupiter," said he, "appeared to me, and commanded me to tell you, that you should not suffer your consuls to lay down their charge before they are made friends." When he had spoken, the people cried out that they should be reconciled. Pompey stood still and said nothing, but Crassus, first offering him his hand, said, "I cannot think, my countrymen, that I do any thing humiliating or unworthy of myself, if I make the first offers of accommodation and friendship with Pompey, whom you yourselves styled the Great, before he was of man's estate, and decreed him a triumph before he was capable of sitting in the senate."

This is what was memorable in Crassus's consulship, but as for his censorship, that was altogether idle and inactive, for he neither made a scrutiny of the senate, nor took a review of the horsemen, nor a census of the people, though he had as mild a man as could be desired for his colleague, Lutatius Catulus. It is said, indeed, that when Crassus intended a violent and unjust measure, which was the reducing Egypt to be tributary to Rome, Catulus strongly opposed it, and falling out about it, they laid down their office by consent. In the great conspiracy of Catiline, which was very near subverting the government, Crassus was not without some suspicion of being concerned, and one man came forward and declared him to be in the plot; but nobody credited him. Yet Cicero, in one of his orations, clearly charges both Crassus and Caesar with the guilt of it, though that speech was not published till they were both dead. But in his speech upon his consulship, he declares that Crassus came to him by night, and brought a letter concerning Catiline, stating the details of the conspiracy. Crassus hated him ever after, but was hindered by his son from doing him any open injury; for Publius was a great lover of learning and eloquence, and a constant follower of Cicero, insomuch that he put himself into mourning when he was accused, and induced the other young men to do the same. And at last he reconciled him to his father.

Caesar now returning from his command, and designing to get the consulship, and seeing that Crassus and Pompey were again at variance, was unwilling to disoblige one by making application to the other, and despaired of success without the help of one of them; he therefore made it his business to reconcile them, making it appear that by weakening each other's influence they were promoting the interest of the Ciceros, the Catuli, and the Catos, who would really be of no account if they would join their interests and their factions, and act together in public with one policy and one united power. And so reconciling them by his persuasions, out of the three parties he set up one irresistible power, which utterly subverted the government both of senate and people. Not that he made either Pompey or Crassus greater than they were before, but by their means made himself greatest of all; for by the help of the adherents of both, he was at once gloriously declared consul, which office when he administered with credit, they decreed him the command of an army, and allotted him Gaul for his province, and so placed him as it were in the citadel, not doubting but they should divide the rest at their pleasure between themselves, when they had confirmed him in his allotted command. Pompey was actuated in all this by an immoderate desire of ruling, but Crassus, adding to his old disease of covetousness, a new passion after trophies and triumphs, emulous of Caesar's exploits, not content to be beneath him in these points, though above him in all others, could not be at rest, till it ended in an ignominious overthrow, and a public calamity. When Caesar came out of Gaul to Lucca, a great many went thither from Rome to meet him. Pompey and Crassus had various conferences with him in secret, in which they came to the resolution to proceed to still more decisive steps, and to get the whole management of affairs into their hands, Caesar to keep his army, and Pompey and Crassus to obtain new ones and new provinces. To effect all which there was but one way, the getting the consulate a second time, which they were to stand for, and Caesar to assist them by writing to his friends, and sending many of his soldiers to vote.

But when they returned to Rome, their design was presently suspected, and a report was soon spread that this interview had been for no good. When Marcellinus and Domitius asked Pompey in the senate if he intended to stand for the consulship, he answered, perhaps he would, perhaps not; and being urged again, replied, he would ask it of the honest citizens, but not of the dishonest. Which answer appearing too haughty and arrogant, Crassus said, more modestly, that he would desire it if it might be for the advantage of the public, otherwise he would decline it. Upon this some others took confidence and came forward as candidates, among them Domitius. But when Pompey and Crassus now openly appeared for it, the rest were afraid and drew back; only Cato encouraged Domitius, who was his friend and relation, to proceed, exciting him to persist, as though he was now defending the public liberty, as these men, he said, did not so much aim at the consulate, as at arbitrary government, and it was not a petition for office, but a seizure of provinces and armies. Thus spoke and thought Cato, and almost forcibly compelled Domitius to appear in the forum, where many sided with them. For there was, indeed, much wonder and question among the people, "Why should Pompey and Crassus want another consulship? and why they two together, and not with some third person? We have a great many men not unworthy to be fellow-consuls with either the one or the other." Pompey's party, being apprehensive of this, committed all manner of indecencies and violences, and amongst other things lay in wait for Domitius, as he was coming thither before daybreak with his friends; his torchbearer they killed, and wounded several others, of whom Cato was one. And these being beaten back and driven into a house, Pompey and Crassus were proclaimed consuls. Not long after, they surrounded the house with armed men, thrust Cato out of the forum, killed some that made resistance, and decreed Caesar his command for five years longer, and provinces for themselves, Syria, and both the Spains, which being divided by lots, Syria fell to Crassus, and the Spains to Pompey.

All were well pleased with the chance, for the people were desirous that Pompey should not go far from the city, and he, being extremely fond of his wife, was very glad to continue there; but Crassus was so transported with his fortune, that it was manifest he thought he had never had such good luck befall him as now, so that he had much to do to contain himself before company and strangers; but amongst his private friends he let fall many vain and childish words, which were unworthy of his age, and contrary to his usual character, for he had been very little given to boasting hitherto. But then being strangely puffed up, and his head heated, he would not limit his fortune with Parthia and Syria; but looking on the actions of Lucullus against Tigranes and the exploits of Pompey against Mithridates as but child's play, he proposed to himself in his hopes to pass as far as Bactria and India, and the utmost ocean. Not that he was called upon by the decree which appointed him to his office to undertake any expedition against the Parthians, but it was well known that he was eager for it, and Caesar wrote to him out of Gaul, commending his resolution, and inciting him to the war. And when Ateius, the tribune of the people, designed to stop his journey, and many others murmured that one man should undertake a war against a people that had done them no injury, and were at amity with them, he desired Pompey to stand by him and accompany him out of the town, as he had a great name amongst the common people. And when several were ready prepared to interfere and raise an outcry, Pompey appeared with a pleasing countenance, and so mollified the people, that they let Crassus pass quietly. Ateius, however, met him, and first by word of mouth warned and conjured him not to proceed, and then commanded his attendant officer to seize him and detain him; but the other tribunes not permitting it, the officer released Crassus. Ateius, therefore, running to the gate, when Crassus was come thither, set down a chafing-dish with lighted fire in it, and burning incense and pouring libations on it, cursed him with dreadful imprecations, calling upon and naming several strange and horrible deities. In the Roman belief there is so much virtue in these sacred and ancient rites, that no man can escape the effects of them, and that the utterer himself seldom prospers; so that they are not often made use of, and but upon a great occasion. And Ateius was blamed at the time for resorting to them, as the city itself, in whose cause he used them, would be the first to feel the ill effects of these curses and supernatural terrors.

Crassus arrived at Brundusium, and though the sea was very rough, he had not patience to wait, but went on board, and lost many of his ships. With the remnant of his army he marched rapidly through Galatia, where meeting with king Deiotarus, who, though he was very old, was about building a new city, Crassus scoffingly told him, "Your majesty begins to build at the twelfth hour." "Neither do you," said he, "O general, undertake your Parthian expedition very early." For Crassus was then sixty years old, and he seemed older than he was. At his first coming, things went as he would have them, for he made a bridge over Euphrates without much difficulty, and passed over his army in safety, and occupied many cities of Mesopotamia, which yielded voluntarily. But a hundred of his men were killed in one, in which Apollonius was tyrant; therefore, bringing his forces against it, he took it by storm, plundered the goods, and sold the inhabitants. The Greeks call this city Zenodotia, upon the taking of which, he permitted the army to salute him Imperator, but this was very ill thought of, and it looked as if he despaired a nobler achievement, that he made so much of this little success. Putting garrisons of seven thousand foot and one thousand horse in the new conquests, he returned to take up his winter quarters in Syria, where his son was to meet him coming from Caesar out of Gaul, decorated with rewards for his valor, and bringing with him one thousand select horse. Here Crassus seemed to commit his first error, and except, indeed, the whole expedition, his greatest; for, whereas he ought to have gone forward and seized Babylon and Seleucia, cities that were ever at enmity with the Parthians, he gave the enemy time to provide against him. Besides, he spent his time in Syria more like an usurer than a general, not in taking an account of the arms, and in improving the skill and discipline of his soldiers, but in computing the revenue of the cities, wasting many days in weighing by scale and balance the treasure that was in the temple of Hierapolis, issuing requisitions for levies of soldiers upon particular towns and kingdoms, and then again withdrawing them on payment of sums of money, by which he lost his credit and became despised. Here, too, he met with the first ill-omen from that goddess, whom some call Venus, others Juno, others Nature, or the Cause that produces out of moisture the first principles and seeds of all things, and gives mankind their earliest knowledge of all that is good for them. For as they were going out of the temple, young Crassus stumbled, and his father fell upon him.

When he drew his army out of winter quarters, ambassadors came to him from Arsaces, with this short speech: If the army was sent by the people of Rome, he denounced mortal war, but if, as he understood was the case, against the consent of his country, Crassus for his own private profit had invaded his territory, then their king would be more merciful, and taking pity upon Crassus's dotage, would send those soldiers back, who had been left not so truly to keep guard on him as to be his prisoners. Crassus boastfully told them he would return his answer at Seleucia, upon which Vagises, the eldest of them, laughed and showed the palm of his hand, saying, "Hail will grow here before you will see Seleucia;" so they returned to their king, Hyrodes, telling him it was war. Several of the Romans that were in garrison in Mesopotamia with great hazard made their escape, and brought word that the danger was worth consideration, urging their own eye-witness of the numbers of the enemy, and the manner of their fighting, when they assaulted their towns; and, as men's manner is, made all seem greater than really it was. By flight it was impossible to escape them, and as impossible to overtake them when they fled, and they had a new and strange sort of darts, as swift as sight, for they pierced whatever they met with, before you could see who threw; their men-at-arms were so provided that their weapons would cut through anything, and their armor give way to nothing. All which when the soldiers heard, their hearts failed them; for till now they thought there was no difference between the Parthians and the Armenians or Cappadocians, whom Lucullus grew weary with plundering, and had been persuaded that the main difficulty of the war consisted only in the tediousness of the march, and the trouble of chasing men that durst not come to blows, so that the danger of a battle was beyond their expectation; accordingly, some of the officers advised Crassus to proceed no further at present, but reconsider the whole enterprise, amongst whom in particular was Cassius, the quaestor. The soothsayers, also, told him privately the signs found in the sacrifices were continually adverse and unfavorable. But he paid no heed to them, or to anybody who gave any other advice than to proceed. Nor did Artabazes, king of Armenia, confirm him a little, who came to his aid with six thousand horse; who, however, were said to be only the king's life-guard and suite, for he promised ten thousand cuirassiers more, and thirty thousand foot, at his own charge. He urged Crassus to invade Parthia by the way of Armenia, for not only would he be able there to supply his army with abundant provision, which he would give him, but his passage would be more secure in the mountains and hills, with which the whole country was covered, making it almost impassable to horse, in which the main strength of the Parthians consisted. Crassus returned him but cold thanks for his readiness to serve him, and for the splendor of his assistance, and told him he was resolved to pass through Mesopotamia, where he had left a great many brave Roman soldiers; whereupon the Armenian went his way. As Crassus was taking the army over the river at Zeugma, he encountered preternaturally violent thunder, and the lightning flashed in the faces of the troops, and during the storm a hurricane broke upon the bridge, and carried part of it away; two thunderbolts fell upon the very place where the army was going to encamp; and one of the general's horses, magnificently caparisoned, dragged away the groom into the river and was drowned. It is said, too, that when they went to take up the first standard, the eagle of itself turned its head backward; and after he had passed over his army, as they were distributing provisions, the first thing they gave was lentils and salt, which with the Romans are the food proper to funerals, and are offered to the dead. And as Crassus was haranguing his soldiers, he let fall a word which was thought very ominous in the army; for "I am going," he said, "to break down the bridge, that none of you may return;" and whereas he ought, when he had perceived his blunder, to have corrected himself, and explained his meaning, seeing the men alarmed at the expression, he would not do it out of mere stubbornness. And when at the last general sacrifice the priest gave him the entrails, they slipped out of his hand, and when he saw the standers-by concerned at it, he laughed and said, "See what it is to be an old man; but I shall hold my sword fast enough."

So he marched his army along the river with seven legions, little less than four thousand horse, and as many light-armed soldiers, and the scouts returning declared that not one man appeared, but that they saw the footing of a great many horses which seemed to be retiring in flight, whereupon Crassus conceived great hopes, and the Romans began to despise the Parthians, as men that would not come to combat, hand to hand. But Cassius spoke with him again, and advised him to refresh his army in some of the garrison towns, and remain there till they could get some certain intelligence of the enemy, or at least to make toward Seleucia, and keep by the river, that so they might have the convenience of having provision constantly supplied by the boats, which might always accompany the army, and the river would secure them from being environed, and, if they should fight, it might be upon equal terms.

While Crassus was still considering, and as yet undetermined, there came to the camp an Arab chief named Ariamnes, a cunning and wily fellow, who, of all the evil chances which combined to lead them on to destruction, was the chief and the most fatal. Some of Pompey's old soldiers knew him, and remembered him to have received some kindnesses of Pompey, and to have been looked upon as a friend to the Romans, but he was now suborned by the king's generals, and sent to Crassus to entice him if possible from the river and hills into the wide open plain, where he might be surrounded. For the Parthians desired anything, rather than to be obliged to meet the Romans face to face. He, therefore, coming to Crassus, (and he had a persuasive tongue,) highly commended Pompey as his benefactor, and admired the forces that Crassus had with him, but seemed to wonder why he delayed and made preparations, as if he should not use his feet more than any arms, against men that, taking with them their best goods and chattels, had designed long ago to fly for refuge to the Scythians or Hyrcanians. "If you meant to fight, you should have made all possible haste, before the king should recover courage, and collect his forces together; at present you see Surena and Sillaces opposed to you, to draw you off in pursuit of them, while the king himself keeps out of the way." But this was all a lie, for Hyrodes had divided his army in two parts, with one he in person wasted Armenia, revenging himself upon Artavasdes, and sent Surena against the Romans, not out of contempt, as some pretend, for there is no likelihood that he should despise Crassus, one of the chiefest men of Rome, to go and fight with Artavasdes, and invade Armenia; but much more probably he really apprehended the danger, and therefore waited to see the event, intending that Surena should first run the hazard of a battle, and draw the enemy on. Nor was this Surena an ordinary person, but in wealth, family, and reputation, the second man in the kingdom, and in courage and prowess the first, and for bodily stature and beauty no man like him. Whenever he traveled privately, he had one thousand camels to carry his baggage, two hundred chariots for his concubines, one thousand completely armed men for his life-guards, and a great many more light-armed; and he had at least ten thousand horsemen altogether, of his servants and retinue. The honor had long belonged to his family, that at the king's coronation he put the crown upon his head, and when this very king Hyrodes had been exiled, he brought him in; it was he, also, that took the great city of Seleucia, was the first man that scaled the walls, and with his own hand beat off the defenders. And though at this time he was not above thirty years old, he had a great name for wisdom and sagacity, and, indeed, by these qualities chiefly, he overthrew Crassus, who first through his overweening confidence, and afterwards because he was cowed by his calamities, fell a ready victim to his subtlety. When Ariamnes had thus worked upon him, he drew him from the river into vast plains, by a way that at first was pleasant and easy, but afterwards very troublesome by reason of the depth of the sand; no tree, nor any water, and no end of this to be seen; so that they were not only spent with thirst, and the difficulty of the passage, but were dismayed with the uncomfortable prospect of not a bough, not a stream, not a hillock, not a green herb, but in fact a sea of sand, which encompassed the army with its waves. They began to suspect some treachery, and at the same time came messengers from Artavasdes, that he was fiercely attacked by Hyrodes, who had invaded his country, so that now it was impossible for him to send any succors, and that he therefore advised Crassus to turn back, and with joint forces to give Hyrodes battle, or at least that he should march and encamp where horses could not easily come, and keep to the mountains. Crassus, out of anger and perverseness, wrote him no answer, but told them, at present he was not at leisure to mind the Armenians, but he would call upon them another time, and revenge himself upon Artavasdes for his treachery. Cassius and his friends began again to complain, but when they perceived that it merely displeased Crassus, they gave over, but privately railed at the barbarian, "What evil genius, O thou worst of men, brought thee to our camp, and with what charms and potions hast thou bewitched Crassus, that he should march his army through a vast and deep desert, through ways which are rather fit for a captain of Arabian robbers, than for the general of a Roman army?" But the barbarian being a wily fellow, very submissively exhorted them, and encouraged them to sustain it a little further, and ran about the camp, and, professing to cheer up the soldiers, asked them, jokingly, "What, do you think you march through Campania, expecting everywhere to find springs, and shady trees, and baths, and inns of entertainment? Consider you now travel through the confines of Arabia and Assyria." Thus he managed them like children, and before the cheat was discovered, he rode away; not but that Crassus was aware of his going, but he had persuaded him that he would go and contrive how to disorder the affairs of the enemy.

It is related that Crassus came abroad that day not in his scarlet robe, which Roman generals usually wear, but in a black one, which, as soon as he perceived, he changed. And the standard-bearers had much ado to take up their eagles, which seemed to be fixed to the place. Crassus laughed at it, and hastened their march, and compelled his infantry to keep pace with his cavalry, till some few of the scouts returned and told them that their fellows were slain and they hardly escaped, that the enemy was at hand in full force, and resolved to give them battle. On this all was in an uproar; Crassus was struck with amazement, and for haste could scarcely put his army in good order. First, as Cassius advised, he opened their ranks and files that they might take up as much space as could be, to prevent their being surrounded, and distributed the horse upon the wings, but afterwards changing his mind, he drew up his army in a square, and made a front every way, each of which consisted of twelve cohorts, to every one of which he allotted a troop of horse, that no part might be destitute of the assistance that the horse might give, and that they might be ready to assist everywhere, as need should require. Cassius commanded one of the wings, young Crassus the other, and he himself was in the middle. Thus they marched on till they came to a little river named Balissus, a very inconsiderable one in itself, but very grateful to the soldiers, who had suffered so much by drought and heat all along their march. Most of the commanders were of the opinion that they ought to remain there that night, and to inform themselves as much as possible of the number of the enemies, and their order, and so march against them at break of day; but Crassus was so carried away by the eagerness of his son, and the horsemen that were with him, who desired and urged him to lead them on and engage, that he commanded those that had a mind to it to eat and drink as they stood in their ranks, and before they had all well done, he led them on, not leisurely and with halts to take breath, as if he was going to battle, but kept on his pace as if he had been in haste, till they saw the enemy, contrary to their expectation, neither so many nor so magnificently armed as the Romans expected. For Surena had hid his main force behind the first ranks, and ordered them to hide the glittering of their armor with coats and skins. But when they approached and the general gave the signal, immediately all the field rung with a hideous noise and terrible clamor. For the Parthians do not encourage themselves to war with cornets and trumpets, but with a kind of kettle-drum, which they strike all at once in various quarters. With these they make a dead hollow noise like the bellowing of beasts, mixed with sounds resembling thunder, having, it would seem, very correctly observed, that of all our senses hearing most confounds and disorders us, and that the feelings excited through it most quickly disturb, and most entirely overpower the understanding.

When they had sufficiently terrified the Romans with their noise, they threw off the covering of their armor, and shone like lightning in their breastplates and helmets of polished Margianian steel, and with their horses covered with brass and steel trappings. Surena was the tallest and finest looking man himself, but the delicacy of his looks and effeminacy of his dress did not promise so much manhood as he really was master of; for his face was painted, and his hair parted after the fashion of the Medes, whereas the other Parthians made a more terrible appearance, with their shaggy hair gathered in a mass upon their foreheads after the Scythian mode. Their first design was with their lances to beat down and force back the first ranks of the Romans, but when they perceived the depth of their battle, and that the soldiers firmly kept their ground, they made a retreat, and pretending to break their order and disperse, they encompassed the Roman square before they were aware of it. Crassus commanded his light-armed soldiers to charge, but they had not gone far before they were received with such a shower of arrows that they were glad to retire amongst the heavy-armed, with whom this was the first occasion of disorder and terror, when they perceived the strength and force of their darts, which pierced their arms, and passed through every kind of covering, hard and soft alike. The Parthians now placing themselves at distances began to shoot from all sides, not aiming at any particular mark, (for, indeed, the order of the Romans was so close, that they could not miss if they would,) but simply sent their arrows with great force out of strong bent bows, the strokes from which came with extreme violence. The position of the Romans was a very bad one from the first; for if they kept their ranks, they were wounded, and if they tried to charge, they hurt the enemy none the more, and themselves suffered none the less. For the Parthians threw their darts as they fled, an art in which none but the Scythians excel them, and it is, indeed, a cunning practice, for while they thus fight to make their escape, they avoid the dishonor of a flight.

However, the Romans had some comfort to think that when they had spent all their arrows, they would either give over or come to blows; but when they presently understood that there were numerous camels loaded with arrows, and that when the first ranks had discharged those they had, they wheeled off and took more, Crassus seeing no end of it, was out of all heart, and sent to his son that he should endeavor to fall in upon them before he was quite surrounded; for the enemy advanced most upon that quarter, and seemed to be trying to ride round and come upon the rear. Therefore the young man, taking with him thirteen hundred horse, one thousand of which he had from Caesar, five hundred archers, and eight cohorts of the full-armed soldiers that stood next him, led them up with design to charge the Parthians. Whether it was that they found themselves in a piece of marshy ground, as some think, or else designing to entice young Crassus as far as they could from his father, they turned and began to fly; whereupon he crying out that they durst not stand, pursued them, and with him Censorinus and Megabacchus, both famous, the latter for his courage and prowess, the other for being of a senator's family, and an excellent orator, both intimates of Crassus, and of about the same age. The horse thus pushing on, the infantry stayed little behind, being exalted with hopes and joy, for they supposed they had already conquered, and now were only pursuing; till when they were gone too far, they perceived the deceit, for they that seemed to fly, now turned again, and a great many fresh ones came on. Upon this they made an halt, for they doubted not but now the enemy would attack them, because they were so few. But they merely placed their cuirassiers to face the Romans, and with the rest of their horse rode about scouring the field, and thus stirring up the sand, they raised such a dust that the Romans could neither see nor speak to one another, and being driven in upon one another in one close body, they were thus hit and killed, dying, not by a quick and easy death, but with miserable pains and convulsions; for writhing upon the darts in their bodies, they broke them in their wounds, and when they would by force pluck out the barbed points, they caught the nerves and veins, so that they tore and tortured themselves. Many of them died thus, and those that survived were disabled for any service, and when Publius exhorted them to charge the cuirassiers, they showed him their hands nailed to their shields, and their feet stuck to the ground, so that they could neither fly nor fight. He charged in himself boldly, however, with his horse, and came to close quarters with them, but was very unequal, whether as to the offensive or defensive part; for with his weak and little javelins, he struck against targets that were of tough raw hides and iron, whereas the lightly clad bodies of his Gaulish horsemen were exposed to the strong spears of the enemy. For upon these he mostly depended, and with them he wrought wonders; for they would catch hold of the great spears, and close upon the enemy, and so pull them off from their horses, where they could scarce stir by reason of the heaviness of their armor, and many of the Gauls quitting their own horses, would creep under those of the enemy, and stick them in the belly; which, growing unruly with the pain, trampled upon their riders and upon the enemies promiscuously. The Gauls were chiefly tormented by the heat and drought being not accustomed to either, and most of their horses were slain by being spurred on against the spears, so that they were forced to retire among the foot, bearing off Publius grievously wounded. Observing a sandy hillock not far off, they made to it, and tying their horses to one another, and placing them in the midst, and joining all their shields together before them, they thought they might make some defense against the barbarians. But it fell out quite contrary, for when they were drawn up in a plain, the front in some measure secured those that were behind; but when they were upon the hill, one being of necessity higher up than another, none were in shelter, but all alike stood equally exposed, bewailing their inglorious and useless fate. There were with Publius two Greeks that lived near there at Carrhae, Hieronymus and Nicomachus; these men urged him to retire with them and fly to Ichnae, a town not far from thence, and friendly to the Romans. "No," said he, "there is no death so terrible, for the fear of which Publius would leave his friends that die upon his account;" and bidding them to take care of themselves, he embraced them and sent them away, and, because he could not use his arm, for he was run through with a dart, he opened his side to his armor-bearer, and commanded him to run him through. It is said that Censorinus fell in the same manner. Megabacchus slew himself, as did also the rest of best note. The Parthians coming upon the rest with their lances, killed them fighting, nor were there above five hundred taken prisoners. Cutting off the head of Publius, they rode off directly towards Crassus.

His condition was thus. When he had commanded his son to fall upon the enemy, and word was brought him that they fled and that there was a distant pursuit, and perceiving also that the enemy did not press upon him so hard as formerly, for they were mostly gone to fall upon Publius, he began to take heart a little; and drawing his army towards some sloping ground, expected when his son would return from the pursuit. Of the messengers whom Publius sent to him, (as soon as he saw his danger,) the first were intercepted by the enemy, and slain; the last hardly escaping, came and declared that Publius was lost, unless he had speedy succors. Crassus was terribly distracted, not knowing what counsel to take, and indeed no longer capable of taking any; overpowered now by fear for the whole army, now by desire to help his son. At last he resolved to move with his forces. Just upon this, up came the enemy with their shouts and noises more terrible than before, their drums sounding again in the ears of the Romans, who now feared a fresh engagement. And they who brought Publius's head upon the point of a spear, riding up near enough that it could be known, scoffingly inquired where were his parents and what family he was of, for it was impossible that so brave and gallant a warrior should be the son of so pitiful a coward as Crassus. This sight above all the rest dismayed the Romans, for it did not incite them to anger as it might have done, but to horror and trembling, though they say Crassus outdid himself in this calamity, for he passed through the ranks and cried out to them, "This, O my countrymen, is my own peculiar loss, but the fortune and the glory of Rome is safe and untainted so long as you are safe. But if any one be concerned for my loss of the best of sons, let him show it in revenging him upon the enemy. Take away their joy, revenge their cruelty, nor be dismayed at what is past; for whoever tries for great objects must suffer something. Neither did Lucullus overthrow Tigranes without bloodshed, nor Scipio Antiochus; our ancestors lost one thousand ships about Sicily, and how many generals and captains in Italy? no one of which losses hindered them from overthrowing their conquerors; for the State of Rome did not arrive to this height by fortune, but by perseverance and virtue in confronting danger."

While Crassus thus spoke exhorting them, he saw but few that gave much heed to him, and when he ordered them to shout for the battle, he could no longer mistake the despondency of his army, which made but a faint and unsteady noise, while the shout of the enemy was clear and bold. And when they came to the business, the Parthian servants and dependents riding about shot their arrows, and the horsemen in the foremost ranks with their spears drove the Romans close together, except those who rushed upon them for fear of being killed by their arrows. Neither did these do much execution, being quickly dispatched; for the strong thick spear made large and mortal wounds, and often run through two men at once. As they were thus fighting, the night coming on parted them, the Parthians boasting that they would indulge Crassus with one night to mourn his son, unless upon better consideration he would rather go to Arsaces, than be carried to him. These, therefore, took up their quarters near them, being flushed with their victory. But the Romans had a sad night of it; for neither taking care for the burial of their dead, nor the cure of the wounded, nor the groans of the expiring, everyone bewailed his own fate. For there was no means of escaping, whether they should stay for the light, or venture to retreat into the vast desert in the dark. And now the wounded men gave them new trouble, since to take them with them would retard their flight, and if they should leave them, they might serve as guides to the enemy by their cries. However, they were all desirous to see and hear Crassus, though they were sensible that he was the cause of all their mischief. But he wrapped his cloak around him, and hid himself, where he lay as an example, to ordinary minds, of the caprice of fortune, but to the wise, of inconsiderateness and ambition; who, not content to be superior to so many millions of men, being inferior to two, esteemed himself as the lowest of all. Then came Octavius, his lieutenant, and Cassius, to comfort him, but he being altogether past helping, they themselves called together the centurions and tribunes, and agreeing that the best way was to fly, they ordered the army out, without sound of trumpet, and at first with silence. But before long, when the disabled men found they were left behind, strange confusion and disorder, with an outcry and lamentation, seized the camp, and a trembling and dread presently fell upon them, as if the enemy were at their heels. By which means, now and then fuming out of their way, now and then standing to their ranks, sometimes taking up the wounded that followed, sometimes laying them down, they wasted the time, except three hundred horse, whom Egnatius brought safe to Carrhae about midnight; where calling, in the Roman tongue, to the watch, as soon as they heard him, he bade them tell Coponius, the governor, that Crassus had fought a very great battle with the Parthians; and having said but this, and not so much as telling his name, he rode away at full speed to Zeugma. And by this means he saved himself and his men, but lost his reputation by deserting his general. However, his message to Coponius was for the advantage of Crassus; for he, suspecting by this hasty and confused delivery of the message that all was not well, immediately ordered the garrison to be in arms, and as soon as he understood that Crassus was upon the way towards him, he went out to meet him, and received him with his army into the town.

The Parthians, although they perceived their dislodgement in the night, yet did not pursue them, but as soon as it was day, they came upon those that were left in the camp, and put no less than four thousand to the sword, and with their light; horse picked up a great many stragglers. Varguntinus, the lieutenant, while it was yet dark, had broken off from the main body with four cohorts which had strayed out of the way; and the Parthians, encompassing these on a small hill, slew every man of them excepting twenty, who with their drawn swords forced their way through the thickest, and they admiring their courage, opened their ranks to the right and left, and let them pass without molestation to Carrhae.

Soon after a false report was brought to Surena, that Crassus, with his principal officers, had escaped, and that those who were got into Carrhae were but a confused rout of insignificant people, not worth further pursuit. Supposing, therefore, that he had lost the very crown and glory of his victory, and yet being uncertain whether it were so or not, and anxious to ascertain the fact, that so he should either stay and besiege Carrhae or follow Crassus, he sent one of his interpreters to the walls, commanding him in Latin to call for Crassus or Cassius, for that the general, Surena, desired a conference. As soon as Crassus heard this, he embraced the proposal, and soon after there came up a band of Arabians, who very well knew the faces of Crassus and Cassius, as having been frequently in the Roman camp before the battle. They having espied Cassius from the wall, told him that Surena desired a peace, and would give them safe convoy, if they would make a treaty with the king his master, and withdraw all their troops out of Mesopotamia; and this he thought most advisable for them both, before things came to the last extremity; Cassius, embracing the proposal, desired that a time and place might be appointed where Crassus and Surena might have an interview. The Arabians, having charged themselves with the message, went back to Surena, who wee not a little rejoiced that Crassus was there to be besieged.

Next day, therefore, he came up with his army, insulting over the Romans, and haughtily demanding of them Crassus and Cassius bound, if they expected any mercy. The Romans, seeing themselves deluded and mocked, were much troubled at it, but advising Crassus to lay aside his distant and empty hopes of aid from the Armenians, resolved to fly for it; and this design ought to have been kept private, till they were upon their way, and not have been told to any of the people of Carrhae. But Crassus let this also be known to Andromachus, the most faithless of men, nay he was so infatuated as to choose him for his guide. The Parthians then, to be sure, had punctual intelligence of all that passed; but it being contrary to their usage, and also difficult for them to fight by night, and Crassus having chosen that time to set out, Andromachus, lest he should get the start too far of his pursuers, led him hither and thither, and at last conveyed him into the midst of morasses and places full of ditches, so that the Romans had a troublesome and perplexing journey of it, and some there were who, supposing by these windings and turnings of Andromachus that no good was intended, resolved to follow him no further. And at last Cassius himself returned to Carrhae, and his guides, the Arabians, advising him to tarry there till the moon was got out of Scorpio, he told them that he was most afraid of Sagittarius, and so with five hundred horse went off to Syria. Others there were, who having got honest guides, took their way by the mountains called Sinnaca, and got into places of security by daybreak; these were five thousand under the command of Octavius, a very gallant man. But Crassus fared worse; day overtook him still deceived by Andromachus, and entangled in the fens and the difficult country. There were with him four cohorts of legionary soldiers, a very few horsemen, and five lictors, with whom having with great difficulty got into the way, and not being a mile and a half from Octavius, instead of going to join him, although the enemy were already upon him, he retreated to another hill, neither so defensible nor impassable for the horse, but lying under the hills of Sinnaca, and continued so as to join them in a long ridge through the plain. Octavius could see in what danger the general was, and himself, at first but slenderly followed, hurried to the rescue. Soon after, the rest, upbraiding one another with baseness in forsaking their officers, marched down, and falling upon the Parthians, drove them from the hill, and compassing Crassus about, and fencing him with their shields, declared proudly, that no arrow in Parthia should ever touch their general, so long as there was a man of them left alive to protect him.

Surena, therefore, perceiving his soldiers less inclined to expose themselves, and knowing that if the Romans should prolong the battle till night, they might then gain the mountains and be out of his reach, betook himself to his usual craft. Some of the prisoners were set free, who had, as it was contrived, been in hearing, while some of the barbarians spoke of a set purpose in the camp to the effect that the king did not design the war to be pursued to extremity against the Romans, but rather desired, by his gentle treatment of Crassus, to make a step towards reconciliation. And the barbarians desisted from fighting, and Surena himself, with his chief officers, riding gently to the hill, unbent his bow and held out his hand, inviting Crassus to an agreement, and saying that it was beside the king's intentions, that they had thus had experience of the courage and the strength of his soldiers; that now he desired no other contention but that of kindness and friendship, by making a truce, and permitting them to go away in safety. These words of Surena the rest received joyfully, and were eager to accept the offer; but Crassus, who had had sufficient experience of their perfidiousness, and was unable to see any reason for the sudden change, would give no ear to them, and only took time to consider. But the soldiers cried out and advised him to treat, and then went on to upbraid and affront him, saying that it was very unreasonable that he should bring them to fight with such men armed, whom himself, without their arms, durst not look in the face. He tried first to prevail with them by entreaties, and told them that if they would have patience till evening, they might get into the mountains and passes, inaccessible for horse, and be out of danger, and withal he pointed out the way with his hand, entreating them not to abandon their preservation, now close before them. But when they mutinied and clashed their targets in a threatening manner, he was overpowered and forced to go, and only turning about at parting, said, "You, Octavius and Petronius, and the rest of the officers who are present, see the necessity of going which I lie under, and cannot but be sensible of the indignities and violence offered to me. Tell all men when you have escaped, that Crassus perished rather by the subtlety of his enemies, than by the disobedience of his countrymen."

Octavius, however, would not stay there, but with Petronius went down from the hill; as for the lictors, Crassus bade them be gone. The first that met him were two half-blood Greeks, who, leaping from their horses, made a profound reverence to Crassus, and desired him, in Greek, to send some before him, who might see that Surena himself was coming towards them, his retinue disarmed, and not having so much as their wearing swords along with them. But Crassus answered, that if he had the least concern for his life, he would never have entrusted himself in their hands, but sent two brothers of the name of Roscius, to inquire on what terms, and in what numbers they should meet. These Surena ordered immediately to be seized, and himself with his principal officers came up on horseback, and greetings him, said, "How is this, then? A Roman commander is on foot, whilst I and my train are mounted." But Crassus replied, that there was no error committed on either side, for they both met according to the custom of their own country. Surena told him that from that time there was a league between the king his master and the Romans, but that Crassus must go with him to the river to sign it, "for you Romans," said he, "have not good memories for conditions," and so saying, reached out his hand to him. Crassus, therefore, gave order that one of his horses should be brought; but Surena told him there was no need, "the king, my master, presents you with this;" and immediately a horse with a golden bit was brought up to him, and himself was forcibly put into the saddle by the grooms, who ran by the side and struck the horse to make the more haste. But Octavius running up, got hold of the bridle, and soon after one of the officers, Petronius, and the rest of the company came up, striving to stop the horse, and pulling back those who on both sides of him forced Crassus forward. Thus from pulling and thrusting one another, they came to a tumult, and soon after to blows. Octavius, drawing his sword, killed a groom of one of the barbarians, and one of them, getting behind Octavius, killed him. Petronius was not armed, but being struck on the breastplate, fell down from his horse, though without hurt. Crassus was killed by a Parthian, called Pomaxathres; others say, by a different man, and that Pomaxathres only cut off his head and right hand after he had fallen. But this is conjecture rather than certain knowledge, for those that were by had not leisure to observe particulars, and were either killed fighting about Crassus, or ran off at once to get to their comrades on the hill. But the Parthians coming up to them, and saying that Crassus had the punishment he justly deserved, and that Surena bade the rest come down from the hill without fear, some of them came down and surrendered themselves, others were scattered up and down in the night, a very few of whom got safe home, and others the Arabians, beating through the country, hunted down and put to death. It is generally said, that in all twenty thousand men were slain, and ten thousand taken prisoners.

 Surena sent the head and hand of Crassus to Hyrodes, the king, into Armenia, but himself by his messengers scattering a report that he was bringing Crassus alive to Seleucia, made a ridiculous procession, which by way of scorn, he called a triumph. For one Caius Paccianus, who of all the prisoners was most like Crassus, being put into a woman's dress of the fashion of the barbarians, and instructed to answer to the title of Crassus and Imperator, was brought sitting upon his horse, while before him went a parcel of trumpeters and lictors upon camels. Purses were hung at the end of the bundles of rods, and the heads of the slain fresh bleeding at the end of their axes. After them followed the Seleucian singing women, repeating scurrilous and abusive songs upon the effeminacy and cowardliness of Crassus. This show was seen by everybody; but Surena, calling together the senate of Seleucia, laid before them certain wanton books, of the writings of Aristides, the Milesian; neither, indeed, was this any forgery, for they had been found among the baggage of Rustius, and were a good subject to supply Surena with insulting remarks upon the Romans, who were not able even in the time of war to forget such writings and practices. But the people of Seleucia had reason to commend the wisdom of Aesop's fable of the wallet, seeing their general Surena carrying a bag full of loose Milesian stories before him, but keeping behind him a whole Parthian Sybaris in his many wagons full of concubines; like the vipers and asps people talk of, all the foremost and more visible parts fierce and terrible with spears and arrows and horsemen, but the rear terminating in loose women and castanets, music of the lute, and midnight revellings. Rustius, indeed, is not to be excused, but the Parthians had forgot, when they mocked at the Milesian stories, that many of the royal line of their Arsacidae had been born of Milesian and Ionian mistresses.

Whilst these things were doing, Hyrodes had struck up a peace with the king of Armenia, and made a match between his son Pacorus and the king of Armenia's sister. Their feastings and entertainments in consequence were very sumptuous, and various Grecian compositions, suitable to the occasion, were recited before them. For Hyrodes was not ignorant of the Greek language and literature, and Artavasdes was so expert in it, that he wrote tragedies and orations and histories, some of which are still extant. When the head of Crassus was brought to the door, the tables were just taken away, and one Jason, a tragic actor, of the town of Tralles, was singing the scene in the Bacchae of Euripides concerning Agave. He was receiving much applause, when Sillaces coming to the room, and having made obeisance to the king, threw down the head of Crassus into the midst of the company. The Parthians receiving it with joy and acclamations, Sillaces, by the king's command, was made to sit down, while Jason handed over the costume of Pentheus to one of the dancers in the chorus, and taking up the head of Crassus, and acting the part of a bacchante in her frenzy, in a rapturous impassioned manner, sang the lyric passages,

> *We've hunted down a mighty chase to-day,*
> *And from the mountain bring the noble prey;*

to the great delight of all the company; but when the verses of the dialogue followed,

> *What happy hand the glorious victim slew?*
> *I claim that honor to my courage due;*

Pomaxathres, who happened to be there at the supper, started up and would have got the head into his own hands, "for it is my due," said he, "and no man's else." The king was greatly pleased, and gave presents, according to the custom of the Parthians, to them, and to Jason, the actor, a talent. Such was the burlesque that was played, they tell us, as the afterpiece to the tragedy of Crassus's expedition. But divine justice failed not to punish both Hyrodes, for his cruelty, and Surena for his perjury; for Surena not long after was put to death by Hyrodes, out of mere envy to his glory; and Hyrodes himself, having lost his son Pacorus, who was beaten in a battle with the Romans, falling into a disease which turned to a dropsy, had aconite given him by his second son, Phraates; but the poison working only upon the disease, and carrying away the dropsical matter with itself, the king began suddenly to recover, so that Phraates at length was forced to take the shortest course, and strangled him.

9
COMPARISON OF CRASSUS WITH NICIAS

*I*n the comparison of these two, first, if we compare the estate of Nicias with that of Crassus, we must acknowledge Nicias's to have been more honestly got. In itself, indeed, one cannot much approve of gaining riches by working mines, the greatest part of which is done by malefactors and barbarians, some of them, too, bound, and perishing in those close and unwholesome places. But if we compare this with the sequestrations of Sylla, and the contracts for houses ruined by fire, we shall then think Nicias came very honestly by his money. For Crassus publicly and avowedly made use of these arts, as other men do of husbandry, and putting out money to interest; while as for other matters which he used to deny, when taxed with them, as, namely, selling his voice in the senate for gain's sake, and injuring allies, and courting women, and conniving at criminals, these are things which Nicias was never so much as falsely accused of; nay, he was rather laughed at for giving money to those who made a trade of impeachments, merely out of timorousness, a course, indeed, that would by no means become Pericles and Aristides, but necessary for him who by nature was wanting in assurance, even as Lycurgus, the orator, frankly acknowledged to the people; for when he was accused for buying off an evidence, he said that he was very much pleased that having administered their affairs for some time, he was at last accused, rather for giving, than receiving. Again, Nicias, in his expenses, was of a more public spirit than Crassus, priding himself much on the dedication of gifts in temples, on presiding at gymnastic games, and furnishing choruses for the plays, and adorning processions, while the expenses of Crassus, in feasting and afterwards providing food for so many myriads of people, were much greater than all that Nicias possessed as well as spent, put together. So that one might wonder at anyone's failing to see that vice is a certain inconsistency and incongruity of habit, after such an example of money dishonorably obtained, and wastefully lavished away.

Let so much be said of their estates; as for their management of public affairs, I see not that any dishonesty, injustice, or arbitrary action can be objected to Nicias, who was rather the victim of Alcibiades's tricks, and was always careful and scrupulous in his dealings with the people. But Crassus is very generally blamed for his changeableness in his friendships and enmities, for his unfaithfulness, and his mean and underhand proceedings; since he himself could not deny that to compass the consulship, he hired men to lay violent hands upon Domitius and Cato. Then at the assembly held for assigning the provinces, many were wounded and four actually killed, and he himself, which I had omitted in the narrative of his life, struck with his fist one Lucius Analius, a senator, for contradicting him, so that he left the place bleeding. But as Crassus was to be blamed for his violent and arbitrary courses, so is Nicias no less to be blamed for his timorousness and meanness of spirit, which made him submit and give in to the basest people, whereas in this respect Crassus showed himself lofty spirited and magnanimous, who having to do not with such as Cleon or Hyperbolus, but with the splendid acts of Caesar and the three triumphs of Pompey, would not stoop, but bravely bore up against their joint interests, and in obtaining the office of censor, surpassed even Pompey himself For a statesman ought not to regard how invidious the thing is, but how noble, and by his greatness to overpower envy; but if he will be always aiming at security and quiet, and dread Alcibiades upon the hustings, and the Lacedaemonians at Pylos, and Perdiccas in Thrace, there is room and opportunity enough for retirement, and he may sit out of the noise of business, and weave himself, as one of the sophists says, his triumphal garland of inactivity. His desire of peace, indeed, and of finishing the war, was a divine and truly Grecian ambition, nor in this respect would Crassus deserve to be compared to him, though he had enlarged the Roman empire to the Caspian Sea or the Indian Ocean.

In a State where there is a sense of virtue, a powerful man ought not to give way to the ill-affected, or expose the government to those that are incapable of it, nor suffer high trusts to be committed to those who want common honesty. Yet Nicias, by his connivance, raised Cleon, a fellow remarkable for nothing but his loud voice and brazen face, to the command of an army. Indeed, I do not commend Crassus, who in the war with Spartacus was more forward to fight than became a discreet general, though he was urged into it by a point of honor, lest Pompey by his coming should rob him of the glory of the action, as Mummius did Metellus at the taking of Corinth, but Nicias's proceedings are inexcusable. For he did not yield up a mere opportunity of getting honor and advantage to his competitor, but believing that the expedition would be very hazardous, was thankful to take care of himself, and left the Commonwealth to shift for itself. And whereas Themistocles, lest a mean and incapable fellow should ruin the State by holding command in the Persian war, bought him off, and Cato, in a most dangerous and critical conjuncture, stood for the tribuneship for the sake of his country, Nicias, reserving himself for trifling expeditions against Minoa and Cythera, and the miserable Melians, if there be occasion to come to blows with the Lacedaemonians, slips off his general's cloak and hands over to the unskillfulness and rashness of Cleon, fleet, men, and arms, and the whole command, where the utmost possible skill was called for. Such conduct, I say, is not to be thought so much carelessness of his own fame, as of the interest and preservation of his country. By this means it came to pass he was compelled to the Sicilian war, men generally believing that he was not so much honestly convinced of the difficulty of the enterprise, as ready out of mere love of ease and cowardice to lose the city the conquest of Sicily. But yet it is a great sign of his integrity, that though he was always averse from war, and unwilling to command, yet they always continued to appoint him as the best experienced and ablest general they had. On the other hand Crassus, though always ambitious of command, never attained to it, except by mere necessity in the servile war, Pompey and Metellus and the two brothers Lucullus being absent, although at that time he was at his highest pitch of interest and reputation. Even those who thought most of him seem to have thought him, as the comic poet says:

A brave man anywhere but in the field.

There was no help, however, for the Romans, against his passion for command and for distinction. The Athenians sent out Nicias against his will to the war, and Crassus led out the Romans against theirs; Crassus brought misfortune on Rome, as Athens brought it on Nicias.

Still this is rather ground for praising Nicias, than for finding fault with Crassus. His experience and sound judgment as a general saved him from being carried away by the delusive hopes of his fellow-citizens, and made him refuse to entertain any prospect of conquering Sicily. Crassus, on the other hand, mistook, in entering on a Parthian war as an easy matter. He was eager, while Caesar was subduing the west, Gaul, Germany, and Britain, to advance for his part to the east and the Indian Sea, by the conquest of Asia, to complete the incursions of Pompey and the attempts of Lucullus, men of prudent temper and of unimpeachable worth, who, nevertheless, entertained the same projects as Crassus, and acted under the same convictions. When Pompey was appointed to the like command, the senate was opposed to it; and after Caesar had routed three hundred thousand Germans, Cato recommended that he should be surrendered to the defeated enemy, to expiate in his own person the guilt of breach of faith. The people, meantime, (their service to Cato!) kept holiday for fifteen days, and were overjoyed. What would have been their feelings, and how many holidays would they have celebrated, if Crassus had sent news from Babylon of victory, and thence marching onward had converted Media and Persia, the Hyrcanians, Susa, and Bactra, into Roman provinces?

If wrong we must do, as Euripides says, and cannot be content with peace and present good things, let it not be for such results as destroying Mende or Scandea, or beating up the exiled Aeginetans in the coverts to which like hunted birds they had fled, when expelled from their homes, but let it be for some really great remuneration; nor let us part with justice, like a cheap and common thing, for a small and trifling price. Those who praise Alexander's enterprise and blame that of Crassus, judge of the beginning unfairly by the results.

In actual service, Nicias did much that deserves high praise. He frequently defeated the enemy in battle, and was on the very point of capturing Syracuse; nor should he bear the whole blame of the disaster, which may fairly be ascribed in part to his want of health and to the jealousy entertained of him at home. Crassus, on the other hand, committed so many errors as not to leave fortune room to show him favor. It is no surprise to find such imbecility fall a victim to the power of Parthia; the only wonder is to see it prevailing over the wonted good-fortune of Rome. One scrupulously observed, the other entirely slighted the arts of divination; and as both equally perished, it is difficult to see what inference we should draw. Yet the fault of over-caution, supported by old and general opinion, better deserves forgiveness than that of self-willed and lawless transgression.

In his death, however, Crassus has the advantage, as he did not surrender himself, nor submit to bondage, or let himself be taken in by trickery, but was the victim only of the entreaties of his friends and the perfidy of his enemies; whereas Nicias enhanced the shame of his death by yielding himself up in the hope of a disgraceful and inglorious escape.

10
AGESILAUS

*A*rchidamus, the son of Zeuxidamus, having reigned gloriously over the Lacedaemonians, left behind him two sons, Agis the elder, begotten of Lampido, a noble lady, Agesilaus, much the younger, born of Eupolia, the daughter of Melesippidas. Now the succession belonging to Agis by law, Agesilaus, who in all probability was to be but a private man, was educated according to the usual discipline of the country, hard and severe, and meant to teach young men to obey their superiors. Whence it was that, men say, Simonides called Sparta "the tamer of men," because by early strictness of education, they, more than any nation, trained the citizens to obedience to the laws, and made them tractable and patient of subjection, as horses that are broken in while colts. The law did not impose this harsh rule on the heirs apparent of the kingdom. But Agesilaus, whose good fortune it was to be born a younger brother, was consequently bred to all the arts of obedience, and so the better fitted for the government, when it fell to his share; hence it was that he proved the most popular-tempered of the Spartan kings, his early life having added to his natural kingly and commanding qualities the gentle and humane feelings of a citizen.

While he was yet a boy, bred up in one of what are called the flocks, or classes, he attracted the attachment of Lysander, who was particularly struck with the orderly temper that he manifested. For though he was one of the highest spirits, emulous above any of his companions, ambitious of preeminence in everything, and showed an impetuosity and fervor of mind which irresistibly carried him through all opposition or difficulty he could meet with; yet, on the other side, he was so easy and gentle in his nature, and so apt to yield to authority, that though he would do nothing on compulsion, upon ingenuous motives he would obey any commands, and was more hurt by the least rebuke or disgrace, than he was distressed by any toil or hardship.

He had one leg shorter than the other, but this deformity was little observed in the general beauty of his person in youth. And the easy way in which he bore it, (he being the first always to pass a jest upon himself,) went far to make it disregarded. And indeed his high spirit and eagerness to distinguish himself were all the more conspicuous by it, since he never let his lameness withhold him from any toil or any brave action. Neither his statue nor picture are extant, he never allowing them in his life, and utterly forbidding them to be made after his death. He is said to have been a little man, of a contemptible presence; but the goodness of his humor, and his constant cheerfulness and playfulness of temper, always free from anything of moroseness or haughtiness, made him more attractive, even to his old age, than the most beautiful and youthful men of the nation. Theophrastus writes, that the Ephors laid a fine upon Archidamus for marrying a little wife, "For" said they, "she will bring us a race of kinglets, instead of kings."

Whilst Agis, the elder brother, reigned, Alcibiades, being then an exile from Athens, came from Sicily to Sparta; nor had he stayed long there, before his familiarity with Timaea, the king's wife, grew suspected, insomuch that Agis refused to own a child of hers, which, he said, was Alcibiades's, not his. Nor, if we may believe Duris, the historian, was Timaea much concerned at it, being herself forward enough to whisper among her helot maid-servants, that the infant's true name was Alcibiades, not Leotychides. Meanwhile it was believed, that the amour he had with her was not the effect of his love but of his ambition, that he might have Spartan kings of his posterity. This affair being grown public, it became needful for Alcibiades to withdraw from Sparta. But the child Leotychides had not the honors due to a legitimate son paid him, nor was he ever owned by Agis, till by his prayers and tears he prevailed with him to declare him his son before several witnesses upon his death-bed. But this did not avail to fix him in the throne of Agis, after whose death Lysander, who had lately achieved his conquest of Athens by sea, and was of the greatest power in Sparta, promoted Agesilaus, urging Leotychides's bastardy as a bar to his pretensions. Many of the other citizens, also, were favorable to Agesilaus and zealously joined his party, induced by the opinion they had of his merits, of which they themselves had been spectators, in the time that he had been bred up among them. But there was a man, named Diopithes, at Sparta, who had a great knowledge of ancient oracles, and was thought particularly skillful and clever in all points of religion and divination. He alleged, that it was unlawful to make a lame man king of Lacedaemon, citing in the debate the following oracle:

> *—Beware, great Sparta, lest there come of thee*
> *Though sound thyself; an halting sovereignty;*
> *Troubles, both long and unexpected too,*
> *And storms of deadly warfare shall ensue.*

But Lysander was not wanting with an evasion, alleging that if the Spartans were really apprehensive of the oracle, they must have a care of Leotychides; for it was not the limping foot of a king that the gods cared about, but the purity of the Herculean family, into whose sights if a spurious issue were admitted, it would make the kingdom to halt indeed. Agesilaus likewise alleged, that the bastardy of Leotychides was witnessed to by Neptune, who threw Agis out of bed by a violent earthquake, after which time he ceased to visit his wife, yet Leotychides was born above ten months after this.

Agesilaus was upon these allegations declared king, and soon possessed himself of the private estate of Agis, as well as his throne, Leotychides being wholly rejected as a bastard. He now turned his attention to his kindred by the mother's side, persons of worth and virtue, but miserably poor. To them he gave half his brother's estate, and by this popular act gained general good-will and reputation, in the place of the envy and ill-feeling which the inheritance might otherwise have procured him. What Xenophon tells us of him, that by complying with, and, as it were, being ruled by his country, he grew into such great power with them, that he could do what he pleased, is meant to apply to the power he gained in the following manner with the Ephors and Elders. These were at that time of the greatest authority in the State; the former, officers annually chosen; the Elders, holding their places during life; both instituted, as already told in the life of Lycurgus, to restrain the power of the kings. Hence it was that there was always from generation to generation, a feud and contention between them and the kings. But Agesilaus took another course. Instead of contending with them, he courted them; in all proceedings he commenced by taking their advice, was always ready to go, nay almost run, when they called him; if he were upon his royal seat hearing causes and the Ephors came in, he rose to them; whenever any man was elected into the Council of Elders, he presented him with a gown and an ox. Thus, whilst he made show of deference to them, and of a desire to extend their authority, he secretly advanced his own, and enlarged the prerogatives of the kings by several liberties which their friendship to his person conceded.

To other citizens he so behaved himself, as to be less blamable in his enmities than in his friendships; for against his enemy he forbore to take any unjust advantage, but his friends he would assist, even in what was unjust. If an enemy had done anything praiseworthy, he felt it shameful to detract from his due, but his friends he knew not how to reprove when they did ill, nay, he would eagerly join with them, and assist them in their misdeed, and thought all offices of friendship commendable, let the matter in which they were employed be what it would. Again, when any of his adversaries was overtaken in a fault, he would be the first to pity him, and be soon entreated to procure his pardon, by which he won the hearts of all men. Insomuch that his popularity grew at last suspected by the Ephors, who laid a fine on him, professing that he was appropriating the citizens to himself, who ought to be the common property of the State. For as it is the opinion of philosophers, that could you take away strife and opposition out of the universe, all the heavenly bodies would stand still, generation and motion would cease in the mutual concord and agreement of all things, so the Spartan legislator seems to have admitted ambition and emulation, among the ingredients of his Commonwealth as the incentives of virtue, distinctly wishing that there should be some dispute and competition among his men of worth, and pronouncing the mere idle, uncontested, mutual compliance to unproved deserts to be but a false sort of concord. And some think Homer had an eye to this, when he introduces Agamemnon well pleased with the quarrel arising between Ulysses and Achilles, and with the "terrible words" that passed between them, which he would never have done, unless he had thought emulations and dissensions between the noblest men to be of great public benefit. Yet this maxim is not simply to be granted, without restriction, for if animosities go too far, they are very dangerous to cities, and of most pernicious consequence.

When Agesilaus was newly entered upon the government, there came news from Asia, that the Persian king was making great naval preparations, resolving with a high hand to dispossess the Spartans of their maritime supremacy. Lysander was eager for the opportunity of going over and succoring his friends in Asia, whom he had there left governors and masters of the cities, whose mal-administration and tyrannical behavior was causing them to be driven out, and in some cases put to death. He therefore persuaded Agesilaus to claim the command of the expedition, and by carrying the war far from Greece into Persia, to anticipate the designs of the barbarian. He also wrote to his friends in Asia, that by embassy they should demand Agesilaus for their captain. Agesilaus, therefore, coming into the public assembly, offered his service, upon condition that he might have thirty Spartans for captains and counselors, two thousand chosen men of the newly enfranchised helots, and allies to the number of six thousand. Lysander's authority and assistance soon obtained his request, so that he was sent away with the thirty Spartans, of whom Lysander was at once the chief, not only because of his power and reputation, but also on account of his friendship with Agesilaus, who esteemed his procuring him this charge a greater obligation, than that of preferring him to the kingdom.

Whilst the army was collecting to the rendezvous at Geraestus, Agesilaus went with some of his friends to Aulis, where in a dream he saw a man approach him, and speak to him after this manner: "O king of the Lacedaemonians, you cannot but know that, before yourself, there hath been but one general captain of the whole of the Greeks, namely, Agamemnon; now, since you succeed him in the same office and command of the same men, since you war against the same enemies, and begin your expedition from the same place, you ought also to offer such a sacrifice, as he offered before he weighed anchor." Agesilaus at the same moment remembered that the sacrifice which Agamemnon offered was his own daughter, he being so directed by the oracle. Yet was he not at all disturbed at it, but as soon as he arose, he told his dream to his friends, adding, that he would propitiate the goddess with the sacrifices a goddess must delight in, and would not follow the ignorant example of his predecessor. He therefore ordered a hind to be crowned with chaplets, and bade his own soothsayer perform the rite, not the usual person whom the Boeotians, in ordinary course, appointed to that office. When the Boeotian magistrates understood it, they were much offended, and sent officers to Agesilaus, to forbid his sacrificing contrary to the laws of the country. These having delivered their message to him, immediately went to the altar, and threw down the quarters of the hind that lay upon it. Agesilaus took this very ill, and without further sacrifice immediately sailed away, highly displeased with the Boeotians, and much discouraged in his mind at the omen, boding to himself an unsuccessful voyage, and an imperfect issue of the whole expedition.

When he came to Ephesus, he found the power and interest of Lysander, and the honors paid to him, insufferably great; all applications were made to him, crowds of suitors attended at his door, and followed upon his steps, as if nothing but the mere name of commander belonged, to satisfy the usage, to Agesilaus, the whole power of it being devolved upon Lysander. None of all the commanders that had been sent into Asia was either so powerful or so formidable as he; no one had rewarded his friends better, or had been more severe against his enemies; which things having been lately done, made the greater impression on men's minds, especially when they compared the simple and popular behavior of Agesilaus, with the harsh and violent and brief-spoken demeanor which Lysander still retained. Universal deference was yielded to this, and little regard shown to Agesilaus. This first occasioned offense to the other Spartan captains, who resented that they should rather seem the attendants of Lysander, than the councilors of Agesilaus. And at length Agesilaus himself, though not perhaps all envious man in his nature, nor apt to be troubled at the honors redounding upon other men, yet eager for honor and jealous of his glory, began to apprehend that Lysander's greatness would carry away from him the reputation of whatever great action should happen. He therefore went this way to work. He first opposed him in all his counsels; whatever Lysander specially advised was rejected, and other proposals followed. Then whoever made any address to him, if he found him attached to Lysander, certainly lost his suit. So also in judicial cases, anyone whom he spoke strongly against was sure to come off with success, and any man whom he was particularly solicitous to procure some benefit for, might think it well if he got away without an actual loss. These things being clearly not done by chance, but constantly and of a set purpose, Lysander was soon sensible of them, and hesitated not to tell his friends, that they suffered for his sake, bidding them apply themselves to the king, and such as were more powerful with him than he was. Such sayings of his seeming to be designed purposely to excite ill feeling, Agesilaus went on to offer him a yet more open affront, appointing him his meat-carver; and would in public companies scornfully say, "Let them go now and pay their court to my carver." Lysander, no longer able to brook these indignities, complained at last to Agesilaus himself, telling him, that he knew very well how to humble his friends. Agesilaus answered, "I know certainly how to humble those who pretend to more power than myself." "That," replied Lysander, "is perhaps rather said by you, than done by me; I desire only, that you will assign me some office and place, in which I may serve you without incurring your displeasure."

Upon this Agesilaus sent him to the Hellespont, whence he procured Spithridates, a Persian of the province of Pharnabazus, to come to the assistance of the Greeks with two hundred horse, and a great supply of money. Yet his anger did not so come down, but he thenceforward pursued the design of wresting the kingdom out of the hands of the two families which then enjoyed it, and making it wholly elective; and it is thought that he would on account of this quarrel have excited a great commotion in Sparta, if he had not died in the Boeotian war. Thus ambitious spirits in a commonwealth, when they transgress their bounds, are apt to do more harm than good. For though Lysander's pride and assumption was most ill-timed and insufferable in its display, yet Agesilaus surely could have found some other way of setting him right, less offensive to a man of his reputation and ambitious temper. Indeed they were both blinded with the same passion, so as one not to recognize the authority of his superior, the other not to bear with the imperfections of his friend.

Tisaphernes being at first afraid of Agesilaus, treated with him about setting the Grecian cities at liberty, which was agreed on. But soon after finding a sufficient force drawn together, he resolved upon war, for which Agesilaus was not sorry. For the expectation of this expedition was great, and he did not think it for his honor, that Xenophon with ten thousand men should march through the heart of Asia to the sea, beating the Persian forces when and how he pleased, and that he at the head of the Spartans, then sovereigns both at sea and land, should not achieve some memorable action for Greece. And so to be even with Tisaphernes, he requites his perjury by a fair stratagem. He pretends to march into Caria, whither when he had drawn Tisaphernes and his army, he suddenly turns back, and falls upon Phrygia, takes many of their cities, and carries away great booty, showing his allies, that to break a solemn league was a downright contempt of the gods, but the circumvention of an enemy in war was not only just but glorious, a gratification at once and an advantage.

Being weak in horse, and discouraged by ill omens in the sacrifices, he retired to Ephesus, and there raised cavalry. He obliged the rich men, that were not inclined to serve in person, to find each of them a horseman armed and mounted; and there being many who preferred doing this, the army was quickly reinforced by a body, not of unwilling recruits for the infantry, but of brave and numerous horsemen. For those that were not good at fighting themselves, hired such as were more military in their inclinations, and such as loved not horse-service substituted in their places such as did. Agamemnon's example had been a good one, when he took the present of an excellent mare, to dismiss a rich coward from the army.

When by Agesilaus's order the prisoners he had taken in Phrygia were exposed to sale, they were first stripped of their garments, and then sold naked. The clothes found many customers to buy them, but the bodies being, from the want of all exposure and exercise, white and tender-skinned, were derided and scorned as unserviceable. Agesilaus, who stood by at the auction, told his Greeks, "These are the men against whom ye fight, and these the things you will gain by it."

The season of the year being come, he boldly gave out that he would invade Lydia; and this plaindealing of his was now mistaken for a stratagem by Tisaphernes, who, by not believing Agesilaus, having been already deceived by him, overreached himself. He expected that he should have made choice of Caria, as a rough country, not fit for horse, in which he deemed Agesilaus to be weak, and directed his own marches accordingly. But when he found him to be as good as his word, and to have entered into the country of Sardis, he made great haste after him, and by great marches of his horse, overtaking the loose stragglers who were pillaging the country, he cut them off. Agesilaus meanwhile, considering that the horse had outridden the foot, but that he himself had the whole body of his own army entire, made haste to engage them. He mingled his light-armed foot, carrying targets, with the horse, commanding them to advance at full speed and begin the battle, whilst he brought up the heavier-armed men in the rear. The success was answerable to the design; the barbarians were put to the rout, the Grecians pursued hard, took their camp, and put many of them to the sword. The consequence of this victory was very great; for they had not only the liberty of foraging the Persian country, and plundering at pleasure, but also saw Tisaphernes pay dearly for all the cruelty he had showed the Greeks, to whom he was a professed enemy. For the king of Persia sent Tithraustes, who took off his head, and presently dealt with Agesilaus about his return into Greece, sending to him ambassadors to that purpose, with commission to offer him great sums of money. Agesilaus's answer was, that the making of peace belonged to the Lacedaemonians, not to him; as for wealth, he had rather see it in his soldiers' hands than his own; that the Grecians thought it not honorable to enrich themselves with the bribes of their enemies, but with their spoils only. Yet, that he might gratify Tithraustes for the justice he had done upon Tisaphernes, the common enemy of the Greeks, he removed his quarters into Phrygia, accepting thirty talents for his expenses. Whilst he was upon his march, he received a staff from the government at Sparta, appointing him admiral as well as general. This was an honor which was never done to any but Agesilaus, who being now undoubtedly the greatest and most illustrious man of his time, still, as Theopompus has said, gave himself more occasion of glory in his own virtue and merit than was given him in this authority and power. Yet he committed a fault in preferring Pisander to the command of the navy, when there were others at hand both older and more experienced; in this not so much consulting the public good, as the gratification of his kindred, and especially his wife, whose brother Pisander was.

Having removed his camp into Pharnabazus's province, he not only met with great plenty of provisions, but also raised great sums of money, and marching on to the bounds of Paphlagonia, he soon drew Cotys, the king of it, into a league, to which he of his own accord inclined, out of the opinion he had of Agesilaus's honor and virtue. Spithridates, from the time of his abandoning Pharnabazus, constantly attended Agesilaus in the camp whithersoever he went. This Spithridates had a son, a very handsome boy, called Megabates, of whom Agesilaus was extremely fond, and also a very beautiful daughter, that was marriageable. Her Agesilaus matched to Cotys, and taking of him a thousand horse, with two thousand light-armed foot, he returned into Phrygia, and there pillaged the country of Pharnabazus, who durst not meet him in the field, nor yet trust to his garrisons, but getting his valuables together, got out of the way and moved about up and down with a flying army, till Spithridates joining with Herippidas the Spartan, took his camp, and all his property. Herippidas being too severe an inquirer into the plunder with which the barbarian soldiers had enriched themselves, and forcing them to deliver it up with too much strictness, so disobliged Spithridates with his questioning and examining, that he changed sides again, and went off with the Paphlagonians to Sardis. This was a very great vexation to Agesilaus, not only that he had lost the friendship of a valiant commander, and with him a considerable part of his army, but still more that it had been done with the disrepute of a sordid and petty covetousness, of which he always had made it a point of honor to keep both himself and his country clear. Besides these public causes, he had a private one, his excessive fondness for the son, which touched him to the quick, though he endeavored to master it, and, especially in presence of the boy, to suppress all appearance of it; so much so that when Megabates, for that was his name, came once to receive a kiss from him, he declined it. At which when the young boy blushed and drew back, and afterward saluted him at a more reserved distance, Agesilaus soon repenting his coldness, and changing his mind, pretended to wonder why he did not salute him with the same familiarity as formerly. His friends about him answered, "You are in the fault, who would not accept the kiss of the boy, but turned away in alarm; he would come to you again, if you would have the courage to let him do so." Upon this Agesilaus paused a while, and at length answered, "You need not encourage him to it; I think I had rather be master of myself in that refusal, than see all things that are now before my eyes turned into gold." Thus he demeaned himself to Megabates when present, but he had so great a passion for him in his absence, that it may be questioned whether if the boy had returned again, all the courage he had would have sustained him in such another refusal.

After this, Pharnabazus sought an opportunity of conferring with Agesilaus, which Apollophanes of Cyzicus, the common host of them both, procured for him. Agesilaus coming first to the appointed place, threw himself down upon the grass under a tree, lying there in expectation of Pharnabazus, who, bringing with him soft skins and wrought carpets to lie down upon, when he saw Agesilaus's posture, grew ashamed of his luxuries and made no use of them, but laid himself down upon the grass also, without regard for his delicate and richly dyed clothing. Pharnabazus had matter enough of complaint against Agesilaus, and therefore, after the mutual civilities were over, he put him in mind of the great services he had done the Lacedaemonians in the Attic war, of which he thought it an ill recompense to have his country thus harassed and spoiled, by those men who owed so much to him. The Spartans that were present hung down their heads, as conscious of the wrong they had done to their ally. But Agesilaus said, "We, O Pharnabazus, when we were in amity with your master the king, behaved ourselves like friends, and now that we are at war with him, we behave ourselves as enemies. As for you, we must look upon you as a part of his property, and must do these outrages upon you, not intending the harm to you, but to him whom we wound through you. But whenever you will choose rather to be a friend to the Grecians, than a slave of the king of Persia, you may then reckon this army and navy to be all at your command, to defend both you, your country, and your liberties, without which there is nothing honorable, or indeed desirable among men." Upon this Pharnabazus discovered his mind, and answered, "If the king sends another governor in my room, I will certainly come over to you, but as long as he trusts me with the government, I shall be just to him, and not fail to do my utmost endeavors in opposing you." Agesilaus was taken with the answer, and shook hands with him; and rising, said, "How much rather had I have so brave a man my friend than mine enemy."

Pharnabazus being gone off, his son, staying behind, ran up to Agesilaus, and smilingly said, "Agesilaus, I make you my guest;" and thereupon presented him with a javelin which he had in his hand. Agesilaus received it, and being much taken with the good mien and the courtesy of the youth, looked about to see if there were anything in his train fit to offer him in return; and observing the horse of Idaeus, the secretary, to have very fine trappings on, he took them off, and bestowed them upon the young gentleman. Nor did his kindness rest there, but he continued ever after to be mindful of him, so that when he was driven out of his country by his brothers, and lived an exile in Peloponnesus, he took great care of him, and condescended even to assist him in some love-matters. He had an attachment for a youth of Athenian birth, who was bred up as an athlete; and when at the Olympic games this boy, on account of his great size and general strong and full-grown appearance, was in some danger of not being admitted into the list, the Persian betook himself to Agesilaus, and made use of his friendship. Agesilaus readily assisted him, and not without a great deal of difficulty effected his desires. He was in all other things a man of great and exact justice, but when the case concerned a friend, to be straitlaced in point of justice, he said, was only a colorable presence of denying him. There is an epistle written to Idrieus, prince of Caria, that is ascribed to Agesilaus; it is this: "If Nicias be innocent, absolve him; if he be guilty, absolve him upon my account; however be sure to absolve him." This was his usual character in his deportment towards his friends. Yet his rule was not without exception; for sometimes he considered the necessity of his affairs more than his friend, of which he once gave an example, when upon a sudden and disorderly removal of his camp, he left a sick friend behind him, and when he called loudly after him, and implored his help, turned his back, and said it was hard to be compassionate and wise too. This story is related by Hieronymus, the philosopher.

Another year of the war being spent, Agesilaus's fame still increased, insomuch that the Persian king received daily information concerning his many virtues, and the great esteem the world had of his temperance, his plain living, and his moderation. When he made any journey, he would usually take up his lodging in a temple, and there make the gods witnesses of his most private actions, which others would scarce permit men to be acquainted with. In so great an army, you should scarce find common soldier lie on a coarser mattress, than Agesilaus; he was so indifferent to the varieties of heat and cold, that all the seasons, as the gods sent them, seemed natural to him. The Greeks that inhabited Asia were much pleased to see the great lords and governors of Persia, with all the pride, cruelty, and luxury in which they lived, trembling and bowing before a man in a poor threadbare cloak, and at one laconic word out of his mouth, obsequiously deferring and changing their wishes and purposes. So that it brought to the minds of many the verses of Timotheus,

> *Mars is the tyrant, gold Greece does not fear.*

Many parts of Asia now revolting from the Persians, Agesilaus restored order in the cities, and without bloodshed or banishment of any of their members, reestablished the proper constitution in the governments, and now resolved to carry away the war from the seaside, and to march further up into the country, and to attack the king of Persia himself in his own home in Susa and Ecbatana; not willing to let the monarch sit idle in his chair, playing umpire in the conflicts of the Greeks, and bribing their popular leaders. But these great thoughts were interrupted by unhappy news from Sparta; Epicydidas is from thence sent to remand him home, to assist his own country, which was then involved in a great war;

> *Greece to herself doth a barbarian grow,*
> *Others could not, she doth herself o'erthrow.*

What better can we say of those jealousies, and that league and conspiracy of the Greeks for their own mischief, which arrested fortune in full career, and turned back arms that were already uplifted against the barbarians, to be used upon themselves, and recalled into Greece the war which had been banished out of her? I by no means assent to Demaratus of Corinth, who said, that those Greeks lost a great satisfaction, that did not live to see Alexander sit in the throne of Darius. That sight should rather have drawn tears from them, when they considered, that they had left that glory to Alexander and the Macedonians, whilst they spent all their own great commanders in playing them against each other in the fields of Leuctra, Coronea, Corinth, and Arcadia.

Nothing was greater or nobler than the behavior of Agesilaus on this occasion, nor can a nobler instance be found in story, of a ready obedience and just deference to orders. Hannibal, though in a bad condition himself, and almost driven out of Italy, could scarcely be induced to obey, when he was called home to serve his country. Alexander made a jest of the battle between Agis and Antipater, laughing and saying, "So, whilst we were conquering Darius in Asia, it seems there was a battle of mice in Arcadia." Happy Sparta, meanwhile, in the justice and modesty of Agesilaus, and in the deference he paid to the laws of his country; who, immediately upon receipt of his orders, though in the midst of his high fortune and power, and in full hope of great and glorious success, gave all up and instantly departed, "his object unachieved," leaving many regrets behind him among his allies in Asia, and proving by his example the falseness of that saying of Demostratus, the son of Phaeax, "That the Lacedaemonians were better in public, but the Athenians in private." For while approving himself an excellent king and general, he likewise showed himself in private an excellent friend, and a most agreeable companion.

The coin of Persia was stamped with the figure of an archer; Agesilaus said, That a thousand Persian archers had driven him out of Asia; meaning the money that had been laid out in bribing the demagogues and the orators in Thebes and Athens, and thus inciting those two States to hostility against Sparta.

Having passed the Hellespont, he marched by land through Thrace, not begging or entreating a passage anywhere, only he sent his messengers to them, to demand whether they would have him pass as a friend or as an enemy. All the rest received him as a friend, and assisted him on his journey. But the Trallians, to whom Xerxes also is said to have given money, demanded a price of him, namely, one hundred talents of silver, and one hundred women. Agesilaus in scorn asked, Why they were not ready to receive them? He marched on, and finding the Trallians in arms to oppose him, fought them, and slew great numbers of them. He sent the like embassy to the king of Macedonia, who replied, He would take time to deliberate: "Let him deliberate," said Agesilaus, "we will go forward in the meantime." The Macedonian, being surprised and daunted at the resolution of the Spartan, gave orders to let him pass as friend. When he came into Thessaly, he wasted the country, because they were in league with the enemy. To Larissa, the chief city of Thessaly, he sent Xenocles and Scythes to treat of a peace, whom when the Larissaeans had laid hold of, and put into custody, others were enraged, and advised the siege of the town; but he answered, That he valued either of those men at more than the whole country of Thessaly. He therefore made terms with them, and received his men again upon composition. Nor need we wonder at this saying of Agesilaus, since when he had news brought him from Sparta, of several great captains slain in a battle near Corinth, in which the slaughter fell upon other Greeks, and the Lacedaemonians obtained a great victory with small loss, he did not appear at all satisfied; but with a great sigh cried out, "O Greece, how many brave men hast thou destroyed; who, if they had been preserved to so good an use, had sufficed to have conquered all Persia!" Yet when the Pharsalians grew troublesome to him, by pressing upon his army, and incommoding his passage, he led out five hundred horse, and in person fought and routed them, setting up a trophy under the mount Narthacius. He valued himself very much upon that victory, that with so small a number of his own training, he had vanquished a body of men that thought themselves the best horsemen of Greece.

Here Diphridas, the Ephor, met him, and delivered his message from Sparta, which ordered him immediately to make an inroad into Boeotia; and though he thought this fitter to have been done at another time, and with greater force, he yet obeyed the magistrates. He thereupon told his soldiers that the day was come, on which they were to enter upon that employment, for the performance of which they were brought out of Asia. He sent for two divisions of the army near Corinth to his assistance. The Lacedaemonians at home, in honor to him, made proclamation for volunteers that would serve under the king, to come in and be enlisted. Finding all the young men in the city ready to offer themselves, they chose fifty of the strongest, and sent them.

Agesilaus having gained Thermopylae, and passed quietly through Phocis, as soon as he had entered Boeotia, and pitched his camp near Chaeronea, at once met with an eclipse of the sun, and with ill news from the navy, Pisander, the Spartan admiral, being beaten and slain at Cnidos, by Pharnabazus and Conon. He was much moved at it, both upon his own and the public account. Yet lest his army, being now near engaging, should meet with any discouragement, he ordered the messengers to give out, that the Spartans were the conquerors, and he himself putting on a garland, solemnly sacrificed for the good news, and sent portions of the sacrifices to his friends.

When he came near to Coronea, and was within view of the enemy, he drew up his army, and giving the left wing to the Orchomenians, he himself led the right. The Thebans took the right wing of their army, leaving the left to the Argives. Xenophon, who was present, and fought on Agesilaus's side, reports it to be the hardest fought battle that he had seen. The beginning of it was not so, for the Thebans soon put the Orchomenians to rout, as also did Agesilaus the Argives. But both parties having news of the misfortune of their left wings, they betook themselves to their relief. Here Agesilaus might have been sure of his victory, had he contented himself not to charge them in the front, but in the flank or rear; but being angry and heated in the fight, he would not wait the opportunity, but fell on at once, thinking to bear them down before him. The Thebans were not behind him in courage, so that the battle was fiercely carried on on both sides, especially near Agesilaus's person, whose new guard of fifty volunteers stood him in great stead that day, and saved his life. They fought with great valor, and interposed their bodies frequently between him and danger, yet could they not so preserve him, but that he received many wounds through his armor with lances and swords, and was with much difficulty gotten off alive by their making a ring about him, and so guarding him, with the slaughter of many of the enemy and the loss of many of their own number. At length finding it too hard a task to break the front of the Theban troops, they opened their own files, and let the enemy march through them, (an artifice which in the beginning they scorned,) watching in the meantime the posture of the enemy, who having passed through, grew careless, as esteeming themselves past danger; in which position they were immediately set upon by the Spartans. Yet were they not then put to rout, but marched on to Helicon, proud of what they had done, being able to say, that they themselves, as to their part of the army, were not worsted.

Agesilaus, sore wounded as he was, would not be borne to his tent, till he had been first carried about the field, and had seen the dead conveyed within his encampment. As many of his enemies as had taken sanctuary in the temple, he dismissed. For there stood near the battlefield, the temple of Minerva the Itonian, and before it a trophy erected by the Boeotians, for the victory which under the conduct of Sparton, their general, they obtained over the Athenians under Tolmides, who himself fell in the battle. And next morning early, to make trial of the Theban courage, whether they had any mind to a second encounter, he commanded his soldiers to put on garlands on their heads, and play with their flutes, and raise a trophy before their faces; but when they, instead of fighting, sent for leave to bury their dead, he gave it them; and having so assured himself of the victory, after this he went to Delphi, to the Pythian games, which were then celebrating, at which feast he assisted, and there solemnly offered the tenth part of the spoils he had brought from Asia, which amounted to a hundred talents.

Thence he returned to his own country, where his way and habits of life quickly excited the affection and admiration of the Spartans; for, unlike other generals, he came home from foreign lands the same man that he went out, having not so learned the fashions of other countries, as to forget his own, much less to dislike or despise them. He followed and respected all the Spartan customs, without any change either in the manner of his supping, or bathing, or his wife's apparel, as if he had never traveled over the river Eurotas. So also with his household furniture and his own armor; nay, the very gates of his house were so old, that they might well be thought of Aristodemus's setting up. His daughter's Canathrum, says Xenophon, was no richer than that of any one else. The Canathrum, as they call it, is a chair or chariot made of wood, in the shape of a griffin, or tragelaphus, on which the children and young virgins are carried in processions. Xenophon has not left us the name of this daughter of Agesilaus; and Dicaearchus expresses some indignation, because we do not know, he says, the name of Agesilaus's daughter, nor of Epaminondas's mother. But in the records of Laconia, we ourselves found his wife's name to have been Cleora, and his two daughters to have been called Eupolia and Prolyta. And you may also to this day see Agesilaus's spear kept in Sparta, nothing differing from that of other men.

There was a vanity he observed among the Spartans, about keeping running horses for the Olympic games, upon which he found they much valued themselves. Agesilaus regarded it as a display not of any real virtue, but of wealth and expense; and to make this evident to the Greeks, induced his sister, Cynisca, to send a chariot into the course. He kept with him Xenophon, the philosopher, and made much of him, and proposed to him to send for his children, and educate them at Sparta, where they would be taught the best of all learning; how to obey, and how to command. Finding on Lysander's death a large faction formed, which he on his return from Asia had established against Agesilaus, he thought it advisable to expose both him and it, by showing what manner of a citizen he had been whilst he lived. To that end, finding among his writings all oration, composed by Cleon the Halicarnassean, but to have been spoken by Lysander in a public assembly, to excite the people to innovations and changes in the government, he resolved to publish it, as an evidence of Lysander's practices. But one of the Elders having the perusal of it, and finding it powerfully written, advised him to have a care of digging up Lysander again, and rather bury that oration in the grave with him; and this advice he wisely hearkened to, and hushed the whole thing up; and ever after forbore publicly to affront any of his adversaries, but took occasions of picking out the ringleaders, and sending them away upon foreign services. He thus had means for exposing the avarice and the injustice of many of them in their employments; and again when they were by others brought into question, he made it his business to bring them off, obliging them, by that means, of enemies to become his friends, and so by degrees left none remaining.

Agesipolis, his fellow king, was under the disadvantage of being born of an exiled father, and himself young, modest, and inactive, meddled not much in affairs. Agesilaus took a course of gaining him over, and making him entirely tractable. According to the custom of Sparta, the kings, if they were in town, always dined together. This was Agesilaus's opportunity of dealing with Agesipolis, whom he found quick, as he himself was, in forming attachments for young men, and accordingly talked with him always on such subjects, joining and aiding him, and acting as his confidant, such attachments in Sparta being entirely honorable, and attended always with lively feeling of modesty, love of virtue, and a noble emulation; of which more is said in Lycurgus's life.

Having thus established his power in the city, he easily obtained that his half-brother Teleutias might be chosen admiral, and thereupon making all expedition against the Corinthians, he made himself master of the long walls by land, through the assistance of his brother at sea. Coming thus upon the Argives, who then held Corinth, in the midst of their Isthmian festival, he made them fly from the sacrifice they had just commenced, and leave all their festive provision behind them. The exiled Corinthians that were in the Spartan army, desired him to keep the feast, and to preside in the celebration of it. This he refused, but gave them leave to carry on the solemnity if they pleased, and he in the meantime stayed and guarded them. When Agesilaus marched off, the Argives returned and celebrated the games over again, when some who were victors before, became victors a second time, others lost the prizes which before they had gained. Agesilaus thus made it clear to everybody, that the Argives must in their own eyes have been guilty of great cowardice, since they set such a value on presiding at the games, and yet had not dared to fight for it. He himself was of opinion, that to keep a mean in such things was best; he assisted at the sports and dances usual in his own country, and was always ready and eager to be present at the exercises either of the young men, or of the girls, but things that many men used to be highly taken with, he seemed not at all concerned about. Callippides, the tragic actor, who had a great name in all Greece and was made much of, once met and saluted him; of which when he found no notice taken, he confidently thrust himself into his train, expecting that Agesilaus would pay him some attention. When all that failed, he boldly accosted him, and asked him, whether he did not remember him? Agesilaus turned, and looking him in the face, "Are you not," said he, "Callippides the showman?" Being invited once to hear a man who admirably imitated the nightingale, he declined, saying, he had heard the nightingale itself. Menecrates, the physician, having had great success in some desperate diseases, was by way of flattery called Jupiter; he was so vain as to take the name, and having occasion to write a letter to Agesilaus, thus addressed it:

"Jupiter Menecrates to King Agesilaus, greeting."

The king returned answer:

"Agesilaus to Menecrates, health and a sound mind."

Whilst Agesilaus was in the Corinthian territories, having just taken the Heraeum, he was looking on while his soldiers were carrying away the prisoners and the plunder, when ambassadors from Thebes came to him to treat of peace. Having a great aversion for that city, and thinking it then advantageous to his affairs publicly to slight them, he took the opportunity, and would not seem either to see them, or hear them speak. But as if on purpose to punish him in his pride, before they parted from him, messengers came with news of the complete slaughter of one of the Spartan divisions by Iphicrates, a greater disaster than had befallen them for many years; and that the more grievous, because it was a choice regiment of full-armed Lacedaemonians overthrown by a parcel of mere mercenary targeteers. Agesilaus leapt from his seat, to go at once to their rescue, but found it too late, the business being over. He therefore returned to the Heraeum, and sent for the Theban ambassadors to give them audience. They now resolved to be even with him for the affront he gave them, and without speaking one word of the peace, only desired leave to go into Corinth. Agesilaus, irritated with this proposal, told them in scorn, that if they were anxious to go and see how proud their friends were of their success, they should do it tomorrow with safety. Next morning, taking the ambassadors with him, he ravaged the Corinthian territories, up to the very gates of the city, where having made a stand, and let the ambassadors see that the Corinthians durst not come out to defend themselves, he dismissed them. Then gathering up the small remainders of the shattered regiment, he marched homewards, always removing his camp before day, and always pitching his tents after night, that he might prevent their enemies among the Arcadians from taking any opportunity of insulting over their loss.

After this, at the request of the Achaeans, he marched with them into Acarnania, and there collected great spoils, and defeated the Acarnanians in battle. The Achaeans would have persuaded him to keep his winter quarters there, to hinder the Acarnanians from sowing their corn; but he was of the contrary opinion, alleging, that they would be more afraid of a war next summer, when their fields were sown, than they would be if they lay fallow. The event justified his opinion; for next summer, when the Achaeans began their expedition again, the Acarnanians immediately made peace with them.

When Conon and Pharnabazus with the Persian navy were grown masters of the sea, and had not only infested the coast of Laconia, but also rebuilt the walls of Athens at the cost of Pharnabazus, the Lacedaemonians thought fit to treat of peace with the king of Persia. To that end, they sent Antalcidas to Tiribazus, basely and wickedly betraying the Asiatic Greeks, on whose behalf Agesilaus had made the war. But no part of this dishonor fell upon Agesilaus, the whole being transacted by Antalcidas, who was his bitter enemy, and was urgent for peace upon any terms, because war was sure to increase his power and reputation. Nevertheless once being told by way of reproach, that the Lacedaemonians had gone over to the Medes, he replied, "No, the Medes have come over to the Lacedaemonians." And when the Greeks were backward to submit to the agreement, he threatened them with war, unless they fulfilled the king of Persia's conditions, his particular end in this being to weaken the Thebans; for it was made one of the articles of peace, that the country of Boeotia should be left independent. This feeling of his to Thebes appeared further afterwards, when Phoebidas, in full peace, most unjustifiably seized upon the Cadmea. The thing was much resented by all Greece, and not well liked by the Lacedaemonians themselves; those especially who were enemies to Agesilaus, required an account of the action, and by whose authority it was done, laying the suspicion of it at his door. Agesilaus resolutely answered, on the behalf of Phoebidas, that the profitableness of the act was chiefly to be considered; if it were for the advantage of the commonwealth, it was no matter whether it were done with or without authority. This was the more remarkable in him, because in his ordinary language, he was always observed to be a great maintainer of justice, and would commend it as the chief of virtues, saying, that valor without justice was useless, and if all the world were just, there would be no need of valor. When any would say to him, the Great King will have it so; he would reply, "How is he greater than I, unless he be juster?" nobly and rightly taking, as a sort of royal measure of greatness, justice, and not force. And thus when, on the conclusion of the peace, the king of Persia wrote to Agesilaus, desiring a private friendship and relations of hospitality, he refused it, saying, that the public friendship was enough; whilst that lasted there was no need of private. Yet in his acts he was not constant to his doctrine, but sometimes out of ambition, and sometimes out of private pique, he let himself be carried away; and particularly in this case of the Thebans, he not only saved Phoebidas, but persuaded the Lacedaemonians to take the fault upon themselves, and to retain the Cadmea, putting a garrison into it, and to put the government of Thebes into the hands of Archias and Leontidas, who had been betrayers of the castle to them.

This excited strong suspicion that what Phoebidas did was by Agesilaus's order, which was corroborated by after occurrences. For when the Thebans had expelled the garrison, and asserted their liberty, he, accusing them of the murder of Archias and Leontidas, who indeed were tyrants, though in name holding the office of Polemarchs, made war upon them. He sent Cleombrotus on that errand, who was now his fellow king, in the place of Agesipolis, who was dead, excusing himself by reason of his age; for it was forty years since he had first borne arms, and he was consequently exempt by the law; meanwhile the true reason was, that he was ashamed, having so lately fought against tyranny in behalf of the Phliasians, to fight now in defense of a tyranny against the Thebans.

One Sphodrias, of Lacedaemon, of the contrary faction to Agesilaus, was governor in Thespiae, a bold and enterprising man, though he had perhaps more of confidence than wisdom. This action of Phoebidas fired him, and incited his ambition to attempt some great enterprise, which might render him as famous as he perceived the taking of the Cadmea had made Phoebidas. He thought the sudden capture of the Piraeus, and the cutting off thereby the Athenians from the sea, would be a matter of far more glory. It is said, too, that Pelopidas and Melon, the chief captains of Boeotia, put him upon it; that they privily sent men to him, pretending to be of the Spartan faction, who, highly commending Sphodrias, filled him with a great opinion of himself, protesting him to be the only man in the world that was fit for so great an enterprise. Being thus stimulated, he could hold no longer, but hurried into an attempt as dishonorable and treacherous as that of the Cadmea, but executed with less valor and less success; for the day broke whilst he was yet in the Thriasian plain, whereas he designed the whole exploit to have been done in the night. As soon as the soldiers perceived the rays of light reflecting from the temples of Eleusis, upon the first rising of the sun, it is said that their hearts failed them; nay, he himself, when he saw that he could not have the benefit of the night, had not courage enough to go on with his enterprise; but, having pillaged the country, he returned with shame to Thespiae. An embassy was upon this sent from Athens to Sparta, to complain of the breach of peace; but the ambassadors found their journey needless, Sphodrias being then under process by the magistrates of Sparta. Sphodrias durst not stay to expect judgment, which he found would be capital, the city being highly incensed against him, out of the shame they felt at the business, and their desire to appear in the eyes of the Athenians as fellow-sufferers; in the wrong, rather than accomplices in its being done.

This Sphodrias had a son of great beauty named Cleonymus, to whom Archidamus, the son of Agesilaus, was extremely attached. Archidamus, as became him, was concerned for the danger of his friend's father, but yet he durst not do anything openly for his assistance, he being one of the professed enemies of Agesilaus. But Cleonymus having solicited him with tears about it, as knowing Agesilaus to be of all his father's enemies the most formidable, the young man for two or three days followed after his father with such fear and confusion, that he durst not speak to him. At last, the day of sentence being at hand, he ventured to tell him, that Cleonymus had entreated him to intercede for his father Agesilaus, though well aware of the love between the two young men, yet did not prohibit it, because Cleonymus from his earliest years had been looked upon as a youth of very great promise; yet he gave not his son any kind or hopeful answer in the case, but coldly told him, that he would consider what he could honestly and honorably do in it, and so dismissed him. Archidamus, being ashamed of his want of success, forbore the company of Cleonymus, whom he usually saw several times every day. This made the friends of Sphodrias to think his case desperate, till Etymocles, one of Agesilaus's friends, discovered to them the king's mind, namely, that he abhorred the fact, but yet he thought Sphodrias a gallant man, such as the commonwealth much wanted at that time. For Agesilaus used to talk thus concerning the cause, out of a desire to gratify his son. And now Cleonymus quickly understood, that Archidamus had been true to him, in using all his interest with his father; and Sphodrias's friends ventured to be forward in his defense. The truth is, that Agesilaus was excessively fond of his children; and it is to him the story belongs, that when they were little ones, he used to make a horse of a stick, and ride with them; and being caught at this sport by a friend, he desired him not to mention it, till he himself were the father of children.

Meanwhile, Sphodrias being acquitted, the Athenians betook themselves to arms, and Agesilaus fell into disgrace with the people; since to gratify the whims of a boy, he had been willing to pervert justice, and make the city accessory to the crimes of private men, whose most unjustifiable actions had broken the peace of Greece. He also found his colleague, Cleombrotus, little inclined to the Theban war; so that it became necessary for him to waive the privilege of his age, which he before had claimed, and to lead the army himself into Boeotia; which he did with variety of success, sometimes conquering, and sometimes conquered; insomuch that receiving a wound in a battle, he was reproached by Antalcidas, that the Thebans had paid him well for the lessons he had given them in fighting. And, indeed, they were now grown far better soldiers than ever they had been, being so continually kept in training, by the frequency of the Lacedaemonian expeditions against them. Out of the foresight of which it was, that anciently Lycurgus, in three several laws, forbade them to make many wars with the same nation, as this would be to instruct their enemies in the art of it. Meanwhile, the allies of Sparta were not a little discontented at Agesilaus, because this war was commenced not upon any fair public ground of quarrel, but merely out of his private hatred to the Thebans; and they complained with indignation, that they, being the majority of the army, should from year to year be thus exposed to danger and hardship here and there, at the will of a few persons. It was at this time, we are told, that Agesilaus, to obviate the objection, devised this expedient, to show the allies were not the greater number. He gave orders that all the allies, of whatever country, should sit down promiscuously on one side, and all the Lacedaemonians on the other: which being done, he commanded a herald to proclaim, that all the potters of both divisions should stand out; then all the blacksmiths; then all the masons; next the carpenters; and so he went through all the handicrafts. By this time almost all the allies were risen, but of the Lacedaemonians not a man, they being by law forbidden to learn any mechanical business; and now Agesilaus laughed and said, "You see, my friends, how many more soldiers we send out than you do."

When he brought back his army from Boeotia through Megara, as he was going up to the magistrate's office in the Acropolis, he was suddenly seized with pain and cramp in his sound leg, and great swelling and inflammation ensued. He was treated by a Syracusan physician, who let him blood below the ankle; this soon eased his pain, but then the blood could not be stopped, till the loss of it brought on fainting and swooning; at length, with much trouble, he stopped it. Agesilaus was carried home to Sparta in a very weak condition, and did not recover strength enough to appear in the field for a long time after.

Meanwhile, the Spartan fortune was but ill; they received many losses both by sea and land; but the greatest was that at Tegyrae, when for the first time they were beaten by the Thebans in a set battle.

All the Greeks were, accordingly, disposed to a general peace, and to that end ambassadors came to Sparta. Among these was Epaminondas, the Theban, famous at that time for his philosophy and learning, but he had not yet given proof of his capacity as a general. He, seeing all the others crouch to

Agesilaus, and court favor with him, alone maintained the dignity of an ambassador, and with that freedom that became his character, made a speech in behalf not of Thebes only, from whence he came, but of all Greece, remonstrating, that Sparta alone grew great by war, to the distress and suffering of all her neighbors. He urged, that a peace should be made upon just and equal terms, such as alone would be a lasting one, which could not otherwise be done, than by reducing all to equality. Agesilaus, perceiving all the other Greeks to give much attention to this discourse, and to be pleased with it, presently asked him, whether he thought it a part of this justice and equality that the Boeotian towns should enjoy their independence. Epaminondas instantly and without wavering asked him in return, whether he thought it just and equal that the Laconian towns should enjoy theirs. Agesilaus started from his seat and bade him once for all speak out and say whether or not Boeotia should be independent. And when Epaminondas replied once again with the same inquiry, whether Laconia should be so, Agesilaus was so enraged that, availing himself of the pretext he immediately struck the name of the Thebans out of the league, and declared war against them. With the rest of the Greeks he made a peace, and dismissed them with this saying, that what could be peaceably adjusted, should; what was otherwise incurable, must be committed to the success of war, it being a thing of too great difficulty to provide for all things by treaty. The Ephors upon this dispatched their orders to Cleombrotus, who was at that time in Phocis, to march directly into Boeotia, and at the same time sent to their allies for aid. The confederates were very tardy in the business, and unwilling to engage, but as yet they feared the Spartans too much to dare to refuse. And although many portents, and prodigies of ill presage, which I have mentioned in the life of Epaminondas, had appeared; and though Prothous, the Laconian, did all he could to hinder it, yet Agesilaus would needs go forward, and prevailed so, that the war was decreed. He thought the present juncture of affairs very advantageous for their revenge, the rest of Greece being wholly free, and the Thebans excluded from the peace. But that this war was undertaken more upon passion than judgment, the event may prove; for the treaty was finished but the fourteenth of Scirophorion, and the Lacedaemonians received their great overthrow at Leuctra, on the fifth of Hecatombaeon, within twenty days. There fell at that time a thousand, Spartans, and Cleombrotus their king, and around him the bravest men of the nation; particularly, the beautiful youth, Cleonymus the son of Sphodrias, who was thrice struck down at the feet of the king, and as often rose, but was slain at the last.

    This unexpected blow, which fell so heavy upon the Lacedaemonians, brought greater glory to Thebes than ever was acquired by any other of the Grecian republics, in their civil wars against each other. The behavior, notwithstanding, of the Spartans, though beaten, was as great, and as highly to be admired, as that of the Thebans. And indeed, if, as Xenophon says, in conversation good men even in their sports and at their wine let fall many sayings that are worth the preserving; how much more worthy to be recorded, is an exemplary constancy of mind, as shown both in the words and in the acts of brave men, when they are pressed by adverse fortune! It happened that the Spartans were celebrating a solemn feast, at which many strangers were present from other countries, and the town full of them, when this news of the overthrow came. It was the gymnopaediae, and the boys were dancing in the theater, when the messengers arrived from Leuctra. The Ephors, though they were sufficiently aware that this blow had ruined the Spartan power, and that their primacy over the rest of Greece was gone for ever, yet gave orders that the dances should not break off, nor any of the celebration of the festival abate; but privately sending the names of the slain to each family, out of which they were lost, they continued the public spectacles. The next morning, when they had full intelligence concerning it, and everybody knew who were slain, and who survived, the fathers, relatives, and friends of the slain came out rejoicing in the market-place, saluting each other with a kind of exultation; on the contrary, the fathers of the survivors hid themselves at home among the women. If necessity drove any of them abroad, they went very dejectedly, with downcast looks, and sorrowful countenances. The women outdid the men in it; those whose sons were slain, openly rejoicing, cheerfully making visits to one another, and meeting triumphantly in the temples; they who expected their children home, being very silent, and much troubled.

But the people in general, when their allies now began to desert them, and Epaminondas, in all the confidence of victory, was expected with an invading army in Peloponnesus, began to think again of Agesilaus's lameness, and to entertain feelings of religious fear and despondency, as if their having rejected the sound-footed, and having chosen the halting king, which the oracle had specially warned them against, was the occasion of all their distresses. Yet the regard they had to the merit and reputation of Agesilaus, so far stilled this murmuring of the people, that notwithstanding it, they entrusted themselves to him in this distress, as the only man that was fit to heal the public malady, the arbiter of all their difficulties, whether relating to the affairs of war or peace. One great one was then before them, concerning the runaways (as their name is for them) that had fled out of the battle, who being many and powerful, it was feared that they might make some commotion in the republic, to prevent the execution of the law upon them for their cowardice. The law in that case was very severe; for they were not only to be debarred from all honors, but also it was a disgrace to intermarry with them; whoever met any of them in the streets, might beat him if he chose, nor was it lawful for him to resist; they in the meanwhile were obliged to go about unwashed and meanly dressed, with their clothes patched with divers colors, and to wear their beards half shaved half unshaven. To execute so rigid a law as this, in a case where the offenders were so many, and many of them of such distinction, and that in a time when the commonwealth wanted soldiers so much as then it did, was of dangerous consequence. Therefore they chose Agesilaus as a sort of new lawgiver for the occasion. But he, without adding to or diminishing from or any way changing the law, came out into the public assembly, and said, that the law should sleep for today, but from this day forth be vigorously executed. By this means he at once preserved the law from abrogation, and the citizens from infamy; and that he might alleviate the despondency and self-distrust of the young men, he made an inroad into Arcadia, where carefully avoiding all fighting, he contented himself with spoiling the territory, and taking a small town belonging to the Mantineans, thus reviving the hearts of the people, letting them see that they were not everywhere unsuccessful.

Epaminondas now invaded Laconia, with an army of forty thousand, besides light-armed men and others that followed the camp only for plunder, so that in all they were at least seventy thousand. It was now six hundred years since the Dorians had possessed Laconia, and in all that time the face of an enemy had not been seen within their territories, no man daring to invade them; but now they made their entrance, and burnt and plundered without resistance the hitherto untouched and sacred territory, up to Eurotas, and the very suburbs of Sparta; for Agesilaus would not permit them to encounter so impetuous a torrent, as Theopompus calls it, of war. He contented himself with fortifying the chief parts of the city, and with placing guards in convenient places, enduring meanwhile the taunts of the Thebans, who reproached him by name as the kindler of the war, and the author of all that mischief to his country, bidding him defend himself if he could. But this was not all; he was equally disturbed at home with the tumults of the city, the outcries and running about of the old men, who were enraged at their present condition, and the women, yet worse, out of their senses with the clamors, and the fires of the enemy in the field. He was also himself afflicted by the sense of his lost glory; who having come to the throne of Sparta when it was in its most flourishing and powerful condition, now lived to see it laid low in esteem, and all its great vaunts cut down, even that which he himself had been accustomed to use, that the women of Sparta had never seen the smoke of the enemy's fire. As it is said, also, that when Antalcidas once being in dispute with an Athenian about the valor of the two nations, the Athenian boasted, that they had often driven the Spartans from the river Cephisus, "Yes," said Antalcidas, "but we never had occasion to drive you from Eurotas." And a common Spartan of less note, being in company with an Argive, who was bragging how many Spartans lay buried in the fields of Argos, replied, "None of you are buried in the country of Laconia." Yet now the case was so altered, that

Antalcidas, being one of the Ephors, out of fear sent away his children privately to the island of Cythera.

When the enemy essayed to get over the river, and thence to attack the town, Agesilaus, abandoning the rest, betook himself to the high places and strong-holds of it. But it happened, that Eurotas at that time was swollen to a great height with the snow that had fallen, and made the passage very difficult to the Thebans, not only by its depth, but much more by its extreme coldness. Whilst this was doing, Epaminondas was seen in the front of the phalanx, and was pointed out to Agesilaus, who looked long at him, and said but these words, "O, bold man!" But when he came to the city, and would have fain attempted something within the limits of it that might raise him a trophy there, he could not tempt Agesilaus out of his hold, but was forced to march off again, wasting the country as he went.

Meanwhile, a body of long discontented and bad citizens, about two hundred in number, having got into a strong part of the town called the Issorion, where the temple of Diana stands, seized and garrisoned it. The Spartans would have fallen upon them instantly; but Agesilaus, not knowing how far the sedition might reach, bade them forbear, and going himself in his ordinary dress, with but one servant, when he came near the rebels, called out, and told them, that they mistook their orders; this was not the right place; they were to go, one part of them thither, showing them another place in the city, and part to another, which he also showed. The conspirators gladly heard this, thinking themselves unsuspected of treason, and readily went off to the places which he showed them. Whereupon Agesilaus placed in their room a guard of his own; and of the conspirators he apprehended fifteen, and put them to death in the night. But after this, a much more dangerous conspiracy was discovered of Spartan citizens, who had privately met in each other's houses, plotting a revolution. These were men whom it was equally dangerous to prosecute publicly according to law, and to connive at. Agesilaus took counsel with the Ephors, and put these also to death privately without process; a thing never before known in the case of any born Spartan.

At this time, also, many of the Helots and country people, who were in the army, ran away to the enemy, which was matter of great consternation to the city. He therefore caused some officers of his, every morning before day, to search the quarters of the soldiers, and where any man was gone, to hide his arms, that so the greatness of the number might not appear.

Historians differ about the cause of the Thebans' departure from Sparta. Some say, the winter forced them; as also that the Arcadian soldiers disbanding, made it necessary for the rest to retire. Others say, that they stayed there three months, till they had laid the whole country waste. Theopompus is the only author who says that when the Boeotian generals had already resolved upon the retreat, Phrixus, the Spartan, came to them, and offered them from

Agesilaus ten talents to be gone, so hiring them to do what they were already doing of their own accord. How he alone should come to be aware of this, I know not; only in this all authors agree, that the saving of Sparta from ruin was wholly due to the wisdom of Agesilaus, who in this extremity of affairs quitted all his ambition and his haughtiness, and resolved to play a saving game. But all his wisdom and courage was not sufficient to recover the glory of it, and to raise it to its ancient greatness. For as we see in human bodies, long used to a very strict and too exquisitely regular diet, any single great disorder is usually fatal; so here one stroke overthrew the whole State's long prosperity. Nor can we be surprised at this. Lycurgus had formed a polity admirably designed for the peace, harmony, and virtuous life of the citizens; and their fall came from their assuming foreign dominion and arbitrary sway, things wholly undesirable, in the judgment of Lycurgus, for a well-conducted and happy State.

Agesilaus being now in years, gave over all military employments; but his son Archidamus, having received help from Dionysius of Sicily, gave a great defeat to the Arcadians, in the fight known by the name of the Tearless Battle, in which there was a great slaughter of the enemy, without the loss of one Spartan. Yet this victory, more than anything else, discovered the present weakness of Sparta; for heretofore victory was esteemed so usual a thing with them, that for their greatest successes, they merely sacrificed a cock to the gods. The soldiers never vaunted, nor did the citizens display any great joy at the news; even when the great victory, described by Thucydides, was obtained at Mantinea, the messenger that brought the news had no other reward than a piece of meat, sent by the magistrates from the common table. But at the news of this Arcadian victory, they were not able to contain themselves; Agesilaus went out in procession with tears of joy in his eyes, to meet and embrace his son, and all the magistrates and public officers attended him. The old men and the women marched out as far as the river Eurotas, lifting up their hands, and thanking the gods, that Sparta was now cleared again of the disgrace and indignity that had befallen her, and once more saw the light of day. Since before, they tell us, the Spartan men, out of shame at their disasters, did not dare so much as to look their wives in the face.

When Epaminondas restored Messene, and recalled from all quarters the ancient citizens to inhabit it, they were not able to obstruct the design, being not in condition of appearing in the field against them. But it went greatly against Agesilaus in the minds of his countrymen, when they found so large a territory, equal to their own in compass, and for fertility the richest of all Greece, which they had enjoyed so long, taken from them in his reign. Therefore it was that the king broke off treaty with the Thebans, when they offered him peace, rather than set his hand to the passing away of that country, though it was already taken from him. Which point of honor had like to have cost him dear; for not long after he was overreached by a stratagem, which had almost amounted to the loss of Sparta. For when the Mantineans again revolted from Thebes to Sparta, and Epaminondas understood that Agesilaus was come to their assistance with a powerful army, he privately in the night quitted his quarters at Tegea, and unknown to the Mantineans, passing by Agesilaus, marched towards Sparta, insomuch that he failed very little of taking it empty and unarmed. Agesilaus had intelligence sent him by Euthynus, the Thespian, as Callisthenes says, but Xenophon says by a Cretan; and immediately dispatched a horseman to Lacedaemon, to apprise them of it, and to let them know that he was hastening to them. Shortly after his arrival the Thebans crossed the Eurotas. They made an assault upon the town, and were received by Agesilaus with great courage, and with exertions beyond what was to be expected at his years. For he did not now fight with that caution and cunning which he formerly made use of, but put all upon a desperate push; which, though not his usual method, succeeded so well, that he rescued the city out of the very hands of Epaminondas, and forced him to retire, and, at the erection of a trophy, was able, in the presence of their wives and children, to declare that the Lacedaemonians had nobly paid their debt to their country, and particularly his son Archidamus, who had that day made himself illustrious, both by his courage and agility of body, rapidly passing about by the short lanes to every endangered point, and everywhere maintaining the town against the enemy with but few to help him. Isadas, however, the son of Phoebidas, must have been, I think, the admiration of the enemy as well as of his friends. He was a youth of remarkable beauty and stature, in the very flower of the most attractive time of life, when the boy is just rising into the man. He had no arms upon him, and scarcely clothes; he had just anointed himself at home, when upon the alarm, without further waiting, in that undress, he snatched a spear in one hand, and a sword in the other, and broke his way through the combatants to the enemies, striking at all he met. He received no wound, whether it were that a special divine care rewarded his valor with an extraordinary protection, or whether his shape being so large and beautiful, and his dress so unusual, they thought him more than a man. The Ephors gave him a garland; but as soon as they had done so, they fined him a thousand drachmas, for going out to battle unarmed.

A few days after this there was another battle fought near Mantinea, in which Epaminondas, having routed the van of the Lacedaemonians, was eager in the pursuit of them, when Anticrates, the Laconian, wounded him with a spear, says Dioscorides; but the Spartans to this day call the posterity of this Anticrates, swordsmen, because he wounded Epaminondas with a sword. They so dreaded Epaminondas when living, that the slayer of him was embraced and admired by all; they decreed honors and gifts to him, and an exemption from taxes to his posterity, a privilege enjoyed at this day by Callicrates, one of his descendants.

Epaminondas being slain, there was a general peace again concluded, from which Agesilaus's party excluded the Messenians, as men that had no city, and therefore would not let them swear to the league; to which when the rest of the Greeks admitted them, the Lacedaemonians broke off, and continued the war alone, in hopes of subduing the Messenians. In this Agesilaus was esteemed a stubborn and headstrong man, and insatiable of war, who took such pains to undermine the general peace, and to protract the war at a time when he had not money to carry it on with, but was forced to borrow of his friends and raise subscriptions, with much difficulty, while the city, above all things, needed repose. And all this to recover the one poor town of Messene, after he had lost so great an empire both by sea and land, as the Spartans were possessed of, when he began to reign.

But it added still more to his ill-repute when he put himself into the service of Tachos, the Egyptian. They thought it too unworthy of a man of his high station, who was then looked upon as the first commander in all Greece, who had filled all countries with his renown, to let himself out to hire to a barbarian, an Egyptian rebel, (for Tachos was no better) and to fight for pay, as captain only of a band of mercenaries. If, they said, at those years of eighty and odd, after his body had been worn out with age, and enfeebled with wounds, he had resumed that noble undertaking, the liberation of the Greeks from Persia, it had been worthy of some reproof. To make an action honorable, it ought to be agreeable to the age, and other circumstances of the person; since it is circumstance and proper measure that give an action its character, and make it either good or bad. But Agesilaus valued not other men's discourses; he thought no public employment dishonorable; the ignoblest thing in his esteem, was for a man to sit idle and useless at home, waiting for his death to come and take him. The money, therefore, that he received from Tachos, he laid out in raising men, with whom having filled his ships, he took also thirty Spartan counselors with him, as formerly he had done in his Asiatic expedition, and set sail for Egypt.

As soon as he arrived in Egypt, all the great officers of the kingdom came to pay their compliments to him at his landing. His reputation being so great had raised the expectation of the whole country, and crowds flocked in to see him; but when they found, instead of the splendid prince whom they looked for, a little old man of contemptible appearance, without all ceremony lying down upon the grass, in coarse and threadbare clothes, they fell into laughter and scorn of him, crying out, that the old proverb was; now made good, "The mountain had brought forth a mouse." They were yet more astonished at his stupidity, as they thought it, who, when presents were made him of all sorts of provisions, took only the meal, the calves, and the geese, but rejected the sweetmeats, the confections and perfumes; and when they urged him to the acceptance of them, took them and gave them to the helots in his army. Yet he was taken, Theophrastus tells us, with the garlands they made of the papyrus, because of their simplicity, and when he returned home, he demanded one of the king, which he carried with him.

When he joined with Tachos, he found his expectation of being general-in-chief disappointed. Tachos reserved that place for himself, making Agesilaus only captain of the mercenaries, and Chabrias, the Athenian, commander of the fleet. This was the first occasion of his discontent, but there followed others; he was compelled daily to submit to the insolence and vanity of this Egyptian, and was at length forced to attend him into Phoenicia, in a condition much below his character and dignity, which he bore and put up with for a time, till he had opportunity of showing his feelings. It was afforded him by Nectanabis, the cousin of Tachos, who commanded a large force under him, and shortly after deserted him, and was proclaimed king by the Egyptians. This man invited Agesilaus to join his party, and the like he did to Chabrias, offering great rewards to both. Tachos, suspecting it, immediately applied himself both to Agesilaus and Chabrias, with great humility beseeching their continuance in his friendship. Chabrias consented to it, and did what he could by persuasion and good words to keep Agesilaus with them. But he gave this short reply, "You, O Chabrias, came hither a volunteer, and may go and stay as you see cause; but I am the servant of Sparta, appointed to head the Egyptians, and therefore I cannot fight against those to whom I was sent as a friend, unless I am commanded to do so by my country." This being said, he dispatched messengers to Sparta, who were sufficiently supplied with matter both for dispraise of Tachos, and commendation of Nectanabis. The two Egyptians also sent their ambassadors to Lacedaemon, the one to claim continuance of the league already made, the other to make great offers for the breaking of it, and making a new one. The Spartans having heard both sides, gave in their public answer, that they referred the whole matter to Agesilaus; but privately wrote to him, to act as he should find it best for the profit of the commonwealth. Upon receipt of his orders, he at once changed sides, carrying all the mercenaries with him to Nectanabis, covering with the plausible presence of acting for the benefit of his country, a most questionable piece of conduct, which, stripped of that disguise, in real truth was no better than downright treachery. But the Lacedaemonians, who make it their first principle of action to serve their country's interest, know not anything to be just or unjust by any measure but that.

Tachos, being thus deserted by the mercenaries, fled for it; upon which a new king of the Mendesian province was proclaimed his successor, and came against Nectanabis with an army of one hundred thousand men. Nectanabis, in his talk with Agesilaus, professed to despise them as newly raised men, who, though many in number, were of no skill in war, being most of them mechanics and tradesmen, never bred to war. To whom Agesilaus answered, that he did not fear their numbers, but did fear their ignorance, which gave no room for employing stratagem against them. Stratagem only avails with men who are alive to suspicion, and expecting to be assailed, expose themselves by their attempts at defense; but one who has no thought or expectation of anything, gives as little opportunity to the enemy, as he who stands stock-still does to a wrestler. The Mendesian was not wanting in solicitations of Agesilaus, insomuch that Nectanabis grew jealous. But when Agesilaus advised to fight the enemy at once, saying, it was folly to protract the war and rely on time, in a contest with men who had no experience in fighting battles, but with their great numbers might be able to surround them, and cut off their communications by entrenchments, and anticipate them in many matters of advantage, this altogether confirmed him in his fears and suspicions. He took quite the contrary course, and retreated into a large and strongly fortified town. Agesilaus, finding himself mistrusted, took it very ill, and was full of indignation, yet was ashamed to change sides back again, or to go away without effecting anything, so that he was forced to follow Nectanabis into the town.

When the enemy came up, and began to draw lines about the town, and to entrench, the Egyptian now resolved upon a battle, out of fear of a siege. And the Greeks were eager for it, provisions growing already scarce in the town. When Agesilaus opposed it, the Egyptians then suspected him much more, publicly calling him the betrayer of the king. But Agesilaus, being now satisfied within himself, bore these reproaches patiently, and followed the design which he had laid, of overreaching the enemy, which was this.

The enemy were forming a deep ditch and high wall, resolving to shut up the garrison and starve it. When the ditch was brought almost quite round, and the two ends had all but met, he took the advantage of the night, and armed all his Greeks. Then going to the Egyptian, "This, young man, is your opportunity," said he, "of saving yourself, which I all this while durst not announce, lest discovery should prevent it; but now the enemy has, at his own cost, and the pains and labor of his own men, provided for our security. As much of this wall as is built will prevent them from surrounding us with their multitude, the gap yet left will be sufficient for us to sally out by; now play the man, and follow the example the Greeks will give you, and by fighting valiantly, save yourself and your army; their front will not be able to stand against us, and their rear we are sufficiently secured from, by a wall of their own making." Nectanabis, admiring the sagacity of Agesilaus, immediately placed himself in the middle of the Greek troops, and fought with them; and upon the first charge soon routed the enemy. Agesilaus having now gained credit with the king, proceeded to use, like a trick in wrestling, the same stratagem over again. He sometimes pretended a retreat, at other times advanced to attack their flanks, and by this means at last drew them into a place enclosed between two ditches that were very deep, and full of water. When he had them at this advantage, he soon charged them, drawing up the front of his battle equal to the space between the two ditches, so that they had no way of surrounding him, being enclosed themselves on both sides. They made but little resistance; many fell, others fled and were dispersed.

Nectanabis, being thus settled and fixed in his kingdom, with much kindness and affection invited Agesilaus to spend his winter in Egypt, but he made haste home to assist in the wars of his own country, which was he knew in want of money, and forced to hire mercenaries, whilst their own men were fighting abroad. The king, therefore, dismissed him very honorably, and among other gifts presented him with two hundred and thirty talents of silver toward the charge of the war. But the weather being tempestuous, his ships kept in shore, and passing along the coast of Africa he reached an uninhabited spot called the Port of Menelaus, and here, when his ships were just upon landing, he expired, being eighty-four years old, and having reigned in Lacedaemon forty-one. Thirty of which years he passed with the reputation of being the greatest and most powerful man of all Greece, and was looked upon as, in a manner, general and king of it, until the battle of Leuctra. It was the custom of the Spartans to bury their common dead in the place where they died, whatsoever country it was, but their kings they carried home. The followers of Agesilaus, for want of honey, enclosed his body in wax, and so conveyed him to Lacedaemon.

His son Archidamus succeeded him on his throne; so did his posterity successively to Agis, the fifth from Agesilaus; who was slain by Leonidas, while attempting to restore the ancient discipline of Sparta.

11
POMPEY

The people of Rome seem to have entertained for Pompey from his childhood, the same affection that Prometheus in the tragedy of Aeschylus expresses for Hercules, speaking of him as the author of his deliverance, in these words,

> *Ah cruel Sire! how dear thy son to me!*
> *The generous offspring of my enemy!*

For on the one hand, never did the Romans give such demonstrations of a vehement and fierce hatred against any of their generals, as they did against Strabo, the father of Pompey; during whose lifetime, it is true, they stood in awe of his military power, as indeed he was a formidable warrior, but immediately upon his death, which happened by a stroke of thunder, they treated him with the utmost contumely, dragging his corpse from the bier, as it was carried to his funeral. On the other side, never had any Roman the people's good-will and devotion more zealous throughout all the changes of fortune, more early in its first springing up, or more steadily rising with his prosperity, or more constant in his adversity, than Pompey had. In Strabo, there was one great cause of their hatred, his insatiable covetousness; in Pompey, there were many that helped to make him the object of their love; his temperance, his skill, and exercise in war, his eloquence of speech, integrity of mind and affability in conversation and address; insomuch that no man ever asked a favor with less offense, or conferred one with a better grace. When he gave, it was without assumption, when he received, it was with dignity and honor.

In his youth, his countenance pleaded for him, seeming to anticipate his eloquence, and win upon the affections of the people before he spoke. His beauty even in his bloom of youth had something in it at once of gentleness and dignity; and when his prime of manhood came, the majesty kingliness of his character at once became visible in it. His hair sat somewhat hollow or rising a little; and this, with the languishing motion of his eyes, seemed to form a resemblance in his face, though perhaps more talked of than really apparent, to the statues of king Alexander. And because many applied that name to him in his youth, Pompey himself did not decline it, insomuch that some called him so in derision. And Lucius Philippus, a man of consular dignity, when he was pleading in favor of him, thought it not unfit to say, that people could not be surprised if Philip was a lover of Alexander.

It is related of Flora, the courtesan, that when she was now pretty old; she took great delight in speaking of her early familiarity with Pompey, and was wont to say, that she could never part after being with him without a bite. She would further tell, that Geminius, a companion of Pompey's, fell in love with her, and made his court with great importunity; and on her refusing, and telling him, however her inclinations were, yet she could not gratify his desires for Pompey's sake, he therefore made his request to Pompey, and Pompey frankly gave his consent, but never afterwards would have any converse with her, notwithstanding, that he seemed to have a great passion for her; and Flora, on this occasion, showed none of the levity that might have been expected of her, but languished for some time after under a sickness brought on by grief and desire. This Flora, we are told, was such a celebrated beauty, that Caecilius Metellus, when he adorned the temple of Castor and Pollux with paintings and statues, among the rest dedicated hers for her singular beauty. In his conduct also to the wife of Demetrius, his freed servant, (who had great influence with him in his lifetime, and left an estate of four thousand talents,) Pompey acted contrary to his usual habits, not quite fairly or generously, fearing lest he should fall under the common censure of being enamored and charmed with her beauty, which was irresistible, and became famous everywhere. Nevertheless, though he seemed to be so extremely circumspect and cautious, yet even in matters of this nature, he could not avoid the calumnies of his enemies, but upon the score of married women, they accused him, as if he had connived at many things, and embezzled the public revenue to gratify their luxury.

Of his easiness of temper and plainness, in what related to eating and drinking, the story is told, that once in a sickness, when his stomach nauseated common meats, his physician prescribed him a thrush to eat; but upon search, there was none to be bought, for they were not then in season, and one telling him they were to be had at Lucullus's, who kept them all the year round, "So then," said he, "if it were not for Lucullus's luxury, Pompey should not live;"

and thereupon not minding the prescription of the physician, he contented himself with such meat as could easily be procured. But this was at a later time.

Being as yet a very young man, and upon an expedition in which his father was commanding against Cinna, he had in his tent with him one Lucius Terentius, as his companion and comrade, who, being corrupted by Cinna, entered into an engagement to kill Pompey, as others had done, to set the general's tent on fire. This conspiracy being discovered to Pompey at supper, he showed no discomposure at it, but on the contrary drank more liberally than usual, and expressed great kindness to Terentius; but about bedtime, pretending to go to his repose, he stole away secretly out of the tent, and setting a guard about his father, quietly expected the event. Terentius, when he thought the proper time come, rose with his naked sword, and coming to Pompey's bedside, stabbed several strokes through the bedclothes, as if he were lying there. Immediately after this there was a great uproar throughout all the camp, arising from the hatred they bore to the general, and a universal movement of the soldiers to revolt, all tearing down their tents, and betaking themselves to their arms. The general himself all this while durst not venture out because of the tumult; but Pompey, going about in the midst of them, besought them with tears; and at last threw himself prostrate upon his face before the gate of the camp, and lay there in the passage at their feet, shedding tears, and bidding those that were marching off, if they would go, trample upon him. Upon which, none could help going back again, and all, except eight hundred, either through shame or compassion, repented, and were reconciled to the general.

Immediately upon the death of Strabo, there was an action commenced against Pompey, as his heir, for that his father had embezzled the public treasure. But Pompey, having traced the principal thefts, charged them upon one Alexander, a freed slave of his father's, and proved before the judges that he had been the appropriator. But he himself was accused of having in his possession some hunting tackle, and books, that were taken at Asculum. To this he confessed thus far, that he received them from his father when he took Asculum, but pleaded further, that he had lost them since, upon Cinna's return to Rome when his home was broken open and plundered by Cinna's guards. In this cause he had a great many preparatory pleadings against his accuser, in which he showed an activity and steadfastness beyond his years, and gained great reputation and favor; insomuch that Antistius, the praetor and judge of the cause, took a great liking to him, and offered him his daughter in marriage, having had some communications with his friends about it. Pompey accepted the proposal, and they were privately contracted; however, the secret was not so closely kept as to escape the multitude, but it was discernible enough from the favor shown him by Antistius in his cause. And at last, when Antistius pronounced the absolutory sentence of the judges, the people, as if it had been upon a signal given, made the acclamation used according to ancient custom, at marriages, Talasio. The origin of which custom is related to be this. At the time when the daughters of the Sabines came to Rome, to see the shows and sports there, and were violently seized upon by the most distinguished and bravest of the Romans for wives, it happened that some goatswains and herdsmen of the meaner rank were carrying off a beautiful and tall maiden; and lest any of their betters should meet them, and take her away, as they ran, they cried out with one voice, Talasio, Talasius being a well-known and popular person among them, insomuch that all that heard the name, clapped their hands for joy, and joined with them in the shout, as applauding and congratulating the chance. Now, say they, because this proved a fortunate match to Talasius, hence it is that this acclamation is sportively used as a nuptial cry at all weddings. This is the most credible of the accounts that are given of the Talasio. And some few days after this judgment, Pompey married Antistia.

After this he went to Cinna's camp, where finding some false suggestions and calumnies prevailing against him, he began to be afraid and presently withdrew himself secretly; which sudden disappearance occasioned great suspicion. And there went a rumor and speech through all the camp, that Cinna had murdered the young man; upon which all that had been anyways disobliged, and bore any malice to him, resolved to make an assault upon him. He, endeavoring to make his escape, was seized by a centurion, who pursued him with his naked sword. Cinna, in this distress, fell upon his knees, and offered him his seal-ring, of great value, for his ransom; but the centurion repulsed him insolently, saying, "I did not come to seal a covenant, but to be revenged upon a lawless and wicked tyrant;" and so dispatched him immediately.

Thus Cinna being slain, Carbo, a tyrant yet more senseless than he, took the command and exercised it, while Sylla meantime was approaching, much to the joy and satisfaction of most people, who in their present evils were ready to find some comfort if it were but in the exchange of a master. For the city was brought to that pass by oppression and calamities, that being utterly in despair of liberty, men were only anxious for the mildest and most tolerable bondage. At that time Pompey was in Picenum in Italy, where he spent some time amusing himself, as he had estates in the country there, though the chief motive of his stay was the liking he felt for the towns of that district, which all regarded him with hereditary feelings of kindness and attachment. But when he now saw that the noblest and best of the city began to forsake their homes and property, and fly from all quarters to Sylla's camp, as to their haven, he likewise was desirous to go; not, however, as a fugitive, alone and with nothing to offer, but as a friend rather than a suppliant, in a way that would gain him honor, bringing help along with him, and at the head of a body of troops. Accordingly he solicited the Picentines for their assistance, who as cordially embraced his motion, and rejected the messengers sent from Carbo; insomuch that a certain Vindius taking upon him to say, that Pompey was come from the school-room to put himself at the head of the people, they were so incensed that they fell forthwith upon this Vindius and killed him. From henceforward Pompey, finding a spirit of government upon him, though not above twenty-three years of age, nor deriving, an authority by commission from any man, took the privilege to grant himself full power, and causing a tribunal to be erected in the market-place of Auximum, a populous city, expelled two of their principal men, brothers, of the name of Ventidius, who were acting against him in Carbo's interest, commanding them by a public edict to depart the city; and then proceeded to levy soldiers, issuing out commissions to centurions, and other officers, according to the form of military discipline. And in this manner he went round all the rest of the cities in the district. So that those of Carbo's faction flying, and all others cheerfully submitting to his command, in a little time he mustered three entire legions, having supplied himself beside with all manner of provisions, beasts of burden, carriages, and other necessaries of war. And with this equipage he set forward on his march towards Sylla, not as if he were in haste, or desirous of escaping observation, but by small journeys, making several halts upon the road, to distress and annoy the enemy, and exerting himself to detach from Carbo's interest every part of Italy that he passed through.

Three commanders of the enemy encountered him at once, Carinna, Cloelius, and Brutus, and drew up their forces, not all in the front, nor yet together on any one part, but encamping three several armies in a circle about him, they resolved to encompass and overpower him. Pompey was no way alarmed at this, but collecting all his troops into one body, and placing his horse in the front of the battle, where he himself was in person, he singled out and bent all his forces against Brutus, and when the Celtic horsemen from the enemy's side rode out to meet him, Pompey himself encountering hand to hand with the foremost and stoutest among them, killed him with his spear. The rest seeing this turned their backs, and fled, and breaking the ranks of their own foot, presently caused a general rout; whereupon the commanders fell out among themselves, and marched off, some one way, some another, as their fortunes led them, and the towns round about came in and surrendered themselves to Pompey, concluding that the enemy was dispersed for fear. Next after these, Scipio, the consul, came to attack him, and with as little success; for before the armies could join, or be within the throw of their javelins, Scipio's soldiers saluted Pompey's, and came over to them, while Scipio made his escape by flight. Last of all, Carbo himself sent down several troops of horse against him by the river Arsis, which Pompey assailed with the same courage and success as before; and having routed and put them to flight, he forced them in the pursuit into difficult ground, unpassable for horse, where seeing no hopes of escape, they yielded themselves with their horses and armor, all to his mercy.

Sylla was hitherto unacquainted with all these actions; and on the first intelligence he received of his movements was in great anxiety about him, fearing lest he should be cut off among so many and such experienced commanders of the enemy, and marched therefore with all speed to his aid. Now Pompey, having advice of his approach, sent out orders to his officers, to marshal and draw up all his forces in full array, that they might make the finest and noblest appearance before the commander-in-chief; for he expected indeed great honors from him, but met with even greater. For as soon as Sylla saw him thus advancing, his army so well appointed, his men so young and strong, and their spirits so high and hopeful with their successes, he alighted from his horse, and being first, as was his due, saluted by them with the title of Imperator, he returned the salutation upon Pompey, in the same term and style of Imperator, which might well cause surprise, as none could have ever anticipated that he would have imparted, to one so young in years and not yet a senator, a title which was the object of contention between him and the Scipios and Marii. And indeed all the rest of his deportment was agreeable to this first compliment; whenever Pompey came into his presence, he paid some sort of respect to him, either in rising and being uncovered, or the like, which he was rarely seen to do to anyone else, notwithstanding that there were many about him of great rank and honor. Yet Pompey was not puffed up at all, or exalted with these favors. And when Sylla would have sent him with all expedition into Gaul, a province in which it was thought Metellus who commanded in it had done nothing worthy of the large forces at his disposal, Pompey urged, that it could not be fair or honorable for him, to take a province out of the hands of his senior in command and superior in reputation; however, if Metellus were willing, and should request his service, he should be very ready to accompany and assist him in the war. Which when Metellus came to understand, he approved of the proposal, and invited him over by letter. And on this Pompey fell immediately into Gaul, where he not only achieved wonderful exploits of himself, but also fired up and kindled again that bold and warlike spirit, which old age had in a manner extinguished in Metellus, into a new heat; just as molten copper, they say, when poured upon that which is cold and solid, will dissolve and melt it faster than fire itself. But as when a famous wrestler has gained the first place among men, and borne away the prizes at all the games, it is not usual to take account of his victories as a boy, or to enter them upon record among the rest; so with the exploits of Pompey in his youth, though they were extraordinary in themselves, yet because they were obscured and buried in the multitude and greatness of his later wars and conquests, I dare not be particular in them, lest, by trifling away time in the lesser moments of his youth, we should be driven to omit those greater actions and fortunes which best illustrate his character.

Now, when Sylla had brought all Italy under his dominion, and was proclaimed dictator, he began to reward the rest of his followers, by giving them wealth, appointing them to offices in the State, and granting them freely and without restriction any favors they asked for. But as for Pompey, admiring his valor and conduct, and thinking that he might prove a great stay and support to him hereafter in his affairs, he sought means to attach him to himself by some personal alliance, and his wife Metella joining in his wishes, they two persuaded Pompey to put away Antistia, and marry Aemilia, the step-daughter of Sylla, borne by Metella to Scaurus her former husband, she being at that very time the wife of another man, living with him, and with child by him. These were the very tyrannies of marriage, and much more agreeable to the times under Sylla, than to the nature and habits of Pompey; that Aemilia great with child should be, as it were, ravished from the embraces of another for him, and that Antistia should be divorced with dishonor and misery by him, for whose sake she had been but just before bereft of her father. For Antistius was murdered in the senate, because he was suspected to be a favorer of Sylla for Pompey's sake; and her mother, likewise, after she had seen all these indignities, made away with herself; a new calamity to be added to the tragic accompaniments of this marriage, and that there might be nothing wanting to complete them, Aemilia herself died, almost immediately after entering Pompey's house, in childbed.

About this time news came to Sylla, that Perpenna was fortifying himself in Sicily, that the island was now become a refuge and receptacle for the relics of the adverse party; that Carbo was hovering about those seas with a navy, that Domitius had fallen in upon Africa and that many of the exiled men of note who had escaped from the proscriptions were daily flocking into those parts. Against these, therefore, Pompey was sent with a large force; and no sooner was he arrived in Sicily but Perpenna immediately departed, leaving the whole island to him. Pompey received the distressed cities into favor, and treated all with great humanity, except the Mamertines in Messena; for when they protested against his court and jurisdiction, alleging their privilege and exemption founded upon an ancient charter or grant of the Romans, he replied sharply, "What! will you never cease prating of laws to us that have swords by our sides?" It was thought, likewise, that he showed some inhumanity to Carbo, seeming rather to insult over his misfortunes, than to chastise his crimes. For if there had been a necessity, as perhaps there was, that he should be taken off, that might have been done at first, as soon as he was taken prisoner, for then it would have been the act of him that commanded it. But here Pompey commended a man that had been thrice consul of Rome, to be brought in fetters to stand at the bar, he himself sitting upon the bench in judgment, examining the cause with the formalities of law, to the offense and indignation of all that were present, and afterwards ordered him to be taken away and put to death. It is related, by the way, of Carbo, that as soon as he was brought to the place, and saw the sword drawn for execution, he was suddenly seized with a looseness or pain in his bowels, and desired a little respite of the executioner, and a convenient place to relieve himself. And yet further, Caius Oppius, the friend of Caesar, tells us, that Pompey dealt cruelly with Quintus Valerius, a man of singular learning and science. For when he was brought to him, he walked aside, and drew him into conversation, and after putting a variety of questions to him, and receiving answers from him, he ordered his officers to take him away, and put him to death. But we must not be too credulous in the case of narratives told by Oppius, especially when he undertakes to relate anything touching the friends or foes of Caesar. This is certain, that there lay a necessity upon Pompey to be severe upon many of Sylla's enemies, those at least that were eminent persons in themselves, and notoriously known to be taken; but for the rest, he acted with all the clemency possible for him, conniving at the concealment of some, and himself being the instrument in the escape of others. So in the case of the Himeraeans; for when Pompey had determined on severely punishing their city, as they had been abettors of the enemy, Sthenis, the leader of the people there, craving liberty of speech, told him, that what he was about to do was not at all consistent with justice, for that he would pass by the guilty, and destroy the innocent; and on Pompey demanding, who that guilty person was that would assume the offenses of them all, Sthenis replied, it was himself, who had engaged his friends by persuasion to what they had done, and his enemies by force; whereupon Pompey being much taken with the frank speech and noble spirit of the man, first forgave his crime, and then pardoned all the rest of the Himeraeans. Hearing, likewise, that his soldiers were very disorderly their march, doing violence upon the roads, he ordered their swords to be sealed up in their scabbards, and whosoever kept them not so, were severely punished.

Whilst Pompey was thus busy in the affairs and government of Sicily, he received a decree of the senate, and a commission from Sylla, commanding him forthwith to sail into Africa, and make war upon Domitius with all his forces: for Domitius had rallied up a far greater army than Marius had had not long since, when he sailed out of Africa into Italy, and caused a revolution in Rome, and himself, of a fugitive outlaw, became a tyrant. Pompey, therefore, having prepared everything with the utmost speed, left Memmius, his sister's husband, governor of Sicily, and set sail with one hundred and twenty galleys, and eight hundred other vessels laden with provisions, money, ammunition, and engines of battery. He arrived with his fleet, part at the port of Utica, part at Carthage; and no sooner was he landed, but seven thousand of the enemy revolted and came over to him, while his own forces that he brought with him consisted of six entire legions. Here they tell us of a pleasant incident that happened to him at his first arrival. For some of his soldiers having by accident stumbled upon a treasure, by which they got a good sum of money, the rest of the army hearing this, began to fancy that the field was full of gold and silver, which had been hid there of old by the Carthaginians in the time of their calamities, and thereupon fell to work, so that the army was useless to Pompey for many days, being totally engaged in digging for the fancied treasure, he himself all the while walking up and down only, and laughing to see so many thousands together, digging and turning up the earth. Until at last, growing weary and hopeless, they came to themselves, and returned to their general, begging him to lead them where he pleased, for that they had already received the punishment of their folly. By this time Domitius had prepared himself; and drawn out his army in array against Pompey; but there was a watercourse betwixt them, craggy, and difficult to pass over; and this, together with a great storm of wind and rain pouring down even from break of day, seemed to leave but little possibility of their coming together, so that Domitius, not expecting any engagement that day, commanded his forces to draw off and retire to the camp. Now Pompey, who was watchful upon every occasion, making use of the opportunity, ordered a march forthwith, and having passed over the torrent, fell in immediately upon their quarters. The enemy was in a great disorder and tumult, and in that confusion attempted a resistance; but they neither were all there, nor supported one another; besides, the wind having veered about, beat the rain full in their faces. Neither indeed was the storm less troublesome to the Romans, for that they could not clearly discern one another, insomuch that even Pompey himself, being unknown, escaped narrowly; for when one of his soldiers demanded of him the word of battle, it happened that he was somewhat slow in his answer, which might have cost him his life.

The enemy being routed with a great slaughter, (for it is said, that of twenty thousand there escaped but three thousand,) the army saluted Pompey by the name of Imperator; but he declined it, telling them, that he could not by any means accept of that title, as long as he saw the camp of the enemy standing; but if they designed to make him worthy of the honor, they must first demolish that. The soldiers on hearing this, went at once and made an assault upon the works and trenches, and there Pompey fought without his helmet, in memory of his former danger, and to avoid the like. The camp was thus taken by storm, and among the rest, Domitius was slain. After that overthrow, the cities of the country thereabouts were all either secured by surrender, or taken by storm. King Iarbas, likewise, a confederate and auxiliary of Domitius, was taken prisoner, and his kingdom was given to Hiempsal.

Pompey could not rest here, but being ambitious to follow the good fortune and use the valor of his army, entered Numidia; and marching forward many days' journey up into the country, he conquered all wherever he came. And having revived the terror of the Roman power, which was now almost obliterated among the barbarous nations, he said likewise, that the wild beasts of Africa ought not to be left without some experience of the courage and success of the Romans; and therefore he bestowed some few days in hunting lions and elephants. And it is said, that it was not above the space of forty days at the utmost, in which he gave a total overthrow to the enemy, reduced Africa, and established the affairs of the kings and kingdoms of all that country, being then in the twenty-fourth year of his age.

When Pompey returned back to the city of Utica, there were presented to him letters and orders from Sylla, commanding him to disband the rest of his army, and himself with one legion only to wait there the coming of another general, to succeed him in the government. This, inwardly, was extremely grievous to Pompey, though he made no show of it. But the army resented it openly, and when Pompey besought them to depart and go home before him, they began to revile Sylla, and declared broadly, that they were resolved not to forsake him, neither did they think it safe for him to trust the tyrant. Pompey at first endeavored to appease and pacify them by fair speeches; but when he saw that his persuasions were vain, he left the bench, and retired to his tent with tears in his eyes. But the soldiers followed him, and seizing upon him, by force brought him again, and placed him in his tribunal; where great part of that day was spent in dispute, they on their part persuading him to stay and command them, he, on the other side, pressing upon them obedience, and the danger of mutiny. At last, when they grew yet more importunate and clamorous, he swore that he would kill himself if they attempted to force him; and scarcely even thus appeased them. Nevertheless, the first tidings brought to Sylla were, that Pompey was up in rebellion; on which he remarked to some of his friends, "I see, then, it is my destiny to contend with children in my old age;" alluding at the same time to Marius, who, being but a mere youth, had given him great trouble, and brought him into extreme danger. But being undeceived afterwards by better intelligence, and finding the whole city prepared to meet Pompey, and receive him with every display of kindness and honor, he resolved to exceed them all. And, therefore, going out foremost to meet him, and embracing him with great cordiality, he gave him his welcome aloud in the title of Magnus, or the Great, and bade all that were present call him by that name. Others say that he had this title first given him by a general acclamation of all the army in Africa, but that it was fixed upon him by this ratification of Sylla. It is certain that he himself was the last that owned the title; for it was a long time after, when he was sent proconsul into Spain against Sertorius, that he began to write himself in his letters and commissions by the name of Pompeius Magnus; common and familiar use having then worn off the invidiousness of the title. And one cannot but accord respect and admiration to the ancient Romans, who did not reward the successes of action and conduct in war alone with such honorable titles, but adorned likewise the virtues and services of eminent men in civil government with the same distinctions and marks of honor. Two persons received from the people the name of Maximus, or the Greatest, Valerius, for reconciling the senate and people, and Fabius Rullus, because he put out of the senate certain sons of freed slaves who had been admitted into it because of their wealth.

Pompey now desired the honor of a triumph, which Sylla opposed, alleging that the law allowed that honor to none but consuls and praetors, and therefore Scipio the elder, who subdued the Carthaginians in Spain in far greater and nobler conflicts, never petitioned for a triumph, because he had never been consul or praetor; and if Pompey, who had scarcely yet fully grown a beard, and was not of age to be a senator, should enter the city in triumph, what a weight of envy would it bring, he said, at once upon his government and Pompey's honor. This was his language to Pompey, intimating that he could not by any means yield to his request, but if he would persist in his ambition, that he was resolved to interpose his power to humble him. Pompey, however, was not daunted; but bade Sylla recollect, that more worshiped the rising than the setting sun; as if to tell him that his power was increasing, and Sylla's in the wane. Sylla did not perfectly hear the words, but observing a sort of amazement and wonder in the looks and gestures of those that did hear them, he asked what it was that he said. When it was told him, he seemed astounded at Pompey's boldness, and cried out twice together, "Let him triumph," and when others began to show their disapprobation and offense at it, Pompey, it is said, to gall and vex them the more, designed to have his triumphant chariot drawn with four elephants, (having brought over several which belonged to the African kings,) but the gates of the city being too narrow, he was forced to desist from that project, and be content with horses. And when his soldiers, who had not received as large rewards as they had expected, began to clamor, and interrupt the triumph, Pompey regarded these as little as the rest, and plainly told them that he had rather lose the honor of his triumph, than flatter them. Upon which Servilius, a man of great distinction, and at first one of the chief opposers of Pompey's triumph, said, he now perceived that Pompey was truly great and worthy of a triumph. It is clear that he might easily have been a senator, also, if he had wished, but he did not sue for that, being ambitious, it seems, only of unusual honors. For what wonder had it been for Pompey, to sit in the senate before his time? But to triumph before he was in the senate, was really an excess of glory.

And moreover, it did not a little ingratiate him with the people; who were much pleased to see him after his triumph take his place again among the Roman knights. On the other side, it was no less distasteful to Sylla to see how fast he came on, and to what a height of glory and power he was advancing; yet being ashamed to hinder him, he kept quiet. But when, against his direct wishes, Pompey got Lepidus made consul, having openly joined in the canvass and, by the good-will the people felt for himself, conciliated their favor for Lepidus, Sylla could forbear no longer; but when he saw him coming away from the election through the forum with a great train after him, cried out to him, "Well, young man, I see you rejoice in your victory. And, indeed, is it not a most generous and worthy act, that the consulship should be given to Lepidus, the vilest of men, in preference to Catulus, the best and most deserving in the city, and all by your influence with the people? It will be well, however, for you to be wakeful and look to your interests; as you have been making your enemy stronger than yourself." But that which gave the clearest demonstration of Sylla's ill-will to Pompey, was his last will and testament; for whereas he had bequeathed several legacies to all the rest of his friends, and appointed some of them guardians to his eon, he passed by Pompey without the least remembrance. However, Pompey bore this with great moderation and temper; and when Lepidus and others were disposed to obstruct his interment in the Campus Martius, and to prevent any public funeral taking place, came forward in support of it, and saw his obsequies performed with all honor and security.

Shortly after the death of Sylla, his prophetic words were fulfilled; and Lepidus proposing to be the successor to all his power and authority, without any ambiguities or pretences, immediately appeared in arms, rousing once more and gathering about him all the long dangerous remains of the old factions, which had escaped the hand of Sylla. Catulus, his colleague, who was followed by the sounder part of the senate and people, was a man of the greatest esteem among the Romans for wisdom and justice; but his talent lay in the government of the city rather than the camp, whereas the exigency required the skill of Pompey. Pompey, therefore, was not long in suspense which way to dispose of himself, but joining with the nobility, was presently appointed general of the army against Lepidus, who had already raised up war in great part of Italy, and held Cisalpine Gaul in subjection with an army under Brutus. As for the rest of his garrisons, Pompey subdued them with ease in his march, but Mutina in Gaul resisted in a formal siege, and he lay here a long time encamped against Brutus. In the meantime Lepidus marched in all haste against Rome, and sitting down before it with a crowd of followers, to the terror of those within, demanded a second consulship. But that fear quickly vanished upon letters sent from Pompey, announcing that he had ended the war without a battle; for Brutus, either betraying his army, or being betrayed by their revolt, surrendered himself to Pompey, and receiving a guard of horse, was conducted to a little town upon the river Po; where he was slain the next day by Geminius, in execution of Pompey's commands. And for this Pompey was much censured; for, having at the beginning of the revolt written to the senate that Brutus had voluntarily surrendered himself, immediately afterward he sent other letters, with matter of accusation against the man, after he was taken off. Brutus, who with Cassius slew Caesar, was son to this Brutus; neither in war nor in his death like his father, as appears at large in his life. Lepidus upon this being driven out of Italy, fled to Sardinia, where he fell sick and died of sorrow, not for his public misfortunes, as they say, but, upon the discovery of a letter, proving his wife to have been unfaithful to him.

There yet remained Sertorius, a very different general from Lepidus, in possession of Spain, and making himself formidable to Rome; the final disease, as it were, in which the scattered evils of the civil wars had now collected. He had already cut off various inferior commanders, and was at this time coping with Metellus Pius, a man of repute and a good soldier, though perhaps he might now seem too slow, by reason of his age, to second and improve the happier moments of war, and might be sometimes wanting to those advantages which Sertorius by his quickness and dexterity would wrest out of his hands. For Sertorius was always hovering about, and coming upon him unawares, like a captain of thieves rather than soldiers, disturbing him perpetually with ambuscades and light skirmishes; whereas Metellus was accustomed to regular conduct, and fighting in battle array with full-armed soldiers. Pompey, therefore, keeping his army in readiness, made it his object to be sent in aid to Metellus; neither would he be induced to disband his forces, notwithstanding that Catulus called upon him to do so, but by some colorable device or other he still kept them in arms about the city, until the senate at last thought fit, upon the report of Lucius Philippus, to decree him that government. At that time, they say, one of the senators there expressing his wonder and demanding of Philippus whether his meaning was that Pompey should be sent into Spain as proconsul, "No," replied Philippus, "but as proconsuls," as if both consuls for that year were in his opinion wholly useless.

When Pompey was arrived in Spain, as is usual upon the fame of a new leader, men began to be inspired with new hopes, and those nations that had not entered into a very strict alliance with Sertorius, began to waver and revolt; whereupon Sertorius uttered various arrogant and scornful speeches against Pompey, saying in derision, that he should want no other weapon but a ferula and rod to chastise this boy with, if he were not afraid of that old woman, meaning Metellus. Yet in deed and reality he stood in awe of Pompey, and kept on his guard against him, as appeared by his whole management of the war, which he was observed to conduct much more warily than before; for Metellus, which one would not have imagined, was grown excessively luxurious in his habits having given himself over to self-indulgence and pleasure, and from a moderate and temperate, became suddenly a sumptuous and ostentatious liver, so that this very thing gained Pompey great reputation and good-will, as he made himself somewhat specially an example of frugality, although that virtue was habitual in him, and required no great industry to exercise it, as he was naturally inclined to temperance, and no ways inordinate in his desires. The fortune of the war was very various; nothing however annoyed Pompey so much as the taking of the town of Lauron by Sertorius. For when Pompey thought he had him safe inclosed, and had boasted somewhat largely of raising the siege, he found himself all of a sudden encompassed; insomuch that he durst not move out of his camp, but was forced to sit still whilst the city was taken and burnt before his face. However, afterwards in a battle near Valentia, he gave great defeat to Herennius and Perpenna, two commanders among the refugees who had fled to Sertorius, and now lieutenants under him, in which he slew above ten thousand men.

Pompey, being elated and filled with confidence by this victory, made all haste to engage Sertorius himself, and the rather lest Metellus should come in for a share in the honor of the victory. Late in the day, towards sunset, they joined battle near the river Sucro, both being in fear lest Metellus should come; Pompey, that he might engage alone, Sertorius, that he might have one alone to engage with. The issue of the battle proved doubtful, for a wing of each side had the better; but of the generals, Sertorius had the greater honor, for that he maintained his post, having put to flight the entire division that was opposed to him, whereas Pompey was himself almost made a prisoner; for being set upon by a strong man at arms that fought on foot, (he being on horseback,) as they were closely engaged hand to hand, the strokes of their swords chanced to light upon their hands, but with a different success; for Pompey's was a slight wound only, whereas he cut off the other's hand. However, it happened so, that many now falling upon Pompey together, and his own forces there being put to the rout, he made his escape beyond expectation, by quitting his horse, and turning him out among the enemy. For the horse being richly adorned with golden trappings, and having a caparison of great value, the soldiers quarreled among themselves for the booty, so that while they were fighting with one another, and dividing the spoil, Pompey made his escape. By break of day the next morning, each drew out his forces into the field to claim the victory; but Metellus coming up, Sertorius vanished, having broken up and dispersed his army. For this was the way in which he used to raise and disband his armies, so that sometimes he would be wandering up and down all alone, and at other times again he would come pouring into the field at the head of no less than one hundred and fifty thousand fighting-men, swelling of a sudden like a winter torrent.

When Pompey was going after the battle to meet and welcome Metellus, and when they were near one another, he commanded his attendants to lower their rods in honor of Metellus, as his senior and superior. But Metellus on the other side forbade it, and behaved himself in general very obligingly to him, not claiming any prerogative either in respect of his consular rank or seniority; excepting only that when they encamped together, the watchword was given to the whole camp by Metellus. But generally they had their camps asunder, being divided and distracted by the enemy, who took all shapes, and being always in motion, would by some skillful artifice appear in a variety of places almost in the same instant, drawing them from one attack to another, and at last keeping them from foraging, wasting the country, and holding the dominion of the sea, Sertorius drove them both out of that part of Spain which was under his control, and forced them for want of necessaries to retreat into provinces that did not belong to them.

Pompey, having made use of and expended the greatest part of his own private revenues upon the war, sent and demanded moneys of the senate, adding, that in case they did not furnish him speedily, he should be forced to return into Italy with his army. Lucullus being consul at that time, though at variance with Pompey, yet in consideration that he himself was a candidate for the command against Mithridates, procured and hastened these supplies, fearing lest there should be any presence or occasion given to Pompey of returning home, who of himself was no less desirous of leaving Sertorius, and of undertaking the war against Mithridates, as an enterprise which by all appearance would prove much more honorable and not so dangerous. In the meantime Sertorius died, being treacherously murdered by some of his own party; and Perpenna, the chief among them, took the command, and attempted to carry on the same enterprises with Sertorius, having indeed the same forces and the same means, only wanting the same skill and conduct in the use of them. Pompey therefore marched directly against, Perpenna, and finding him acting merely at random in his affairs, had a decoy ready for him, and sent out a detachment of ten cohorts into the level country with orders to range up and down and disperse themselves abroad. The bait took accordingly, and no sooner had Perpenna turned upon the prey and had them in chase, but Pompey appeared suddenly with all his army and joining battle, gave him a total overthrow. Most of his officers were slain in the field, and he himself being brought prisoner to Pompey, was by his order put to death. Neither was Pompey guilty in this of ingratitude or unmindfulness of what had occurred in Sicily, which some have laid to his charge, but was guided by a high minded policy and a deliberate counsel for the security of his country. For Perpenna, having in his custody all Sertorius's papers, offered to produce several letters from the greatest men in Rome, who, desirous of a change and subversion of the government, had invited Sertorius into Italy. And Pompey, fearing that these might be the occasion of worse wars than those which were now ended, thought it advisable to put Perpenna to death, and burnt the letters without reading them.

Pompey continued in Spain after this so long a time as was necessary for the suppression of all the greatest disorders in the province; and after moderating and allaying the more violent heats of affairs there, returned with his army into Italy, where he arrived, as chance would have it, in the height of the servile war. Accordingly, upon his arrival, Crassus, the commander in that war, at some hazard precipitated a battle, in which he had great success, and slew upon the place twelve thousand three hundred of the insurgents. Nor yet was he so quick, but that fortune reserved to Pompey some share of honor in the success of this war, for five thousand of those that had escaped out of the battle fell into his hands; and when he had totally cut them off, he wrote to the senate, that Crassus had overthrown the slaves in battle, but that he had plucked up the whole war by the roots. And it was agreeable to the people in Rome both thus to say, and thus to hear said, because of the general favor of Pompey. But of the Spanish war and the conquest of Sertorius, no one, even in jest, could have ascribed the honor to anyone else. Nevertheless, all this high respect for him, and this desire to see him come home, were not unmixed with apprehensions and suspicions that he might perhaps not disband his army, but take his way by the force of arms and a supreme command to the seat of Sylla. And so in the number of all those that ran out to meet him and congratulate his return, as many went out of fear as affection. But after Pompey had removed this alarm, by declaring beforehand that he would discharge the army after his triumph, those that envied him could now only complain that he affected popularity, courting the common people more than the nobility, and that whereas Sylla had abolished the tribuneship of the people, he designed to gratify the people by restoring that office, which was indeed the fact. For there was not any one thing that the people of Rome were more wildly eager for, or more passionately desired, than the restoration of that office, insomuch that Pompey thought himself extremely fortunate in this opportunity, despairing (if he were anticipated by someone else in this) of ever meeting with any other sufficient means of expressing his gratitude for the favors which he had received from the people.

Though a second triumph was decreed him, and he was declared consul, yet all these honors did not seem so great an evidence of his power and glory, as the ascendant which he had over Crassus; for he, the wealthiest among all the statesmen of his time, and the most eloquent and greatest too, who had looked down on Pompey himself, and on all others as beneath him, durst not appear a candidate for the consulship before he had applied to Pompey. The request was made accordingly, and was eagerly embraced by Pompey, who had long sought an occasion to oblige him in some friendly office; so that he solicited for Crassus, and entreated the people heartily, declaring, that their favor would be no less to him in choosing Crassus his colleague, than in making himself consul. Yet for all this, when they were created consuls, they were always at variance, and opposing one another. Crassus prevailed most in the senate, and Pompey's power was no less with the people, he having restored to them the office of tribune, and having allowed the courts of judicature to be transferred back to the knights by a new law. He himself in person, too, afforded them a most grateful spectacle, when he appeared and craved his discharge from the military service. For it is an ancient custom among the Romans, that the knights, when they had served out their legal time in the wars, should lead their horses into the market-place before the two officers, called censors, and having given an account of the commanders and generals under whom they served, as also of the places and actions of their service, should be discharged, every man with honor or disgrace, according to his deserts. There were then sitting in state upon the bench two censors, Gellius and Lentulus, inspecting the knights, who were passing by in muster before them, when Pompey was seen coming down into the forum, with all the ensigns of a consul, but leading his horse in his hand. When he came up, he bade his lictors make way for him, and so he led his horse to the bench; the people being all this while in a sort of amaze, and all in silence, and the censors themselves regarding the sight with a mixture of respect and gratification. Then the senior censor examined him: "Pompeius Magnus, I demand of you whether you have served the full time in the wars that is prescribed by the law?" "Yes," replied Pompey with a loud voice, "I have served all, and all under myself as general." The people hearing this gave a great shout, and made such an outcry for delight, that there was no appeasing it; and the censors rising from their judgment-seat, accompanied him home to gratify the multitude, who followed after, clapping their hands and shouting.

Pompey's consulship was now expiring, and yet his difference with Crassus increasing, when one Caius Aurelius, a knight, a man who had declined public business all his lifetime, mounted the hustings, and addressed himself in an oration to the assembly, declaring that Jupiter had appeared to him in a dream, commanding him to tell the consuls, that they should not give up office until they were friends. After this was said, Pompey stood silent, but Crassus took him by the hand, and spoke in this manner: "I do not think, fellow-citizens, that I shall do anything mean or dishonorable, in yielding first to Pompey, whom you were pleased to ennoble with the title of Great, when as yet he scarce had a hair on his face; and granted the honor of two triumphs, before he had a place in the senate." Hereupon they were reconciled and laid down their office. Crassus resumed the manner of life which he had always pursued before; but Pompey in the great generality of causes for judgment declined appearing on either side, and by degrees withdrew himself totally from the forum, showing himself but seldom in public; and whenever he did, it was with a great train after him. Neither was it easy to meet or visit him without a crowd of people about him; he was most pleased to make his appearance before large numbers at once, as though he wished to maintain in this way his state and majesty, and as if he held himself bound to preserve his dignity from contact with the addresses and conversation of common people. And life in the robe of peace is only too apt to lower the reputation of men that have grown great by arms, who naturally find difficulty in adapting themselves to the habits of civil equality. They expect to be treated as the first in the city, even as they were in the camp; and on the other hand, men who in war were nobody, think it intolerable if in the city at any rate they are not to take the lead. And so, when a warrior renowned for victories and triumphs shall turn advocate and appear among them in the forum, they endeavor their utmost to obscure and depress him; whereas, if he gives up any pretensions here and retires, they will maintain his military honor and authority beyond the reach of envy. Events themselves not long after showed the truth of this.

The power of the pirates first commenced in Cilicia, having in truth but a precarious and obscure beginning, but gained life and boldness afterwards in the wars of Mithridates, where they hired themselves out, and took employment in the king's service. Afterwards, whilst the Romans were embroiled in their civil wars, being engaged against one another even before the very gates of Rome, the seas lay waste and unguarded, and by degrees enticed and drew them on not only to seize upon and spoil the merchants and ships upon the seas, but also to lay waste the islands and seaport towns. So that now there embarked with these pirates men of wealth and noble birth and superior abilities, as if it had been a natural occupation to gain distinction in. They had divers arsenals, or piratic harbors, as likewise watch towers and beacons, all along the sea-coast; and fleets were here received that were well manned with the finest mariners, and well served with the expertest pilots, and composed of swift sailing and light-built vessels adapted for their special purpose. Nor was it merely their being thus formidable that excited indignation; they were even more odious for their ostentation than they were feared for their force. Their ships had gilded masts at their stems; the sails woven of purple, and the oars plated with silver, as if their delight were to glory in their iniquity. There was nothing but music and dancing, banqueting and revels, all along the shore. Officers in command were taken prisoners, and cities put under contribution, to the reproach and dishonor of the Roman supremacy. There were of these corsairs above one thousand sail, and they had taken no less than four hundred cities, committing sacrilege upon the temples of the gods, and enriching themselves with the spoils of many never violated before, such as were those of Claros, Didyma, and Samothrace; and the temple of the Earth in Hermione, and that of Aesculapius in Epidaurus, those of Neptune at the Isthmus, at Taenarus, and at Calauria; those of Apollo at Actium and Leucas, and those of Juno, in Samos, at Argos, and at Lacinium. They themselves offered strange sacrifices upon Mount Olympus, and performed certain secret rites or religious mysteries, among which those of Mithras have been preserved to our own time, having received their previous institution from them. But besides these insolencies by sea, they were also injurious to the Romans by land; for they would often go inland up the roads, plundering and destroying their villages and country-houses. And once they seized upon two Roman praetors, Sextilius and Bellinus, in their purple-edged robes, and carried them off together with their officers and lictors. The daughter also of Antonius, a man that had had the honor of a triumph, taking a journey into the country, was seized, and redeemed upon payment of a large ransom. But it was most abusive of all, that when any of the captives declared himself to be a Roman and told his name, they affected to be surprised, and feigning fear, smote their thighs and fell down at his feet, humbly beseeching him to be gracious and forgive them. The captive seeing them so humble and suppliant, believed them to be in earnest; and some of them now would proceed to put Roman shoes on his feet, and to dress him in a Roman gown, to prevent, they said, his being mistaken another time. After all this pageantry, when they had thus deluded and mocked him long enough, at last putting out a ship's ladder, when they were in the midst of the sea, they told him he was free to go, and wished him a pleasant journey; and if he resisted, they themselves threw him overboard, and drowned him.

This piratic power having got the dominion and control of all the Mediterranean, there was left no place for navigation or commerce. And this it was which most of all made the Romans, finding themselves to be extremely straitened in their markets, and considering that if it should continue, there would be a dearth and famine in the land, determine at last to send out Pompey to recover the seas from the pirates. Gabinius, one of Pompey's friends, preferred a law, whereby there was granted to him, not only the government of the seas as admiral, but in direct words, sole and irresponsible sovereignty over all men. For the decree gave him absolute power and authority in all the seas within the pillars of Hercules, and in the adjacent mainland for the space of four hundred furlongs from the sea. Now there were but few regions in the Roman empire out of that compass; and the greatest of the nations and most powerful of the kings were included in the limit. Moreover by this decree he had a power of selecting fifteen lieutenants out of the senate, and of assigning to each his province in charge; then he might take likewise out of the treasury and out of the hands of the revenue-farmers what moneys he pleased; as also two hundred sail of ships, with a power to press and levy what soldiers and seamen he thought fit. When this law was read, the common people approved of it exceedingly, but the chief men and most important among the senators looked upon it as an exorbitant power, even beyond the reach of envy, but well deserving their fears. Therefore concluding with themselves that such unlimited authority was dangerous, they agreed unanimously to oppose the bill, and all went against it, except Caesar, who gave his vote for the law, not to gratify Pompey, but the people, whose favor he had courted underhand from the beginning, and hoped to compass for himself. The rest inveighed bitterly against Pompey, insomuch that one of the consuls told him, that if he was ambitious of the place of Romulus, he would scarce avoid his end, but he was in danger of being torn in pieces by the multitude for his speech. Yet when Catulus stood up to speak against the law, the people in reverence to him were silent and attentive. And when, after saying much in the most honorable terms in favor of Pompey, he proceeded to advise the people in kindness to spare him, and not to expose a man of his value to such a succession of dangers and wars, "For," said he, "where could you find another Pompey, or whom would you have in case you should chance to lose him?" they all cried out with one voice, "Yourself." And so Catulus, finding all his rhetoric ineffectual, desisted. Then Roscius attempted to speak, but could obtain no hearing, and made signs with his fingers, intimating, "Not him alone," but that there might be a second Pompey or colleague in authority with him. Upon this, it is said, the multitude being extremely incensed, made such a loud outcry, that a crow flying over the market-place at that instant was struck, and drops down among the crowd; whence it would appear that the cause of birds falling down to the ground, is not any rupture or division of the air causing a vacuum, but purely the actual stroke of the voice, which when carried up in a great mass and with violence, raises a sort of tempest and billow, as it were, in the air.

The assembly broke up for that day; and when the day was come, on which the bill was to pass by suffrage into a decree, Pompey went privately into the country; but hearing that it was passed and confirmed, he resumed again into the city by night, to avoid the envy that might be occasioned by the concourse of people that would meet and congratulate him. The next morning he came abroad and sacrificed to the gods, and having audience at an open assembly, so handled the matter that they enlarged his power, giving him many things besides what was already granted, and almost doubling the preparation appointed in the former decree. Five hundred ships were manned for him, and an army raised of one hundred and twenty thousand foot, and five thousand horse. Twenty-four senators that had been generals of armies were appointed to serve as lieutenants under him, and to these were added two quaestors. Now it happened within this time that the prices of provisions were much reduced, which gave an occasion to the joyful people of saying, that the very name of Pompey had ended the war. However, Pompey in pursuance of his charge divided all the seas, and the whole Mediterranean into thirteen parts, allotting a squadron to each, under the command of his officers; and having thus dispersed his power into all quarters, and encompassed the pirates everywhere, they began to fall into his hands by whole shoals, which he seized and brought into his harbors. As for those that withdrew themselves betimes, or otherwise escaped his general chase, they all made to Cilicia, where they hid themselves as in their hive; against whom Pompey now proceeded in person with sixty of his best ships, not however until he had first scoured and cleared all the seas near Rome, the Tyrrhenian, and the African, and all the waters of Sardinia, Corsica, and Sicily; all which he performed in the space of forty days, by his own indefatigable industry and the zeal of his lieutenants.

Pompey met with some interruption in Rome, through the malice and envy of Piso, the consul, who had given some check to his proceedings, by withholding his stores and discharging his seamen; whereupon he sent his fleet round to Brundusium, himself going the nearest way by land through Tuscany to Rome; which was no sooner known by the people, than they all flocked out to meet him upon the way, as if they had not sent him out but few days before. What chiefly excited their joy, was the unexpectedly rapid change in the markets, which abounded now with the greatest plenty, so that Piso was in great danger to have been deprived of his consulship, Gabinius having a law ready prepared for that purpose; but Pompey forbade it, behaving himself as in that, so in all things else, with great moderation, and when he had made sure of all that he wanted or desired, he departed for Brundusium, whence he set sail in pursuit of the pirates. And though he was straitened in time, and his hasty voyage forced him to sail by several cities without touching, yet he would not pass by the city of Athens unsaluted; but landing there, after he had sacrificed to the gods, and made an address to the people, as he was returning out of the city, he read at the gates two epigrams, each in a single line, written in his own praise; one within the gate:—

Thy humbler thoughts make thee a god the more;

the other without:—

Adieu we bid, who welcome bade before.

Now because Pompey had shown himself merciful to some of these pirates that were yet roving in bodies about the seas, having upon their supplication ordered a seizure of their ships and persons only, without any further process or severity, therefore the rest of their comrades in hopes of mercy too, made their escape from his other commanders, and surrendered themselves with their wives and children into his protection. He continued to pardon all that came in, and the rather because by them he might make discovery of those who fled from his justice, as conscious that their crimes were beyond an act of indemnity. The most numerous and important part of these conveyed their families and treasures, with all their people that were unfit for war, into castles and strong forts about Mount Taurus; but they themselves having well manned their galleys, embarked for Coracesium in Cilicia, where they received Pompey and gave him battle. Here they had a final overthrow, and retired to the land, where they were besieged. At last, having dispatched their heralds to him with a submission, they delivered up to his mercy themselves, their towns, islands, and strong-holds, all which they had so fortified that they were almost impregnable, and scarcely even accessible.

Thus was this war ended, and the whole power of the pirates at sea dissolved everywhere in the space of three months, wherein, besides a great number of other vessels, he took ninety men-of-war with brazen beaks; and likewise prisoners of war to the number of no less than twenty thousand.

As regarded the disposal of these prisoners, he never so much as entertained the thought of putting them to death; and yet it might be no less dangerous on the other hand to disperse them, as they might reunite and make head again, being numerous, poor, and warlike. Therefore wisely weighing with himself, that man by nature is not a wild or unsocial creature, neither was he born so, but makes himself what he naturally is not, by vicious habit; and that again on the other side, he is civilized and grows gentle by a change of place, occupation, and manner of life, as beasts themselves that are wild by nature, become tame and tractable by housing and gentler usage, upon this consideration he determined to translate these pirates from sea to land, and give them a taste of an honest and innocent course of life, by living in towns, and tilling the ground. Some therefore were admitted into the small and half-peopled towns of the Cilicians, who for an enlargement of their territories, were willing to receive them. Others he planted in the city of the Solians, which had been lately laid waste by Tigranes, king of Armenia, and which he now restored. But the largest number were settled in Dyme, the town of Achaea, at that time extremely depopulated, and possessing an abundance of good land.

However, these proceedings could not escape the envy and censure of his enemies; and the course he took against Metellus in Crete was disapproved of even by the chiefest of his friends. For Metellus, a relation of Pompey's former colleague in Spain, had been sent praetor into Crete, before this province of the seas was assigned to Pompey. Now Crete was the second source of pirates next to Cilicia, and Metellus having shut up a number of them in their strong-holds there, was engaged in reducing and extirpating them. Those that were yet remaining and besieged sent their supplications to Pompey, and invited him into the island as a part of his province, alleging it to fall, every part of it, within the distance from the sea specified in his commission, and so within the precincts of his charge. Pompey receiving the submission, sent letters to Metellus, commanding him to leave off the war; and others in like manner to the cities, in which he charged them not to yield any obedience to the commands of Metellus. And after these, he sent Lucius Octavius, one of his lieutenants, to act as general, who entering the besieged fortifications, and fighting in defense of the pirates, rendered Pompey not odious only, but even ridiculous too; that he should lend his name as a guard to a nest of thieves, that knew neither god nor law, and make his reputation serve as a sanctuary to them, only out of pure envy and emulation to Metellus. For neither was Achilles thought to act the part of a man, but rather of a mere boy, mad after glory, when by signs he forbade the rest of the Greeks to strike at Hector:—

> *"for fear*
> *Some other hand should give the blow, and he*
> *Lose the first honor of the victory."*

Whereas Pompey even sought to preserve the common enemies of the world, only that he might deprive a Roman praetor, after all his labors, of the honor of a triumph. Metellus however was not daunted, but prosecuted the war against the pirates, expelled them from their strongholds and punished them; and dismissed Octavius with the insults and reproaches of the whole camp.

When the news came to Rome that the war with the pirates was at an end, and that Pompey was unoccupied, diverting himself in visits to the cities for want of employment, one Manlius, a tribune of the people, preferred a law that Pompey should have all the forces of Lucullus, and the provinces under his government, together with Bithynia, which was under the command of Glabrio; and that he should forthwith conduct the war against the two kings, Mithridates and Tigranes, retaining still the same naval forces and the sovereignty of the seas as before. But this was nothing less than to constitute one absolute monarch of all the Roman empire. For the provinces which seemed to be exempt from his commission by the former decree, such as were Phrygia, Lycaonia, Galatia, Cappadocia, Cilicia, the upper Colchis, and Armenia, were all added in by this latter law, together with all the troops and forces with which Lucullus had defeated Mithridates and Tigranes. And though Lucullus was thus simply robbed of the glory of his achievements in having a successor assigned him, rather to the honor of his triumph, than the danger of the war; yet this was of less moment in the eyes of the aristocratical party, though they could not but admit the injustice and ingratitude to Lucullus. But their great grievance was, that the power of Pompey should be converted into a manifest tyranny; and they therefore exhorted and encouraged one another privately to bend all their forces in opposition to this law, and not tamely to cast away their liberty; yet when the day came on which it was to pass into a decree, their hearts failed them for fear of the people, and all were silent except Catulus, who boldly inveighed against the law and its proposer, and when he found that he could do nothing with the people, turned to the senate, crying out and bidding them seek out some mountain as their forefathers had done, and fly to the rocks where they might preserve their liberty. The law passed into a decree, as it is said, by the suffrages of all the tribes. And Pompey in his absence was made lord of almost all that power, which Sylla only obtained by force of arms, after a conquest of the very city itself. When Pompey had advice by letters of the decree, it is said that in the presence of his friends, who came to give him joy of his honor, he seemed displeased, frowning and smiting his thigh, and exclaimed as one overburdened, and weary of government, "Alas, what a series of labors upon labors! If I am never to end my service as a soldier, nor to escape from this invidious greatness, and live at home in the country with my wife, I had better have been an unknown man." But all this was looked upon as mere trifling, neither indeed could the best of his friends call it anything else, well knowing that his enmity with Lucullus, setting a flame just now to his natural passion for glory and empire, made him feel more than usually gratified.

As indeed appeared not long afterwards by his actions, which clearly unmasked him; for in the first place, he sent out his proclamations into all quarters, commanding the soldiers to join him, and summoned all the tributary kings and princes within his charge; and in short, as soon as he had entered upon his province, he left nothing unaltered that had been done and established by Lucullus. To some he remitted their penalties, and deprived others of their rewards, and acted in all respects as if with the express design that the admirers of Lucullus might know that all his authority was at an end. Lucullus expostulated by friends, and it was thought fitting that there should be a meeting betwixt them; and accordingly they met in the country of Galatia. As they were both great and successful generals, their officers bore their rods before them all wreathed with branches of laurel; Lucullus came through a country full of green trees and shady woods, but Pompey's march was through a cold and barren district. Therefore the lictors of Lucullus, perceiving that Pompey's laurels were withered and dry, helped him to some of their own, and adorned and crowned his rods with fresh laurels. This was thought ominous, and looked as if Pompey came to take away the reward and honor of Lucullus's victories. Lucullus had the priority in the order of consulships, and also in age; but Pompey's two triumphs made him the greater man. Their first addresses in this interview were dignified and friendly, each magnifying the other's actions, and offering congratulations upon his success. But when they came to the matter of their conference or treaty, they could agree on no fair or equitable terms of any kind, but even came to harsh words against each other, Pompey upbraiding Lucullus with avarice, and Lucullus retorting ambition upon Pompey, so that their friends could hardly part them. Lucullus, remaining in Galatia, made a distribution of the lands within his conquests, and gave presents to whom he pleased; and Pompey encamping not far distant from him, sent out his prohibitions, forbidding the execution of any of the orders of Lucullus, and commanded away all his soldiers, except sixteen hundred, whom he thought likely to be unserviceable to himself, being disorderly and mutinous, and whom he knew to be hostile to Lucullus; and to these acts he added satirical speeches, detracting openly from the glory of his actions, and giving out, that the battles of Lucullus had been but with the mere stage-shows and idle pictures of royal pomp, whereas the real war against a genuine army, disciplined by defeat, was reserved to him, Mithridates having now begun to be in earnest, and having betaken himself to his shields, swords, and horses. Lucullus, on the other side, to be even with him, replied, that Pompey came to fight with the mere image and shadow of war, it being his usual practice, like a lazy bird of prey, to come upon the carcass, when others had slain the dead, and to tear in pieces the relics of a war. Thus he had appropriated to himself the victories over Sertorius, over Lepidus, and over the insurgents under Spartacus; whereas this last had been achieved by Crassus, that obtained by Catulus, and the first won by Metellus. And therefore it was no great wonder, that the glory of the Pontic and Armenian war should be usurped by a man who had condescended to any artifices to work himself into the honor of a triumph over a few runaway slaves.

After this Lucullus went away, and Pompey having placed his whole navy in guard upon the seas betwixt Phoenicia and Bosporus, himself marched against Mithridates, who had a phalanx of thirty thousand foot, with two thousand horse, yet durst not bid him battle. He had encamped upon a strong mountain where it would have been hard to attack him, but abandoned it in no long time, as destitute of water. No sooner was he gone but Pompey occupied it, and observing the plants that were thriving there, together with the hollows which he found in several places, conjectured that such a plot could not be without springs, and therefore ordered his men to sink wells in every corner. After which there was, in a little time, great plenty of water throughout all the camp, insomuch that he wondered how it was possible for Mithridates to be ignorant of this, during all that time of his encampment there. After this Pompey followed him to his next camp, and there drawing lines round about him, shut him in. But he, after having endured a siege of forty-five days, made his escape secretly, and fled away with all the best part of his army, having first put to death all the sick and unserviceable. Not long after Pompey overtook him again near the banks of the river Euphrates, and encamped close by him; but fearing lest he should pass over the river and give him the slip there too, he drew up his army to attack him at midnight. And at that very time Mithridates, it is said, saw a vision in his dream foreshowing what should come to pass. For he seemed to be under sail in the Euxine Sea with a prosperous gale, and just in view of Bosporus, discoursing pleasantly with the ship's company, as one overjoyed for his past danger and present security, when on a sudden he found himself deserted of all, and floating upon a broken plank of the ship at the mercy of the sea. Whilst he was thus laboring under these passions and phantasms, his friends came and awaked him with the news of Pompey's approach; who was now indeed so near at hand, that the fight must be for the camp itself, and the commanders accordingly drew up the forces in battle array. Pompey perceiving how ready they were and well prepared for defense, began to doubt with himself whether he should put it to the hazard of a fight in the dark, judging it more prudent to encompass them only at present, lest they should fly, and to give them battle with the advantage of numbers the next day. But his oldest officers were of another opinion, and by entreaties and encouragements obtained permission that they might charge them immediately. Neither was the night so very dark, but that, though the moon was going down, it yet gave light enough to discern a body. And indeed this was one especial disadvantage to the king's army. For the Romans coming upon them with the moon on their backs, the moon, being very low, and just upon setting, cast the shadows a long way before their bodies, reaching almost to the enemy, whose eyes were thus so much deceived that not exactly discerning the distance, but imagining them to be near at hand, they threw their darts at the shadows, without the least execution. The Romans therefore perceiving this, ran in upon them with a great shout; but the barbarians, all in a panic, unable to endure the charge, turned and fled, and were put to great slaughter, above ten thousand being slain; the camp also was taken. As for Mithridates himself, he at the beginning of the onset, with a body of eight hundred horse charged through the Roman army, and made his escape. But before long all the rest dispersed, some one way, some another, and he was left only with three persons, among whom was his concubine, Hypsicratia, a girl always of a manly and daring spirit, and the king called her on that account Hypsicrates. She being attired and mounted like a Persian horseman, accompanied the king in all his flight, never weary even in the longest journey, nor ever failing to attend the king in person, and look after his horse too, until they came to Inora, a castle of the king's, well stored with gold and treasure. From thence Mithridates took his richest apparel, and gave it among those that had resorted to him in their flight; and to every one of his friends he gave a deadly poison, that they might not fall into the power of the enemy against their wills. From thence he designed to have gone to Tigranes in Armenia, but being prohibited by Tigranes, who put out a proclamation with a reward of one hundred talents to any one that should apprehend him, he passed by the head-waters of the river Euphrates, and fled through the country of Colchis.

Pompey in the meantime made an invasion into Armenia, upon the invitation of young Tigranes, who was now in rebellion against his father, and gave

Pompey a meeting about the river Araxes, which rises near the head of Euphrates, but turning its course and bending towards the east, falls into the Caspian Sea. They two, therefore, marched together through the country, taking in all the cities by the way, and receiving their submission. But king Tigranes, having lately suffered much in the war with Lucullus, and understanding that Pompey was of a kind and gentle disposition, admitted Roman troops into his royal palaces, and taking along with him his friends and relations, went in person to surrender himself into the hands of Pompey. He came as far as the trenches on horseback, but there he was met by two of Pompey's lictors, who commanded him to alight and walk on foot, for no man ever was seen on horseback within a Roman camp. Tigranes submitted to this immediately, and not only so, but loosing his sword, delivered up that too; and last of all, as soon as he appeared before Pompey, he pulled off his royal turban, and attempted to have laid it at his feet. Nay, worst of all, even he himself had fallen prostrate as an humble suppliant at his knees, had not Pompey prevented it, taking him by the hand and placing him near him, Tigranes himself on one side of him and his son upon the other. Pompey now told him that the rest of his losses were chargeable upon Lucullus, by whom he had been dispossessed of Syria, Phoenicia, Cilicia, Galatia, and Sophene; but all that he had preserved to himself entire till that time he should peaceably enjoy, paying the sum of six thousand talents as a fine or penalty for injuries done to the Romans, and that his son should have the kingdom of Sophene. Tigranes himself was well pleased with these conditions of peace, and when the Romans saluted him king, seemed to be overjoyed, and promised to every common soldier half a mina of silver, to every centurion ten minas, and to every tribune a talent; but the son was displeased, insomuch that when he was invited to supper, he replied, that he did not stand in need of Pompey for that sort of honor, for he would find out some other Roman to sup with. Upon this he was put into close arrest, and reserved for the triumph.

Not long after this Phraates, king of Parthia, sent to Pompey, and demanded to have young Tigranes, as his son-in-law, given up to him, and that the river Euphrates should be the boundary of the empires. Pompey replied, that for Tigranes, he belonged more to his own natural father than his father-in-law, and for the boundaries, he would take care that they should be according to right and justice.

So Pompey, leaving Armenia in the custody of Afranius, went himself in chase of Mithridates; to do which he was forced of necessity to march through several nations inhabiting about Mount Caucasus. Of these the Albanians and Iberians were the two chiefest. The Iberians stretch out as far as the Moschian mountains and the Pontus; the Albanians lie more eastwardly, and towards the Caspian Sea. These Albanians at first permitted Pompey, upon his request, to pass through the country; but when winter had stolen upon the Romans whilst they were still in the country, and they were busy celebrating the festival of Saturn, they mustered a body of no less than forty thousand fighting men, and set upon them, having passed over the river Cyrnus, which rising from the mountains of Iberia, and receiving the river Araxes in its course from Armenia, discharges itself by twelve mouths into the Caspian. Or, according to others, the Araxes does not fall into it, but they flow near one another, and so discharge themselves as neighbors into the same sea. It was in the power of Pompey to have obstructed the enemy's passage over the river, but he suffered them to pass over quietly; and then leading on his forces and giving battle, he routed them, and slew great numbers of them in the field. The king sent ambassadors with his submission, and Pompey upon his supplication pardoned the offense, and making a treaty with him, he marched directly against the Iberians, a nation no less in number than the other, but much more warlike, and extremely desirous of gratifying Mithridates, and driving out Pompey. These Iberians were never subject to the Medes or Persians, and they happened likewise to escape the dominion of the Macedonians, because Alexander was so quick in his march through Hyrcania. But these also Pompey subdued in a great battle, where there were slain nine thousand upon the spot, and more than ten thousand taken prisoners. From thence he entered into the country of Colchis, where Servilius met him by the river Phasis, bringing the fleet with which he was guarding the Pontus.

The pursuit of Mithridates, who had thrown himself among the tribes inhabiting Bosporus and the shores of the Maeotian Sea, presented great difficulties. News was also brought to Pompey that the Albanians had again revolted. This made him turn back, out of anger and determination not to be beaten by them, and with difficulty and great danger he passed back over the Cyrnus, which the barbarous people had fortified a great way down the banks with palisadoes. And after this, having a tedious march to make through a waterless and difficult country, he ordered ten thousand skins to be filled with water, and so advanced towards the enemy; whom he found drawn up in order of battle near the river Abas, to the number of sixty thousand horse, and twelve thousand foot, ill armed generally, and most of them covered only with the skins of wild beasts. Their general was Cosis, the king's brother, who as soon as the battle was begun, singled out Pompey, and rushing in upon him, darted his javelin into the joints of his breastplate; while Pompey, in return, struck him through the body with his lance, and slew him. It is related that in this battle there were Amazons fighting as auxiliaries with the barbarians, and that they came down from the mountains by the river Thermodon. For that after the battle, when the Romans were taking the spoil and plunder of the field, they met with several targets and buskins of the Amazons; but no woman's body was found among the dead. They inhabit the parts of Mount Caucasus that reach down to the Hyrcanian Sea, not immediately bordering upon the Albanians, for the Gelae and the Leges lie betwixt; and they keep company with these people yearly, for two months only, near the river Thermodon; after which they retire to their own habitations, and live alone all the rest of the year.

After this engagement, Pompey was eager to advance with his forces upon the Hyrcanian and Caspian Sea, but was forced to retreat at a distance of three days' march from it, by the number of venomous serpents, and so he retreated into Armenia the Less. Whilst he was there, kings of the Elymaeans and Medes sent ambassadors to him, to whom he gave friendly answer by letter; and sent against the king of Parthia, who had made incursions upon Gordyene, and despoiled the subjects of Tigranes, an army under the command of Afranius, who put him to the rout, and followed him in chase as far as the district of Arbela.

Of the concubines of king Mithridates that were brought before Pompey, he took none to himself, but sent them all away to their parents and relations; most of them being either the daughters or wives of princes and great commanders. Stratonice, however, who had the greatest power and influence with him, and to whom he had committed the custody of his best and richest fortress, had been, it seems, the daughter of a musician, an old man, and of no great fortune, and happening to sing one night before Mithridates at a banquet, she struck his fancy so, that immediately he took her with him, and sent away the old man much dissatisfied, the king having not so much as said one kind word to himself. But when he rose in the morning, and saw tables in his house richly covered with gold and silver plate, a great retinue of servants, eunuchs, and pages, bringing him rich garments, and a horse standing before the door richly caparisoned, in all respects as was usual with the king's favorites, he looked upon it all as a piece of mockery, and thinking himself trifled with, attempted to make off and run away. But the servants laying hold upon him, and informing him really that the king had bestowed on him the house and furniture of a rich man lately deceased, and that these were but the first-fruits or earnests of greater riches and possessions that were to come, he was persuaded at last with much difficulty to believe them. And so putting on his purple robes, and mounting his horse, he rode through the city, crying out, "All this is mine;" and to those that laughed at him, he said, there was no such wonder in this, but it was a wonder rather that he did not throw stones at all he met, he was so transported with joy. Such was the parentage and blood of Stratonice. She now delivered up this castle into the hands of Pompey, and offered him many presents of great value, of which he accepted only such as he thought might serve to adorn the temples of the gods, and add to the splendor of his triumph; the rest he left to Stratonice's disposal, bidding her please herself in the enjoyment of them.

And in the same manner he dealt with the presents offered him by the king of Iberia, who sent him a bedstead, table, and a chair of state, all of gold, desiring him to accept of them; but he delivered them all into the custody of the public treasurers, for the use of the Commonwealth.

In another castle called Caenum, Pompey found and read with pleasure several secret writings of Mithridates, containing much that threw light on his character. For there were memoirs by which it appeared that besides others, he had made away with his son Ariarathes by poison, as also with Alcaeus the Sardian, for having robbed him of the first honors in a horse-race. There were several judgments upon the interpretation of dreams, which either he himself or some of his mistresses had had; and besides these, there was a series of wanton letters to and from his concubine Monime. Theophanes tells us that there was found also an address by Rutilius, in which he attempted to exasperate him to the laughter of all the Romans in Asia; though most men justly conjecture this to be a malicious invention of Theophanes, who probably hated Rutilius because he was a man in nothing like himself; or perhaps it might be to gratify Pompey, whose father is described by Rutilius in his history, as the vilest man alive.

From thence Pompey came to the city of Amisus, where his passion for glory put him into a position which might be called a punishment on himself. For whereas he had often sharply reproached Lucullus, in that while the enemy was still living, he had taken upon him to issue decrees, and distribute rewards and honors, as conquerors usually do only when the war is brought to an end, yet now was he himself, while Mithridates was paramount in the kingdom of Bosporus, and at the head of a powerful army, as if all were ended, just doing the same thing, regulating the provinces, and distributing rewards, many great commanders and princes having flocked to him, together with no less than twelve barbarian kings; insomuch that to gratify these other kings, when he wrote to the king of Parthia, he would not condescend, as others used to do, in the superscription of his letter, to give him his title of king of kings.

Moreover, he had a great desire and emulation to occupy Syria, and to march through Arabia to the Red Sea, that he might thus extend his conquests every way to the great ocean that encompasses the habitable earth; as in Africa he was the first Roman that advanced his victories to the ocean; and again in Spain he made the Atlantic Sea the limit of the empire; and then thirdly, in his late pursuit of the Albanians, he had wanted but little of reaching the Hyrcanian Sea. Accordingly he raised his camp, designing to bring the Red Sea within the circuit of his expedition, especially as he saw how difficult it was to hunt after Mithridates with an army, and that he would prove a worse enemy flying than fighting. But yet he declared, that he would leave a sharper enemy behind him than himself, namely, famine; and therefore he appointed a guard of ships to lie in wait for the merchants that sailed to

Bosporus, death being the penalty for any who should attempt to carry provisions thither.

Then he set forward with the greatest part of his army, and in his march casually fell in with several dead bodies still uninterred, of those soldiers who were slain with Triarius in his unfortunate engagement with Mithridates; these he buried splendidly and honorably. The neglect of whom, it is thought, caused, as much as anything, the hatred that was felt against Lucullus, and alienated the affections of the soldiers from him. Pompey having now by his forces under the command of Afranius, subdued the Arabians about the mountain Amanus, himself entered Syria, and finding it destitute of any natural and lawful prince, reduced it into the form of a province, as a possession of the people of Rome. He conquered also Judaea, and took its king, Aristobulus, captive. Some cities he built anew, and to others he gave their liberty, chastising their tyrants. Most part of the time that he spent there was employed in the administration of justice, In deciding controversies of kings and States; and where he himself could not be present in person, he gave commissions to his friends, and sent them. Thus when there arose a difference betwixt the Armenians and Parthians about some territory, and the judgment was referred to him, he gave a power by commission to three judges and arbiters to hear and determine the controversy. For the reputation of his power was great; nor was the fame of his justice and clemency inferior to that of his power, and served indeed as a veil for a multitude of faults committed by his friends and familiars. For although it was not in his nature to check or chastise wrongdoers, yet he himself always treated those that had to do with him in such a manner, that they submitted to endure with patience the acts of covetousness and oppression done by others.

Among these friends of his, there was one Demetrius who had the greatest influence with him of all; he was a freed slave, a youth of good understanding, but somewhat too insolent in his good fortune, of whom there goes this story. Cato, the philosopher, being as yet a very young man, but of great repute and a noble mind, took a journey of pleasure to Antioch, at a time when Pompey was not there, having a great desire to see the city. He, as his custom was, walked on foot, and his friends accompanied him on horseback; and seeing before the gates of the city a multitude dressed in white, the young men on one side of the road, and the boys on the other, he was somewhat offended at it, imagining that it was officiously done in honor of him, which was more than he had any wish for. However, he desired his companions to alight and walk with him; but when they drew near, the master of the ceremonies in this procession came out with a garland and a rod in his hand, and met them, inquiring, where they had left Demetrius, and when he would come? Upon which Cato's companions burst out into laughter, but Cato said only, "Alas, poor city!" and passed by without any other answer. However, Pompey rendered Demetrius less odious to others by enduring his presumption and impertinence to himself. For it is reported how that Pompey, when he had invited his friends to an entertainment, would be very ceremonious in waiting, till they all came and were placed, while Demetrius would be already stretched upon the couch as if he cared for no one, with his dress over his ears, hanging down from his head. Before his return into Italy, he had purchased the pleasantest country-seat about Rome, with the finest walks and places for exercise, and there were sumptuous gardens, called by the name of Demetrius, while Pompey his master, up to his third triumph, was contented with an ordinary and simple habitation. Afterwards, it is true, when he had erected his famous and stately theater for the people of Rome, he built as a sort of appendix to it, a house for himself, much more splendid than his former, and yet no object even this to excite men's envy, since he who came to be master of it after Pompey could not but express wonder and inquire where Pompey the Great used to sup. Such is the story told us.

The king of the Arabs near Petra, who had hitherto despised the power of the Romans, now began to be in great alarm at it, and sent letters to him promising to be at his commands, and to do whatever he should see fit to order. However, Pompey having a desire to confirm and keep him in the same mind, marched forwards for Petra, an expedition not altogether irreprehensible in the opinion of many; who thought it a mere running away from their proper duty, the pursuit of Mithridates, Rome's ancient and inveterate enemy, who was now rekindling the war once more, and making preparations, it was reported, to lead his army through Scythia and Paeonia, into Italy. Pompey, on the other side, judging it easier to destroy his forces in battle, than to seize his person in flight, resolved not to tire himself out in a vain pursuit, but rather to spend his leisure upon another enemy, as a sort of digression in the meanwhile. But fortune resolved the doubt; for when he was now not far from Petra, and had pitched his tents and encamped for that day, as he was talking exercise with his horse outside the camp, couriers came riding up from Pontus, bringing good news, as was known at once by the heads of their javelins, which it is the custom to carry crowned with branches of laurel. The soldiers, as soon as they saw them, flocked immediately to Pompey, who notwithstanding was minded to finish his exercise; but when they began to be clamorous and importunate, he alighted from his horse, and taking the letters went before them into the camp. Now there being no tribunal erected there, not even that military substitute for one which they make by cutting up thick turfs of earth and piling them one upon another, they, through eagerness and impatience, heaped up a pile of pack-saddles, and Pompey standing upon that, told them the news of Mithridates's death, how that he had himself put an end to his life upon the revolt of his son Pharnaces, and that Pharnaces had taken all things there into his hands and possession, which he did, his letters said, in right of himself and the Romans. Upon this news, the whole army expressing their joy, as was to be expected, fell to sacrificing to the gods, and feasting, as if in the person of Mithridates alone there had died many thousands of their enemies.

Pompey by this event having brought this war to its completion, with much more ease than was expected, departed forthwith out of Arabia, and passing rapidly through the intermediate provinces, he came at length to the city Amisus. There he received many presents brought from Pharnaces, with several dead bodies of the royal blood, and the corpse of Mithridates himself, which was not easy to be known by the face, for the physicians that embalmed him had not dried up his brain, but those who were curious to see him knew him by the scars there. Pompey himself would not endure to see him, but to deprecate the divine jealousy, sent it away to the city of Sinope. He admired the richness of his robes, no less than the size and splendor of his armor. His swordbelt, however, which had cost four hundred talents, was stolen by Publius, and sold to Ariarathes; his tiara also, a piece of admirable workmanship, Gaius, the foster brother of Mithridates, gave secretly to Faustus, the son of Sylla, at his request. All which Pompey was ignorant of, but afterwards, when Pharnaces came to understand it, he severely punished those that embezzled them.

Pompey now having ordered all things, and established that province, took his journey homewards in greater pomp and with more festivity. For when he came to Mitylene, he gave the city their freedom upon the intercession of Theophanes, and was present at the contest, there periodically held, of the poets, who took at that time no other theme or subject than the actions of Pompey. He was extremely pleased with the theater itself, and had a model of it taken, intending to erect one in Rome on the same design, but larger and more magnificent. When he came to Rhodes, he attended the lectures of all the philosophers there, and gave to every one of them a talent. Posidonius has published the disputation which he held before him against Hermagoras the rhetorician, upon the subject of Invention in general. At Athens, also, he showed similar, munificence to the philosophers, and gave fifty talents towards the repairing and beautifying the city. So that now by all these acts he well hoped to return into Italy in the greatest splendor and glory possible to man, and find his family as desirous to see him, as he felt himself to come home to them. But that supernatural agency, whose province and charge it is always to mix some ingredient of evil with the greatest and most glorious goods of fortune, had for some time back been busy in his household, preparing him a sad welcome. For Mucia during his absence had dishonored his bed. Whilst he was abroad at a distance, he had refused all credence to the report; but when he drew nearer to Italy, where his thoughts were more at leisure to give consideration to the charge, he sent her a bill of divorce; but neither then in writing, nor afterwards by word of mouth, did he ever give a reason why he discharged her; the cause of it is mentioned in Cicero's epistles.

Rumors of every kind were scattered abroad about Pompey, and were carried to Rome before him, so that there was a great tumult and stir, as if he designed forthwith to march with his army into the city, and establish himself securely as sole ruler. Crassus withdrew himself, together with his children and property, out of the city, either that he was really afraid, or that he counterfeited rather, as is most probable, to give credit to the calumny and exasperate the jealousy of the people. Pompey, therefore, as soon as he entered Italy, called a general muster of the army; and having made a suitable address and exchanged a kind farewell with his soldiers, he commanded them to depart every man to his country and place of habitation, only taking care that they should not fail to meet again at his triumph. Thus the army being disbanded, and the news commonly reported, a wonderful result ensued. For when the cities saw Pompey the Great passing through the country unarmed, and with a small train of familiar friends only, as if he was returning from a journey of pleasure, not from his conquests, they came pouring out to display their affection for him, attending and conducting him to Rome with far greater forces than he disbanded; insomuch that if he had designed any movement or innovation in the State, he might have done it without his army.

Now, because the law permitted no commander to enter into the city before his triumph, he sent to the senate, entreating them as a favor to him to prorogue the election of consuls, that thus he might be able to attend and give countenance to Piso, one of the candidates. The request was resisted by Cato, and met with a refusal. However, Pompey could not but admire the liberty and boldness of speech which Cato alone had dared to use in the maintenance of law and justice. He therefore had a great desire to win him over, and purchase his friendship at any rate; and to that end, Cato having two nieces, Pompey asked for one in marriage for himself, the other for his son. But Cato looked unfavorably on the proposal, regarding it as a design for undermining his honesty, and in a manner bribing him by a family alliance; much to the displeasure of his wife and sister, who were indignant that he should reject a connection with Pompey the Great. About that time Pompey having a design of setting up Afranius for the consulship, gave a sum of money among the tribes for their votes, and people came and received it in his own gardens a proceeding which, when it came to be generally known, excited great disapprobation, that he should thus for the sake of men who could not obtain the honor by their own merits, make merchandise of an office which had been given to himself as the highest reward of his services. "Now," said Cato to his wife and sister, "had we contracted an alliance with Pompey, we had been allied to this dishonor too;" and this they could not but acknowledge, and allow his judgment of what was right and fitting to have been wiser and better than theirs.

The splendor and magnificence of Pompey's triumph was such that though it took up the space of two days, yet they were extremely straitened in time, so that of what was prepared for that pageantry, there was as much withdrawn as would have set out and adorned another triumph. In the first place, there were tables carried, inscribed with the names and titles of the nations over whom he triumphed, Pontus, Armenia, Cappadocia, Paphlagonia, Media, Colchis, the Iberians, the Albanians, Syria, Cilicia, and Mesopotamia, together with Phoenicia and Palestine, Judaea, Arabia, and all the power of the pirates subdued by sea and land. And in these different countries there appeared the capture of no less than one thousand fortified places, nor much less than nine hundred cities, together with eight hundred ships of the pirates, and the foundation of thirty-nine towns. Besides, there was set forth in these tables an account of all the tributes throughout the empire, and how that before these conquests the revenue amounted but to fifty millions, whereas from his acquisitions they had a revenue of eighty-five millions; and that in present payment he was bringing into the common treasury ready money, and gold and silver plate, and ornaments, to the value of twenty thousand talents, over and above what had been distributed among the soldiers, of whom he that had least had fifteen hundred drachmas for his share. The prisoners of war that were led in triumph, besides the chief pirates, were the son of Tigranes, king of Armenia, with his wife and daughter; as also Zosime, wife of king Tigranes himself, and Aristobulus, king of Judaea, the sister of king Mithridates and her five sons, and some Scythian women. There were likewise the hostages of the Albanians and Iberians, and of the king of Commagene, besides a vast number of trophies, one for every battle in which he was conqueror, either himself in person, or by his lieutenants. But that which seemed to be his greatest glory, being one which no other Roman ever attained to, was this, that he made his third triumph over the third division of the world. For others among the Romans had the honor of triumphing thrice, but his first triumph was over Africa, his second, over Europe, and this last, over Asia; so that he seemed in these three triumphs to have led the whole world captive.

As for his age, those who affect to make the parallel exact in all things betwixt him and Alexander the Great, do not allow him to have been quite thirty-four, whereas in truth at that time he was near forty. And well had it been for him had he terminated his life at this date, while he still enjoyed Alexander's fortune, since all his aftertime served only either to bring him prosperity that made him odious, or calamities too great to be retrieved. For that great authority which he had gained in the city by his merits, he made use of only in patronizing the iniquities of others, so that by advancing their fortunes, he detracted from his own glory, till at last he was overthrown even by the force and greatness of his own power. And as the strongest citadel or fort in a town, when it is taken by an enemy, does then afford the same strength to the foe, as it had done to friends before; so Caesar, after Pompey's aid had made him strong enough to defy his country, ruined and overthrew at last the power which had availed him against the rest. The course of things was as follows. Lucullus, when he returned out of Asia, where he had been treated with insult by Pompey, was received by the senate with great honor, which was yet increased when Pompey came home; to check whose ambition they encouraged him to assume the administration of the government, whereas he was now grown cold and disinclined to business, having given himself over to the pleasures of ease and the enjoyment of a splendid fortune. However, he began for the time to exert himself against Pompey, attacked him sharply, and succeeded in having his own acts and decrees, which were repealed by Pompey, reestablished, and with the assistance of Cato, gained the superiority in the senate. Pompey having fallen from his hopes in such an unworthy repulse, was forced to fly to the tribunes of the people for refuge, and to attach himself to the young men, among whom was Clodius, the vilest and most impudent wretch alive, who took him about, and exposed him as a tool to the people, carrying him up and down among the throngs in the market-place, to countenance those laws and speeches which he made to cajole the people and ingratiate himself. And at last for his reward, he demanded of Pompey, as if he had not disgraced, but done him great kindness, that he should forsake (as in the end he did forsake) Cicero, his friend, who on many public occasions had done him the greatest service. And so when Cicero was in danger, and implored his aid, he would not admit him into his presence, but shutting up his gates against those that came to mediate for him, slips out at a back door, whereupon Cicero fearing the result of his trial, departed privately from Rome.

About that time Caesar, returning from military service, started a course of policy which brought him great present favor, and much increased his power for the future, and proved extremely destructive both to Pompey and the commonwealth. For now he stood candidate for his first consulship, and well observing the enmity betwixt Pompey and Crassus, and finding that by joining with one he should make the other his enemy, he endeavored by all means to reconcile them, an object in itself honorable and tending to the public good, but as he undertook it, a mischievous and subtle intrigue. For he well knew that opposite parties or factions in a commonwealth, like passengers in a boat, serve to trim and balance the unready motions of power there; whereas if they combine and come all over to one side, they cause a shock which will be sure to overset the vessel and carry down everything. And therefore Cato wisely told those who charged all the calamities of Rome upon the disagreement betwixt Pompey and Caesar, that they were in error in charging all the crime upon the last cause; for it was not their discord and enmity, but their unanimity and I friendship, that gave the first and greatest blow to the commonwealth.

Caesar being thus elected consul, began at once to make an interest with the poor and meaner sort, by preferring and establishing laws for planting colonies and dividing lands, lowering the dignity of his office, and turning his consulship into a sort of tribuneship rather. And when Bibulus, his colleague, opposed him, and Cato was prepared to second Bibulus, and assist him vigorously, Caesar brought Pompey upon the hustings, and addressing him in the sight of the people, demanded his opinion upon the laws that were proposed. Pompey gave his approbation. "Then," said Caesar, "in case any man should offer violence to these laws, will you be reedy to give assistance to the people?" "Yes," replied Pompey, "I shall be ready, and against those that threaten the sword, I will appear with sword and buckler." Nothing ever was said or done by Pompey up to that day, that seemed more insolent or overbearing; so that his friends endeavored to apologize for it as a word spoken inadvertently; but by his actions afterwards it appeared plainly that he was totally devoted to Caesar's service. For on a sudden, contrary to all expectation, he married Julia, the daughter of Caesar, who had been affianced before and was to be married within a few days to Caepio. And to appease Caepio's wrath, he gave him his own daughter in marriage, who had been espoused before to Faustus, the son of Sylla. Caesar himself married Calpurnia, the daughter of Piso.

Upon this Pompey, filling the city with soldiers, carried all things by force as he pleased. As Bibulus, the consul, was going to the forum, accompanied by Lucullus and Cato, they fell upon him on a sudden and broke his rods; and somebody threw a vessel of ordure upon the head of Bibulus himself; and two tribunes of the people, who escorted him, were desperately wounded in the fray. And thus having cleared the forum of all their adversaries, they got their bill for the division of lands established and passed into an act; and not only so, but the whole populace being taken with this bait, became totally at their devotion, inquiring into nothing and without a word giving their suffrages to whatever they propounded. Thus they confirmed all those acts and decrees of Pompey, which were questioned and contested by Lucullus; and to Caesar they granted the provinces of Gaul, both within and without the Alps, together with Illyricum, for five years, and likewise an army of four entire legions; then they created consuls for the year ensuing, Piso, the father-in-law of Caesar, and Gabinius, the most extravagant of Pompey's flatterers.

During all these transactions, Bibulus kept close within doors, nor did he appear publicly in person for the space of eight months together, notwithstanding he was consul, but sent out proclamations full of bitter invectives and accusations against them both. Cato turned prophet, and, as if he had been possessed with a spirit of divination, did nothing else in the senate but foretell what evils should befall the Commonwealth and Pompey. Lucullus pleaded old age, and retired to take his ease, as superannuated for affairs of State; which gave occasion to the saying of Pompey, that the fatigues of luxury were not more seasonable for an old man than those of government. Which in truth proved a reflection upon himself; for he not long after let his fondness for his young wife seduce him also into effeminate habits. He gave all his time to her, and passed his days in her company in country-houses and gardens, paying no heed to what was going on in the forum. Insomuch that Clodius, who was then tribune of the people, began to despise him, and engage in the most audacious attempts. For when he had banished Cicero, and sent away Cato into Cyprus under pretence of military duty, and when Caesar was gone upon his expedition to Gaul, finding the populace now looking to him as the leader who did everything according to their pleasure, he attempted forthwith to repeal some of Pompey's decrees; he took Tigranes, the captive, out of prison, and kept him about him as his companion; and commenced actions against several of Pompey's friends, thus designing to try the extent of his power. At last, upon a time when Pompey was present at the hearing of a certain cause, Clodius, accompanied with a crowd of profligate and impudent ruffians, standing up in a place above the rest, put questions to the populace as follows: "Who is the dissolute general? who is the man that seeks another man? who scratches his head with one finger?" and the rabble, upon the signal of his shaking his gown, with a great shout to every question, like singers making, responses in a chorus, made answer, "Pompey."

This indeed was no small annoyance to Pompey, who was quite unaccustomed to hear anything ill of himself, and unexperienced altogether in such encounters; and he was yet more vexed, when he saw that the senate rejoiced at this foul usage, and regarded it as a just punishment upon him for his treachery to Cicero. But when it came even to blows and wounds in the forum, and that one of Clodius's bondslaves was apprehended, creeping through the crowd towards Pompey with a sword in his hand, Pompey laid hold of this pretence, though perhaps otherwise apprehensive of Clodius's insolence and bad language, and never appeared again in the forum during all the time he was tribune, but kept close at home, and passed his time in consulting with his friends, by what means he might best allay the displeasure of the senate and nobles against him. Among other expedients, Culleo advised the divorce of Julia, and to abandon Caesar's friendship to gain that of the senate; this he would not hearken to. Others again advised him to call home Cicero from banishment, a man who was always the great adversary of Clodius, and as great a favorite of the senate; to this he was easily persuaded. And therefore he brought Cicero's brother into the forum, attended with a strong party, to petition for his return; where, after a warm dispute, in which several were wounded and some slain, he got the victory over Clodius. No sooner was Cicero returned home upon this decree, but immediately he used his efforts to reconcile the senate to Pompey; and by speaking in favor of the law upon the importation of corn, did again, in effect, make Pompey sovereign lord of all the Roman possessions by sea and land. For by that law, there were placed under his control all ports, markets, and storehouses, and in short, all the concerns both of the merchants and the husbandmen; which gave occasion to the charge brought against it by Clodius, that the law was not made because of the scarcity of corn, but the scarcity of corn was made, that they might pass a law, whereby that power of his, which was now grown feeble and consumptive, might be revived again, and Pompey reinstated in a new empire. Others look upon it as a politic device of Spinther, the consul, whose design it was to secure Pompey in a greater authority, that he himself might be sent in assistance to king Ptolemy. However, it is certain that Canidius, the tribune, preferred a law to dispatch Pompey in the character of an ambassador, without an army, attended only with two lictors, as a mediator betwixt the king and his subjects of Alexandria. Neither did this proposal seem unacceptable to Pompey, though the senate cast it out upon the specious pretence, that they were unwilling to hazard his person. However, there were found several writings scattered about the forum and near the senate-house, intimating how grateful it would be to Ptolemy to have Pompey appointed for his general instead of Spinther. And Timagenes even asserts that Ptolemy went away and left Egypt, not out of necessity, but purely upon the persuasion of Theophanes, who was anxious to give Pompey the opportunity for holding a new command, and gaining further wealth. But Theophanes's want of honesty does not go so far to make this story credible as does Pompey's own nature, which was averse, with all its ambition, to such base and disingenuous acts, to render it improbable.

 Thus Pompey being appointed chief purveyor, and having within his administration and management all the corn trade, sent abroad his factors and agents into all quarters, and he himself sailing into Sicily, Sardinia, and Africa, collected vast stores of corn. He was just ready to set sail upon his voyage home, when a great storm arose upon the sea, and the ships' commanders doubted whether it were safe. Upon which Pompey himself went first aboard, and bid the mariners weigh anchor, declaring with a loud voice, that there was a necessity to sail, but no necessity to live. So that with this spirit and courage, and having met with favorable fortune, he made a prosperous return, and filled the markets with corn, and the sea with ships. So much so that this great plenty and abundance of provisions yielded a sufficient supply, not only to the city of Rome, but even to other places too, dispersing itself; like waters from a spring, into all quarters.

 Meantime Caesar grew great and famous with his wars in Gaul, and while in appearance he seemed far distant from Rome, entangled in the affairs of the Belgians, Suevians, and Britons, in truth he was working craftily by secret practices in the midst of the people, and countermining Pompey in all political matters of most importance. He himself with his army close about him, as if it had been his own body, not with mere views of conquest over the barbarians, but as though his contests with them were but mere sports and exercises of the chase, did his utmost with this training and discipline to make it invincible and alarming. And in the meantime his gold and silver and other spoils and treasure which he took from the enemy in his conquests, he sent to Rome in presents, tempting people with his gifts, and aiding aediles, praetors, and consuls, as also their wives, in their expenses, and thus purchasing himself numerous friends. Insomuch, that when he passed back again over the Alps, and took up his winter quarters in the city of Luca, there flocked to him an infinite number of men and women, striving who should get first to him, two hundred senators included, among whom were Pompey and Crassus; so that there were to be seen at once before Caesar's door no less than six score rods of proconsuls and praetors. The rest of his addressers he sent all away full fraught with hopes and money; but with Crassus and Pompey, he entered into special articles of agreement, that they should stand candidates for the consulship next year; that Caesar on his part should send a number of his soldiers to give their votes at the election; that as soon as they were elected, they should use their interest to have the command of some provinces and legions assigned to themselves, and that Caesar should have his present charge confirmed to him for five years more. When these arrangements came to be generally known, great indignation was excited among the chief men in Rome; and Marcellinus, in an open assembly of the people, demanded of them both, whether they designed to sue for the consulship or no. And being urged by the people for their answer, Pompey spoke first, and told them, perhaps he would sue for it, perhaps he would not. Crassus was more temperate, and said, that he would do what should be judged most agreeable with the interest of the Commonwealth; and when Marcellinus persisted in his attack on Pompey, and spoke, as it was thought, with some vehemence, Pompey remarked that Marcellinus was certainly the unfairest of men, to show him no gratitude for having thus made him an orator out of a mute, and converted him from a hungry starveling into a man so full-fed that he could not contain himself.

Most of the candidates nevertheless abandoned their canvass for the consulship; Cato alone persuaded and encouraged Lucius Domitius not to desist, "since," said he, "the contest now is not for office, but for liberty against tyrants and usurpers." Therefore those of Pompey's party, fearing this inflexible constancy in Cato, by which he kept with him the whole senate, lest by this he should likewise pervert and draw after him all the well-affected part of the commonalty, resolved to withstand Domitius at once, and to prevent his entrance into the forum. To this end, therefore, they sent in a band of armed men, who slew the torchbearer of Domitius, as he was leading the way before him, and put all the rest to flight; last of all, Cato himself retired, having received a wound in his right arm while defending Domitius. Thus by these means and practices they obtained the consulship; neither did they behave themselves with more decency in their further proceedings; but in the first place, when the people were choosing Cato praetor, and just ready with their votes for the poll, Pompey broke up the assembly, upon a pretext of some inauspicious appearance, and having gained the tribes by money, they publicly proclaimed Vatinius praetor. Then, in pursuance of their covenants with Caesar, they introduced several laws by Trebonius, the tribune, continuing Caesar's commission to another five years' charge of his province; to Crassus there were appointed Syria, and the Parthian war; and to Pompey himself, all Africa, together with both Spains, and four legions of soldiers, two of which he lent to Caesar upon his request, for the wars in Gaul.

Crassus, upon the expiration of his consulship, departed forthwith into his province; but Pompey spent some time in Rome, upon the opening or dedication of his theater, where he treated the people with all sorts of games, shows, and exercises, in gymnastics alike and in music. There was likewise the hunting or baiting of wild beasts, and combats with them, in which five hundred lions were slain; but above all, the battle of elephants was a spectacle full of horror and amazement.

These entertainments brought him great honor and popularity; but on the other side he created no less envy to himself, in that he committed the government of his provinces and legions into the hands of friends as his lieutenants, whilst he himself was going about and spending his time with his wife in all the places of amusement in Italy; whether it were he was so fond of her himself, or she so fond of him, and he unable to distress her by going away, for this also is stated. And the love displayed by this young wife for her elderly husband was a matter of general note, to be attributed, it would seem, to his constancy in married life, and to his dignity of manner, which in familiar intercourse was tempered with grace and gentleness, and was particularly attractive to women, as even Flora, the courtesan, may be thought good enough evidence to prove. It once happened in a public assembly, as they were at an election of the aediles, that the people came to blows, and several about Pompey were slain, so that he, finding himself all bloody, ordered a change of apparel; but the servants who brought home his clothes, making a great bustle and hurry about the house, it chanced that the young lady, who was then with child, saw his gown all stained with blood; upon which she dropped immediately into a swoon, and was hardly brought to life again; however, what with her fright and suffering, she fell into labor and miscarried; even those who chiefly censured Pompey for his friendship to Caesar, could not reprove him for his affection to so attached a wife. Afterwards she was great again, and brought to bed of a daughter, but died in childbed; neither did the infant outlive her mother many days. Pompey had prepared all things for the interment of her corpse at his house near Alba, but the people seized upon it by force, and performed the solemnities in the field of Mars, rather in compassion for the young lady, than in favor either for Pompey or Caesar; and yet of these two, the people seemed at that time to pay Caesar a greater share of honor in his absence, than to Pompey, though he was present.

For the city now at once began to roll and swell, so to say, with the stir of the coming storm. Things everywhere were in a state of agitation, and everybody's discourse tended to division, now that death had put an end to that relation which hitherto had been a disguise rather than restraint to the ambition of these men. Besides, not long after came messengers from Parthia with intelligence of the death of Crassus there, by which another safeguard against civil war was removed, since both Caesar and Pompey kept their eyes on Crassus, and awe of him held them together more or less within the bounds of fair-dealing all his lifetime. But when fortune had taken away this second, whose province it might have been to revenge the quarrel of the conquered, you might then say with the comic poet,

> *The combatants are waiting to begin,*
> *Smearing their hands with dust and oiling each his skin.*

So inconsiderable a thing is fortune in respect of human nature, and so insufficient to give content to a covetous mind, that an empire of that mighty extent and sway could not satisfy the ambition of two men; and though they knew and had read, that

> *The gods, when they divided out 'twixt three,*
> *This massive universe, heaven, hell, and sea,*
> *Each one sat down contented on his throne*
> *And undisturbed each god enjoys his own,*

yet they thought the whole Roman empire not sufficient to contain them, though they were but two.

Pompey once in an oration to the people, told them, that he had always come into office before he expected he should, and that he had always left it sooner than they expected he would; and, indeed, the disbanding of all his armies witnessed as much. Yet when he perceived that Caesar would not so willingly discharge his forces, he endeavored to strengthen himself against him by offices and commands in the city; but beyond this he showed no desire for any change, and would not seem to distrust, but rather to disregard and contemn him. And when he saw how they bestowed the places of government quite contrary to his wishes, because the citizens were bribed in their elections, he let things take their course, and allowed the city to be left without any government at all. Hereupon there was mention straightaway made of appointing a dictator. Lucilius, a tribune of the people, was the man who first adventured to propose it, urging the people to make Pompey dictator. But the tribune was in danger of being turned out of his office, by the opposition that Cato made against it. And for Pompey, many of his friends appeared and excused him, alleging that he never was desirous of that government, neither would he accept of it. And when Cato therefore made a speech in commendation of Pompey, and exhorted him to support the cause of good order in the Commonwealth, he could not for shame but yield to it, and so for the present Domitius and Messala were elected consuls. But shortly afterwards, when there was another anarchy, or vacancy in the government, and the talk of a dictator was much louder and more general than before, those of Cato's party, fearing lest they should be forced to appoint Pompey, thought it policy to keep him from that arbitrary and tyrannical power, by giving him an office of more legal authority. Bibulus himself, who was Pompey's enemy, first gave his vote in the senate, that Pompey should be created consul alone; alleging, that by these means either the Commonwealth would be freed from its present confusion, or that its bondage should be lessened by serving the worthiest. This was looked upon as a very strange opinion, considering the man that spoke it; and therefore on Cato's standing up, everybody expected that he would have opposed it; but after silence made, he said that he would never have been the author of that advice himself, but since it was propounded by another, his advice was to follow it, adding, that any form of government was better than none at all; and that in a time so full of distraction, he thought no man fitter to govern than Pompey. This counsel was unanimously approved of, and a decree passed that Pompey should be made sole consul, with this clause, that if he thought it necessary to have a colleague, he might choose whom he pleased, provided it were not till after two months expired.

Thus was Pompey created and declared sole consul by Sulpicius, regent in this vacancy; upon which he made very cordial acknowledgments to Cato, professing himself much his debtor, and requesting his good advice in conducting the government; to this Cato replied, that Pompey had no reason to thank him, for all that he had said was for the service of the commonwealth, not of Pompey; but that he would be always ready to give his advice privately, if he were asked for it; and if not, he should not fail to say what he thought in public. Such was Cato's conduct on all occasions.

On his return into the city Pompey married Cornelia, the daughter of Metellus Scipio, not a maiden, but lately left a widow by Publius, the son of Crassus, her first husband, who had been killed in Parthia. The young lady had other attractions besides those of youth and beauty; for she was highly educated, played well upon the lute, understood geometry, and had been accustomed to listen with profit to lectures on philosophy; all this, too, without in any degree becoming unamiable or pretentious, as sometimes young women do when they pursue such studies. Nor could any fault be found either with her father's family or reputation. The disparity of their ages was however not liked by everybody; Cornelia being in this respect a fitter match for Pompey's son. And wiser judges thought it rather a slight upon the commonwealth when he, to whom alone they had committed their broken fortunes, and from whom alone, as from their physician, they expected a cure to these distractions, went about crowned with garlands and celebrating his nuptial feasts; never considering, that his very consulship was a public calamity, which would never have been given him, contrary to the rules of law, had his country been in a flourishing state. Afterwards, however, he took cognizance of the cases of those that had obtained offices by gifts and bribery, and enacted laws and ordinances, setting forth the rules of judgment by which they should be arraigned; and regulating all things with gravity and justice, he restored security, order, and silence to their courts of judicature, himself giving his presence there with a band of soldiers. But when his father-in-law Scipio was accused, he sent for the three hundred and sixty judges to his house, and entreated them to be favorable to him; whereupon his accuser, seeing Scipio come into the court, accompanied by the judges themselves, withdrew the prosecution. Upon this Pompey was very ill spoken of, and much worse in the case of Plancus; for whereas he himself had made a law, putting a stop to the practice of making speeches in praise of persons under trial, yet notwithstanding this prohibition, he came into court, and spoke openly in commendation of Plancus, insomuch that Cato, who happened to be one of the judges at that time, stopping his ears with his hands, told him, he could not in conscience listen to commendations contrary to law. Cato upon this was refused, and set aside from being a judge, before sentence was given, but Plancus was condemned by the rest of the judges, to Pompey's dishonor. Shortly after, Hypsaeus, a man of consular dignity, who was under accusation, waited for Pompey's return from his bath to his supper, and falling down at his feet, implored his favor; but he disdainfully passed him by, saying, that he did nothing else but spoil his supper. Such partiality was looked upon as a great fault in Pompey, and highly condemned; however, he managed all things else discreetly, and having put the government in very good order, he chose his father-in-law to be his colleague in the consulship for the last five months. His provinces were continued to him for the term of four years longer, with a commission to take one thousand talents yearly out of the treasury for the payment of his army.

This gave occasion to some of Caesar's friends to think it reasonable, that some consideration should be had of him too, who had done such signal services in war, and fought so many battles for the empire, alleging, that he deserved at least a second consulship, or to have the government of his province continued, that so he might command and enjoy in peace what he had obtained in war, and no successor come in to reap the fruits of his labor, and carry off the glory of his actions. There arising some debate about this matter, Pompey took upon him, as it were out of kindness to Caesar, to plead his cause, and allay any jealousy that was conceived against him, telling them, that he had letters from Caesar, expressing his desire for a successor, and his own discharge from the command; but it would be only right that they should give him leave to stand for the consulship though in his absence. But those of Cato's party withstood this, saying, that if he expected any favor from the citizens, he ought to leave his army, and come in a private capacity to canvas for it. And Pompey's making no rejoinder, but letting it pass as a matter in which he was overruled, increased the suspicion of his real feelings towards Caesar. Presently, also, under presence of a war with Parthia, he sent for his two legions which he had lent him. However, Caesar, though he well knew why they were asked for, sent them home very liberally rewarded.

About that time Pompey recovered of a dangerous fit of sickness which seized him at Naples, where the whole city, upon the suggestion of Praxagoras, made sacrifices of thanksgiving to the gods for his recovery. The neighboring towns likewise happening to follow their example, the thing then went its course throughout all Italy, so that there was not a city either great or small, that did not feast and rejoice for many days together. And the company of those that came from all parts to meet him was so numerous, that no place was able to contain them, but the villages, seaport towns, and the very highways, were all full of people, feasting and sacrificing to the gods. Nay, many went to meet him with garlands on their heads, and flambeaux in their hands, casting flowers and nosegays upon him as he went along; so that this progress of his, and reception, was one of the noblest and most glorious sights imaginable. And yet it is thought that this very thing was not one of the least causes and occasions of the civil war. For Pompey, yielding to a feeling of exultation, which in the greatness of the present display of joy lost sight of more solid grounds of consideration, and abandoning that prudent temper which had guided him hitherto to a safe use of all his good fortune and his successes, gave himself up to an extravagant confidence in his own, and contempt of Caesar's power; insomuch that he thought neither force of arms nor care necessary against him, but that he could pull him down much easier than he had set him up. Besides this, Appius, under whose command those legions which Pompey lent to Caesar were returned, coming lately out of Gaul, spoke slightingly of Caesar's actions there, and spread scandalous reports about him, at the same time telling Pompey, that he was unacquainted with his own strength and reputation, if he made use of any other forces against Caesar than Caesar's own; for such was the soldiers' hatred to Caesar, and their love to Pompey so great, that they would all come over to him upon his first appearance. By these flatteries Pompey was so puffed up, and led on into such a careless security, that he could not choose but laugh at those who seemed to fear a war; and when some were saying, that if Caesar should march against the city, they could not see what forces there were to resist him, he replied with a smile, bidding them be in no concern, "for," said he, "whenever I stamp with my foot in any part of Italy, there will rise up forces enough in an instant, both horse and foot."

Caesar, on the other side, was more and more vigorous in his proceedings, himself always at hand about the frontiers of Italy, and sending his soldiers continually into the city to attend all elections with their votes. Besides, he corrupted several of the magistrates, and kept them in his pay; among others, Paulus, the consul, who was brought over by a bribe of one thousand and five hundred talents; and Curio, tribune of the people, by a discharge of the debts with which he was overwhelmed; together with Mark Antony, who, out of friendship to Curio, had become bound with him in the same obligations for them all. And it was stated as a fact, that a centurion of Caesar's waiting at the senate-house, and hearing that the senate refused to give him a longer term of his government, clapped his hand upon his sword, and said, "But this shall give it." And indeed all his practices and preparations seemed to bear this appearance. Curio's demands, however, and requests in favor of Caesar, were more popular in appearance; for he desired one of these two things, either that Pompey also should be called upon to resign his army, or that Caesar's should not be taken away from him; for if both of them became private persons, both would be satisfied with simple justice; or if both retained their present power, each being a match for the other, they would be contented with what they already had; but he that weakens one, does at the same time strengthen the other, and so doubles that very strength and power which he stood in fear of before. Marcellus, the consul, replied nothing to all this, but that Caesar was a robber, and should be proclaimed an enemy to the state, if he did not disband his army. However, Curio, with the assistance of Antony and Piso, prevailed, that the matter in debate should be put to the question, and decided by vote in the senate. So that it being ordered upon the question for those to withdraw, who were of opinion that Caesar only should lay down his army and Pompey command, the majority withdrew. But when it was ordered again for those to withdraw, whose vote was that both should lay down their arms and neither command, there were but twenty-two for Pompey, all the rest remained on Curio's side. Whereupon he, as one proud of his conquest, leaped out in triumph among the people, who received him with as great tokens of joy, clapping their hands, and crowning him with garlands and flowers. Pompey was not then present in the senate, because it is not lawful for generals in command of an army to come into the city. But Marcellus rising up, said, that he would not sit there hearing speeches, when he saw ten legions already passing the Alps on their march toward the city, but on his own authority would send someone to oppose them in defense of the country.

Upon this the city went into mourning, as in a public calamity, and Marcellus, accompanied by the senate, went solemnly through the forum to meet Pompey, and made him this address. "I hereby give you orders, O Pompey, to defend your country, to employ the troops you now command, and to levy more." Lentulus, consul elect for the year following, spoke to the same purpose. Antony, however, contrary to the will of the senate, having in a public assembly read a letter of Caesar's, containing various plausible overtures such as were likely to gain the common people, proposing, namely, that both Pompey and he quitting their governments, and dismissing their armies, should submit to the judgment of the people, and give an account of their actions before them, the consequence was that when Pompey began to make his levies, he found himself disappointed in his expectations. Some few, indeed, came in, but those very unwillingly; others would not answer to their names, and the generality cried out for peace. Lentulus, notwithstanding he was now entered upon his consulship, would not assemble the senate; but Cicero, who was lately returned from Cilicia, labored for a reconciliation, proposing that Caesar should leave his province of Gaul and army, reserving two legions only, together with the government of Illyricum, and should thus be put in nomination for a second consulship. Pompey disliking this motion, Caesar's friends were contented that he should surrender one of the two; but Lentulus still opposing, and Cato crying out that Pompey did ill to be deceived again, the reconciliation did not take effect.

In the meantime, news was brought that Caesar had occupied Ariminum, a great city in Italy, and was marching directly towards Rome with all his forces. But this latter was altogether false, for he had no more with him at that time than three hundred horse and five thousand foot; and he did not mean to tarry for the body of his army, which lay beyond the Alps, choosing rather to fall in on a sudden upon his enemies, while they were in confusion, and did not expect him, than to give them time, and fight them after they had made preparations. For when he came to the banks of the Rubicon, a river that made the bounds of his province, there he made a halt, pausing a little, and considering, we may suppose, with himself the greatness of the enterprise which he had undertaken; then, at last, like men that are throwing themselves headlong from some precipice into a vast abyss, having shut, as it were, his mind's eyes and put away from his sight the idea of danger, he merely uttered to those near him in Greek the words, "Anerriphtho kubos," (let the die be cast,) and led his army through it. No sooner was the news arrived, but there was an uproar throughout all the city, and a consternation in the people even to astonishment, such as never was known in Rome before; all the senate ran immediately to Pompey, and the magistrates followed. And when Tullus made inquiry about his legions and forces, Pompey seemed to pause a little, and answered with some hesitation, that he had those two legions ready that Caesar sent back, and that out of the men who had been previously enrolled he believed he could shortly make up a body of thirty thousand men. On which Tullus crying out aloud, "O Pompey, you have deceived us," gave his advice to send off a deputation to Caesar. Favonius, a man of fair character, except that he used to suppose his own petulance and abusive talking a copy of Cato's straightforwardness, bade Pompey stamp upon the ground, and call forth the forces he had promised. But Pompey bore patiently with this unseasonable raillery; and on Cato putting him in mind of what he had foretold from the very beginning about Caesar, made this answer only, that Cato indeed had spoken more like a prophet, but he had acted more like a friend. Cato then advised them to choose Pompey general with absolute power and authority, saying that the same men who do great evils, know best how to cure them. He himself went his way forthwith into Sicily, the province that was allotted him, and all the rest of the senators likewise departed every one to his respective government.

Thus all Italy in a manner being up in arms, no one could say what was best to be done. For those that were without, came from all parts flocking into the city; and they who were within, seeing the confusion and disorder so great there, all good things impotent, and disobedience and insubordination grown too strong to be controlled by the magistrates, were quitting it as fast as the others came in. Nay, it was so far from being possible to allay their fears, that they would not suffer Pompey to follow out his own judgment, but every man pressed and urged him according to his particular fancy, whether it proceeded from doubt, fear, grief, or any meaner passion; so that even in the same day quite contrary counsels were acted upon. Then, again, it was as impossible to have any good intelligence of the enemy; for what each man heard by chance upon a flying rumor, he would report for truth, and exclaim against Pompey if he did not believe it. Pompey, at length, seeing such a confusion in Rome, determined with himself to put an end to their clamors by his departure, and therefore commanding all the senate to follow him, and declaring, that whosoever tarried behind, should be judged a confederate of Caesar's, about the dusk of the evening he went out and left the city. The consuls also followed after in a hurry, without offering the sacrifices to the gods, usual before a war. But in all this, Pompey himself had the glory, that in the midst of such calamities, he had so much of men's love and good-will. For though many found fault with the conduct of the war, yet no man hated the general; and there were more to be found of those that went out of Rome, because that they could not forsake Pompey, than of those that fled for love of liberty.

Some few days after Pompey was gone out, Caesar came into the city, and made himself master of it, treating everyone with a great deal of courtesy, and appeasing their fears, except only Metellus, one of the tribunes; on whose refusing to let him take any money out of the treasury, Caesar threatened him with death, adding words yet harsher than the threat, that it was far easier for him to do it than say it. By this means removing Metellus, and taking what moneys were of use for his occasions, he set forwards in pursuit of Pompey, endeavoring with all speed to drive him out of Italy before his army, that was in Spain, could join him.

But Pompey arriving at Brundusium, and having plenty of ships there, bade the two consuls embark immediately, and with them shipped thirty cohorts of foot, bound before him for Dyrrhachium. He sent likewise his father-in-law Scipio, and Cnaeus his son, into Syria, to provide and fit out a fleet there; himself in the meantime having blocked up the gates, placed his lightest soldiers as guards upon the walls; and giving express orders that the citizens should keep within doors, he dug up all the ground inside the city, cutting trenches, and fixing stakes and palisades throughout all the streets of the city, except only two that led down to the sea-side. Thus in three days space having with ease put all the rest of his army on shipboard, he suddenly gave the signal to those that guarded the walls, who nimbly repairing to the ships, were received on board and carried off. Caesar meantime perceiving their departure by seeing the walls unguarded, hastened after, and in the heat of pursuit was all but entangled himself among the stakes and trenches. But the Brundusians discovering the danger to him, and showing him the way, he wheeled about, and taking a circuit round the city, made towards the haven, where he found all the ships on their way, excepting only two vessels that had but a few soldiers aboard.

Most are of opinion, that this departure of Pompey's is to be counted among the best of his military performances, but Caesar himself could not but wonder that he, who was thus ingarrisoned in a city well fortified, who was in expectation of his forces from Spain, and was master of the sea besides, should leave and abandon Italy. Cicero accuses him of imitating the conduct of Themistocles, rather than of Pericles, when the circumstances were more like those of Pericles than they were like those of Themistocles. However, it appeared plainly, and Caesar showed it by his actions, that he was in great fear of delay, for when he had taken Numerius, a friend of Pompey's, prisoner, he sent him as an ambassador to Brundusium, with offers of peace and reconciliation upon equal terms; but Numerius sailed away with Pompey. And now Caesar having become master of all Italy in sixty days, without a drop of blood shed, had a great desire forthwith to follow Pompey; but being destitute of shipping, he was forced to divert his course, and march into Spain, designing to bring over Pompey's forces there to his own.

In the meantime Pompey raised a mighty army both by sea and land. As for his navy, it was irresistible. For there were five hundred men of war, besides an infinite company of light vessels, Liburnians, and others; and for his land forces, the cavalry made up a body of seven thousand horse, the very flower of Rome and Italy, men of family, wealth, and high spirit; but the infantry was a mixture of unexperienced soldiers drawn from different quarters, and these he exercised and trained near Beroea, where he quartered his army; himself noways slothful, but performing all his exercises as if he had been in the flower of his youth, conduct which raised the spirits of his soldiers extremely. For it was no small encouragement for them to see Pompey the Great, sixty years of age wanting two, at one time handling his arms among the foot, then again mounted among the horse, drawing out his sword with ease in full career, and sheathing it up as easily; and in darting the javelin, showing not only skill and dexterity in hitting the mark, but also strength and activity in throwing it so far that few of the young men went beyond him.

Several kings and princes of nations came thither to him, and there was a concourse of Roman citizens who had held the magistracies, so numerous that they made up a complete senate. Labienus forsook his old friend Caesar, whom he had served throughout all his wars in Gaul, and came over to Pompey; and Brutus, son to that Brutus that was put to death in Gaul, a man of a high spirit, and one that to that day had never so much as saluted or spoke to Pompey, looking upon him as the murderer of his father, came then and submitted himself to him as the defender of their liberty. Cicero likewise, though he had written and advised otherwise, yet was ashamed not to be accounted in the number of those that would hazard their lives and fortunes for the safeguard of their country. There came to him also into Macedonia, Tidius Sextius, a man extremely old, and lame of one leg; so that others indeed mocked and laughed at the spectacle, but Pompey, as soon as he saw him, rose and ran to meet him, esteeming it no small testimony in his favor, when men of such age and infirmities should rather choose to be with him in danger, than in safety at home. Afterwards in a meeting of their senate they passed a decree, on the motion of Cato, that no Roman citizen should be put to death but in battle, and that they should not sack or plunder any city that was subject to the Roman empire, a resolution which gained Pompey's party still greater reputation, insomuch that those who were noways at all concerned in the war, either because they dwelt afar off, or were thought incapable of giving help, were yet, in their good wishes, upon his side, and in all their words, so far as that went, supported the good or just cause, as they called it; esteeming those as enemies to the gods and men, that wished not victory to Pompey.

Neither was Pompey's clemency such, but that Caesar likewise showed himself as merciful a conqueror; for when he had taken and overthrown all

Pompey's forces in Spain, he gave them easy terms, leaving the commanders at their liberty, and taking the common soldiers into his own pay. Then repassing the Alps, and making a running march through Italy, he came to Brundusium about the winter solstice, and crossing the sea there, landed at the port of Oricum. And having Jubius, an intimate friend of Pompey's, with him as his prisoner, he dispatched him to Pompey with an invitation, that they, meeting together in a conference, should disband both their armies within three days, and renewing their former friendship with solemn oaths, should return together into Italy. Pompey looked upon this again as some new stratagem, and therefore marching down in all haste to the sea-coast, possessed himself of all forts and places of strength suitable to encamp in, and to secure his laud forces, as likewise of all ports and harbors commodious to receive any that came by sea, so that what wind soever blew, it must needs in some way or other be favorable to him, bringing in either provision, men, or money; while Caesar, on the contrary, was so hemmed in both by sea and land, that he was forced to desire battle, daily provoking the enemy, and assailing them in their very forts; and in these light skirmishes for the most part had the better. Once only he was dangerously overthrown, and was within a little of losing his whole army, Pompey having fought nobly, routing the whole force, and killing two thousand on the spot. But either he was not able, or was afraid, to go on and force his way into their camp with them, so that Caesar made the remark, that "Today the victory had been the enemy's, had there been anyone among them to gain it." Pompey's soldiers were so encouraged by this victory that they were eager now to have all put to the decision of a battle; but Pompey himself, though he wrote to distant kings, generals, and states in confederacy with him, as a conqueror, yet was afraid to hazard the success of a battle, choosing rather by delays, and distress of provisions, to tire out a body of men, who had never yet been conquered by force of arms, and had long been used to fight and conquer together; while their time of life, now an advanced one, which made them quickly weary of those other hardships of war, such as were long marches, and frequent decampings, making trenches, and building fortifications, made them eager to come to close combat and venture a battle with all speed.

Pompey had all along hitherto by his persuasions pretty well quieted his soldiers; but after this last engagement, when Caesar for want of provisions was forced to raise his camp, and passed through Athamania into Thessaly, it was impossible to curb or allay the heat of their spirits any longer. For all crying out with a general voice, that Caesar was fled, some were for pursuing and pressing upon him, others for returning into Italy; some there were that sent their friends and servants beforehand to Rome, to hire houses near the forum, that they might be in readiness to sue for offices; several of their own motion sailed off at once to Lesbos to carry to Cornelia, (whom Pompey had conveyed thither to be in safety,) the joyful news, that the war was ended. And a senate being called, and the matter being under debate, Afranius was of opinion, that Italy should first be regained, for that it was the grand prize and crown of all the war; and they who were masters of that, would quickly have at their devotion all the provinces of Sicily, Sardinia, Corsica, Spain, and Gaul; but what was of greatest weight and moment to Pompey, it was his own native country that lay near, reaching out her hand for his help; and certainly it could not be consistent with his honor to leave her thus exposed to all indignities, and in bondage under slaves and the flatterers of a tyrant. But Pompey himself, on the contrary, thought it neither honorable to fly a second time before Caesar, and be pursued, when fortune had given him the advantage of a pursuit; nor indeed lawful before the gods to forsake Scipio and divers other men of consular dignity dispersed throughout Greece and Thessaly, who must necessarily fall into Caesar's hands, together with large sums of money and numerous forces; and as to his care for the city of Rome, that would most eminently appear, by removing the scene of war to a greater distance, and leaving her, without feeling the distress or even hearing the sound of these evils, to await in peace the return of whichever should be the victor.

With this determination, Pompey marched forwards in pursuit of Caesar, firmly resolved with himself not to give him battle, but rather to besiege and distress him, by keeping close at his heels, and cutting him short. There were other reasons that made him continue this resolution, but especially because a saying that was current among the Romans serving in the cavalry came to his ear, to the effect, that they ought to beat Caesar as soon as possible, and then humble Pompey too. And some report, it was for this reason that Pompey never employed Cato in any matter of consequence during the whole war, but now when he pursued Caesar, left him to guard his baggage by sea, fearing lest, if Caesar should be taken off, he himself also by Cato's means not long after should be forced to give up his power.

Whilst he was thus slowly attending the motions of the enemy, he was exposed on all sides to outcries, and imputations of using his generalship to defeat, not Caesar, but his country and the senate, that he might always continue in authority, and never cease to keep those for his guards and servants, who themselves claimed to govern the world. Domitius Aenobarbus, continually calling him Agamemnon, and king of kings, excited jealousy against him; and Favonius, by his unseasonable raillery, did him no less injury than those who openly attacked him, as when he cried out, "Good friends, you must not expect to gather any figs in Tusculum this year." But Lucius Afranius, who had lain under an imputation of treachery for the loss of the army in Spain, when he saw Pompey purposely declining an engagement, declared openly, that he could not but admire, why those who were so ready to accuse him, did not go themselves and fight this buyer and seller of their provinces.

With these and many such speeches they wrought upon Pompey, who never could bear reproach, or resist the expectations of his friends; and thus they forced him to break his measures, so that he forsook his own prudent resolution to follow their vain hopes and desires: weakness that would have been blamable ill the pilot of a ship, how much more in the sovereign commander of such an army, and so many nations. But he, though he had often commended those physicians who did not comply with the capricious appetites of their patients, yet himself could not but yield to the malady and disease of his companions and advisers in the war, rather than use some severity in their cure. Truly who could have said that health was not disordered and a cure not required in the case of men who went up and down the camp, suing already for the consulship and office of praetor, while Spinther, Domitius, and Scipio made friends, raised factions, and quarrelled among themselves, who should succeed Caesar in the dignity of his high-priesthood, esteeming all as lightly, as if they were to engage only with Tigranes, king of Armenia, or some petty Nabathaean king, not with that Caesar and his army that had stormed a thousand towns, and subdued more than three hundred several nations; that had fought innumerable battles with the Germans and Gauls, and always carried the victory; that had taken a million of men prisoners, and slain as many upon the spot in pitched battles?

But they went on soliciting and clamoring, and on reaching the plain of Pharsalia, they forced Pompey by their pressure and importunities to call a council of war, where Labienus, general of the horse, stood up first and swore that he would not return out of the battle if he did not rout the enemies; and all the rest took the same oath. That night Pompey dreamed that as he went into the theater, the people received him with great applause, and that he himself adorned the temple of Venus the Victorious, with many spoils. This vision partly encouraged, but partly also disheartened him, fearing lest that splendor and ornament to Venus should be made with spoils furnished by himself to Caesar, who derived his family from that goddess. Besides there were some panic fears and alarms that ran through the camp, with such a noise that it awaked him out of his sleep. And about the time of renewing the watch towards morning, there appeared a great light over Caesar's camp, whilst they were all at rest, and from thence a ball of flaming fire was carried into Pompey's camp, which Caesar himself says he saw, as he was walking his rounds.

Now Caesar having designed to raise his camp with the morning and move to Scotussa, whilst the soldiers were busy in pulling down their tents, and sending on their cattle and servants before them with their baggage, there came in scouts who brought word that they saw arms carried to and fro in the enemy's camp, and heard a noise and running up and down, as of men preparing for battle; not long after there came in other scouts with further intelligence, that the first ranks were already set in battle array. Thereupon Caesar, when he had told them that the wished for day was come at last, when they should fight with men, not with hunger and famine, instantly gave orders for the red colors to be set up before his tent, that being the ordinary signal of battle among the Romans. As soon as the soldiers saw that, they left their tents, and with great shouts of joy ran to their arms; the officers, likewise, on their parts drawing up their companies in order of battle, every man fell into his proper rank without any trouble or noise, as quietly and orderly as if they had been in a dance.

Pompey himself led the right wing of his army against Antony, and placed his father-in-law Scipio in the middle against Lucius Calvinus. The left wing was commanded by Lucius Domitius; and supported by the great mass of the horse. For almost the whole cavalry was posted there, in the hope of crushing Caesar, and cutting off the tenth legion, which was spoken of as the stoutest in all the army, and in which Caesar himself usually fought in person. Caesar observing the left wing of the enemy to be lined and fortified with such a mighty guard of horse, and alarmed at the gallantry of their appearance, sent for a detachment of six cohorts out of the reserves, and placed them in the rear of the tenth legion, commanding them not to stir, lest they should be discovered by the enemy; but when the enemy's horse should begin to charge, and press upon them, that they should make up with all speed to the front through the foremost ranks, and not throw their javelins at a distance, as is usual with brave soldiers, that they may come to a close fight with their swords the sooner, but that they should strike them upwards into the eyes and faces of the enemy; telling them that those fine young dancers would never endure the steel shining in their eyes, but would fly to save their handsome faces. This was Caesar's employment at that time. But while he was thus instructing his soldiers, Pompey on horseback was viewing the order of both armies, and when he saw how well the enemy kept their ranks, expecting quietly the signal of battle; and, on the contrary, how impatient and unsteady his own men were, waving up and down in disorder for want of experience, he was very much afraid that their ranks would be broken upon the first onset; and therefore he gave out orders that the van should make a stand, and keeping close in their ranks, should receive the enemy's charge. Caesar much condemns this command; which he says not only took off from the strength of the blows, which would otherwise have been made with a spring; but also lost the men the impetus, which, more than anything, in the moment of their coming upon the enemy, fills soldiers with impulse and inspiration, the very shouts and rapid pace adding to their fury; of which Pompey deprived his men, arresting them in their course and cooling down their heat.

Caesar's army consisted of twenty-two thousand, and Pompey's of somewhat above twice as many. When the signal of battle was given on both sides, and the trumpets began to sound a charge, most men of course were fully occupied with their own matters; only some few of the noblest Romans, together with certain Greeks there present, standing as spectators without the battle, seeing the armies now ready to join, could not but consider in themselves to what a pass private ambition and emulation had brought the empire. Common arms, and kindred ranks drawn up under the self-same standards, the whole flower and strength of the same single city here meeting in collision with itself, offered plain proof how blind and how mad a thing human nature is, when once possessed with any passion; for if they had been desirous only to rule, and enjoy in peace what they had conquered in war, the greatest and best part of the world was subject to them both by sea and land. But if there was yet a thirst in their ambition, that must still be fed with new trophies and triumphs, the Parthian and German wars would yield matter enough to satisfy the most covetous of honor. Scythia, moreover, was yet unconquered, and the Indians too, where their ambition might be colored over with the specious pretext of civilizing barbarous nations. And what Scythian horse, Parthian arrows, or Indian riches, could be able to resist seventy thousand Roman soldiers, well appointed in arms, under the command of two such generals as Pompey and Caesar, whose names they had heard of before that of the Romans, and whose prowess, by their conquests of such wild, remote, savage, and brutish nations, was spread further than the fame of the Romans themselves? Today they met in conflict, and could no longer be induced to spare their country, even out of regard for their own glory or the fear of losing the name which till this day both had held, of having never yet been defeated. As for their former private ties, and the charms of Julia, and the marriage that had made them near connections, these could now only be looked upon as tricks of state, the mere securities of a treaty made to serve the needs of an occasion, not the pledges of any real friendship.

Now, therefore, as soon as the plains of Pharsalia were covered with men, horse, and armor, and that the signal of battle was raised on either side, Caius Crassianus, a centurion, who commanded a company of one hundred and twenty men, was the first that advanced out of Caesar's army, to give the charge, and acquit himself of a solemn engagement that he had made to Caesar. He had been the first man that Caesar had seen going out of the camp in the morning, and Caesar, after saluting him, had asked him what he thought of the coming battle. To which he, stretching out his right hand, replied aloud, "Thine is the victory, O Caesar, thou shalt conquer gloriously, and I myself this day will be the subject of thy praise either alive or dead." In pursuance of this promise he hastened forward, and being followed by many more, charged into the midst of the enemy. There they came at once to a close fight with their swords, and made a great slaughter; but as he was still pressing forward, and breaking the ranks of the vanguard, one of Pompey's soldiers ran him in at the mouth, so that the point of the sword came out behind at his neck; and Crassianus being thus slain, the fight became doubtful, and continued equal on that part of the battle.

Pompey had not yet brought on the right wing, but stayed and looked about, waiting to see what execution his cavalry would do on the left. They had already drawn out their squadrons in form, designing to turn Caesar's flank, and force those few horse, which he had placed in the front, to give back upon the battalion of foot. But Caesar, on the other side, having given the signal, his horse retreated back a little, and gave way to those six subsidiary cohorts, which had been posted in the rear, as a reserve to cover the flank; and which now came out, three thousand men in number, and met the enemy; and when they came up, standing by the horses, struck their javelins upwards, according to their instructions, and hit the horsemen full in their faces. They, unskillful in any manner of fight, and least of all expecting or understanding such a kind as this, had not courage enough to endure the blows upon their faces, but turning their backs, and covering their eyes with their hands, shamefully took to flight. Caesar's men, however, did not follow them, but marched upon the foot, and attacked the wing, which the flight of the cavalry had left unprotected, and liable to be turned and taken in the rear, so that this wing now being attacked in the flank by these, and charged in the front by the tenth legion, was not able to abide the charge, or make any longer resistance, especially when they saw themselves surrounded and circumvented in the very way in which they had designed to invest the enemy. Thus these being likewise routed and put to flight, when Pompey, by the dust flying in the air, conjectured the fate of his horse, it were very hard to say what his thoughts or intentions were, but looking like one distracted and beside himself, and without any recollection or reflection that he was Pompey the Great, he retired slowly towards his camp, without speaking a word to any man, exactly according to the description in the verses,

> *But Jove from heaven struck Ajax with a fear;*
> *Ajax the bold then stood astonished there,*
> *Flung o'er his back the mighty sevenfold shield,*
> *And trembling gazed and spied about the field.*

In this state and condition he went into his own tent, and sat down, speechless still, until some of the enemy fell in together with his men that were flying into the camp, and then he let fall only this one word, "What? into the very camp?" and said no more; but rose up, and putting on a dress suitable to his present fortune, made his way secretly out.

By this time the rest of the army was put to flight, and there was a great slaughter in the camp among the servants and those that guarded the tents, but of the soldiers themselves there were not above six thousand slain, as is stated by Asinius Pollio, who himself fought in this battle on Caesar's side. When Caesar's soldiers had taken the camp, they saw clearly the folly and vanity of the enemy; for all their tents and pavilions were richly set out with garlands of myrtle, embroidered carpets and hangings, and tables laid and covered with goblets. There were large bowls of wine ready, and everything prepared and put in array, in the manner rather of people who had offered sacrifice and were going to celebrate a holiday, than of soldiers who had armed themselves to go out to battle, so possessed with the expectation of success and so full of empty confidence had they gone out that morning.

When Pompey had got a little way from the camp, he dismounted and forsook his horse, having but a small retinue with him; and finding that no man pursued him, walked on softly afoot, taken up altogether with thoughts, such as probably might possess a man that for the space of thirty-four years together had been accustomed to conquest and victory, and was then at last, in his old age, learning for the first time what defeat and flight were. And it was no small affliction to consider, that he had lost in one hour all that glory and power, which he had been getting in so many wars, and bloody battles; and that he who but a little before was guarded with such an army of foot, so many squadrons of horse, and such a mighty fleet, was now flying in so mean a condition, and with such a slender retinue, that his very enemies who fought him could not know him. Thus, when he had passed by the city of Larissa, and came into the pass of Tempe, being very thirsty, he kneeled down and drank out of the river; then rising up again, he passed through Tempe, until he came to the seaside, and there he betook himself to a poor fisherman's cottage, where he rested the remainder of the night. The next morning about break of day he went into one of the river boats, and taking none of those that followed him except such as were free, dismissed his servants, advising them to go boldly to Caesar, and not be afraid. As he was rowing up and down near the shore, he chanced to spy a large merchant-ship, lying off, just ready to set sail; the master of which was a Roman citizen, named Peticius, who, though he was not familiarly acquainted with Pompey, yet knew him well by sight. Now it happened that this Peticius dreamed, the night before, that he saw Pompey, not like the man he had often seen him, but in a humble and dejected condition, and in that posture discoursing with him. He was then telling his dream to the people on board, as men do when at leisure, and especially dreams of that consequence, when of a sudden one of the mariners told him, he saw a river boat with oars putting off from shore, and that some of the men there shook their garments, and held out their hands, with signs to take them in; thereupon Peticius looking attentively, at once recognized Pompey, just as he appeared in his dream, and smiting his hand on his head, ordered the mariners to let down the ship's boat, he himself waving his hand, and calling to him by his name, already assured of his change and the change of his fortune by that of his garb. So that without waiting for any further entreaty or discourse, he took him into his ship, together with as many of his company as he thought fit, and hoisted sail. There were with him the two Lentuli, and Favonius; and a little after they spied king Deiotarus, making up towards them from the shore; so they stayed and took him in along with them. At supper time, the master of the ship having made ready such provisions as he had aboard, Pompey, for want of his servants, began to undo his shoes himself; which Favonius noticing ran to him and undid them, and helped him to anoint himself, and always after continued to wait upon, and attend him in all things, as servants do their masters, even to the washing of his feet, and preparing his supper. Insomuch that anyone there present, observing the free and unaffected courtesy of these services, might have well exclaimed,

> *O heavens, in those that noble are,*
> *Whate'er they do is fit and fair.*

Pompey, sailing by the city of Amphipolis, crossed over from thence to Mitylene, with a design to take in Cornelia and his son; and as soon as he arrived at the port in that island, he dispatched a messenger into the city, with news very different from Cornelia's expectation. For she, by all the former messages and letters sent to please her, had been put in hopes that the war was ended at Dyrrhachium, and that there was nothing more remaining for Pompey, but the pursuit of Caesar. The messenger finding her in the same hopes still, was not able to salute or speak to her, but declaring the greatness of her misfortune by his tears rather than by his words, desired her to make haste if she would see Pompey, with one ship only, and that not of his own. The young lady hearing this, fell down in a swoon, and continued a long time senseless and speechless. And when with some trouble she was brought to her senses again, being conscious to herself that this was no time for lamentation and tears, she started up and ran through the city towards the seaside, where Pompey meeting and embracing her, as she sank down, supported by his arms, "This, sir," she exclaimed, "is the effect of my fortune, not of yours, that I see you thus reduced to one poor vessel, who before your marriage with Cornelia, were wont to sail in these seas with a fleet of five hundred ships. Why therefore should you come to see me, or why not rather have left to her evil genius one who has brought upon you her own ill-fortune? How happy a woman had I been, if I had breathed out my last, before the news came from Parthia of the death of Publius, the husband of my youth, and how prudent if I had followed his destiny, as I designed! But I was reserved for a greater mischief, even the ruin of Pompey the Great."

Thus, they say, Cornelia spoke to him, and this was Pompey's reply: "You have had, Cornelia, but one season of a better fortune, which it may be, gave you unfounded hopes, by attending me a longer time than is usual. It behoves us, who are mortals born, to endure these events, and to try fortune yet again; neither is it any less possible to recover our former state, than it was to fall from that into this." Thereupon Cornelia sent for her servants and baggage out of the city. The citizens also of Mitylene came out to salute and invite Pompey into the city, but he refused, advising them to be obedient to the conqueror, and fear not, for that Caesar was a man of great goodness and clemency. Then turning to Cratippus, the philosopher, who came among the rest out of the city to visit him, he began to find some fault, and briefly argued with him upon Providence, but Cratippus modestly declined the dispute, putting him in better hopes only, lest by opposing, he might seem too austere or unseasonable. For he might have put Pompey a question in his turn, in defense of Providence; and might have demonstrated the necessity there was that the commonwealth should be turned into a monarchy, because of their ill government in the state; and could have asked, "How, O Pompey, and by what token or assurance can we ascertain, that if the victory had been yours, you would have used your fortune better than Caesar? We must leave the divine power to act as we find it do."

Pompey having taken his wife and friends aboard, set sail, making no port, nor touching anywhere, but when he was necessitated to take in provisions, or fresh water. The first city he entered was Attalia, in Pamphylia, and whilst he was there, there came some galleys thither to him out of Cilicia, together with a small body of soldiers, and he had almost sixty senators with him again; then hearing that his navy was safe too, and that Cato had rallied a considerable body of soldiers after their overthrow, and was crossing with them over into Africa, he began to complain and blame himself to his friends that he had allowed himself to be driven into engaging by land, without making use of his other forces, in which he was irresistibly the stronger, and had not kept near enough to his fleet, that failing by land, he might have reinforced himself from the sea, and would have been again at the head of a power quite sufficient to encounter the enemy on equal terms. And in truth, neither did Pompey during all the war commit a greater oversight, nor Caesar use a more subtle stratagem, than in drawing the fight so far off from the naval forces.

As it now was, however, since he must come to some decision, and try some plan within his present ability, he dispatched his agents to the neighboring cities, and himself sailed about in person to others, requiring their aid in money and men for his ships. But, fearing lest the rapid approach of the enemy might cut off all his preparations, he began to consider what place would yield him the safest refuge and retreat at present. A consultation was held, and it was generally agreed that no province of the Romans was secure enough. As for foreign kingdoms, he himself was of opinion, that Parthia would be the fittest to receive and defend them in their present weakness, and best able to furnish them with new means and send them out again with large forces. Others of the council were for going into Africa, and to king Juba. But Theophanes the Lesbian, thought it madness to leave Egypt, that was but at a distance of three days' sailing, and make no use of Ptolemy, who was still a boy, and was highly indebted to Pompey for the friendship and favor he had shown to his father, only to put himself under the Parthian, and trust the most treacherous nation in the world; and rather than make any trial of the clemency of a Roman, and his own near connection, to whom if he would but yield to be second, he might be the first and chief over all the rest, to go and place himself at the mercy of Arsaces, which even Crassus had not submitted to, while alive; and, moreover, to expose his young wife, of the family of the Scipios, among a barbarous people, who govern by their lusts, and measure their greatness by their power to commit affronts and insolencies; from whom, though she suffered no dishonor, yet it might be thought she did, being in the hands of those who had the power to do it. This argument alone, they say, was persuasive enough to divert his course, that was designed towards Euphrates, if it were so indeed that any counsel of Pompey's, and not some superior power, made him take this other way.

As soon, therefore, as it was resolved upon, that he should fly into Egypt, setting sail from Cyprus in a galley of Seleucia, together with Cornelia, while the rest of his company sailed along near him, some in ships of war, and others in merchant vessels, he passed over sea without danger. But on hearing that king Ptolemy was posted with his army at the city of Pelusium, making war against his sister, he steered his course that way, and sent a messenger before to acquaint the king with his arrival, and to crave his protection. Ptolemy himself was quite young, and therefore Pothinus, who had the principal administration of all affairs, called a council of the chief men, those being the greatest whom he pleased to make so, and commanded them every man to deliver his opinion touching the reception of Pompey. It was, indeed, a miserable thing, that the fate of the great Pompey should be left to the determinations of Pothinus the eunuch, Theodotus of Chios, the paid rhetoric master, and Achillas the Egyptian. For these, among the chamberlains and menial domestics, that made up the rest of the council, were the chief and leading men. Pompey, who thought it dishonorable for him to owe his safety to Caesar, riding at anchor at a distance from shore, was forced to wait the sentence of this tribunal. It seems they were so far different in their opinions that some were for sending the man away, and others again for inviting and receiving him; but Theodotus, to show his cleverness and the cogency of his rhetoric, undertook to demonstrate, that neither the one nor the other was safe in that juncture of affairs. For if they entertained him, they would be sure to make Caesar their enemy, and Pompey their master; or if they dismissed him, they might render themselves hereafter obnoxious to Pompey, for that inhospitable expulsion, and to Caesar, for the escape; so that the most expedient course would be to send for him and take away his life, for by that means they would ingratiate themselves with the one, and have no reason to fear the other; adding, it is related, with a smile, that "a dead man cannot bite."

This advice being approved of, they committed the execution of it to Achillas. He, therefore, taking with him as his accomplices one Septimius, a man that had formerly held a command under Pompey, and Salvius, another centurion, with three or four attendants, made up towards Pompey's galley. In the meantime, all the chiefest of those who accompanied Pompey in this voyage, were come into his ship to learn the event of their embassy. But when they saw the manner of their reception, that in appearance it was neither princely nor honorable, nor indeed in any way answerable to the hopes of Theophanes, or their expectation, (for there came but a few men in a fisherman's boat to meet them,) they began to suspect the meanness of their entertainment, and gave warning to Pompey that he should row back his galley, whilst he was out of their reach, and make for the sea. By this time, the Egyptian boat drew near, and Septimius standing up first, saluted Pompey in the Latin tongue, by the title of imperator. Then Achillas, saluting him in the Greek language, desired him to come aboard his vessel, telling him, that the sea was very shallow towards the shore, and that a galley of that burden could not avoid striking upon the sands. At the same time they saw several of the king's galleys getting their men on board, and all the shore covered with soldiers; so that even if they changed their minds, it seemed impossible for them to escape, and besides, their distrust would have given the assassins a pretence for their cruelty. Pompey, therefore, taking his leave of Cornelia, who was already lamenting his death before it came, bade two centurions, with Philip, one of his freedmen, and a slave called Scythes, go on board the boat before him. And as some of the crew with Achillas were reaching out their hands to help him, he turned about towards his wife and son, and repeated those iambics of Sophocles,

> *He that once enters at a tyrant's door,*
> *Becomes a slave, though he were free before.*

These were the last words he spoke to his friends, and so he went aboard. Observing presently that notwithstanding there was a considerable distance betwixt his galley and the shore, yet none of the company addressed any words of friendliness or welcome to him all the way, he looked earnestly upon Septimius, and said, "I am not mistaken, surely, in believing you to have been formerly my fellow-soldier." But he only nodded with his head, making no reply at all, nor showing any other courtesy. Since, therefore, they continued silent, Pompey took a little book in his hand, in which was written out an address in Greek, which he intended to make to king Ptolemy, and began to read it. When they drew near to the shore, Cornelia, together with the rest of his friends in the galley, was very impatient to see the event, and began to take courage at last, when she saw several of the royal escort coming to meet him, apparently to give him a more honorable reception; but in the meantime, as Pompey took Philip by the hand to rise up more easily, Septimius first stabbed him from behind with his sword; and after him likewise Salvius and Achillas drew out their swords. He, therefore, taking up his gown with both hands, drew it over his face, and neither saying nor doing anything unworthy of himself, only groaning a little, endured the wounds they gave him, and so ended his life, in the fifty-ninth year of his age, the very next day after the day of his birth.

Cornelia, with her company from the galley, seeing him murdered, gave such a cry that it was heard to the shore, and weighing anchor with all speed, they hoisted sail, and fled. A strong breeze from the shore assisted their flight into the open sea, so that the Egyptians, though desirous to overtake them, desisted from the pursuit. But they cut off Pompey's head, and threw the rest of his body overboard, leaving it naked upon the shore, to be viewed by any that had the curiosity to see so sad a spectacle. Philip stayed by and watched till they had glutted their eyes in viewing it; and then washing it with sea-water, having nothing else, he wrapped it up in a shirt of his own for a winding-sheet. Then seeking up and down about the sands, at last he found some rotten planks of a little fisher-boat, not much, but yet enough to make up a funeral pile for a naked body, and that not quite entire. As Philip was busy in gathering and putting these old planks together, an old Roman citizen, who in his youth had served in the wars under Pompey, came up to him and demanded, who he was that was preparing the funeral of Pompey the Great. And Philip making answer, that he was his freedman, "Nay, then," said he, "you shall not have this honor alone; let even me, too, I pray you, have my share in such a pious office. that I may not altogether repent me of this pilgrimage in a strange land, but in compensation of many misfortunes, may obtain this happiness at last, even with mine own hands to touch the body of Pompey, and do the last duties to the greatest general among the Romans." And in this manner were the obsequies of Pompey performed. The next day Lucius Lentulus, not knowing what had passed, came sailing from Cyprus along the shore of that coast, and seeing a funeral pile, and Philip standing by, exclaimed, before he was yet seen by any one, "Who is this that has found his end here?" adding, after a short pause, with a sigh, "Possibly even thou, Pompeius Magnus!" and so going ashore, he was presently apprehended and slain. This was the end of Pompey.

Not long after, Caesar arrived in the country that was polluted with this foul act, and when one of the Egyptians was sent to present him with Pompey's head, he turned away from him with abhorrence as from a murderer; and on receiving his seal, on which was engraved a lion holding a sword in his paw, he burst into tears. Achillas and Pothinus he put to death; and king Ptolemy himself, being overthrown in battle upon the banks of the Nile, fled away and was never heard of afterwards. Theodotus, the rhetorician, flying out of Egypt, escaped the hands of Caesar's justice, but lived a vagabond in banishment; wandering up and down, despised and hated of all men, till at last Marcus Brutus, after he had killed Caesar, finding him in his province of Asia, put him to death, with every kind of ignominy. The ashes of Pompey were carried to his wife Cornelia, who deposited them at his country house near Alba.

12

COMPARISON OF POMPEY AND AGESILAUS

Thus having drawn out the history of the lives of Agesilaus and Pompey, the next thing is to compare them; and in order to this, to take a cursory view, and bring together the points in which they chiefly disagree; which are these. In the first place, Pompey attained to all his greatness and glory by the fairest and justest means, owing his advancement to his own efforts, and to the frequent and important aid which he rendered Sylla, in delivering Italy from its tyrants. But Agesilaus appears to have obtained his kingdom, not without offense both towards gods and towards men, towards these, by procuring judgment of bastardy against Leotychides, whom his brother had declared his lawful son, and towards those, by putting a false gloss upon the oracle, and eluding its sentence against his lameness. Secondly, Pompey never ceased to display his respect for Sylla during his lifetime, and expressed it also after his death, by enforcing the honorable interment of his corpse, in despite of Lepidus, and by giving his daughter in marriage to his son Faustus. But Agesilaus, upon a slight presence, cast off Lysander with reproach and dishonor. Yet Sylla in fact had owed to Pompey's services, as much as Pompey ever received from him, whereas Lysander made Agesilaus king of Sparta, and general of all Greece. Thirdly, Pompey's transgressions of right and justice in his political life were occasioned chiefly by his relations with other people, and most of his errors had some affinity, as well as himself, to Caesar and Scipio, his fathers-in-law. But Agesilaus, to gratify the fondness of his son, saved the life of Sphodrias by a sort of violence, when he deserved death for the wrong he had done to the Athenians; and when Phoebidas treacherously broke the peace with Thebes, zealously abetted him for the sake, it was clear, of the unjust act itself. In short, what mischief soever Pompey might be said to have brought on Rome through compliance with the wishes of his friends or through inadvertency, Agesilaus may be said to have brought on Sparta out of obstinacy and malice, by kindling the Boeotian war. And if, moreover, we are to attribute any part of these disasters to some personal ill-fortune attaching to the men themselves, in the case of Pompey, certainly, the Romans had no reason to anticipate it. Whereas Agesilaus would not suffer the Lacedaemonians to avoid what they foresaw and were forewarned must attend the "lame sovereignty." For had Leotychides been chargeable ten thousand times as foreign and spurious, yet the race of the Eurypontidae was still in being, and could easily have furnished Sparta with a lawful king, that was sound in his limbs, had not Lysander darkened and disguised the true sense of the oracle in favor of Agesilaus.

Such a politic piece of sophistry as was devised by Agesilaus, in that great perplexity of the people as to the treatment to be given to those who had played the coward at the battle of Leuctra, when after that unhappy defeat, he decreed, that the laws should sleep for that day, it would be hard to find any parallel to; neither indeed have we the fellow of it in all Pompey's story. But on the contrary, Pompey for a friend thought it no sin to break those very laws which he himself had made; as if to show at once the force of his friendship, and the greatness of his power; whereas Agesilaus, under the necessity, as it seemed, of either rescinding the laws, or not saving the citizens, contrived an expedient by the help of which the laws should not touch these citizens, and yet should not, to avoid it, be overthrown. Then I must commend it as an incomparable act of civil virtue and obedience in Agesilaus, that immediately upon the receipt of the scytala, he left the wars in Asia, and returned into his country. For he did not like Pompey merely advance his country's interest by acts that contributed at the same time to promote his own greatness, but looking to his country's good, for its sake laid aside as great authority and honor as ever any man had before or since, except Alexander the Great.

But now to take another point of view, if we sum up Pompey's military expeditions and exploits of war, the number of his trophies, and the greatness of the powers which he subdued, and the multitude of battles in which he triumphed, I am persuaded even Xenophon himself would not put the victories of Agesilaus in balance with his, though Xenophon has this privilege allowed him, as a sort of special reward for his other excellences, that he may write and speak, in favor of his hero, whatever he pleases. Methinks, too, there is a great deal of difference betwixt these men, in their clemency and moderation towards their enemies. For Agesilaus, while attempting to enslave Thebes and exterminate Messene, the latter, his country's ancient associate, and Thebes, the mother-city of his own royal house, almost lost Sparta itself, and did really lose the government of Greece; whereas Pompey gave cities to those of the pirates who were willing to change their manner of life; and when it was in his power to lead Tigranes, king of Armenia, in triumph, he chose rather to make him a confederate of the Romans, saying, that a single day was worth less than all future time. But if the preeminence in that which relates to the office and virtues of a general, should be determined by the greatest and most important acts and counsels of war, the Lacedaemonian would not a little exceed the Roman. For Agesilaus never deserted his city, though it was besieged by an army of seventy thousand men, when there were very few soldiers within to defend it, and those had been defeated too, but a little before, at the battle of Leuctra. But Pompey, when Caesar with a body only of fifty-three hundred men, had taken but one town in Italy, departed in a panic out of Rome, either through cowardice, when there were so few, or at least through a false and mistaken belief that there were more; and having conveyed away his wife and children, he left all the rest of the citizens defenseless, and fled; whereas he ought either to have conquered in fight for the defense of his country, or yielded upon terms to the conqueror, who was moreover his fellow-citizen, and allied to him; but now to the same man to whom he refused a prolongation of the term of his government, and thought it intolerable to grant another consulship, to him he gave the power, by letting him take the city, to tell Metellus, together with all the rest, that they were his prisoners.

That which is chiefly the office of a general, to force the enemy into fighting when he finds himself the stronger, and to avoid being driven into it himself when he is the weaker, this excellence Agesilaus always displayed, and by it kept himself invincible; whereas in contending with Pompey, Caesar, who was the weaker, successfully declined the danger, and his own strength being in his land forces. drove him into putting the conflict to issue with these, and thus made himself master of the treasure, stores, and the sea too, which were all in his enemy's hands, and by the help of which the victory could have been secured without fighting. And what is alleged as an apology in vindication of Pompey, is to a general of his age and standing the greatest of disgraces. For, granting that a young commander might by clamor and outcry be deprived of his fortitude and strength of mind, and weakly forsake his better judgment, and the thing be neither strange nor altogether unpardonable, yet for Pompey the Great, whose camp the Romans called their country, and his tent the senate, styling the consuls, praetors, and all other magistrates who were conducting, the government at Rome, by no better title than that of rebels and traitors, for him, whom they well knew never to have been under the command of any but himself, having served all his campaigns under himself as sole general, for him upon so small a provocation as the scoffs of Favonius and Domitius, and lest he should bear the nickname of Agamemnon, to be wrought upon, and even forced to hazard the whole empire and liberty of Rome upon the cast of a die, was surely indeed intolerable. Who, if he had so much regarded a present infamy, should have guarded the city at first with his arms, and fought the battle in defense of Rome, not have left it as he did; nor while declaring his flight from Italy an artifice in the manner of Themistocles, nevertheless be ashamed in Thessaly of a prudent delay before engaging. Heaven had not appointed the Pharsalian fields to be the stage and theater upon which they should contend for the empire of Rome, neither was he summoned thither by any herald upon challenge, with intimation that he must either undergo the combat, or surrender the prize to another. There were many other fields, thousands of cities, and even the whole earth placed at his command, by the advantage of his fleet, and his superiority at sea, if he would but have followed the examples of Maximus, Marius, Lucullus, and even Agesilaus himself, who endured no less tumults within the city of Sparta, when the Thebans provoked him to come out and fight in defense of the land, and sustained in Egypt also numerous calumnies, slanders, and suspicions on the part of the king, whom he counseled to abstain from a battle. And thus following always what he had determined in his own judgment upon mature advice, by that means he not only preserved the Egyptians, against their wills, not only kept Sparta, in those desperate convulsions, by his sole act, safe from overthrow, but even was able to set up trophies likewise in the city over the Thebans, having given his countrymen an occasion of being victorious afterwards by not at first leading them out, as they tried to force him to do to their own destruction. The consequence was that in the end Agesilaus was commended by the very men, when they found themselves saved, upon whom he had put this compulsion, whereas Pompey, whose error had been occasioned by others, found those his accusers whose advice had misled him. Some indeed profess that he was deceived by his father-in-law Scipio, who, designing to conceal and keep to himself the greatest part of that treasure which he had brought out of Asia, pressed Pompey to battle, upon the pretence that there would be a want of money. Yet admitting he was deceived, one in his place ought not to have been so, nor should have allowed so slight an artifice to cause the hazard of such mighty interests. And thus we have taken a view of each, by comparing together their conduct, and actions in war.

As to their voyages into Egypt, one steered his course thither out of necessity in flight; the other neither honorably, nor of necessity, but as a mercenary soldier, having enlisted himself into the service of a barbarous nation for pay, that he might be able afterwards to wage war upon the Greeks. And secondly, what we charge upon the Egyptians in the name of Pompey, the Egyptians lay to the charge of Agesilaus. Pompey trusted them and was betrayed and murdered by them; Agesilaus accepted their confidence and deserted them, transferring his aid to the very enemies who were now attacking those whom be had been brought over to assist.

13

ALEXANDER

It being my purpose to write the lives of Alexander the king, and of Caesar, by whom Pompey was destroyed, the multitude of their great actions affords so large a field that I were to blame if I should not by way of apology forewarn my reader that I have chosen rather to epitomize the most celebrated parts of their story, than to insist at large on every particular circumstance of it. It must be borne in mind that my design is not to write histories, but lives. And the most glorious exploits do not always furnish us with the clearest discoveries of virtue or vice in men; sometimes a matter of less moment, an expression or a jest, informs us better of their characters and inclinations, than the most famous sieges, the greatest armaments, or the bloodiest battles whatsoever. Therefore as portrait-painters are more exact in the lines and features of the face in which the character is seen, than in the other parts of the body, so I must be allowed to give my more particular attention to the marks and indications of the souls of men, and while I endeavor by these to portray their lives, may be free to leave more weighty matters and great battles to be treated of by others.

It is agreed on by all hands, that on the father's side, Alexander descended from Hercules by Caranus, and from Aeacus by Neoptolemus on the mother's side. His father Philip, being in Samothrace, when he was quite young, fell in love there with Olympias, in company with whom he was initiated in the religious ceremonies of the country, and her father and mother being both dead, soon after, with the consent of her brother Arymbas, he married her. The night before the consummation of their marriage, she dreamed that a thunderbolt fell upon her body, which kindled a great fire, whose divided flames dispersed themselves all about, and then were extinguished. And Philip some time after he was married, dreamt that he sealed up his wife's body with a seal, whose impression, as he fancied, was the figure of a lion. Some of the diviners interpreted this as a warning to Philip to look narrowly to his wife; but Aristander of Telmessus, considering how unusual it was to seal up anything that was empty, assured him the meaning of his dream was, that the queen was with child of a boy, who would one day prove as stout and courageous as a lion. Once, moreover, a serpent was found lying by Olympias as she slept, which more than anything else, it is said, abated Philip's passion for her; and whether he feared her as an enchantress, or thought she had commerce with some god, and so looked on himself as excluded, he was ever after less fond of her conversation. Others say, that the women of this country having always been extremely addicted to the enthusiastic Orphic rites, and the wild worship of Bacchus, (upon which account they were called Clodones, and Mimallones,) imitated in many things the practices of the Edonian and Thracian women about Mount Haemus, from whom the word threskeuein, seems to have been derived, as a special term for superfluous and over-curious forms of adoration; and that Olympias, zealously affecting these fanatical and enthusiastic inspirations, to perform them with more barbaric dread, was wont in the dances proper to these ceremonies to have great tame serpents about her, which sometimes creeping out of the ivy and the mystic fans, sometimes winding themselves about the sacred spears, and the women's chaplets, made a spectacle which the men could not look upon without terror.

Philip, after this vision, sent Chaeron of Megalopolis to consult the oracle of Apollo at Delphi, by which he was commanded to perform sacrifice, and henceforth pay particular honor, above all other gods, to Ammon; and was told he should one day lose that eye with which he presumed to peep through the chink of the door, when he saw the god, under the form of a serpent, in the company of his wife. Eratosthenes says that Olympias, when she attended Alexander on his way to the army in his first expedition, told him the secret of his birth, and bade him behave himself with courage suitable to his divine extraction. Others again affirm that she wholly disclaimed any pretensions of the kind, and was wont to say, "When will Alexander leave off slandering me to Juno?"

Alexander was born the sixth of Hecatombaeon, which month the Macedonians call Lous, the same day that the temple of Diana at Ephesus was burnt; which Hegesias of Magnesia makes the occasion of a conceit, frigid enough to have stopped the conflagration. The temple, he says, took fire and was burnt while its mistress was absent, assisting at the birth of Alexander. And all the Eastern soothsayers who happened to be then at Ephesus, looking upon the ruin of this temple to be the forerunner of some other calamity, ran about the town, beating their faces, and crying, that this day had brought forth something that would prove fatal and destructive to all Asia.

Just after Philip had taken Potidaea, he received these three messages at one time, that Parmenio had overthrown the Illyrians in a great battle, that his race-horse had won the course at the Olympic games, and that his wife had given birth to Alexander; with which being naturally well pleased, as an addition to his satisfaction, he was assured by the diviners that a son, whose birth was accompanied with three such successes, could not fail of being invincible.

The statues that gave the best representation of Alexander's person, were those of Lysippus, (by whom alone he would suffer his image to be made,) those peculiarities which many of his successors afterwards and his friends used to affect to imitate, the inclination of his head a little on one side towards his left shoulder, and his melting eye, having been expressed by this artist with great exactness. But Apelles, who drew him with thunderbolts in his hand, made his complexion browner and darker than it was naturally; for he was fair and of a light color, passing into ruddiness in his face and upon his breast. Aristoxenus in his Memoirs tells us that a most agreeable odor exhaled from his skin, and that his breath and body all over was so fragrant as to perfume the clothes which he wore next him; the cause of which might probably be the hot and adjust temperament of his body. For sweet smells, Theophrastus conceives, are produced by the concoction of moist humors by heat, which is the reason that those parts of the world which are driest and most burnt up, afford spices of the best kind, and in the greatest quantity; for the heat of the sun exhausts all the superfluous moisture which lies in the surface of bodies, ready to generate putrefaction. And this hot constitution, it may be, rendered Alexander so addicted to drinking, and so choleric. His temperance, as to the pleasures of the body, was apparent in him in his very childhood, as he was with much difficulty incited to them, and always used them with great moderation; though in other things he was extremely eager and vehement, and in his love of glory, and the pursuit of it, he showed a solidity of high spirit and magnanimity far above his age. For he neither sought nor valued it upon every occasion, as his father Philip did, (who affected to show his eloquence almost to a degree of pedantry, and took care to have the victories of his racing chariots at the Olympic games engraved on his coin,) but when he was asked by some about him, whether he would run a race in the Olympic games, as he was very swift-footed, he answered, he would, if he might have kings to run with him. Indeed, he seems in general to have looked with indifference, if not with dislike, upon the professed athletes. He often appointed prizes, for which not only tragedians and musicians, pipers and harpers, but rhapsodists also, strove to outvie one another; and delighted in all manner of hunting and cudgel-playing, but never gave any encouragement to contests either of boxing or of the pancratium.

While he was yet very young, he entertained the ambassadors from the king of Persia, in the absence of his father, and entering much into conversation with them, gained so much upon them by his affability, and the questions he asked them, which were far from being childish or trifling, (for he inquired of them the length of the ways, the nature of the road into inner Asia, the character of their king, how he carried himself to his enemies, and what forces he was able to bring, into the field,) that they were struck with admiration of him, and looked upon the ability so much famed of Philip, to be nothing in comparison with the forwardness and high purpose that appeared thus early in his son. Whenever he heard Philip had taken any town of importance, or won any signal victory, instead of rejoicing at it altogether, he would tell his companions that his father would anticipate everything, and leave him and them no opportunities of performing great and illustrious actions. For being more bent upon action and glory than either upon pleasure or riches, he esteemed all that he should receive from his father as a diminution and prevention of his own future achievements; and would have chosen rather to succeed to a kingdom involved in troubles and wars, which would have afforded him frequent exercise of his courage, and a large field of honor, than to one already flourishing and settled, where his inheritance would be an inactive life, and the mere enjoyment of wealth and luxury.

The care of his education, as it might be presumed, was committed to a great many attendants, preceptors, and teachers, over the whole of whom Leonidas, a near kinsman of Olympias, a man of an austere temper, presided, who did not indeed himself decline the name of what in reality is a noble and honorable office, but in general his dignity, and his near relationship, obtained him from other people the title of Alexander's foster father and governor. But he who took upon him the actual place and style of his pedagogue, was Lysimachus the Acarnanian, who, though he had nothing specially to recommend him, but his lucky fancy of calling himself Phoenix, Alexander Achilles, and Philip Peleus, was therefore well enough esteemed, and ranked in the next degree after Leonidas.

Philonicus the Thessalian brought the horse Bucephalas to Philip, offering to sell him for thirteen talents; but when they went into the field to try him, they found him so very vicious and unmanageable, that he reared up when they endeavored to mount him, and would not so much as endure the voice of any of Philip's attendants. Upon which, as they were leading him away as wholly useless and untractable, Alexander, who stood by, said, "What an excellent horse do they lose, for want of address and boldness to manage him!" Philip at first took no notice of what he said; but when he heard him repeat the same thing several times, and saw he was much vexed to see the horse sent away, "Do you reproach," said he to him, "those who are older than yourself, as if you knew more, and were better able to manage him than they?" "I could manage this horse," replied he, "better than others do." "And if you do not," said Philip, "what will you forfeit for your rashness?" "I will pay," answered Alexander, "the whole price of the horse." At this the whole company fell a laughing; and as soon as the wager was settled amongst them, he immediately ran to the horse, and taking hold of the bridle, turned him directly towards the sun, having, it seems, observed that he was disturbed at and afraid of the motion of his own shadow; then letting him go forward a little, still keeping the reins in his hand, and stroking him gently when he found him begin to grow eager and fiery, he let fall his upper garment softly, and with one nimble leap securely mounted him, and when he was seated, by little and little drew in the bridle, and curbed him without either striking or spurring him. Presently, when he found him free from all rebelliousness, and on]y impatient for the course, he let him go at full speed, inciting him now with a commanding voice, and urging him also with his heel. Philip and his friends looked on at first in silence and anxiety for the result, till seeing him turn at the end of his career, and come back rejoicing and triumphing for what he had performed, they all burst out into acclamations of applause; and his father, shedding tears, it is said, for joy, kissed him as he came down from his horse, and in his transport, said, "O my son, look thee out a kingdom equal to and worthy of thyself, for Macedonia is too little for thee."

After this, considering him to be of a temper easy to be led to his duty by reason, but by no means to be compelled, he always endeavored to persuade rather than to command or force him to anything; and now looking upon the instruction and tuition of his youth to be of greater difficulty and importance, than to be wholly trusted to the ordinary masters in music and poetry, and the common school subjects, and to require, as Sophocles says,

The bridle and the rudder too,

he sent for Aristotle, the most learned and most cerebrated philosopher of his time, and rewarded him with a munificence proportionable to and becoming the care he took to instruct his son. For he repeopled his native city Stagira, which he had caused to be demolished a little before, and restored all the citizens who were in exile or slavery, to their habitations. As a place for the pursuit of their studies and exercises, he assigned the temple of the Nymphs, near Mieza, where, to this very day, they show you Aristotle's stone seats, and the shady walks which he was wont to frequent. It would appear that Alexander received from him not only his doctrines of Morals, and of Politics, but also something of those more abstruse and profound theories which these philosophers, by the very names they gave them, professed to reserve for oral communication to the initiated, and did not allow many to become acquainted with. For when he was in Asia, and heard Aristotle had published some treatises of that kind, he wrote to him, using very plain language to him in behalf of philosophy, the following letter. "Alexander to Aristotle greeting. You have not done well to publish your books of oral doctrine; for what is there now that we excel others in, if those things which we have been particularly instructed in be laid open to all? For my part, I assure you, I had rather excel others in the knowledge of what is excellent, than in the extent of my power and dominion. Farewell." And Aristotle, soothing this passion for preeminence, speaks, in his excuse for himself, of these doctrines, as in fact both published and not published: as indeed, to say the truth, his books on metaphysics are written in a style which makes them useless for ordinary teaching, and instructive only, in the way of memoranda, for those who have been already conversant in that sort of learning.

Doubtless also it was to Aristotle, that he owed the inclination he had, not to the theory only, but likewise to the practice of the art of medicine. For when any of his friends were sick, he would often prescribe them their course of diet, and medicines proper to their disease, as we may find in his epistles. He was naturally a great lover of all kinds of learning and reading; and Onesicritus informs us, that he constantly laid Homer's Iliads, according to the copy corrected by Aristotle, called the casket copy, with his dagger under his pillow, declaring that he esteemed it a perfect portable treasure of all military virtue and knowledge. When he was in the upper Asia, being destitute of other books, he ordered Harpalus to send him some; who furnished him with Philistus's History, a great many of the plays of Euripides, Sophocles, and Aeschylus, and some dithyrambic odes, composed by Telestes and Philoxenus. For awhile he loved and cherished Aristotle no less, as he was wont to say himself, than if he had been his father, giving this reason for it, that as he had received life from the one, so the other had taught him to live well. But afterwards, upon some mistrust of him, yet not so great as to make him do him any hurt, his familiarity and friendly kindness to him abated so much of its former force and affectionateness, as to make it evident he was alienated from him. However, his violent thirst after and passion for learning, which were once implanted, still grew up with him, and never decayed; as appears by his veneration of Anaxarchus, by the present of fifty talents which he sent to Xenocrates, and his particular care and esteem of Dandamis and Calanus.

While Philip went on his expedition against the Byzantines, he left Alexander, then sixteen years old, his lieutenant in Macedonia, committing the charge of his seal to him; who, not to sit idle, reduced the rebellious Maedi, and having taken their chief town by storm, drove out the barbarous inhabitants, and planting a colony of several nations in their room, called the place after his own name, Alexandropolis. At the battle of Chaeronea, which his father fought against the Grecians, he is said to have been the first man that charged the Thebans' sacred band. And even in my remembrance, there stood an old oak near the river Cephisus, which people called Alexander's oak, because his tent was pitched under it. And not far off are to be seen the graves of the Macedonians who fell in that battle. This early bravery made Philip so fond of him, that nothing pleased him more than to hear his subjects call himself their general and Alexander their king.

But the disorders of his family, chiefly caused by his new marriages and attachments, (the troubles that began in the women's chambers spreading, so to say, to the whole kingdom,) raised various complaints and differences between them, which the violence of Olympias, a woman of a jealous and implacable temper, made wider, by exasperating Alexander against his father. Among the rest, this accident contributed most to their falling out. At the wedding of Cleopatra, whom Philip fell in love with and married, she being much too young for him, her uncle Attalus in his drink desired the Macedonians would implore the gods to give them a lawful successor to the kingdom by his niece. This so irritated Alexander, that throwing one of the cups at his head, "You villain," said he, "what, am I then a bastard?" Then Philip taking Attalus's part, rose up and would have run his son through; but by good fortune for them both, either his over-hasty rage, or the wine he had drunk, made his foot slip, so that he fell down on the floor. At which Alexander reproachfully insulted over him: "See there," said he, "the man, who makes preparations to pass out of Europe into Asia, overturned in passing from one seat to another." After this debauch, he and his mother Olympias withdrew from Philip's company, and when he had placed her in Epirus, he himself retired into Illyria.

About this time, Demaratus the Corinthian, an old friend of the family, who had the freedom to say anything among them without offense, coming to visit Philip, after the first compliments and embraces were over, Philip asked him, whether the Grecians were at amity with one another. "It ill becomes you," replied Demaratus, "to be so solicitous about Greece, when you have involved your own house in so many dissensions and calamities." He was so convinced by this seasonable reproach, that he immediately sent for his son home, and by Demartatus's mediation prevailed with him to return. But this reconciliation lasted not long; for when Pixodorus, viceroy of Caria, sent Aristocritus to treat for a match between his eldest daughter and Philip's son Arrhidaeus, hoping by this alliance to secure his assistance upon occasion, Alexander's mother, and some who pretended to be his friends, presently filled his head with tales and calumnies, as if Philip, by a splendid marriage and important alliance, were preparing the way for settling the kingdom upon Arrhidaeus. In alarm at this, he dispatched Thessalus, the tragic actor, into Caria, to dispose Pixodorus to slight Arrhidaeus, both as illegitimate and a fool, and rather to accept of himself for his son-in-law. This proposition was much more agreeable to Pixodorus than the former. But Philip, as soon as he was made acquainted with this transaction, went to his son's apartment, taking with him Philotas, the son of Parmenio, one of Alexander's intimate friends and companions, and there reproved him severely, and reproached him bitterly, that he should be so degenerate, and unworthy of the power he was to leave him, as to desire the alliance of a mean Carian, who was at best but the slave of a barbarous prince. Nor did this satisfy his resentment, for he wrote to the Corinthians, to send Thessalus to him in chains, and banished Harpalus, Nearchus, Erigyius, and Ptolemy, his son's friends and favorites, whom Alexander afterwards recalled, and raised to great honor and preferment.

Not long after this, Pausanias, having had an outrage done to him at the instance of Attalus and Cleopatra, when he found he could get no reparation for his disgrace at Philip's hands, watched his opportunity and murdered him. The guilt of which fact was laid for the most part upon Olympias, who was said to have encouraged and exasperated the enraged youth to revenge; and some sort of suspicion attached even to Alexander himself, who, it was said, when Pausanias came and complained to him of the injury he had received, repeated the verse out of Euripides's Medea:—

On husband, and on father, and on bride.

However, he took care to find out and punish the accomplices of the conspiracy severely, and was very angry with Olympias for treating Cleopatra inhumanly in his absence.

Alexander was but twenty years old when his father was murdered, and succeeded to a kingdom beset on all sides with great dangers, and rancorous enemies. For not only the barbarous nations that bordered on Macedonia, were impatient of being governed by any but their own native princes; but Philip likewise, though he had been victorious over the Grecians, yet, as the time had not been sufficient for him to complete his conquest and accustom them to his sway, had simply left all things in a general disorder and confusion. It seemed to the Macedonians a very critical time; and some would have persuaded Alexander to give up all thought of retaining the Grecians in subjection by force of arms, and rather to apply himself to win back by gentle means the allegiance of the tribes who were designing revolt, and try the effect of indulgence in arresting the first motions towards revolution. But he rejected this counsel as weak and timorous, and looked upon it to be more prudence to secure himself by resolution and magnanimity, than, by seeming to buckle to any, to encourage all to trample on him. In pursuit of this opinion, he reduced the barbarians to tranquility, and put an end to all fear of war from them, by a rapid expedition into their country as far as the river Danube, where he gave Syrmus, king of the Triballians, an entire overthrow. And hearing the Thebans were in revolt, and the Athenians in correspondence with them, he immediately marched through the pass of Thermopylae, saying that to Demosthenes who had called him a child while he was in Illyria and in the country of the Triballians, and a youth when he was in Thessaly, he would appear a man before the walls of Athens.

When he came to Thebes, to show how willing he was to accept of their repentance for what was past, he only demanded of them Phoenix and Prothytes, the authors of the rebellion, and proclaimed a general pardon to those who would come over to him. But when the Thebans merely retorted by demanding Philotas and Antipater to be delivered into their hands, and by a proclamation on their part, invited all who would assert the liberty of Greece to come over to them, he presently applied himself to make them feel the last extremities of war. The Thebans indeed defended themselves with a zeal and courage beyond their strength, being much outnumbered by their enemies. But when the Macedonian garrison sallied out upon them from the citadel, they were so hemmed in on all sides, that the greater part of them fell in the battle; the city itself being taken by storm, was sacked and razed, Alexander's hope being that so severe an example might terrify the rest of Greece into obedience, and also in order to gratify the hostility of his confederates, the Phocians and Plataeans. So that, except the priests, and some few who had heretofore been the friends and connections of the Macedonians, the family of the poet Pindar, and those who were known to have opposed the public vote for the war, all the rest, to the number of thirty thousand, were publicly sold for slaves; and it is computed that upwards of six thousand were put to the sword. Among the other calamities that befell the city, it happened that some Thracian soldiers having broken into the house of a matron of high character and repute, named Timoclea, their captain, after he had used violence with her, to satisfy his avarice as well as lust, asked her, if she knew of any money concealed; to which she readily answered she did, and bade him follow her into a garden, where she showed him a well, into which, she told him, upon the taking of the city she had thrown what she had of most value. The greedy Thracian presently stooping down to view the place where he thought the treasure lay, she came behind him, and pushed him into the well, and then flung great stones in upon him, till she had killed him. After which, when the soldiers led her away bound to Alexander, her very mien and gait showed her to be a woman of dignity, and of a mind no less elevated, not betraying the least sign of fear or astonishment. And when the king asked her who she was, "I am," said she, "the sister of Theagenes, who fought the battle of Chaeronea with your father Philip, and fell there in command for the liberty of Greece." Alexander was so surprised, both at what she had done, and what she said, that he could not choose but give her and her children their freedom to go whither they pleased.

After this he received the Athenians into favor, although they had shown themselves so much concerned at the calamity of Thebes that out of sorrow they omitted the celebration of the Mysteries, and entertained those who escaped with all possible humanity. Whether it were, like the lion, that his passion was now satisfied, or that after an example of extreme cruelty, he had a mind to appear merciful, it happened well for the Athenians; for he not only forgave them all past offenses, but bade them to look to their affairs with vigilance, remembering that if he should miscarry, they were likely to be the arbiters of Greece. Certain it is, too, that in after-time he often repented of his severity to the Thebans, and his remorse had such influence on his temper as to make him ever after less rigorous to all others. He imputed also the murder of Clitus, which he committed in his wine, and the unwillingness of the Macedonians to follow him against the Indians, by which his enterprise and glory was left imperfect, to the wrath and vengeance of Bacchus, the protector of Thebes. And it was observed that whatsoever any Theban, who had the good fortune to survive this victory, asked of him, he was sure to grant without the least difficulty.

Soon after, the Grecians, being assembled at the Isthmus, declared their resolution of joining with Alexander in the war against the Persians, and proclaimed him their general. While he stayed here, many public ministers and philosophers came from all parts to visit him, and congratulated him on his election, but contrary to his expectation, Diogenes of Sinope, who then was living at Corinth, thought so little of him, that instead of coming to compliment him, he never so much as stirred out of the suburb called the Cranium, where Alexander found him lying along in the sun. When he saw so much company near him, he raised himself a little, and vouchsafed to look upon Alexander; and when he kindly asked him whether he wanted anything, "Yes," said he, "I would have you stand from between me and the sun." Alexander was so struck at this answer, and surprised at the greatness of the man, who had taken so little notice of him, that as he went away, he told his followers who were laughing at the moroseness of the philosopher, that if he were not Alexander, he would choose to be Diogenes.

Then he went to Delphi, to consult Apollo concerning the success of the war he had undertaken, and happening to come on one of the forbidden days, when it was esteemed improper to give any answers from the oracle, he sent messengers to desire the priestess to do her office; and when she refused, on the plea of a law to the contrary, he went up himself, and began to draw her by force into the temple, until tired and overcome with his importunity, "My son," said she, "thou art invincible." Alexander taking hold of what she spoke, declared he had received such an answer as he wished for, and that it was needless to consult the god any further. Among other prodigies that attended the departure of his army, the image of Orpheus at Libethra, made of cypresswood, was seen to sweat in great abundance, to the discouragement of many.

But Aristander told him, that far from presaging any ill to him, it signified he should perform acts so important and glorious as would make the poets and musicians of future ages labor and sweat to describe and celebrate them.

His army, by their computation who make the smallest amount, consisted of thirty thousand foot, and four thousand horse; and those who make the most of it, speak but of forty-three thousand foot, and three thousand horse. Aristobulus says, he had not a fund of above seventy talents for their pay, nor had he more than thirty days' provision, if we may believe Duris; Onesicritus tells us, he was two hundred talents in debt. However narrow and disproportionable the beginnings of so vast an undertaking might seem to be, yet he would not embark his army until he had informed himself particularly what means his friends had to enable them to follow him, and supplied what they wanted, by giving good farms to some, a village to one, and the revenue of some hamlet or harbor town to another. So that at last he had portioned out or engaged almost all the royal property; which giving Perdiccas an occasion to ask him what he would leave himself, he replied, his hopes. "Your soldiers," replied Perdiccas, "will be your partners in those," and refused to accept of the estate he had assigned him. Some others of his friends did the like, but to those who willingly received, or desired assistance of him, he liberally granted it, as far as his patrimony in Macedonia would reach, the most part of which was spent in these donations.

With such vigorous resolutions, and his mind thus disposed, he passed the Hellespont, and at Troy sacrificed to Minerva, and honored the memory of the heroes who were buried there, with solemn libations; especially Achilles, whose gravestone he anointed, and with his friends, as the ancient custom is, ran naked about his sepulchre, and crowned it with garlands, declaring how happy he esteemed him, in having while he lived so faithful a friend, and when he was dead, so famous a poet to proclaim his actions. While he was viewing the rest of the antiquities and curiosities of the place, being told he might see Paris's harp, if he pleased, he said, he thought it not worth looking on, but he should be glad to see that of Achilles, to which he used to sing the glories and great actions of brave men.

In the meantime Darius's captains having collected large forces, were encamped on the further bank of the river Granicus, and it was necessary to fight, as it were, in the gate of Asia for an entrance into it. The depth of the river, with the unevenness and difficult ascent of the opposite bank, which was to be gained by main force, was apprehended by most, and some pronounced it an improper time to engage, because it was unusual for the kings of Macedonia to march with their forces in the month called Daesius. But Alexander broke through these scruples, telling; them they should call it a second Artemisius. And when Parmenio advised him not to attempt anything that day, because it was late, he told him that he should disgrace the Hellespont, should he fear the Granicus. And so without more saying, he immediately took the river with thirteen troops of horse, and advanced against whole showers of darts thrown from the steep opposite side, which was covered with armed multitudes of the enemy's horse and foot, notwithstanding the disadvantage of the ground and the rapidity of the stream; so that the action seemed to have more of frenzy and desperation in it, than of prudent conduct. However, he persisted obstinately to gain the passage, and at last with much ado making his way up the banks, which were extremely muddy and slippery, he had instantly to join in a mere confused hand-to-hand combat with the enemy, before he could draw up his men, who were still passing over, into any order. For the enemy pressed upon him with loud and warlike outcries; and charging horse against horse, with their lances, after they had broken and spent these, they fell to it with their swords. And Alexander, being easily known by his buckler, and a large plume of white feathers on each side of his helmet, was attacked on all sides, yet escaped wounding, though his cuirass was pierced by a javelin in one of the joinings. And Rhoesaces and Spithridates, two Persian commanders, falling upon him at once, he avoided one of them, and struck at Rhoesaces, who had a good cuirass on, with such force, that his spear breaking in his hand, he was glad to betake himself to his dagger. While they were thus engaged, Spithridates came up on one side of him, and raising himself upon his horse, gave him such a blow with his battle-axe on the helmet, that he cut off the crest of it, with one of his plumes, and the helmet was only just so far strong enough to save him, that the edge of the weapon touched the hair of his head. But as he was about to repeat his stroke, Clitus, called the black Clitus, prevented him, by running him through the body with his spear. At the same time Alexander dispatched Rhoesaces with his sword. While the horse were thus dangerously engaged, the Macedonian phalanx passed the river, and the foot on each side advanced to fight. But the enemy hardly sustaining the first onset, soon gave ground and fled, all but the mercenary Greeks, who, making a stand upon a rising ground, desired quarter, which Alexander, guided rather by passion than judgment, refused to grant, and charging them himself first, had his horse (not Bucephalas, but another) killed under him. And this obstinacy of his to cut off these experienced desperate men, cost him the lives of more of his own soldiers than all the battle before, besides those who were wounded. The Persians lost in this battle twenty thousand foot, and two thousand five hundred horse. On Alexander's side, Aristobulus says there were not wanting above four and thirty, of whom nine were foot-soldiers; and in memory of them he caused so many statues of brass, of Lysippus's making, to be erected. And that the Grecians might participate the honor of his victory, he sent a portion of the spoils home to them, particularly to the Athenians three hundred bucklers, and upon all the rest he ordered this inscription to be set: "Alexander the son of Philip, and the

Grecians, except the Lacedaemonians, won these from the barbarians who inhabit Asia." All the plate and purple garments, and other things of the same kind that he took from the Persians, except a very small quantity which he reserved for himself, he sent as a present to his mother.

This battle presently made a great change of affairs to Alexander's advantage. For Sardis itself, the chief seat of the barbarian's power in the maritime provinces, and many other considerable places were surrendered to him; only Halicarnassus and Miletus stood out, which he took by force, together with the territory about them. After which he was a little unsettled in his opinion how to proceed. Sometimes he thought it best to find out Darius as soon as he could, and put all to the hazard of a battle; another while he looked upon it as a more prudent course to make an entire reduction of the sea-coast, and not to seek the enemy till he had first exercised his power here and made himself secure of the resources of these provinces. While he was thus deliberating what to do, it happened that a spring of water near the city of Xanthus in Lycia, of its own accord swelled over its banks, and threw up a copper plate upon the margin, in which was engraven in ancient characters, that the time would come, when the Persian empire should be destroyed by the Grecians. Encouraged by this accident, he proceeded to reduce the maritime parts of Cilicia and Phoenicia, and passed his army along the sea-coasts of Pamphylia with such expedition that many historians have described and extolled it with that height of admiration, as if it were no less than a miracle, and an extraordinary effect of divine favor, that the waves which usually come rolling in violently from the main, and hardly ever leave so much as a narrow beach under the steep, broken cliffs at any time uncovered, should on a sudden retire to afford him passage. Menander, in one of his comedies, alludes to this marvel when he says,

> *Was Alexander ever favored more?*
> *Each man I wish for meets me at my door,*
> *And should I ask for passage through the sea,*
> *The sea I doubt not would retire for me.*

But Alexander himself in his epistles mentions nothing unusual in this at all, but says he went from Phaselis, and passed through what they call the Ladders. At Phaselis he stayed some time, and finding the statue of Theodectes, who was a native of this town and was now dead, erected in the marketplace, after he had supped, having drunk pretty plentifully, he went and danced about it, and crowned it with garlands, honoring not ungracefully in his sport, the memory of a philosopher whose conversation he had formerly enjoyed, when he was Aristotle's scholar.

Then he subdued the Pisidians who made head against him, and conquered the Phrygians, at whose chief city Gordium, which is said to be the seat of the ancient Midas, he saw the famous chariot fastened with cords made of the rind of the corner-tree, which whosoever should untie, the inhabitants had a tradition, that for him was reserved the empire of the world. Most authors tell the story that Alexander, finding himself unable to untie the knot, the ends of which were secretly twisted round and folded up within it, cut it asunder with his sword. But Aristobulus tells us it was easy for him to undo it, by only pulling the pin out of the pole, to which the yoke was tied, and afterwards drawing off the yoke itself from below. From hence he advanced into Paphlagonia and Cappadocia, both which countries he soon reduced to obedience, and then hearing of the death of Memnon, the best commander Darius had upon the sea-coasts, who, if he had lived, might, it was supposed, have put many impediments and difficulties in the way of the progress of his arms, he was the rather encouraged to carry the war into the upper provinces of Asia.

Darius was by this time upon his march from Susa, very confident, not only in the number of his men, which amounted to six hundred thousand, but likewise in a dream, which the Persian soothsayers interpreted rather in flattery to him, than according to the natural probability. He dreamed that he saw the Macedonian phalanx all on fire, and Alexander waiting on him, clad in the same dress which he himself had been used to wear when he was courier to the late king; after which, going into the temple of Belus, he vanished out of his sight. The dream would appear to have supernaturally signified to him the illustrious actions the Macedonians were to perform, and that as he from a courier's place had risen to the throne, so Alexander should come to be master of Asia, and not long surviving his conquests, conclude his life with glory. Darius's confidence increased the more, because Alexander spent so much time in Cilicia, which he imputed to his cowardice. But it was sickness that detained him there, which some say he contracted from his fatigues, others from bathing in the river Cydnus, whose waters were exceedingly cold. However it happened, none of his physicians would venture to give him any remedies, they thought his case so desperate, and were so afraid of the suspicions and ill-will of the Macedonians if they should fail in the cure; till Philip, the Acarnanian, seeing how critical his case was, but relying on his own well-known friendship for him, resolved to try the last efforts of his art, and rather hazard his own credit and life, than suffer him to perish for want of physic, which he confidently administered to him, encouraging him to take it boldly, if he desired a speedy recovery, in order to prosecute the war. At this very time, Parmenio wrote to Alexander from the camp, bidding him have a care of Philip, as one who was bribed by Darius to kill him, with great sums of money, and a promise of his daughter in marriage. When he had perused the letter, he put it under his pillow, without showing it so much as to any of his most intimate friends, and when Philip came in with the potion, he took it with great cheerfulness and assurance, giving him meantime the letter to read. This was a spectacle well worth being present at, to see Alexander take the draught, and Philip read the letter at the same time, and then turn and look upon one another, but with different sentiments; for Alexander's looks were cheerful and open, to show his kindness to and confidence in his physician, while the other was full of surprise and alarm at the accusation, appealing to the gods to witness his innocence, sometimes lifting up his hands to heaven, and then throwing himself down by the bedside, and beseeching Alexander to lay aside all fear, and follow his directions without apprehension. For the medicine at first worked so strongly as to drive, so to say, the vital forces into the interior; he lost his speech, and falling into a swoon, had scarce any sense or pulse left. However, in no long time, by Philip's means, his health and strength returned, and he showed himself in public to the Macedonians, who were in continual fear and dejection until they saw him abroad again.

There was at this time in Darius's army a Macedonian refugee, named Amyntas, one who was pretty well acquainted with Alexander's character. This man, when he saw Darius intended to fall upon the enemy in the passes and defiles, advised him earnestly to keep where he was, in the open and extensive plains, it being the advantage of a numerous army to have field-room enough when it engages with a lesser force. Darius, instead of taking his counsel, told him he was afraid the enemy would endeavor to run away, and so Alexander would escape out of his hands. "That fear," replied Amyntas, "is needless, for assure yourself that far from avoiding, you, he will make all the speed he can to meet you, and is now most likely on his march towards you." But Amyntas's counsel was to no purpose, for Darius immediately decamping, marched into Cilicia, at the same time that Alexander advanced into Syria to meet him; and missing one another in the night, they both turned back again. Alexander, greatly pleased with the event, made all the haste he could to fight in the defiles, and Darius to recover his former ground, and draw his army out of so disadvantageous a place. For now he began to perceive his error in engaging himself too far in a country in which the sea, the mountains, and the river Pinarus running through the midst of it, would necessitate him to divide his forces, render his horse almost unserviceable, and only cover and support the weakness of the enemy. Fortune was not kinder to Alexander in the choice of the ground, than he was careful to improve it to his advantage. For being much inferior in numbers, so far from allowing himself to be outflanked, he stretched his right wing much further out than the left wing of his enemies, and fighting there himself in the very foremost ranks, put the barbarians to flight. In this battle he was wounded in the thigh, Chares says by Darius, with whom he fought hand to hand. But in the account which he gave Antipater of the battle though indeed he owns he was wounded in the thigh with sword, though not dangerously, yet he takes no notice who it was that wounded him.

Nothing was wanting to complete this victory, in which he overthrew above a hundred and ten thousand of his enemies, but the taking the person of Darius, who escaped very narrowly by flight. However, having taken his chariot and his bow, he returned from pursuing him, and found his own men busy in pillaging the barbarians' camp, which (though to disburden themselves, they had left most of their baggage at Damascus) was exceedingly rich. But Darius's tent, which was full of splendid furniture, and quantities of gold and silver, they reserved for Alexander himself, who after he had put off his arms, went to bathe himself, saying, "Let us now cleanse ourselves from the toils of war in the bath of Darius." "Not so," replied one of his followers, "but in Alexander's rather; for the property of the conquered is, and should be called the conqueror's." Here, when he beheld the bathing vessels, the waterpots, the pans, and the ointment boxes, all of gold, curiously wrought, and smelt the fragrant odors with which the whole place was exquisitely perfumed, and from thence passed into a pavilion of great size and height, where the couches and tables and preparations for an entertainment were perfectly magnificent, he turned to those about him and said, "This, it seems, is royalty."

But as he was going to supper, word was brought him that Darius's mother and wife and two unmarried daughters, being taken among the rest of the prisoners, upon the sight of his chariot and bow were all in mourning and sorrow, imagining him to be dead. After a little pause, more livelily affected with their affliction than with his own success he sent Leonnatus to them to let them know Darius was not dead, and that they need not fear any harm from Alexander, who made war upon him only for dominion; they should themselves be provided with everything they had been used to receive from Darius. This kind message could not but be very welcome to the captive ladies, especially being made good by actions no less humane and generous. For he gave them leave to bury whom they pleased of the Persians, and to make use for this purpose of what garments and furniture they thought fit out of the booty. He diminished nothing of their equipage, or of the attentions and respect formerly paid them, and allowed larger pensions for their maintenance than they had before. But the noblest and most royal part of their usage was, that he treated these illustrious prisoners according to their virtue and character, not suffering them to hear, or receive, or so much as to apprehend anything that was unbecoming. So that they seemed rather lodged in some temple, or some holy virgin chambers, where they enjoyed their privacy sacred and uninterrupted, than in the camp of an enemy. Nevertheless Darius's wife was accounted the most beautiful princess then living, as her husband the tallest and handsomest man of his time, and the daughters were not unworthy of their parents. But Alexander, esteeming it more kingly to govern himself than to conquer his enemies, sought no intimacy with any one of them, nor indeed with any other woman before marriage, except Barsine, Memnon's widow, who was taken prisoner at Damascus. She had been instructed in the Grecian learning, was of a gentle temper, and, by her father Artabazus, royally descended, which good qualities, added to the solicitations and encouragement of Parmenio, as Aristobulus tells us, made him the more willing to attach himself to so agreeable and illustrious a woman. Of the rest of the female captives though remarkably handsome and well proportioned, he took no further notice than to say jestingly, that Persian women were terrible eye-sores. And he himself, retaliating, as it were, by the display of the beauty of his own temperance and self-control, bade them be removed, as he would have done so many lifeless images. When Philoxenus, his lieutenant on the sea-coast, wrote to him to know if he would buy two young boys, of great beauty, whom one Theodorus, a Tarentine, had to sell, he was so offended, that he often expostulated with his friends, what baseness Philoxenus had ever observed in him, that he should presume to make him such a reproachful offer. And he immediately wrote him a very sharp letter, telling him Theodorus and his merchandise might go with his good-will to destruction. Nor was he less severe to Hagnon, who sent him word he would buy a Corinthian youth named Crobylus, as a present for him. And hearing that Damon and Timotheus, two of Parmenio's Macedonian soldiers, had abused the wives of some strangers who were in his pay, he wrote to Parmenio, charging him strictly, if he found them guilty, to put them to death, as wild beasts that were only made for the mischief of mankind. In the same letter he added, that he had not so much as seen or desired to see the wife of Darius, no, nor suffered anybody to speak of her beauty before him. He was wont to say, that sleep and the act of generation chiefly made him sensible that he was mortal; as much as to say, that weariness and pleasure proceed both from the same frailty and imbecility of human nature.

In his diet, also, he was most temperate, as appears, omitting many other circumstances, by what he said to Ada, whom he adopted, with the title of mother, and afterwards created queen of Caria. For when she out of kindness sent him every day many curious dishes, and sweetmeats, and would have furnished him with some cooks and pastry-men, who were thought to have great skill, he told her he wanted none of them, his preceptor, Leonidas, having already given him the best, which were a night march to prepare for breakfast, and a moderate breakfast to create an appetite for supper. Leonidas also, he added, used to open and search the furniture of his chamber, and his wardrobe, to see if his mother had left him anything that was delicate or superfluous. He was much less addicted to wine than was generally believed; that which gave people occasion to think so of him was, that when he had nothing else to do, he loved to sit long and talk, rather than drink, and over every cup hold a long conversation. For when his affairs called upon him, he would not be detained, as other generals often were, either by wine, or sleep, nuptial solemnities, spectacles, or any other diversion whatsoever; a convincing argument of which is, that in the short time he lived, he accomplished so many and so great actions. When he was free from employment, after he was up, and had sacrificed to the gods, he used to sit down to breakfast, and then spend the rest of the day in hunting, or writing memoirs, giving decisions on some military questions, or reading. In marches that required no great haste, he would practice shooting as he went along, or to mount a chariot, and alight from it in full speed. Sometimes, for sport's sake, as his journals tell us, he would hunt foxes and go fowling. When he came in for the evening, after he had bathed and was anointed, he would call for his bakers and chief cooks, to know if they had his dinner ready. He never cared to dine till it was pretty late and beginning to be dark, and was wonderfully circumspect at meals that everyone who sat with him should be served alike and with proper attention; and his love of talking, as was said before, made him delight to sit long at his wine. And then, though otherwise no prince's conversation was ever so agreeable, he would fall into a temper of ostentation and soldierly boasting, which gave his flatterers a great advantage to ride him, and made his better friends very uneasy. For though they thought it too base to strive who should flatter him most, yet they found it hazardous not to do it; so that between the shame and the danger, they were in a great strait how to behave themselves. After such an entertainment, he was wont to bathe, and then perhaps he would sleep till noon, and sometimes all day long. He was so very temperate in his eating, that when any rare fish or fruits were sent him, he would distribute them among his friends, and often reserve nothing for himself. His table, however, was always magnificent, the expense of it still increasing with his good fortune, till it amounted to ten thousand drachmas a day, to which sum he limited it, and beyond this he would suffer none to lay out in any entertainment where he himself was the guest.

 After the battle of Issus, he sent to Damascus to seize upon the money and baggage, the wives and children of the Persians, of which spoil the Thessalian horsemen had the greatest share; for he had taken particular notice of their gallantry in the fight, and sent them thither on purpose to make their reward suitable to their courage. Not but that the rest of the army had so considerable a part of the booty as was sufficient to enrich them all. This first gave the Macedonians such a taste of the Persian wealth and women and barbaric splendor of living, that they were ready to pursue and follow upon it with all the eagerness of hounds upon a scent. But Alexander, before he proceeded any further, thought it necessary to assure himself of the sea-coast. Those who governed in Cyprus, put that island into his possession, and Phoenicia, Tyre only excepted, was surrendered to him. During the siege of this city, which with mounds of earth cast up, and battering engines, and two hundred galleys by sea, was carried on for seven months together, he dreamt that he saw

Hercules upon the walls, reaching, out his hand, and calling to him. And many of the Tyrians in their sleep, fancied that Apollo told them he was displeased with their actions, and was about to leave them and go over to Alexander. Upon which, as if the god had been a deserting soldier, they seized him, so to say, in the act, tied down the statue with ropes, and nailed it to the pedestal, reproaching him, that he was a favorer of Alexander. Another time, Alexander dreamed he saw a Satyr mocking him at a distance, and when he endeavored to catch him, he still escaped from him, till at last with much perseverance, and running about after him, he got him into his power. The soothsayers making two words of Satyrus, assured him, that Tyre should he his own. The inhabitants at this time show a spring of water, near which they say Alexander slept, when he fancied the Satyr appeared to him.

While the body of the army lay before Tyre, he made an excursion against the Arabians who inhabit the Mount Antilibanus, in which he hazarded his life extremely to bring off his master Lysimachus, who would needs go along with him, declaring he was neither older nor inferior in courage to Phoenix, Achilles's guardian. For when, quitting their horses, they began to march up the hills on foot, the rest of the soldiers outwent them a great deal, so that night drawing on, and the enemy near, Alexander was fain to stay behind so long, to encourage and help up the lagging and tired old man, that before he was aware, he was left behind, a great way from his soldiers, with a slender attendance, and forced to pass an extremely cold night in the dark, and in a very inconvenient place; till seeing a great many scattered fires of the enemy at some distance, and trusting to his agility of body, and as he was always wont by undergoing toils and labors himself to cheer and support the Macedonians in any distress, he ran straight to one of the nearest fires, and with his dagger dispatching two of the barbarians that sat by it, snatched up a lighted brand, and returned with it to his own men. They immediately made a great fire, which so alarmed the enemy that most of them fled, and those that assaulted them were soon routed, and thus they rested securely the remainder of the night. Thus Chares writes.

But to return to the siege, it had this issue. Alexander, that he might refresh his army, harassed with many former encounters, had led only a small party towards the walls, rather to keep the enemy busy, than with any prospect of much advantage. It happened at this time that Aristander, the soothsayer, after he had sacrificed, upon view of the entrails, affirmed confidently to those who stood by, that the city should be certainly taken that very month, upon which there was a laugh and some mockery among the soldiers, as this was the last day of it. The king seeing him in perplexity, and always anxious to support the credit of the predictions, gave order that they should not count it as the thirtieth, but as the twenty-third of the month, and ordering the trumpets to sound, attacked the walls more seriously than he at first intended. The sharpness of the assault so inflamed the rest of his forces who were left in the camp, that they could not hold from advancing to second it, which they performed with so much vigor, that the Tyrians retired, and the town was carried that very day. The next place he sat down before was Gaza, one of the largest cities of Syria, where this accident befell him. A large bird flying over him, let a clod of earth fall upon his shoulder, and then settling upon one of the battering engines, was suddenly entangled and caught in the nets composed of sinews, which protected the ropes with which the machine was managed. This fell out exactly according to Aristander's prediction, which was, that Alexander should be wounded, and the city reduced.

From hence he sent great part of the spoils to Olympias, Cleopatra, and the rest of his friends, not omitting his preceptor Leonidas, on whom he bestowed five hundred talents weight of frankincense, and a hundred of myrrh, in remembrance of the hopes he had once expressed of him when he was but a child. For Leonidas, it seems, standing by him one day while he was sacrificing, and seeing him take both his hands full of incense to throw into the fire, told him it became him to be more sparing in his offerings, and not be so profuse till he was master of the countries which those sweet gums and spices came from. So Alexander now wrote to him, saying, "We have sent you abundance of myrrh and frankincense, that for the future you may not be stingy to the gods." Among the treasures and other booty that was taken from Darius, there was a very precious casket, which being brought to Alexander for a great rarity, he asked those about him what they thought fittest to be laid up in it; and when they had delivered their various opinions, he told them he should keep Homer's Iliad in it. This is attested by many credible authors, and if what those of Alexandria tell us, relying upon the authority of Heraclides, be true, Homer was neither an idle, nor an unprofitable companion to him in his expedition. For when he was master of Egypt, designing to settle a colony of Grecians there, he resolved to build a large and populous city, and give it his own name. In order to which, after he had measured and staked out the ground with the advice of the best architects, he chanced one night in his sleep to see a wonderful vision; a grey-headed old man, of a venerable aspect, appeared to stand by him, and pronounce these verses:—

> *An island lies, where loud the billows roar,*
> *Pharos they call it, on the Egyptian shore.*

Alexander upon this immediately rose up and went to Pharos, which, at that time, was an island lying a little above the Canobic mouth of the river Nile, though it has now been joined to the main land by a mole. As soon as he saw the commodious situation of the place, it being a long neck of land, stretching like an isthmus between large lagoons and shallow waters on one side, and the sea on the other, the latter at the end of it making a spacious harbor, he said, Homer, besides his other excellencies, was a very good architect, and ordered the plan of a city to be drawn out answerable to the place. To do which, for want of chalk, the soil being black, they laid out their lines with flour, taking in a pretty large compass of ground in a semicircular figure, and drawing into the inside of the circumference equal straight lines from each end, thus giving it something of the form of a cloak or cape. While he was pleasing himself with his design, on a sudden an infinite number of great birds of several kinds, rising like a black cloud out of the river and the lake, devoured every morsel of the flour that had been used in setting out the lines; at which omen even Alexander himself was troubled, till the augurs restored his confidence again by telling him, it was a sign the city he was about to build would not only abound in all things within itself, but also be the nurse and feeder of many nations. He commanded the workmen to proceed, while he went to visit the temple of Ammon.

This was a long and painful, and, in two respects, a dangerous journey; first, if they should lose their provision of water, as for several days none could be obtained; and, secondly, if a violent south wind should rise upon them, while they were traveling through the wide extent of deep sands, as it is said to have done when Cambyses led his army that way, blowing the sand together in heaps, and raising, as it were, the whole desert like a sea upon them, till fifty thousand were swallowed up and destroyed by it. All these difficulties were weighed and represented to him; but Alexander was not easily to be diverted from anything he was bent upon. For fortune having hitherto seconded him in his designs, made him resolute and firm in his opinions, and the boldness of his temper raised a sort of passion in him for surmounting difficulties; as if it were not enough to be always victorious in the field, unless places and seasons and nature herself submitted to him. In this journey, the relief and assistance the gods afforded him in his distresses, were more remarkable, and obtained greater belief than the oracles he received afterwards, which, however, were valued and credited the more on account of those occurrences. For first, plentiful rains that fell, preserved them from any fear of perishing by drought, and, allaying the extreme dryness of the sand, which now became moist and firm to travel on, cleared and purified the air. Besides this, when they were out of their way, and were wandering up and down, because the marks which were wont to direct the guides were disordered and lost, they were set right again by some ravens, which flew before them when on their march, and waited for them when they lingered and fell behind; and the greatest miracle, as Callisthenes tells us, was that if any of the company went astray in the night, they never ceased croaking and making a noise, till by that means they had brought them into the right way again. Having passed through the wilderness, they came to the place; where the high-priest at the first salutation bade Alexander welcome from his father Ammon. And being asked by him whether any of his father's murderers had escaped punishment, he charged him to speak with more respect, since his was not a mortal father. Then Alexander, changing his expression, desired to know of him if any of those who murdered Philip were yet unpunished, and further concerning dominion, whether the empire of the world was reserved for him? This, the god answered, he should obtain, and that Philip's death was fully revenged, which gave him so much satisfaction, that he made splendid offerings to Jupiter, and gave the priests very rich presents. This is what most authors write concerning the oracles. But Alexander, in a letter to his mother, tells her there were some secret answers, which at his return he would communicate to her only. Others say that the priest, desirous as a piece of courtesy to address him in Greek, "O Paidion," by a slip in pronunciation ended with the s instead of the n, and said, "O Paidios," which mistake Alexander was well enough pleased with, and it went for current that the oracle had called him so.

Among the sayings of one Psammon, a philosopher, whom he heard in Egypt, he most approved of this, that all men are governed by God, because in everything, that which is chief and commands, is divine. But what he pronounced himself upon this subject, was even more like a philosopher, for he said, God was the common father of us all, but more particularly of the best of us. To the barbarians he carried himself very haughtily, as if he were fully persuaded of his divine birth and parentage; but to the Grecians more moderately, and with less affectation of divinity, except it were once in writing to the Athenians about Samos, when he tells them that he should not himself have bestowed upon them that free and glorious city; "You received it," he says, "from the bounty of him who at that time was called my lord and father," meaning Philip. However, afterwards being wounded with an arrow, and feeling much pain, he turned to those about him, and told them, "This, my friends, is real flowing blood, not Ichor,

'Such as immortal gods are wont to shed.'"

And another time, when it thundered so much that everybody was afraid, and Anaxarchus, the sophist, asked him if he who was Jupiter's son could do anything like this, "Nay," said Alexander, laughing, "I have no desire to be formidable to my friends, as you would have me, who despised my table for being furnished with fish, and not with the heads of governors of provinces." For in fact it is related as true, that Anaxarchus seeing a present of small fishes, which the king sent to Hephaestion, had used this expression, in a sort of irony, and disparagement of those who undergo vast labors and encounter great hazards in pursuit of magnificent objects, which after all bring them little more pleasure or enjoyment than what others have. From what I have said upon this subject, it is apparent that Alexander in himself was not foolishly affected, or had the vanity to think himself really a god, but merely used his claims to divinity as a means of maintaining among other people the sense of his superiority.

At his return out of Egypt into Phoenicia, he sacrificed and made solemn processions, to which were added shows of lyric dances and tragedies, remarkable not merely for the splendor of the equipage and decorations, but for the competition among those who exhibited them. For the kings of Cyprus were here the exhibitors, just in the same manner as at Athens those who are chosen by lot out of the tribes. And, indeed, they showed the greatest emulation to outvie each other; especially Nicocreon, king of Salamis, and Pasicrates of Soli, who furnished the chorus, and defrayed the expenses of the two most celebrated actors, Athenodorus and Thessalus, the former performing for Pasicrates, and the latter for Nicocreon. Thessalus was most favored by Alexander, though it did not appear till Athenodorus was declared victor by the plurality of votes. For then at his going away, he said the judges deserved to be commended for what they had done, but that he would willingly have lost part of his kingdom, rather than to have seen Thessalus overcome. However, when he understood Athenodorus was fined by the Athenians for being absent at the festivals of Bacchus, though he refused his request that he would write a letter in his behalf, he gave him a sufficient sum to satisfy the penalty. Another time, when Lycon of Scarphia happened to act with great applause in the theater, and in a verse which he introduced into the comic part which he was acting, begged for a present of ten talents, he laughed and gave him the money.

Darius wrote him a letter, and sent friends to intercede with him, requesting him to accept as a ransom of his captives the sum of a thousand talents, and offering him in exchange for his amity and alliance, all the countries on this side the river Euphrates, together with one of his daughters in marriage. These propositions he communicated to his friends, and when Parmenio told him, that for his part, if he were Alexander, he should readily embrace them, "So would I," said Alexander, "if I were Parmenio." Accordingly, his answer to Darius was, that if he would come and yield himself up into his power, he would treat him with all possible kindness; if not, he was resolved immediately to go himself and seek him. But the death of Darius's wife in childbirth made him soon after regret one part of this answer, and he showed evident marks of grief, at being thus deprived of a further opportunity of exercising his clemency and good nature, which he manifested, however, as far as he could, by giving her a most sumptuous funeral.

Among the eunuchs who waited in the queen's chamber, and were taken prisoners with the women, there was one Tireus, who getting out of the camp, fled away on horseback to Darius, to inform him of his wife's death. He, when he heard it, beating his head, and bursting into tears and lamentations, said,

"Alas! how great is the calamity of the Persians! Was it not enough that their king's consort and sister was a prisoner in her lifetime, but she must, now she is dead also, be but meanly and obscurely buried?" "Oh king," replied the eunuch, "as to her funeral rites, or any respect or honor that should have been shown in them, you have not the least reason to accuse the ill-fortune of your country; for to my knowledge neither your queen Statira when alive, nor your mother, nor children, wanted anything of their former happy condition, unless it were the light of your countenance, which I doubt not but the lord Oromasdes will yet restore to its former glory. And after her decease, I assure you, she had not only all due funeral ornaments, but was honored also with the tears of your very enemies; for Alexander is as gentle after victory, as he is terrible in the field." At the hearing of these words, such was the grief and emotion of Darius's mind, that they carried him into extravagant suspicions; and taking Tireus aside into a more private part of his tent, "Unless thou likewise," said he to him, "hast deserted me, together with the good fortune of Persia, and art become a Macedonian in thy heart; if thou yet ownest me for thy master Darius, tell me, I charge thee, by the veneration thou payest the light of Mithras, and this right hand of thy king, do I not lament the least of Statira's misfortunes in her captivity and death? Have I not suffered something more injurious and deplorable in her lifetime? And had I not been miserable with less dishonor, if I had met with a more severe and inhuman enemy? For how is it possible a young man as he is, should treat the wife of his opponent with so much distinction, were it not from some motive that does me disgrace?" Whilst he was yet speaking, Tireus threw himself at his feet, and besought him neither to wrong Alexander so much, nor his dead wife and sister, as to give utterance to any such thoughts, which deprived him of the greatest consolation left him in his adversity, the belief that he was overcome by a man whose virtues raised him above human nature; that he ought to look upon Alexander with love and admiration, who had given no less proofs of his continence towards the Persian women, than of his valor among the men. The eunuch confirmed all he said with solemn and dreadful oaths, and was further enlarging upon Alexander's moderation and magnanimity on other occasions, when Darius, breaking away from him into the other division of the tent, where his friends and courtiers were, lifted up his hands to heaven, and uttered this prayer, "Ye gods," said he, "of my family, and of my kingdom, if it be possible, I beseech you to restore the declining affairs of Persia, that I may leave them in as flourishing a condition as I found them, and have it in my power to make a grateful return to Alexander for the kindness which in my adversity he has shown to those who are dearest to me. But if, indeed, the fatal time be come, which is to give a period to the Persian monarchy, if our ruin be a debt that must be paid to the divine jealousy and the vicissitude of things, then I beseech you grant that no other man but Alexander may sit upon the throne of Cyrus." Such is the narrative given by the greater number of the historians.

But to return to Alexander. After he had reduced all Asia on this side the Euphrates, he advanced towards Darius, who was coming down against him with a million of men. In his march, a very ridiculous passage happened. The servants who followed the camp, for sport's sake divided themselves into two parties, and named the commander of one of them Alexander, and of the other Darius. At first they only pelted one another with clods of earth, but presently took to their fists, and at last, heated with the contention, they fought in good earnest with stones and clubs, so that they had much ado to part them; till Alexander, upon hearing of it, ordered the two captains to decide the quarrel by single combat, and armed him who bore his name himself, while Philotas did the same to him who represented Darius. The whole army were spectators of this encounter, willing from the event of it to derive an omen of their own future success. After they had fought stoutly a pretty long while, at last he who was called Alexander had the better, and for a reward of his prowess, had twelve villages given him, with leave to wear the Persian dress. So we are told by Eratosthenes.

But the great battle of all that was fought with Darius, was not, as most writers tell us, at Arbela, but at Gaugamela, which, in their language, signifies the camel's house, forasmuch as one of their ancient kings having escaped the pursuit of his enemies on a swift camel, in gratitude to his beast, settled him at this place, with an allowance of certain villages and rents for his maintenance. It came to pass that in the month Boedromion, about the beginning of the feast of Mysteries at Athens, there was an eclipse of the moon, the eleventh night after which, the two armies being now in view of one another, Darius kept his men in arms, and by torchlight took a general review of them. But Alexander, while his soldiers slept, spent the night before his tent with his diviner Aristander, performing certain mysterious ceremonies, and sacrificing to the god Fear. In the meanwhile the oldest of his commanders, and chiefly Parmenio, when they beheld all the plain between Niphates and the Gordyaean mountains shining with the lights and fires which were made by the barbarians, and heard the uncertain and confused sound of voices out of their camp, like the distant roaring of a vast ocean, were so amazed at the thoughts of such a multitude, that after some conference among themselves, they concluded it an enterprise too difficult and hazardous for them to engage so numerous an enemy in the day, and therefore meeting the king as he came from sacrificing, besought him to attack Darius by night, that the darkness might conceal the danger of the ensuing battle. To this he gave them the celebrated answer, "I will not steal a victory," which though some at the time thought a boyish and inconsiderate speech, as if he played with danger, others, however, regarded as an evidence that he confided in his present condition, and acted on a true judgment of the future, not wishing to leave Darius, in case he were worsted, the pretext of trying his fortune again, which he might suppose himself to have, if he could impute his overthrow to the disadvantage of the night, as he did before to the mountains, the narrow passages, and the sea. For while he had such numerous forces and large dominions still remaining, it was not any want of men or arms that could induce him to give up the war, but only the loss of all courage and hope upon the conviction of an undeniable and manifest defeat.

After they were gone from him with this answer, he laid himself down in his tent and slept the rest of the night more soundly than was usual with him, to the astonishment of the commanders, who came to him early in the morning, and were fain themselves to give order that the soldiers should breakfast. But at last, time not giving them leave to wait any longer, Parmenio went to his bedside, and called him twice or thrice by his name, till he waked him, and then asked him how it was possible, when he was to fight the most important battle of all, he could sleep as soundly as if he were already victorious. "And are we not so, indeed," replied Alexander, smiling, "since we are at last relieved from the trouble of wandering in pursuit of Darius through a wide and wasted country, hoping in vain that he would fight us?" And not only before the battle, but in the height of the danger, he showed himself great, and manifested the self-possession of a just foresight and confidence. For the battle for some time fluctuated and was dubious. The left wing, where Parmenio commanded, was so impetuously charged by the Bactrian horse that it was disordered and forced to give ground, at the same time that Mazaeus had sent a detachment round about to fall upon those who guarded the baggage, which so disturbed Parmenio, that he sent messengers to acquaint Alexander that the camp and baggage would be all lost unless he immediately believed the rear by a considerable reinforcement drawn out of the front. This message being brought him just as he was giving the signal to those about him for the onset, he bade them tell Parmenio that he must have surely lost the use of his reason, and had forgotten, in his alarm, that soldiers, if victorious, become masters of their enemies' baggage; and if defeated, instead of taking care of their wealth or their slaves, have nothing more to do but to fight gallantly and die with honor. When he had said this, he put on his helmet, having the rest of his arms on before he came out of his tent, which were coat of the Sicilian make, girt close about him, and over that a breastpiece of thickly quilted linen, which was taken among other booty at the battle of Issus. The helmet, which was made by Theophilus, though of iron, was so well wrought and polished, that it was as bright as the most refined silver. To this was fitted a gorget of the same metal, set with precious stones. His sword, which was the weapon he most used in fight, was given him by the king of the Citieans, and was of an admirable temper and lightness. The belt which he also wore in all engagements, was of much richer workmanship than the rest of his armor. It was a work of the ancient Helicon, and had been presented to him by the Rhodians, as mark of their respect to him. So long as he was engaged in drawing up his men, or riding about to give orders or directions, or to view them, he spared Bucephalas, who was now growing old, and made use of another horse; but when he was actually to fight, he sent for him again, and as soon as he was mounted, commenced the attack.

He made the longest address that day to the Thessalians and other Greeks, who answered him with loud shouts, desiring him to lead them on against the barbarians, upon which he shifted his javelin into his left hand, and with his right lifted up towards heaven, besought the gods, as Callisthenes tells us, that if he was of a truth the son of Jupiter, they would he pleased to assist and strengthen the Grecians. At the same time the augur Aristander, who had a white mantle about him, and a crown of gold on his head, rode by and showed them an eagle that soared just over Alexander, and directed his Right towards the enemy; which so animated the beholders, that after mutual encouragements and exhortations, the horse charged at full speed, and were followed in a mass by the whole phalanx of the foot. But before they could well come to blows with the first ranks, the barbarians shrunk back, and were hotly pursued by Alexander, who drove those that fled before him into the middle of the battle, where Darius himself was in person, whom he saw from a distance over the foremost ranks, conspicuous in the midst of his life-guard, a tall and fine-looking man, drawn in a lofty chariot, defended by an abundance of the best horse, who stood close in order about it, ready to receive the enemy. But Alexander's approach was so terrible, forcing those who gave back upon those who yet maintained their ground, that he beat down and dispersed them almost all. Only a few of the bravest and valiantest opposed the pursuit, who were slain in their king's presence, falling in heaps upon one another, and in the very pangs of death striving to catch hold of the horses. Darius now seeing all was lost, that those who were placed in front to defend him were broken and beat back upon him, that he could not turn or disengage his chariot without great difficulty, the wheels being clogged and entangled among the dead bodies, which lay in such heaps as not only stopped, but almost covered the horses, and made them rear and grow so unruly, that the frighted charioteer could govern them no longer, in this extremity was glad to quit his chariot and his arms, and mounting, it is said, upon a mare that had been taken from her foal, betook himself to flight. But he had not escaped so either, if Parmenio had not sent fresh messengers to Alexander, to desire him to return and assist him against a considerable body of the enemy which yet stood together, and would not give ground. For, indeed, Parmenio is on all hands accused of having been sluggish and unserviceable in this battle, whether age had impaired his courage, or that, as Callisthenes says, he secretly disliked and envied Alexander's growing greatness. Alexander, though he was not a little vexed to be so recalled and hindered from pursuing his victory, yet concealed the true reason from his men, and causing a retreat to be sounded, as if it were too late to continue the execution any longer, marched back towards the place of danger, and by the way met with the news of the enemy's total overthrow and flight.

This battle being thus over, seemed to put a period to the Persian empire; and Alexander, who was now proclaimed king of Asia, returned thanks to the gods in magnificent sacrifices, and rewarded his friends and followers with great sums of money, and places, and governments of provinces. And eager to gain honor with the Grecians, he wrote to them that he would have all tyrannies abolished, that they might live free according to their own laws, and specially to the Plataeans, that their city should be rebuilt, because their ancestors had permitted their countrymen of old to make their territory the seat of the war, when they fought with the barbarians for their common liberty. He sent also part of the spoils into Italy, to the Crotoniats, to honor the zeal and courage of their citizen Phayllus, the wrestler, who, in the Median war, when the other Grecian colonies in Italy disowned Greece, that he might have a share in the danger, joined the fleet at Salamis, with a vessel set forth at his own charge. So affectionate was Alexander to all kind of virtue, and so desirous to preserve the memory of laudable actions.

From hence he marched through the province of Babylon, which immediately submitted to him, and in Ecbatana was much surprised at the sight of the place where fire issues in a continuous stream, like a spring of water, out of a cleft in the earth, and the stream of naphtha, which, not far from this spot, flows out so abundantly as to form a sort of lake. This naphtha, in other respects resembling bitumen, is so subject to take fire, that before it touches the flame, it will kindle at the very light that surrounds it, and often inflame the intermediate air also. The barbarians, to show the power and nature of it, sprinkled the street that led to the king's lodgings with little drops of it, and when it was almost night, stood at the further end with torches, which being applied to the moistened places, the first at once taking fire, instantly, as quick as a man could think of it, it caught from one end to another, in such a manner that the whole street was one continued flame. Among those who used to wait on the king and find occasion to amuse him when he anointed and washed himself, there was one Athenophanes, an Athenian, who desired him to make an experiment of the naphtha upon Stephanus, who stood by in the bathing place, a youth with a ridiculously ugly face, whose talent was singing well, "For," said he, "if it take hold of him and is not put out, it must undeniably be allowed to be of the most invincible strength." The youth, as it happened, readily consented to undergo the trial, and as soon as he was anointed and rubbed with it, his whole body broke out into such a flame, and was so seized by the fire, that Alexander was in the greatest perplexity and alarm for him, and not without reason; for nothing could have prevented his being consumed by it, if by good chance there had not been people at hand with a great many vessels of water for the service of the bath, with all which they had much ado to extinguish the fire; and his body was so burned all over, that he was not cured of it a good while after. And thus it is not without some plausibility that they endeavor to reconcile the fable to truth, who say this was the drug in the tragedies with which Medea anointed the crown and veil which she gave to Creon's daughter. For neither the things themselves, nor the fire could kindle of its own accord, but being prepared for it by the naphtha, they imperceptibly attracted and caught a flame which happened to be brought near them. For the rays and emanations of fire at a distance have no other effect upon some bodies than bare light and heat, but in others, where they meet with airy dryness, and also sufficient rich moisture, they collect themselves and soon kindle and create a transformation. The manner, however, of the production of naphtha admits of a diversity of opinion on whether this liquid substance that feeds the flame does not rather proceed from a soil that is unctuous and productive of fire, as that of the province of Babylon is, where the ground is so very hot, that oftentimes the grains of barley leap up, and are thrown out, as if the violent inflammation had made the earth throb; and in the extreme heats the inhabitants are wont to sleep upon skins filled with water. Harpalus, who was left governor of this country, and was desirous to adorn the palace gardens and walks with Grecian plants, succeeded in raising all but ivy, which the earth would not bear, but constantly killed. For being a plant that loves a cold soil, the temper of this hot and fiery earth was improper for it. But such digressions as these the impatient reader will be more willing to pardon, if they are kept within a moderate compass.

    At the taking of Susa, Alexander found in the palace forty thousand talents in money ready coined, besides an unspeakable quantity of other furniture and treasure; amongst which was five thousand talents' worth of Hermionian purple, that had been laid up there a hundred and ninety years, and yet kept its color as fresh and lively as at first. The reason of which, they say, is that in dyeing the purple they made use of honey, and of white oil in the white tincture, both which after the like space of time preserve the clearness and brightness of their luster. Dinon also relates that the Persian kings had water fetched from the Nile and the Danube, which they laid up in their treasuries as a sort of testimony of the greatness of their power and universal empire.

    The entrance into Persia was through a most difficult country, and was guarded by the noblest of the Persians, Darius himself having escaped further. Alexander, however, chanced to find a guide in exact correspondence with what the Pythia had foretold when he was a child, that a lycus should conduct him into Persia. For by such an one, whose father was a Lycian, and his mother a Persian, and who spoke both languages, he was now led into the country, by a way something about, yet without fetching any considerable compass. Here a great many of the prisoners were put to the sword, of which himself gives this account, that he commanded them to be killed in the belief that it would be for his advantage. Nor was the money found here less, he says, than at Susa, besides other movables and treasure, as much as ten thousand pair of mules and five thousand camels could well carry away. Amongst other things he happened to observe a large statue of Xerxes thrown carelessly down to the ground in the confusion made by the multitude of soldiers pressing; into the palace. He stood still, and accosting it as if it had been alive, "Shall we," said he, "neglectfully pass thee by, now thou art prostrate on the ground, because thou once invadedst Greece, or shall we erect thee again in consideration of the greatness of thy mind and thy other virtues?" But at last, after he had paused some time, and silently considered with himself, he went on without taking any further notice of it. In this place he took up his winter quarters, and stayed four months to refresh his soldiers. It is related that the first time he sat on the royal throne of Persia, under the canopy of gold, Demaratus, the Corinthian, who was much attached to him and had been one of his father's friends, wept, in an old man's manner, and deplored the misfortune of those Creeks whom death had deprived of the satisfaction of seeing Alexander seated on the throne of Darius.

From hence designing to march against Darius, before he set out, he diverted himself with his officers at an entertainment of drinking and other pastimes, and indulged so far as to let every one's mistress sit by and drink with them. The most celebrated of them was Thais, an Athenian, mistress of Ptolemy, who was afterwards king of Egypt. She, partly as a sort of well-turned compliment to Alexander, partly out of sport, as the drinking went on, at last was carried so far as to utter a saying, not misbecoming her native country's character, though somewhat too lofty for her own condition. She said it was indeed some recompense for the toils she had undergone in following the camp all over Asia, that she was that day treated in, and could insult over, the stately palace of the Persian monarchs. But, she added, it would please her much better, if while the king looked on, she might in sport, with her own hands, set fire to the court of that Xerxes who reduced the city of Athens to ashes, that it might be recorded to posterity, that the women who followed Alexander had taken a severer revenge on the Persians for the sufferings and affronts of Greece, than all the famed commanders had been able to do by sea or land. What she said was received with such universal liking and murmurs of applause, and so seconded by the encouragement and eagerness of the company, that the king himself, persuaded to be of the party, started from his seat, and with a chaplet of flowers on his head, and a lighted torch in his hand, led them the way, while they went after him in a riotous manner, dancing and making loud cries about the place; which when the rest of the Macedonians perceived, they also in great delight ran thither with torches; for they hoped the burning and destruction of the royal palace was an argument that he looked homeward, and had no design to reside among the barbarians. Thus some writers give their account of this action, while others say it was done deliberately; however, all agree that he soon repented of it, and gave order to put out the fire.

Alexander was naturally most munificent, and grew more so as his fortune increased, accompanying what he gave with that courtesy and freedom, which, to speak truth, is necessary to make a benefit really obliging. I will give a few instances of this kind. Ariston, the captain of the Paeonians, having killed an enemy, brought his head to show him, and told him that in his country, such a present was recompensed with a cup of gold. "With an empty one," said Alexander, smiling, "but I drink to you in this, which I give you full of wine." Another time, as one of the common soldier was driving a mule laden with some of the king's treasure, the beast grew tired, and the soldier took it upon his own back, and began to march with it, till Alexander seeing the man so overcharged, asked what was the matter; and when he was informed, just as he was ready to lay down his burden for weariness, "Do not faint now," said he to him, "but finish the journey, and carry what you have there to your own tent for yourself." He was always more displeased with those who would not accept of what he gave than with those who begged of him. And therefore he wrote to Phocion, that he would not own him for his friend any longer, if he refused his presents. He had never given anything to Serapion, one of the youths that played at ball with him, because he did not ask of him, till one day, it coming to Serapion's turn to play, he still threw the ball to others, and when the king asked him why he did not direct it to him, "Because you do not ask for it," said he; which answer pleased him so, that he was very liberal to him afterwards. One Proteas, a pleasant, jesting, drinking fellow, having incurred his displeasure, got his friends to intercede for him, and begged his pardon himself with tears, which at last prevailed, and Alexander declared he was friends with him. "I cannot believe it," said Proteas, "unless you first give me some pledge of it." The king understood his meaning, and presently ordered five talents to be given him. How magnificent he was in enriching his friends, and those who attended on his person, appears by a letter which Olympias wrote to him, where she tells him he should reward and honor those about him in a more moderate way, For now," said she, "you make them all equal to kings, you give them power and opportunity of making many friends of their own, and in the meantime you leave yourself destitute." She often wrote to him to this purpose, and he never communicated her letters to anybody, unless it were one which he opened when Hephaestion was by, whom he permitted, as his custom was, to read it along with him; but then as soon as he had done, he took off his ring, and set the seal upon Hephaestion's lips. Mazaeus, who was the most considerable man in Darius's court, had a son who was already governor of a province. Alexander bestowed another upon him that was better; he, however, modestly refused, and told him, instead of one Darius, he went the way to make many Alexanders. To Parmenio he gave Bagoas's house, in which he found a wardrobe of apparel worth more than a thousand talents. He wrote to Antipater, commanding him to keep a life-guard about him for the security of his person against conspiracies. To his mother he sent many presents, but would never suffer her to meddle with matters of state or war, not indulging her busy temper, and when she fell out with him upon this account, he bore her ill-humor very patiently. Nay more, when he read a long letter from Antipater, full of accusations against her, "Antipater," he said, "does not know that one tear of a mother effaces a thousand such letters as these."

But when he perceived his favorites grow so luxurious and extravagant in their way of living and expenses, that Hagnon, the Teian, wore silver nails in his shoes, that Leonnatus employed several camels, only to bring him powder out of Egypt to use when he wrestled, and that Philotas had hunting nets a hundred furlongs in length, that more used precious ointment than plain oil when they went to bathe, and that they carried about servants everywhere with them to rub them and wait upon them in their chambers, he reproved them in gentle and reasonable terms, telling them he wondered that they who had been engaged in so many signal battles did not know by experience, that those who labor sleep more sweetly and soundly than those who are labored for, and could fail to see by comparing the Persians' manner of living with their own, that it was the most abject and slavish condition to be voluptuous, but the most noble arid royal to undergo pain and labor. He argued with them further, how it was possible for anyone who pretended to be a soldier, either to look well after his horse, or to keep his armor bright and in good order, who thought it much to let his hands be serviceable to what was nearest to him, his own body. "Are you still to learn," said he, "that the end and perfection of our victories is to avoid the vices and infirmities of those whom we subdue?" And to strengthen his precepts by example, he applied himself now more vigorously than ever to hunting and warlike expeditions, embracing all opportunities of hardship and danger, insomuch that a Lacedaemonian, who was there on an embassy to him, and chanced to be by when he encountered with and mastered a huge lion, told him he had fought gallantly with the beast, which of the two should be king. Craterus caused a representation to be made of this adventure, consisting of the lion and the dogs, of the king engaged with the lion, and himself coming in to his assistance, all expressed in figures of brass, some of which were by Lysippus, and the rest by Leochares; and had it dedicated in the temple of Apollo at Delphi. Alexander exposed his person to danger in this manner, with the object both of inuring himself, and inciting others to the performance of brave and virtuous actions.

But his followers, who were grown rich, and consequently proud, longed to indulge themselves in pleasure and idleness, and were weary of marches and expeditions, and at last went on so far as to censure and speak ill of him. All which at first he bore very patiently, saying, it became a king well to do good to others, and be evil spoken of. Meantime, on the smallest occasions that called for a show of kindness to his friends, there was every indication on his part of tenderness and respect. Hearing Peucestes was bitten by a bear, he wrote to him, that he took it unkindly he should send others notice of it, and not make him acquainted with it; "But now," said he, "since it is so, let me know how you do, and whether any of your companions forsook you when you were in danger, that I may punish them." He sent Hephaestion, who was absent about some business, word how while they were fighting for their diversion with an ichneumon, Craterus was by chance run through both thighs with Perdiccas's javelin. And upon Peucestes's recovery from a fit of sickness, he sent a letter of thanks to his physician Alexippus. When Craterus was ill, he saw a vision in his sleep, after which he offered sacrifices for his health, and bade him to do so likewise. He wrote also to Pausanias, the physician, who was about to purge Craterus with hellebore, partly out of an anxious concern for him, and partly to give him a caution how he used that medicine. He was so tender of his friends' reputation that he imprisoned Ephialtes and Cissus, who brought him the first news of Harpalus's flight and withdrawal from his service, as if they had falsely accused him. When he sent the old and infirm soldiers home, Eurylochus, a citizen of Aegae, got his name enrolled among the sick, though he ailed nothing, which being discovered, he confessed he was in love with a young woman named Telesippa, and wanted to go along with her to the seaside. Alexander inquired to whom the woman belonged, and being told she was a free courtesan, "I will assist you," said he to Eurylochus, "in your amour, if your mistress be to be gained either by presents or persuasions; but we must use no other means, because she is free-born."

It is surprising to consider upon what slight occasions he would write letters to serve his friends. As when he wrote one in which he gave order to search for a youth that belonged to Seleucus, who was run away into Cilicia; and in another, thanked and commended Peucestes for apprehending Nicon, a servant of Craterus; and in one to Megabyzus, concerning a slave that had taken sanctuary in a temple, gave direction that he should not meddle with him while he was there, but if he could entice him out by fair means, then he gave him leave to seize him. It is reported of him that when he first sat in judgment upon capital causes, he would lay his hand upon one of his ears while the accuser spoke, to keep it free and unprejudiced in behalf of the party accused. But afterwards such a multitude of accusations were brought before him, and so many proved true, that he lost his tenderness of heart, and gave credit to those also that were false; and especially when anybody spoke ill of him, he would be transported out of his reason, and show himself cruel and inexorable, valuing his glory and reputation beyond his life or kingdom.

He now, as we said, set forth to seek Darius, expecting he should be put to the hazard of another battle, but heard he was taken and secured by Bessus, upon which news he sent home the Thessalians, and gave them a largess of two thousand talents over and above the pay that was due to them. This long and painful pursuit of Darius, for in eleven days he marched thirty-three hundred furlongs, harassed his soldiers so that most of them were ready to give it up, chiefly for want of water. While they were in this distress, it happened that some Macedonians who had fetched water in skins upon their mules from a river they had found out, came about noon to the place where Alexander was, and seeing him almost choked with thirst, presently filled a helmet and offered it him. He asked them to whom they were carrying the water; they told him to their children, adding, that if his life were but saved, it was no matter for them, they should be able well enough to repair that loss, though they all perished. Then he took the helmet into his hands, and looking round about, when he saw all those who were near him stretching their heads out and looking, earnestly after the drink, he returned it again with thanks without tasting a drop of it, "For," said he, "if I alone should drink, the rest will be out of heart." The soldiers no sooner took notice of his temperance and magnanimity upon this occasion, but they one and all cried out to him to lead them forward boldly, and began whipping on their horses. For whilst they had such a king, they said they defied both weariness and thirst, and looked upon themselves to be little less than immortal. But though they were all equally cheerful and willing, yet not above threescore horse were able, it is said, to keep up, and to fall in with Alexander upon the enemy's camp, where they rode over abundance of gold and silver that lay scattered about, and passing by a great many chariots full of women that wandered here and there for want of drivers, they endeavored to overtake the first of those that fled, in hopes to meet with Darius among them. And at last, after much trouble, they found him lying in a chariot, wounded all over with darts, just at the point of death. However, he desired they would give him some drink, and when he had drunk a little cold water, he told Polystratus, who gave it him, that it had become the last extremity of his ill fortune, to receive benefits and not be able to return them. "But Alexander," said he, "whose kindness to my mother, my wife, and my children I hope the gods will recompense, will doubtless thank you for your humanity to me. Tell him, therefore, in token of my acknowledgment, I give him this right hand," with which words he took hold of Polystratus's hand and died. When Alexander came up to them, he showed manifest tokens of sorrow, and taking off his own cloak, threw it upon the body to cover it.

And sometime afterwards, when Bessus was taken, he ordered him to be torn in pieces in this manner. They fastened him to a couple of trees which were bound down so as to meet, and then being let loose, with a great force returned to their places, each of them carrying that part of the body along with it that was tied to it. Darius's body was laid in state, and sent to his mother with pomp suitable to his quality. His brother Exathres, Alexander received into the number of his intimate friends.

And now with the flower of his army he marched into Hyrcania, where he saw a large bay of an open sea, apparently not much less than the Euxine, with water, however, sweeter than that of other seas, but could learn nothing of certainty concerning it, further than that in all probability it seemed to him to be an arm issuing from the lake of Maeotis. However, the naturalists were better informed of the truth, and had given an account of it many years before Alexander's expedition; that of four gulfs which out of the main sea enter into the continent, this, known indifferently as the Caspian and as the Hyrcanian sea, is the most northern. Here the barbarians, unexpectedly meeting with those who led Bucephalas, took them prisoners, and carried the horse away with them, at which Alexander was so much vexed, that he sent a herald to let them know he would put them all to the sword, men, women, and children, without mercy, if they did not restore him. But on their doing so, and at the same time surrendering their cities into his hands, he not only treated them kindly, but also paid a ramsom for his horse to those who took him.

From hence he marched into Parthia, where not having much to do, he first put on the barbaric dress, perhaps with the view of making the work of civilizing them the easier, as nothing gains more upon men than a conformity to their fashions and customs. Or it may have been as a first trial, whether the Macedonians might be brought to adore him, as the Persians did their kings, by accustoming them by little and little to bear with the alteration of his rule and course of life in other things. However, he followed not the Median fashion, which was altogether foreign and uncouth, and adopted neither the trousers nor the sleeved vest, nor the tiara for the head, but taking a middle way between the Persian mode and the Macedonian, so contrived his habit that it was not so flaunting as the one, and yet more pompous and magnificent than the other. At first he wore this habit only when he conversed with the barbarians, or within doors, among his intimate friends and companions, but afterwards he appeared in it abroad, when he rode out, and at public audiences, a sight which the Macedonians beheld with grief; but they so respected his other virtues and good qualities, that they felt it reasonable in some things to gratify his fancies and his passion of glory, in pursuit of which he hazarded himself so far, that, besides his other adventures, he had but lately been wounded in the leg by an arrow, which had so shattered the shank-bone that splinters were taken out. And on another occasion he received a violent blow with a stone upon the nape of the neck, which dimmed his sight for a good while afterwards. And yet all this could not hinder him from exposing himself freely to any dangers, insomuch that he passed the river Orexartes, which he took to be the Tanais, and putting the Scythians to flight, followed them above a hundred furlongs, though suffering all the time from a diarrhea.

Here many affirm that the Amazon came to give him a visit. So Clitarchus, Polyclitus, Onesicritus, Antigenes, and Ister, tell us. But Aristobulus and Chares, who held the office of reporter of requests, Ptolemy and Anticlides, Philon the Theban, Philip of Theangela, Hecataeus the Eretrian, Philip the Chalcidian, and Duris the Samian, say it is wholly a fiction. And truly Alexander himself seems to confirm the latter statement, for in a letter in which he gives Antipater an account of all that happened, he tells him that the king of Scythia offered him his daughter in marriage, but makes no mention at all of the Amazon. And many years after, when Onesicritus read this story in his fourth book to Lysimachus, who then reigned, the king laughed quietly and asked, "Where could I have been at that time?"

But it signifies little to Alexander whether this be credited or no. Certain it is, that apprehending the Macedonians would be weary of pursuing the war, he left the greater part of them in their quarters; and having with him in Hyrcania the choice of his men only, amounting to twenty thousand foot, and three thousand horse, he spoke to them to this effect: That hitherto the barbarians had seen them no otherwise than as it were in a dream, and if they should think of returning when they had only alarmed Asia, and not conquered it, their enemies would set upon them as upon so many women. However, he told them he would keep none of them with him against their will, they might go if they pleased; he should merely enter his protest, that when on his way to make the Macedonians the masters of the world, he was left alone with a few friends and volunteers. This is almost word for word, as he wrote in a letter to Antipater, where he adds, that when he had thus spoken to them, they all cried out, they would go along with him whithersoever it was his pleasure to lead them. After succeeding with these, it was no hard matter for him to bring over the multitude, which easily followed the example of their betters. Now, also, he more and more accommodated himself in his way of living to that of the natives, and tried to bring them, also, as near as he could to the Macedonian customs, wisely considering that whilst he was engaged in an expedition which would carry him far from thence, it would be wiser to depend upon the goodwill which might arise from intermixture and association as a means of maintaining tranquillity, than upon force and compulsion. In order to this, he chose out thirty thousand boys, whom he put under masters to teach them the Greek tongue, and to train them up to arms in the Macedonian discipline. As for his marriage with Roxana, whose youthfulness and beauty had charmed him at a drinking entertainment, where he first happened to see her, taking part in a dance, it was, indeed, a love affair, yet it seemed at the same time to be conducive to the object he had in hand. For it gratified the conquered people to see him choose a wife from among themselves, and it made them feel the most lively affection for him, to find that in the only passion which he, the most temperate of men, was overcome by, he yet forbore till he could obtain her in a lawful and honorable way.

Noticing, also, that among his chief friends and favorites, Hephaestion most approved all that he did, and complied with and imitated him in his change of habits, while Craterus continued strict in the observation of the customs and fashions of his own country, he made it his practice to employ the first in all transactions with the Persians, and the latter when he had to do with the Greeks or Macedonians. And in general he showed more affection for Hephaestion, and more respect for Craterus; Hephaestion, as he used to say, being Alexander's, and Craterus the king's friend. And so these two friends always bore in secret a grudge to each other, and at times quarreled openly, so much so, that once in India they drew upon one another, and were proceeding in good earnest, with their friends on each side to second them, when Alexander rode up and publicly reproved Hephaestion, calling him fool and madman, not to be sensible that without his favor he was nothing. He rebuked Craterus, also, in private, severely, and then causing them both to come into his presence, he reconciled them, at the same time swearing by Ammon and the rest of the gods, that he loved them two above all other men, but if ever he perceived them fall out again he would be sure to put both of them to death, or at least the aggressor. After which they neither ever did or said anything, so much as in jest, to offend one another.

There was scarcely anyone who had greater repute among the Macedonians than Philotas, the son of Parmenio. For besides that he was valiant and able to endure any fatigue of war, he was also next to Alexander himself the most munificent, and the greatest lover of his friends, one of whom asking him for some money, he commanded his steward to give it him; and when he told him he had not wherewith, "Have you not any plate then," said he, "or any clothes of mine to sell?" But he carried his arrogance and his pride of wealth and his habits of display and luxury to a degree of assumption unbecoming a private man, and affecting all the loftiness without succeeding in showing any of the grace or gentleness of true greatness, by this mistaken and spurious majesty he gained so much envy and ill-will, that Parmenio would sometimes tell him, "My son, to be not quite so great would be better." For he had long before been complained of, and accused to Alexander. Particularly when Darius was defeated in Cilicia, and an immense booty was taken at Damascus, among the rest of the prisoners who were brought into the camp, there was one Antigone of Pydna, a very handsome woman, who fell to Philotas's share. The young man one day in his cups, in the vaunting, outspoken, soldier's manner, declared to his mistress, that all the great actions were performed by him and his father, the glory and benefit of which, he said, together with the title of king, the boy Alexander reaped and enjoyed by their means. She could not hold, but discovered what he had said to one of her acquaintance, and he, as is usual in such cases, to another, till at last the story came to the ears of Craterus, who brought the woman secretly to the king. When Alexander had heard what she had to say, he commanded her to continue her intrigue with Philotas, and give him an account from time to time of all that should fall from him to this purpose. He thus unwittingly caught in a snare, to gratify some times a fit of anger, sometimes a mere love of vainglory, let himself utter numerous foolish, indiscreet speeches against the king in Antigone's hearing, of which though Alexander was informed and convinced by strong evidence, yet he would take no notice of it at present, whether it was that he confided in Parmenio's affection and loyalty, or that he apprehended their authority and interest in the army. But about this time one Limnus, a Macedonian of Chalastra, conspired against Alexander's life, and communicated his design to a youth whom he was fond of, named Nicomachus, inviting him to be of the party. But he not relishing the thing, revealed it to his brother Balinus, who immediately addressed himself to Philotas, requiring him to introduce them both to Alexander, to whom they had something of great moment to impart which very nearly concerned him. But he, for what reason is uncertain, went not with them, professing that the king was engaged with affairs of more importance. And when they had urged him a second time, and were still slighted by him, they applied themselves to another, by whose means being admitted into Alexander's presence, they first told about Limnus's conspiracy, and by the way let Philotas's negligence appear, who had twice disregarded their application to him. Alexander was greatly incensed, and on finding that Limnus had defended himself, and had been killed by the soldier who was sent to seize him, he was still more discomposed, thinking he had thus lost the means of detecting the plot. As soon as his displeasure against Philotas began to appear, presently all his old enemies showed themselves, and said openly, the king was too easily imposed on, to imagine that one so inconsiderable as Limnus, a Chalastrian, should of his own head undertake such an enterprise; that in all likelihood he was but subservient to the design, an instrument that was moved by some greater spring; that those ought to be more strictly examined about the matter whose interest it was so much to conceal it. When they had once gained the king's ear for insinuations of this sort, they went on to show a thousand grounds of suspicion against Philotas, till at last they prevailed to have him seized and put to the torture, which was done in the presence of the principal officers, Alexander himself being placed behind some tapestry to understand what passed. Where, when he heard in what a miserable tone, and with what abject submissions Philotas applied himself to Hephaestion, he broke out, it is said, in this manner: "Are you so mean-spirited and effeminate, Philotas, and yet can engage in so desperate a design?" After his death, he presently sent into Media, and put also Parmenio, his father, to death, who had done brave service under Philip, and was the only man, of his older friends and counselors, who had encouraged Alexander to invade Asia. Of three sons whom he had had in the army, he had already lost two, and now was himself put to death with the third. These actions rendered Alexander an object of terror to many of his friends, and chiefly to Antipater, who, to strengthen himself, sent messengers privately to treat for an alliance with the Aetolians, who stood in fear of Alexander, because they had destroyed the town of the Oeniadae; on being informed of which, Alexander had said the children of the Oeniadae need not revenge their fathers' quarrel, for he would himself take care to punish the Aetolians.

Not long after this happened the deplorable end of Clitus, which to those who barely hear the matter-of-fact, may seem more inhuman than that of Philotas; but if we consider the story with its circumstance of time, and weigh the cause, we shall find it to have occurred rather through a sort of mischance of the king's, whose anger and over-drinking offered an occasion to the evil genius of Clitus. The king had a present of Grecian fruit brought him from the sea-coast, which was so fresh and beautiful, that he was surprised at it, and called Clitus to him to see it, and to give him a share of it. Clitus was then sacrificing, but he immediately left off and came, followed by three sheep, on whom the drink-offering had been already poured preparatory to sacrificing them. Alexander, being informed of this, told his diviners, Aristander and Cleomantis the Lacedaemonian, and asked them what it meant; on whose assuring him, it was an ill omen, he commanded them in all haste to offer sacrifices for Clitus's safety, forasmuch as three days before he himself had seen a strange vision in his sleep, of Clitus all in mourning, sitting by Parmenio's sons who were dead. Clitus, however, stayed not to finish his devotions, but came straight to supper with the king, who had sacrificed to Castor and Pollux. And when they had drunk pretty hard, some of the company fell a singing the verses of one Pranichus, or as others say of Pierion, which were made upon those captains who had been lately worsted by the barbarians, on purpose to disgrace and turn them to ridicule. This gave offense to the older men who were there, and they upbraided both the author and the singer of the verses, though Alexander and the younger men about him were much amused to hear them, and encouraged them to go on, till at last Clitus, who had drunk too much, and was besides of a froward and willful temper, was so nettled that he could hold no longer, saying, it was not well done to expose the Macedonians so before the barbarians and their enemies, since though it was their unhappiness to be overcome, yet they were much better men than those who laughed at them. And when Alexander remarked, that Clitus was pleading his own cause, giving cowardice the name of misfortune, Clitus started up; "This cowardice, as you are pleased to term it," said he to him, "saved the life of a son of the gods, when in flight from Spithridates's sword; and it is by the expense of Macedonian blood, and by these wounds, that you are now raised to such a height, as to be able to disown your father Philip, and call yourself the Son of Ammon." "Thou base fellow," said Alexander, who was now thoroughly exasperated, "dost thou think to utter these things everywhere of me, and stir up the Macedonians to sedition, and not be punished for it?" "We are sufficiently punished already," answered Clitus, "if this be the recompense of our toils, and we must esteem theirs a happy lot, who have not lived to see their countrymen scourged with Median rods, and forced to sue to the Persians to have access to their king." While he talked thus at random, and those near Alexander got up from their seats and began to revile him in turn, the elder men did what they could to compose the disorder. Alexander, in the meantime turning about to Xenodochus, the Cardian, and Artemius, the Colophonian, asked them if they were not of opinion that the Greeks, in comparison with the Macedonians, behaved themselves like so many demi-gods among wild beasts. But Clitus for all this would not give over, desiring Alexander to speak out if he had anything more to say, or else why did he invite men who were freeborn and accustomed to speak their minds openly without restraint, to sup with him. He had better live and converse with barbarians and slaves who would not scruple to bow the knee to his Persian girdle and his white tunic. Which words so provoked Alexander, that not able to suppress his anger any longer, he threw one of the apples that lay upon the table at him, and hit him, and then looked about for his sword. But Aristophanes, one of his life-guard, had hid that out of the way, and others came about him and besought him, but in vain. For breaking from them, he called out aloud to his guards in the Macedonian language, which was a certain sign of some great disturbance in him, and commanded a trumpeter to sound, giving him a blow with his clenched fist for not instantly obeying him; though afterwards the same man was commended for disobeying an order which would have put the whole army into tumult and confusion. Clitus still refusing to yield, was with much trouble forced by his friends out of the room. But he came in again immediately at another door, very irreverently and confidently singing the verses out of Euripides's Andromache, —

> *In Greece, alas! how ill things ordered are!*

Upon this, at last, Alexander, snatching a spear from one of the soldiers, met Clitus as he was coming forward and was putting by the curtain that hung before the door, and ran him through the body. He fell at once with a cry and a groan. Upon which the king's anger immediately vanishing, he came perfectly to himself, and when he saw his friends about him all in a profound silence, he pulled the spear out of the dead body, and would have thrust it into his own throat, if the guards had not held his hands, and by main force carried him away into his chamber, where all that night and the next day he wept bitterly, till being quite spent with lamenting and exclaiming, he lay as it were speechless, only fetching deep sighs. His friends apprehending some harm from his silence, broke into the room, but he took no notice of what any of them said, till Aristander putting him in mind of the vision he had seen concerning Clitus, and the prodigy that followed, as if all had come to pass by an unavoidable fatality, he then seemed to moderate his grief. They now brought Callisthenes, the philosopher, who was the near friend of Aristotle, and Anaxarchus of Abdera, to him. Callisthenes used moral language, and gentle and soothing means, hoping to find access for words of reason, and get a hold upon the passion. But Anaxarchus, who had always taken a course of his own in philosophy, and had a name for despising and slighting his contemporaries, as soon as he came in, cried out aloud, "Is this the Alexander whom the whole world looks to, lying here weeping like a slave, for fear of the censure and reproach of men, to whom he himself ought to be a law and measure of equity, if he would use the right his conquests have given him as supreme lord and governor of all, and not be the victim of a vain and idle opinion? Do not you know," said he, "that Jupiter is represented to have Justice and Law on each hand of him, to signify that all the actions of a conqueror are lawful and just?" With these and the like speeches, Anaxarchus indeed allayed the king's grief, but withal corrupted his character, rendering him more audacious and lawless than he had been. Nor did he fail by these means to insinuate himself into his favor, and to make Callisthenes's company, which at all times, because of his austerity, was not very acceptable, more uneasy and disagreeable to him.

It happened that these two philosophers meeting at an entertainment, where conversation turned on the subject of climate and the temperature of the air, Callisthenes joined with their opinion, who held that those countries were colder, and the winter sharper there than in Greece. Anaxarchus would by no means allow this, but argued against it with some heat. "Surely," said Callisthenes, "you cannot but admit this country to be colder than Greece, for there you used to have but one threadbare cloak to keep out the coldest winter, and here you have three good warm mantles one over another." This piece of raillery irritated Anaxarchus and the other pretenders to learning, and the crowd of flatterers in general could not endure to see Callisthenes so much admired and followed by the youth, and no less esteemed by the older men for his orderly life, and his gravity, and for being contented with his condition; all confirming what he had professed about the object he had in his journey to Alexander, that it was only to get his countrymen recalled from banishment, and to rebuild and repeople his native town. Besides the envy which his great reputation raised, he also, by his own deportment, gave those who wished him ill, opportunity to do him mischief. For when he was invited to public entertainments, he would most times refuse to come, or if he were present at any, he put a constraint upon the company by his austerity and silence, which seemed to intimate his disapproval of what he saw. So that Alexander himself said in application to him,

> *That vain pretense to wisdom I detest,*
> *Where a man's blind to his own interest.*

Being with many more invited to sup with the king, he was called upon when the cup came to him, to make an oration extempore in praise of the Macedonians; and he did it with such a flow of eloquence, that all who heard it rose from their seats to clap and applaud him, and threw their garland upon him; only Alexander told him out of Euripides,

> *I wonder not that you have spoke so well,*
> *'Tis easy on good subjects to excel.*

"Therefore," said he, "if you will show the force of your eloquence, tell my Macedonians their faults, and dispraise them, that by hearing their errors they may learn to he better for the future." Callisthenes presently obeyed him, retracting all he had said before, and, inveighing against the Macedonians with great freedom, added, that Philip thrived and grew powerful, chiefly by the discord of the Grecians, applying this verse to him:—

> *In civil strife e'en villains rise to fame;*

which so offended the Macedonians, that he was odious to them ever after. And Alexander said, that instead of his eloquence, he had only made his ill-will appear in what he had spoken. Hermippus assures us, that one Stroebus, a servant whom Callisthenes kept to read to him, gave this account of these passages afterwards to Aristotle; and that when he perceived the king grow more and more averse to him, two or three times, as he was going away, he repeated the verses, —

> *Death seiz'd at last on great Patroclus too,*
> *Though he in virtue far exceeded you.*

Not without reason, therefore, did Aristotle give this character of Callisthenes, that he was, indeed, a powerful speaker, but had no judgment. He acted certainly a true philosopher's part in positively refusing, as he did, to pay adoration; and by speaking out openly against that which the best and gravest of the Macedonians only repined at in secret, he delivered the Grecians and Alexander himself from a great disgrace, when the practice was given up. But he ruined himself by it, because he went too roughly to work, as if he would have forced the king to that which he should have effected by reason and persuasion. Chares of Mitylene writes, that at a banquet, Alexander, after he had drunk, reached the cup to one of his friends, who, on receiving it, rose up towards the domestic altar, and when he had drunk, first adored, and then kissed Alexander, and afterwards laid himself down at the table with the rest. Which they all did one after another, till it came to Callisthenes's turn, who took the cup and drank, while the king who was engaged in conversation with Hephaestion was not observing, and then came and offered to kiss him. But Demetrius, surnamed Phidon, interposed, saying, "Sir, by no means let him kiss you, for he only of us all has refused to adore you;" upon which the king declined it, and all the concern Callisthenes showed was, that he said aloud, "Then I go away with a kiss less than the rest." The displeasure he incurred by this action procured credit for Hephaestion's declaration that he had broken his word to him in not paying the king the same veneration that others did, as he had faithfully promised to do. And to finish his disgrace, a number of such men as Lysimachus and Hagnon now came in with their asseverations that the sophist went about everywhere boasting of his resistance to arbitrary power, and that the young men all ran after him, and honored him as the only man among so many thousands who had the courage to preserve his liberty. Therefore when Hermolaus's conspiracy came to be discovered, the charges which his enemies brought against him were the more easily believed, particularly that when the young man asked him what he should do to be the most illustrious person on earth, he told him the readiest way was to kill him who was already so; and that to incite him to commit the deed, he bade him not be awed by the golden couch, but remember Alexander was a man equally infirm and vulnerable as another. However, none of Hermolaus's accomplices, in the utmost extremity, made any mention of Callisthenes's being engaged in the design. Nay, Alexander himself, in the letters which he wrote soon after to Craterus, Attalus, and Alcetas, tells them that the young men who were put to the torture, declared they had entered into the conspiracy of themselves, without any others being privy to, or guilty of it. But yet afterwards, in a letter to Antipater, he accuses Callisthenes. "The young men," he says, "were stoned to death by the Macedonians, but for the sophist," (meaning Callisthenes,) "I will take care to punish him with them too who sent him to me, and who harbor those in their cities who conspire against my life," an unequivocal declaration against Aristotle, in whose house Callisthenes, for his relationship's sake, being his niece Hero's son, had been educated. His death is variously related. Some say he was hanged by Alexander's orders; others, that he died of sickness in prison; but Chares writes he was kept in chains seven months after he was apprehended, on purpose that he might be proceeded against in full council, when Aristotle should be present; and that growing very fat, and contracting a disease of vermin, he there died, about the time that Alexander was wounded in India, in the country of the Malli Oxydracae, all which came to pass afterwards.

For to go on in order, Demaratus of Corinth, now quite an old man, had made a great effort, about this time, to pay Alexander a visit; and when he had seen him, said he pitied the misfortune of those Grecians, who were so unhappy as to die before they had beheld Alexander seated on the throne of Darius. But he did not long enjoy the benefit of the king's kindness for him, any otherwise than that soon after falling sick and dying, he had a magnificent funeral, and the army raised him a monument of earth, fourscore cubits high, and of a vast circumference. His ashes were conveyed in a very rich chariot, drawn by four horses, to the seaside.

Alexander now intent upon his expedition into India, took notice that his soldiers were so charged with booty that it hindered their marching. Therefore, at break of day, as soon as the baggage wagons were laden, first he set fire to his own, and to those of his friends, and then commanded those to be burnt which belonged to the rest of the army. An act which in the deliberation of it had seemed more dangerous and difficult than it proved in the execution, with which few were dissatisfied; for most of the soldiers, as if they had been inspired, uttering loud outcries and warlike shoutings, supplied one another with what was absolutely necessary, and burnt and destroyed all that was superfluous, the sight of which redoubled Alexander's zeal and eagerness for his design. And, indeed, he was now grown very severe and inexorable in punishing those who committed any fault. For he put Menander, one of his friends, to death, for deserting a fortress where he had placed him in garrison, and shot Orsodates, one of the barbarians who revolted from him, with his own hand.

At this time a sheep happened to yean a lamb, with the perfect shape and color of a tiara upon the head, and testicles on each side; which portent Alexander regarded with such dislike, that he immediately caused his Babylonian priests, whom he usually carried about with him for such purposes, to purify him, and told his friends he was not so much concerned for his own sake as for theirs, out of an apprehension that after his death the divine power might suffer his empire to fall into the hands of some degenerate, impotent person. But this fear was soon removed by a wonderful thing that happened not long after, and was thought to presage better. For Proxenus, a Macedonian, who was the chief of those who looked to the king's furniture, as he was breaking up the ground near the river Oxus, to set up the royal pavilion, discovered a spring of a fat, oily liquor, which after the top was taken off, ran pure, clear oil, without any difference either of taste or smell, having exactly the same smoothness and brightness, and that, too, in a country where no olives grew. The water, indeed, of the river Oxus, is said to be the smoothest to the feeling of all waters, and to leave a gloss on the skins of those who bathe themselves in it. Whatever might be the cause, certain it is that Alexander was wonderfully pleased with it, as appears by his letters to Antipater, where he speaks of it as one of the most remarkable presages that God had ever favored him with. The diviners told him it signified his expedition would be glorious in the event, but very painful, and attended with many difficulties; for oil, they said, was bestowed on mankind by God as a refreshment of their labors.

Nor did they judge amiss, for he exposed himself to many hazards in the battles which he fought, and received very severe wounds, but the greatest loss in his army was occasioned through the unwholesomeness of the air, and the want of necessary provisions. But he still applied himself to overcome fortune and whatever opposed him, by resolution and virtue, and thought nothing impossible to true intrepidity, and on the other hand nothing secure or strong for cowardice. It is told of him that when he besieged Sisimithres, who held an inaccessible, impregnable rock against him, and his soldiers began to despair of taking it, he asked Oxyartes whether Sisimithres was a man of courage, who assuring him he was the greatest coward alive, "Then you tell me," said he, "that the place may easily be taken, since what is in command of it is weak." And in a little time he so terrified Sisimithres, that he took it without any difficulty. At an attack which he made upon such another precipitous place with some of his Macedonian soldiers, he called to one whose name was Alexander, and told him, he at any rate must fight bravely, if it were but for his name's sake. The youth fought gallantly and was killed in the action, at which he was sensibly afflicted. Another time, seeing his men march slowly and unwillingly to the siege of the place called Nysa, because of a deep river between them and the town, he advanced before them, and standing upon the bank, "What a miserable man," said he, "am I, that I have not learned to swim!" and then was hardly dissuaded from endeavoring to pass it upon his shield. Here, after the assault was over, the ambassadors who from several towns which he had blocked up, came to submit to him and make their peace, were surprised to find him still in his armor, without anyone in waiting or attendance upon him, and when at last some one brought him a cushion, he made the eldest of them, named Acuphis, take it and sit down upon it. The old man, marveling at his magnanimity and courtesy, asked him what his countrymen should do to merit his friendship. "I would have them," said Alexander, "choose you to govern them, and send one hundred of the most worthy men among them to remain with me as hostages." Acuphis laughed and answered, "I shall govern them with more ease, Sir, if I send you so many of the worst, rather than the best of my subjects."

The extent of king Taxiles's dominions in India was thought to be as large as Egypt, abounding in good pastures, and producing beautiful fruits. The king himself had the reputation of a wise man, and at his first interview with Alexander, he spoke to him in these terms: "To what purpose," said he, "should we make war upon one another, if the design of your coming into these parts be not to rob us of our water or our necessary food, which are the only things that wise men are indispensably obliged to fight for? As for other riches and possessions, as they are accounted in the eye of the world, if I am better provided of them than you, I am ready to let you share with me; but if fortune has been more liberal to you than me, I have no objection to be obliged to you." This discourse pleased Alexander so much, that embracing him, "Do you think," said he to him, "your kind words and courteous behavior will bring you off in this interview without a contest? No, you shall not escape so. I shall contend and do battle with you so far, that how obliging soever you are, you shall not have the better of me." Then receiving some presents from him, he returned him others of greater value, and to complete his bounty, gave him in money ready coined one thousand talents; at which his old friends were much displeased, but it gained him the hearts of many of the barbarians. But the best soldiers of the Indians now entering into the pay of several of the cities, undertook to defend them, and did it so bravely, that they put Alexander to a great deal of trouble, till at last, after a capitulation, upon the surrender of the place, he fell upon them as they were marching away, and put them all to the sword. This one breach of his word remains as a blemish upon his achievements in war, which he otherwise had performed throughout with that justice and honor that became a king. Nor was he less incommoded by the Indian philosophers, who inveighed against those princes who joined his party, and solicited the free nations to oppose him. He took several of these also, and caused them to be hanged.

Alexander, in his own letters, has given us an account of his war with Porus. He says the two armies were separated by the river Hydaspes, on whose opposite bank Porus continually kept his elephants in order of battle, with their heads towards their enemies, to guard the passage; that he, on the other hand, made every day a great noise and clamor in his camp, to dissipate the apprehensions of the barbarians; that one stormy dark night he passed the river, at a distance from the place where the enemy lay, into a little island, with part of his foot, and the best of his horse. Here there fell a most violent storm of rain, accompanied with lightning and whirlwinds, and seeing some of his men burnt and dying with the lightning, he nevertheless quitted the island and made over to the other side. The Hydaspes, he says, now after the storm, was so swollen and grown so rapid, as to have made a breach in the bank, and a part of the river was now pouring in here, so that when he came across, it was with difficulty he got a footing on the land, which was slippery and unsteady, and exposed to the force of the currents on both sides. This is the occasion when he is related to have said, "O ye Athenians, will ye believe what dangers I incur to merit your praise?" This, however, is Onesicritus's story. Alexander says, here the men left their boats, and passed the breach in their armor, up to the breast in water, and that then he advanced with his horse about twenty furlongs before his foot, concluding that if the enemy charged him with their cavalry, he should be too strong for them; if with their foot, his own would come up time enough to his assistance. Nor did he judge amiss; for being charged by a thousand horse, and sixty armed chariots, which advanced before their main body, he took all the chariots, and killed four hundred horse upon the place. Porus, by this time guessing that Alexander himself had crossed over, came on with his whole army, except a party which he left behind, to hold the rest of the Macedonians in play, if they should attempt to pass the river. But he, apprehending the multitude of the enemy, and to avoid the shock of their elephants, dividing his forces, attacked their left wing himself, and commanded Coenus to fall upon the right, which was performed with good success. For by this means both wings being broken, the enemies fell back in their retreat upon the center, and crowded in upon their elephants. There rallying, they fought a hand to hand battle, and it was the eighth hour of the day before they were entirely defeated. This description the conqueror himself has left us in his own epistles.

Almost all the historians agree in relating that Porus was four cubits and a span high, and that when he was upon his elephant, which was of the largest size, his stature and bulk were so answerable, that he appeared to be proportionably mounted, as a horseman on his horse. This elephant, during the whole battle, gave many singular proofs of sagacity and of particular care of the king, whom as long as he was strong and in a condition to fight, he defended with great courage, repelling those who set upon him; and as soon as he perceived him overpowered with his numerous wounds and the multitude of darts that were thrown at him, to prevent his falling off, he softly knelt down and began to draw out the darts with his proboscis. When Porus was taken prisoner; and Alexander asked him how he expected to be used, he answered, "As a king." For that expression, he said, when the same question was put to him a second time, comprehended everything. And Alexander, accordingly, not only suffered him to govern his own kingdom as satrap under himself, but gave him also the additional territory of various independent tribes whom he subdued, a district which, it is said, contained fifteen several nations and five thousand considerable towns, besides abundance of villages. To another government, three times as large as this, he appointed Philip, one of his friends.

Some little time after the battle with Porus, Bucephalas died, as most of the authorities state, under cure of his wounds, or as Onesicritus says, of fatigue and age, being thirty years old. Alexander was no less concerned at his death, than if he had lost an old companion or an intimate friend, and built a city, which he named Bucephalia, in memory of him, on the bank of the river Hydaspes. He also, we are told, built another city, and called it after the name of a favorite dog, Peritas, which he had brought up himself. So Sotion assures us he was informed by Potamon of Lesbos.

But this last combat with Porus took off the edge of the Macedonians' courage, and stayed their further progress into India. For having found it hard enough to defeat an enemy who brought but twenty thousand foot and two thousand horse into the field, they thought they had reason to oppose Alexander's design of leading them on to pass the Ganges too, which they were told was thirty-two furlongs broad and a hundred fathoms deep, and the banks on the further side covered with multitudes of enemies. For they were told that the kings of the Gandaritans and Praesians expected them there with eighty thousand horse, two hundred thousand foot, eight thousand armed chariots, and six thousand fighting elephants. Nor was this a mere vain report, spread to discourage them. For Androcottus, who not long after reigned in those parts, made a present of five hundred elephants at once to Seleucus, and with an army of six hundred thousand men subdued all India. Alexander at first was so grieved and enraged at his men's reluctancy, that he shut himself up in his tent, and threw himself upon the ground, declaring, if they would not pass the Ganges, he owed them no thanks for anything they had hitherto done, and that to retreat now, was plainly to confess himself vanquished. But at last the reasonable persuasions of his friends and the cries and lamentations of his soldiers, who in a suppliant manner crowded about the entrance of his tent, prevailed with him to think of returning. Yet he could not refrain from leaving behind him various deceptive memorials of his expedition, to impose upon after-times, and to exaggerate his glory with posterity, such as arms larger than were really worn, and mangers for horses, with bits of bridles above the usual size, which he set up, and distributed in several places. He erected altars, also, to the gods, which the kings of the Praesians even in our time do honor to when they pass the river, and offer sacrifice upon them after the Grecian manner. Androcottus, then a boy, saw Alexander there, and is said often afterwards to have been heard to say, that he missed but little of making himself master of those countries; their king, who then reigned, was so hated and despised for the viciousness of his life, and the meanness of his extraction.

Alexander was now eager to see the ocean. To which purpose he caused a great many row-boats and rafts to be built, in which he fell gently down the rivers at his leisure, yet so that his navigation was neither unprofitable nor inactive. For by several descents upon the banks, he made himself master of the fortified towns, and consequently of the country on both sides. But at a siege of a town of the Mallians, who have the repute of being the bravest people of India, he ran in great danger of his life. For having beaten off the defendants with showers of arrows, he was the first man that mounted the wall by a scaling ladder, which, as soon as he was up, broke and left him almost alone, exposed to the darts which the barbarians threw at him in great numbers from below. In this distress, turning himself as well as he could, he leaped down in the midst of his enemies, and had the good fortune to light upon his feet. The brightness and clattering of his armor when he came to the ground, made the barbarians think they saw rays of light, or some bright phantom playing before his body, which frightened them so at first, that they ran away and dispersed. Till seeing him seconded but by two of his guards, they fell upon him hand to hand, and some, while he bravely defended himself, tried to wound him through his armor with their swords and spears. And one who stood further off, drew a bow with such just strength, that the arrow finding its way through his cuirass, stuck in his ribs under the breast. This stroke was so violent, that it made him give back, and set one knee to the ground, upon which the man ran up with his drawn scimitar, thinking to dispatch him, and had done it, if Peucestes and Limnaeus had not interposed, who were both wounded, Limnaeus mortally, but Peucestes stood his ground, while Alexander killed the barbarian. But this did not free him from danger; for besides many other wounds, at last he received so weighty a stroke of a club upon his neck, that he was forced to lean his body against the wall, still, however, facing the enemy. At this extremity, the Macedonians made their way in and gathered round him. They took him up, just as he was fainting away, having lost all sense of what was done near him, and conveyed him to his tent, upon which it was presently reported all over the camp that he was dead. But when they had with great difficulty and pains sawed off the shaft of the arrow, which was of wood, and so with much trouble got off his cuirass, they came to cut out the head of it, which was three fingers broad and four long, and stuck fast in the bone. During the operation, he was taken with almost mortal swoonings, but when it was out he came to himself again. Yet though all danger was past, he continued very weak, and confined himself a great while to a regular diet and the method of his cure, till one day hearing the Macedonians clamoring outside in their eagerness to see him, he took his cloak and went out. And having sacrificed to the gods, without more delay he went on board again, and as he coasted along, subdued a great deal of the country on both sides, and several considerable cities.

In this voyage, he took ten of the Indian philosophers prisoners, who had been most active in persuading Sabbas to revolt, and had caused the Macedonians a great deal of trouble. These men, called Gymnosophists, were reputed to be extremely ready and succinct in their answers, which he made trial of, by putting difficult questions to them, letting them know that those whose answers were not pertinent, should be put to death, of which he made the eldest of them judge. The first being asked which he thought most numerous, the dead or the living, answered, "The living, because those who are dead are not at all." Of the second, he desired to know whether the earth or the sea produced the largest beast; who told him, "The earth, for the sea is but a part of it." His question to the third was, Which is the cunningest of beasts? "That," said he, "which men have not yet found out." He bade the fourth tell him what argument he used to Sabbas to persuade him to revolt. "No other," said he, "than that he should either live or die nobly." Of the fifth he asked, Which was eldest, night or day? The philosopher replied, "Day was eldest, by one day at least." But perceiving Alexander not well satisfied with that account, he added, that he ought not to wonder if strange questions had as strange answers made to them. Then he went on and inquired of the next, what a man should do to be exceedingly beloved. "He must be very powerful," said he, "without making himself too much feared." The answer of the seventh to his question, how a man might become a god, was, "By doing that which was impossible for men to do." The eighth told him, "Life is stronger than death, because it supports so many miseries." And the last being asked, how long he thought it decent for a man to live, said, "Till death appeared more desirable than life." Then Alexander turned to him whom he had made judge, and commanded him to give sentence. "All that I can determine," said he, "is, that they have every one answered worse than another." "Nay," said the king, "then you shall die first, for giving such a sentence." "Not so, O king," replied the gymnosophist, "unless you said falsely that he should die first who made the worst answer." In conclusion he gave them presents and dismissed them.

But to those who were in greatest reputation among them, and lived a private quiet life, he sent Onesicritus, one of Diogenes the Cynic's disciples, desiring them to come to him. Calanus, it is said, very arrogantly and roughly commanded him to strip himself, and hear what he said, naked, otherwise he would not speak a word to him, though he came from Jupiter himself. But Dandamis received him with more civility, and hearing him discourse of Socrates, Pythagoras, and Diogenes, told him he thought them men of great parts, and to have erred in nothing so much as in having too great respect for the laws and customs of their country. Others say, Dandamis only asked him the reason why Alexander undertook so long a journey to come into those parts. Taxiles, however, persuaded Calanus to wait upon Alexander. His proper name was Sphines, but because he was wont to say Cale, which in the Indian tongue is a form of salutation, to those he met with anywhere, the Greeks called him Calanus. He is said to have shown Alexander an instructive emblem of government, which was this. He threw a dry shriveled hide upon the ground, and trod upon the edges of it. The skin when it was pressed in one place, still rose up in another, wheresoever he trod round about it, till he set his foot in the middle, which made all the parts lie even and quiet. The meaning of this similitude being that he ought to reside most in the middle of his empire, and not spend too much time on the borders of it.

His voyage down the rivers took up seven months' time, and when he came to the sea, he sailed to an island which he himself called Scillustis, others Psiltucis, where going ashore, he sacrificed, and made what observations he could as to the nature of the sea and the sea-coast. Then having besought the gods that no other man might ever go beyond the bounds of this expedition, he ordered his fleet of which he made Nearchus admiral, and Onesicritus pilot, to sail round about, keeping the Indian shore on the right hand, and returned himself by land through the country of the Orites, where he was reduced to great straits for want of provisions, and lost a vast number of men, so that of an army of one hundred and twenty thousand foot and fifteen thousand horse, he scarcely brought back above a fourth part out of India, they were so diminished by diseases, ill diet, and the scorching heats, but most by famine. For their march was through an uncultivated country whose inhabitants fared hardly, possessing only a few sheep, and those of a wretched kind, whose flesh was rank and unsavory, by their continual feeding upon sea-fish.

After sixty days march he came into Gedrosia, where he found great plenty of all things, which the neighboring kings and governors of provinces, hearing of his approach, had taken care to provide. When he had here refreshed his army, he continued his march through Carmania, feasting all the way for seven days together. He with his most intimate friends banqueted and reveled night and day upon a platform erected on a lofty, conspicuous scaffold, which was slowly drawn by eight horses. This was followed by a great many chariots, some covered with purple and embroidered canopies, and some with green boughs, which were continually supplied afresh, and in them the rest of his friends and commanders drinking, and crowned with garlands of flowers. Here was now no target or helmet or spear to be seen; instead of armor, the soldiers handled nothing but cups and goblets and Thericlean drinking vessels, which, along the whole way, they dipped into large bowls and jars, and drank healths to one another, some seating themselves to it, others as they went along. All places resounded with music of pipes and flutes, with harping and singing, and women dancing as in the rites of Bacchus. For this disorderly, wandering march, besides the drinking part of it, was accompanied with all the sportiveness and insolence of bacchanals, as much as if the god himself had been there to countenance and lead the procession. As soon as he came to the royal palace of Gedrosia, he again refreshed and feasted his army; and one day after he had drunk pretty hard, it is said, he went to see a prize of dancing contended for, in which his favorite Bagoas, having gained the victory, crossed the theater in his dancing habit, and sat down close by him, which so pleased the Macedonians, that they made loud acclamations for him to kiss Bagoas, and never stopped clapping their hands and shouting till Alexander put his arms round him and kissed him.

Here his admiral, Nearchus, came to him and delighted him so with the narrative of his voyage, that he resolved himself to sail out of the mouth of Euphrates with a great fleet, with which he designed to go round by Arabia and Africa, and so by Hercules's Pillars into the Mediterranean; in order for which, he directed all sorts of vessels to be built at Thapsacus, and made great provision everywhere of seamen and pilots. But the tidings of the difficulties he had gone through in his Indian expedition, the danger of his person among the Mallians, the reported loss of a considerable part of his forces, and a general doubt as to his own safety, had begun to give occasion for revolt among many of the conquered nations, and for acts of great injustice, avarice, and insolence on the part of the satraps and commanders in the provinces, so that there seemed to be an universal fluctuation and disposition to change. Even at home, Olympias and Cleopatra had raised a faction against Antipater, and divided his government between them, Olympias seizing upon Epirus, and Cleopatra upon Macedonia. When Alexander was told of it, he said his mother had made the best choice, for the Macedonians would never endure to be ruled by a woman. Upon this he dispatched Nearchus again to his fleet, to carry the war into the maritime provinces, and as he marched that way himself, he punished those commanders who had behaved ill, particularly Oxyartes, one of the sons of Abuletes, whom he killed with his own hand, thrusting him through the body with his spear. And when Abuletes, instead of the necessary provisions which he ought to have furnished, brought him three thousand talents in coined money, he ordered it to be thrown to his horses, and when they would not touch it, "What good," he said, "will this provision do us?" and sent him away to prison.

When he came into Persia, he distributed money among the women, as their own kings had been wont to do, who as often as they came thither, gave every one of them a piece of gold; on account of which custom, some of them, it is said, had come but seldom, and Ochus was so sordidly covetous, that to avoid this expense, he never visited his native country once in all his reign. Then finding Cyrus's sepulchre opened and rifled, he put Polymachus, who did it, to death, though he was a man of some distinction, a born Macedonian of Pella. And after he had read the inscription, he caused it to be cut again below the old one in Greek characters; the words being these: "O man, whosoever thou art, and from whencesoever thou comest (for I know thou wilt come), I am Cyrus, the founder of the Persian empire; do not grudge me this little earth which covers my body." The reading of this sensibly touched Alexander, filling him with the thought of the uncertainty and mutability of human affairs. At the same time, Calanus having been a little while troubled with a disease in the bowels, requested that he might have a funeral pile erected, to which he came on horseback, and after he had said some prayers and sprinkled himself and cut off some of his hair to throw into the fire, before he ascended it, he embraced and took leave of the Macedonians who stood by, desiring them to pass that day in mirth and good-fellowship with their king, whom in a little time, he said, he doubted not but to see again at Babylon. Having thus said, he lay down, and covering up his face, he stirred not when the fire came near him, but continued still in the same posture as at first, and so sacrificed himself, as it was the ancient custom of the philosophers in those countries to do. The same thing was done long after by another Indian, who came with Caesar to Athens, where they still show you "the Indian's monument." At his return from the funeral pile, Alexander invited a great many of his friends and principal officers to supper, and proposed a drinking match, in which the victor should receive a crown. Promachus drank twelve quarts of wine, and won the prize, which was a talent, from them all; but he survived his victory but three days, and was followed, as Chares says, by forty-one more, who died of the same debauch, some extremely cold weather having set in shortly after.

At Susa, he married Darius's daughter Statira, and celebrated also the nuptials of his friends, bestowing the noblest of the Persian ladies upon the worthiest of them, at the same time making in an entertainment in honor of the other Macedonians whose marriages had already taken place. At this magnificent festival, it is reported, there were no less than nine thousand guests, to each of whom he gave a golden cup for the libations. Not to mention other instances of his wonderful magnificence, he paid the debts of his army, which amounted to nine thousand eight hundred and seventy talents. But Antigenes, who had lost one of his eyes, though he owed nothing, got his name set down in the list of those who were in debt, and bringing one who pretended to be his creditor, and to have supplied him from the bank, received the money. But when the cheat was found out, the king was so incensed at it, that he banished him from court, and took away his command, though he was an excellent soldier, and a man of great courage. For when he was but a youth, and served under Philip at the siege of Perinthus, where he was wounded in the eye by an arrow shot out of an engine, he would neither let the arrow be taken out, nor be persuaded to quit the field, till he had bravely repulsed the enemy and forced them to retire into the town. Accordingly he was not able to support such a disgrace with any patience, and it was plain that grief and despair would have made him kill himself, but that the king fearing it, not only pardoned him, but let him also enjoy the benefit of his deceit.

The thirty thousand boys whom he left behind him to be taught and disciplined, were so improved at his return, both in strength and beauty, and performed their exercises with such dexterity and wonderful agility, that he was extremely pleased with them, which grieved the Macedonians, and made them fear he would have the less value for them. And when he proceeded to send down the infirm and maimed soldiers to the sea, they said they were unjustly and infamously dealt with, after they were worn out in his service upon all occasions, now to be turned away with disgrace and sent home into their country among their friends and relations, in a worse condition than when they came out; therefore they desired him to dismiss them one and all, and to account his Macedonians useless, now he was so well furnished with a set of dancing boys, with whom, if he pleased, he might go on and conquer the world. These speeches so incensed Alexander, that after he had given them a great deal of reproachful language in his passion, he drove them away, and committed the watch to Persians, out of whom he chose his guards and attendants. When the Macedonians saw him escorted by these men, and themselves excluded and shamefully disgraced, their high spirits fell, and conferring with one another, they found that jealousy and rage had almost distracted them. But at last coming to themselves again, they went without their arms, with only their under garments on, crying and weeping, to offer themselves at his tent, and desired him to deal with them as their baseness and ingratitude deserved. However, this would not prevail; for though his anger was already something mollified, yet he would not admit them into his presence, nor would they stir from thence, but continued two days and nights before his tent, bewailing themselves, and imploring him as their lord to have compassion on them. But the third day he came out to them, and seeing them very humble and penitent, he wept himself a great while, and after a gentle reproof spoke kindly to them, and dismissed those who were unserviceable with magnificent rewards, and with this recommendation to Antipater, that when they came home, at all public shows and in the theaters, they should sit on the best and foremost seats, crowned with chaplets of flowers. He ordered, also, that the children of those who had lost their lives in his service, should have their fathers' pay continued to them.

When he came to Ecbatana in Media, and had dispatched his most urgent affairs, he began to divert himself again with spectacles and public entertainments, to carry on which he had a supply of three thousand actors and artists, newly arrived out of Greece. But they were soon interrupted by Hephaestion's falling sick of a fever, in which, being a young man and a soldier too, he could not confine himself to so exact a diet as was necessary; for whilst his physician Glaucus was gone to the theater, he ate a fowl for his dinner, and drank a large draught of wine, upon which he became very ill, and shortly after died. At this misfortune, Alexander was so beyond all reason transported, that to express his sorrow, he immediately ordered the manes and tails of all his horses and mules to be cut, and threw down the battlements of the neighboring cities. The poor physician he crucified, and forbade playing on the flute, or any other musical instrument in the camp a great while, till directions came from the oracle of Ammon, and enjoined him to honor Hephaestion, and sacrifice to him as to a hero. Then seeking to alleviate his grief in war, he set out, as it were, to a hunt and chase of men, for he fell upon the Cossaeans, and put the whole nation to the sword. This was called a sacrifice to Hephaestion's ghost. In his sepulchre and monument and the adorning of them, he intended to bestow ten thousand talents; and designing that the excellence of the workmanship and the singularity of the design might outdo the expense, his wishes turned, above all other artists, to Stasicrates, because he always promised something very bold, unusual, and magnificent in his projects. Once when they had met before, he had told him, that of all the mountains he knew, that of Athos in Thrace was the most capable of being adapted to represent the shape and lineaments of a man; that if he pleased to command him, he would make it the noblest and most durable statue in the world, which in its left hand should hold a city of ten thousand inhabitants, and out of its right should pour a copious river into the sea. Though Alexander declined this proposal, yet now he spent a great deal of time with workmen to invent and contrive others even more extravagant and sumptuous.

As he was upon his way to Babylon, Nearchus, who had sailed back out of the ocean up the mouth of the river Euphrates, came to tell him he had met with some Chaldaean diviners, who had warned him against Alexander's going thither. Alexander, however, took no thought of it, and went on, and when he came near the walls of the place, he saw a great many crows fighting with one another, some of whom fell down just by him. After this, being privately informed that Apollodorus, the governor of Babylon, had sacrificed, to know what would become of him, he sent for Pythagoras, the soothsayer, and on his admitting the thing, asked him, in what condition he found the victim; and when he told him the liver was defective in its lobe, "A great presage indeed!" said Alexander. However, he offered Pythagoras no injury, but was sorry that he had neglected Nearchus's advice, and stayed for the most part outside the town, removing his tent from place to place, and sailing up and down the Euphrates. Besides this, he was disturbed by many other prodigies. A tame ass fell upon the biggest and handsomest lion that he kept, and killed him by a kick. And one day after he had undressed himself to be anointed, and was playing at ball, just as they were going to bring his clothes again, the young men who played with him perceived a man clad in the king's robes, with a diadem upon his head, sitting silently upon his throne. They asked him who he was, to which he gave no answer a good while, till at last coming to himself, he told them his name was Dionysius, that he was of Messenia, that for some crime of which he was accused, he was brought thither from the sea-side, and had been kept long in prison, that Serapis appeared to him, had freed him from his chains, conducted him to that place, and commanded him to put on the king's robe and diadem, and to sit where they found him, and to say nothing. Alexander, when he heard this, by the direction of his soothsayers, put the fellow to death, but he lost his spirits, and grew diffident of the protection and assistance of the gods, and suspicious of his friends. His greatest apprehension was of Antipater and his sons, one of whom, Iolaus, was his chief cupbearer; and Cassander, who had lately arrived, and had been bred up in Greek manners, the first time he saw some of the barbarians adore the king, could not forbear laughing at it aloud, which so incensed Alexander, that he took him by the hair with both hands, and dashed his head against the wall. Another time, Cassander would have said something in defense of Antipater to those who accused him, but Alexander interrupting him said, "What is it you say? Do you think people, if they had received no injury, would come such a journey only to calumniate your father?" To which when Cassander replied, that their coming so far from the evidence was a great proof of the falseness of their charges, Alexander smiled, and said those were some of Aristotle's sophisms, which would serve equally on both sides; and added, that both he and his father should be severely punished, if they were found guilty of the least injustice towards those who complained. All which made such a deep impression of terror in Cassander's mind, that long after when he was king of Macedonia, and master of Greece, as he was walking up and down at Delphi, and looking at the statues, at the sight of that of Alexander he was suddenly struck with alarm, and shook all over, his eyes rolled, his head grew dizzy, and it was long before he recovered himself.

When once Alexander had given way to fears of supernatural influence, his mind grew so disturbed and so easily alarmed, that if the least unusual or extraordinary thing happened, he thought it a prodigy or a presage, and his court was thronged with diviners and priests whose business was to sacrifice and purify and foretell the future. So miserable a thing is incredulity and contempt of divine power on the one hand, and so miserable, also, superstition on the other, which like water, where the level has been lowered, flowing in and never stopping, fills the mind with slavish fears and follies, as now in Alexander's case. But upon some answers which were brought him from the oracle concerning Hephaestion, he laid aside his sorrow, and fell again to sacrificing and drinking; and having given Nearchus a splendid entertainment, after he had bathed, as was his custom, just as he was going to bed, at Medius's request he went to supper with him. Here he drank all the next day, and was attacked with a fever, which seized him, not as some write, after he had drunk of the bowl of Hercules; nor was he taken with any sudden pain in his back, as if he had been struck with lance, for these are the inventions of some authors who thought it their duty to make the last scene of so great an action as tragical and moving as they could. Aristobulus tells us, that in the rage of his fever and a violent thirst, he took a draught of wine, upon which he fell into delirium, and died on the thirtieth day of the month Daesius.

But the journals give the following record. On the eighteenth of the month, he slept in the bathing-room on account of his fever. The next day he bathed and removed into his chamber, and spent his time in playing dice with Medius. In the evening he bathed and sacrificed, and ate freely, and had the fever on him through the night. On the twentieth, after the usual sacrifices and bathing, he lay in the bathing-room and heard Nearchus's narrative of his voyage, and the observations he had made in the great sea. The twenty-first he passed in the same manner, his fever still increasing, and suffered much during the night. The next day the fever was very violent, and he had himself removed and his bed set by the great bath, and discoursed with his principal officers about finding fit men to fill up the vacant places in the army. On the twenty-fourth he was much worse, and was carried out of his bed to assist at the sacrifices, and gave order that the general officers should wait within the court, whilst the inferior officers kept watch without doors. On the twenty-fifth he was removed to his palace on the other side the river, where he slept a little, but his fever did not abate, and when the generals came into his chamber, he was speechless, and continued so the following day. The Macedonians, therefore, supposing he was dead, came with great clamors to the gates, and menaced his friends so that they were forced to admit them, and let them all pass through unarmed along by his bedside. The same day Python and Seleucus were dispatched to the temple of Serapis to inquire if they should bring Alexander thither, and were answered by the god, that they should not remove him. On the twenty-eighth, in the evening, he died. This account is most of it word for word as it is written in the diary.

At the time, nobody had any suspicion of his being poisoned, but upon some information given six years after, they say Olympias put many to death, and scattered the ashes of Iolaus, then dead, as if he had given it him. But those who affirm that Aristotle counseled Antipater to do it, and that by his means the poison was brought, adduce one Hagnothemis as their authority, who, they say, heard king Antigonus speak of it, and tell us that the poison was water, deadly cold as ice, distilling from a rock in the district of Nonacris, which they gathered like a thin dew, and kept in an ass's hoof; for it was so very cold and penetrating that no other vessel would hold it. However, most are of opinion that all this is a mere made-up story, no slight evidence of which is, that during the dissensions among the commanders, which lasted several days, the body continued clear and fresh, without any sign of such taint or corruption, though it lay neglected in a close, sultry place.

Roxana, who was now with child, and upon that account much honored by the Macedonians, being jealous of Statira, sent for her by a counterfeit letter, as if Alexander had been still alive; and when she had her in her power, killed her and her sister, and threw their bodies into a well, which they filled up with earth, not without the privity and assistance of Perdiccas, who in the time immediately following the king's death, under cover of the name of Arrhidaeus, whom he carried about him as a sort of guard to his person, exercised the chief authority Arrhidaeus, who was Philip's son by an obscure woman of the name of Philinna, was himself of weak intellect, not that he had been originally deficient either in body or mind; on the contrary, in his childhood, he had showed a happy and promising character enough. But a diseased habit of body, caused by drugs which Olympias gave him, had ruined not only his health, but his understanding.

14
CAESAR

After Sylla became master of Rome, he wished to make Caesar put away his wife Cornelia, daughter of Cinna, the late sole ruler of the commonwealth, but was unable to effect it either by promises or intimidation, and so contented himself with confiscating her dowry. The ground of Sylla's hostility to Caesar, was the relationship between him and Marius; for Marius, the elder, married Julia, the sister of Caesar's father, and had by her the younger Marius, who consequently was Caesar's first cousin. And though at the beginning, while so many were to be put to death and there was so much to do, Caesar was overlooked by Sylla, yet he would not keep quiet, but presented himself to the people as a candidate for the priesthood, though he was yet a mere boy. Sylla, without any open opposition, took measures to have him rejected, and in consultation whether he should be put to death, when it was urged by some that it was not worth his while to contrive the death of a boy, he answered, that they knew little who did not see more than one Marius in that boy. Caesar, on being informed of this saying, concealed himself, and for a considerable time kept out of the way in the country of the Sabines, often changing his quarters, till one night, as he was removing from one house to another on account of his health, he fell into the hands of Sylla's soldiers, who were searching those parts in order to apprehend any who had absconded. Caesar, by a bribe of two talents, prevailed with Cornelius, their captain, to let him go, and was no sooner dismissed but he put to sea, and made for Bithynia. After a short stay there with Nicomedes, the king, in his passage back he was taken near the island Pharmacusa by some of the pirates, who, at that time, with large fleets of ships and innumerable smaller vessels infested the seas everywhere.

When these men at first demanded of him twenty talents for his ransom, he laughed at them for not understanding the value of their prisoner, and voluntarily engaged to give them fifty. He presently dispatched those about him to several places to raise the money, till at last he was left among a set of the most bloodthirsty people in the world, the Cilicians, only with one friend and two attendants. Yet he made so little of them, that when he had a mind to sleep, he would send to them, and order them to make no noise. For thirty-eight days, with all the freedom in the world, he amused himself with joining in their exercises and games, as if they had not been his keepers, but his guards. He wrote verses and speeches, and made them his auditors, and those who did not admire them, he called to their faces illiterate and barbarous, and would often, in raillery, threaten to hang them. They were greatly taken with this, and attributed his free talking to a kind of simplicity and boyish playfulness. As soon as his ransom was come from Miletus, he paid it, and was discharged, and proceeded at once to man some ships at the port of Miletus, and went in pursuit of the pirates, whom he surprised with their ships still stationed at the island, and took most of them. Their money he made his prize, and the men he secured in prison at Pergamus, and made application to Junius, who was then governor of Asia, to whose office it belonged, as praetor, to determine their punishment. Junius, having his eye upon the money, for the sum was considerable, said he would think at his leisure what to do with the prisoners, upon which Caesar took his leave of him, and went off to Pergamus, where he ordered the pirates to be brought forth and crucified; the punishment he had often threatened them with whilst he was in their hands, and they little dreamed he was in earnest.

In the meantime Sylla's power being now on the decline, Caesar's friends advised him to return to Rome, but he went to Rhodes, and entered himself in the school of Apollonius, Molon's son, a famous rhetorician, one who had the reputation of a worthy man, and had Cicero for one of his scholars. Caesar is said to have been admirably fitted by nature to make a great statesman and orator, and to have taken such pains to improve his genius this way, that without dispute he might challenge the second place. More he did not aim at, as choosing to be first rather amongst men of arms and power, and, therefore, never rose to that height of eloquence to which nature would have carried him, his attention being diverted to those expeditions and designs, which at length gained him the empire. And he himself, in his answer to Cicero's panegyric on Cato, desires his reader not to compare the plain discourse of a soldier with the harangues of an orator who had not only fine parts, but had employed his life in this study.

When he was returned to Rome, he accused Dolabella of maladministration, and many cities of Greece came in to attest it. Dolabella was acquitted, and Caesar, in return for the support he had received from the Greeks, assisted them in their prosecution of Publius Antonius for corrupt practices, before Marcus Lucullus, praetor of Macedonia. In this cause he so far succeeded, that Antonius was forced to appeal to the tribunes at Rome, alleging that in Greece he could not have fair play against Grecians. In his pleadings at Rome, his eloquence soon obtained him great credit and favor, and he won no less upon the affections of the people by the affability of his manners and address, in which he slowed a tact and consideration beyond what could have been expected at his age; and the open house he kept, the entertainments he gave, and the general splendor of his manner of life contributed little by little to create and increase his political influence. His enemies slighted the growth of it at first, presuming it would soon fail when his money was gone; whilst in the meantime it was growing up and flourishing among the common people. When his power at last was established and not to be overthrown, and now openly tended to the altering of the whole constitution, they were aware too late, that there is no beginning so mean, which continued application will not make considerable, and that despising a danger at first, will make it at last irresistible. Cicero was the first who had any suspicions of his designs upon the government, and, as a good pilot is apprehensive of a storm when the sea is most smiling, saw the designing temper of the man through this disguise of good-humor and affability, and said, that in general, in all he did and undertook, he detected the ambition for absolute power, "but when I see his hair so carefully arranged, and observe him adjusting it with one finger, I cannot imagine it should enter into such a man's thoughts to subvert the Roman state." But of this more hereafter.

The first proof he had of the people's good-will to him, was when he received by their suffrages a tribuneship in the army, and came out on the list with a higher place than Caius Popilius. A second and clearer instance of their favor appeared upon his making a magnificent oration in praise of his aunt Julia, wife to Marius, publicly in the forum, at whose funeral he was so bold as to bring forth the images of Marius, which nobody had dared to produce since the government came into Sylla's hands, Marius's party having from that time been declared enemies of the State. When some who were present had begun to raise a cry against Caesar, the people answered with loud shouts and clapping in his favor, expressing their joyful surprise and satisfaction at his having, as it were, brought up again from the grave those honors of Marius, which for so long a time had been lost to the city. It had always been the custom at Rome to make funeral orations in praise of elderly matrons, but there was no precedent of any upon young women till Caesar first made one upon the death of his own wife. This also procured him favor, and by this show of affection he won upon the feelings of the people, who looked upon him as a man of great tenderness and kindness of heart. After he had buried his wife, he went as quaestor into Spain under one of the praetors, named Vetus, whom he honored ever after, and made his son his own quaestor, when he himself came to be praetor. After this employment was ended, he married Pompeia, his third wife, having then a daughter by Cornelia, his first wife, whom he afterwards married to Pompey the Great. He was so profuse in his expenses, that before he had any public employment, he was in debt thirteen hundred talents, and many thought that by incurring such expense to be popular, he changed a solid good for what would prove but short and uncertain return; but in truth he was purchasing what was of the greatest value at an inconsiderable rate. When he was made surveyor of the Appian Way, he disbursed, besides the public money, a great sum out of his private purse; and when he was aedile, be provided such a number of gladiators, that he entertained the people with three hundred and twenty single combats, and by his great liberality and magnificence in theatrical shows, in processions, and public feastings, he threw into the shade all the attempts that had been made before him, and gained so much upon the people, that everyone was eager to find out new offices and new honors for him in return for his munificence.

There being two factions in the city, one that of Sylla, which was very powerful, the other that of Marius, which was then broken and in a very low condition, he undertook to revive this and to make it his own. And to this end, whilst he was in the height of his repute with the people for the magnificent shows he gave as aedile, he ordered images of Marius, and figures of Victory, with trophies in their hands, to be carried privately in the night and placed in the capitol. Next morning, when some saw them bright with gold and beautifully made, with inscriptions upon them, referring them to Marius's exploits over the Cimbrians, they were surprised at the boldness of him who had set them up, nor was it difficult to guess who it was. The fame of this soon spread and brought together a great concourse of people. Some cried out that it was an open attempt against the established government thus to revive those honors which had been buried by the laws and decrees of the senate; that Caesar had done it to sound the temper of the people whom he had prepared before, and to try whether they were tame enough to bear his humor, and would quietly give way to his innovations. On the other hand, Marius's party took courage, and it was incredible how numerous they were suddenly seen to be, and what a multitude of them appeared and came shouting into the capitol. Many, when they saw Marius's likeness, cried for joy, and Caesar was highly extolled as the one man, in the place of all others, who was a relation worthy of Marius. Upon this the senate met, and Catulus Lutatius, one of the most eminent Romans of that time, stood up and inveighed against Caesar, closing his speech with the remarkable saying, that Caesar was now not working mines, but planting batteries to overthrow the state. But when Caesar had made an apology for himself, and satisfied the senate, his admirers were very much animated, and advised him not to depart from his own thoughts for anyone, since with the people's good favor he would erelong get the better of them all, and be the first man in the commonwealth.

At this time, Metellus, the High-Priest, died, and Catulus and Isauricus, persons of the highest reputation, and who had great influence in the senate, were competitors for the office; yet Caesar would not give way to them, but presented himself to the people as a candidate against them. The several parties seeming very equal, Catulus, who, because he had the most honor to lose, was the most apprehensive of the event, sent to Caesar to buy him off, with offers of a great sum of money. But his answer was, that he was ready to borrow a larger sum than that, to carry on the contest. Upon the day of election, as his mother conducted him out of doors with tears, after embracing her, "My mother," he said, "today you will see me either High-Priest, or an exile." When the votes were taken, after a great struggle, he carried it, and excited among the senate and nobility great alarm lest he might now urge on the people to every kind of insolence. And Piso and Catulus found fault with Cicero for having let Caesar escape, when in the conspiracy of Catiline he had given the government such advantage against him. For Catiline, who had designed not only to change the present state of affairs, but to subvert the whole empire and confound all, had himself taken to flight, while the evidence was yet incomplete against him, before his ultimate purposes had been properly discovered. But he had left Lentulus and Cethegus in the city to supply his place in the conspiracy, and whether they received any secret encouragement and assistance from Caesar is uncertain; all that is certain, is, that they were fully convicted in the senate, and when Cicero, the consul, asked the several opinions of the senators, how they would have them punished, all who spoke before Caesar sentenced them to death; but Caesar stood up and made a set speech, in which he told them, that he thought it without precedent and not just to take away the lives of persons of their birth and distinction before they were fairly tried, unless there was an absolute necessity for it; but that if they were kept confined in any towns of Italy Cicero himself should choose, till Catiline was defeated, then the senate might in peace and at their leisure determine what was best to be done.

This sentence of his carried so much appearance of humanity, and he gave it such advantage by the eloquence with which he urged it, that not only those who spoke after him closed with it, but even they who had before given a contrary opinion, now came over to his, till it came about to Catulus's and Cato's turn to speak. They warmly opposed it, and Cato intimated in his speech the suspicion of Caesar himself, and pressed the matter so strongly, that the criminals were given up to suffer execution. As Caesar was going out of the senate, many of the young men who at that time acted as guards to Cicero, ran in with their naked swords to assault him. But Curio, it is said, threw his gown over him, and conveyed him away, and Cicero himself, when the young men looked up to see his wishes, gave a sign not to kill him, either for fear of the people, or because he thought the murder unjust and illegal. If this be true, I wonder how Cicero came to omit all mention of it in his book about his consulship. He was blamed, however, afterwards, for not having made use of so fortunate an opportunity against Caesar, as if he had let it escape him out of fear of the populace, who, indeed, showed remarkable solicitude about Caesar, and some time after, when he went into the senate to clear himself of the suspicions he lay under, and found great clamors raised against him, upon the senate in consequence sitting longer than ordinary, they went up to the house in a tumult, and beset it, demanding Caesar, and requiring them to dismiss him. Upon this, Cato, much fearing some movement among the poor citizens, who were always the first to kindle the flame among the people, and placed all their hopes in Caesar, persuaded the senate to give them a monthly allowance of corn, an expedient which put the commonwealth to the extraordinary charge of seven million five hundred thousand drachmas in the year, but quite succeeded in removing the great cause of terror for the present, and very much weakened Caesar's power, who at that time was just going to be made praetor, and consequently would have been more formidable by his office.

But there was no disturbance during his praetorship, only what misfortune he met with in his own domestic affairs. Publius Clodius was a patrician by descent, eminent both for his riches and eloquence, but in licentiousness of life and audacity exceeded the most noted profligates of the day. He was in love with Pompeia, Caesar's wife, and she had no aversion to him. But there was strict watch kept on her apartment, and Caesar's mother, Aurelia, who was a discreet woman, being continually about her, made any interview very dangerous and difficult. The Romans have a goddess whom they call Bona, the same whom the Greeks call Gynaecea. The Phrygians, who claim a peculiar title to her, say she was mother to Midas. The Romans profess she was one of the Dryads, and married to Faunus. The Grecians affirm that she is that mother of Bacchus whose name is not to be uttered, and, for this reason, the women who celebrate her festival, cover the tents with vine-branches, and, in accordance with the fable, a consecrated serpent is placed by the goddess. It is not lawful for a man to be by, nor so much as in the house, whilst the rites are celebrated, but the women by themselves perform the sacred offices, which are said to be much the same with those used in the solemnities of Orpheus. When the festival comes, the husband, who is either consul or praetor; and with him every male creature, quits the house. The wife then taking it under her care, sets it in order, and the principal ceremonies are performed during the night, the women playing together amongst themselves as they keep watch, and music of various kinds going on.

As Pompeia was at that time celebrating this feast, Clodius, who as yet had no beard, and so thought to pass undiscovered, took upon him the dress and ornaments of a singing woman, and so came thither, having the air of a young girl. Finding the doors open, he was without any stop introduced by the maid, who was in the intrigue. She presently ran to tell Pompeia, but as she was away a long time, he grew uneasy in waiting for her, and left his post and traversed the house from one room to another, still taking care to avoid the lights, till at last Aurelia's woman met him, and invited him to play with her, as the women did among themselves. He refused to comply, and she presently pulled him forward, and asked him who he was, and whence he came. Clodius told her he was waiting for Pompeia's own maid, Abra, being in fact her own name also, and as he said so, betrayed himself by his voice. Upon which the woman shrieking, ran into the company where there were lights, and cried out, she had discovered a man. The women were all in a fright. Aurelia covered up the sacred things and stopped the proceedings, and having ordered the doors to be shut, went about with lights to find Clodius, who was got into the maid's room that he had come in with, and was seized there. The women knew him, and drove him out of doors, and at once, that same night, went home and told their husbands the story. In the morning, it was all about the town, what an impious attempt Clodius had made, and how he ought to be punished as an offender, not only against those whom he had affronted, but also against the public and the gods. Upon which one of the tribunes impeached him for profaning the holy rites, and some of the principal senators combined together and gave evidence against him, that besides many other horrible crimes, he had been guilty of incest with his own sister, who was married to Lucullus. But the people set themselves against this combination of the nobility, and defended Clodius, which was of great service to him with the judges, who took alarm and were afraid to provoke the multitude. Caesar at once dismissed Pompeia, but being summoned as a witness against Clodius, said he had nothing to charge him with. This looking like a paradox, the accuser asked him why he parted with his wife. Caesar replied, "I wished my wife to be not so much as suspected." Some say that Caesar spoke this as his real thought; others, that he did it to gratify the people, who were very earnest to save Clodius. Clodius, at any rate, escaped; most of the judges giving their opinions so written as to be illegible, that they might not be in danger from the people by condemning him, nor in disgrace with the nobility by acquitting him.

Caesar, in the meantime, being out of his praetorship, had got the province of Spain, but was in great embarrassment with his creditors, who, as he was going off, came upon him, and were very pressing and importunate. This led him to apply himself to Crassus, who was the richest man in Rome, but wanted Caesar's youthful vigor and heat to sustain the opposition against Pompey. Crassus took upon him to satisfy those creditors who were most uneasy to him, and would not be put off any longer, and engaged himself to the amount of eight hundred and thirty talents, upon which Caesar was now at liberty to go to his province. In his journey, as he was crossing the Alps, and passing by a small village of the barbarians with but few inhabitants and those wretchedly poor, his companions asked the question among themselves by way of mockery, if there were any canvassing for offices there; any contention which should be uppermost, or feuds of great men one against another. To which Caesar made answer seriously, "For my part, I had rather be the first man among these fellows, than the second man in Rome." It is said that another time, when free from business in Spain, after reading some part of the history of Alexander, he sat a great while very thoughtful, and at last burst out into tears. His friends were surprised, and asked him the reason of it. "Do you think," said he, "I have not just cause to weep, when I consider that Alexander at my age had conquered so many nations, and I have all this time done nothing that is memorable?" As soon as he came into Spain he was very active, and in a few days had got together ten new cohorts of foot in addition to the twenty which were there before. With these he marched against the Calaici and Lusitani and conquered them, and advancing as far as the ocean, subdued the tribes which never before had been subject to the Romans. Having managed his military affairs with good success, he was equally happy in the course of his civil government. He took pains to establish a good understanding amongst the several states, and no less care to heal the differences between debtors and creditors. He ordered that the creditor should receive two parts of the debtor's yearly income, and that the other part should be managed by the debtor himself, till by this method the whole debt was at last discharged. This conduct made him leave his province with a fair reputation; being rich himself, and having enriched his soldiers, and having received from them the honorable name of Imperator.

There is a law among the Romans, that whoever desires the honor of a triumph must stay without the city and expect his answer. And another, that those who stand for the consulship shall appear personally upon the place. Caesar was come home at the very time of choosing consuls, and being in a difficulty between these two opposite laws, sent to the senate to desire that since he was obliged to be absent, he might sue for the consulship by his friends. Cato, being backed by the law, at first opposed his request; afterwards perceiving that Caesar had prevailed with a great part of the senate to comply with it, he made it his business to gain time, and went on wasting the whole day in speaking. Upon which Caesar thought fit to let the triumph fall, and pursued the consulship. Entering the town and coming forward immediately, he had recourse to a piece of state-policy by which everybody was deceived but Cato. This was the reconciling of Crassus and Pompey, the two men who then were most powerful in Rome. There had been a quarrel between them, which he now succeeded in making up, and by this means strengthened himself by the united power of both, and so under the cover of an action which carried all the appearance of a piece of kindness and good-nature, caused what was in effect a revolution in the government. For it was not the quarrel between Pompey and Caesar, as most men imagine, which was the origin of the civil wars, but their union, their conspiring together at first to subvert the aristocracy, and so quarreling afterwards between themselves. Cato, who often foretold what the consequence of this alliance would be, had then the character of a sullen, interfering man, but in the end the reputation of a wise but unsuccessful counselor.

Thus Caesar being doubly supported by the interests of Crassus and Pompey, was promoted to the consulship, and triumphantly proclaimed with Calpurnius Bibulus. When he entered on his office, he brought in bills which would have been preferred with better grace by the most audacious of the tribunes than by a consul, in which he proposed the plantation of colonies and division of lands, simply to please the commonalty. The best and most honorable of the senators opposed it, upon which, as he had long wished for nothing more than for such a colorable pretext, he loudly protested how much against his will it was to be driven to seek support from the people, and how the senate's insulting and harsh conduct left no other course possible for him, than to devote himself henceforth to the popular cause and interest. And so he hurried out of the senate, and presenting himself to the people, and there placing Crassus and Pompey, one on each side of him, he asked them whether they consented to the bills he had proposed. They owned their assent, upon which he desired them to assist him against those who had threatened to oppose him with their swords. They engaged they would, and Pompey added further, that he would meet their swords with a sword and buckler too. These words the nobles much resented, as neither suitable to his own dignity, nor becoming the reverence due to the senate, but resembling rather the vehemence of a boy, or the fury of a madman. But the people were pleased with it. In order to get a yet firmer hold upon Pompey, Caesar having a daughter, Julia, who had been before contracted to Servilius Caepio, now betrothed her to Pompey, and told Servilius he should have Pompey's daughter, who was not unengaged either, but promised to Sylla's son, Faustus. A little time after, Caesar married Calpurnia, the daughter of Piso, and got Piso made consul for the year following. Cato exclaimed loudly against this, and protested with a great deal of warmth, that it was intolerable the government should be prostituted by marriages, and that they should advance one another to the commands of armies, provinces, and other great posts, by means of women.

Bibulus, Caesar's colleague, finding it was to no purpose to oppose his bills, but that he was in danger of being murdered in the forum, as also was Cato, confined himself to his house, and there let the remaining part of his consulship expire. Pompey, when he was married, at once filled the forum with soldiers, and gave the people his help in passing the new laws, and secured Caesar the government of all Gaul, both on this and the other side of the Alps, together with Illyricum, and the command of four legions for five years. Cato made some attempts against these proceedings, but was seized and led off on the way to prison by Caesar, who expected he would appeal to the tribunes. But when he saw that Cato went along without speaking a word, and not only the nobility were indignant, but that the people, also, out of respect for Cato's virtue, were following in silence, and with dejected looks, he himself privately desired one of the tribunes to rescue Cato. As for the other senators, some few of them attended the house, the rest being disgusted, absented themselves. Hence Considius, a very old man, took occasion one day to tell Caesar, that the senators did not meet because they were afraid of his soldiers. Caesar asked, "Why don't you then, out of the same fear, keep at home?" To which Considius replied, that age was his guard against fear, and that the small remains of his life were not worth much caution. But the most disgraceful thing that was done in Caesar's consulship, was his assisting to gain the tribuneship for the same Clodius who had made the attempt upon his wife's chastity, and intruded upon the secret vigils. He was elected on purpose to effect Cicero's downfall; nor did Caesar leave the city to join his army, till they two had overpowered Cicero, and driven him out of Italy.

Thus far have we followed Caesar's actions before the wars of Gaul. After this, he seems to begin his course afresh, and to enter upon a new life and scene of action. And the period of those wars which he now fought, and those many expeditions in which he subdued Gaul, showed him to be a soldier and general not in the least inferior to any of the greatest and most admired commanders who had ever appeared at the head of armies. For if we compare him with the Fabii, the Metelli, the Scipios, and with those who were his contemporaries, or not long before him, Sylla, Marius, the two Luculli, or even Pompey himself, whose glory, it may be said, went up at that time to heaven for every excellence in war, we shall find Caesar's actions to have surpassed them all. One he may be held to have outdone in consideration of the difficulty of the country in which he fought, another in the extent of territory which he conquered; some, in the number and strength of the enemies whom he defeated; one man, because of the wildness and perfidiousness of the tribes whose good-will he conciliated, another in his humanity and clemency to those he overpowered; others, again in his gifts and kindnesses to his soldiers; all alike in the number of the battles which he fought and the enemies whom he killed. For he had not pursued the wars in Gaul full ten years, when he had taken by storm above eight hundred towns, subdued three hundred states, and of the three millions of men, who made up the gross sum of those with whom at several times he engaged, he had killed one million, and taken captive a second.

He was so much master of the good-will and hearty service of his soldiers, that those who in other expeditions were but ordinary men, displayed a courage past defeating or withstanding when they went upon any danger where Caesar's glory was concerned. Such a one was Acilius, who, in the sea-fight before Marseilles, had his right hand struck off with a sword, yet did not quit his buckler out of his left, but struck the enemies in the face with it, till he drove them off, and made himself master of the vessel. Such another was Cassius Scaeva, who, in a battle near Dyrrhachium, had one of his eyes shot out with an arrow, his shoulder pierced with one javelin, and his thigh with another; and having received one hundred and thirty darts upon his target, called to the enemy, as though he would surrender himself. But when two of them came up to him, he cut off the shoulder of one with a sword, and by a blow over the face forced the other to retire, and so with the assistance of his friends, who now came up, made his escape. Again, in Britain, when some of the foremost officers had accidentally got into a morass full of water, and there were assaulted by the enemy, a common soldier, whilst Caesar stood and looked on, threw himself into the midst of them, and after many signal demonstrations of his valor, rescued the officers, and beat off the barbarians. He himself, in the end, took to the water, and with much difficulty, partly by swimming, partly by wading, passed it, but in the passage lost his shield. Caesar and his officers saw it and admired, and went to meet him with joy and acclamation. But the soldier, much dejected and in tears, threw himself down at Caesar's feet, and begged his pardon for having let go his buckler. Another time in Africa, Scipio having taken a ship of Caesar's in which Granius Petro, lately appointed quaestor, was sailing, gave the other passengers as free prize to his soldiers, but thought fit to offer the quaestor his life. But he said it was not usual for Caesar's soldiers to take, but give mercy, and having said so, fell upon his sword and killed himself.

This love of honor and passion for distinction were inspired into them and cherished in them by Caesar himself, who, by his unsparing distribution of money and honors, showed them that he did not heap up wealth from the wars for his own luxury, or the gratifying his private pleasures, but that all he received was but a public fund laid by for the reward and encouragement of valor, and that he looked upon all he gave to deserving soldiers as so much increase to his own riches. Added to this, also, there was no danger to which he did not willingly expose himself, no labor from which he pleaded all exemption. His contempt of danger was not so much wondered at by his soldiers, because they knew how much he coveted honor. But his enduring so much hardship, which he did to all appearance beyond his natural strength, very much astonished them. For he was a spare man, had a soft and white skin, was distempered in the head, and subject to an epilepsy, which, it is said, first seized him at Corduba. But he did not make the weakness of his constitution a pretext for his ease, but rather used war as the best physic against his indispositions; whilst by indefatigable journeys, coarse diet, frequent lodging in the field, and continual laborious exercise, he struggled with his diseases, and fortified his body against all attacks. He slept generally in his chariots or litters, employing even his rest in pursuit of action. In the day he was thus carried to the forts, garrisons, and camps, one servant sitting with him, who used to write down what he dictated as he went, and a soldier attending behind with his sword drawn. He drove so rapidly, that when he first left Rome, he arrived at the river Rhone within eight days. He had been an expert rider from his childhood; for it was usual with him to sit with his hands joined together behind his back, and so to put his horse to its full speed. And in this war he disciplined himself so far as to be able to dictate letters from on horseback, and to give directions to two who took notes at the same time, or, as Oppius says, to more. And it is thought that he was the first who contrived means for communicating with friends by cipher, when either press of business, or the large extent of the city, left him no time for a personal conference about matters that required dispatch. How little nice he was in his diet, may be seen in the following instance. When at the table of Valerius Leo, who entertained him at supper at Milan, a dish of asparagus was put before him, on which his host instead of oil had poured sweet ointment. Caesar partook of it without any disgust, and reprimanded his friends for finding fault with it. "For it was enough," said he, "not to eat what you did not like; but he who reflects on another man's want of breeding, shows he wants it as much himself." Another time upon the road he was driven by a storm into a poor man's cottage, where he found but one room, and that such as would afford but a mean reception to a single person, and therefore told his companions, places of honor should be given up to the greater men, and necessary accommodations to the weaker, and accordingly ordered that Oppius, who was in bad health, should lodge within, whilst he and the rest slept under a shed at the door.

His first war in Gaul was against the Helvetians and Tigurini, who having burnt their own towns, twelve in number, and four hundred villages, would have marched forward through that part of Gaul which was included in the Roman province, as the Cimbrians and Teutons formerly had done. Nor were they inferior to these in courage; and in numbers they were equal, being in all three hundred thousand, of which one hundred and ninety thousand were fighting men. Caesar did not engage the Tigurini in person, but Labienus, under his directions, routed them near the river Arar. The Helvetians surprised Caesar, and unexpectedly set upon him as he was conducting his army to a confederate town. He succeeded, however, in making his retreat into a strong position, where, when he had mustered and marshalled his men, his horse was brought to him; upon which he said, "When I have won the battle, I will use my horse for the chase, but at present let us go against the enemy," and accordingly charged them on foot. After a long and severe combat, he drove the main army out of the field, but found the hardest work at their carriages and ramparts, where not only the men stood and fought, but the women also and children defended themselves, till they were cut to pieces; insomuch that the fight was scarcely ended till midnight. This action, glorious in itself, Caesar crowned with another yet more noble, by gathering in a body all the barbarians that had escaped out of the battle, above one hundred thousand in number, and obliging them to reoccupy the country which they had deserted, and the cities which they had burnt. This he did for fear the Germans should pass in and possess themselves of the land whilst it lay uninhabited.

His second war was in defense of the Gauls against the Germans, though some time before he had made Ariovistus, their king, recognized at Rome as an ally. But they were very insufferable neighbors to those under his government; and it was probable, when occasion offered, they would renounce the present arrangements, and march on to occupy Gaul. But finding his officers timorous, and especially those of the young nobility who came along with him in hopes of turning their campaigns with him into a means for their own pleasure or profit, he called them together, and advised them to march off, and not run the hazard of a battle against their inclinations, since they had such weak and unmanly feelings; telling them that he would take only the tenth legion, and march against the barbarians, whom he did not expect to find an enemy more formidable than the Cimbri, nor, he added, should they find him a general inferior to Marius. Upon this, the tenth legion deputed some of their body to pay him their acknowledgments and thanks, and the other legions blamed their officers, and all, with great vigor and zeal, followed him many days' journey, till they encamped within two hundred furlongs of the enemy. Ariovistus's courage to some extent was cooled upon their very approach; for never expecting the Romans would attack the Germans, whom he had thought it more likely they would not venture to withstand even in defense of their own subjects, he was the more surprised at Caesar's conduct, and saw his army to be in consternation. They were still more discouraged by the prophecies of their holy women, who foretell the future by observing the eddies of rivers, and taking signs from the windings and noise of streams, and who now warned them not to engage before the next new moon appeared. Caesar having had intimation of this, and seeing the Germans lie still, thought it expedient to attack them whilst they were under these apprehensions, rather than sit still and wait their time. Accordingly he made his approaches to the strongholds and hills on which they lay encamped, and so galled and fretted them, that at last they came down with great fury to engage. But he gained a signal victory, and pursued them for four hundred furlongs, as far as the Rhine; all which space was covered with spoils and bodies of the slain. Ariovistus made shift to pass the Rhine with the small remains of an army, for it is said the number of the slain amounted to eighty thousand.

After this action, Caesar left his army at their winter-quarters in the country of the Sequani, and in order to attend to affairs at Rome, went into that part of Gaul which lies on the Po, and was part of his province; for the river Rubicon divides Gaul, which is on this side the Alps, from the rest of Italy. There he sat down and employed himself in courting people's favor; great numbers coming to him continually, and always finding their requests answered; for he never failed to dismiss all with present pledges of his kindness in hand, and further hopes for the future. And during all this time of the war in Gaul, Pompey never observed how Caesar was on the one hand using the arms of Rome to effect his conquests, and on the other was gaining over and securing to himself the favor of the Romans, with the wealth which those conquests obtained him. But when he heard that the Belgae, who were the most powerful of all the Gauls, and inhabited a third part of the country, were revolted, and had got together a great many thousand men in arms, he immediately set out and took his way thither with great expedition, and falling upon the enemy as they were ravaging the Gauls, his allies, he soon defeated and put to flight the largest and least scattered division of them. For though their numbers were great, yet they made but a slender defense, and the marshes and deep rivers were made passable to the Roman foot by the vast quantity of dead bodies. Of those who revolted, all the tribes that lived near the ocean came over without fighting, and he, therefore, led his army against the Nervii, the fiercest and most warlike people of all in those parts. These live in a country covered with continuous woods, and having lodged their children and property out of the way in the depth of the forest, fell upon Caesar with a body of sixty thousand men, before he was prepared for them, while he was making his encampment. They soon routed his cavalry, and having surrounded the twelfth and seventh legions, killed all the officers, and had not Caesar himself snatched up a buckler, and forced his way through his own men to come up to the barbarians, or had not the tenth legion, when they saw him in danger, run in from the tops of the hills, where they lay, and broken through the enemy's ranks to rescue him, in all probability not a Roman would have been saved. But now, under the influence of Caesar's bold example, they fought a battle, as the phrase is, of more than human courage, and yet with their utmost efforts they were not able to drive the enemy out of the field, but cut them down fighting in their defense. For out of sixty thousand men, it is stated that not above five hundred survived the battle, and of four hundred of their senators not above three.

When the Roman senate had received news of this, they voted sacrifices and festivals to the gods, to be strictly observed for the space of fifteen days, a longer space than ever was observed for any victory before. The danger to which they had been exposed by the joint outbreak of such a number of nations was felt to have been great; and the people's fondness for Caesar gave additional luster to successes achieved by him. He now, after settling everything in Gaul, came back again, and spent the winter by the Po, in order to carry on the designs he had in hand at Rome. All who were candidates for offices used his assistance, and were supplied with money from him to corrupt the people and buy their votes, in return of which, when they were chosen, they did all things to advance his power. But what was more considerable, the most eminent and powerful men in Rome in great numbers came to visit him at Lucca, Pompey, and Crassus, and Appius, the governor of Sardinia, and Nepos, the proconsul of Spain, so that there were in the place at one time one hundred and twenty lictors, and more than two hundred senators. In deliberation here held, it was determined that Pompey and Crassus should be consuls again for the following year; that Caesar should have a fresh supply of money, and that his command should be renewed to him for five years more. It seemed very extravagant to all thinking men, that those very persons who had received so much money from Caesar should persuade the senate to grant him more, as if he were in want. Though in truth it was not so much upon persuasion as compulsion, that, with sorrow and groans for their own acts, they passed the measure. Cato was not present, for they had sent him seasonably out of the way into Cyprus; but Favonius, who was a zealous imitator of Cato, when he found he could do no good by opposing it, broke out of the house, and loudly declaimed against these proceedings to the people, but none gave him any hearing; some slighting him out of respect to Crassus and Pompey, and the greater part to gratify Caesar, on whom depended their hopes.

After this, Caesar returned again to his forces in Gaul, where he found that country involved in a dangerous war, two strong nations of the Germans having lately passed the Rhine, to conquer it; one of them called the Usipes, the other the Tenteritae. Of the war with this people, Caesar himself has given this account in his commentaries, that the barbarians, having sent ambassadors to treat with him, did, during the treaty, set upon him in his march, by which means with eight hundred men they routed five thousand of his horse, who did not suspect their coming; that afterwards they sent other ambassadors to renew the same fraudulent practices, whom he kept in custody, and led on his army against the barbarians, as judging it mere simplicity to keep faith with those who had so faithlessly broken the terms they had agreed to. But Tanusius states, that when the senate decreed festivals and sacrifices for this victory, Cato declared it to be his opinion that Caesar ought to be given into the hands of the barbarians, that so the guilt which this breach of faith might otherwise bring upon the state, might be expiated by transferring the curse on him, who was the occasion of it. Of those who passed the Rhine, there were four hundred thousand cut off; those few who escaped were sheltered by the Sugambri, a people of Germany. Caesar took hold of this pretense to invade the Germans, being at the same time ambitious of the honor of being the first man that should pass the Rhine with an army. He carried a bridge across it, though it was very wide, and the current at that particular point very full, strong, and violent, bringing down with its waters trunks of trees, and other lumber, which much shook and weakened the foundations of his bridge. But he drove great piles of wood into the bottom of the river above the passage, to catch and stop these as they floated down, and thus fixing his bridle upon the stream, successfully finished this bridge, which no one who saw could believe to be the work but of ten days.

In the passage of his army over it, he met with no opposition; the Suevi themselves, who are the most warlike people of all Germany, flying with their effects into the deepest and most densely wooded valleys. When he had burnt all the enemy's country, and encouraged those who embraced the Roman interest, he went back into Gaul, after eighteen days' stay in Germany. But his expedition into Britain was the most famous testimony of his courage. For he was the first who brought a navy into the western ocean, or who sailed into the Atlantic with an army to make war; and by invading an island, the reported extent of which had made its existence a matter of controversy among historians, many of whom questioned whether it were not a mere name and fiction, not a real place, he might be said to have carried the Roman empire beyond the limits of the known world. He passed thither twice from that part of Gaul which lies over against it, and in several battles which he fought, did more hurt to the enemy than service to himself, for the islanders were so miserably poor, that they had nothing worth being plundered of. When he found himself unable to put such an end to the war as he wished, he was content to take hostages from the king, and to impose a tribute, and then quitted the island. At his arrival in Gaul, he found letters which lay ready to be conveyed over the water to him from his friends at Rome, announcing his daughter's death, who died in labor of a child by Pompey. Caesar and Pompey both were much afflicted with her death, nor were their friends less disturbed, believing that the alliance was now broken, which had hitherto kept the sickly commonwealth in peace, for the child also died within a few days after the mother. The people took the body of Julia, in spite of the opposition of the tribunes, and carried it into the field of Mars, and there her funeral rites were performed, and her remains are laid.

Caesar's army was now grown very numerous, so that he was forced to disperse them into various camps for their winter-quarters, and he having gone himself to Italy as he used to do, in his absence a general outbreak throughout the whole of Gaul commenced, and large armies marched about the country, and attacked the Roman quarters, and attempted to make themselves masters of the forts where they lay. The greatest and strongest party of the rebels, under the command of Abriorix, cut off Costa and Titurius with all their men, while a force sixty thousand strong besieged the legion under the command of Cicero, and had almost taken it by storm, the Roman soldiers being all wounded, and having quite spent themselves by a defense beyond their natural strength. But Caesar, who was at a great distance, having received the news, quickly got together seven thousand men, and hastened to relieve Cicero. The besiegers were aware of it, and went to meet him, with great confidence that they should easily overpower such an handful of men. Caesar, to increase their presumption, seemed to avoid fighting, and still marched off, till he found a place conveniently situated for a few to engage against many, where he encamped. He kept his soldiers from making any attack upon the enemy, and commanded them to raise the ramparts higher, and barricade the gates, that by show of fear, they might heighten the enemy's contempt of them. Till at last they came without any order in great security to make an assault, when he issued forth, and put them to flight with the loss of many men.

This quieted the greater part of the commotions in these parts of Gaul, and Caesar, in the course of the winter, visited every part of the country, and with great vigilance took precautions against all innovations. For there were three legions now come to him to supply the place of the men he had lost, of which Pompey furnished him with two, out of those under his command; the other was newly raised in the part of Gaul by the Po. But in a while the seeds of war, which had long since been secretly sown and scattered by the most powerful men in those warlike nations, broke forth into the greatest and most dangerous war that ever was in those parts, both as regards the number of men in the vigor of their youth who were gathered and armed from all quarters, the vast funds of money collected to maintain it, the strength of the towns, and the difficulty of the country where it was carried on. It being winter, the rivers were frozen, the woods covered with snow, and the level country flooded, so that in some places the ways were lost through the depth of the snow; in others, the overflowing of marshes and streams made every kind of passage uncertain. All which difficulties made it seem impracticable for Caesar to make any attempt upon the insurgents. Many tribes had revolted together, the chief of them being the Arverni and Carnutini; the general who had the supreme command in war was Vergentorix, whose father the Gauls had put to death on suspicion of his aiming at absolute government.

He having disposed his army in several bodies, and set officers over them, drew over to him all the country round about as far as those that lie upon the Arar, and having intelligence of the opposition which Caesar now experienced at Rome, thought to engage all Gaul in the war. Which if he had done a little later, when Caesar was taken up with the civil wars, Italy had been put into as great a terror as before it was by the Cimbri. But Caesar, who above all men was gifted with the faculty of making the right use of everything in war, and most especially of seizing the right moment, as soon as he heard of the revolt, returned immediately the same way he went, and showed the barbarians, by the quickness of his march in such a severe season, that an army was advancing against them which was invincible. For in the time that one would have thought it scarce credible that a courier or express should have come with a message from him, he himself appeared with all his army, ravaging the country, reducing their posts, subduing their towns, receiving into his protection those who declared for him. Till at last the Edui, who hitherto had styled themselves brethren to the Romans, and had been much honored by them, declared against him, and joined the rebels, to the great discouragement of his army. Accordingly he removed thence, and passed the country of the Lingones, desiring to reach the territories of the Sequani, who were his friends, and who lay like a bulwark in front of Italy against the other tribes of Gaul. There the enemy came upon him, and surrounded him with many myriads, whom he also was eager to engage; and at last, after some time and with much slaughter, gained on the whole a complete victory; though at first he appears to have met with some reverse, and the Aruveni show you a small sword hanging up in a temple, which they say was taken from Caesar. Caesar saw this afterwards himself, and smiled, and when his friends advised it should be taken down, would not permit it, because he looked upon it as consecrated.

After the defeat a great part of those who had escaped, fled with their king into a town called Alesia, which Caesar besieged, though the height of the walls, and number of those who defended them, made it appear impregnable; and meantime, from without the walls, he was assailed by a greater danger than can be expressed. For the choice men of Gaul, picked out of each nation, and well armed, came to relieve Alesia, to the number of three hundred thousand; nor were there in the town less than one hundred and seventy thousand. So that Caesar being shut up betwixt two such forces, was compelled to protect himself by two walls, one towards the town, the other against the relieving army, as knowing it these forces should join, his affairs would be entirely ruined. The danger that he underwent before Alesia, justly gained him great honor on many accounts, and gave him an opportunity of showing greater instances of his valor and conduct than any other contest had done. One wonders much how he should be able to engage and defeat so many thousands of men without the town, and not be perceived by those within, but yet more, that the Romans themselves, who guarded their wall which was next the town, should be strangers to it. For even they knew nothing of the victory, till they heard the cries of the men and lamentations of the women who were in the town, and had from thence seen the Romans at a distance carrying into their camp a great quantity of bucklers, adorned with gold and silver, many breastplates stained with blood, besides cups and tents made in the Gallic fashion. So soon did so vast an army dissolve and vanish like a ghost or dream, the greatest part of them being killed upon the spot. Those who were in Alesia, having given themselves and Caesar much trouble, surrendered at last; and Vergentorix, who was the chief spring of all the war, putting his best armor on, and adorning his horse, rode out of the gates, and made a turn about Caesar as he was sitting, then quitted his horse, threw off his armor, and remained seated quietly at Caesar's feet until he was led away to be reserved for the triumph.

Caesar had long ago resolved upon the overthrow of Pompey, as had Pompey, for that matter, upon his. For Crassus, the fear of whom had hitherto kept them in peace, having now been killed in Parthia, if the one of them wished to make himself the greatest man in Rome, he had only to overthrow the other; and if he again wished to prevent his own fall, he had nothing for it but to be beforehand with him whom he feared. Pompey had not been long under any such apprehensions, having till lately despised Caesar, as thinking it no difficult matter to put down him whom he himself had advanced. But Caesar had entertained this design from the beginning against his rivals, and had retired, like an expert wrestler, to prepare himself apart for the combat. Making the Gallic wars his exercise-ground, he had at once improved the strength of his soldiery, and had heightened his own glory by his great actions, so that he was looked on as one who might challenge comparison with Pompey. Nor did he let go any of those advantages which were now given him both by Pompey himself and the times, and the ill government of Rome, where all who were candidates for offices publicly gave money, and without any shame bribed the people, who having received their pay, did not contend for their benefactors with their bare suffrages, but with bows, swords, and slings. So that after having many times stained the place of election with the blood of men killed upon the spot, they left the city at last without a government at all, to be carried about like a ship without a pilot to steer her; while all who had any wisdom could only be thankful if a course of such wild and stormy disorder and madness might end no worse than in a monarchy. Some were so bold as to declare openly, that the government was incurable but by a monarchy, and that they ought to take that remedy from the hands of the gentlest physician, meaning Pompey, who, though in words he pretended to decline it, yet in reality made his utmost efforts to be declared dictator. Cato perceiving his design, prevailed with the senate to make him sole consul, that with the offer of a more legal sort of monarchy he might be withheld from demanding the dictatorship. They over and above voted him the continuance of his provinces, for he had two, Spain and all Africa, which he governed by his lieutenants, and maintained armies under him, at the yearly charge of a thousand talents out of the public treasury.

Upon this Caesar also sent and petitioned for the consulship, and the continuance of his provinces. Pompey at first did not stir in it, but Marcellus and Lentulus opposed it, who had always hated Caesar, and now did every thing, whether fit or unfit, which might disgrace and affront him. For they took away the privilege of Roman citizens from the people of New Comum, who were a colony that Caesar had lately planted in Gaul; and Marcellus, who was then consul, ordered one of the senators of that town, then at Rome, to be whipped, and told him he laid that mark upon him to signify he was no citizen of Rome, bidding him, when he went back again, to show it to Caesar. After Marcellus's consulship, Caesar began to lavish gifts upon all the public men out of the riches he had taken from the Gauls; discharged Curio, the tribune, from his great debts; gave Paulus, then consul, fifteen hundred talents, with which he built the noble court of justice adjoining the forum, to supply the place of that called the Fulvian. Pompey, alarmed at these preparations, now openly took steps, both by himself and his friends, to have a successor appointed in Caesar's room, and sent to demand back the soldiers whom he had lent him to carry on the wars in Gaul. Caesar returned them, and made each soldier a present of two hundred and fifty drachmas. The officer who brought them home to Pompey, spread amongst the people no very fair or favorable report of Caesar, and flattered Pompey himself with false suggestions that he was wished for by Caesar's army; and though his affairs here were in some embarrassment through the envy of some, and the ill state of the government, yet there the army was at his command, and if they once crossed into Italy, would presently declare for him; so weary were they of Caesar's endless expeditions, and so suspicious of his designs for a monarchy. Upon this Pompey grew presumptuous, and neglected all warlike preparations, as fearing no danger, and used no other means against him than mere speeches and votes, for which Caesar cared nothing. And one of his captains, it is said, who was sent by him to Rome, standing before the senate-house one day, and being told that the senate would not give Caesar a longer time in his government, clapped his hand on the hilt of his sword, and said, "But this shall."

Yet the demands which Caesar made had the fairest colors of equity imaginable. For he proposed to lay down his arms, and that Pompey should do the same, and both together should become private men, and each expect a reward of his services from the public. For that those who proposed to disarm him, and at the same time to confirm Pompey in all the power he held, were simply establishing the one in the tyranny which they accused the other of aiming at. When Curio made these proposals to the people in Caesar's name, he was loudly applauded, and some threw garlands towards him, and dismissed him as they do successful wrestlers, crowned with flowers. Antony, being tribune, produced a letter sent from Caesar on this occasion, and read it, though the consuls did what they could to oppose it. But Scipio, Pompey's father-in-law, proposed in the senate, that if Caesar did not lay down his arms within such a time, he should be voted an enemy; and the consuls putting it to the question, whether Pompey should dismiss his soldiers, and again, whether Caesar should disband his, very few assented to the first, but almost all to the latter. But Antony proposing again, that both should lay down their commissions, all but a very few agreed to it. Scipio was upon this very violent, and Lentulus the consul cried aloud, that they had need of arms, and not of suffrages, against a robber; so that the senators for the present adjourned, and appeared in mourning as a mark of their grief for the dissension.

Afterwards there came other letters from Caesar, which seemed yet more moderate, for he proposed to quit everything else, and only to retain Gaul within the Alps, Illyricum, and two legions, till he should stand a second time for consul. Cicero, the orator, who was lately returned from Cilicia, endeavored to reconcile differences, and softened Pompey, who was willing to comply in other things, but not to allow him the soldiers. At last Cicero used his persuasions with Caesar's friends to accept of the provinces, and six thousand soldiers only, and so to make up the quarrel. And Pompey was inclined to give way to this, but Lentulus, the consul, would not hearken to it, but drove Antony and Curio out of the senate-house with insults, by which he afforded Caesar the most plausible pretense that could be, and one which he could readily use to inflame the soldiers, by showing them two persons of such repute and authority, who were forced to escape in a hired carriage in the dress of slaves. For so they were glad to disguise themselves, when they fled out of Rome.

There were not about him at that time above three hundred horse, and five thousand foot; for the rest of his army, which was left behind the Alps, was to be brought after him by officers who had received orders for that purpose. But he thought the first motion towards the design which he had on foot did not require large forces at present, and that what was wanted was to make this first step suddenly, and so as to astound his enemies with the boldness of it; as it would be easier, he thought, to throw them into consternation by doing what they never anticipated, than fairly to conquer them, if he had alarmed them by his preparations. And therefore, he commanded his captains and other officers to go only with their swords in their hands, without any other arms, and make themselves masters of Ariminum, a large city of Gaul, with as little disturbance and bloodshed as possible. He committed the care of these forces to Hortensius, and himself spent the day in public as a stander-by and spectator of the gladiators, who exercised before him. A little before night he attended to his person, and then went into the hall, and conversed for some time with those he had invited to supper, till it began to grow dusk, when he rose from table, and made his excuses to the company, begging them to stay till he came back, having already given private directions to a few immediate friends, that they should follow him, not all the same way, but some one way, some another. He himself got into one of the hired carriages, and drove at first another way, but presently turned towards Ariminum. When he came to the river Rubicon, which parts Gaul within the Alps from the rest of Italy, his thoughts began to work, now he was just entering upon the danger, and he wavered much in his mind, when he considered the greatness of the enterprise into which he was throwing himself. He checked his course, and ordered a halt, while he revolved with himself, and often changed his opinion one way and the other, without speaking a word. This was when his purposes fluctuated most; presently he also discussed the matter with his friends who were about him, (of which number Asinius Pollio was one,) computing how many calamities his passing that river would bring upon mankind, and what a relation of it would be transmitted to posterity. At last, in a sort of passion, casting aside calculation, and abandoning himself to what might come, and using the proverb frequently in their mouths who enter upon dangerous and bold attempts, "The die is cast," with these words he took the river. Once over, he used all expedition possible, and before it was day reached Ariminum, and took it. It is said that the night before he passed the river, he had an impious dream, that he was unnaturally familiar with his own mother.

As soon as Ariminum was taken, wide gates, so to say, were thrown open, to let in war upon every land alike and sea, and with the limits of the province, the boundaries of the laws were transgressed. Nor would one have thought that, as at other times, the mere men and women fled from one town of Italy to another in their consternation, but that the very towns themselves left their sites, and fled for succor to each other. The city of Rome was overrun as it were with a deluge, by the conflux of people flying in from all the neighboring places. Magistrates could no longer govern, nor the eloquence of any orator quiet it; it was all but suffering shipwreck by the violence of its own tempestuous agitation. The most vehement contrary passions and impulses were at work everywhere. Nor did those who rejoiced at the prospect of the change altogether conceal their feelings, but when they met, as in so great a city they frequently must, with the alarmed and dejected of the other party, they provoked quarrels by their bold expressions of confidence in the event. Pompey, sufficiently disturbed of himself, was yet more perplexed by the clamors of others; some telling him that he justly suffered for having armed Caesar against himself and the government; others blaming him for permitting Caesar to be insolently used by Lentulus, when he made such ample concessions, and offered such reasonable proposals towards an accommodation. Favonius bade him now stamp upon the ground; for once talking big in the senate, he desired them not to trouble themselves about making any preparations for the war, for that he himself, with one stamp of his foot, would fill all Italy with soldiers. Yet still Pompey at that time had more forces than Caesar; but he was not permitted to pursue his own thoughts, but being continually disturbed with false reports and alarms, as if the enemy was close upon him and carrying all before him, he gave way, and let himself be borne down by the general cry. He put forth an edict declaring the city to be in a state of anarchy, and left it with orders that the senate should follow him, and that no one should stay behind who did not prefer tyranny to their country and liberty.

The consuls at once fled, without making even the usual sacrifices; so did most of the senators, carrying off their own goods in as much haste as if they had been robbing their neighbors. Some, who had formerly much favored Caesar's cause, in the prevailing alarm, quitted their own sentiments, and without any prospect of good to themselves, were carried along by the common stream. It was a melancholy thing to see the city tossed in these tumults, like a ship given up by her pilots, and left to run, as chance guides her, upon any rock in her way. Yet, in spite of their sad condition, people still esteemed the place of their exile to be their country for Pompey's sake, and fled from Rome, as if it had been Caesar's camp. Labienus even, who had been one of Caesar's nearest friends, and his lieutenant, and who had fought by him zealously in the Gallic wars, now deserted him, and went over to Pompey. Caesar sent all his money and equipage after him, and then sat down before Corfinium, which was garrisoned with thirty cohorts under the command of Domitius. He, in despair of maintaining the defense, requested a physician, whom he had among his attendants, to give him poison; and taking the dose, drank it, in hopes of being dispatched by it. But soon after, when he was told that Caesar showed the utmost clemency towards those he took prisoners, he lamented his misfortune, and blamed the hastiness of his resolution. His physician consoled him, by informing him that he had taken a sleeping draught, not a poison; upon which, much rejoiced, and rising from his bed, he went presently to Caesar, and gave him the pledge of his hand, yet afterwards again went over to Pompey. The report of these actions at Rome, quieted those who were there, and some who had fled thence returned.

Caesar took into his army Domitius's soldiers, as he did all those whom he found in any town enlisted for Pompey's service. Being now strong and formidable enough, he advanced against Pompey himself, who did not stay to receive him, but fled to Brundisium, having sent the consuls before with a body of troops to Dyrrhachium. Soon after, upon Caesar's approach, he set to sea, as shall be more particularly related in his Life. Caesar would have immediately pursued him, but wanted shipping, and therefore went back to Rome, having made himself master of all Italy without bloodshed in the space of sixty days. When he came thither, he found the city more quiet than he expected, and many senators present, to whom he addressed himself with courtesy and deference, desiring them to send to Pompey about any reasonable accommodations towards a peace. But nobody complied with this proposal; whether out of fear of Pompey, whom they had deserted, or that they thought Caesar did not mean what he said, but thought it his interest to talk plausibly. Afterwards, when Metellus, the tribune, would have hindered him from taking money out of the public treasure, and adduced some laws against it, Caesar replied, that arms and laws had each their own time; "If what I do displeases you, leave the place; war allows no free talking. When I have laid down my arms, and made peace, come back and make what speeches you please. And this," he added, "I tell you in diminution of my own just right, as indeed you and all others who have appeared against me and are now in my power, may be treated as I please." Having said this to Metellus, he went to the doors of the treasury, and the keys being not to be found, sent for smiths to force them open. Metellus again making resistance, and some encouraging him in it, Caesar, in a louder tone, told him he would put him to death, if he gave him any further disturbance. "And this," said he, "you know, young man, is more disagreeable for me to say, than to do." These words made Metellus withdraw for fear, and obtained speedy execution henceforth for all orders that Caesar gave for procuring necessaries for the war.

He was now proceeding to Spain, with the determination of first crushing Afranius and Varro, Pompey's lieutenants, and making himself master of the armies and provinces under them, that he might then more securely advance against Pompey, when he had no enemy left behind him. In this expedition his person was often in danger from ambuscades, and his army by want of provisions, yet he did not desist from pursuing the enemy, provoking them to fight, and hemming them with his fortifications, till by main force he made himself master of their camps and their forces.

Only the generals got off, and fled to Pompey.

When Caesar came back to Rome, Piso, his father-in-law, advised him to send men to Pompey, to treat of a peace; but Isauricus, to ingratiate himself with Caesar, spoke against it. After this, being created dictator by the senate, he called home the exiles, and gave back then rights as citizens to the children of those who had suffered under Sylla; he relieved the debtors by an act remitting some part of the interest on their debts, and passed some other measures of the same sort, but not many. For within eleven days he resigned his dictatorship, and having declared himself consul, with Servilius Isauricus, hastened again to the war. He marched so fast, that he left all his army behind him, except six hundred chosen horse, and five legions, with which he put to sea in the very middle of winter, about the beginning of the month January, (which corresponds pretty nearly with the Athenian month Posideon,) and having past the Ionian Sea, took Oricum and Apollonia, and then sent back the ships to

Brundisium, to bring over the soldiers who were left behind in the march. They, while yet on the march, their bodies now no longer in the full vigor of youth, and they themselves weary with such a multitude of wars, could not but exclaim against Caesar, "When at last, and where, will this Caesar let us be quiet? He carries us from place to place, and uses us as if we were not to be worn out, and had no sense of labor. Even our iron itself is spent by blows, and we ought to have some pity on our bucklers and breastplates, which have been used so long. Our wounds, if nothing else, should make him see that we are mortal men, whom he commands, subject to the same pains and sufferings as other human beings. The very gods themselves cannot force the winter season, or hinder the storms in their time; yet he pushes forward, as if he were not pursuing, but flying from an enemy." So they talked as they marched leisurely towards Brundisium. But when they came thither, and found Caesar gone off before them, their feelings changed, and they blamed themselves as traitors to their general. They now railed at their officers for marching so slowly, and placing themselves on the heights overlooking the sea towards Epirus, they kept watch to see if they could espy the vessels which were to transport them to Caesar.

He in the meantime was posted in Apollonia, but had not an army with him able to fight the enemy, the forces from Brundisium being so long in coming, which put him to great suspense and embarrassment what to do. At last he resolved upon a most hazardous experiment, and embarked, without anyone's knowledge, in a boat of twelve oars, to cross over to Brundisium, though the sea was at that time covered with a vast fleet of the enemies. He got on board in the night time, in the dress of a slave, and throwing himself down like a person of no consequence, lay along at the bottom of the vessel. The river Anius was to carry them down to sea, and there used to blow a gentle gale every morning from the land, which made it calm at the mouth of the river, by driving the waves forward; but this night there had blown a strong wind from the sea, which overpowered that from the land, so that where the river met the influx of the sea-water and the opposition of the waves, it was extremely rough and angry; and the current was beaten back with such a violent swell, that the master of the boat could not make good his passage, but ordered his sailors to tack about and return. Caesar, upon this, discovers himself, and taking the man by the hand, who was surprised to see him there, said, "Go on, my friend, and fear nothing; you carry Caesar and his fortune in your boat." The mariners, when they heard that, forgot the storm, and laying all their strength to their oars, did what they could to force their way down the river. But when it was to no purpose, and the vessel now took in much water, Caesar finding himself in such danger in the very mouth of the river, much against his will permitted the master to turn back. When he was come to land, his soldiers ran to him in a multitude, reproaching him for what he had done, and indignant that he should think himself not strong enough to get a victory by their sole assistance, but must disturb himself, and expose his life for those who were absent, as if he could not trust those who were with him.

After this, Antony came over with the forces from Brundisium, which encouraged Caesar to give Pompey battle, though he was encamped very advantageously, and furnished with plenty of provisions both by sea and land, whilst he himself was at the beginning but ill-supplied, and before the end was extremely pinched for want of necessaries, so that his soldiers were forced to dig up a kind of root which grew there, and tempering it with milk, to feed on it. Sometimes they made a kind of bread of it, and advancing up to the enemy's outposts, would throw in these loaves, telling them, that as long as the earth produced such roots they would not give up blockading Pompey. But Pompey took what care he could, that neither the loaves nor the words should reach his men, who were out of heart and despondent, through terror at the fierceness and hardiness of their enemies, whom they looked upon as a sort of wild beasts. There were continual skirmishes about Pompey's outworks, in all which Caesar had the better, except one, when his men were forced to fly in such a manner that he had like to have lost his camp. For Pompey made such a vigorous sally on them that not a man stood his ground; the trenches were filled with the slaughter, many fell upon their own ramparts and bulwarks, whither they were driven in flight by the enemy. Caesar met them, and would have turned them back, but could not. When he went to lay hold of the ensigns, those who carried them threw them down, so that the enemies took thirty-two of them. He himself narrowly escaped; for taking hold of one of his soldiers, a big and strong man, that was flying by him, he bade him stand and face about; but the fellow, full of apprehensions from the danger he was in, laid hold of his sword, as if he would strike Caesar, but Caesar's armor-bearer cut off his arm. Caesar's affairs were so desperate at that time, that when Pompey, either through over-cautiousness, or his ill fortune, did not give the finishing stroke to that great success, but retreated after he had driven the routed enemy within their camp, Caesar, upon seeing his withdrawal, said to his friends, "The victory to-day had been on the enemies' side, if they had had a general who knew how to gain it." When he was retired into his tent, he laid himself down to sleep, but spent that night as miserably as ever he did any, in perplexity and consideration with himself, coming to the conclusion that he had conducted the war amiss. For when he had a fertile country before him, and all the wealthy cities of Macedonia and Thessaly, he had neglected to carry the war thither, and had sat down by the seaside, where his enemies had such a powerful fleet, so that he was in fact rather besieged by the want of necessaries, than besieging others with his arms. Being thus distracted in his thoughts with the view of the difficulty and distress he was in, he raised his camp, with the intention of advancing towards Scipio, who lay in Macedonia; hoping either to entice Pompey into a country where he should fight without the advantage he now had of supplies from the sea, or to overpower Scipio, if not assisted.

This set all Pompey's army and officers on fire to hasten and pursue Caesar, whom they concluded to be beaten and flying. But Pompey was afraid to hazard a battle on which so much depended, and being himself provided with all necessaries for any length of time, thought to tire out and waste the vigor of Caesar's army, which could not last long. For the best part of his men, though they had great experience and showed an irresistible courage in all engagements, yet by their frequent marches, changing their camps, attacking fortifications, and keeping long night-watches, were getting worn-out and broken; they being now old, their bodies less fit for labor, and their courage, also, beginning to give way with the failure of their strength. Besides, it was said that an infectious disease, occasioned by their irregular diet, was prevailing in Caesar's army, and what was of greatest moment, he was neither furnished with money nor provisions, so that in a little time he must needs fall of himself.

For these reasons Pompey had no mind to fight him, but was thanked for it by none but Cato, who rejoiced at the prospect of sparing his fellow-citizens. For he when he saw the dead bodies of those who had fallen in the last battle on Caesar's side, to the number of a thousand, turned away, covered his face, and shed tears. But everyone else upbraided Pompey for being reluctant to fight, and tried to goad him on by such nicknames as Agamemnon, and king of kings, as if he were in no hurry to lay down his sovereign authority, but was pleased to see so many commanders attending on him, and paying their attendance at his tent. Favonius, who affected Cato's free way of speaking his mind, complained bitterly that they should eat no figs even this year at Tusculum, because of Pompey's love of command. Afranius, who was lately returned out of Spain, and on account of his ill success there, labored under the suspicion of having been bribed to betray the army, asked why they did not fight this purchaser of provinces. Pompey was driven, against his own will, by this kind of language, into offering battle, and proceeded to follow Caesar. Caesar had found great difficulties in his march, for no country would supply him with provisions, his reputation being very much fallen since his late defeat. But after he took Gomphi, a town of Thessaly, he not only found provisions for his army, but physic too. For there they met with plenty of wine, which they took very freely, and heated with this, sporting and reveling on their march in bacchanalian fashion, they shook off the disease, and their whole constitution was relieved and changed into another habit.

When the two armies were come into Pharsalia, and both encamped there, Pompey's thoughts ran the same way as they had done before, against fighting, and the more because of some unlucky presages, and a vision he had in a dream. But those who were about him were so confident of success, that Domitius, and Spinther, and Scipio, as if they had already conquered, quarreled which should succeed Caesar in the pontificate. And many sent to Rome to take houses fit to accommodate consuls and praetors, as being sure of entering upon those offices, as soon as the battle was over. The cavalry especially were obstinate for fighting, being splendidly armed and bravely mounted, and valuing themselves upon the fine horses they kept, and upon their own handsome persons; as also upon the advantage of their numbers, for they were five thousand against one thousand of Caesar's. Nor were the numbers of the infantry less disproportionate, there being forty-five thousand of Pompey's, against twenty-two thousand of the enemy.

Caesar, collecting his soldiers together, told them that Corfinius was coming up to them with two legions, and that fifteen cohorts more under Calenus were posted at Megara and Athens; he then asked them whether they would stay till these joined them, or would hazard the battle by themselves. They all cried out to him not to wait, but on the contrary to do whatever he could to bring about an engagement as soon as possible. When he sacrificed to the gods for the lustration of his army, upon the death of the first victim, the augur told him, within three days he should come to a decisive action. Caesar asked him whether he saw anything in the entrails, which promised a happy event. "That," said the priest, "you can best answer yourself; for the gods signify a great alteration from the present posture of affairs. If, therefore, you think yourself well off now, expect worse fortune; if unhappy, hope for better." The night before the battle, as he walked the rounds about midnight, there was a light seen in the heaven, very bright and flaming, which seemed to pass over Caesar's camp, and fall into Pompey's. And when Caesar's soldiers came to relieve the watch in the morning, they perceived a panic disorder among the enemies. However, he did not expect to fight that day, but set about raising his camp with the intention of marching towards Scotussa.

But when the tents were now taken down, his scouts rode up to him, and told him the enemy would give him battle. With this news he was extremely pleased, and having performed his devotions to the gods, set his army in battle array, dividing them into three bodies. Over the middlemost he placed Domitius Calvinus; Antony commanded the left wing, and he himself the right, being resolved to fight at the head of the tenth legion. But when he saw the enemies' cavalry taking position against him, being struck with their fine appearance and their number, he gave private orders that six cohorts from the rear of the army should come round and join him, whom he posted behind the right wing, and instructed them what they should do, when the enemy's horse came to charge. On the other side, Pompey commanded the right wing, Domitius the left, and Scipio, Pompey's father-in-law, the center. The whole weight of the cavalry was collected on the left wing, with the intent that they should outflank the right wing of the enemy, and rout that part where the general himself commanded. For they thought no phalanx of infantry could be solid enough to sustain such a shock, but that they must necessarily be broken and shattered all to pieces upon the onset of so immense a force of cavalry. When they were ready on both sides to give the signal for battle, Pompey commended his foot who were in the front to stand their ground, and without breaking their order, receive quietly the enemy's first attack, till they came within javelin's cast. Caesar, in this respect, also, blames Pompey's generalship, as if he had not been aware how the first encounter, when made with an impetus and upon the run, gives weight and force to the strokes, and fires the men's spirits into a flame, which the general concurrence fans to full heat. He himself was just putting the troops into motion and advancing to the action, when he found one of his captains, a trusty and experienced soldier, encouraging his men to exert their utmost. Caesar called him by his name, and said, "What hopes, Caius Crassinius, and what grounds for encouragement?" Crassinius stretched out his hand, and cried in a loud voice, "We shall conquer nobly, Caesar; and I this day will deserve your praises, either alive or dead." So he said, and was the first man to run in upon the enemy, followed by the hundred and twenty soldiers about him, and breaking through the first rank, still pressed on forwards with much slaughter of the enemy, till at last he was struck back by the wound of a sword, which went in at his mouth with such force that it came out at his neck behind.

Whilst the foot was thus sharply engaged in the main battle, on the flank Pompey's horse rode up confidently, and opened their ranks very wide, that they might surround the Fight wing of Caesar. But before they engaged, Caesar's cohorts rushed out and attacked them, and did not dart their javelins at a distance, nor strike at the thighs and legs, as they usually did in close battle, but aimed at their faces. For thus Caesar had instructed them, in hopes that young gentlemen, who had not known much of battles and wounds, but came wearing their hair long, in the flower of their age and height of their beauty, would be more apprehensive of such blows, and not care for hazarding both a danger at present and a blemish for the future. And so it proved, for they were so far from bearing the stroke of the javelins, that they could not stand the sight of them, but turned about, and covered their faces to secure them. Once in disorder, presently they turned about to fly; and so most shamefully ruined all. For those who had beat them back, at once outflanked the infantry, and falling on their rear, cut them to pieces. Pompey, who commanded the other wing of the army, when he saw his cavalry thus broken and flying, was no longer himself, nor did he now remember that he was Pompey the Great, but like one whom some god had deprived of his senses, retired to his tent without speaking; a word, and there sat to expect the event, till the whole army was routed, and the enemy appeared upon the works which were thrown up before the camp, where they closely engaged with his men, who were posted there to defend it. Then first he seemed to have recovered his senses, and uttering, it is said, only these words, "What, into the camp too?" he laid aside his general's habit, and putting on such clothes as might best favor his flight, stole off. What fortune he met with afterwards, how he took shelter in Egypt, and was murdered there, we tell you in his Life.

Caesar, when he came to view Pompey's camp, and saw some of his opponents dead upon the ground, others dying, said, with a groan, "This they would have; they brought me to this necessity. I, Caius Caesar, after succeeding in so many wars, had been condemned, had I dismissed my army." These words, Pollio says, Caesar spoke in Latin at that time, and that he himself wrote them in Greek; adding, that those who were killed at the taking of the camp, were most of them servants; and that not above six thousand soldiers fell. Caesar incorporated most of the foot whom he took prisoners, with his own legions, and gave a free pardon to many of the distinguished persons, and amongst the rest, to Brutus, who afterwards killed him. He did not immediately appear after the battle was over, which put Caesar, it is said, into great anxiety for him; nor was his pleasure less when he saw him present himself alive.

There were many prodigies that foreshowed this victory, but the most remarkable that we are told of, was that at Tralles. In the temple of Victory stood Caesar's statue. The ground on which it stood was naturally hard and solid, and the stone with which it was paved still harder; yet it is said that a palm-tree shot itself up near the pedestal of this statue. In the city of Padua, one Caius Cornelius, who had the character of a good augur, the fellow-citizen and acquaintance of Livy, the historian, happened to be making some augural observations that very day when the battle was fought. And first, as Livy tells us, he pointed out the time of the fight, and said to those who were by him, that just then the battle was begun, and the men engaged. When he looked a second time, and observed the omens, he leaped up as if he had been inspired, and cried out, "Caesar, you are victorious." This much surprised the standers by, but he took the garland which he had on from his head, and swore he would never wear it again till the event should give authority to his art. This Livy positively states for a truth.

Caesar, as a memorial of his victory, gave the Thessalians their freedom, and then went in pursuit of Pompey. When he was come into Asia, to gratify Theopompus, the author of the collection of fables, he enfranchised the Cnidians, and remitted one third of their tribute to all the people of the province of Asia. When he came to Alexandria, where Pompey was already murdered, he would not look upon Theodotus, who presented him with his head, but taking only his signet, shed tears. Those of Pompey's friends who had been arrested by the king of Egypt, as they were wandering in those parts, he relieved, and offered them his own friendship. In his letter to his friends at Rome, he told them that the greatest and most signal pleasure his victory had given him, was to be able continually to save the lives of fellow-citizens who had fought against him. As to the war in Egypt, some say it was at once dangerous and dishonorable, and noways necessary, but occasioned only by his passion for Cleopatra. Others blame the ministers of the king, and especially the eunuch Pothinus, who was the chief favorite, and had lately killed Pompey, who had banished Cleopatra, and was now secretly plotting Caesar's destruction, (to prevent which, Caesar from that time began to sit up whole nights, under pretense of drinking, for the security of his person,) while openly he was intolerable in his affronts to Caesar, both by his words and actions. For when Caesar's soldiers had musty and unwholesome corn measured out to them, Pothinus told them they must be content with it, since they were fed at another's cost. He ordered that his table should be served with wooden and earthen dishes, and said Caesar had carried off all the gold and silver plate, under pretense of arrears of debt. For the present king's father owed Caesar one thousand seven hundred and fifty myriads of money; Caesar had formerly remitted to his children the rest, but thought fit to demand the thousand myriads at that time, to maintain his army. Pothinus told him that he had better go now and attend to his other affairs of greater consequence, and that he should receive his money at another time with thanks. Caesar replied that he did not want Egyptians to be his counselors, and soon after, privately sent for Cleopatra from her retirement.

 She took a small boat, and one only of her confidents, Apollodorus, the Sicilian, along with her, and in the dusk of the evening landed near the palace. She was at a loss how to get in undiscovered, till she thought of putting herself into the coverlet of a bed and lying at length, whilst Apollodorus tied up the bedding and carried it on his back through the gates to Caesar's apartment. Caesar was first captivated by this proof of Cleopatra's bold wit, and was afterwards so overcome by the charm of her society, that he made a reconciliation between her and her brother, on condition that she should rule as his colleague in the kingdom. A festival was kept to celebrate this reconciliation, where Caesar's barber, a busy, listening fellow, whose excessive timidity made him inquisitive into everything, discovered that there was a plot carrying on against Caesar by Achillas, general of the king's forces, and Pothinus, the eunuch. Caesar, upon the first intelligence of it, set a guard upon the hall where the feast was kept, and killed Pothinus. Achillas escaped to the army, and raised a troublesome and embarrassing war against Caesar, which it was not easy for him to manage with his few soldiers against so powerful a city and so large an army. The first difficulty he met with was want of water, for the enemies had turned the canals. Another was, when the enemy endeavored to cut off his communication by sea, he was forced to divert that danger by setting fire to his own ships, which, after burning the docks, thence spread on and destroyed the great library. A third was, when in an engagement near Pharos, he leaped from the mole into a small boat, to assist his soldiers who were in danger, and when the Egyptians pressed him on every side, he threw himself into the sea, and with much difficulty swam off. This was the time when, according to the story, he had a number of manuscripts in his hand, which, though he was continually darted at, and forced to keep his head often under water, yet he did not let go, but held them up safe from wetting in one hand, whilst he swam with the other. His boat, in the meantime, was quickly sunk. At last, the king having gone off to Achillas and his party, Caesar engaged and conquered them. Many fell in that battle, and the king himself was never seen after. Upon this, he left Cleopatra queen of Egypt, who soon after had a son by him, whom the Alexandrians called Caesarion, and then departed for Syria.

Thence he passed to Asia, where he heard that Domitius was beaten by Pharnaces, son of Mithridates, and had fled out of Pontus with a handful of men; and that Pharnaces pursued the victory so eagerly, that though he was already master of Bithynia and Cappadocia, he had a further design of attempting the Lesser Armenia, and was inviting all the kings and tetrarchs there to rise. Caesar immediately marched against him with three legions, fought him near Zela, drove him out of Pontus, and totally defeated his army. When he gave Amantius, a friend of his at Rome, an account of this action, to express the promptness and rapidity of it, he used three words, I came, saw, and conquered, which in Latin having all the same cadence, carry with them a very suitable air of brevity.

Hence he crossed into Italy, and came to Rome at the end of that year, for which he had been a second time chosen dictator, though that office had never before lasted a whole year, and was elected consul for the next. He was ill spoken of, because upon a mutiny of some soldiers, who killed Cosconius and Galba, who had been praetors, he gave them only the slight reprimand of calling them Citizens, instead of Fellow-Soldiers, and afterwards assigned to each man a thousand drachmas, besides a share of lands in Italy. He was also reflected on for Dolabella's extravagance, Amantius's covetousness, Antony's debauchery, and Corfinius's profuseness, who pulled down Pompey's house, and rebuilt it, as not magnificent enough; for the Romans were much displeased with all these. But Caesar, for the prosecution of his own scheme of government, though he knew their characters and disapproved them, was forced to make use of those who would serve him.

After the battle of Pharsalia, Cato and Scipio fled into Africa, and there, with the assistance of king Juba, got together a considerable force, which Caesar resolved to engage. He, accordingly, passed into Sicily about the winter-solstice, and to remove from his officers' minds all hopes of delay there, encamped by the sea-shore, and as soon as ever he had a fair wind, put to sea with three thousand foot and a few horse. When he had landed them, he went back secretly, under some apprehensions for the larger part of his army, but met them upon the sea, and brought them all to the same camp. There he was informed that the enemies relied much upon an ancient oracle, that the family of the Scipios should be always victorious in Africa. There was in his army a man, otherwise mean and contemptible, but of the house of the Africani, and his name Scipio Sallutio. This man Caesar, (whether in raillery, to ridicule Scipio, who commended the enemy, or seriously to bring over the omen to his side, it were hard to say,) put at the head of his troops, as if he were general, in all the frequent battles which he was compelled to fight. For he was in such want both of victualing for his men, and forage for his horses, that he was forced to feed the horses with sea-weed, which he washed thoroughly to take off its saltiness, and mixed with a little grass, to give it a more agreeable taste. The Numidians, in great numbers, and well horsed, whenever he went, came up and commanded the country. Caesar's cavalry being one day unemployed, diverted themselves with seeing an African, who entertained them with dancing and at the same time playing upon the pipe to admiration. They were so taken with this, that they alighted, and gave their horses to some boys, when on a sudden the enemy surrounded them, killed some, pursued the rest, and fell in with them into their camp; and had not Caesar himself and Asinius Pollio come to their assistance, and put a stop to their flight, the war had been then at an end. In another engagement, also, the enemy had again the better, when Caesar, it is said, seized a standard-bearer, who was running away, by the neck, and forcing him to face about, said, "Look, that is the way to the enemy."

Scipio, flushed with this success at first, had a mind to come to one decisive action. He therefore left Afranius and Juba in two distinct bodies not far distant, and marched himself towards Thapsus, where he proceeded to build a fortified camp above a lake, to serve as a center-point for their operations, and also as a place of refuge. Whilst Scipio was thus employed, Caesar with incredible dispatch made his way through thick woods, and a country supposed to be impassable, cut off one party of the enemy, and attacked another in the front. Having routed these, he followed up his opportunity and the current of his good fortune, and on the first onset carried Afranius's camp, and ravaged that of the Numidians, Juba, their king, being glad to save himself by flight; so that in a small part of a single day he made himself master of three camps, and killed fifty thousand of the enemy, with the loss only of fifty of his own men. This is the account some give of that fight. Others say, he was not in the action, but that he was taken with his usual distemper just as he was setting his army in order. He perceived the approaches of it, and before it had too far disordered his senses, when he was already beginning to shake under its influence, withdrew into a neighboring fort, where he reposed himself. Of the men of consular and praetorian dignity that were taken after the fight, several Caesar put to death, others anticipated him by killing themselves.

Cato had undertaken to defend Utica, and for that reason was not in the battle. The desire which Caesar had to take him alive, made him hasten thither; and upon the intelligence that he had dispatched himself, he was much discomposed, for what reason is not so well agreed. He certainly said, "Cato, I must grudge you your death, as you grudged me the honor of saving your life." Yet the discourse he wrote against Cato after his death, is no great sign of his kindness, or that he was inclined to be reconciled to him. For how is it probable that he would have been tender of his life, when he was so bitter against his memory? But from his clemency to Cicero, Brutus, and many others who fought against him, it may be divined that Caesar's book was not written so much out of animosity to Cato, as in his own vindication. Cicero had written an encomium upon Cato, and called it by his name. A composition by so great a master upon so excellent a subject, was sure to be in everyone's hands. This touched Caesar, who looked upon a panegyric on his enemy, as no better than an invective against himself; and therefore he made in his Anti-Cato, a collection of whatever could be said in his derogation. The two compositions, like Cato and Caesar themselves, have each of them their several admirers.

Caesar, upon his return to Rome, did not omit to pronounce before the people a magnificent account of his victory, telling them that he had subdued a country which would supply the public every year with two hundred thousand attic bushels of corn, and three million pounds weight of oil. He then led three triumphs for Egypt, Pontus, and Africa, the last for the victory over, not Scipio, but king Juba, as it was professed, whose little son was then carried in the triumph, the happiest captive that ever was, who of a barbarian Numidian, came by this means to obtain a place among the most learned historians of Greece. After the triumphs, he distributed rewards to his soldiers, and treated the people with feasting and shows. He entertained the whole people together at one feast, where twenty-two thousand dining couches were laid out; and he made a display of gladiators, and of battles by sea, in honor, as he said, of his daughter Julia, though she had been long since dead. When these shows were over, an account was taken of the people, who from three hundred and twenty thousand, were now reduced to one hundred and fifty thousand. So great a waste had the civil war made in Rome alone, not to mention what the other parts of Italy and the provinces suffered.

He was now chosen a fourth time consul, and went into Spain against Pompey's sons. They were but young, yet had gathered together a very numerous army, and showed they had courage and conduct to command it, so that Caesar was in extreme danger. The great battle was near the town of Munda, in which Caesar seeing his men hard pressed, and making but a weak resistance, ran through the ranks among the soldiers, and crying out, asked them whether they were not ashamed to deliver him into the hands of boys? At last, with great difficulty, and the best efforts he could make, he forced back the enemy, killing thirty thousand of them, though with the loss of one thousand of his best men. When he came back from the fight, he told his friends that he had often fought for victory, but this was the first time that he had ever fought for life. This battle was won on the feast of Bacchus, the very day in which Pompey, four years before. had set out for the war. The younger of Pompey's sons escaped; but Didius, some days after the fight, brought the head of the elder to Caesar. This was the last war he was engaged in. The triumph which he celebrated for this victory, displeased the Romans beyond any thing. For he had not defeated foreign generals, or barbarian kings, but had destroyed the children and family of one of the greatest men of Rome, though unfortunate; and it did not look well to lead a procession in celebration of the calamities of his country, and to rejoice in those things for which no other apology could be made either to gods or men, than their being absolutely necessary. Besides that, hitherto he had never sent letters or messengers to announce any victory over his fellow-citizens, but had seemed rather to be ashamed of the action, than to expect honor from it.

Nevertheless his countrymen, conceding all to his fortune, and accepting the bit, in the hope that the government of a single person would give them time to breathe after so many civil wars and calamities, made him dictator for life. This was indeed a tyranny avowed, since his power now was not only absolute, but perpetual too. Cicero made the first proposals to the senate for conferring honors upon him, which might in some sort be said not to exceed the limits of ordinary human moderation. But others, striving which should deserve most, carried them so excessively high, that they made Caesar odious to the most indifferent and moderate sort of men, by the pretension and the extravagance of the titles which they decreed him. His enemies, too, are thought to have had some share in this, as well as his flatterers. It gave them advantage against him, and would be their justification for any attempt they should make upon him; for since the civil wars were ended, he had nothing else that he could be charged with. And they had good reason to decree a temple to Clemency, in token of their thanks for the mild use he made of his victory. For he not only pardoned many of those who fought against him, but, further, to some gave honors and offices; as particularly to Brutus and Cassius, who both of them were praetors. Pompey's images that were thrown down, he set up again, upon which Cicero also said that by raising Pompey's statues he had fixed his own. When his friends advised him to have a guard, and several offered their service, he would not hear of it; but said it was better to suffer death once, than always to live in fear of it. He looked upon the affections of the people to be the best and surest guard, and entertained them again with public feasting, and general distributions of corn; and to gratify his army, he sent out colonies to several places, of which the most remarkable were Carthage and Corinth; which as before they had been ruined at the same time, so now were restored and repeopled together.

As for the men of high rank, he promised to some of them future consulships and praetorships, some he consoled with other offices and honors, and to all held out hopes of favor by the solicitude he showed to rule with the general good-will; insomuch that upon the death of Maximus one day before his consulship was ended, he made Caninius Revilius consul for that day. And when many went to pay the usual compliments and attentions to the new consul, "Let us make haste," said Cicero, "lest the man be gone out of his office before we come."

Caesar was born to do great things, and had a passion after honor, and the many noble exploits he had done did not now serve as an inducement to him to sit still and reap the fruit of his past labors, but were incentives and encouragments to go on, and raised in him ideas of still greater actions, and a desire of new glory, as if the present were all spent. It was in fact a sort of emulous struggle with himself, as it had been with another, how he might outdo his past actions by his future. In pursuit of these thoughts, he resolved to make war upon the Parthians, and when he had subdued them, to pass through Hyrcania; thence to march along by the Caspian Sea to Mount Caucasus, and so on about Pontus, till he came into Scythia; then to overrun all the countries bordering upon Germany, and Germany itself; and so to return through Gaul into Italy, after completing the whole circle of his intended empire, and bounding it on every side by the ocean. While preparations were making for this expedition, he proposed to dig through the isthmus on which Corinth stands; and appointed Anienus to superintend the work. He had also a design of diverting the Tiber, and carrying it by a deep channel directly from Rome to Circeii, and so into the sea near Tarracina, that there might be a safe and easy passage for all merchants who traded to Rome. Besides this, he intended to drain all the marshes by Pomentium and Setia, and gain ground enough from the water to employ many thousands of men in tillage. He proposed further to make great mounds on the shore nearest Rome, to hinder the sea from breaking in upon the land, to clear the coast at Ostia of all the hidden rocks and shoals that made it unsafe for shipping, and to form ports and harbors fit to receive the large number of vessels that would frequent them.

These things were designed without being carried into effect; but his reformation of the calendar, in order to rectify the irregularity of time, was not only projected with great scientific ingenuity, but was brought to its completion, and proved of very great use. For it was not only in ancient times that the

Romans had wanted a certain rule to make the revolutions of their months fall in with the course of the year, so that their festivals and solemn days for sacrifice were removed by little and little, till at last they came to be kept at seasons quite the contrary to what was at first intended, but even at this time the people had no way of computing the solar year; only the priests could say the time, and they, at their pleasure, without giving any notice, slipped in the intercalary month, which they called Mercedonius. Numa was the first who put in this month, but his expedient was but a poor one and quite inadequate to correct all the errors that arose in the returns of the annual cycles, as we have shown in his life. Caesar called in the best philosophers and mathematicians of his time to settle the point, and out of the systems he had before him, formed a new and more exact method of correcting the calendar, which the Romans use to this day, and seem to succeed better than any nation in avoiding the errors occasioned by the inequality of the cycles. Yet even this gave offense to those who looked with an evil eye on his position, and felt oppressed by his power. Cicero, the orator, when someone in his company chanced to say, the next morning Lyra would rise, replied, "Yes, in accordance with the edict," as if even this were a matter of compulsion.

But that which brought upon him the most apparent and mortal hatred, was his desire of being king; which gave the common people the first occasion to quarrel with him, and proved the most specious pretense to those who had been his secret enemies all along. Those, who would have procured him that title, gave it out, that it was foretold in the Sybils' books that the Romans should conquer the Parthians when they fought against them under the conduct of a king, but not before. And one day, as Caesar was coming down from Alba to Rome, some were so bold as to salute him by the name of king; but he finding the people disrelish it, seemed to resent it himself, and said his name was Caesar, not king. Upon this, there was a general silence, and he passed on looking not very well pleased or contented. Another time, when the senate had conferred on him some extravagant honors, he chanced to receive the message as he was sitting on the rostra, where, though the consuls and praetors themselves waited on him, attended by the whole body of the senate, he did not rise, but behaved himself to them as if they had been private men, and told them his honors wanted rather to be retrenched than increased. This treatment offended not only the senate, but the commonalty too, as if they thought the affront upon the senate equally reflected upon the whole republic; so that all who could decently leave him went off, looking much discomposed. Caesar, perceiving the false step he had made, immediately retired home; and laying his throat bare, told his friends that he was ready to offer this to anyone who would give the stroke. But afterwards he made the malady from which he suffered, the excuse for his sitting, saying that those who are attacked by it, lose their presence of mind, if they talk much standing; that they presently grow giddy, fall into convulsions, and quite lose their reason. But this was not the reality, for he would willingly have stood up to the senate, had not Cornelius Balbus, one of his friends, or rather flatterers, hindered him. "Will you not remember," said he, "you are Caesar, and claim the honor which is due to your merit?"

He gave a fresh occasion of resentment by his affront to the tribunes. The Lupercalia were then celebrated, a feast at the first institution belonging, as some writers say, to the shepherds, and having some connection with the Arcadian Lycaea. Many young noblemen and magistrates run up and down the city with their upper garments off, striking all they meet with thongs of hide, by way of sport; and many women, even of the highest rank, place themselves in the way, and hold out their hands to the lash, as boys in a school do to the master, out of a belief that it procures an easy labor to those who are with child, and makes those conceive who are barren. Caesar, dressed in a triumphal robe, seated himself in a golden chair at the rostra, to view this ceremony. Antony, as consul, was one of those who ran this course, and when he came into the forum, and the people made way for him, he went up and reached to Caesar a diadem wreathed with laurel. Upon this, there was a shout, but only a slight one, made by the few who were planted there for that purpose; but when Caesar refused it, there was universal applause. Upon the second offer, very few, and upon the second refusal, all again applauded. Caesar finding it would not take, rose up, and ordered the crown to be carried into the capitol. Caesar's statues were afterwards found with royal diadems on their heads. Flavius and Marullus, two tribunes of the people, went presently and pulled them off, and having apprehended those who first saluted Caesar as king, committed them to prison. The people followed them with acclamations, and called them by the name of Brutus, because Brutus was the first who ended the succession of kings, and transferred the power which before was lodged in one man into the hands of the senate and people. Caesar so far resented this, that he displaced Marullus and Flavius; and in urging his charges against them, at the same time ridiculed the people, by himself giving the men more than once the names of Bruti, and Cumaei.

This made the multitude turn their thoughts to Marcus Brutus, who, by his father's side, was thought to be descended from that first Brutus, and by his mother's side from the Servilii, another noble family, being besides nephew and son-in-law to Cato. But the honors and favors he had received from Caesar, took off the edge from the desires he might himself have felt for overthrowing the new monarchy. For he had not only been pardoned himself after Pompey's defeat at Pharsalia, and had procured the same grace for many of his friends, but was one in whom Caesar had a particular confidence. He had at that time the most honorable praetorship of the year, and was named for the consulship four years after, being preferred before Cassius, his competitor.

Upon the question as to the choice, Caesar, it is related, said that Cassius had the fairer pretensions, but that he could not pass by Brutus. Nor would he afterwards listen to some who spoke against Brutus, when the conspiracy against him was already afoot, but laying his hand on his body, said to the informers, "Brutus will wait for this skin of mine," intimating that he was worthy to bear rule on account of his virtue, but would not be base and ungrateful to gain it. Those who desired a change, and looked on him as the only, or at least the most proper, person to effect it, did not venture to speak with him; but in the night time laid papers about his chair of state, where he used to sit and determine causes, with such sentences in them as, "You are asleep, Brutus," "You are no longer Brutus." Cassius, when he perceived his ambition a little raised upon this, was more instant than before to work him yet further, having himself a private grudge against Caesar, for some reasons that we have mentioned in the Life of Brutus. Nor was Caesar without suspicions of him, and said once to his friends, "What do you think Cassius is aiming at? I don't like him, he looks so pale." And when it was told him that Antony and Dolabella were in a plot against him, he said he did not fear such fat, luxurious men, but rather the pale, lean fellows, meaning Cassius and Brutus.

Fate, however, is to all appearance more unavoidable than unexpected. For many strange prodigies and apparitions are said to have been observed shortly before the event. As to the lights in the heavens, the noises heard in the night, and the wild birds which perched in the forum, these are not perhaps worth taking notice of in so great a case as this. Strabo, the philosopher, tells us that a number of men were seen, looking as if they were heated through with fire, contending with each other; that a quantity of flame issued from the hand of a soldier's servant, so that they who saw it thought he must be burnt, but that after all he had no hurt. As Caesar was sacrificing, the victim's heart was missing, a very bad omen, because no living creature can subsist without a heart. One finds it also related by many, that a soothsayer bade him prepare for some great danger on the ides of March. When the day was come, Caesar, as he went to the senate, met this soothsayer, and said to him by way of raillery, "The ides of March are come;" who answered him calmly, "Yes, they are come, but they are not past." The day before this assassination, he supped with Marcus Lepidus; and as he was signing some letters, according to his custom, as he reclined at table, there arose a question what sort of death was the best. At which he immediately, before anyone could speak, said, "A sudden one."

After this, as he was in bed with his wife, all the doors and windows of the house flew open together; he was startled at the noise, and the light which broke into the room, and sat up in his bed, where by the moonshine he perceived Calpurnia fast asleep, but heard her utter in her dream some indistinct words and inarticulate groans. She fancied at that time she was weeping over Caesar, and holding him butchered in her arms. Others say this was not her dream, but that she dreamed that a pinnacle which the senate, as Livy relates, had ordered to be raised on Caesar's house by way of ornament and grandeur, was tumbling down, which was the occasion of her tears and ejaculations. When it was day, she begged of Caesar, if it were possible, not to stir out, but to adjourn the senate to another time; and if he slighted her dreams, that he would be pleased to consult his fate by sacrifices, and other kinds of divination. Nor was he himself without some suspicion and fears; for he never before discovered any womanish superstition in Calpurnia, whom he now saw in such great alarm. Upon the report which the priests made to him, that they had killed several sacrifices, and still found them inauspicious, he resolved to send Antony to dismiss the senate.

In this juncture, Decimus Brutus, surnamed Albinus, one whom Caesar had such confidence in that he made him his second heir, who nevertheless was engaged in the conspiracy with the other Brutus and Cassius, fearing lest if Caesar should put off the senate to another day, the business might get wind, spoke scoffingly and in mockery of the diviners, and blamed Caesar for giving the senate so fair an occasion of saying he had put a slight upon them, for that they were met upon his summons, and were ready to vote unanimously, that he should be declared king of all the provinces out of Italy, and might wear a diadem in any other place but Italy, by sea or land. If anyone should be sent to tell them they might break up for the present, and meet again when Calpurnia should chance to have better dreams, what would his enemies say? Or who would with any patience hear his friends, if they should presume to defend his government as not arbitrary and tyrannical? But if he was possessed so far as to think this day unfortunate, yet it were more decent to go himself to the senate, and to adjourn it in his own person. Brutus, as he spoke these words, took Caesar by the hand, and conducted him forth. He was not gone far from the door, when a servant of some other person's made towards him, but not being able to come up to him, on account of the crowd of those who pressed about him, he made his way into the house, and committed himself to Calpurnia, begging of her to secure him till Caesar returned, because he had matters of great importance to communicate to him.

Artemidorus, a Cnidian, a teacher of Greek logic, and by that means so far acquainted with Brutus and his friends as to have got into the secret, brought Caesar in a small written memorial, the heads of what he had to depose. He had observed that Caesar, as he received any papers, presently gave them to the servants who attended on him; and therefore came as near to him as he could, and said, "Read this, Caesar, alone, and quickly, for it contains matter of great importance which nearly concerns you." Caesar received it, and tried several times to read it, but was still hindered by the crowd of those who came to speak to him. However, he kept it in his hand by itself till he came into the senate. Some say it was another who gave Caesar this note, and that Artemidorus could not get to him, being all along kept off by the crowd.

All these things might happen by chance. But the place which was destined for the scene of this murder, in which the senate met that day, was the same in which Pompey's statue stood, and was one of the edifices which Pompey had raised and dedicated with his theater to the use of the public, plainly showing that there was something of a supernatural influence which guided the action, and ordered it to that particular place. Cassius, just before the act, is said to have looked towards Pompey's statue, and silently implored his assistance, though he had been inclined to the doctrines of Epicurus. But this occasion, and the instant danger, carried him away out of all his reasonings, and filled him for the time with a sort of inspiration. As for Antony, who was firm to Caesar, and a strong man, Brutus Albinus kept him outside the house, and delayed him with a long conversation contrived on purpose. When Caesar entered, the senate stood up to show their respect to him, and of Brutus's confederates, some came about his chair and stood behind it, others met him, pretending to add their petitions to those of Tillius Cimber, in behalf of his brother, who was in exile; and they followed him with their joint supplications till he came to his seat. When he was sat down, he refused to comply with their requests, and upon their urging him further, began to reproach them severally for their importunities, when Tillius, laying hold of his robe with both his hands, pulled it down from his neck, which was the signal for the assault. Casca gave him the first cut, in the neck, which was not mortal nor dangerous, as coming from one who at the beginning of such a bold action was probably very much disturbed. Caesar immediately turned about, and laid his hand upon the dagger and kept hold of it. And both of them at the same time cried out, he that received the blow, in Latin, "Vile Casca, what does this mean?" and he that gave it, in Greek, to his brother, "Brother, help!" Upon this first onset, those who were not privy to the design were astonished and their horror and amazement at what they saw were so great, that they durst not fly nor assist Caesar, nor so much as speak a word. But those who came prepared for the business enclosed him on every side, with their naked daggers in their hands. Which way soever he turned, he met with blows, and saw their swords leveled at his face and eyes, and was encompassed, like a wild beast in the toils, on every side. For it had been agreed they should each of them make a thrust at him, and flesh themselves with his blood; for which reason Brutus also gave him one stab in the groin. Some say that he fought and resisted all the rest, shifting his body to avoid the blows, and calling out for help, but that when he saw Brutus's sword drawn, he covered his face with his robe and submitted, letting himself fall, whether it were by chance, or that he was pushed in that direction by his murderers, at the foot of the pedestal on which Pompey's statue stood, and which was thus wetted with his blood. So that Pompey himself seemed to have presided, as it were, over the revenge done upon his adversary, who lay here at his feet, and breathed out his soul through his multitude of wounds, for they say he received three and twenty. And the conspirators themselves were many of them wounded by each other, whilst they all leveled their blows at the same person.

When Caesar was dispatched, Brutus stood forth to give a reason for what they had done, but the senate would not hear him, but flew out of doors in all haste, and filled the people with so much alarm and distraction, that some shut up their houses, others left their counters and shops. All ran one way or the other, some to the place to see the sad spectacle, others back again after they had seen it. Antony and Lepidus, Caesar's most faithful friends, got off privately, and hid themselves in some friends' houses. Brutus and his followers, being yet hot from the deed, marched in a body from the senate-house to the capitol with their drawn swords, not like persons who thought of escaping, but with an air of confidence and assurance, and as they went along, called to the people to resume their liberty, and invited the company of any more distinguished people whom they met. And some of these joined the procession and went up along with them, as if they also had been of the conspiracy, and could claim a share in the honor of what had been done. As, for example, Caius Octavius and Lentulus Spinther, who suffered afterwards for their vanity, being taken off by Antony and the young Caesar, and lost the honor they desired, as well as their lives, which it cost them, since no one believed they had any share in the action. For neither did those who punished them profess to revenge the fact, but the ill-will. The day after, Brutus with the rest came down from the capitol, and made a speech to the people, who listened without expressing either any pleasure or resentment, but showed by their silence that they pitied Caesar, and respected Brutus. The senate passed acts of oblivion for what was past, and took measures to reconcile all parties. They ordered that Caesar should be worshipped as a divinity, and nothing, even of the slightest consequence, should be revoked, which he had enacted during his government. At the same time they gave Brutus and his followers the command of provinces, and other considerable posts. So that all people now thought things were well settled, and brought to the happiest adjustment.

But when Caesar's will was opened, and it was found that he had left a considerable legacy to each one of the Roman citizens, and when his body was seen carried through the market-place all mangled with wounds, the multitude could no longer contain themselves within the bounds of tranquillity and order, but heaped together a pile of benches, bars, and tables, which they placed the corpse on, and setting fire to it, burnt it on them. Then they took brands from the pile, and ran some to fire the houses of the conspirators, others up and down the city, to find out the men and tear them to pieces, but met, however, with none of them, they having taken effectual care to secure themselves.

One Cinna, a friend of Caesar's, chanced the night before to have an odd dream. He fancied that Caesar invited him to supper, and that upon his refusal to go with him, Caesar took him by the hand and forced him, though he hung back. Upon hearing the report that Caesar's body was burning in the marketplace, he got up and went thither, out of respect to his memory, though his dream gave him some ill apprehensions, and though he was suffering from a fever. One of the crowd who saw him there, asked another who that was, and having learned his name, told it to his next neighbor. It presently passed for a certainty that he was one of Caesar's murderers, as, indeed, there was another Cinna, a conspirator, and they, taking this to be the man, immediately seized him, and tore him limb from limb upon the spot.

Brutus and Cassius, frightened at this, within a few days retired out of the city. What they afterwards did and suffered, and how they died, is written in the Life of Brutus. Caesar died in his fifty-sixth year, not having survived Pompey above four years. That empire and power which he had pursued through the whole course of his life with so much hazard, he did at last with much difficulty compass, but reaped no other fruits from it than the empty name and invidious glory. But the great genius which attended him through his lifetime, even after his death remained as the avenger of his murder, pursuing through every sea and land all those who were concerned in it, and suffering none to escape, but reaching all who in any sort or kind were either actually engaged in the fact, or by their counsels any way promoted it.

The most remarkable of mere human coincidences was that which befell Cassius, who, when he was defeated at Philippi, killed himself with the same dagger which he had made use of against Caesar. The most signal preternatural appearances were the great comet, which shone very bright for seven nights after Caesar's death, and then disappeared, and the dimness of the sun, whose orb continued pale and dull for the whole of that year, never showing its ordinary radiance at its rising, and giving but a weak and feeble heat. The air consequently was damp and gross, for want of stronger rays to open and rarify it. The fruits, for that reason, never properly ripened, and began to wither and fall off for want of heat, before they were fully formed. But above all, the phantom which appeared to Brutus showed the murder was not pleasing to the gods. The story of it is this.

Brutus being to pass his army from Abydos to the continent on the other side, laid himself down one night, as he used to do, in his tent, and was not asleep, but thinking of his affairs, and what events he might expect. For he is related to have been the least inclined to sleep of all men who have commanded armies, and to have had the greatest natural capacity for continuing awake, and employing himself without need of rest. He thought he heard a noise at the door of his tent, and looking that way, by the light of his lamp, which was almost out, saw a terrible figure, like that of a man, but of unusual stature and severe countenance. He was somewhat frightened at first, but seeing it neither did nor spoke anything to him, only stood silently by his bedside, he asked who it was. The specter answered him, "Thy evil genius, Brutus, thou shalt see me at Philippi." Brutus answered courageously, "Well, I shall see you," and immediately the appearance vanished. When the time was come, he drew up his army near Philippi against Antony and Caesar, and in the first battle won the day, routed the enemy, and plundered Caesar's camp. The night before the second battle, the same phantom appeared to him again, but spoke not a word. He presently understood his destiny was at hand, and exposed himself to all the danger of the battle. Yet he did not die in the fight, but seeing his men defeated, got up to the top of a rock, and there presenting his sword to his naked breast, and assisted, as they say, by a friend, who helped him to give the thrust, met his death.

15

CATO THE YOUNGER

The family of Cato derived its first luster from his great-grandfather Cato, whose virtue gained him such great reputation and authority among the Romans, as we have written in his life.

This Cato was, by the loss of both his parents, left an orphan, together with his brother Caepio, and his sister Porcia. He had also a half-sister, Servilia, by the mother's side. All these lived together, and were bred up in the house of Livius Drusus, their uncle by the mother who, at that time, had a great share in the government, being a very eloquent speaker, a man of the greatest temperance, and yielding in dignity to none of the Romans.

It is said of Cato, that even from his infancy, in his speech, his countenance, and all his childish pastimes, he discovered an inflexible temper, unmoved by any passion, and firm in everything. He was resolute in his purposes, much beyond the strength of his age, to go through with whatever he undertook. He was rough and ungentle toward those that flattered him, and still more unyielding to those who threatened him. It was difficult to excite him to laughter; his countenance seldom relaxed even into a smile; he was not quickly or easily provoked to anger, but if once incensed, he was no less difficult to pacify.

When he began to learn, he proved dull, and slow to apprehend, but of what he once received, his memory was remarkably tenacious. And such, in fact, we find generally to be the course of nature; men of fine genius are readily reminded of things, but those who receive with most pains and difficulty, remember best; every new thing they learn, being, as it were, burnt and branded in on their minds. Cato's natural stubbornness and slowness to be persuaded, may also have made it more difficult for him to be taught. For to learn, is to submit to have something done to one; and persuasion comes soonest to those who have least strength to resist it. Hence young men are sooner persuaded than those that are more in years, and sick men, than those that are well in health In fine, where there is least previous doubt and difficulty the new impression is most easily accepted. Yet Cato, they say, was very obedient to his preceptor, and would do whatever he was commanded; but he would also ask the reason, and inquire the cause of everything. And, indeed, his teacher was a very well-bred man, more ready to instruct, than to beat his scholars. His name was Sarpedon.

When Cato was a child, the allies of the Romans sued to be made free citizens of Rome. Pompaedius Silo, one of their deputies, a brave soldier, and a man of great repute, who had contracted a friendship with Drusus, lodged at his house for several days, in which time being grown familiar with the children, "Well," said he to them, "will you entreat your uncle to befriend us in our business?" Caepio, smiling, assented, but Cato made no answer, only he looked steadfastly and fiercely on the strangers. Then said Pompaedius, "And you, young sir, what say you to us? will not you, as well as your brother, intercede with your uncle in our behalf?" And when Cato continued to give no answer, by his silence and his countenance seeming to deny their petition, Pompaedius snatched him up to the window as if he would throw him out, and told him to consent, or he would fling him down, and, speaking in a harsher tone, held his body out of the window, and shook him several times. When Cato had suffered this a good while, unmoved and unalarmed, Pompaedius setting him down, said in an under-voice to his friend, "What a blessing for Italy, that he is but a child! If he were a man, I believe we should not gain one voice among the people." Another time, one of his relations, on his birthday, invited Cato and some other children to supper, and some of the company diverted themselves in a separate part of the house, and were at play, the elder and the younger together, their sport being to act the pleadings before the judges, accusing one another, and carrying away the condemned to prison. Among these a very beautiful young child, being bound and carried by a bigger into prison, cried out to Cato, who seeing what was going on, presently ran to the door, and thrusting away those who stood there as guard, took out the child, and went home in anger, followed by some of his companions.

Cato at length grew so famous among them, that when Sylla designed to exhibit the sacred game of young men riding courses on horseback, which they called Troy, having gotten together the youth of good birth, he appointed two for their leaders. One of them they accepted for his mother's sake, being the son of Metella, the wife of Sylla; but as for the other, Sextus, the nephew of Pompey, they would not be led by him, nor exercise under him. Then Sylla asking, whom they would have, they all cried out, Cato; and Sextus willingly yielded the honor to him, as the more worthy.

Sylla, who was a friend of their family, sent at times for Cato and his brother to see them and talk with them; a favor which he showed to very few, after gaining his great power and authority. Sarpedon, full of the advantage it would be, as well for the honor as the safety of his scholars, would often bring Cato to wait upon Sylla at his house, which, for the multitude of those that were being carried off in custody, and tormented there, looked like a place of execution. Cato was then in his fourteenth year, and seeing the heads of men said to be of great distinction brought thither, and observing the secret sighs of those that were present, he asked his preceptor, "Why does nobody kill this man?" "Because," said he, "they fear him, child, more than they hate him." "Why, then," replied Cato, "did you not give me a sword, that I might stab him, and free my country from this slavery?" Sarpedon hearing this, and at the same time seeing his countenance swelling with anger and determination, took care thenceforward to watch him strictly, lest he should hazard any desperate attempt.

While he was yet very young, to some that asked him, whom he loved best, he answered, his brother. And being asked, whom next, he replied, his brother, again. So likewise the third time, and still the same, till they left off to ask any further. As he grew in age, this love to his brother grew yet the stronger. When he was about twenty years old, he never supped, never went out of town, nor into the forum, without Caepio. But when his brother made use of precious ointments and perfumes, Cato declined them; and he was, in all his habits, very strict and austere, so that when Caepio was admired for his moderation and temperance, he would acknowledge that indeed he might be accounted such, in comparison with some other men, "but," said he, "when I compare myself with Cato, I find myself scarcely different from Sippius," one at that time notorious for his luxurious and effeminate living.

Cato being made priest of Apollo, went to another house, took his portion of their paternal inheritance, amounting to a hundred and twenty talents, and began to live yet more strictly than before. Having gained the intimate acquaintance of Antipater the Tyrian, the Stoic philosopher, he devoted himself to the study, above everything, of moral and political doctrine. And though possessed, as it were, by a kind of inspiration for the pursuit of every virtue, yet what most of all virtue and excellence fixed his affection, was that steady and inflexible Justice, which is not to be wrought upon by favor or compassion. He learned also the art of speaking and debating in public, thinking that political philosophy, like a great city, should maintain for its security the military and warlike element. But he would never recite his exercises before company, nor was he ever heard to declaim. And to one that told him, men blamed his silence, "But I hope not my life," he replied, "I will begin to speak, when I have that to say which had not better be unsaid."

The great Porcian Hall, as it was called, had been built and dedicated to the public use by the old Cato, when aedile. Here the tribunes of the people used to transact their business, and because one of the pillars was thought to interfere with the convenience of their seats, they deliberated whether it were best to remove it to another place, or to take it away. This occasion first drew Cato, much against his will, into the forum; for he opposed the demand of the tribunes, and in so doing, gave a specimen both of his courage and his powers of speaking, which gained him great admiration. His speech had nothing youthful or refined in it, but was straightforward, full of matter, and rough, at the same time that there was a certain grace about his rough statements which won the attention; and the speaker's character showing itself in all he said, added to his severe language something that excited feelings of natural pleasure and interest. His voice was full and sounding, and sufficient to be heard by so great a multitude, and its vigor and capacity of endurance quite indefatigable; for he often would speak a whole day, and never stop.

When he had carried this cause, he betook himself again to study and retirement. He employed himself in inuring his body to labor and violent exercise; and habituated himself to go bareheaded in the hottest and the coldest weather, and to walk on foot at all seasons. When he went on a journey with any of his friends, though they were on horseback and he on foot, yet he would often join now one, then another, and converse with them on the way. In sickness, the patience he showed in supporting, and the abstinence he used for curing his distempers, were admirable. When he had an ague, he would remain alone, and suffer nobody to see him, till he began to recover, and found the fit was over. At supper, when he threw dice for the choice of dishes, and lost, and the company offered him nevertheless his choice, he declined to dispute, as he said, the decision of Venus. At first, he was wont to drink only once after supper, and then go away; but in process of time he grew to drink more, insomuch that oftentimes he would continue till morning. This his friends explained by saying that state affairs and public business took him up all day, and being desirous of knowledge, he liked to pass the night at wine in the conversation of philosophers. Hence, upon one Memmius saying in public, that Cato spent whole nights in drinking, "You should add," replied Cicero, "that he spends whole days in gambling." And in general Cato esteemed the customs and manners of men at that time so corrupt, and a reformation in them so necessary, that he thought it requisite, in many things, to go contrary to the ordinary way of the world. Seeing the lightest and gayest purple was then most in fashion, he would always wear that which was nearest black; and he would often go out of doors, after his morning meal, without either shoes or tunic; not that he sought vainglory from such novelties, but he would accustom himself to be ashamed only of what deserves shame, and to despise all other sorts of disgrace.

The estate of one Cato, his cousin, which was worth one hundred talents, falling to him, he turned it all into ready money, which he kept by him for any of his friends that should happen to want, to whom he would lend it without interest. And for some of them, he suffered his own land and his slaves to be mortgaged to the public treasury.

When he thought himself of an age fit to marry, having never before known any woman, he was contracted to Lepida, who had before been contracted to Metellus Scipio, but on Scipio's own withdrawal from it, the contract had been dissolved, and she left at liberty. Yet Scipio afterward repenting himself, did all he could to regain her, before the marriage with Cato was completed, and succeeded in so doing. At which Cato was violently incensed, and resolved at first to go to law about it; but his friends persuaded him to the contrary. However, he was so moved by the heat of youth and passion, that he wrote a quantity of iambic verses against Scipio, in the bitter, sarcastic style of Archilochus, without, however, his license and scurrility. After this, he married Atilia, the daughter of Soranus, the first, but not the only woman he ever knew, less happy thus far than Laelius, the friend of Scipio, who in the whole course of so long a life never knew but the one woman to whom he was united in his first and only marriage.

In the war of the slaves, which took its name from Spartacus, their ringleader, Gellius was general, and Cato went a volunteer, for the sake of his brother Caepio, who was a tribune in the army. Cato could find here no opportunity to show his zeal or exercise his valor, on account of the ill conduct of the general. However, amidst the corruption and disorders of that army, he showed such a love of discipline, so much bravery upon occasion, and so much courage and wisdom in everything, that it appeared he was no way inferior to the old Cato. Gellius offered him great rewards, and would have decreed him the first honors; which, however, he refused, saying, he had done nothing that deserved them. This made him be thought a man of a strange and eccentric temper.

There was a law passed, moreover, that the candidates who stood for any office should not have prompters in their canvass, to tell them the names of the citizens; and Cato, when he sued to be elected tribune, was the only man that obeyed this law. He took great pains to learn by his own knowledge to salute those he had to speak with, and to call them by their names; yet even those who praised him for this, did not do so without some envy and jealousy, for the more they considered the excellence of what he did, the more they were grieved at the difficulty they found to do the like.

Being chosen tribune, he was sent into Macedon to join Rubrius, who was general there. It is said that his wife showing much concern, and weeping at his departure, Munatius, one of Cato's friends, said to her, "Do not trouble yourself, Atilia, I will engage to watch over him for you." "By all means," replied Cato; and when they had gone one day's journey together, "Now," said he to Munatius, after they had supped, "that you may be sure to keep your promise to Atilia, you must not leave me day nor night," and from that time, he ordered two beds to be made in his own chamber, that Munatius might lie there. And so he continued to do, Cato making it his jest to see that he was always there. There went with him fifteen slaves, two freedmen, and four of his friends; these rode on horseback, but Cato always went on foot, yet would he keep by them, and talk with each of them in turn, as they went.

When he came to the army, which consisted of several legions, the general gave him the command of one; and as he looked upon it as a small matter, and not worthy a commander, to give evidence of his own single valor, he resolved to make his soldiers, as far as he could, like himself, not, however, in this, relaxing the terrors of his office, but associating reason with his authority. He persuaded and instructed every one in particular, and bestowed rewards or punishments according to desert; and at length his men were so well disciplined, that it was hard to say, whether they were more peaceable, or more warlike, more valiant, or more just; they were alike formidable to their enemies and courteous to their allies, fearful to do wrong, and forward to gain honor. And Cato himself acquired in the fullest measure, what it had been his least desire to seek, glory and good repute; he was highly esteemed by all men, and entirely beloved by the soldiers. Whatever he commanded to be done, he himself took part in the performing; in his apparel, his diet and mode of traveling, he was more like a common soldier than an officer; but in character, high purpose, and wisdom, he far exceeded all that had the names and titles of commanders, and he made himself, without knowing it, the object of general affection. For the true love of virtue is in all men produced by the love and respect they bear to him that teaches it; and those who praise good men, yet do not love them, may respect their reputation, but do not really admire, and will never imitate their virtue.

There dwelt at that time in Pergamus, Athenodorus, surnamed Cordylio, a man of high repute for his knowledge of the stoic philosophy, who was now grown old, and had always steadily refused the friendship and acquaintance of princes and great men. Cato understood this; so that imagining he should not be able to prevail with him by sending or writing, and being by the laws allowed two months' absence from the army, he resolved to go into Asia to see him in person, trusting to his own good qualities not to lose his labor. And when he had conversed with him, and succeeded in persuading him out of his former resolutions, he returned and brought him to the camp, as joyful and as proud of this victory as if he had done some heroic exploit, greater than any of those of Pompey or Lucullus, who, with their armies, at that time were subduing so many nations and kingdoms.

While Cato was yet in the service, his brother, on a journey towards Asia, fell sick at Aenus in Thrace, letters with intelligence of which were immediately dispatched to him. The sea was very rough, and no convenient ship of any size to be had; so Cato, getting into a small trading-vessel, with only two of his friends and three servants, set sail from Thessalonica, and having very narrowly escaped drowning, he arrived at Aenus just as Caepio expired. Upon this occasion, he was thought to have showed himself more a fond brother than a philosopher, not only in the excess of his grief, bewailing, and embracing the dead body, but also in the extravagant expenses of the funeral, the vast quantity of rich perfumes and costly garments which were burnt with the corpse, and the monument of Thasian marble, which he erected, at the cost of eight talents, in the public place of the town of Aenus. For there were some who took upon them to cavil at all this, as not consistent with his usual calmness and moderation, not discerning that though he were steadfast, firm, and inflexible to pleasure, fear, or foolish entreaties, yet he was full of natural tenderness and brotherly affection. Divers of the cities and princes of the country, sent him many presents, to honor the funeral of his brother; but he took none of their money, only the perfumes and ornaments he received, and paid for them also. And afterwards, when the inheritance was divided between him and Caepio's daughter, he did not require any portion of the funeral expenses to be discharged out of it. Notwithstanding this, it has been affirmed that he made his brother's ashes be passed through a sieve, to find the gold that was melted down when burnt with the body. But he who made this statement appears to have anticipated an exemption for his pen, as much as for his sword, from all question and criticism.

The time of Cato's service in the army being expired, he received, at his departure, not only the prayers and praises, but the tears, and embraces of the soldiers, who spread their clothes at his feet, and kissed his hand as he passed, an honor which the Romans at that time scarcely paid even to a very few of their generals and commander-in-chief. Having left the army, he resolved, before he would return home and apply himself to state affairs, to travel in Asia, and observe the manners, the customs, and the strength of every province. He was also unwilling to refuse the kindness of Deiotarus, king of Galatia, who having had great familiarity and friendship with his father, was very desirous to receive a visit from him. Cato's arrangements in his journey were as follows. Early in the morning he sent out his baker and his cook towards the place where he designed to stay the next night; these went soberly and quietly into the town, in which, if there happened to be no friend or acquaintance of Cato or his family, they provided for him in an inn, and gave no disturbance to anybody; but if there were no inn, then and in this case only, they went to the magistrates, and desiring them to help them to lodgings, took without complaint whatever was allotted to them. His servants thus behaving themselves towards the magistrates, without noise and threatening, were often discredited, or neglected by them, so that Cato many times arrived and found nothing provided for him. And it was all the worse when he appeared himself; still less account was taken of him. When they saw him sitting, without saying anything, on his baggage, they set him down at once as a person of no consequence, who did not venture to make any demand. Sometimes, on such occasions, he would call them to him and tell them, "Foolish people, lay aside this inhospitality. All your visitors will not be Catos. Use your courtesy, to take off the sharp edge of power. There are men enough who desire but a pretense, to take from you by force, what you give with such reluctance."

While he traveled in this manner, a diverting accident befell him in Syria. As he was going into Antioch, he saw a great multitude of people outside the gates, ranged in order on either side the way; here the young men with long cloaks, there the children decently dressed; others wore garlands and white garments, who were the priests and magistrates. Cato, imagining all this could mean nothing but a display in honor of his reception, began to be angry with his servants who had been sent before, for suffering it to be done; then making his friends alight, he walked along with them on foot. As soon as he came near the gate, an elderly man, who seemed to be master of these ceremonies, with a wand and a garland in his hand, came up to Cato, and without saluting him, asked him, where he had left Demetrius, and how soon he thought he would be there. This Demetrius was Pompey's servant, and as at this time the whole world, so to say, had its eyes fixed upon Pompey, this man also was highly honored, on account of his influence with his master. Upon this, Cato's friends fell into such violent laughter, that they could not restrain themselves while they passed through the crowd; and he himself, ashamed and distressed, uttered the words, "Unfortunate city!" and said no more. Afterwards, however, it always made him laugh, when he either told the story or was otherwise reminded of it.

Pompey himself shortly after made the people ashamed of their ignorance and folly in thus neglecting him, for Cato, coming in his journey to Ephesus, went to pay his respects to him, who was the elder man, had gained much honor, and was then general of a great army. Yet Pompey would not receive him sitting, but as soon as he saw him, rose up, and going to meet him, as the more honorable person, gave him his hand, and embraced him with great show of kindness. He said much in commendation of his virtue, both at that time when receiving him, and also yet more, after he had withdrawn. So that now all men began at once to display their respect for Cato, and discovered in the very same things for which they despised him before, an admirable mildness of temper, and greatness of spirit. And indeed the civility that Pompey himself showed him, appeared to come from one that rather respected than loved him; and the general opinion was, that while Cato was there, he paid him admiration, but was not sorry when he was gone. For when other young men came to see him, he usually urged and entreated them to continue with him. Now he did not at all invite Cato to stay, but as if his own power were lessened by the other's presence, he very willingly allowed him to take his leave. Yet to Cato alone, of all those who went for Rome, he recommended his children and his wife, who was indeed connected by relationship with Cato.

After this, all the cities through which he passed, strove and emulated each other in showing him respect and honor. Feasts and entertainments were made for his reception, so that he bade his friends keep strict watch and take care of him, lest he should end by making good what was said by Curio, who though he were his familial friend, yet disliking the austerity of his temper, asked him one day, if when he left the army, he designed to see Asia, and Cato answering, "Yes, by all means," "You do well," replied Curio, "you will bring back with you a better temper and pleasanter manners;" pretty nearly the very words he used.

Deiotarus being now an old man, had sent for Cato, to recommend his children and family to his protection; and as soon as he came, brought him presents of all sorts of things, which he begged and entreated him to accept. And his importunities displeased Cato so much, that though he came but in the evening, he stayed only that night, and went away early the next morning. After he was gone one day's journey, he found at Pessinus a yet greater quantity of presents provided for him there, and also letters from Deiotarus, entreating him to receive them, or at least to permit his friends to take them, who for his sake deserved some gratification, and could not have much done for them out of Cato's own means. Yet he would not suffer it, though he saw some of them very willing to receive such gifts, and ready to complain of his severity; but he answered, that corruption would never want pretense, and his friends should share with him in whatever he should justly and honestly obtain, and so returned the presents to Deiotarus.

When he took ship for Brundusium, his friends would have persuaded him to put his brother's ashes into another vessel; but he said, he would sooner part with his life than leave them, and so set sail. And as it chanced, he, we are told, had a very dangerous passage, though others at the same time went over safely enough.

After he was returned to Rome, he spent his time for the most part either at home, in conversation with Athenodorus, or at the forum, in the service of his friends. Though it was now the time that he should become quaestor, he would not stand for the place till he had studied the laws relating to it, and by inquiry from persons of experience, had attained a distinct understanding of the duty and authority belonging to it. With this knowledge, as soon as he came into the office, he made a great reformation among the clerks and under-officers of the treasury, people who had long practice and familiarity in all the public records and the laws, and, when new magistrates came in year by year, so ignorant and unskillful as to be in absolute need of others to teach them what to do, did not submit and give way, but kept the power in their own hands, and were in effect the treasurers themselves. Till Cato, applying himself roundly to the work, showed that he possessed not only the title and honor of a quaestor, but the knowledge and understanding and full authority of his office. So that he used the clerks and under-officers like servants, as they were, exposing their corrupt practices, and instructing their ignorance. Being bold impudent fellows, they flattered the other quaestors, his colleagues, and by their means endeavored to maintain an opposition against him. But he convicted the chiefest of them of a breach of trust in the charge of an inheritance, and turned him out of his place. A second he brought to trial for dishonesty, who was defended by Lutatius Catulus, at that time censor, a man very considerable for his office, but yet more for his character, as he was eminent above all the Romans of that age for his reputed wisdom and integrity. He was also intimate with Cato, and much commended his way of living. So perceiving he could not bring off his client, if he stood a fair trial, he openly began to beg him off. Cato objected to his doing this. And when he continued still to be importunate, "It would be shameful, Catulus," he said, "that the censor, the judge of all our lives, should incur the dishonor of removal by our officers." At this expression, Catalus looked as if he would have made some answer; but he said nothing, and either through anger or shame went away silent, and out of countenance. Nevertheless, the man was not found guilty, for the voices that acquitted him were but one in number less than those that condemned him, and Marcus Lollius, one of Cato's colleagues, who was absent by reason of sickness, was sent for by Catalus, and entreated to come and save the man. So Lollius was brought into court in a chair, and gave his voice also for acquitting him. Yet Cato never after made use of that clerk, and never paid him his salary, nor would he make any account of the vote given by Lollius. Having thus humbled the clerks, and brought them to be at command, he made use of the books and registers as he thought fit, and in a little while gained the treasury a higher name than the Senate-house itself; and all men said, Cato had made the office of a quaestor equal to the dignity of a consul. When he found many indebted to the state upon old accounts, and the state also in debt to many private persons, he took care that the public might no longer either do or suffer wrong; he strictly and punctually exacted what was due to the treasury, and as freely and speedily paid all those to whom it was indebted. So that the people were filled with sentiments of awe and respect, on seeing those made to pay, who thought to have escaped with their plunder, and others receiving all their due, who despaired of getting anything. And whereas usually those who brought false bills and pretended orders of the senate, could through favor get them accepted, Cato would never be so imposed upon, and in the case of one particular order, question arising, whether it had passed the senate, he would not believe a great many witnesses that attested it, nor would admit of it, till the consuls came and affirmed it upon oath.

There were at that time a great many whom Sylla had made use of as his agents in the proscription, and to whom he had for their service in putting men to death, given twelve thousand drachmas apiece. These men everybody hated as wicked and polluted wretches, but nobody durst be revenged upon them. Cato called everyone to account, as wrongfully possessed of the public money, and exacted it of them, and at the same time sharply reproved them for their unlawful and impious actions. After these proceedings, they were presently accused of murder, and being already in a manner prejudged as guilty, they were easily found so, and accordingly suffered; at which the whole people rejoiced, and thought themselves now to see the old tyranny finally abolished, and Sylla himself, so to say, brought to punishment.

Cato's assiduity also, and indefatigable diligence, won very much upon the people. He always came first of any of his colleagues to the treasury, and went away the last. He never missed any assembly of the people, or sitting of the senate; being always anxious and on the watch for those who lightly, or as a matter of interest, passed votes in favor of this or that person, for remitting debts or granting away customs that were owing to the state. And at length, having kept the exchequer pure and clear from base informers, and yet having filled it with treasure, he made it appear the state might be rich, without oppressing the people. At first he excited feelings of dislike and irritation in some of his colleagues, but after a while they were well contented with him, since he was perfectly willing that they should cast all the odium on him, when they declined to gratify their friends with the public money, or to give dishonest judgments in passing their accounts; and when hard pressed by suitors, they could readily answer it was impossible to do anything, unless Cato would consent. On the last day of his office, he was honorably attended to his house by almost all the people; but on the way he was informed that several powerful friends were in the treasury with Marcellus, using all their interest with him to pass a certain debt to the public revenue, as if it had been a gift. Marcellus had been one of Cato's friends from his childhood, and so long as Cato was with him, was one of the best of his colleagues in this office, but when alone, was unable to resist the importunity of suitors, and prone to do anybody a kindness. So Cato immediately turned back, and finding that Marcellus had yielded to pass the thing, he took the book, and while

Marcellus silently stood by and looked on, struck it out. This done, he brought Marcellus out of the treasury, and took him home with him; who for all this, neither then, nor ever after, complained of him, but always continued his friendship and familiarity with him.

Cato after he had laid down his office, yet did not cease to keep a watch upon the treasury. He had his servants who continually wrote out the details of the expenditure, and he himself kept always by him certain books, which contained the accounts of the revenue from Sylla's time to his own quaestorship, which he had bought for five talents.

He was always first at the senate, and went out last; and often, while the others were slowly collecting, he would sit and read by himself, holding his gown before his book. He was never once out of town when the senate was to meet. And when afterwards Pompey and his party, finding that he could never be either persuaded or compelled to favor their unjust designs, endeavored to keep him from the senate, by engaging him in business for his friends, to plead their causes, or arbitrate in their differences, or the like, he quickly discovered the trick, and to defeat it, fairly told all his acquaintance that he would never meddle in any private business when the senate was assembled. Since it was not in the hope of gaining honor or riches, nor out of mere impulse, or by chance that he engaged himself in politics, but he undertook the service of the state, as the proper business of an honest man, and therefore he thought himself obliged to be as constant to his public duty, as the bee to the honeycomb. To this end, he took care to have his friends and correspondents everywhere, to send him reports of the edicts, decrees, judgments, and all the important proceedings that passed in any of the provinces. Once when Clodius, the seditious orator, to promote his violent and revolutionary projects, traduced to the people some of the priests and priestesses, (among whom Fabia, sister to Cicero's wife, Terentia, ran great danger,) Cato, having boldly interfered, and having made Clodius appear so infamous that he was forced to leave the town, was addressed, when it was over, by Ciccro, who came to thank him for what he had done. "You must thank the commonwealth," said he, for whose sake alone he professed to do everything. Thus he gained a great and wonderful reputation; so that an advocate in a cause, where there was only one witness against him, told the judges they ought not to rely upon a single witness, though it were Cato himself. And it was a sort of proverb with many people, if any very unlikely and incredible thing were asserted, to say, they would not believe it, though Cato himself should affirm it. One day a debauched and sumptuous liver talking in the senate about frugality and temperance, Amnaeus standing up, cried, "Who can endure this, Sir, to have you feast like Crassus, build like Lucullus and talk like Cato." So likewise those who were vicious and dissolute in their manners, yet affected to be grave and severe in their language, were in derision called Catos.

At first, when his friends would have persuaded him to stand to be tribune of the people, he thought it undesirable; for that the power of so great an office ought to be reserved, as the strongest medicines, for occasions of the last necessity. But afterwards in a vacation time, as he was going, accompanied with his books and philosophers, to Lucania, where he had lands with a pleasant residence, they met by the way a great many horses, carriages, and attendants, of whom they understood, that Metellus Nepos was going to Rome, to stand to be tribune of the people. Hereupon Cato stopped, and after a little pause, gave orders to return back immediately; at which the company seeming to wonder, "Don't you know," said he, "how dangerous of itself the madness of Metellus is? and now that he comes armed with the support of Pompey, he will fall like lightning on the state, and bring it to utter disorder; therefore this is no time for idleness and diversion, but we must go and prevent this man in his designs, or bravely die in defense of our liberty." Nevertheless, by the persuasion of his friends, he went first to his country-house, where he stayed but a very little time, and then returned to town.

He arrived in the evening, and went straight the next morning to the forum, where he began to solicit for the tribuneship, in opposition to Metellus. The power of this office consists rather in controlling, than performing any business; for though all the rest except any one tribune should be agreed, yet his denial or intercession could put a stop to the whole matter. Cato, at first, had not many that appeared for him; but as soon as his design was known, all the good and distinguished persons of the city quickly came forward to encourage and support him, looking upon him, not as one that desired a favor of them, but one that proposed to do a great favor to his country and all honest men; who had many times refused the same office, when he might have had it without trouble, but now sought it with danger, that he might defend their liberty and their government. It is reported that so great a number flocked about him, that he was like to be stifled amidst the press, and could scarce get through the crowd. He was declared tribune, with several others, among whom was Metellus.

When Cato was chosen into this office, observing that the election of consuls was become a matter of purchase, he sharply rebuked the people for this corruption, and in the conclusion of his speech protested, he would bring to trial whomever he should find giving money, making an exception only in the case of Silanus, on account of their near connection, he having married Servilia, Cato's sister. He therefore did not prosecute him, but accused Lucius Murena, who had been chosen consul by corrupt means with Silanus. There was a law that the party accused might appoint a person to keep watch upon his accuser, that he might know fairly what means he took in preparing the accusation. He that was set upon Cato by Murena, at first followed and observed him strictly, yet never found him dealing any way unfairly or insidiously, but always generously and candidly going on in the just and open methods of proceeding. And he so admired Cato's great spirit, and so entirely trusted to his integrity, that meeting him in the forum, or going to his house, he would ask him, if he designed to do anything that day in order to the accusation, and if Cato said no, he went away, relying on his word. When the cause was pleaded, Cicero, who was then consul and defended Murena, took occasion to be extremely witty and jocose, in reference to Cato, upon the stoic philosophers, and their paradoxes, as they call them, and so excited great laughter among the judges; upon which Cato, smiling, said to the standers by, "What a pleasant consul we have, my friends." Murena was acquitted, and afterwards showed himself a man of no ill feeling or want of sense; for when he was consul, he always took Cato's advice in the most weighty affairs, and during all the time of his office, paid him much honor and respect. Of which not only Murena's prudence, but also Cato's own behavior, was the cause; for though he were terrible and severe as to matters of justice, in the senate, and at the bar, yet after the thing was over, his manner to all men was perfectly friendly and humane.

Before he entered on the office of tribune, he assisted Cicero, at that time consul, in many contests that concerned his office, but most especially in his great and noble acts at the time of Catiline's conspiracy, which owed their last successful issue to Cato. Catiline had plotted a dreadful and entire subversion of the Roman state by sedition and open war, but being convicted by Cicero, was forced to fly the city. Yet Lentulus and Cethegus remained with several others, to carry on the same plot; and blaming Catiline, as one that wanted courage, and had been timid and petty in his designs, they themselves resolved to set the whole town on fire, and utterly to overthrow the empire, rousing whole nations to revolt and exciting foreign wars. But the design was discovered by Cicero, (as we have written in his life,) and the matter brought before the senate. Silanus, who spoke first, delivered his opinion, that the conspirators ought to suffer the last of punishments, and was therein followed by all who spoke after him; till it came to Caesar, who being an excellent speaker, and looking upon all changes and commotions in the state as materials useful for his own purposes, desired rather to increase than extinguish them; and standing up, he made a very merciful and persuasive speech, that they ought not to suffer death without fair trial according to law, and moved that they might be kept in prison. Thus was the house almost wholly turned by Caesar, apprehending also the anger of the people; insomuch that even Silanus retracted, and said he did not mean to propose death, but imprisonment, for that was the utmost a Roman could suffer. Upon this they were all inclined to the milder and more merciful opinion, when Cato standing up, began at once with great passion and vehemence to reproach Silanus for his change of opinion, and to attack Caesar, who would, he said, ruin the commonwealth by soft words and popular speeches, and was endeavoring to frighten the senate, when he himself ought to fear, and be thankful, if he escaped unpunished or unsuspected, who thus openly and boldly dared to protect the enemies of the state, and while finding no compassion for his own native country, brought, with all its glories, so near to utter ruin, could yet be full of pity for those men, who had better never have been born, and whose death must deliver the commonwealth from bloodshed and destruction. This only of all Cato's speeches, it is said, was preserved; for Cicero, the consul, had disposed, in various parts of the senate-house, several of the most expert and rapid writers, whom he had taught to make figures comprising numerous words in a few short strokes; as up to that time they had not used those we call short-hand writers, who then, as it is said, established the first example of the art. Thus Cato carried it, and so turned the house again, that it was decreed the conspirators should be put to death.

Not to omit any small matters that may serve to show Cato's temper, and add something to the portraiture of his mind, it is reported, that while Caesar and he were in the very heat, and the whole senate regarding them two, a little note was brought in to Caesar, which Cato declared to be suspicious, and urging that some seditious act was going on, bade the letter be read. Upon which Caesar handed the paper to Cato; who discovering it to be a love-letter from his sister Servilia to Caesar, by whom she had been corrupted, threw it to him again, saying, "Take it, drunkard," and so went on with his discourse. And, indeed, it seems Cato had but ill-fortune in women; for this lady was ill spoken of, for her familiarity with Caesar, and the other Servilia, Cato's sister also, was yet more ill-conducted; for being married to Lucullus, one of the greatest men in Rome, and having brought him a son, she was afterwards divorced for incontinency. But what was worst of all, Cato's own wife Atilia was not free from the same fault; and after she had borne him two children, he was forced to put her away for her misconduct. After that he married Marcia, the daughter of Philippus, a woman of good reputation, who yet has occasioned much discourse; and the life of Cato, like a dramatic piece, has this one scene or passage full of perplexity and doubtful meaning.

It is thus related by Thrasea, who refers to the authority of Munatius, Cato's friend and constant companion. Among many that loved and admired Cato, some were more remarkable and conspicuous than others. Of these was Quintus Hortensius, a man of high repute and approved virtue, who desired not only to live in friendship and familiarity with Cato, but also to unite his whole house and family with him by some sort or other of alliance in marriage. Therefore he set himself to persuade Cato, that his daughter Porcia, who was already married to Bibulus, and had borne him two children, might nevertheless be given to him, as a fair plot of land, to bear fruit also for him. "For," said he, "though this in the opinion of men may seem strange, yet in nature it is honest, and profitable for the public, that a woman in the prime of her youth should not lie useless, and lose the fruit of her womb, nor, on the other side, should burden and impoverish one man, by bringing him too many children. Also by this communication of families among worthy men, virtue would increase, and be diffused through their posterity; and the commonwealth would be united and cemented by their alliances." Yet if Bibulus would not part with his wife altogether, he would restore her as soon as she had brought him a child, whereby he might be united to both their families. Cato answered, that he loved Hortensius very well, and much approved of uniting their houses, but he thought it strange to speak of marrying his daughter, when she was already given to another. Then Hortensius, turning the discourse, did not hesitate to speak openly and ask for Cato's own wife, for she was young and fruitful, and he had already children enough. Neither can it be thought that Hortensius did this, as imagining Cato did not care for Marcia; for, it is said, she was then with child. Cato, perceiving his earnest desire, did not deny his request, but said that Philippus, the father of Marcia, ought also to be consulted. Philippus, therefore, being sent for, came; and finding they were well agreed, gave his daughter Marcia to Hortensius in the presence of Cato, who himself also assisted at the marriage. This was done at a later time, but since I was speaking of women, I thought it well to mention it now.

Lentulus and the rest of the conspirators were put to death, but Caesar, finding so much insinuated and charged against him in the senate, betook himself to the people, and proceeded to stir up the most corrupt and dissolute elements of the state to form a party in his support. Cato, apprehensive of what might ensue, persuaded the senate to win over the poor and unprovided-for multitude, by a distribution of corn, the annual charge of which amounted to twelve hundred and fifty talents. This act of humanity and kindness unquestionably dissipated the present danger. But Metellus, coming into his office of tribune, began to hold tumultuous assemblies, and had prepared a decree, that Pompey the Great should presently be called into Italy, with all his forces, to preserve the city from the danger of Catiline's conspiracy. This was the fair pretense; but the true design was, to deliver all into the hands of Pompey, and give him an absolute power. Upon this the senate was assembled, and Cato did not fall sharply upon Metellus, as he often did, but urged his advice in the most reasonable and moderate tone. At last he descended even to entreaty, and extolled the house of Metellus, as having always taken part with the nobility. At this Metellus grew the more insolent, and despising Cato, as if he yielded and were afraid, let himself proceed to the most audacious menaces, openly threatening to do whatever he pleased in spite of the senate. Upon this Cato changed his countenance, his voice, and his language; and after many sharp expressions, boldly concluded, that while he lived, Pompey should never come armed into the city. The senate thought them both extravagant, and not well in their safe senses; for the design of Metellus seemed to be mere rage and frenzy, out of excess of mischief bringing all things to ruin and confusion, and Cato's virtue looked like a kind of ecstasy of contention in the cause of what was good and just.

But when the day came for the people to give their voices for the passing this decree, and Metellus beforehand occupied the forum with armed men, strangers, gladiators, and slaves, those that in hopes of change followed Pompey, were known to be no small part of the people, and besides, they had great assistance from Caesar, who was then praetor; and though the best and chiefest men of the city were no less offended at these proceedings than Cato, they seemed rather likely to suffer with him, than able to assist him. In the meantime Cato's whole family were in extreme fear and apprehension for him; some of his friends neither ate nor slept all the night, passing the whole time in debating and perplexity; his wife and sisters also bewailed and lamented him. But he himself, void of all fear, and full of assurance, comforted and encouraged them by his own words and conversation with them. After supper he went to rest at his usual hour, and was the next day waked out of a profound sleep by Minucius Thermus, one of his colleagues. So soon as he was up, they two went together into the forum, accompanied by very few, but met by a great many, who bade them have a care of themselves. Cato, therefore, when he saw the temple of Castor and Pollux encompassed with armed men, and the steps guarded by gladiators, and at the top Metellus and Caesar seated together, turning to his friends, "Behold," said he, "this audacious coward, who has levied a regiment of soldiers against one unarmed naked man;" and so he went on with Thermus. Those who kept the passages, gave way to these two only, and would not let anybody else pass. Yet Cato taking Munatius by the hand, with much difficulty pulled him through along with him. Then going directly to Metellus and Caesar, he sat himself down between them, to prevent their talking to one another, at which they were both amazed and confounded. And those of the honest party, observing the countenance, and admiring the high spirit and boldness of Cato, went nearer, and cried out to him to have courage, exhorting also one another to stand together, and not betray their liberty, nor the defender of it.

Then the clerk took out the bill, but Cato forbade him to read it, whereupon Metellus took it, and would have read it himself, but Cato snatched away the book. Yet Metellus having the decree by heart, began to recite it without book; but Thermus put his hand to his mouth, and stopped his speech. Metellus seeing them fully bent to withstand him, and the people cowed, and inclining to the better side, sent to his house for armed men. And on their rushing in with great noise and terror, all the rest dispersed and ran away, except Cato, who alone stood still, while the other party threw sticks and stones at him from above, until Murena, whom he had formerly accused, came up to protect him, and holding his gown before him, cried out to them to leave off throwing; and, in fine, persuading and pulling him along, he forced him into the temple of Castor and Pollux. Metellus now seeing the place clear, and all the adverse party fled out of the forum, thought he might easily carry his point; so he commanded the soldiers to retire, and recommencing in an orderly manner, began to proceed to passing the decree. But the other side having recovered themselves, returned very boldly, and with loud shouting, insomuch that Metellus's adherents were seized with a panic, supposing them to be coming with a reinforcement of armed men, and fled every one out of the place. They being thus dispersed, Cato came in again, and confirmed the courage, and commended the resolution of the people; so that now the majority were, by all means, for deposing Metellus from his office. The senate also being assembled, gave orders once more for supporting Cato, and resisting the motion, as of a nature to excite sedition and perhaps civil war in the city.

But Metellus continued still very bold and resolute; and seeing his party stood greatly in fear of Cato, whom they looked upon as invincible, he hurried out of the senate into the forum, and assembled the people, to whom he made a bitter and invidious speech against Cato, crying out, he was forced to fly from his tyranny, and this conspiracy against Pompey; that the city would soon repent their having dishonored so great a man. And from hence he started to go to Asia, with the intention, as would be supposed, of laying before Pompey all the injuries that were done him. Cato was highly extolled for having delivered the state from this dangerous tribuneship, and having in some measure defeated, in the person of Metellus, the power of Pompey; but he was yet more commended when, upon the senate proceeding to disgrace Metellus and depose him from his office, he altogether opposed and at length diverted the design. The common people admired his moderation and humanity, in not trampling wantonly on an enemy whom he had overthrown, and wiser men acknowledged his prudence and policy, in not exasperating Pompey.

Lucullus soon after returned from the war in Asia, the finishing of which, and thereby the glory of the whole, was thus, in all appearance, taken out of his hands by Pompey. And he was also not far from losing his triumph, for Caius Memmius traduced him to the people, and threatened to accuse him; rather, however, out of love to Pompey, than for any particular enmity to him. But Cato, being allied to Lucullus, who had married his sister Servilia, and also thinking it a great injustice, opposed Memmius, thereby exposing himself to much slander and misrepresentation, insomuch that they would have turned him out of his office, pretending that he used his power tyrannically. Yet at length Cato so far prevailed against Memmius, that he was forced to let fall the accusations, and abandon the contest. And Lucullus having thus obtained his triumph, yet more sedulously cultivated Cato's friendship, which he looked upon as a great guard and defense for him against Pompey's power.

And now Pompey also returning with glory from the war, and confiding in the good-will of the people, shown in their splendid reception of him, thought he should be denied nothing, and sent therefore to the senate to put off the assembly for the election of consuls, till he could be present to assist Piso, who stood for that office. To this most of the senators were disposed to yield; Cato, only, not so much thinking that this delay would be of great importance, but, desiring to cut down at once Pompey's high expectations and designs, withstood his request, and so overruled the senate, that it was carried against him. And this not a little disturbed Pompey, who found he should very often fail in his projects, unless he could bring over Cato to his interest. He sent, therefore, for Munatius, his friend; and Cato having two nieces that were marriageable, he offered to marry the eldest himself, and take the youngest for his son. Some say they were not his nieces, but his daughters. Munatius proposed the matter to Cato, in presence of his wife and sisters; the women were full of joy at the prospect of an alliance with so great and important a person. But Cato, without delay or balancing, forming his decision at once, answered, "Go, Munatius, go and tell Pompey, that Cato is not assailable on the side of the women's chamber; I am grateful indeed for the intended kindness, and so long as his actions are upright, I promise him a friendship more sure than any marriage alliance, but I will not give hostages to Pompey's glory, against my country's safety." This answer was very much against the wishes of the women, and to all his friends it seemed somewhat harsh and haughty. But afterwards, when Pompey, endeavoring to get the consulship for one of his friends, gave pay to the people for their votes, and the bribery was notorious, the money being counted out in Pompey's own gardens, Cato then said to the women, they must necessarily have been concerned in the contamination of these misdeeds of Pompey, if they had been allied to his family; and they acknowledged that he did best in refusing it. Yet if we may judge by the event, Cato was much to blame in rejecting that alliance, which thereby fell to Caesar. And then that match was made, which, uniting his and Pompey's power, had well-nigh ruined the Roman empire, and did destroy the commonwealth. Nothing of which perhaps had come to pass, but that Cato was too apprehensive of Pompey's least faults, and did not consider how he forced him into conferring on another man the opportunity of committing the greatest.

These things, however, were yet to come. Lucullus, meantime, and Pompey, had a great dispute concerning their orders and arrangements in Pontus, each endeavoring that his own ordinances might stand. Cato took part with Lucullus, who was manifestly suffering wrong; and Pompey, finding himself the weaker in the senate, had recourse to the people, and to gain votes, he proposed a law for dividing the lands among the soldiers. Cato opposing him in this also, made the bill be rejected. Upon this he joined himself with Clodius, at that time the most violent of all the demagogues; and entered also into friendship with Caesar, upon an occasion of which also Cato was the cause. For Caesar returning from his government in Spain, at the same time sued to be chosen consul, and yet desired not to lose his triumph. Now the law requiring that those who stood for any office should be present, and yet that whoever expected a triumph should continue without the walls, Caesar requested the senate, that his friends might be permitted to canvass for him in his absence. Many of the senators were willing to consent to it, but Cato opposed it, and perceiving them inclined to favor Caesar, spent the whole day in speaking, and so prevented the senate from coming to any conclusion. Caesar, therefore, resolving to let fall his pretensions to the triumph, came into the town, and immediately made a friendship with Pompey, and stood for the consulship. And so soon as he was declared consul elect, he married his daughter Julia to Pompey. And having thus combined themselves together against the commonwealth, the one proposed laws for dividing the lands among the poor people, and the other was present to support the proposals Lucullus, Cicero, and their friends, joined with Bibulus, the other consul, to hinder their passing, and, foremost of them all, Cato, who already looked upon the friendship and alliance of Pompey and Caesar as very dangerous, and declared he did not so much dislike the advantage the people should get by this division of the lands, as he feared the reward these men would gain, by thus courting and cozening the people. And in this he gained over the senate to his opinion, as likewise many who were not senators, who were offended at Caesar's ill conduct, that he, in the office of consul, should thus basely and dishonorably flatter the people; practicing, to win their favor, the same means that were wont to be used only by the most rash and rebellious tribunes. Caesar, therefore, and his party, fearing they should not carry it by fair dealing, fell to open force. First a basket of dung was thrown upon Bibulus as he was going to the forum; then they set upon his lictors and broke their rods; at length several darts were thrown, and many men wounded; so that all that were against those laws, fled out of the forum, the rest with what haste they could, and Cato, last of all, walking out slowly, often turning back and calling down vengeance upon them.

 Thus the other party not only carried their point of dividing the lands, but also ordained, that all the senate should swear to confirm this law, and to defend it against whoever should attempt to alter it, indicting great penalties on those that should refuse the oath. All the senators seeing the necessity they were in, took the oath, remembering the example of Metellus in old time, who refusing to swear upon the like occasion, was forced to leave Italy. As for Cato, his wife and children with tears besought him, his friends and familiars persuaded and entreated him, to yield and take the oath; but he that principally prevailed with him was Cicero, the orator, who urged upon him that it was perhaps not even right in itself, that a private man should oppose what the public had decreed; that the thing being already past altering, it were folly and madness to throw himself into danger, without the chance of doing his country any good; it would be the greatest of all evils, to embrace, as it were, the opportunity to abandon the commonwealth, for whose sake he did everything, and to let it fall into the hands of those who designed nothing but its ruin, as if he were glad to be saved from the trouble of defending it. "For," said he, "though Cato have no need of Rome, yet Rome has need of Cato, and so likewise have all his friends." Of whom Cicero professed he himself was the chief, being; at that time aimed at by Clodius, who openly threatened to fall upon him, as soon as ever he should get to be tribune. Thus Cato, they say, moved by the entreaties and the arguments of his friends, went unwillingly to take the oath, which he did the last of all, except only Favonius, one of his intimate acquaintance.

Caesar, exalted with this success, proposed another law, for dividing almost all the country of Campania among the poor and needy citizens. Nobody durst speak against it but Cato, whom Caesar therefore pulled from the rostra, and dragged to prison: yet Cato did not even thus remit his freedom of speech, but as he went along, continued to speak against the law, and advised the people to put down all legislators who proposed the like. The senate and the best of the citizens followed him with sad and dejected looks, showing their grief and indignation by their silence, so that Caesar could not be ignorant how much they were offended; but for contention's sake, he still persisted, expecting Cato should either supplicate him, or make an appeal. But when he saw that he did not so much as think of doing either, ashamed of what he was doing and of what people thought of it, he himself privately bade one of the tribunes interpose and procure his release. However, having won the multitude by these laws and gratifications, they decreed that Caesar should have the government of Illyricum, and all Gaul, with an army of four legions, for the space of five years, though Cato still cried out they were, by their own vote, placing a tyrant in their citadel. Publius Clodius, who illegally of a patrician became a plebeian, was declared tribune of the people, as he had promised to do all things according to their pleasure, on condition he might banish Cicero. And for consuls, they set up Calpurnius Piso, the father of Caesar's wife, and Aulus Gabinius, one of Pompey's creatures, as they tell us, who best knew his life and manners.

Yet when they had thus firmly established all things, having mastered one part of the city by favor, and the other by fear, they themselves were still afraid of Cato, and remembered with vexation what pains and trouble their success over him had cost them, and indeed what shame and disgrace, when at last they were driven to use violence to him. This made Clodius despair of driving Cicero out of Italy while Cato stayed at home. Therefore, having first laid his design, as soon as he came into his office, he sent for Cato, and told him, that he looked upon him as the most incorrupt of all the Romans, and was ready to show he did so. "For whereas," said he, "many have applied to be sent to Cyprus on the commission in the case of Ptolemy, and have solicited to have the appointment, I think you alone are deserving of it, and I desire to give you the favor of the appointment." Cato at once cried out, it was a mere design upon him, and no favor, but an injury. Then Clodius proudly and fiercely answered, "If you will not take it as a kindness, you shall go, though never so unwillingly;" and immediately going into the assembly of the people, he made them pass a decree, that Cato should be sent to Cyprus. But they ordered him neither ship, nor soldier, nor any attendant, except two secretaries; one of whom was a thief and a rascal, and the other a retainer to Clodius. Besides, as if Cyprus and Ptolemy were not work sufficient, he was ordered also to restore the refugees of Byzantium. For Clodius was resolved to keep him far enough off, whilst himself continued tribune.

Cato being in this necessity of going away, advised Cicero, who was next to be set upon, to make no resistance, lest he should throw the state into civil war and confusion, but to give way to the times, and thus become once more the preserver of his country. He himself sent forward Canidius, one of his friends, to Cyprus, to persuade Ptolemy to yield, without being forced; which if he did, he should want neither riches nor honor, for the Romans would give him the priesthood of the goddess at Paphos. He himself stayed at Rhodes, making some preparations, and expecting an answer from Cyprus. In the meantime, Ptolemy, king of Egypt, who had left Alexandria, upon some quarrel between him and his subjects, and was sailing for Rome, in hopes that Pompey and Caesar would send troops to restore him, in his way thither desired to see Cato, to whom he sent, supposing he would come to him. Cato had taken purging medicine at the time when the messenger came, and made answer, that Ptolemy had better come to him, if he thought fit. And when he came, he neither went forward to meet him, nor so much as rose up to him, but saluting him as an ordinary person, bade him sit down. This at once threw Ptolemy into some confusion, who was surprised to see such stern and haughty manners in one who made so plain and unpretending an appearance; but afterwards, when he began to talk about his affairs, he was no less astonished at the wisdom and freedom of his discourse. For Cato blamed his conduct, and pointed out to him what honor and happiness he was abandoning, and what humiliations and troubles he would run himself into; what bribery he must resort to and what cupidity he would have to satisfy, when he came to the leading men at Rome, whom all Egypt turned into silver would scarcely content. He therefore advised him to return home, and be reconciled to his subjects, offering to go along with him, and assist him in composing the differences. And by this language Ptolemy being brought to himself, as it might be out of a fit of madness or delirium and discerning the truth and wisdom of what Cato said, resolved to follow his advice; but he was again over-persuaded by his friends to the contrary, and so, according to his first design, went to Rome. When he came there, and was forced to wait at the gate of one of the magistrates, he began to lament his folly, in having rejected, rather, as it seemed to him, the oracle of a god, than the advice merely of a good and wise man.

In the meantime, the other Ptolemy, in Cyprus, very luckily for Cato, poisoned himself. It was reported he had left great riches; therefore Cato designing to go first to Byzantium, sent his nephew Brutus to Cyprus, as he would not wholly trust Canidius. Then, having reconciled the refugees and the people of Byzantium, he left the city in peace and quietness; and so sailed to Cyprus, where he found a royal treasure of plate, tables, precious stones and purple, all which was to be turned into ready money. And being determined to do everything with the greatest exactness, and to raise the price of everything to the utmost, to this end he was always present at selling the things, and went carefully into all the accounts. Nor would he trust to the usual customs of the market, but looked doubtfully upon all alike, the officers, criers, purchasers, and even his own friends; and so in fine he himself talked with the buyers, and urged them to bid high, and conducted in this manner the greatest part of the sales.

This mistrustfulness offended others of his friends, and, in particular, Munatius, the most intimate of them all, became almost irreconcilable. And this afforded Caesar the subject of his severest censures in the book he wrote against Cato. Yet Munatius himself relates, that the quarrel was not so much occasioned by Cato's mistrust, as by his neglect of him, and by his own jealousy of Canidius. For Munatius also wrote a book concerning Cato, which is the chief authority followed by Thrasea. Munatius says, that coming to Cyprus after the other, and having a very poor lodging provided for him, he went to Cato's house, but was not admitted, because he was engaged in private with Canidius; of which he afterwards complained in very gentle terms to Cato, but received a very harsh answer, that too much love, according to Theophrastus, often causes hatred; "and you," he said, "because you bear me much love, think you receive too little honor, and presently grow angry. I employ Canidius on account of his industry and his fidelity; he has been with me from the first, and I have found him to be trusted." These things were said in private between them two; but Cato afterwards told Canidius what had passed; on being informed of which, Munatius would no more go to sup with him, and when he was invited to give his counsel, refused to come. Then Cato threatened to seize his goods, as was the custom in the case of those who were

PARALLEL LIVES

disobedient; but Munatius not regarding his threats, returned to Rome, and continued a long time thus discontented. But afterwards, when Cato was come back also, Marcia, who as yet lived with him, contrived to have them both invited to sup together at the house of one Barca; Cato came in last of all, when the rest were laid down, and asked, where he should be. Barca answered him, where he pleased; then looking about, he said, he would be near Munatius, and went and placed himself next to him; yet he showed him no other mark of kindness, all the time they were at table together. But another time, at the entreaty of Marcia, Cato wrote to Munatius, that he desired to speak with him. Munatius went to his house in the morning, and was kept by Marcia till all the company was gone; then Cato came, threw both his arms about him, and embraced him very kindly, and they were reconciled. I have the more fully related this passage, for that I think the manners and tempers of men are more clearly discovered by things of this nature, than by great and conspicuous actions.

Cato got together little less than seven thousand talents of silver; but apprehensive of what might happen in so long a voyage by sea, he provided a great many coffers, that held two talents and five hundred drachmas apiece; to each of these he fastened a long rope, and to the other end of the rope a piece of cork, so that if the ship should miscarry, it might be discovered thereabout the chests lay under water. Thus all the money, except a very little, was safely transported. But he had made two books, in which all the accounts of his commission were carefully written out, and neither of these was preserved. For his freedman Philargyrus, who had the charge of one of them, setting sail from Cenchreae was lost, together with the ship and all her freight. And the other Cato himself kept safe, till he came to Corcyra, but there he set up his tent in the market-place, and the sailors being very cold in the night, made a great many fires, some of which caught the tents, so that they were burnt, and the book lost. And though he had brought with him several of Ptolemy's stewards, who could testify to his integrity, and stop the mouths of enemies and false accusers, yet the loss annoyed him, and he was vexed with himself about the matter, as he had designed them not so much for a proof of his own fidelity, as for a pattern of exactness to others.

The news did not fail to reach Rome, that he was coming up the river. All the magistrates, the priests, and the whole senate, with great part of the people, went out to meet him; both the banks of the Tiber were covered with people; so that his entrance was in solemnity and honor not inferior to a triumph. But it was thought somewhat strange, and looked like willfulness and pride, that when the consuls and praetors appeared, he did not disembark, nor stay to salute them, but rowed up the stream in a royal galley of six banks of oars, and stopped not till he brought his vessels to the dock. However, when the money was carried through the streets, the people much wondered at the vast quantity of it, and the senate being assembled, decreed him in honorable terms an extraordinary praetorship, and also the privilege of appearing at the public spectacles in a robe faced with purple. Cato declined all these honors, but declaring what diligence and fidelity he had found in Nicias, the steward of Ptolemy, he requested the senate to give him his freedom.

Philippus, the father of Marcia, was that year consul, and the authority and power of the office rested in a manner in Cato; for the other consul paid him no less regard for his virtue's sake, than Philippus did on account of the connection between them. And Cicero now being returned from his banishment, into which he was driven by Clodius, and having again obtained great credit among the people, went, in the absence of Clodius, and by force took away the records of his tribuneship, which had been laid up in the capitol. Hereupon the senate was assembled, and Clodius complained of Cicero, who answered, that Clodius was never legally tribune, and therefore whatever he had done, was void, and of no authority. But Cato interrupted him while he spoke, and at last standing up said, that indeed he in no way justified or approved of Clodius's proceedings; but if they questioned the validity of what had been done in his tribuneship, they might also question what himself had done at Cyprus, for the expedition was unlawful, if he that sent him had no lawful authority: for himself, he thought Clodius wee legally made tribune, who, by permission of the law, was from a patrician adopted into a plebeian family; if he had done ill in his office, he ought to be called to account for it; but the authority of the magistracy ought not to suffer for the faults of the magistrate. Cicero took this ill, and for a long time discontinued his friendship with Cato; but they were afterwards reconciled.

Pompey and Crassus, by agreement with Caesar, who crossed the Alps to see them, had formed a design, that they two should stand to be chosen consuls a second time, and when they should be in their office, they would continue to Caesar his government for five years more, and take to themselves the greatest provinces, with armies and money to maintain them. This seemed a plain conspiracy to subvert the constitution and parcel out the empire. Several men of high character had intended to stand to be consuls that year, but upon the appearance of these great competitors, they all desisted, except only Lucius Domitius, who had married Porcia, the sister of Cato, and was by him persuaded to stand it out, and not abandon such an undertaking, which, he said, was not merely to gain the consulship, but to save the liberty of Rome. In the meantime, it was the common topic among the more prudent part of the citizens, that they ought not to suffer the power of Pompey and Crassus to be united, which would then be carried beyond all bounds, and become dangerous to the state; that therefore one of them must be denied. For these reasons they took part with Domitius, whom they exhorted and encouraged to go on, assuring him, that many who feared openly to appear for him, would privately assist him. Pompey's party fearing this, laid wait for Domitius, and set upon him as he was going before daylight, with torches, into the Field. First he that bore the light next before Domitius, was knocked down and killed; then several others being wounded, all the rest fled, except Cato and Domitius, whom Cato held, though himself were wounded in the arm, and crying out, conjured the others to stay, and not while they had any breath, forsake the defense of their liberty against those tyrants, who plainly showed with what moderation they were likely to use the power, which they endeavored to gain by such violence. But at length Domitius also, no longer willing to face the danger, fled to his own house, and so Pompey and Crassus were declared consuls.

Nevertheless, Cato would not give over, but resolved to stand himself to be praetor that year, which he thought would be some help to him in his design of opposing them; that he might not act as a private man, when he was to contend with public magistrates. Pompey and Crassus apprehended this; and fearing that the office of praetor in the person of Cato might be equal in authority to that of consul, they assembled the senate unexpectedly, without giving any notice to a great many of the senators, and made an order, that those who were chosen praetors, should immediately enter upon their office, without attending the usual time, in which, according to law, they might be accused, if they had corrupted the people with gifts. When by this order they had got leave to bribe freely, without being called to account, they set up their own friends and dependents to stand for the praetorship, giving money, and watching the people as they voted. Yet the virtue and reputation of Cato was like to triumph over all these stratagems; for the people generally felt it to be shameful that a price should be paid for the rejection of Cato, who ought rather to be paid himself to take upon him the office. So he carried it by the voices of the first tribe. Hereupon Pompey immediately framed a lie, crying out, it thundered; and straight broke up the assembly; for the Romans religiously observed this as a bad omen, and never concluded any matter after it had thundered. Before the next time, they had distributed larger bribes, and driving also the best men out of the Field, by these foul means they procured Vatinius to be chosen praetor, instead of Cato. It is said, that those who had thus corruptly and dishonestly given their voices, at once, when it was done, hurried, as if it were in flight, out of the Field. The others staying together, and exclaiming at the event, one of the tribunes continued the assembly, and Cato standing up, as it were by inspiration, foretold all the miseries that afterward befell the state, exhorted them to beware of Pompey and Crassus, who were guilty of such things, and had laid such designs, that they might well fear to have Cato praetor. When he had ended this speech, he was followed to his house by a greater number of people than were all the new praetors elect put together.

Caius Trebonius now proposed the law for allotting provinces to the consuls, one of whom was to have Spain and Africa, the other Egypt and Syria, with full power of making war, and carrying it on both by sea and land, as they should think fit. When this was proposed, all others despaired of putting any stop to it, and neither did nor said anything against it. But Cato, before the voting began, went up into the place of speaking, and desiring to be heard, was with much difficulty allowed two hours to speak. Having spent that time in informing them and reasoning with them, and in foretelling to them much that was to come, he was not suffered to speak any longer; but as he was going on, a sergeant came and pulled him down; yet when he was down, he still continued speaking in a loud voice, and finding many to listen to him, and join in his indignation. Then the sergeant took him, and forced him out of the forum; but as soon as he got loose, he returned again to the place of speaking, crying out to the people to stand by him. When he had done thus several times, Trebonius grew very angry, and commanded him to be carried to prison; but the multitude followed him, and listened to the speech which he made to them, as he went along, so that Trebonius began to be afraid again, and ordered him to be released. Thus that day was expended, and the business staved off by Cato. But in the days succeeding, many of the citizens being overawed by fears and threats, and others won by gifts and favors, Aquillius, one of the tribunes, they kept by an armed force within the senate-house; Cato, who cried, it thundered, they drove out of the forum; many were wounded, and some slain; and at length by open force they passed the law. At this many were so incensed, that they got together, and were going to throw down the statues of Pompey; but Cato went, and diverted them from that design.

Again, another law was proposed, concerning the provinces and legions for Caesar. Upon this occasion Cato did not apply himself to the people, but appealed to Pompey himself; and told him, he did not consider now, that he was setting Caesar upon his own shoulders, who would shortly grow too weighty for him, and at length, not able to lay down the burden, nor yet to bear it any longer, he would precipitate both it and himself with it upon the commonwealth; and then he would remember Cato's advice, which was no less advantageous to him, than just and honest in itself. Thus was Pompey often warned, but still disregarded and slighted it, never mistrusting Caesar's change, and always confiding in his own power and good fortune.

Cato was made praetor the following year; but, it seems, he did not do more honor and credit to the office by his signal integrity, than he disgraced and diminished it by his strange behavior. For he would often come to the court without his shoes, and sit upon the bench without any under garment, and in this attire would give judgment in capital causes, and upon persons of the highest rank. It is said, also, he used to drink wine after his morning meal, and then transact the business of his office; but this was wrongfully reported of him. The people were at that time extremely corrupted by the gifts of those who sought offices, and most made a constant trade of selling their voices. Cato was eager utterly to root this corruption out of the commonwealth; he therefore persuaded the senate to make an order, that those who were chosen into any office, though nobody should accuse them, should be obliged to come into the court, and give account upon oath of their proceedings in their election. This was extremely obnoxious to those who stood for the offices, and yet more to those vast numbers who took the bribes. Insomuch that one morning, as Cato was going to the tribunal, a great multitude of people flocked together, and with loud cries and maledictions reviled him, and threw stones at him. Those that were about the tribunal presently fled, and Cato himself being forced thence, and jostled about in the throng, very narrowly escaped the stones that were thrown at him, and with much difficulty got hold of the Rostra, where, standing up with a bold and undaunted countenance, he at once mastered the tumult, and silenced the clamor; and addressing them in fit terms for the occasion, was heard with great attention, and perfectly quelled the sedition. Afterwards, on the senate commending him for this, "But I," said he, "do not commend you for abandoning your praetor in danger, and bringing him no assistance."

In the meantime, the candidates were in great perplexity; for every one dreaded to give money himself, and yet feared lest his competitors should. At length they agreed to lay down one hundred and twenty-five thousand drachmas apiece, and then all of them to canvass fairly and honestly, on condition, that if any one was found to make use of bribery, he should forfeit the money. Being thus agreed, they chose Cato to keep the stakes, and arbitrate the matter; to him they brought the sum concluded on, and before him subscribed the agreement. The money he did not choose to have paid for them, but took their securities who stood bound for them. Upon the day of election, he placed himself by the tribune who took the votes, and very watchfully observing all that passed, he discovered one who had broken the agreement, and immediately ordered him to pay his money to the rest. They, however, commending his justice highly, remitted the penalty, as thinking the discovery a sufficient punishment. It raised, however, as much envy against Cato as it gained him reputation, and many were offended at his thus taking upon himself the whole authority of the senate, the courts of judicature, and the magistracies. For there is no virtue, the honor and credit for which procures a man more odium than that of justice; and this, because more than any other, it acquires a man power and authority among the common people. For they only honor the valiant and admire the wise, while in addition they also love just men, and put entire trust and confidence in them. They fear the bold man, and mistrust the clever man, and moreover think them rather beholding; to their natural complexion, than to any goodness of their will, for these excellences; they look upon valor as a certain natural strength of the mind, and wisdom as a constitutional acuteness; whereas a man has it in his power to be just, if he have but the will to be so, and therefore injustice is thought the most dishonorable, because it is least excusable.

Cato upon this account was opposed by all the great men, who thought themselves reproved by his virtue. Pompey especially looked upon the increase of Cato's credit, as the ruin of his own power, and therefore continually set up men to rail against him. Among these was the seditious Clodius, now again united to Pompey; who declared openly, that Cato had conveyed away a great deal of the treasure that was found in Cyprus; and that he hated Pompey, only because he refused to marry his daughter. Cato answered, that although they had allowed him neither horse nor man, he had brought more treasure from Cyprus alone, than Pompey had, after so many wars and triumphs, from the ransacked world; that he never sought the alliance of Pompey; not that he thought him unworthy of being related to him, but because he differed so much from him, in things that concerned the commonwealth. "For," said he, "I laid down the province that was given me, when I went out of my praetorship; Pompey, on the contrary, retains many provinces for himself; and he bestows many on others; and but now he sent Caesar a force of six thousand men into Gaul, which Caesar never asked the people for, nor had Pompey obtained their consent to give. Men, and horse, and arms in any number, are become the mutual gifts of private men to one another; and Pompey keeping the titles of commander and general, hands over the armies and provinces to others to govern, while he himself stays at home to preside at the contests of the canvass, and to stir up tumults at elections; out of the anarchy he thus creates amongst us, seeking, we see well enough, a monarchy for himself." Thus he retorted on Pompey.

He had an intimate friend and admirer of the name of Marcus Favonius, much the same to Cato as we are told Apollodorus, the Phalerian, was in old time to Socrates, whose words used to throw him into perfect transports and ecstasies, getting into his head, like strong wine, and intoxicating him to a sort of frenzy. This Favonius stood to be chosen aedile, and was like to lose it; but Cato, who was there to assist him, observed that all the votes were written in one hand, and discovering the cheat, appealed to the tribunes, who stopped the election. Favonius was afterward chosen aedile, and Cato, who assisted him in all things that belonged to his office, also undertook the care of the spectacles that were exhibited in the theater; giving the actors crowns, not of gold, but of wild olive, such as used to be given at the Olympic games; and instead of the magnificent presents that were usually made, he offered to the Greeks beet root, lettuces, radishes, and pears; and to the Romans, earthen pots of wine, pork, figs, cucumbers, and little fagots of wood. Some ridiculed Cato for his economy, others looked with respect on this gentle relaxation of his usual rigor and austerity. In fine, Favonius himself mingled with the crowd, and sitting among the spectators, clapped and applauded Cato, bade him bestow rewards on those who did well, and called on the people to pay their honors to him, as for himself he had placed his whole authority in Cato's hands. At the same time, Curio, the colleague of Favonius, gave very magnificent entertainments in another theater; but the people left his, and went to those of Favonius, which they much applauded, and joined heartily in the diversion, seeing him act the private man, and Cato the master of the shows, who, in fact, did all this in derision of the great expenses that others incurred, and to teach them that in amusements men ought to seek amusement only, and the display of a decent cheerfulness, not great preparations and costly magnificence, demanding the expenditure of endless care and trouble about things of little concern.

After this Scipio, Hypsaeus, and Milo, stood to be consuls, and that not only with the usual and now recognized disorders of bribery and corruption, but with arms and slaughter, and every appearance of carrying their audacity and desperation to the length of actual civil war. Whereupon it was proposed, that Pompey might be empowered to preside over that election. This Cato at first opposed, saying that the laws ought not to seek protection from Pompey, but Pompey from the laws. Yet the confusion lasting a long time, the forum continually, as it were, besieged with three armies, and no possibility appearing of a stop being put to these disorders, Cato at length agreed, that rather than fall into the last extremity, the senate should freely confer all on Pompey, since it was necessary to make use of a lesser illegality as a remedy against the greatest of all, and better to set up a monarchy themselves, than to suffer a sedition to continue, that must certainly end in one. Bibulus, therefore, a friend of Cato's, moved the senate to create Pompey sole consul; for that either he would reestablish the lawful government, or they should serve under the best master. Cato stood up, and, contrary to all expectation, seconded this motion, concluding, that any government was better than mere confusion, and that he did not question but Pompey would deal honorably, and take care of the commonwealth, thus committed to his charge. Pompey being hereupon declared consul, invited Cato to see him in the suburbs. When he came, he saluted and embraced him very kindly, acknowledged the favor he had done him, and desired his counsel and assistance, in the management of this office. Cato made answer, that what he had spoken on any former occasion was not out of hate to Pompey, nor what he had now done, out of love to him, but all for the good of the commonwealth; that in private, if he asked him, he would freely give his advice; and in public, though he asked him not, he would always speak his opinion. And he did accordingly. For first, when Pompey made severe laws for punishing and laying great fines on those who had corrupted the people with gifts, Cato advised him to let alone what was already passed, and to provide for the future; for if he should look up past misdemeanors, it would be difficult to know where to stop; and if he would ordain new penalties, it would be unreasonable to punish men by a law, which at that time they had not the opportunity of breaking. Afterwards, when many considerable men, and some of Pompey's own relations were accused, and he grew remiss, and disinclined to the prosecution, Cato sharply reproved him, and urged him to proceed. Pompey had made a law, also, to forbid the custom of making commendatory orations in behalf of those that were accused; yet he himself wrote one for Munatius Plancus, and sent it while the cause was pleading; upon which Cato, who was sitting as one of the judges, stopped his ears with his hands, and would not hear it read. Whereupon Plancus, before sentence was given, excepted against him, but was condemned notwithstanding. And indeed Cato was a great trouble and perplexity to almost all that were accused of anything, as they feared to have him one of their judges, yet did not dare to demand his exclusion. And many had been condemned, because by refusing him, they seemed to show that they could not trust their own innocence; and it was a reproach thrown in the teeth of some by their enemies, that they had not accepted Cato for their judge.

In the meanwhile, Caesar kept close with his forces in Gaul, and continued in arms; and at the same time employed his gifts, his riches, and his friends above all things, to increase his power in the city. And now Cato's old admonitions began to rouse Pompey out of the negligent security in which he lay, into a sort of imagination of danger at hand; but seeing him slow and unwilling, and timorous to undertake any measures of prevention against Caesar, Cato resolved himself to stand for the consulship, and presently force Caesar either to lay down his arms or discover his intentions. Both Cato's competitors were persons of good position; Sulpicius, who was one, owed much to Cato's credit and authority in the city, and it was thought unhandsome and ungratefully done, to stand against him; not that Cato himself took it ill, "For it is no wonder," said he, "if a man will not yield to another, in that which he esteems the greatest good." He had persuaded the senate to make an order, that those who stood for offices, should themselves ask the people for their votes, and not solicit by others, nor take others about with them, to speak for them, in their canvass. And this made the common people very hostile to him, if they were to lose not only the means of receiving money, but also the opportunity of obliging several persons, and so to become by his means both poor and less regarded. Besides this, Cato himself was by nature altogether unfit for the business of canvassing, as he was more anxious to sustain the dignity of his life and character, than to obtain the office. Thus by following his own way of soliciting, and not suffering his friends to do those things which take with the multitude, he was rejected, and lost the consulship.

But whereas, upon such occasions, not only those who missed the office, but even their friends and relations, used to feel themselves disgraced and humiliated, and observed a sort of mourning for several days after, Cato took it so unconcernedly, that he anointed himself, and played at ball in the Field, and after breakfasting, went into the forum, as he used to do, without his shoes or his tunic, and there walked about with his acquaintance. Cicero blames him, for that when affairs required such a consul, he would not take more pains, nor condescend to pay some court to the people, as also because that he afterwards neglected to try again; whereas he had stood a second time to be chosen praetor. Cato answered, that he lost the praetorship the first time, not by the voice of the people, but by the violence and corrupt dealing of his adversaries; whereas in the election of consuls, there had been no foul play. So that he plainly saw the people did not like his manners, which an honest man ought not to alter for their sake; nor yet would a wise man attempt the same thing again, while liable to the same prejudices.

Caesar was at this time engaged with many warlike nations, and was subduing them at great hazards. Among the rest, it was believed he had set upon the Germans, in a time of truce, and had thus slain three hundred thousand of them. Upon which, some of his friends moved the senate for a public thanksgiving; but Cato declared, they ought to deliver Caesar into the hands of those who had been thus unjustly treated, and so expiate the offense and not bring a curse upon the city; "Yet we have reason," said he, "to thank the gods, for that they spared the commonwealth, and did not take vengeance upon the army, for the madness and folly of the general." Hereupon Caesar wrote a letter to the senate, which was read openly, and was full of reproachful language and accusations against Cato; who, standing up, seemed not at all concerned, and without any heat or passion, but in a calm and, as it were, premeditated discourse, made all Caesar's charges against him show like mere common scolding and abuse, and in fact a sort of pleasantry and play on Caesar's part; and proceeding then to go into all Caesar's political courses, and to explain and reveal (as though he had been not his constant opponent, but his fellow-conspirator,) his whole conduct and purpose from its commencement, he concluded by telling the senate, it was not the sons of the Britons or the Gauls they need fear, but Caesar himself, if they were wise. And this discourse so moved and awakened the senate, that Caesar's friends repented they had had a letter read, which had given Cato an opportunity of saying so many reasonable things, and such severe truths against him. However, nothing was then decided upon; it was merely said, that it would be well to send him a successor. Upon that Caesar's friends required, that Pompey also should lay down his arms, and resign his provinces, or else that Caesar might not be obliged to either. Then Cato cried out, what he had foretold was come to pass; now it was manifest he was using his forces to compel their judgment, and was turning against the state those armies he had got from it by imposture and trickery. But out of the Senate-house Cato could do but little, as the people were ever ready to magnify Caesar and the senate, though convinced by Cato, were afraid of the people.

But when the news was brought that Caesar had seized Ariminum, and was marching with his army toward Rome, then all men, even Pompey, and the common people too, cast their eyes on Cato, who had alone foreseen and first clearly declared Caesar's intentions. He, therefore, told them, "If you had believed me, or regarded my advice, you would not now have been reduced to stand in fear of one man, or to put all your hopes in one alone." Pompey acknowledged, that Cato indeed had spoken most like a prophet, while he himself had acted too much like a friend. And Cato advised the senate to put all into the hands of Pompey; "For those who can raise up great evils," said he, "can best allay them."

Pompey, finding he had not sufficient forces, and that those he could raise, were not very resolute, forsook the city. Cato, resolving to follow Pompey into exile, sent his younger son to Munatius, who was then in the country of Bruttium, and took his eldest with him; but wanting somebody to keep his house and take care of his daughters, he took Marcia again, who was now a rich widow, Hortensius being dead, and having left her all his estate. Caesar afterward made use of this action also, to reproach him with covetousness, and a mercenary design in his marriage. "For," said he, "if he had need of wife, why did he part with her? And if he had not, why did he take her again? Unless he gave her only as a bait to Hortensius; and lent her when she was young, to have her again when she was rich." But in answer to this, we might fairly apply the saying of Euripides.

> *To speak of mysteries — the chief of these*
> *Surely were cowardice in Hercules.*

For it is much the same thing to reproach Hercules for cowardice, and to accuse Cato of covetousness; though otherwise, whether he did altogether right in this marriage, might be disputed. As soon, however, as he had again taken Marcia, he committed his house and his daughters to her, and himself followed Pompey. And it is said, that from that day he never cut his hair, nor shaved his beard, nor wore a garland, but was always full of sadness, grief, and dejectedness for the calamities of his country, and continually showed the same feeling to the last, whatever party had misfortune or success.

The government of Sicily being allotted to him, he passed over to Syracuse; where understanding that Asinius Pollio was arrived at Messena, with forces from the enemy, Cato sent to him, to know the reason of his coming thither: Pollio, on the other side, called upon him to show reason for the present convulsions. And being at the same time informed how Pompey had quite abandoned Italy, and lay encamped at Dyrrhachium, he spoke of the strangeness and incomprehensibility of the divine government of things; "Pompey, when he did nothing wisely nor honestly, was always successful; and now that he would preserve his country, and defend her liberty, he is altogether unfortunate." As for Asinius, he said, he could drive him out of Sicily, but as there were larger forces coming to his assistance, he would not engage the island in a war. He therefore advised the Syracusans to join the conquering party and provide for their own safety; and so set sail from thence.

When he came to Pompey, he uniformly gave advice to protract the war; as he always hoped to compose matters, and was by no means desirous that they should come to action; for the commonwealth would suffer extremely, and be the certain cause of its own ruin, whoever were conqueror by the sword. In like manner, he persuaded Pompey and the council to ordain, that no city should be sacked that was subject to the people of Rome; and that no Roman should be killed, but in the heat of battle; and hereby he got himself great honor, and brought over many to Pompey's party, whom his moderation and humanity attracted. Afterwards being sent into Asia, to assist those who were raising men, and preparing ships in those parts, he took with him his sister Servilia, and a little boy whom she had by Lucullus. For since her widowhood, she had lived with her brother, and much recovered her reputation, having put herself under his care, followed him in his voyages, and complied with his severe way of living. Yet Caesar did not fail to asperse him upon her account also.

Pompey's officers in Asia, it seems, had no great need of Cato; but he brought over the people of Rhodes by his persuasions, and leaving his sister Servilia and her child there, he returned to Pompey, who had now collected very great forces both by sea and land. And here Pompey, more than in any other act, betrayed his intentions. For at first he designed to give Cato the command of the navy, which consisted of no less than five hundred ships of war, besides a vast number of light galleys, scouts, and open boats. But presently bethinking himself, or put in mind by his friends, that Cato's principal and only aim being to free his country from all usurpation, if he were master of such great forces, as soon as ever Caesar should be conquered, he would certainly call upon Pompey, also, to lay down his arms, and be subject to the laws, he changed his mind, and though he had already mentioned it to Cato, nevertheless made Bibulus admiral. Notwithstanding this, he had no reason to suppose that Cato's zeal in the cause was in any way diminished. For before one of the battles at Dyrrhachium, when Pompey himself, we are told, made an address to the soldiers and bade the officers do the like, the men listened to them but coldly, and with silence, until Cato, last of all, came forward, and in the language of philosophy, spoke to them, as the occasion required, concerning liberty, manly virtue, death, and a good name; upon all which he delivered himself with strong natural passion, and concluded with calling in the aid of the gods, to whom he directed his speech, as if they were present to behold them fight for their country. And at this the army gave such a shout and showed such excitement, that their officers led them on full of hope and confidence to the danger. Caesar's party were routed, and put to flight; but his presiding fortune used the advantage of Pompey's cautiousness and diffidence, to render the victory incomplete. But of this we have spoken in the life of Pompey. While, however, all the rest rejoiced, and magnified their success, Cato alone bewailed his country, and cursed that fatal ambition, which made so many brave Romans murder one another.

After this, Pompey following Caesar into Thessaly, left at Dyrrhachium a quantity of munitions, money, and stores, and many of his domestics and relations; the charge of all which he gave to Cato, with the command only of fifteen cohorts. For though he trusted him much, yet he was afraid of him too, knowing full well, that if he had bad success, Cato would be the last to forsake him, but if he conquered, would never let him use his victory at his pleasure. There were, likewise, many persons of high rank that stayed with Cato at Dyrrhachium. When they heard of the overthrow at Pharsalia, Cato resolved with himself, that if Pompey were slain, he would conduct those that were with him into Italy, and then retire as far from the tyranny of Caesar as he could, and live in exile; but if Pompey were safe, he would keep the army together for him. With this resolution he passed over to Corcyra, where the navy lay, there he would have resigned his command to Cicero, because he had been consul, and himself only a praetor: but Cicero refused it, and was going for Italy. At which Pompey's son being incensed, would rashly and in heat have punished all those who were going away, and in the first place have laid hands on Cicero; but Cato spoke with him in private, and diverted him from that design. And thus he clearly saved the life of Cicero, and rescued several others also from ill-treatment.

Conjecturing that Pompey the Great was fled toward Egypt or Africa, Cato resolved to hasten after him; and having taken all his men aboard, he set sail; but first to those who were not zealous to continue the contest, he gave free liberty to depart. When they came to the coast of Africa, they met with Sextus, Pompey's younger son, who told them of the death of his father in Egypt; at which they were all exceedingly grieved, and declared that after Pompey they would follow no other leader but Cato. Out of compassion therefore to so many worthy persons, who had given such testimonies of their fidelity, and whom he could not for shame leave in a desert country, amidst so many difficulties, he took upon him the command, and marched toward the city of Cyrene, which presently received him, though not long before they had shut their gates against Labienus. Here he was informed that Scipio, Pompey's father-in-law, was received by king Juba, and that Attius Varus, whom Pompey had made governor of Africa, had joined them with his forces. Cato therefore resolved to march toward them by land, it being now winter; and got together a number of asses to carry water, and furnished himself likewise with plenty of all other provision, and a number of carriages. He took also with him some of those they call Psylli, who cure the biting of serpents, by sucking out the poison with their mouths, and have likewise certain charms, by which they stupefy and lay asleep the serpents.

Thus they marched seven days together, Cato all the time going on foot at the head of his men, and never making use of any horse or chariot. Ever since the battle of Pharsalia, he used to sit at table, and added this to his other ways of mourning, that he never lay down but to sleep.

Having passed the winter in Africa, Cato drew out his army, which amounted to little less than ten thousand. The affairs of Scipio and Varus went very ill, by reason of their dissensions and quarrels among themselves, and their submissions and flatteries to king Juba, who was insupportable for his vanity, and the pride he took in his strength and riches. The first time he came to a conference with Cato, he had ordered his own seat to be placed in the middle, between Scipio and Cato; which Cato observing, took up his chair, and set himself on the other side of Scipio, to whom he thus gave the honor of sitting in the middle, though he were his enemy, and had formerly published some scandalous writing against him. There are people who speak as if this were quite an insignificant matter, and who nevertheless find fault with Cato, because in Sicily, walking one day with Philostratus, he gave him the middle place, to show his respect for philosophy. However, he now succeeded both in humbling the pride of Juba, who was treating Scipio and Varus much like a pair of satraps under his orders, and also in reconciling them to each other. All the troops desired him to be their leader; Scipio, likewise, and Varus gave way to it, and offered him the command; but he said, he would not break those laws, which he sought to defend, and he, being, but propraetor, ought not to command in the presence of a proconsul, (for Scipio had been created proconsul,) besides that people took it as a good omen; to see a Scipio command in Africa, and the very name inspired the soldiers with hopes of success.

Scipio, having taken upon him the command, presently resolved, at the instigation of Juba, to put all the inhabitants of Utica to the sword, and to raze the city, for having, as they professed, taken part with Caesar. Cato would by no means suffer this; but invoking the gods, exclaiming and protesting against it in the council of war, he with much difficulty delivered the poor people from this cruelty. And afterwards, upon the entreaty of the inhabitants, and at the instance of Scipio, Cato took upon himself the government of Utica, lest, one way or other, it should fall into Caesar's hands; for it was a strong place, and very advantageous for either party. And it was yet better provided and more strongly fortified by Cato, who brought in great store of corn, repaired the walls, erected towers, and made deep trenches and palisades around the town. The young men of Utica he lodged among these works, having first taken their arms from them; the rest of the inhabitants he kept within the town, and took the greatest care, that no injury should be done nor affront offered them by the Romans. From hence he sent great quantity of arms, money, and provision to the camp, and made this city their chief magazine.

He advised Scipio, as he had before done Pompey, by no means to hazard a battle against a man experienced in war, and formidable in the field, but to use delay; for time would gradually abate the violence of the crisis, which is the strength of usurpation. But Scipio out of pride rejected this counsel, and wrote a letter to Cato, in which he reproached him with cowardice; and that he could not be content to lie secure himself within walls and trenches, but he must hinder others from boldly using their own good-sense to seize the right opportunity. In answer to this, Cato wrote word again, that he would take the horse and foot which he had brought into Africa, and go over into Italy, to make a diversion there, and draw Caesar off from them. But Scipio derided this proposition also. Then Cato openly let it be seen that he was sorry he had yielded the command to Scipio, who he saw would not carry on the war with any wisdom, and if, contrary to all appearance, he should succeed, he would use his success as unjustly at home. For Cato had then made up his mind, and so he told his friends, that he could have but slender hopes in those generals that had so much boldness, and so little conduct; yet if anything should happen beyond expectation, and Caesar should be overthrown, for his part he would not stay at Rome, but would retire from the cruelty and inhumanity of Scipio, who had already uttered fierce and proud threats against many.

But what Cato had looked for, fell out sooner than he expected. Late in the evening came one from the army, whence he had been three days coming, who brought word there had been a great battle near Thapsus; that all was utterly lost; Caesar had taken the camps, Scipio and Juba were fled with a few only, and all the rest of the army was lost. This news arriving in time of war, and in the night, so alarmed the people, that they were almost out of their wits, and could scarce keep themselves within the walls of the city. But Cato came forward, and meeting the people in this hurry and clamor, did all he could to comfort and encourage them, and somewhat appeased the fear and amazement they were in, telling them that very likely things were not so bad in truth, but much exaggerated in the report. And so he pacified the tumult for the present. The next morning, he sent for the three hundred, whom he used as his council; these were Romans, who were in Africa upon business, in commerce and money-lending; there were also several senators and their sons. They were summoned to meet in the temple of Jupiter. While they were coming together, Cato walked about very quietly and unconcerned, as if nothing new had happened. He had a book in his hand, which he was reading; in this book was an account of what provision he had for war, armor, corn, ammunition and soldiers.

When they were assembled, he began his discourse; first, as regarded the three hundred themselves, and very much commended the courage and fidelity they had shown, and their having very well served their country with their persons, money, and counsel. Then he entreated them by no means to separate, as if each single man could hope for any safety in forsaking his companions; on the contrary, while they kept together, Caesar would have less reason to despise them, if they fought against him, and be more forward to pardon them, if they submitted to him. Therefore, he advised them to consult among themselves, nor should he find fault, whichever course they adopted. If they thought fit to submit to fortune, he would impute their change to necessity; but if they resolved to stand firm, and undertake the danger for the sake of liberty, he should not only commend, but admire their courage, and would himself be their leader and companion too, till they had put to the proof the utmost fortune of their country; which was not Utica or Adrumetum, but Rome, and she had often, by her own greatness, raised herself after worse disasters. Besides, as there were many things that would conduce to their safety, so chiefly this, that they were to fight against one whose affairs urgently claimed his presence in various quarters. Spain was already revolted to the younger Pompey; Rome was unaccustomed to the bridle, and impatient of it, and would therefore be ready to rise in insurrection upon any turn of affairs. As for themselves, they ought not to shrink from the danger; and in this might take example from their enemy, who so freely exposes his life to effect the most unrighteous designs, yet never can hope for so happy a conclusion, as they may promise themselves; for notwithstanding the uncertainty of war, they will be sure of a most happy life, if they succeed, or a most glorious death, if they miscarry. However, he said, they ought to deliberate among themselves, and he joined with them in praying the gods that in recompense of their former courage and goodwill, they would prosper their present determinations. When Cato had thus spoken, many were moved and encouraged by his arguments, but the greatest part were so animated by the sense of his intrepidity, generosity, and goodness, that they forgot the present danger, and as if he were the only invincible leader, and above all fortune, they entreated him to employ their persons, arms, and estates, as he thought fit; for they esteemed it far better to meet death in following his counsel, than to find their safety in betraying one of so great virtue. One of the assembly proposed the making a decree, to set the slaves at liberty; and most of the rest approved the motion. Cato said, that it ought not to be done, for it was neither just nor lawful; but if any of their masters would willingly set them free, those that were fit for service should be received. Many promised so to do; whose names he ordered to be enrolled, and then withdrew.

Presently after this, he received letters from Juba and Scipio. Juba, with some few of his men, was retired to a mountain, where he waited to hear what Cato would resolve upon; and intended to stay there for him, if he thought fit to leave Utica, or to come to his aid with his troops, if he were besieged. Scipio was on shipboard, near a certain promontory, not far from Utica, expecting an answer upon the same account. But Cato thought fit to retain the messengers, till the three hundred should come to some resolution,

As for the senators that were there, they showed great forwardness, and at once set free their slaves, and furnished them with arms. But the three hundred being men occupied in merchandise and money-lending, much of their substance also consisting in slaves, the enthusiasm that Cato's speech had raised in them, did not long continue. As there are substances that easily admit heat, and as suddenly lose it, when the fire is removed, so these men were heated and inflamed, while Cato was present; but when they began to reason among themselves, the fear they had of Caesar, soon overcame their reverence for Cato and for virtue. "For who are we," said they, "and who is it we refuse to obey? Is it not that Caesar, who is now invested with all the power of Rome? and which of us is a Scipio, a Pompey, or a Cato? But now that all men make their honor give way to their fear, shall we alone engage for the liberty of Rome, and in Utica declare war against him, before whom Cato and Pompey the Great fled out of Italy? Shall we set free our slaves against Caesar, who have ourselves no more liberty than he is pleased to allow? No, let us, poor creatures, know ourselves, submit to the victor, and send deputies to implore his mercy." Thus said the most moderate of them; but the greatest part were for seizing the senators, that by securing them, they might appease Caesar's anger. Cato, though he perceived the change, took no notice of it; but wrote to Juba and Scipio to keep away from Utica, because he mistrusted the three hundred.

A considerable body of horse, which had escaped from the late fight, riding up towards Utica, sent three men before to Cato, who yet did not all bring the same message; for one party was for going to Juba, another for joining with Cato, and some again were afraid to go into Utica. When Cato heard this, he ordered Marcus Rubrius to attend upon the three hundred, and quietly take the names of those who of their own accord set their slaves at liberty, but by no means to force anybody. Then, taking with him the senators, he went out of the town, and met the principal officers of these horsemen, whom he entreated not to abandon so many Roman senators, nor to prefer Juba for their commander before Cato, but consult the common safety, and to come into the city, which was impregnable, and well furnished with corn and other provision, sufficient for many years. The senators, likewise, with tears besought them to stay. Hereupon the officers went to consult their soldiers, and Cato with the senators sat down upon an embankment, expecting their resolution. In the meantime comes Rubrius in great disorder, crying out, the three hundred were all in commotion, and exciting revolt and tumult in the city. At this all the rest fell into despair, lamenting and bewailing their condition. Cato endeavored to comfort them, and sent to the three hundred, desiring them to have patience. Then the officers of the horse returned with no very reasonable demands. They said, they did not desire to serve Juba, for his pay, nor should they fear Caesar, while they followed Cato, but they dreaded to be shut up with the Uticans, men of traitorous temper, and Carthaginian blood; for though they were quiet at present, yet as soon as Caesar should appear, without doubt they would conspire together, and betray the Romans. Therefore, if he expected they should join with him, he must drive out of the town or destroy all the Uticans, that he might receive them into a place clear both of enemies and barbarians. This Cato thought utterly cruel and barbarous; but he mildly answered, he would consult the three hundred.

Then he returned to the city, where he found the men, not framing excuses, or dissembling out of reverence to him, but openly declaring that no one should compel them to make war against Caesar; which, they said, they were neither able nor willing to do. And some there were who muttered words about retaining the senators till Caesar's coming; but Cato seemed not to hear this, as indeed he had the excuse of being a little deaf. At the same time came one to him, and told him the horse were going away. And now, fearing lest the three hundred should take some desperate resolution concerning the senators, he presently went out with some of his friends, and seeing they were gone some way, he took horse, and rode after them. They, when they saw him coming, were very glad, and received him very kindly, entreating him to save himself with them. At this time, it is said, Cato shed tears, while entreating them on behalf of the senators, and stretching out his hands in supplication. He turned some of their horses' heads, and laid hold of the men by their armor, till in fine he prevailed with them, out of compassion, to stay only that one day, to procure a safe retreat for the senators. Having thus persuaded them to go along with him, some he placed at the gates of the town, and to others gave the charge of the citadel. The three hundred began to fear they should suffer for their inconstancy, and sent to Cato, entreating him by all means to come to them; but the senators flocking about him, would not suffer him to go, and said they would not trust their guardian and savior to the hands of perfidious traitors.

For there had never, perhaps, been a time when Cato's virtue appeared more manifestly; and every class of men in Utica could clearly see, with sorrow and admiration, how entirely free was everything that he was doing from any secret motives or any mixture of self-regard; he, namely, who had long before resolved on his own death, was taking such extreme pains, toil, and care, only for the sake of others, that when he had secured their lives, he might put an end to his own. For it was easily perceived, that he had determined to die, though he did not let it appear.

Therefore, having pacified the senators, he complied with the request of the three hundred, and went to them alone without any attendance. They gave him many thanks, and entreated him to employ and trust them for the future; and if they were not Catos, and could not aspire to his greatness of mind, they begged he would pity their weakness; and told him, they had determined to send to Caesar and entreat him, chiefly and in the first place, for Cato, and if they could not prevail for him, they would not accept of pardon for themselves, but as long as they had breath, would fight in his defense. Cato commended their good intentions, and advised them to send speedily, for their own safety, but by no means to ask anything in his behalf; for those who are conquered, entreat, and those who have done wrong, beg pardon; for himself, he did not confess to any defeat in all his life, but rather, so far as he had thought fit, he had got the victory, and had conquered Caesar in all points of justice and honesty. It was Caesar that ought to be looked upon as one surprised and vanquished; for he was now convicted and found guilty of those designs against his country, which he had so long practiced and so constantly denied. When he had thus spoken, he went out of the assembly, and being informed that Caesar was coming with his whole army, "Ah," said he, "he expects to find us brave men." Then he went to the senators, and urged them to make no delay, but hasten to be gone, while the horsemen were yet in the city. So ordering all the gates to be shut, except one towards the sea, he assigned their several ships to those that were to depart, and gave money and provision to those that wanted; all which he did with great order and exactness, taking care to suppress all tumults, and that no wrong should be done to the people.

Marcus Octavius, coming with two legions, now encamped near Utica, and sent to Cato, to arrange about the chief command. Cato returned him no answer; but said to his friends, "Can we wonder all has gone ill with us, when our love of office survives even in our very ruin?" In the meantime, word was brought him, that the horse were going away, and were beginning to spoil and plunder the citizens. Cato ran to them, and from the first he met, snatched what they had taken; the rest threw down all they had gotten, and went away silent, and ashamed of what they had done. Then he called together all the people of Utica, and requested them upon the behalf of the three hundred, not to exasperate Caesar against them, but all to seek their common safety together with them. After that, he went again to the port, to see those who were about to embark; and there he embraced and dismissed those of his friends and acquaintance whom he had persuaded to go. As for his son, he did not counsel him to be gone, nor did he think fit to persuade him to forsake his father. But there was one Statyllius, a young man, in the flower of his age, of a brave spirit, and very desirous to imitate the constancy of Cato. Cato entreated him to go away, as he was a noted enemy to Caesar, but without success. Then Cato looked at Apollonides, the stoic philosopher, and Demetrius, the peripatetic; "It belongs to you," said he, "to cool the fever of this young man's spirit, and to make him know what is good for him." And thus, in setting his friends upon their way, and in dispatching the business of any that applied to him, he spent that night, and the greatest part of the next day.

Lucius Caesar, a kinsman of Caesar's, being appointed to go deputy for the three hundred, came to Cato, and desired he would assist him to prepare a persuasive speech for them; "And as to you yourself," said he, "it will be an honor for me to kiss the hands and fall at the knees of Caesar, in your behalf." But Cato would by no means permit him to do any such thing; "For as to myself," said he, "if I would be preserved by Caesar's favor, I should myself go to him; but I would not be beholden to a tyrant, for his acts of tyranny. For it is but usurpation in him to save, as their rightful lord, the lives of men over whom he has no title to reign. But if you please, let us consider what you had best say for the three hundred." And when they had continued some time together, as Lucius was going away, Cato recommended to him his son, and the rest of his friends; and taking him by the hand, bade him farewell.

Then he retired to his house again, and called together his son and his friends, to whom he conversed on various subjects; among the rest, he forbade his son to engage himself in the affairs of state. For to act therein as became him, was now impossible; and to do otherwise, would be dishonorable. Toward evening he went into his bath. As he was bathing, he remembered Statyllius, and called out aloud, "Apollonides, have you tamed the high spirit of Statyllius, and is he gone without bidding us farewell?" "No," said Apollonides, "I have said much to him, but to little purpose; he is still resolute and unalterable, and declares he is determined to follow your example." At this, it is said, Cato smiled, and answered, "That will soon be tried."

After he had bathed, he went to supper, with a great deal of company; at which he sat up, as he had always used to do ever since the battle of Pharsalia; for since that time he never lay down, but when he went to sleep. There supped with him all his own friends and the magistrates of Utica.

After supper, the wine produced a great deal of lively and agreeable discourse, and a whole series of philosophical questions was discussed. At length they came to the strange dogmas of the stoics, called their Paradoxes; and to this in particular, That the good man only is free, and that all wicked men are slaves. The peripatetic, as was to be expected, opposing this, Cato fell upon him very warmly; and somewhat raising his voice, he argued the matter at great length, and urged the point with such vehemence, that it was apparent to everybody, he was resolved to put an end to his life, and set himself at liberty. And so, when he had done speaking, there was a great silence, and evident dejection. Cato, therefore, to divert them from any suspicion of his design, turned the conversation, and began again to talk of matters of present interest and expectation, showing great concern for those that were at sea, as also for the others, who, traveling by land, were to pass through a dry and barbarous desert.

When the company was broke up, he walked with his friends, as he used to do after supper, gave the necessary orders to the officers of the watch, and going into his chamber, he embraced his son and every one of his friends with more than usual warmth, which again renewed their suspicion of his design. Then laying himself down, he took into his hand Plato's dialogue concerning the soul. Having read more than half the book, he looked up, and missing his sword, which his son had taken away while he was at supper, he called his servant, and asked, who had taken away his sword. The servant making no answer, he fell to reading again; and a little after, not seeming importunate, or hasty for it, but as if he would only know what was become of it, he bade it be brought. But having waited some time, when he had read through the book, and still nobody brought the sword, he called up all his servants, and in a louder tone demanded his sword. To one of them he gave such a blow in the mouth, that he hurt his own hand; and now grew more angry, exclaiming that he was betrayed and delivered naked to the enemy by his son and his servants. Then his son, with the rest of his friends, came running, into the room, and falling at his feet, began to lament and beseech him. But Cato raising up himself, and looking fiercely, "When," said he, "and how did I become deranged, and out of my senses, that thus no one tries to persuade me by reason, or show me what is better, if I am supposed to be ill-advised? Must I be disarmed, and hindered from using my own reason? And you, young man, why do not you bind your father's hands behind him, that when Caesar comes, he may find me unable to defend myself? To dispatch myself I want no sword; I need but hold my breath awhile, or strike my head against the wall."

When he had thus spoken, his son went weeping out of the chamber, and with him all the rest, except Demetrius and Apollollides, to whom, being left alone with him, he began to speak more calmly. "And you," said he, "do you also think to keep a man of my age alive by force, and to sit here and silently watch me? Or do you bring me some reasons to prove, that it will not be base and unworthy for Cato, when he can find his safety no other way, to seek it from his enemy? If so, adduce your arguments, and show cause why we should now unlearn what we formerly were taught, in order that rejecting all the convictions in which we lived, we may now by Caesar's help grow wiser, and be yet more obliged to him, than for life only. Not that I have determined aught concerning myself, but I would have it in my power to perform what I shall think fit to resolve; and I shall not fail to take you as my advisers, in holding counsel, as I shall do, with the doctrines which your philosophy teaches; in the meantime, do not trouble yourselves; but go tell my son, that he should not compel his father to what he cannot persuade him to." They made him no answer, but went weeping out of the chamber. Then the sword being brought in by a little boy, Cato took it, drew it out, and looked at it; and when he saw the point was good, "Now," said he, "I am master of myself;" and laying down the sword, he took his book again, which, it is related, he read twice over. After this he slept so soundly, that he was heard to snore by those that were without.

About midnight, he called up two of his freedmen, Cleanthes, his physician, and Butas, whom he chiefly employed in public business. Him he sent to the port, to see if all his friends had sailed; to the physician he gave his hand to be dressed, as it was swollen with the blow he had struck one of his servants. At this they all rejoiced, hoping that now he designed to live.

Butas, after a while, returned, and brought word they were all gone except Crassus, who had stayed about some business, but was just ready to depart; he said, also, that the wind was high, and the sea very rough. Cato, on hearing this, sighed, out of compassion to those who were at sea, and sent Butas again, to see if any of them should happen to return for anything they wanted, and to acquaint him therewith.

Now the birds began to sing, and he again fell into a little slumber. At length Butas came back, and told him, all was quiet in the port. Then Cato, laying himself down, as if he would sleep out the rest of the night, bade him shut the door after him. But as soon as Butas was gone out, he took his sword, and stabbed it into his breast; yet not being able to use his hand so well, on account of the swelling, he did not immediately die of the wound; but struggling, fell off the bed, and throwing down a little mathematical table that stood by, made such a noise, that the servants, hearing it, cried out. And immediately his son and all his friends came into the chamber, where seeing him lie weltering in his blood, great part of his bowels out of his body, but himself still alive and able to look at them, they all stood in horror. The physician went to him, and would have put in his bowels, which were not pierced, and sewed up the wound; but Cato, recovering himself, and understanding the intention, thrust away the physician, plucked out his own bowels, and tearing open the wound, immediately expired.

In less time than one would think his own family could have known this accident, all the three hundred were at the door. And a little after, the people of Utica flocked thither, crying out with one voice, he was their benefactor and their savior, the only free and only undefeated man. At the very same time, they had news that Caesar was coming; yet neither fear of the present danger, nor desire to flatter the conqueror, nor the commotions and discord among themselves, could divert them from doing honor to Cato. For they sumptuously set out his body, made him a magnificent funeral, and buried him by the seaside, where now stands his statue, holding a sword. And only when this had been done, they returned to consider of preserving themselves and their city.

Caesar had been informed that Cato stayed at Utica, and did not seek to fly; that he had sent away the rest of the Romans, but himself, with his son and a few of his friends, continued there very unconcernedly, so that he could not imagine what might be his design. But having a great consideration for the man, he hastened thither with his army. When he heard of his death, it is related he said these words, "Cato, I grudge you your death, as you have grudged me the preservation of your life." And, indeed, if Cato would have suffered himself to owe his life to Caesar, he would not so much have impaired his own honor, as augmented the other's glory. What would have been done, of course we cannot know, but from Caesar's usual clemency, we may guess what was most likely.

Cato was forty-eight years old when he died. His son suffered no injury from Caesar; but, it is said, he grew idle, and was thought to be dissipated among women. In Cappadocia, he stayed at the house of Marphadates, one of the royal family there, who had a very handsome wife; and continuing his visit longer than was suitable, he made himself the subject of various epigrams; such as, for example,

> *Tomorrow, (being the thirtieth day),*
> *Cato, 't is thought, will go away;*

> *Porcius and Marphadates, friends so true,*
> *One Soul, they say, suffices for the two,*

that being the name of the woman, and so again,

> *To Cato's greatness every one confesses,*
> *A royal Soul he certainly possesses.*

But all these stains were entirely wiped off by the bravery of his death. For in the battle of Philippi, where he fought for his country's liberty against Caesar and Antony, when the ranks were breaking, he, scorning to fly, or to escape unknown, called out to the enemy, showed himself to them in the front, and encouraged those of his party who stayed; and at length fell, and left his enemies full of admiration of his valor.

Nor was the daughter of Cato inferior to the rest of her family, for sober-living and greatness of spirit. She was married to Brutus, who killed Caesar;

was acquainted with the conspiracy, and ended her life as became one of her birth and virtue. All which is related in the life of Brutus.

Statyllius, who said he would imitate Cato, was at that time hindered by the philosophers, when he would have put an end to his life. He afterward followed Brutus, to whom he was very faithful and very serviceable, and died in the field of Philippi.

16
DEMOSTHENES

Whoever it was, Sosius, that wrote the poem in honor of Alcibiades, upon his winning the chariot race at the Olympian Games, whether it were Euripides, as is most commonly thought, or some other person, he tells us, that to a man's being happy it is in the first place requisite he should be born in "some famous city." But for him that would attain to true happiness, which for the most part is placed in the qualities and disposition of the mind, it is, in my opinion, of no other disadvantage to be of a mean, obscure country, than to be born of a small or plain-looking woman. For it were ridiculous to think that Iulis, a little part of Ceos, which itself is no great island, and Aegina, which an Athenian once said ought to be removed, like a small eye-sore, from the port of Piraeus, should breed good actors and poets, and yet should never be able to produce a just, temperate, wise, and high-minded man. Other arts, whose end it is to acquire riches or honor, are likely enough to wither and decay in poor and undistinguished towns; but virtue, like a strong and durable plant, may take root and thrive in any place where it can lay hold of an ingenuous nature, and a mind that is industrious. I, for my part, shall desire that for any deficiency of mine in right judgment or action, I myself may be, as in fairness, held accountable, and shall not attribute it to the obscurity of my birthplace.

But if any man undertake to write a history, that has to be collected from materials gathered by observation and the reading of works not easy to be got in all places, nor written always in his own language, but many of them foreign and dispersed in other hands, for him, undoubtedly, it is in the first place and above all things most necessary, to reside in some city of good note, addicted to liberal arts, and populous; where he may have plenty of all sorts of books, and upon inquiry may hear and inform himself of such particulars as, having escaped the pens of writers, are more faithfully preserved in the memories of men, lest his work be deficient in many things, even those which it can least dispense with.

But for me, I live in a little town, where I am willing to continue, lest it should grow less; and having had no leisure, while I was in Rome and other parts of Italy, to exercise myself in the Roman language, on account of public business and of those who came to be instructed by me in philosophy, it was very late, and in the decline of my age, before I applied myself to the reading of Latin authors. Upon which that which happened to me, may seem strange, though it be true; for it was not so much by the knowledge of words, that I came to the understanding of things, as by my experience of things I was enabled to follow the meaning of words. But to appreciate the graceful and ready pronunciation of the Roman tongue, to understand the various figures and connection of words, and such other ornaments, in which the beauty of speaking consists, is, I doubt not, an admirable and delightful accomplishment; but it requires a degree of practice and study, which is not easy, and will better suit those who have more leisure, and time enough yet before them for the occupation.

And so in this fifth book of my Parallel Lives, in giving an account of Demosthenes and Cicero, my comparison of their natural dispositions and their characters will be formed upon their actions and their lives as statesmen, and I shall not pretend to criticize their orations one against the other, to show which of the two was the more charming or the more powerful speaker. For there, as Ion says,

We are but like a fish upon dry land;

a proverb which Caecilius perhaps forgot, when he employed his always adventurous talents in so ambitious an attempt as a comparison of Demosthenes and Cicero: and, possibly, if it were a thing obvious and easy for every man to know himself, the precept had not passed for an oracle.

The divine power seems originally to have designed Demosthenes and Cicero upon the same plan, giving them many similarities in their natural characters, as their passion for distinction and their love of liberty in civil life, and their want of courage in dangers and war, and at the same time also to have added many accidental resemblances. I think there can hardly be found two other orators, who, from small and obscure beginnings, became so great and mighty; who both contested with kings and tyrants; both lost their daughters, were driven out of their country, and returned with honor; who, flying from thence again, were both seized upon by their enemies, and at last ended their lives with the liberty of their countrymen. So that if we were to suppose there had been a trial of skill between nature and fortune, as there is sometimes between artists, it would be hard to judge, whether that succeeded best in making them alike in their dispositions and manners, or this, in the coincidences of their lives. We will speak of the eldest first.

Demosthenes, the father of Demosthenes, was a citizen of good rank and quality, as Theopompus informs us, surnamed the Sword-maker, because he had a large workhouse, and kept servants skillful in that art at work. But of that which Aeschines, the orator, said of his mother, that she was descended of one Gylon, who fled his country upon an accusation of treason, and of a barbarian woman, I can affirm nothing, whether he spoke true, or slandered and maligned her. This is certain, that Demosthenes, being as yet but seven years old, was left by his father in affluent circumstances, the whole value of his estate being little short of fifteen talents, and that he was wronged by his guardians, part of his fortune being embezzled by them, and the rest neglected; insomuch that even his teachers were defrauded of their salaries. This was the reason that he did not obtain the liberal education that he should have had; besides that on account of weakness and delicate health, his mother would not let him exert himself, and his teachers forbore to urge him. He was meager and sickly from the first, and hence had his nickname of Batalus, given him, it is said, by the boys, in derision of his appearance; Batalus being, as some tell us, a certain enervated flute-player, in ridicule of whom Antiphanes wrote a play. Others speak of Batalus as a writer of wanton verses and drinking songs. And it would seem that some part of the body, not decent to be named, was at that time called batalus by the Athenians. But the name of Argas, which also they say was a nickname of Demosthenes, was given him for his behavior, as being savage and spiteful, argas being one of the poetical words for a snake; or for his disagreeable way of speaking, Argas being the name of a poet, who composed very harshly and disagreeably. So much, as Plato says, for such matters.

The first occasion of his eager inclination to oratory they say, was this. Callistratus, the orator, being to plead in open court for Oropus, the expectation of the issue of that cause was very great, as well for the ability of the orator, who was then at the height of his reputation, as also for the fame of the action itself. Therefore, Demosthenes, having heard the tutors and schoolmasters agreeing among themselves to be present at this trial, with much importunity persuades his tutor to take him along with him to the hearing; who, having some acquaintance with the doorkeepers, procured a place where the boy might sit unseen, and hear what was said. Callistratus having got the day, and being much admired, the boy began to look upon his glory with a kind of emulation, observing how he was courted on all hands, and attended on his way by the multitude; but his wonder was more than all excited by the power of his eloquence, which seemed able to subdue and win over anything. From this time, therefore, bidding farewell to other sorts of learning and study, he now began to exercise himself, and to take pains in declaiming, as one that meant to be himself also an orator. He made use of Isaeus as his guide to the art of speaking, though Isocrates at that time was giving lessons; whether, as some say, because he was an orphan, and was not able to pay Isocrates his appointed fee of ten minae, or because he preferred Isaeus's speaking, as being more business-like and effective in actual use. Hermippus says, that he met with certain memoirs without any author's name, in which it was written that Demosthenes was a scholar to Plato, and learnt much of his eloquence from him; and he also mentions Ctesibius, as reporting from Callias of Syracuse and some others, that Demosthenes secretly obtained a knowledge of the systems of Isocrates and Alcidamas, and mastered them thoroughly.

As soon, therefore, as he was grown up to man's estate, he began to go to law with his guardians, and to write orations against them; who, in the meantime, had recourse to various subterfuges and pleas for new trials, and Demosthenes, though he was thus, as Thucydides says, taught his business in dangers, and by his own exertions was successful in his suit, was yet unable for all this to recover so much as a small fraction of his patrimony. He only attained some degree of confidence in speaking, and some competent experience in it. And having got a taste of the honor and power which are acquired by pleadings, he now ventured to come forth, and to undertake public business. And, as it is said of Laomedon, the Orchomenian, that by advice of his physician, he used to run long distances to keep off some disease of his spleen, and by that means having, through labor and exercise, framed the habit of his body, he betook himself to the great garland games, and became one of the best runners at the long race; so it happened to Demosthenes, who, first venturing upon oratory for the recovery of his own private property, by this acquired ability in speaking, and at length, in public business, as it were in the great games, came to have the preeminence of all competitors in the assembly. But when he first addressed himself to the people, he met with great discouragements, and was derided for his strange and uncouth style, which was cumbered with long sentences and tortured with formal arguments to a most harsh and disagreeable excess. Besides, he had, it seems, a weakness in his voice, a perplexed and indistinct utterance and a shortness of breath, which, by breaking and disjointing his sentences much obscured the sense and meaning of what he spoke. So that in the end, being quite disheartened, he forsook the assembly; and as he was walking carelessly and sauntering about the Piraeus, Eunomus, the Thriasian, then a very old man, seeing him, upbraided him, saying that his diction was very much like that of Pericles, and that he was wanting to himself through cowardice and meanness of spirit, neither bearing up with courage against popular outcry, nor fitting his body for action, but suffering it to languish through mere sloth and negligence.

Another time, when the assembly had refused to hear him, and he was going home with his head muffled up, taking it very heavily, they relate that Satyrus, the actor, followed him, and being his familiar acquaintance, entered into conversation with him. To whom, when Demosthenes bemoaned himself, that having been the most industrious of all the pleaders, and having almost spent the whole strength and vigor of his body in that employment, he could not yet find any acceptance with the people, that drunken sots, mariners, and illiterate fellows were heard, and had the hustings for their own, while he himself was despised, "You say true, Demosthenes," replied Satyrus, "but I will quickly remedy the cause of all this, if you will repeat to me some passage out of Euripides or Sophocles." Which when Demosthenes had pronounced, Satyrus presently taking it up after him gave the same passage, in his rendering of it, such a new form, by accompanying it with the proper mien and gesture, that to Demosthenes it seemed quite another thing. By this being convinced how much grace and ornament language acquires from action, he began to esteem it a small matter, and as good as nothing for a man to exercise himself in declaiming, if he neglected enunciation and delivery. Hereupon he built himself a place to study in underground, (which was still remaining in our time,) and hither he would come constantly every day to form his action, and to exercise his voice; and here he would continue, oftentimes without intermission, two or three months together, shaving one half of his head, that so for shame he might not go abroad, though he desired it ever so much.

Nor was this all, but he also made his conversation with people abroad, his common speech, and his business, subservient to his studies, taking from hence occasions and arguments as matter to work upon. For as soon as he was parted from his company, down he would go at once into his study, and run over everything in order that had passed, and the reasons that might be alleged for and against it. Any speeches, also, that he was present at, he would go over again with himself, and reduce into periods; and whatever others spoke to him, or he to them, he would correct, transform, and vary several ways. Hence it was, that he was looked upon as a person of no great natural genius, but one who owed all the power and ability he had in speaking to labor and industry. Of the truth of which it was thought to be no small sign, that he was very rarely heard to speak upon the occasion, but though he were by name frequently called upon by the people, as he sat in the assembly, yet he would not rise unless he had previously considered the subject, and came prepared for it. So that many of the popular pleaders used to make it a jest against him; and Pytheas once, scoffing at him, said that his arguments smelt of the lamp. To which Demosthenes gave the sharp answer, "It is true, indeed, Pytheas, that your lamp and mine are not conscious of the same things." To others, however, he would not much deny it, but would admit frankly enough, that he neither entirely wrote his speeches beforehand, nor yet spoke wholly extempore. And he would affirm, that it was the more truly popular act to use premeditation, such preparation being a kind of respect to the people; whereas, to slight and take no care how what is said is likely to be received by the audience, shows something of an oligarchical temper, and is the course of one that intends force rather than persuasion. Of his want of courage and assurance to speak off-hand, they make it also another argument, that when he was at a loss, and discomposed, Demades would often rise up on the sudden to support him, but he was never observed to do the same for Demades.

Whence then, may some say, was it, that Aeschines speaks of him as a person so much to be wondered at for his boldness in speaking? Or, how could it be, when Python, the Byzantine, "with so much confidence and such a torrent of words inveighed against" the Athenians, that Demosthenes alone stood up to oppose him? Or, when Lamachus, the Myrinaean, had written a panegyric upon king Philip and Alexander, in which he uttered many things in reproach of the Thebans and Olynthians, and at the Olympic Games recited it publicly, how was it, that he, rising up, and recounting historically and demonstratively what benefits and advantages all Greece had received from the Thebans and Chalcidians, and on the contrary, what mischiefs the flatterers of the Macedonians had brought upon it, so turned the minds of all that were present that the sophist, in alarm at the outcry against him, secretly made his way out of the assembly? But Demosthenes, it should seem, regarded other points in the character of Pericles to be unsuited to him; but his reserve and his sustained manner, and his forbearing to speak on the sudden, or upon every occasion, as being the things to which principally he owed his greatness, these he followed, and endeavored to imitate, neither wholly neglecting the glory which present occasion offered, nor yet willing too often to expose his faculty to the mercy of chance. For, in fact, the orations which were spoken by him had much more of boldness and confidence in them than those that he wrote, if we may believe Eratosthenes, Demetrius the Phalerian, and the Comedians. Eratosthenes says that often in his speaking he would be transported into a kind of ecstasy, and Demetrius, that he uttered the famous metrical adjuration to the people,

By the earth, the springs, the rivers, and the streams,

as a man inspired, and beside himself. One of the comedians calls him a rhopoperperethras, and another scoffs at him for his use of antithesis:—

And what he took, took back; a phrase to please
The very fancy of Demosthenes.

Unless, indeed, this also is meant by Antiphanes for a jest upon the speech on Halonesus, which Demosthenes advised the Athenians not to take at Philip's hands, but to take back.

All, however, used to consider Demades, in the mere use of his natural gifts, an orator impossible to surpass, and that in what he spoke on the sudden, he excelled all the study and preparation of Demosthenes. And Ariston the Chian, has recorded a judgment which Theophrastus passed upon the orators; for being asked what kind of orator he accounted Demosthenes, he answered, "Worthy of the city of Athens;" and then, what he thought of Demades, he answered, "Above it." And the same philosopher reports, that Polyeuctus, the Sphettian, one of the Athenian politicians about that time, was wont to say that Demosthenes was the greatest orator, but Phocion the ablest, as he expressed the most sense in the fewest words. And, indeed, it is related, that Demosthenes himself, as often as Phocion stood up to plead against him, would say to his acquaintance, "Here comes the knife to my speech." Yet it does not appear whether he had this feeling for his powers of speaking, or for his life and character, and meant to say that one word or nod from a man who was really trusted, would go further than a thousand lengthy periods from others.

Demetrius, the Phalerian, tells us, that he was informed by Demosthenes himself, now grown old, that the ways he made use of to remedy his natural bodily infirmities and defects were such as these; his inarticulate and stammering pronunciation he overcame and rendered more distinct by speaking with pebbles in his mouth; his voice he disciplined by declaiming and reciting speeches or verses when he was out of breath, while running or going up steep places; and that in his house he had a large looking-glass, before which he would stand and go through his exercises. It is told that someone once came to request his assistance as a pleader, and related how he had been assaulted and beaten. "Certainly," said Demosthenes, "nothing of the kind can have happened to you." Upon which the other, raising his voice, exclaimed loudly, "What, Demosthenes, nothing has been done to me?" "Ah," replied Demosthenes, "now I hear the voice of one that has been injured and beaten." Of so great consequence towards the gaining of belief did he esteem the tone and action of the speaker. The action which he used himself was wonderfully pleasing to the common people; but by well-educated people, as, for example, by Demetrius, the Phalerian, it was looked upon as mean, humiliating, and unmanly. And Hermippus says of Aesion, that, being asked his opinion concerning the ancient orators and those of his own time, he answered that it was admirable to see with what composure and in what high style they addressed themselves to the people; but that the orations of Demosthenes, when they are read, certainly appear to be superior in point of construction, and more effective. His written speeches, beyond all question, are characterized by austere tone and by their severity. In his extempore retorts and rejoinders, he allowed himself the use of jest and mockery. When Demades said, "Demosthenes teach me! So might the sow teach Minerva!" he replied, "Was it this Minerva, that was lately found playing the harlot in Collytus?" When a thief, who had the nickname of the Brazen, was attempting to upbraid him for sitting up late, and writing by candlelight, "I know very well," said he, "that you had rather have all lights out; and wonder not, O ye men of Athens, at the many robberies which are committed, since we have thieves of brass and walls of clay." But on these points, though we have much more to mention, we will add nothing at present. We will proceed to take an estimate of his character from his actions and his life as a statesman.

His first entering into public business was much about the time of the Phocian war, as himself affirms, and may be collected from his Philippic orations. For of these, some were made after that action was over, and the earliest of them refer to its concluding events. It is certain that he engaged in the accusation of Midias when he was but two and thirty years old, having as yet no interest or reputation as a politician. And this it was, I consider, that induced him to withdraw the action, and accept a sum of money as a compromise. For of himself

He was no easy or good-natured man,

but of a determined disposition, and resolute to see himself righted; however, finding it a hard matter and above his strength to deal with Midias, a man so well secured on all sides with money, eloquence, and friends, he yielded to the entreaties of those who interceded for him. But had he seen any hopes or possibility of prevailing, I cannot believe that three thousand drachmas could have taken off the edge of his revenge. The object which he chose for himself in the commonwealth was noble and just, the defense of the Grecians against Philip; and in this he behaved himself so worthily that he soon grew famous, and excited attention everywhere for his eloquence and courage in speaking. He was admired through all Greece, the king of Persia courted him, and by Philip himself he was more esteemed than all the other orators. His very enemies were forced to confess that they had to do with a man of mark; for such a character even Aeschines and Hyperides give him, where they accuse and speak against him.

So that I cannot imagine what ground Theopompus had to say, that Demosthenes was of a fickle, unsettled disposition, and could not long continue firm either to the same men or the same affairs; whereas the contrary is most apparent, for the same party and post in politics which he held from the beginning, to these he kept constant to the end; and was so far from leaving them while he lived, that he chose rather to forsake his life than his purpose. He was never heard to apologize for shifting sides like Demades, who would say, he often spoke against himself, but never against the city; nor as Melanopus, who, being generally against Callistratus, but being often bribed off with money, was wont to tell the people, "The man indeed is my enemy, but we must submit for the good of our country;" nor again as Nicodemus, the Messenian, who having first appeared on Cassander's side, and afterwards taken part with Demetrius, said the two things were not in themselves contrary, it being always most advisable to obey the conqueror. We have nothing of this kind to say against Demosthenes, as one who would turn aside or prevaricate, either in word or deed. There could not have been less variation in his public acts if they had all been played, so to say, from first to last, from the same score. Panaetius, the philosopher, said, that most of his orations are so written, as if they were to prove this one conclusion, that what is honest and virtuous is for itself only to be chosen; as that of the Crown, that against Aristocrates, that for the Immunities, and the Philippics; in all which he persuades his fellow-citizens to pursue not that which seems most pleasant, easy, or profitable; but declares over and over again, that they ought in the first place to prefer that which is just and honorable, before their own safety and preservation. So that if he had kept his hands clean, if his courage for the wars had been answerable to the generosity of his principles, and the dignity of his orations, he might deservedly have his name placed, not in the number of such orators as Moerocles, Polyeuctus, and Hyperides, but in the highest rank with Cimon, Thucydides, and Pericles.

Certainly amongst those who were contemporary with him, Phocion, though he appeared on the less commendable side in the commonwealth, and was counted as one of the Macedonian party, nevertheless, by his courage and his honesty, procured himself a name not inferior to those of Ephialtes, Aristides, and Cimon. But Demosthenes, being neither fit to be relied on for courage in arms, as Demetrius says, nor on all sides inaccessible to bribery (for how invincible soever he was against the gifts of Philip and the Macedonians, yet elsewhere he lay open to assault, and was overpowered by the gold which came down from Susa and Ecbatana), was therefore esteemed better able to recommend than to imitate the virtues of past times. And yet (excepting only Phocion), even in his life and manners, he far surpassed the other orators of his time. None of them addressed the people so boldly; he attacked the faults, and opposed himself to the unreasonable desires of the multitude, as may be seen in his orations. Theopompus writes, that the Athenians having by name selected Demosthenes, and called upon him to accuse a certain person, he refused to do it; upon which the assembly being all in an uproar, he rose up and said, "Your counselor, whether you will or no, O ye men of Athens, you shall always have me; but a sycophant or false accuser, though you would have me, I shall never be." And his conduct in the case of

Antiphon was perfectly aristocratical; whom, after he had been acquitted in the assembly, he took and brought before the court of Areopagus, and, setting at naught the displeasure of the people, convicted him there of having promised Philip to burn the arsenal; whereupon the man was condemned by that court, and suffered for it. He accused, also, Theoris, the priestess, amongst other misdemeanors, of having instructed and taught the slaves to deceive and cheat their masters, for which the sentence of death passed upon her, and she was executed.

The oration which Apollodorus made use of, and by it carried the cause against Timotheus, the general, in an action of debt, it is said was written for him by Demosthenes; as also those against Phormion and Stephanus, in which latter case he was thought to have acted dishonorably, for the speech which Phormion used against Apollodorus was also of his making; he, as it were, having simply furnished two adversaries out of the same shop with weapons to wound one another. Of his orations addressed to the public assemblies, that against Androtion, and those against Timocrates and Aristocrates, were written for others, before he had come forward himself as a politician. They were composed, it seems, when he was but seven or eight and twenty years old. That against Aristogiton, and that for the Immunities, he spoke himself, at the request, as he says, of Ctesippus, the son of Chabrias, but, as some say, out of courtship to the young man's mother. Though, in fact, he did not marry her, for his wife was a woman of Samos, as Demetrius, the Magnesian, writes, in his book on Persons of the same Name. It is not certain whether his oration against Aeschines, for Misconduct as Ambassador, was ever spoken; although Idomeneus says that Aeschines wanted only thirty voices to condemn him. But this seems not to be correct, at least so far as may be conjectured from both their orations concerning the Crown; for in these, neither of them speaks clearly or directly of it, as a cause that ever came to trial. But let others decide this controversy.

It was evident, even in time of peace, what course Demosthenes would steer in the commonwealth; for whatever was done by the Macedonian, he criticized and found fault with, and upon all occasions was stirring up the people of Athens, and inflaming them against him. Therefore, in the court of Philip, no man was so much talked of, or of so great account as he; and when he came thither, one of the ten ambassadors who were sent into Macedonia, though all had audience given them, yet his speech was answered with most care and exactness. But in other respects, Philip entertained him not so honorably as the rest, neither did he show him the same kindness and civility with which he applied himself to the party of Aeschines and Philocrates. So that, when the others commended Philip for his able speaking, his beautiful person, nay, and also for his good companionship in drinking, Demosthenes could not refrain from caviling at these praises; the first, he said, was a quality which might well enough become a rhetorician, the second a woman, and the last was only the property of a sponge; no one of them was the proper commendation of a prince.

But when things came at last to war, Philip on the one side being not able to live in peace, and the Athenians, on the other side, being stirred up by Demosthenes, the first action he put them upon was the reducing of Euboea, which, by the treachery of the tyrants, was brought under subjection to Philip. And on his proposition, the decree was voted, and they crossed over thither and chased the Macedonians out of the island. The next, was the relief of the Byzantines and Perinthians, whom the Macedonians at that time were attacking. He persuaded the people to lay aside their enmity against these cities, to forget the offenses committed by them in the Confederate War, and to send them such succors as eventually saved and secured them. Not long after, he undertook an embassy through the States of Greece, which he solicited and so far incensed against Philip, that, a few only excepted, he brought them all into a general league. So that, besides the forces composed of the citizens themselves, there was an army consisting of fifteen thousand foot and two thousand horse, and the money to pay these strangers was levied and brought in with great cheerfulness. On which occasion it was, says Theophrastus, on the allies requesting that their contributions for the war might be ascertained and stated, Crobylus, the orator, made use of the saying, "War can't be fed at so much a day." Now was all Greece up in arms, and in great expectation what would be the event. The Euboeans, the Achaeans, the Corinthians, the Megarians, the Leucadians, and Corcyraeans, their people and their cities, were all joined together in a league. But the hardest task was yet behind, left for Demosthenes, to draw the Thebans into this confederacy with the rest. Their country bordered next upon Attica, they had great forces for the war, and at that time they were accounted the best soldiers of all Greece, but it was no easy matter to make them break with Philip, who, by many good offices, had so lately obliged them in the Phocian war; especially considering how the subjects of dispute and variance between the two cities were continually renewed and exasperated by petty quarrels, arising out of the proximity of their frontiers.

But after Philip, being now grown high and puffed up with his good success at Amphissa, on a sudden surprised Elatea and possessed himself of Phocis, and the Athenians were in a great consternation, none durst venture to rise up to speak, no one knew what to say, all were at a loss, and the whole assembly in silence and perplexity, in this extremity of affairs, Demosthenes was the only man who appeared, his counsel to them being alliance with the Thebans. And having in other ways encouraged the people, and, as his manner was, raised their spirits up with hopes, he, with some others, was sent ambassador to Thebes. To oppose him, as Marsyas says, Philip also sent thither his envoys, Amyntas and Clearellus, two Macedonians, besides Daochus, a Thessalian, and Thrasydaeus. Now the Thebans, in their consultations, were well enough aware what suited best with their own interest, but everyone had before his eyes the terrors of war, and their losses in the Phocian troubles were still recent: but such was the force and power of the orator, fanning up, as Theopompus says, their courage, and firing their emulation, that casting away every thought of prudence, fear, or obligation, in a sort of divine possession, they chose the path of honor, to which his words invited them. And this success, thus accomplished by an orator, was thought to be so glorious and of such consequence, that Philip immediately sent heralds to treat and petition for a peace: all Greece was aroused, and up in arms to help. And the commanders-in-chief, not only of Attica, but of Boeotia, applied themselves to Demosthenes, and observed his directions. He managed all the assemblies of the Thebans, no less than those of the Athenians; he was beloved both by the one and by the other, and exercised the same supreme authority with both; and that not by unfair means, or without just cause, as Theopompus professes, but indeed it was no more than was due to his merit.

But there was, it should seem, some divinely-ordered fortune, commissioned, in the revolution of things, to put a period at this time to the liberty of Greece, which opposed and thwarted all their actions, and by many signs foretold what should happen. Such were the sad predictions uttered by the Pythian priestess, and this old oracle cited out of the Sibyl's verses, —

> *The battle on Thermodon that shall be*
> *Safe at a distance I desire to see,*
> *Far, like an eagle, watching in the air.*
> *Conquered shall weep, and conqueror perish there.*

This Thermodon, they say, is a little rivulet here in our country in Chaeronea, running into the Cephisus. But we know of none that is so called at the present time; and can only conjecture that the streamlet which is now called Haemon, and runs by the Temple of Hercules, where the Grecians were encamped, might perhaps in those days be called Thermodon, and after the fight, being filled with blood and dead bodies, upon this occasion, as we guess, might change its old name for that which it now bears. Yet Duris says that this Thermodon was no river, but that some of the soldiers, as they were pitching their tents and digging trenches about them, found a small stone statue, which, by the inscription, appeared to be the figure of Thermodon, carrying a wounded Amazon in his arms; and that there was another oracle current about it, as follows:—

> *The battle on Thermodon that shall be,*

> *Fail not, black raven, to attend and see;*
> *The flesh of men shall there abound for thee.*

In fine, it is not easy to determine what is the truth. But of Demosthenes it is said, that he had such great confidence in the Grecian forces, and was so excited by the sight of the courage and resolution of so many brave men ready to engage the enemy, that he would by no means endure they should give any heed to oracles, or hearken to prophecies, but gave out that he suspected even the prophetess herself, as if she had been tampered with to speak in favor of Philip. The Thebans he put in mind of Epaminondas, the Athenians, of Pericles, who always took their own measures and governed their actions by reason, looking upon things of this kind as mere pretexts for cowardice. Thus far, therefore, Demosthenes acquitted himself like a brave man. But in the fight he did nothing honorable, nor was his performance answerable to his speeches. For he fled, deserting his place disgracefully, and throwing away his arms, not ashamed, as Pytheas observed, to belie the inscription written on his shield, in letters of gold, "With good fortune."

In the meantime Philip, in the first moment of victory, was so transported with joy, that he grew extravagant, and going out, after he had drunk largely, to visit the dead bodies, he chanted the first words of the decree that had been passed on the motion of Demosthenes,

> *The motion of Demosthenes, Demosthenes's son,*
> *dividing it metrically into feet, and marking the beats.*

But when he came to himself, and had well considered the danger he was lately under, he could not forbear from shuddering at the wonderful ability and power of an orator who had made him hazard his life and empire on the issue of a few brief hours. The fame of it also reached even to the court of Persia, and the king sent letters to his lieutenants, commanding them to supply Demosthenes with money, and to pay every attention to him, as the only man of all the Grecians who was able to give Philip occupation and find employment for his forces near home, in the troubles of Greece. This afterwards came to the knowledge of Alexander, by certain letters of Demosthenes which he found at Sardis, and by other papers of the Persian officers, stating the large sums which had been given him.

At this time, however, upon the ill success which now happened to the Grecians, those of the contrary faction in the commonwealth fell foul upon Demosthenes, and took the opportunity to frame several informations and indictments against him. But the people not only acquitted him of these accusations, but continued towards him their former respect, and still invited him, as a man that meant well, to take a part in public affairs. Insomuch that when the bones of those who had been slain at Chaeronea were brought home to be solemnly interred, Demosthenes was the man they chose to make the funeral oration. They did not show, under the misfortunes which befell them, a base or ignoble mind, as Theopompus writes in his exaggerated style, but, on the contrary, by the honor and respect paid to their counselor, they made it appear that they were noway dissatisfied with the counsels he had given them. The speech, therefore, was spoken by Demosthenes. But the subsequent decrees he would not allow to be passed in his own name, but made use of those of his friends, one after another, looking upon his own as unfortunate and inauspicious; till at length he took courage again after the death of Philip, who did not long outlive his victory at Chaeronea. And this, it seems, was that which was foretold in the last verse of the oracle,

Conquered shall weep, and conqueror perish there.

Demosthenes had secret intelligence of the death of Philip, and laying hold of this opportunity to prepossess the people with courage and better hopes for the future, he came into the assembly with a cheerful countenance, pretending to have had a dream that presaged some great good fortune for Athens; and, not long after, arrived the messengers who brought the news of Philip's death. No sooner had the people received it but immediately they offered sacrifice to the gods, and decreed that Pausanias should be presented with a crown. Demosthenes appeared publicly in a rich dress, with a chaplet on his head, though it were but the seventh day since the death of his daughter, as is said by Aeschines, who upbraids him upon this account, and rails at him as one void of natural affection towards his children. Whereas, indeed, he rather betrays himself to be of a poor, low spirit, and effeminate mind, if he really means to make wailings and lamentation the only signs of a gentle and affectionate nature, and to condemn those who bear such accidents with more temper and less passion. For my own part, I cannot say that the behavior of the Athenians on this occasion was wise or honorable, to crown themselves with garlands and to sacrifice to the Gods for the death of a Prince who, in the midst of his success and victories, when they were a conquered people, had used them with so much clemency and humanity. For besides provoking fortune, it was a base thing, and unworthy in itself, to make him a citizen of Athens, and pay him honors while he lived, and yet as soon as he fell by another's hand, to set no bounds to their jollity, to insult over him dead, and to sing triumphant songs of victory, as if by their own valor they had vanquished him. I must at the same time commend the behavior of Demosthenes, who, leaving tears and lamentations and domestic sorrows to the women, made it his business to attend to the interests of the commonwealth. And I think it the duty of him who would be accounted to have a soul truly valiant, and fit for government, that, standing always firm to the common good, and letting private griefs and troubles find their compensation in public blessings, he should maintain the dignity of his character and station, much more than actors who represent the persons of kings and tyrants, who, we see, when they either laugh or weep on the stage, follow, not their own private inclinations, but the course consistent with the subject and with their position. And if, moreover, when our neighbor is in misfortune, it is not our duty to forbear offering any consolation, but rather to say whatever may tend to cheer him, and to invite his attention to any agreeable objects, just as we tell people who are troubled with sore eyes, to withdraw their sight from bright and offensive colors to green, and those of a softer mixture, from whence can a man seek, in his own case, better arguments of consolation for afflictions in his family, than from the prosperity of his country, by making public and domestic chances count, so to say, together, and the better fortune of the state obscure and conceal the less happy circumstances of the individual. I have been induced to say so much, because I have known many readers melted by Aeschines's language into a soft and unmanly tenderness.

But now to return to my narrative. The cities of Greece were inspirited once more by the efforts of Demosthenes to form a league together. The Thebans, whom he had provided with arms, set upon their garrison, and slew many of them; the Athenians made preparations to join their forces with them; Demosthenes ruled supreme in the popular assembly, and wrote letters to the Persian officers who commanded under the king in Asia, inciting them to make war upon the Macedonian, calling him child and simpleton. But as soon as Alexander had settled matters in his own country, and came in person with his army into Boeotia, down fell the courage of the Athenians, and Demosthenes was hushed; the Thebans, deserted by them, fought by themselves, and lost their city. After which, the people of Athens, all in distress and great perplexity, resolved to send ambassadors to Alexander, and amongst others, made choice of Demosthenes for one; but his heart failing him for fear of the king's anger, he returned back from Cithaeron, and left the embassy. In the meantime, Alexander sent to Athens, requiring ten of their orators to be delivered up to him, as Idomeneus and Duris have reported, but as the most and best historians say, he demanded these eight only: Demosthenes, Polyeuctus, Ephialtes, Lycurgus, Moerocles, Demon, Callisthenes, and Charidemus. It was upon this occasion that Demosthenes related to them the fable in which the sheep are said to deliver up their dogs to the wolves; himself and those who with him contended for the people's safety, being, in his comparison, the dogs that defended the flock, and Alexander "the Macedonian arch wolf." He further told them, "As we see corn-masters sell their whole stock by a few grains of wheat which they carry about with them in a dish, as a sample of the rest, so you, by delivering up us, who are but a few, do at the same time unawares surrender up yourselves all together with us;" so we find it related in the history of Aristobulus, the Cassandrian. The Athenians were deliberating, and at a loss what to do, when Demades, having agreed with the persons whom Alexander had demanded, for five talents, undertook to go ambassador, and to intercede with the king for them; and, whether it was that he relied on his friendship and kindness, or that he hoped to find him satiated, as a lion glutted with slaughter, he certainly went, and prevailed with him both to pardon the men, and to be reconciled to the city.

So he and his friends, when Alexander went away, were great men, and Demosthenes was quite put aside. Yet when Agis, the Spartan, made his insurrection, he also for a short time attempted a movement in his favor; but he soon shrunk back again, as the Athenians would not take any part in it, and, Agis being slain, the Lacedaemonians were vanquished. During this time it was that the indictment against Ctesiphon, concerning the Crown, was brought to trial. The action was commenced a little before the battle in Chaeronea, when Chaerondas was archon, but it was not proceeded with till about ten years after, Aristophon being then archon. Never was any public cause more celebrated than this, alike for the fame of the orators, and for the generous courage of the judges, who, though at that time the accusers of Demosthenes were in the height of power, and supported by all the favor of the Macedonians, yet would not give judgment against him, but acquitted him so honorably, that Aeschines did not obtain the fifth part of their suffrages on his side, so that, immediately after, he left the city, and spent the rest of his life in teaching rhetoric about the island of Rhodes, and upon the continent in Ionia.

It was not long after that Harpalus fled from Alexander, and came to Athens out of Asia; knowing himself guilty of many misdeeds into which his love of luxury had led him, and fearing the king, who was now grown terrible even to his best friends. Yet this man had no sooner addressed himself to the people, and delivered up his goods, his ships, and himself to their disposal, but the other orators of the town had their eyes quickly fixed upon his money, and came in to his assistance, persuading the Athenians to receive and protect their suppliant. Demosthenes at first gave advice to chase him out of the country, and to beware lest they involved their city in a war upon an unnecessary and unjust occasion. But some few days after, as they were taking an account of the treasure, Harpalus, perceiving how much he was pleased with a cup of Persian manufacture, and how curiously he surveyed the sculpture and fashion of it, desired him to poise it in his hand, and consider the weight of the gold. Demosthenes, being amazed to feel how heavy it was, asked him what weight it came to. "To you," said Harpalus, smiling, "it shall come with twenty talents." And presently after, when night drew on, he sent him the cup with so many talents. Harpalus, it seems, was a person of singular skill to discern a man's covetousness by the air of his countenance, and the look and movements of his eyes. For Demosthenes could not resist the temptation, but admitting the present, like an armed garrison, into the citadel of his house, he surrendered himself up to the interest of Harpalus. The next day, he came into the assembly with his neck swathed about with wool and rollers, and when they called on him to rise up and speak, he made signs as if he had lost his voice. But the wits, turning the matter to ridicule, said that certainly the orator had been seized that night with no other than a silver quinsy. And soon after, the people, becoming aware of the bribery, grew angry, and would not suffer him to speak, or make any apology for himself, but ran him down with noise; and one man stood up, and cried out, "What, ye men of Athens, will you not hear the cup-bearer?" So at length they banished Harpalus out of the city; and fearing lest they should be called to account for the treasure which the orators had purloined, they made a strict inquiry, going from house to house; only Callicles, the son of Arrhenidas, who was newly married, they would not suffer to be searched, out of respect, as Theopompus writes, to the bride, who was within.

Demosthenes resisted the inquisition, and proposed a decree to refer the business to the court of Areopagus, and to punish those whom that court should find guilty. But being himself one of the first whom the court condemned, when he came to the bar, he was fined fifty talents, and committed to prison; where, out of shame of the crime for which he was condemned, and through the weakness of his body, growing incapable of supporting the confinement, he made his escape, by the carelessness of some and by the connivance of others of the citizens. We are told, at least, that he had not fled far from the city, when, finding that he was pursued by some of those who had been his adversaries, he endeavored to hide himself. But when they called him by his name, and coming up nearer to him, desired he would accept from them some money which they had brought from home as a provision for his journey, and to that purpose only had followed him, when they entreated him to take courage, and to bear up against his misfortune, he burst out into much greater lamentation, saying, "But how is it possible to support myself under so heavy an affliction, since I leave a city in which I have such enemies, as in any other it is not easy to find friends." He did not show much fortitude in his banishment, spending his time for the most part in Aegina and Troezen, and, with tears in his eyes, looking towards the country of Attica. And there remain upon record some sayings of his, little resembling those sentiments of generosity and bravery which he used to express when he had the management of the commonwealth. For, as he was departing out of the city, it is reported, he lifted up his hands towards the Acropolis, and said, "O Lady Minerva, how is it that thou takest delight in three such fierce untractable beast, the owl, the snake, and the people?" The young men that came to visit and converse with him, he deterred from meddling with state affairs, telling them, that if at first two ways had been proposed to him, the one leading to the speaker's stand and the assembly, the other going direct to destruction, and he could have foreseen the many evils which attend those who deal in public business, such as fears, envies, calumnies, and contentions, he would certainly have taken that which led straight on to his death.

But now happened the death of Alexander, while Demosthenes was in this banishment which we have been speaking of. And the Grecians were once again up in arms, encouraged by the brave attempts of Leosthenes, who was then drawing a circumvallation about Antipater, whom he held close besieged in Lamia. Pytheas, therefore, the orator, and Callimedon, called the Crab, fled from Athens, and taking sides with Antipater, went about with his friends and ambassadors to keep the Grecians from revolting and taking part with the Athenians. But, on the other side, Demosthenes, associating himself with the ambassadors that came from Athens, used his utmost endeavors and gave them his best assistance in persuading the cities to fall unanimously upon the Macedonians, and to drive them out of Greece. Phylarchus says that in Arcadia there happened a rencounter between Pytheas and Demosthenes, which came at last to downright railing, while the one pleaded for the Macedonians, and the other for the Grecians. Pytheas said, that as we always suppose there is some disease in the family to which they bring asses' milk, so wherever there comes an embassy from Athens, that city must needs be indisposed. And Demosthenes answered him, retorting the comparison: "Asses' milk is brought to restore health, and the Athenians come for the safety and recovery of the sick." With this conduct the people of Athens were so well pleased, that they decreed the recall of Demosthenes from banishment. The decree was brought in by Demon the Paeanian, cousin to Demosthenes. So they sent him a ship to Aegina, and he landed at the port of Piraeus, where he was met and joyfully received by all the citizens, not so much as an Archon or a priest staying behind. And Demetrius, the Magnesian, says, that he lifted up his hands towards heaven, and blessed this day of his happy return, as far more honorable than that of Alcibiades; since he was recalled by his countrymen, not through any force or constraint put upon them, but by their own good-will and free inclinations. There remained only his pecuniary fine, which, according to law, could not be remitted by the people. But they found out a way to elude the law. It was a custom with them to allow a certain quantity of silver to those who were to furnish and adorn the altar for the sacrifice of Jupiter Soter. This office, for that turn, they bestowed on Demosthenes, and for the performance of it ordered him fifty talents, the very sum in which he was condemned.

Yet it was no long time that he enjoyed his country after his return, the attempts of the Greeks being soon all utterly defeated. For the battle at Cranon happened in Metagitnion, in Boedromion the garrison entered into Munychia, and in the Pyanepsion following died Demosthenes after this manner.

Upon the report that Antipater and Craterus were coming to Athens, Demosthenes with his party took their opportunity to escape privily out of the city; but sentence of death was, upon the motion of Demades, passed upon them by the people. They dispersed themselves, flying some to one place, some to another; and Antipater sent about his soldiers into all quarters to apprehend them. Archias was their captain, and was thence called the exile-hunter. He was a Thurian born, and is reported to have been an actor of tragedies, and they say that Polus, of Aegina, the best actor of his time, was his scholar; but Hermippus reckons Archias among the disciples of Lacritus, the orator, and Demetrius says, he spent some time with Anaximenes. This Archias finding Hyperides the orator, Aristonicus of Marathon, and Himeraeus, the brother of Demetrius the Phalerian, in Aegina, took them by force out of the temple of Aeacus, whither they were fled for safety, and sent them to Antipater, then at Cleonae, where they were all put to death; and

Hyperides, they say, had his tongue cut out.

Demosthenes, he heard, had taken sanctuary at the temple of Neptune in Calauria, and, crossing over thither in some light vessels, as soon as he had landed himself, and the Thracian spear-men that came with him, he endeavored to persuade Demosthenes to accompany him to Antipater, as if he should meet with no hard usage from him. But Demosthenes, in his sleep the night before, had a strange dream. It seemed to him that he was acting a tragedy, and contended with Archias for the victory; and though he acquitted himself well, and gave good satisfaction to the spectators, yet for want of better furniture and provision for the stage, he lost the day. And so, while Archias was discoursing to him with many expressions of kindness, he sat still in the same posture, and looking up steadfastly upon him, "O Archias," said he, "I am as little affected by your promises now as I used formerly to be by your acting." Archias at this beginning to grow angry and to threaten him, "Now," said Demosthenes, "you speak like the genuine Macedonian oracle; before you were but acting a part. Therefore forbear only a little, while I write a word or two home to my family." Having thus spoken, he withdrew into the temple, and taking a scroll, as if he meant to write, he put the reed into his mouth, and biting it, as he was wont to do when he was thoughtful or writing, he held it there for some time. Then he bowed down his head and covered it. The soldiers that stood at the door, supposing all this to proceed from want of courage and fear of death, in derision called him effeminate, and faint-hearted, and coward. And Archias, drawing near, desired him to rise up, and repeating the same kind things he had spoken before, he once more promised him to make his peace with Antipater. But Demosthenes, perceiving that now the poison had pierced and seized his vitals, uncovered his head, and fixing his eyes upon Archias, "Now," said he, "as soon as you please you may commence the part of Creon in the tragedy, and cast out this body of mine unburied. But, O gracious Neptune, I, for my part, while I am yet alive, arise up and depart out of this sacred place; though Antipater and the Macedonians have not left so much as thy temple unpolluted." After he had thus spoken and desired to be held up, because already he began to tremble and stagger, as he was going forward, and passing by the altar, he fell down, and with a groan gave up the ghost.

Ariston says that he took the poison out of a reed, as we have shown before. But Pappus, a certain historian whose history was recovered by Hermippus, says, that as he fell near the altar, there was found in his scroll this beginning only of a letter, and nothing more, "Demosthenes to Antipater." And that when his sudden death was much wondered at, the Thracians who guarded the doors reported that he took the poison into his hand out of a rag, and put it in his mouth, and that they imagined it had been gold which he swallowed; but the maid that served him, being examined by the followers of Archias, affirmed that he had worn it in a bracelet for a long time, as an amulet. And Eratosthenes also says that he kept the poison in a hollow ring, and that that ring was the bracelet which he wore about his arm. There are various other statements made by the many authors who have related the story, but there is no need to enter into their discrepancies; yet I must not omit what is said by Demochares, the relation of Demosthenes, who is of opinion, it was not by the help of poison that he met with so sudden and so easy a death, but that by the singular favor and providence of the gods he was thus rescued from the cruelty of the Macedonians. He died on the sixteenth of Pyanepsion, the most sad and solemn day of the Thesmophoria, which the women observe by fasting in the temple of the goddess.

Soon after his death, the people of Athens bestowed on him such honors as he had deserved. They erected his statue of brass; they decreed that the eldest of his family should be maintained in the Prytaneum; and on the base of his statue was engraven the famous inscription, —

> *Had you for Greece been strong, as wise you were,*
> *The Macedonian had not conquered her.*

For it is simply ridiculous to say, as some have related, that Demosthenes made these verses himself in Calauria, as he was about to take the poison.

A little before we went to Athens, the following incident was said to have happened. A soldier, being summoned to appear before his superior officer, and answer to an accusation brought against him, put that little gold which he had into the hands of Demosthenes's statue. The fingers of this statue were folded one within another, and near it grew a small plane-tree, from which many leaves, either accidentally blown thither by the wind, or placed so on purpose by the man himself falling together, and lying round about the gold, concealed it for a long time. In the end, the soldier returned, and found his treasure entire, and the fame of this incident was spread abroad. And many ingenious persons of the city competed with each other, on this occasion, to vindicate the integrity of Demosthenes, in several epigrams which they made on the subject.

As for Demades, he did not long enjoy the new honors he now came in for, divine vengeance for the death of Demosthenes pursuing him into Macedonia, where he was justly put to death by those whom he had basely flattered. They were weary of him before, but at this time the guilt he lay under was manifest and undeniable. For some of his letters were intercepted, in which he had encouraged Perdiccas to fall upon Macedonia, and to save the Grecians, who, he said, hung only by an old rotten thread, meaning Antipater. Of this he was accused by Dinarchus, the Corinthian, and Cassander was so enraged, that he first slew his son in his bosom, and then gave orders to execute him; who might-now at last, by his own extreme misfortunes, learn the lesson, that traitors, who make sale of their country, sell themselves first; a truth which Demosthenes had often foretold him, and he would never believe. Thus, Sosius, you have the life of Demosthenes, from such accounts as we have either read or heard concerning him.

17
CICERO

It is generally said, that Helvia, the mother of Cicero, was both well born and lived a fair life; but of his father nothing is reported but in extremes. For whilst some would have him the son of a fuller, and educated in that trade, others carry back the origin of his family to Tullus Attius, an illustrious king of the Volscians, who waged war not without honor against the Romans. However, he who first of that house was surnamed Cicero seems to have been a person worthy to be remembered; since those who succeeded him not only did not reject, but were fond of that name, though vulgarly made a matter of reproach. For the Latins call a vetch Cicer, and a nick or dent at the tip of his nose, which resembled the opening in a vetch, gave him the surname of Cicero.

Cicero, whose story I am writing, is said to have replied with spirit to some of his friends, who recommended him to lay aside or change the name when he first stood for office and engaged in politics, that he would make it his endeavor to render the name of Cicero more glorious than that of the Scauri and Catuli. And when he was quaestor in Sicily, and was making an offering of silver plate to the gods, and had inscribed his two names, Marcus and Tullius, instead of the third he jestingly told the artificer to engrave the figure of a vetch by them. Thus much is told us about his name.

Of his birth it is reported, that his mother was delivered without pain or labor, on the third of the new Calends, the same day on which now the magistrates of Rome pray and sacrifice for the emperor. It is said, also, that a vision appeared to his nurse, and foretold the child she then suckled should afterwards become a great benefit to the Roman States. To such presages, which might in general be thought mere fancies and idle talk, he himself erelong gave the credit of true prophecies. For as soon as he was of an age to begin to have lessons, he became so distinguished for his talent, and got such a name and reputation amongst the boys, that their fathers would often visit the school, that they might see young Cicero, and might be able to say that they themselves had witnessed the quickness and readiness in learning for which he was renowned. And the more rude among them used to be angry with their children, to see them, as they walked together, receiving Cicero with respect into the middle place. And being, as Plato would have, the scholar-like and philosophical temper, eager for every kind of learning, and indisposed to no description of knowledge or instruction, he showed, however, a more peculiar propensity to poetry; and there is a poem now extant, made by him when a boy, in tetrameter verse, called Pontius Glaucus. And afterwards, when he applied himself more curiously to these accomplishments, he had the name of being not only the best orator, but also the best poet of Rome. And the glory of his rhetoric still remains, notwithstanding the many new modes in speaking since his time; but his verses are forgotten and out of all repute, so many ingenious poets having followed him.

Leaving his juvenile studies, he became an auditor of Philo the Academic, whom the Romans, above all the other scholars of Clitomachus, admired for his eloquence and loved for his character. He also sought the company of the Mucii, who were eminent statesmen and leaders in the senate, and acquired from them a knowledge of the laws. For some short time he served in arms under Sylla, in the Marsian war. But perceiving the commonwealth running into factions, and from faction all things tending to an absolute monarchy, he betook himself to a retired and contemplative life, and conversing with the learned Greeks, devoted himself to study, till Sylla had obtained the government, and the commonwealth was in some kind of settlement.

At this time, Chrysogonus, Sylla's emancipated slave, having laid an information about an estate belonging to one who was said to have been put to death by proscription, had bought it himself for two thousand drachmas. And when Roscius, the son and heir of the dead, complained, and demonstrated the estate to be worth two hundred and fifty talents, Sylla took it angrily to have his actions questioned, and preferred a process against Roscius for the murder of his father, Chrysogonus managing the evidence. None of the advocates durst assist him, but fearing the cruelty of Sylla, avoided the cause. The young man, being thus deserted, came for refuge to Cicero. Cicero's friends encouraged him, saying he was not likely ever to have a fairer and more honorable introduction to public life; he therefore undertook the defense, carried the cause, and got much renown for it.

But fearing Sylla, he traveled into Greece, and gave it out that he did so for the benefit of his health. And indeed he was lean and meager, and had such a weakness in his stomach, that he could take nothing but a spare and thin diet, and that not till late in the evening. His voice was loud and good, but so harsh and unmanaged that in vehemence and heat of speaking he always raised it to so high a tone, that there seemed to be reason to fear about his health.

When he came to Athens, he was a hearer of Antiochus of Ascalon, with whose fluency and elegance of diction he was much taken, although he did not approve of his innovations in doctrine. For Antiochus had now fallen off from the New Academy, as they call it, and forsaken the sect of Carneades, whether that he was moved by the argument of manifestness and the senses, or, as some say, had been led by feelings of rivalry and opposition to the followers of Clitomachus and Philo to change his opinions, and in most things to embrace the doctrine of the Stoics. But Cicero rather affected and adhered to the doctrines of the New Academy; and purposed with himself, if he should be disappointed of any employment in the commonwealth, to retire hither from pleading and political affairs, and to pass his life with quiet in the study of philosophy.

But after he had received the news of Sylla's death, and his body, strengthened again by exercise, was come to a vigorous habit, his voice managed and rendered sweet and full to the ear and pretty well brought into keeping with his general constitution, his friends at Rome earnestly soliciting him by letters, and Antiochus also urging him to return to public affairs, he again prepared for use his orator's instrument of rhetoric, and summoned into action his political faculties, diligently exercising himself in declamations, and attending the most celebrated rhetoricians of the time. He sailed from Athens for Asia and Rhodes. Amongst the Asian masters, he conversed with Xenocles of Adramyttium, Dionysius of Magnesia, and Menippus of Caria; at Rhodes, he studied oratory with Apollonius, the son of Molon, and philosophy with Posidonius. Apollonius, we are told, not understanding Latin, requested Cicero to declaim in Greek. He complied willingly, thinking that his faults would thus be better pointed out to him. And after he finished, all his other hearers were astonished, and contended who should praise him most, but Apollonius, who had shown no signs of excitement whilst he was hearing him, so also now, when it was over, sat musing for some considerable time, without any remark. And when Cicero was discomposed at this, he said, "You have my praise and admiration, Cicero, and Greece my pity and commiseration, since those arts and that eloquence which are the only glories that remain to her, will now be transferred by you to Rome."

And now when Cicero, full of expectation, was again bent upon political affairs, a certain oracle blunted the edge of his inclination; for consulting the god of Delphi how he should attain most glory, the Pythoness answered, by making his own genius and not the opinion of the people the guide of his life;

and therefore at first he passed his time in Rome cautiously, and was very backward in pretending to public offices, so that he was at that time in little esteem, and had got the names, so readily given by low and ignorant people in Rome, of Greek and Scholar. But when his own desire of fame and the eagerness of his father and relations had made him take in earnest to pleading, he made no slow or gentle advance to the first place, but shone out in full luster at once, and far surpassed all the advocates of the bar. At first, it is said, he, as well as Demosthenes, was defective in his delivery, and on that account paid much attention to the instructions, sometimes of Roscius the comedian, and sometimes of Aesop the tragedian. They tell of this Aesop, that whilst he was representing on the theater Atreus deliberating the revenge of Thyestes, he was so transported beyond himself in the heat of action, that he struck with his scepter one of the servants, who was running across the stage, so violently, that he laid him dead upon the place. And such afterwards was Cicero's delivery, that it did not a little contribute to render his eloquence persuasive. He used to ridicule loud speakers, saying that they shouted because they could not speak, like lame men who get on horseback because they cannot walk. And his readiness and address in sarcasm, and generally in witty sayings, was thought to suit a pleader very well, and to be highly attractive, but his using it to excess offended many, and gave him the repute of ill nature.

He was appointed quaestor in a great scarcity of corn, and had Sicily for his province, where, though at first he displeased many, by compelling them to send in their provisions to Rome, yet after they had had experience of his care, justice, and clemency, they honored him more than ever they did any of their governors before. It happened, also, that some young Romans of good and noble families, charged with neglect of discipline and misconduct in military service, were brought before the praetor in Sicily. Cicero undertook their defense, which he conducted admirably, and got them acquitted. So returning to Rome with a great opinion of himself for these things, a ludicrous incident befell him, as he tells us himself. Meeting an eminent citizen in Campania, whom he accounted his friend, he asked him what the Romans said and thought of his actions, as if the whole city had been filled with the glory of what he had done. His friend asked him in reply, "Where is it you have been, Cicero?" This for the time utterly mortified and cast him down, to perceive that the report of his actions had sunk into the city of Rome as into an immense ocean, without any visible effect or result in reputation. And afterwards considering with himself that the glory he contended for was an infinite thing, and that there was no fixed end nor measure in its pursuit, he abated much of his ambitious thoughts. Nevertheless, he was always excessively pleased with his own praise, and continued to the very last to be passionately fond of glory; which often interfered with the prosecution of his wisest resolutions.

On beginning to apply himself more resolutely to public business, he remarked it as an unreasonable and absurd thing that artificers, using vessels and instruments inanimate, should know the name, place, and use of every one of them, and yet the statesman, whose instruments for carrying out public measures are men, should be negligent and careless in the knowledge of persons. And so he not only acquainted himself with the names, but also knew the particular place where every one of the more eminent citizens dwelt, what lands he possessed, the friends he made use of, and those that were of his neighborhood, and when he traveled on any road in Italy, he could readily name and show the estates and seats of his friends and acquaintance. Having so small an estate, though a sufficient competency for his own expenses, it was much wondered at that he took neither fees nor gifts from his clients, and more especially, that he did not do so when he undertook the prosecution of Verres. This Verres, who had been praetor of Sicily, and stood charged by the Sicilians of many evil practices during his government there, Cicero succeeded in getting condemned, not by speaking, but in a manner by holding his tongue. For the praetors, favoring Verres, had deferred the trial by several adjournments to the last day, in which it was evident there could not be sufficient time for the advocates to be heard, and the cause brought to an issue. Cicero, therefore, came forward, and said there was no need of speeches; and after producing and examining witnesses, he required the judges to proceed to sentence. However, many witty sayings are on record, as having been used by Cicero on the occasion. When a man named Caecilius, one of the freed slaves, who was said to be given to Jewish practices, would have put by the Sicilians, and undertaken the prosecution of Verres himself, Cicero asked, "What has a Jew to do with swine?" verres being the Roman word for a boar. And when Verres began to reproach Cicero with effeminate living, "You ought," replied he, "to use this language at home, to your sons;" Verres having a son who had fallen into disgraceful courses. Hortensius the orator, not daring directly to undertake the defense of Verres, was yet persuaded to appear for him at the laying on of the fine, and received an ivory sphinx for his reward; and when Cicero, in some passage of his speech, obliquely reflected on him, and Hortensius told him he was not skillful in solving riddles, "No," said Cicero, "and yet you have the Sphinx in your house!"

Verres was thus convicted; though Cicero, who set the fine at seventy-five myriads, lay under the suspicion of being corrupted by bribery to lessen the sum. But the Sicilians, in testimony of their gratitude, came and brought him all sorts of presents from the island, when he was aedile; of which he made no private profit himself, but used their generosity only to reduce the public price of provisions.

He had a very pleasant seat at Arpi, he had also a farm near Naples, and another about Pompeii, but neither of any great value. The portion of his wife,

Terentia, amounted to ten myriads, and he had a bequest valued at nine myriads of denarii; upon these he lived in a liberal but temperate style, with the learned Greeks and Romans that were his familiars. He rarely, if at any time, sat down to meat till sunset, and that not so much on account of business, as for his health and the weakness of his stomach. He was otherwise in the care of his body nice and delicate, appointing himself, for example, a set number of walks and rubbings. And after this manner managing the habit of his body, he brought it in time to be healthful, and capable of supporting many great fatigues and trials. His father's house he made over to his brother, living himself near the Palatine hill, that he might not give the trouble of long journeys to those that made suit to him. And, indeed, there were not fewer daily appearing at his door, to do their court to him, than there were that came to Crassus for his riches, or to Pompey for his power amongst the soldiers, these being at that time the two men of the greatest repute and influence in Rome. Nay, even Pompey himself used to pay court to Cicero, and Cicero's public actions did much to establish Pompey's authority and reputation in the state.

Numerous distinguished competitors stood with him for the praetor's office; but he was chosen before them all, and managed the decision of causes with justice and integrity. It is related that Licinius Macer, a man himself of great power in the city, and supported also by the assistance of Crassus, was accused before him of extortion, and that, in confidence on his own interest and the diligence of his friends, whilst the judges were debating about the sentence, he went to his house, where hastily trimming his hair and putting on a clean gown, as already acquitted, he was setting off again to go to the Forum; but at his hall door meeting Crassus, who told him that he was condemned by all the votes, he went in again, threw himself upon his bed, and died immediately. This verdict was considered very creditable to Cicero, as showing his careful management of the courts of justice. On another occasion, Vatinius, a man of rude manners and often insolent in court to the magistrates, who had large swellings on his neck, came before his tribunal and made some request, and on Cicero's desiring further time to consider it, told him that he himself would have made no question about it, had he been praetor. Cicero, turning quickly upon him, answered, "But I, you see, have not the neck that you have."

When there were but two or three days remaining in his office, Manilius was brought before him, and charged with peculation. Manilius had the good opinion and favor of the common people, and was thought to be prosecuted only for Pompey's sake, whose particular friend he was. And therefore, when he asked a space of time before his trial, and Cicero allowed him but one day, and that the next only, the common people grew highly offended, because it had been the custom of the praetors to allow ten days at least to the accused: and the tribunes of the people having called him before the people, and accused him, he, desiring to be heard, said, that as he had always treated the accused with equity and humanity, as far as the law allowed, so he thought it hard to deny the same to Manilius, and that he had studiously appointed that day of which alone, as praetor, he was master, and that it was not the part of those that were desirous to help him, to cast the judgment of his cause upon another praetor. These things being said made a wonderful change in the people, and, commending him much for it, they desired that he himself would undertake the defense of Manilius; which he willingly consented to, and that principally for the sake of Pompey, who was absent. And, accordingly, taking his place before the people again, he delivered a bold invective upon the oligarchical party and on those who were jealous of Pompey.

Yet he was preferred to the consulship no less by the nobles than the common people, for the good of the city; and both parties jointly assisted his promotion, upon the following reasons. The change of government made by Sylla, which at first seemed a senseless one, by time and usage had now come to be considered by the people no unsatisfactory settlement. But there were some that endeavored to alter and subvert the whole present state of affairs not from any good motives, but for their own private gain; and Pompey being at this time employed in the wars with the kings of Pontus and Armenia, there was no sufficient force at Rome to suppress any attempts at a revolution. These people had for their head a man of bold, daring, and restless character, Lucius Catiline, who was accused, besides other great offenses, of deflowering his virgin daughter, and killing his own brother; for which latter crime, fearing to be prosecuted at law, he persuaded Sylla to set him down, as though he were yet alive, amongst those that were to be put to death by proscription. This man the profligate citizens choosing for their captain, gave faith to one another, amongst other pledges, by sacrificing a man and eating of his flesh; and a great part of the young men of the city were corrupted by him, he providing for everyone pleasures, drink, and women, and profusely supplying the expense of these debauches. Etruria, moreover, had all been excited to revolt, as well as a great part of Gaul within the Alps. But Rome itself was in the most dangerous inclination to change, on account of the unequal distribution of wealth and property, those of highest rank and greatest spirit having impoverished themselves by shows, entertainments, ambition of offices, and sumptuous buildings, and the riches of the city having thus fallen into the hands of mean and low-born persons. So that there wanted but a slight impetus to set all in motion, it being in the power of every daring man to overturn a sickly commonwealth.

Catiline, however, being desirous of procuring a strong position to carry out his designs, stood for the consulship, and had great hopes of success, thinking he should be appointed, with Caius Antonius as his colleague, who was a man fit to lead neither in a good cause nor in a bad one, but might be a valuable accession to another's power. These things the greatest part of the good and honest citizens apprehending, put Cicero upon standing for the consulship; whom the people readily receiving, Catiline was put by, so that he and Caius Antonius were chosen, although amongst the competitors he was the only man descended from a father of the equestrian, and not of the senatorial order.

Though the designs of Catiline were not yet publicly known, yet considerable preliminary troubles immediately followed upon Cicero's entrance upon the consulship. For, on the one side, those who were disqualified by the laws of Sylla from holding any public offices, being neither inconsiderable in power nor in number, came forward as candidates and caressed the people for them; speaking many things truly and justly against the tyranny of Sylla, only that they disturbed the government at an improper and unseasonable time; on the other hand, the tribunes of the people proposed laws to the same purpose, constituting a commission of ten persons, with unlimited powers, in whom as supreme governors should be vested the right of selling the public lands of all Italy and Syria and Pompey's new conquests, of judging and banishing whom they pleased, of planting colonies, of taking moneys out of the treasury, and of levying and paying what soldiers should be thought needful. And several of the nobility favored this law, but especially Caius Antonius, Cicero's colleague, in hopes of being one of the ten. But what gave the greatest fear to the nobles was, that he was thought privy to the conspiracy of Catiline, and not to dislike it, because of his great debts.

Cicero, endeavoring in the first place to provide a remedy against this danger, procured a decree assigning to him the province of Macedonia, he himself declining that of Gaul, which was offered to him. And this piece of favor so completely won over Antonius, that he was ready to second and respond to, like a hired player, whatever Cicero said for the good of the country. And now, having made his colleague thus tame and tractable, he could with greater courage attack the conspirators. And, therefore, in the senate, making an oration against the law of the ten commissioners, he so confounded those who proposed it, that they had nothing to reply. And when they again endeavored, and, having prepared things beforehand, had called the consuls before the assembly of the people, Cicero, fearing nothing, went first out, and commanded the senate to follow him, and not only succeeded in throwing out the law, but so entirely overpowered the tribunes by his oratory, that they abandoned all thought of their other projects.

For Cicero, it may be said, was the one man, above all others, who made the Romans feel how great a charm eloquence lends to what is good, and how invincible justice is, if it be well spoken; and that it is necessary for him who would dexterously govern a commonwealth, in action, always to prefer that which is honest before that which is popular, and in speaking, to free the right and useful measure from everything that may occasion offense. An incident occurred in the theater, during his consulship, which showed what his speaking could do. For whereas formerly the knights of Rome were mingled in the theater with the common people, and took their places amongst them as it happened, Marcus Otho, when he was praetor, was the first who distinguished them from the other citizens, and appointed them a proper seat, which they still enjoy as their special place in the theater. This the common people took as an indignity done to them, and, therefore, when Otho appeared in the theater, they hissed him; the knights, on the contrary, received him with loud clapping. The people repeated and increased their hissing; the knights continued their clapping. Upon this, turning upon one another, they broke out into insulting words, so that the theater was in great disorder. Cicero, being informed of it, came himself to the theater, and summoning the people into the temple of Bellona, he so effectually chid and chastised them for it, that, again returning into the theater, they received Otho with loud applause, contending with the knights who should give him the greatest demonstrations of honor and respect.

The conspirators with Catiline, at first cowed and disheartened, began presently to take courage again. And assembling themselves together, they exhorted one another boldly to undertake the design before Pompey's return, who, as it was said, was now on his march with his forces for Rome. But the old soldiers of Sylla were Catiline's chief stimulus to action. They had been disbanded all about Italy, but the greatest number and the fiercest of them lay scattered among the cities of Etruria, entertaining themselves with dreams of new plunder and rapine amongst the hoarded riches of Italy. These, having for their leader Manlius, who had served with distinction in the wars under Sylla, joined themselves to Catiline, and came to Rome to assist him with their suffrages at the election. For he again pretended to the consulship, having resolved to kill Cicero in a tumult at the elections. Also, the divine powers seemed to give intimation of the coming troubles, by earthquakes, thunderbolts, and strange appearances. Nor was human evidence wanting, certain enough in itself, though not sufficient for the conviction of the noble and powerful Catiline. Therefore Cicero, deferring the day of election, summoned Catiline into the senate, and questioned him as to the charges made against him. Catiline, believing there were many in the senate desirous of change, and to give a specimen of himself to the conspirators present, returned an audacious answer, "What harm," said he, "when I see two bodies, the one lean and consumptive with a head, the other great and strong without one, if I put a head to that body which wants one?" This covert representation of the senate and the people excited yet greater apprehensions in Cicero. He put on armor, and was attended from his house by the noble citizens in a body; and a number of the young men went with him into the Plain. Here, designedly letting his tunic slip partly off from his shoulders, he showed his armor underneath, and discovered his danger to the spectators; who, being much moved at it, gathered round about him for his defense. At length, Catiline was by a general suffrage again put by, and Silanus and Murena chosen consuls.

Not long after this, Catiline's soldiers got together in a body in Etruria, and began to form themselves into companies, the day appointed for the design being near at hand. About midnight, some of the principal and most powerful citizens of Rome, Marcus Crassus, Marcus Marcellus, and Scipio Metellus went to Cicero's house, where, knocking at the gate, and calling up the porter, they commended him to awake Cicero, and tell him they were there. The business was this: Crassus's porter after supper had delivered to him letters brought by an unknown person. Some of them were directed to others, but one to Crassus, without a name; this only Crassus read, which informed him that there was a great slaughter intended by Catiline, and advised him to leave the city. The others he did not open, but went with them immediately to Cicero, being affrighted at the danger, and to free himself of the suspicion he lay under for his familiarity with Catiline. Cicero, considering the matter, summoned the senate at break of day. The letters he brought with him, and delivered them to those to whom they were directed, commanding them to read them publicly; they all alike contained an account of the conspiracy. And when Quintus Arrius, a man of praetorian dignity, recounted to them, how soldiers were collecting in companies in Etruria, and Manlius stated to be in motion with a large force, hovering about those cities, in expectation of intelligence from Rome, the senate made a decree, to place all in the hands of the consuls, who should undertake the conduct of everything, and do their best to save the state. This was not a common thing, but only done by the senate in case of imminent danger.

After Cicero had received this power, he committed all affairs outside to Quintus Metellus, but the management of the city he kept in his own hands. Such a numerous attendance guarded him every day when he went abroad, that the greatest part of the market-place was filled with his train when he entered it. Catiline, impatient of further delay, resolved himself to break forth and go to Manlius, but he commanded Marcius and Cethegus to take their swords, and go early in the morning to Cicero's gates, as if only intending to salute him, and then to fall upon him and slay him. This a noble lady, Fulvia, coming by night, discovered to Cicero, bidding him beware of Cethegus and Marcius. They came by break of day, and being denied entrance, made an outcry and disturbance at the gates, which excited all the more suspicion. But Cicero, going forth, summoned the senate into the temple of Jupiter Stator, which stands at the end of the Sacred Street, going up to the Palatine. And when Catiline with others of his party also came, as intending to make his defense, none of the senators would sit by him, but all of them left the bench where he had placed himself. And when he began to speak, they interrupted him with outcries. At length Cicero, standing up, commanded him to leave the city, for since one governed the commonwealth with words, the other with arms, it was necessary there should be a wall betwixt them. Catiline, therefore, immediately left the town, with three hundred armed men; and assuming, as if he had been a magistrate, the rods, axes, and military ensigns, he went to Manlius, and having got together a body of near twenty thousand men, with these he marched to the several cities, endeavoring to persuade or force them to revolt. So it being now come to open war, Antonius was sent forth to fight him.

The remainder of those in the city whom he had corrupted, Cornelius Lentulus kept together and encouraged. He had the surname Sura, and was a man of a noble family, but a dissolute liver, who for his debauchery was formerly turned out of the senate, and was now holding the office of praetor for the second time, as the custom is with those who desire to regain the dignity of senator. It is said that he got the surname Sura upon this occasion; being quaestor in the time of Sylla, he had lavished away and consumed a great quantity of the public moneys, at which Sylla being provoked, called him to give an account in the senate; he appeared with great coolness and contempt, and said he had no account to give, but they might take this, holding up the calf of his leg, as boys do at ball, when they have missed. Upon which he was surnamed Sura, sura being the Roman word for the calf of the leg. Being at another time prosecuted at law, and having bribed some of the judges, he escaped only by two votes, and complained of the needless expense he had gone to in paying for a second, as one would have sufficed to acquit him. This man, such in his own nature, and now inflamed by Catiline, false prophets and fortune-tellers had also corrupted with vain hopes, quoting to him fictitious verses and oracles, and proving from the Sibylline prophecies that there were three of the name Cornelius designed by fate to be monarchs of Rome; two of whom, Cinna and Sylla, had already fulfilled the decree, and that divine fortune was now advancing with the gift of monarchy for the remaining third Cornelius; and that therefore he ought by all means to accept it, and not lose opportunity by delay, as Catiline had done.

Lentulus, therefore, designed no mean or trivial matter, for he had resolved to kill the whole senate, and as many other citizens as he could, to fire the city, and spare nobody, except only Pompey's children, intending to seize and keep them as pledges of his reconciliation with Pompey. For there was then a common and strong report that Pompey was on his way homeward from his great expedition. The night appointed for the design was one of the Saturnalia; swords, flax, and sulfur they carried and hid in the house of Cethegus; and providing one hundred men, and dividing the city into as many parts, they had allotted to every one singly his proper place, so that in a moment many kindling the fire, the city might be in a flame all together. Others were appointed to stop up the aqueducts, and to kill those who should endeavor to carry water to put it out. Whilst these plans were preparing, it happened there were two ambassadors from the Allobroges staying in Rome; a nation at that time in a distressed condition, and very uneasy under the Roman government. These Lentulus and his party judging useful instruments to move and seduce Gaul to revolt, admitted into the conspiracy, and they gave them letters to their own magistrates, and letters to Catiline; in those they promised liberty, in these they exhorted Catiline to set all slaves free, and to bring them along with him to Rome. They sent also to accompany them to Catiline, one Titus, a native of Croton, who was to carry those letters to him.

These counsels of inconsidering men, who conversed together over wine and with women, Cicero watched with sober industry and forethought, and with most admirable sagacity, having several emissaries abroad, who observed and traced with him all that was done, and keeping also a secret correspondence with many who pretended to join in the conspiracy. He thus knew all the discourse which passed betwixt them and the strangers; and lying in wait for them by night, he took the Crotonian with his letters, the ambassadors of the Allobroges acting secretly in concert with him.

By break of day, he summoned the senate into the temple of Concord, where he read the letters and examined the informers. Junius Silanus further stated, that several persons had heard Cethegus say, that three consuls and four praetors were to be slain; Piso, also, a person of consular dignity, testified other matters of the like nature; and Caius Sulpicius, one of the praetors, being sent to Cethegus's house, found there a quantity of darts and of armor, and a still greater number of swords and daggers, all recently whetted. At length, the senate decreeing indemnity to the Crotonian upon his confession of the whole matter, Lentulus was convicted, abjured his office (for he was then praetor), and put off his robe edged with purple in the senate, changing it for another garment more agreeable to his present circumstances. He, thereupon, with the rest of his confederates present, was committed to the charge of the praetors in free custody.

It being evening, and the common people in crowds expecting without, Cicero went forth to them, and told them what was done, and then, attended by them, went to the house of a friend and near neighbor; for his own was taken up by the women, who were celebrating with secret rites the feast of the goddess whom the Romans call the Good, and the Greeks, the Women's goddess. For a sacrifice is annually performed to her in the consul's house, either by his wife or mother, in the presence of the vestal virgins. And having got into his friend's house privately, a few only being present, he began to deliberate how he should treat these men. The severest, and the only punishment fit for such heinous crimes, he was somewhat shy and fearful of inflicting, as well from the clemency of his nature, as also lest he should be thought to exercise his authority too insolently, and to treat too harshly men of the noblest birth and most powerful friendships in the city; and yet, if he should use them more mildly, he had a dreadful prospect of danger from them. For there was no likelihood, if they suffered less than death, they would be reconciled, but rather, adding new rage to their former wickedness, they would rush into every kind of audacity, while he himself, whose character for courage already did not stand very high with the multitude, would be thought guilty of the greatest cowardice and want of manliness.

Whilst Cicero was doubting what course to take, a portent happened to the women in their sacrificing. For on the altar, where the fire seemed wholly extinguished, a great and bright flame issued forth from the ashes of the burnt wood; at which others were affrighted, but the holy virgins called to Terentia, Cicero's wife, and bade her haste to her husband, and command him to execute what he had resolved for the good of his country, for the goddess had sent a great light to the increase of his safety and glory. Terentia, therefore, as she was otherwise in her own nature neither tender-hearted nor timorous, but a woman eager for distinction (who, as Cicero himself says, would rather thrust herself into his public affairs, than communicate her domestic matters to him), told him these things, and excited him against the conspirators. So also did Quintus his brother, and Publius Nigidius, one of his philosophical friends, whom he often made use of in his greatest and most weighty affairs of state.

The next day, a debate arising in the senate about the punishment of the men, Silanus, being the first who was asked his opinion, said, it was fit they should be all sent to the prison, and there suffer the utmost penalty. To him all consented in order till it came to Caius Caesar, who was afterwards dictator. He was then but a young man, and only at the outset of his career, but had already directed his hopes and policy to that course by which he afterwards changed the Roman state into a monarchy. Of this others foresaw nothing; but Cicero had seen reason for strong suspicion, though without obtaining any sufficient means of proof. And there were some indeed that said that he was very near being discovered, and only just escaped him; others are of opinion that Cicero voluntarily overlooked and neglected the evidence against him, for fear of his friends and power; for it was very evident to everybody, that if Caesar was to be accused with the conspirators, they were more likely to be saved with him, than he to be punished with them.

When, therefore, it came to Caesar's turn to give his opinion, he stood up and proposed that the conspirators should not be put to death, but their estates confiscated, and their persons confined in such cities in Italy as Cicero should approve, there to be kept in custody till Catiline was conquered. To this sentence, as it was the most moderate, and he that delivered it a most powerful speaker, Cicero himself gave no small weight, for he stood up and, turning the scale on either side, spoke in favor partly of the former, partly of Caesar's sentence. And all Cicero's friends, judging Caesar's sentence most expedient for Cicero, because he would incur the less blame if the conspirators were not put to death, chose rather the latter; so that Silanus, also, changing his mind, retracted his opinion, and said he had not declared for capital, but only the utmost punishment, which to a Roman senator is imprisonment. The first man who spoke against Caesar's motion was Catulus Lutatius. Cato followed, and so vehemently urged in his speech the strong suspicion about Caesar himself, and so filled the senate with anger and resolution, that a decree was passed for the execution of the conspirators. But Caesar opposed the confiscation of their goods, not thinking it fair that those who had rejected the mildest part of his sentence should avail themselves of the severest. And when many insisted upon it, he appealed to the tribunes, but they would do nothing; till Cicero himself yielding, remitted that part of the sentence.

After this, Cicero went out with the senate to the conspirators; they were not all together in one place, but the several praetors had them, some one, some another, in custody. And first he took Lentulus from the Palatine, and brought him by the Sacred Street, through the middle of the marketplace, a circle of the most eminent citizens encompassing and protecting him. The people, affrighted at what was doing, passed along in silence, especially the young men; as if, with fear and trembling, they were undergoing a rite of initiation into some ancient, sacred mysteries of aristocratic power. Thus passing from the market-place, and coming to the gaol, he delivered Lentulus to the officer, and commanded him to execute him; and after him Cethegus, and so all the rest in order, he brought and delivered up to execution. And when he saw many of the conspirators in the market-place, still standing together in companies, ignorant of what was done, and waiting for the night, supposing the men were still alive and in a possibility of being rescued, he called out in a loud voice, and said, "They did live;" for so the Romans, to avoid inauspicious language, name those that are dead.

It was now evening, when he returned from the market-place to his own house, the citizens no longer attending him with silence, nor in order, but receiving him, as he passed, with acclamations and applauses, and saluting him as the savior and founder of his country. A bright light shone through the streets from the lamps and torches set up at the doors, and the women showed lights from the tops of the houses, to honor Cicero, and to behold him returning home with a splendid train of the most principal citizens; amongst whom were many who had conducted great wars, celebrated triumphs, and added to the possessions of the Roman empire, both by sea and land. These, as they passed along with him, acknowledged to one another, that though the Roman people were indebted to several officers and commanders of that age for riches, spoils, and power, yet to Cicero alone they owed the safety and security of all these, for delivering them from so great and imminent a danger. For though it might seem no wonderful thing to prevent the design, and punish the conspirators, yet to defeat the greatest of all conspiracies with so little disturbance, trouble, and commotion, was very extraordinary. For the greater part of those who had flocked in to Catiline, as soon as they heard the fate of Lentulus and Cethegus, left and forsook him, and he himself, with his remaining forces, joining battle with Antonius, was destroyed with his army.

And yet there were some who were very ready both to speak ill of Cicero, and to do him hurt for these actions; and they had for their leaders some of the magistrates of the ensuing year, as Caesar, who was one of the praetors, and Metellus and Bestia, the tribunes. These, entering upon their office some few days before Cicero's consulate expired, would not permit him to make any address to the people, but, throwing the benches before the Rostra, hindered his speaking, telling him he might, if he pleased, make the oath of withdrawal from office, and then come down again. Cicero, accordingly, accepting the conditions, came forward to make his withdrawal; and silence being made, he recited his oath, not in the usual, but in a new and peculiar form, namely, that he had saved his country, and preserved the empire; the truth of which oath all the people confirmed with theirs. Caesar and the tribunes, all the more exasperated by this, endeavored to create him further trouble, and for this purpose proposed a law for calling Pompey home with his army, to put an end to Cicero's usurpation. But it was a very great advantage for Cicero and the whole commonwealth that Cato was at that time one of the tribunes. For he, being of equal power with the rest, and of greater reputation, could oppose their designs. He easily defeated their other projects, and, in an oration to the people, so highly extolled Cicero's consulate, that the greatest honors were decreed him, and he was publicly declared the Father of his Country, which title he seems to have obtained, the first man who did so, when Cato gave it him in this address to the people.

At this time, therefore, his authority was very great in the city; but he created himself much envy, and offended very many, not by any evil action, but because he was always lauding and magnifying himself. For neither senate, nor assembly of the people, nor court of judicature could meet, in which he was not heard to talk of Catiline and Lentulus. Indeed, he also filled his books and writings with his own praises, to such an excess as to render a style, in itself most pleasant and delightful, nauseous and irksome to his hearers; this ungrateful humor, like a disease, always cleaving to him. Nevertheless, though he was intemperately fond of his own glory, he was very free from envying others, and was, on the contrary, most liberally profuse in commending both the ancients and his contemporaries, as anyone may see in his writings. And many such sayings of his are also remembered; as that he called Aristotle a river of flowing gold, and said of Plato's

Dialogues, that if Jupiter were to speak, it would be in language like theirs. He used to call Theophrastus his special luxury. And being asked which of Demosthenes's orations he liked best, he answered, the longest. And yet some affected imitators of Demosthenes have complained of some words that occur in one of his letters, to the effect that Demosthenes sometimes falls asleep in his speeches; forgetting the many high encomiums he continually passes upon him, and the compliment he paid him when he named the most elaborate of all his orations, those he wrote against Antony, Philippics. And as for the eminent men of his own time, either in eloquence or philosophy, there was not one of them whom he did not, by writing or speaking favorably of him, render more illustrious. He obtained of Caesar, when in power, the Roman citizenship for Cratippus, the Peripatetic, and got the court of Areopagus, by public decree, to request his stay at Athens, for the instruction of their youth, and the honor of their city. There are letters extant from Cicero to Herodes, and others to his son, in which he recommends the study of philosophy under Cratippus. There is one in which he blames Gorgias, the rhetorician, for enticing his son into luxury and drinking, and, therefore, forbids him his company. And this, and one other to Pelops, the Byzantine, are the only two of his Greek epistles which seem to be written in anger. In the first, he justly reflects on Gorgias, if he were what he was thought to be, a dissolute and profligate character; but in the other, he rather meanly expostulates and complains with Pelops, for neglecting to procure him a decree of certain honors from the Byzantines.

Another illustration of his love of praise is the way in which sometimes, to make his orations more striking, he neglected decorum and dignity. When Munatius, who had escaped conviction by his advocacy, immediately prosecuted his friend Sabinus, he said in the warmth of his resentment, "Do you suppose you were acquitted for your own meets, Munatius, and was it not that I so darkened the case, that the court could not see your guilt?" When from the Rostra he had made an eulogy on Marcus Crassus, with much applause, and within a few days after again as publicly reproached him, Crassus called to him, and said, "Did not you yourself two days ago, in this same place, commend me?" "Yes," said Cicero, "I exercised my eloquence in declaiming upon a bad subject." At another time, Crassus had said that no one of his family had ever lived beyond sixty years of age, and afterwards denied it, and asked, "What should put it into my head to say so?" "It was to gain the people's favor," answered Cicero; "you knew how glad they would be to hear it." When Crassus expressed admiration of the Stoic doctrine, that the good man is always rich, "Do you not mean," said Cicero, "their doctrine that all things belong to the wise?" Crassus being generally accused of covetousness. One of Crassus's sons, who was thought so exceedingly like a man of the name of Axius as to throw some suspicion on his mother's honor, made a successful speech in the senate. Cicero on being asked how he liked it, replied with the Greek words, Axios Crassou.

When Crassus was about to go into Syria, he desired to leave Cicero rather his friend than his enemy, and, therefore, one day saluting him, told him he would come and sup with him, which the other as courteously received. Within a few days after, on some of Cicero's acquaintances interceding for Vatinius, as desirous of reconciliation and friendship, for he was then his enemy, "What," he replied, "does Vatinius also wish to come and sup with me?" Such was his way with Crassus. When Vatinius, who had swellings in his neck, was pleading a cause, he called him the tumid orator; and having been told by someone that Vatinius was dead, on hearing presently after that he was alive, "May the rascal perish," said he, "for his news not being true."

Upon Caesar's bringing forward a law for the division of the lands in Campania amongst the soldiers, many in the senate opposed it; amongst the rest, Lucius Gellius, one of the oldest men in the house, said it should never pass whilst he lived. "Let us postpone it," said Cicero, "Gellius does not ask us to wait long." There was a man of the name of Octavius, suspected to be of African descent. He once said, when Cicero was pleading, that he could not hear him; "Yet there are holes," said Cicero, "in your ears." When Metellus Nepos told him, that he had ruined more as a witness, than he had saved as an advocate, "I admit," said Cicero, "that I have more truth than eloquence." To a young man who was suspected of having given a poisoned cake to his father, and who talked largely of the invectives he meant to deliver against Cicero, "Better these," replied he, "than your cakes." Publius Sextius, having amongst others retained Cicero as his advocate in a certain cause, was yet desirous to say all for himself, and would not allow anybody to speak for him; when he was about to receive his acquittal from the judges, and the ballots were passing, Cicero called to him, "Make haste, Sextius, and use your time; tomorrow you will be nobody." He cited Publius Cotta to bear testimony in a certain cause, one who affected to be thought a lawyer, though ignorant and unlearned; to whom, when he had said, "I know nothing of the matter," he answered, "You think, perhaps, we ask you about a point of law." To Metellus Nepos, who, in a dispute between them, repeated several times, "Who was your father, Cicero?" he replied, "Your mother has made the answer to such a question in your case more difficult;" Nepos's mother having been of ill repute. The son, also, was of a giddy, uncertain temper. At one time, he suddenly threw up his office of tribune, and sailed off into Syria to Pompey; and immediately after, with as little reason, came back again. He gave his tutor, Philagrus, a funeral with more than necessary attention, and then set up the stone figure of a crow over his tomb. "This," said Cicero, "is really appropriate; as he did not teach you to speak, but to fly about." When Marcus Appius, in the opening of some speech in a court of justice, said that his friend had desired him to employ industry, eloquence, and fidelity in that cause, Cicero answered, "And how have you had the heart not to accede to any one of his requests?"

To use this sharp raillery against opponents and antagonists in judicial pleading seems allowable rhetoric. But he excited much ill feeling by his readiness to attack anyone for the sake of a jest. A few anecdotes of this kind may be added. Marcus Aquinius, who had two sons-in-law in exile, received from him the name of king Adrastus. Lucius Cotta, an intemperate lover of wine, was censor when Cicero stood for the consulship. Cicero, being thirsty at the election, his friends stood round about him while he was drinking. "You have reason to be afraid," he said, "lest the censor should be angry with me for drinking water." Meeting one day Voconius with his three very ugly daughters, he quoted the verse,

He reared a race without Apollo's leave.

When Marcus Gellius, who was reputed the son of a slave, had read several letters in the senate with a very shrill, and loud voice, "Wonder not," said Cicero, "he comes of the criers." When Faustus Sylla, the son of Sylla the dictator, who had, during his dictatorship, by public bills proscribed and condemned so many citizens, had so far wasted his estate, and got into debt, that he was forced to publish his bills of sale, Cicero told him that he liked these bills much better than those of his father. By this habit he made himself odious with many people.

But Clodius's faction conspired against him upon the following occasion. Clodius was a member of a noble family, in the flower of his youth, and of a bold and resolute temper. He, being in love with Pompeia, Caesar's wife, got privately into his house in the dress and attire of a music-girl; the women being at that time offering there the sacrifice which must not be seen by men, and there was no man present. Clodius, being a youth and beardless, hoped to get to Pompeia among the women without being taken notice of. But coming into a great house by night, he missed his way in the passages, and a servant belonging to Aurelia, Caesar's mother, spying him wandering up and down, inquired his name. Thus being necessitated to speak, he told her he was seeking for one of Pompeia's maids, Abra by name; and she, perceiving it not to be a woman's voice, shrieked out, and called in the women; who, shutting the gates, and searching every place, at length found Clodius hidden in the chamber of the maid with whom he had come in. This matter being much talked about, Caesar put away his wife, Pompeia, and Clodius was prosecuted for profaning the holy rites.

Cicero was at this time his friend, for he had been useful to him in the conspiracy of Catiline, as one of his forwardest assistants and protectors. But when Clodius rested his defense upon this point, that he was not then at Rome, but at a distance in the country, Cicero testified that he had come to his house that day, and conversed with him on several matters; which thing was indeed true, although Cicero was thought to testify it not so much for the truth's sake as to preserve his quiet with Terentia his wife. For she bore a grudge against Clodius on account of his sister Clodia's wishing, as it was alleged, to marry Cicero, and having employed for this purpose the intervention of Tullus, a very intimate friend of Cicero's; and his frequent visits to Clodia, who lived in their neighborhood, and the attentions he paid to her had excited Terentia's suspicions, and, being a woman of a violent temper, and having the ascendant over Cicero, she urged him on to taking a part against Clodius, and delivering his testimony. Many other good and honest citizens also gave evidence against him, for perjuries, disorders, bribing the people, and debauching women. Lucullus proved, by his women-servants, that he had debauched his youngest sister when she was Lucullus's wife; and there was a general belief that he had done the same with his two other sisters, Tertia, whom Marcius Rex, and Clodia, whom Metellus Celer had married; the latter of whom was called Quadrantia, because one of her lovers had deceived her with a purse of small copper money instead of silver, the smallest copper coin being called a quadrant. Upon this sister's account, in particular, Clodius's character was attacked. Notwithstanding all this, when the common people united against the accusers and witnesses and the whole party, the judges were affrighted, and a guard was placed about them for their defense; and most of them wrote their sentences on the tablets in such a way, that they could not well be read. It was decided, however, that there was a majority for his acquittal, and bribery was reported to have been employed; in reference to which Catulus remarked, when he next met the judges, "You were very right to ask for a guard, to prevent your money being taken from you." And when Clodius upbraided Cicero that the judges had not believed his testimony, "Yes," said he, "five and twenty of them trusted me, and condemned you, and the other thirty did not trust you, for they did not acquit you till they had got your money."

Caesar, though cited, did not give his testimony against Clodius, and declared himself not convinced of his wife's adultery, but that he had put her away because it was fit that Caesar's house should not be only free of the evil fact, but of the fame too.

Clodius, having escaped this danger, and having got himself chosen one of the tribunes, immediately attacked Cicero, heaping up all matters and inciting all persons against him. The common people he gained over with popular laws; to each of the consuls he decreed large provinces, to Piso, Macedonia, and to Gabinius, Syria; he made a strong party among the indigent citizens, to support him in his proceedings, and had always a body of armed slaves about him. Of the three men then in greatest power, Crassus was

Cicero's open enemy, Pompey indifferently made advances to both, and Caesar was going with an army into Gaul. To him, though not his friend (what had occurred in the time of the conspiracy having created suspicions between them), Cicero applied, requesting an appointment as one of his lieutenants in the province. Caesar accepted him, and Clodius, perceiving that Cicero would thus escape his tribunician authority, professed to be inclinable to a reconciliation, laid the greatest fault upon Terentia, made always a favorable mention of him, and addressed him with kind expressions, as one who felt no hatred or ill-will, but who merely wished to urge his complaints in a moderate and friendly way. By these artifices, he so freed Cicero of all his fears, that he resigned his appointment to Caesar, and betook himself again to political affairs. At which Caesar being exasperated, joined the party of Clodius against him, and wholly alienated Pompey from him; he also himself declared in a public assembly of the people, that he did not think Lentulus and Cethegus, with their accomplices, were fairly and legally put to death without being brought to trial. And this, indeed, was the crime charged upon Cicero, and this impeachment he was summoned to answer. And so, as an accused man, and in danger for the result, he changes his dress, and went round with his hair untrimmed, in the attire of a suppliant, to beg the people's grace. But Clodius met him in every corner, having a band of abusive and daring fellows about him, who derided Cicero for his change of dress and his humiliation, and often, by throwing dirt and stones at him, interrupted his supplication to the people.

However, first of all, almost the whole equestrian order changed their dress with him, and no less than twenty thousand young gentlemen followed him with their hair untrimmed, and supplicating with him to the people. And then the senate met, to pass a decree that the people should change their dress as in time of public sorrow. But the consuls opposing it, and Clodius with armed men besetting the senate-house, many of the senators ran out, crying out and tearing their clothes. But this sight moved neither shame nor pity; Cicero must either fly or determine it by the sword with Clodius. He entreated Pompey to aid him, who was on purpose gone out of the way, and was staying at his country-house in the Alban hills; and first he sent his son-in-law Piso to intercede with him, and afterwards set out to go himself. Of which Pompey being informed, would not stay to see him, being ashamed at the remembrance of the many conflicts in the commonwealth which Cicero had undergone in his behalf, and how much of his policy he had directed for his advantage. But being now Caesar's son-in-law, at his instance he had set aside all former kindness, and, slipping out at another door, avoided the interview. Thus being forsaken by Pompey, and left alone to himself, he fled to the consuls. Gabinius was rough with him, as usual, but Piso spoke more courteously, desiring him to yield and give place for a while to the fury of Clodius, and to await a change of times, and to be now, as before, his country's savior from the peril of these troubles and commotions which Clodius was exciting.

Cicero, receiving this answer, consulted with his friends. Lucullus advised him to stay, as being sure to prevail at last; others to fly, because the people would soon desire him again, when they should have enough of the rage and madness of Clodius. This last Cicero approved. But first he took a statue of Minerva, which had been long set up and greatly honored in his house, and carrying it to the capitol, there dedicated it, with the inscription, "To Minerva, Patroness of Rome." And receiving an escort from his friends, about the middle of the night he left the city, and went by land through Lucania, intending to reach Sicily.

But as soon as it was publicly known that he was fled, Clodius proposed to the people a decree of exile, and by his own order interdicted him fire and water, prohibiting any within five hundred miles in Italy to receive him into their houses. Most people, out of respect for Cicero, paid no regard to this edict, offering him every attention and escorting him on his way. But at Hipponium, a city of Lucania, now called Vibo, one Vibius, a Sicilian by birth, who, amongst many other instances of Cicero's friendship, had been made head of the state engineers when he was consul, would not receive him into his house, sending him word he would appoint a place in the country for his reception. Caius Vergilius, the praetor of Sicily, who had been on the most intimate terms with him, wrote to him to forbear coming into Sicily. At these things Cicero being disheartened, went to Brundusium, whence putting forth with a prosperous wind, a contrary gale blowing from the sea carried him back to Italy the next day. He put again to sea, and having reached Dyrrachium, on his coming to shore there, it is reported that an earthquake and a convulsion in the sea happened at the same time, signs which the diviners said intimated that his exile would not be long, for these were prognostics of change. Although many visited him with respect, and the cities of Greece contended which should honor him most, he yet continued disheartened and disconsolate, like an unfortunate lover, often casting his looks back upon Italy; and, indeed, he was become so poor-spirited, so humiliated and dejected by his misfortunes, as none could have expected in a man who had devoted so much of his life to study and learning. And yet he often desired his friends not to call him orator, but philosopher, because he had made philosophy his business, and had only used rhetoric as an instrument for attaining his objects in public life. But the desire of glory has great power in washing the tinctures of philosophy out of the souls of men, and in imprinting the passions of the common people, by custom and conversation, in the minds of those that take a part in governing them, unless the politician be very careful so to engage in public affairs as to interest himself only in the affairs themselves, but not participate in the passions that are consequent to them.

Clodius, having thus driven away Cicero, fell to burning his farms and villas, and afterwards his city house, and built on the site of it a temple to Liberty. The rest of his property he exposed to sale by daily proclamation, but nobody came to buy. By these courses he became formidable to the noble citizens, and, being followed by the commonalty, whom he had filled with insolence and licentiousness, he began at last to try his strength against Pompey, some of whose arrangements in the countries he conquered, he attacked. The disgrace of this made Pompey begin to reproach himself for his cowardice in deserting Cicero, and, changing his mind, he now wholly set himself with his friends to contrive his return. And when Clodius opposed it, the senate made a vote that no public measure should be ratified or passed by them till Cicero was recalled. But when Lentulus was consul, the commotions grew so high upon this matter, that the tribunes were wounded in the Forum, and Quintus, Cicero's brother, was left as dead, lying unobserved amongst the slain. The people began to change in their feelings; and Annius Milo, one of their tribunes, was the first who took confidence to summon Clodius to trial for acts of violence. Many of the common people and out of the neighboring cities formed a party with Pompey, and he went with them, and drove Clodius out of the Forum, and summoned the people to pass their vote. And, it is said, the people never passed any suffrage more unanimously than this. The senate, also, striving to outdo the people, sent letters of thanks to those cities which had received Cicero with respect in his exile, and decreed that his house and his country-places, which Clodius had destroyed, should be rebuilt at the public charge.

Thus Cicero returned sixteen months after his exile, and the cities were so glad, and people so zealous to meet him, that what he boasted of afterwards, that Italy had brought him on her shoulders home to Rome, was rather less than the truth. And Crassus himself, who had been his enemy before his exile, went then voluntarily to meet him, and was reconciled, to please his son Publius, as he said, who was Cicero's affectionate admirer.

Cicero had not been long at Rome, when, taking the opportunity of Clodius's absence, he went, with a great company, to the capitol, and there tore and defaced the tribunician tables, in which were recorded the acts done in the time of Clodius. And on Clodius calling him in question for this, he answered, that he, being of the patrician order, had obtained the office of tribune against law, and, therefore, nothing done by him was valid. Cato was displeased at this, and opposed Cicero, not that he commended Clodius, but rather disapproved of his whole administration; yet, he contended, it was an irregular and violent course for the senate to vote the illegality of so many decrees and acts, including those of Cato's own government in Cyprus and at Byzantium. This occasioned a breach between Cato and Cicero, which, though it came not to open enmity, yet made a more reserved friendship between them.

After this, Milo killed Clodius, and, being arraigned for the murder, he procured Cicero as his advocate. The senate, fearing lest the questioning of so eminent and high-spirited a citizen as Milo might disturb the peace of the city, committed the superintendence of this and of the other trials to Pompey, who should undertake to maintain the security alike of the city and of the courts of justice. Pompey, therefore, went in the night, and occupying the high grounds about it, surrounded the Forum with soldiers. Milo, fearing lest Cicero, being disturbed by such an unusual sight, should conduct his cause the less successfully, persuaded him to come in a litter into the Forum, and there repose himself till the judges were set, and the court filled. For Cicero, it seems, not only wanted courage in arms, but, in his speaking also, began with timidity, and in many cases scarcely left off trembling and shaking when he had got thoroughly into the current and the substance of his speech. Being to defend Licinius Murena against the prosecution of Cato, and being eager to outdo Hortensius, who had made his plea with great applause, he took so little rest that night, and was so disordered with thought and over-watching, that he spoke much worse than usual. And so now, on quitting his litter to commence the cause of Milo, at the sight of Pompey, posted, as it were, and encamped with his troops above, and seeing arms shining round about the Forum, he was so confounded, that he could hardly begin his speech, for the trembling of his body, and hesitance of his tongue; whereas Milo, meantime, was bold and intrepid in his demeanor, disdaining either to let his hair grow, or to put on the mourning habit. And this, indeed, seems to have been one principal cause of his condemnation. Cicero, however, was thought not so much to have shown timidity for himself, as anxiety about his friend.

He was made one of the priests, whom the Romans call Augurs, in the room of Crassus the younger, dead in Parthia. Then he was appointed, by lot, to the province of Cilicia, and set sail thither with twelve thousand foot and two thousand six hundred horse. He had orders to bring back Cappadocia to its allegiance to Ariobarzanes, its king; which settlement he effected very completely without recourse to arms. And perceiving the Cilicians, by the great loss the Romans had suffered in Parthia, and the commotions in Syria, to have become disposed to attempt a revolt, by a gentle course of government he soothed them back into fidelity. He would accept none of the presents that were offered him by the kings; he remitted the charge of public entertainments, but daily, at his own house, received the ingenious and accomplished persons of the province, not sumptuously, but liberally. His house had no porter, nor was he ever found in bed by any man, but early in the morning, standing or walking before his door, he received those who came to offer their salutations.

He is said never once to have ordered any of those under his command to be beaten with rods, or to have their garments rent. He never gave contumelious language in his anger, nor inflicted punishment with reproach. He detected an embezzlement, to a large amount, in the public money, and thus relieved the cities from their burdens, at the same time that he allowed those who made restitution, to retain without further punishment their rights as citizens. He engaged too, in war, so far as to give a defeat to the banditti who infested Mount Amanus, for which he was saluted by his army Imperator. To Caecilius, the orator, who asked him to send him some panthers from Cilicia, to be exhibited on the theater at Rome, he wrote, in commendation of his own actions, that there were no panthers in Cilicia, for they were all fled to Caria, in anger that in so general a peace they had become the sole objects of attack. On leaving his province, he touched at Rhodes, and tarried for some length of time at Athens, longing much to renew his old studies. He visited the eminent men of learning, and saw his former friends and companions; and after receiving in Greece the honors that were due to him, returned to the city, where everything was now just as it were in a flame, breaking out into a civil war.

When the senate would have decreed him a triumph, he told them he had rather, so differences were accommodated, follow the triumphal chariot of Caesar. In private, he gave advice to both, writing many letters to Caesar, and personally entreating Pompey; doing his best to soothe and bring to reason both the one and the other. But when matters became incurable, and Caesar was approaching Rome, and Pompey durst not abide it, but, with many honest citizens, left the city, Cicero, as yet, did not join in the flight, and was reputed to adhere to Caesar. And it is very evident he was in his thoughts much divided, and wavered painfully between both, for he writes in his epistles, "To which side should I turn? Pompey has the fair and honorable plea for war; and Caesar, on the other hand, has managed his affairs better, and is more able to secure himself and his friends. So that I know whom I should fly, not whom I should fly to." But when Trebatius, one of Caesar's friends, by letter signified to him that Caesar thought it was his most desirable course to join his party, and partake his hopes, but if he considered himself too old a man for this, then he should retire into Greece, and stay quietly there, out of the way of either party, Cicero, wondering that Caesar had not written himself, gave an angry reply, that he should not do anything unbecoming his past life. Such is the account to be collected from his letters.

But as soon as Caesar was marched into Spain, he immediately sailed away to join Pompey. And he was welcomed by all but Cato; who, taking him privately, chid him for coming to Pompey. As for himself, he said, it had been indecent to forsake that part in the commonwealth which he had chosen from the beginning; but Cicero might have been more useful to his country and friends, if, remaining neuter, he had attended and used his influence to moderate the result, instead of coming hither to make himself, without reason or necessity, an enemy to Caesar, and a partner in such great dangers. By this language, partly, Cicero's feelings were altered, and partly, also, because Pompey made no great use of him. Although, indeed, he was himself the cause of it, by his not denying that he was sorry he had come, by his depreciating Pompey's resources, finding fault underhand with his counsels, and continually indulging in jests and sarcastic remarks on his fellow-soldiers. Though he went about in the camp with a gloomy and melancholy face himself, he was always trying to raise a laugh in others, whether they wished it or not. It may not be amiss to mention a few instances. To Domitius, on his preferring to a command one who was no soldier, and saying, in his defense, that he was a modest and prudent person, he replied, "Why did not you keep him for a tutor for your children?" On hearing Theophanes, the Lesbian, who was master of the engineers in the army, praised for the admirable way in which he had consoled the Rhodians for the loss of their fleet, "What a thing it is," he said, "to have a Greek in command!" When Caesar had been acting successfully, and in a manner blockading Pompey, Lentulus was saying it was reported that Caesar's friends were out of heart; "Because," said Cicero, "they do not wish Caesar well." To one Marcius, who had just come from Italy, and told them that there was a strong report at Rome that Pompey was blocked up, he said, "And you sailed hither to see it with your own eyes." To Nonius, encouraging them after a defeat to be of good hope, because there were seven eagles still left in Pompey's camp, "Good reason for encouragement," said Cicero, "if we were going to fight with jack-daws." Labienus insisted on some prophecies to the effect that Pompey would gain the victory; "Yes," said Cicero, "and the first step in the campaign has been losing our camp."

After the battle of Pharsalia was over, at which he was not present for want of health, and Pompey was fled, Cato, having considerable forces and a great fleet at Dyrrachium, would have had Cicero commander-in-chief, according to law, and the precedence of his consular dignity. And on his refusing the command, and wholly declining to take part in their plans for continuing the war, he was in the greatest danger of being killed, young Pompey and his friends calling him traitor, and drawing their swords upon him; only that Cato interposed, and hardly rescued and brought him out of the camp.

Afterwards, arriving at Brundusium, he tarried there sometime in expectation of Caesar, who was delayed by his affairs in Asia and Egypt. And when it was told him that he was arrived at Tarentum, and was coming thence by land to Brundusium, he hastened towards him, not altogether without hope, and yet in some fear of making experiment of the temper of an enemy and conqueror in the presence of many witnesses. But there was no necessity for him either to speak or do anything unworthy of himself; for Caesar, as soon as he saw him coming a good way before the rest of the company, came down to meet him, saluted him, and, leading the way, conversed with him alone for some furlongs. And from that time forward he continued to treat him with honor and respect; so that, when Cicero wrote an oration in praise of Cato, Caesar, in writing an answer to it, took occasion to commend Cicero's own life and eloquence, comparing him to Pericles and Theramenes. Cicero's oration was called Cato; Caesar's, anti-Cato.

So also, it is related that when Quintus Ligarius was prosecuted for having been in arms against Caesar, and Cicero had undertaken his defense, Caesar said to his friends, "Why might we not as well once more hear a speech from Cicero? Ligarius, there is no question, is a wicked man and an enemy." But when Cicero began to speak, he wonderfully moved him, and proceeded in his speech with such varied pathos, and such a charm of language, that the color of Caesar's countenance often changed, and it was evident that all the passions of his soul were in commotion. At length, the orator touching upon the Pharsalian battle, he was so affected that his body trembled, and some of the papers he held dropped out of his hands. And thus he was overpowered, and acquitted Ligarius.

Henceforth, the commonwealth being changed into a monarchy, Cicero withdrew himself from public affairs, and employed his leisure in instructing those young men that would, in philosophy; and by the near intercourse he thus had with some of the noblest and highest in rank, he again began to possess great influence in the city. The work and object which he set himself was to compose and translate philosophical dialogues and to render logical and physical terms into the Roman idiom. For he it was, as it is said, who first or principally gave Latin names to phantasia, syncatathesis, epokhe, catalepsis, atomon, ameres, kenon, and other such technical terms, which, either by metaphors or other means of accommodation, he succeeded in making intelligible and expressible to the Romans. For his recreation, he exercised his dexterity in poetry, and when he was set to it, would make five hundred verses in a night. He spent the greatest part of his time at his country-house near Tusculum. He wrote to his friends that he led the life of Laertes, either jestingly, as his custom was, or rather from a feeling of ambition for public employment, which made him impatient under the present state of affairs. He rarely went to the city, unless to pay his court to Caesar. He was commonly the first amongst those who voted him honors, and sought out new terms of praise for himself and for his actions. As, for example, what he said of the statues of Pompey, which had been thrown down, and were afterwards by Caesar's orders set up again: that Caesar, by this act of humanity, had indeed set up Pompey's statues, but he had fixed and established his own.

He had a design, it is said, of writing the history of his country, combining with it much of that of Greece, and incorporating in it all the stories and legends of the past that he had collected. But his purposes were interfered with by various public and various private unhappy occurrences and misfortunes; for most of which he was himself in fault. For first of all, he put away his wife Terentia, by whom he had been neglected in the time of the war, and sent away destitute of necessaries for his journey; neither did he find her kind when he returned into Italy, for she did not join him at Brundusium, where he stayed a long time, nor would allow her young daughter, who undertook so long a journey, decent attendance, or the requisite expenses; besides, she left him a naked and empty house, and yet had involved him in many and great debts. These were alleged as the fairest reasons for the divorce. But Terentia, who denied them all, had the most unmistakable defense furnished her by her husband himself, who not long after married a young maiden for the love of her beauty, as Terentia upbraided him; or as Tiro, his emancipated slave, has written, for her riches, to discharge his debts. For the young woman was very rich, and Cicero had the custody of her estate, being left guardian in trust; and being indebted many myriads of money, he was persuaded by his friends and relations to marry her, notwithstanding his disparity of age, and to use her money to satisfy his creditors. Antony, who mentions this marriage in his answer to the Philippics, reproaches him for putting away a wife with whom he had lived to old age; adding some happy strokes of sarcasm on Cicero's domestic, inactive, unsoldier-like habits. Not long after this marriage, his daughter died in child-bed at Lentulus's house, to whom she had been married after the death of Piso, her former husband. The philosophers from all parts came to comfort Cicero; for his grief was so excessive, that he put away his new-married wife, because she seemed to be pleased at the death of Tullia. And thus stood Cicero's domestic affairs at this time.

He had no concern in the design that was now forming against Caesar, although, in general, he was Brutus's most principal confidant, and one who was as aggrieved at the present, and as desirous of the former state of public affairs, as any other whatsoever. But they feared his temper, as wanting courage, and his old age, in which the most daring dispositions are apt to be timorous.

As soon, therefore, as the act was committed by Brutus and Cassius, and the friends of Caesar were got together, so that there was fear the city would again be involved in a civil war, Antony, being consul, convened the senate, and made a short address recommending concord. And Cicero, following with various remarks such as the occasion called for, persuaded the senate to imitate the Athenians, and decree an amnesty for what had been done in Caesar's case, and to bestow provinces on Brutus and Cassius. But neither of these things took effect. For as soon as the common people, of themselves inclined to pity, saw the dead body of Caesar borne through the marketplace, and Antony showing his clothes filled with blood, and pierced through in every part with swords, enraged to a degree of frenzy, they made a search for the murderers, and with firebrands in their hands ran to their houses to burn them. They, however, being forewarned, avoided this danger; and expecting many more and greater to come, they left the city.

Antony on this was at once in exultation, and everyone was in alarm with the prospect that he would make himself sole ruler, and Cicero in more alarm than anyone. For Antony, seeing his influence reviving in the commonwealth, and knowing how closely he was connected with Brutus, was ill-pleased to have him in the city. Besides, there had been some former jealousy between them, occasioned by the difference of their manners. Cicero, fearing the event, was inclined to go as lieutenant with Dolabella into Syria. But Hirtius and Pansa, consuls elect as successors of Antony, good men and lovers of Cicero, entreated him not to leave them, undertaking to put down Antony if he would stay in Rome. And he, neither distrusting wholly, nor trusting them, let Dolabella go without him, promising Hirtius that he would go and spend his summer at Athens, and return again when he entered upon his office. So he set out on his journey; but some delay occurring in his passage, new intelligence, as often happens, came suddenly from Rome, that Antony had made an astonishing change, and was doing all things and managing all public affairs at the will of the senate, and that there wanted nothing but his presence to bring things to a happy settlement. And therefore, blaming himself for his cowardice, he returned again to Rome, and was not deceived in his hopes at the beginning. For such multitudes flocked out to meet him, that the compliments and civilities which were paid him at the gates, and at his entrance into the city, took up almost one whole day's time.

On the morrow, Antony convened the senate, and summoned Cicero thither. He came not, but kept is bed, pretending to be ill with his journey; but the true reason seemed the fear of some design against him, upon a suspicion and intimation given him on his way to Rome. Antony, however, showed great offense at the affront, and sent soldiers, commanding them to bring him or burn his house; but many interceding and supplicating for him, he was contented to accept sureties. Ever after, when they met, they passed one another with silence, and continued on their guard, till Caesar, the younger, coming from Apollonia, entered on the first Caesar's inheritance, and was engaged in a dispute with Antony about two thousand five hundred myriads of money, which Antony detained from the estate.

Upon this, Philippus, who married the mother, and Marcellus, who married the sister of young Caesar, came with the young man to Cicero, and agreed with him that Cicero should give them the aid of his eloquence and political influence with the senate and people, and Caesar give Cicero the defense of his riches and arms. For the young man had already a great party of the soldiers of Caesar about him. And Cicero's readiness to join him was founded, it is said, on some yet stronger motives; for it seems, while Pompey and Caesar were yet alive, Cicero, in his sleep, had fancied himself engaged in calling some of the sons of the senators into the capitol, Jupiter being about, according to the dream, to declare one of them the chief ruler of Rome. The citizens, running up with curiosity, stood about the temple, and the youths, sitting in their purple-bordered robes, kept silence. On a sudden the doors opened, and the youths, arising one by one in order, passed round the god, who reviewed them all, and, to their sorrow, dismissed them; but when this one was passing by, the god stretched forth his right hand and said, "O ye Romans, this young man, when he shall be lord of Rome, shall put an end to all your civil wars." It is said that Cicero formed from his dream a distinct image of the youth, and retained it afterwards perfectly, but did not know who it was. The next day, going down into the Campus Martius, he met the boys resuming from their gymnastic exercises, and the first was he, just as he had appeared to him in his dream. Being astonished at it, he asked him who were his parents. And it proved to be this young Caesar, whose father was a man of no great eminence, Octavius, and his mother, Attia, Caesar's sister's daughter; for which reason, Caesar, who had no children, made him by will the heir of his house and property. From that time, it is said that Cicero studiously noticed the youth whenever he met him, and he as kindly received the civility; and by fortune he happened to be born when Cicero was consul.

These were the reasons spoken of; but it was principally Cicero's hatred of Antony, and a temper unable to resist honor, which fastened him to Caesar, with the purpose of getting the support of Caesar's power for his own public designs. For the young man went so far in his court to him, that he called him Father; at which Brutus was so highly displeased, that, in his epistles to Atticus he reflected on Cicero saying, it was manifest, by his courting Caesar for fear of Antony, he did not intend liberty to his country, but an indulgent master to himself. Notwithstanding, Brutus took Cicero's son, then studying philosophy at Athens, gave him a command, and employed him in various ways, with a good result. Cicero's own power at this time was at the greatest height in the city, and he did whatsoever he pleased; he completely overpowered and drove out Antony, and sent the two consuls, Hirtius and Pansa, with an army, to reduce him; and, on the other hand, persuaded the senate to allow Caesar the lictors and ensigns of a praetor, as though he were his country's defender. But after Antony was defeated in battle, and the two consuls slain, the armies united, and ranged themselves with Caesar. And the senate, fearing the young man, and his extraordinary fortune, endeavored, by honors and gifts, to call off the soldiers from him, and to lessen his power; professing there was no further need of arms, now Antony was put to flight.

This giving Caesar an affright, he privately sends some friends to entreat and persuade Cicero to procure the consular dignity for them both together;

saying he should manage the affairs as he pleased, should have the supreme power, and govern the young man who was only desirous of name and glory. And Caesar himself confessed, that in fear of ruin, and in danger of being deserted, he had seasonably made use of Cicero's ambition, persuading him to stand with him, and to accept the offer of his aid and interest for the consulship.

And now, more than at any other time, Cicero let himself be carried away and deceived, though an old man, by the persuasions of a boy. He joined him in soliciting votes, and procured the good-will of the senate, not without blame at the time on the part of his friends; and he, too, soon enough after, saw that he had ruined himself, and betrayed the liberty of his country. For the young man, once established, and possessed of the office of consul, bade Cicero farewell; and, reconciling himself to Antony and Lepidus, joined his power with theirs, and divided the government, like a piece of property, with them. Thus united, they made a schedule of above two hundred persons who were to be put to death. But the greatest contention in all their debates was on the question of Cicero's case. Antony would come to no conditions, unless he should be the first man to be killed. Lepidus held with Antony, and Caesar opposed them both. They met secretly and by themselves, for three days together, near the town of Bononia. The spot was not far from the camp, with a river surrounding it. Caesar, it is said, contended earnestly for Cicero the first two days; but on the third day he yielded, and gave him up.

The terms of their mutual concessions were these; that Caesar should desert Cicero, Lepidus his brother Paulus, and Antony, Lucius Caesar, his uncle by his mother's side. Thus they let their anger and fury take from them the sense of humanity, and demonstrated that no beast is more savage than man, when possessed with power answerable to his rage.

Whilst these things were contriving, Cicero was with his brother at his country-house near Tusculum; whence, hearing of the proscriptions, they determined to pass to Astura, a villa of Cicero's near the sea, and to take shipping from thence for Macedonia to Brutus, of whose strength in that province news had already been heard. They traveled together in their separate litters, overwhelmed with sorrow; and often stopping on the way till their litters came together, condoled with one another. But Quintus was the more disheartened, when he reflected on his want of means for his journey; for, as he said, he had brought nothing with him from home. And even Cicero himself had but a slender provision. It was judged, therefore, most expedient that Cicero should make what haste he could to fly, and Quintus return home to provide necessaries, and thus resolved, they mutually embraced, and parted with many tears.

Quintus, within a few days after, betrayed by his servants to those who came to search for him, was slain, together with his young son. But Cicero was carried to Astura, where, finding a vessel, he immediately went on board her, and sailed as far as Circaeum with a prosperous gale; but when the pilots resolved immediately to set sail from thence, whether fearing the sea, or not wholly distrusting the faith of Caesar, he went on shore, and passed by land a hundred furlongs, as if he was going for Rome. But losing resolution and changing his mind, he again returned to the sea, and there spent the night in fearful and perplexed thoughts. Sometimes he resolved to go into Caesar's house privately, and there kill himself upon the altar of his household gods, to bring divine vengeance upon him; but the fear of torture put him off this course. And after passing through a variety of confused and uncertain counsels, at last he let his servants carry him by sea to Capitae, where he had a house, an agreeable place to retire to in the heat of summer, when the Etesian winds are so pleasant.

There was at that place a chapel of Apollo, not far from the sea-side, from which a flight of crows rose with a great noise, and made towards Cicero's vessel as it rowed to land, and lighting on both sides of the yard, some croaked, others pecked the ends of the ropes. This was looked upon by all as an ill omen; and, therefore, Cicero went again ashore, and entering his house, lay down upon his bed to compose himself to rest. Many of the crows settled about the window, making a dismal cawing; but one of them alighted upon the bed where Cicero lay covered up, and with its bill by little and little pecked off the clothes from his face. His servants, seeing this, blamed themselves that they should stay to be spectators of their master's murder, and do nothing in his defense, whilst the brute creatures came to assist and take care of him in his undeserved affliction; and, therefore, partly by entreaty, partly by force, they took him up, and carried him in his litter towards the sea-side.

But in the meantime the assassins were come with a band of soldiers, Herennius, a centurion, and Popillius, a tribune, whom Cicero had formerly defended when prosecuted for the murder of his father. Finding the doors shut, they broke them open, and Cicero not appearing and those within saying they knew not where he was, it is stated that a youth, who had been educated by Cicero in the liberal arts and sciences, an emancipated slave of his brother Quintus, Philologus by name, informed the tribune that the litter was on its way to the sea through the close and shady walks. The tribune, taking a few with him, ran to the place where he was to come out. And Cicero, perceiving Herennius running in the walks, commanded his servants to set down the litter; and stroking his chin, as he used to do, with his left hand, he looked steadfastly upon his murderers, his person covered with dust, his beard and hair untrimmed, and his face worn with his troubles. So that the greatest part of those that stood by covered their faces whilst Herennius slew him. And thus was he murdered, stretching forth his neck out of the litter, being now in his sixty-fourth year. Herennius cut off his head, and, by Antony's command, his hands also, by which his Philippics were written; for so Cicero styled those orations he wrote against Antony, and so they are called to this day.

When these members of Cicero were brought to Rome, Antony was holding an assembly for the choice of public officers; and when he heard it, and saw them, he cried out, "Now let there be an end of our proscriptions." He commanded his head and hands to be fastened up over the Rostra, where the orators spoke; a sight which the Roman people shuddered to behold, and they believed they saw there not the face of Cicero, but the image of Antony's own soul. And yet amidst these actions he did justice in one thing, by delivering up Philologus to Pomponia, the wife of Quintus; who, having got his body into her power, besides other grievous punishments, made him cut off his own flesh by pieces, and roast and eat it; for so some writers have related. But Tiro, Cicero's emancipated slave, has not so much as mentioned the treachery of Philologus.

Some long time after, Caesar, I have been told, visiting one of his daughter's sons, found him with a book of Cicero's in his hand. The boy for fear endeavored to hide it under his gown; which Caesar perceiving, took it from him, and turning over a great part of the book standing, gave it him again, and said, "My child, this was a learned man, and a lover of his country." And immediately after he had vanquished Antony, being then consul, he made Cicero's son his colleague in the office; and under that consulship, the senate took down all the statues of Antony, and abolished all the other honors that had been given him, and decreed that none of that family should thereafter bear the name of Marcus; and thus the final acts of the punishment of Antony were, by the divine powers, devolved upon the family of Cicero.

18
COMPARISON OF DEMOSTHENES AND CICERO

*T*hese are the most memorable circumstances recorded in history of Demosthenes and Cicero which have come to our knowledge. But omitting an exact comparison of their respective faculties in speaking, yet thus much seems fit to be said; that Demosthenes, to make himself a master in rhetoric, applied all the faculties he had, natural or acquired, wholly that way; that he far surpassed in force and strength of eloquence all his contemporaries in political and judicial speaking, in grandeur and majesty all the panegyrical orators, and in accuracy and science all the logicians and rhetoricians of his day; that Cicero was highly educated, and by his diligent study became a most accomplished general scholar in all these branches, having left behind him numerous philosophical treatises of his own on Academic principles; as, indeed, even in his written speeches, both political and judicial, we see him continually trying to show his learning by the way. And one may discover the different temper of each of them in their speeches. For Demosthenes's oratory was without all embellishment and jesting, wholly composed for real effect and seriousness; not smelling of the lamp, as Pytheas scoffingly said, but of the temperance, thoughtfulness, austerity, and grave earnestness of his temper. Whereas Cicero's love of mockery often ran him into scurrility; and in his love of laughing away serious arguments in judicial cases by jests and facetious remarks, with a view to the advantage of his clients, he paid too little regard to what was decent: saying, for example, in his defense of Caelius, that he had done no absurd thing in such plenty and affluence to indulge himself in pleasures, it being a kind of madness not to enjoy the things we possess, especially since the most eminent philosophers have asserted pleasure to be the chiefest good. So also we are told, that when Cicero, being consul, undertook the defense of Murena against Cato's prosecution, by way of bantering Cato, he made a long series of jokes upon the absurd paradoxes, as they are called, of the Stoic sect; so that a loud laughter passing from the crowd to the judges, Cato, with a quiet smile, said to those that sat next him, "My friends, what an amusing consul we have."

And, indeed, Cicero was by natural temper very much disposed to mirth and pleasantry, and always appeared with a smiling and serene countenance. But Demosthenes had constant care and thoughtfulness in his look, and a serious anxiety, which he seldom, if ever, laid aside; and, therefore, was accounted by his enemies, as he himself confessed, morose and ill-mannered.

Also, it is very evident, out of their several writings, that Demosthenes never touched upon his own praises but decently and without offense when there was need of it, and for some weightier end; but, upon other occasions modestly and sparingly. But Cicero's immeasurable boasting of himself in his orations argues him guilty of an uncontrollable appetite for distinction, his cry being evermore that arms should give place to the gown, and the soldier's laurel to the tongue. And at last we find him extolling not only his deeds and actions, but his orations also, as well those that were only spoken, as those that were published; as if he were engaged in a boyish trial of skill, who should speak best, with the rhetoricians, Isocrates and Anaximenes, not as one who could claim the task to guide and instruct the Roman nation, the

Soldier full-armed, terrific to the foe.

It is necessary, indeed, for a political leader to be an able speaker; but it is an ignoble thing for any man to admire and relish the glory of his own eloquence. And, in this matter, Demosthenes had a more than ordinary gravity and magnificence of mind, accounting his talent in speaking nothing more than a mere accomplishment and matter of practice, the success of which must depend greatly on the good-will and candor of his hearers, and regarding those who pride themselves on such accounts to be men of a low and petty disposition.

The power of persuading and governing the people did, indeed, equally belong to both, so that those who had armies and camps at command stood in need of their assistance; as Chares, Diopithes, and Leosthenes of Demosthenes's, Pompey and young Caesar of Cicero's, as the latter himself admits in his Memoirs addressed to Agrippa and Maecenas. But what are thought and commonly said most to demonstrate and try the tempers of men, namely, authority and place, by moving every passion, and discovering every frailty, these are things which Demosthenes never received; nor was he ever in a position to give such proof of himself, having never obtained any eminent office, nor led any of those armies into the field against Philip which he raised by his eloquence. Cicero, on the other hand, was sent quaestor into Sicily, and proconsul into Cilicia and Cappadocia, at a time when avarice was at the height, and the commanders and governors who were employed abroad, as though they thought it a mean thing to steal, set themselves to seize by open force; so that it seemed no heinous matter to take bribes, but he that did it most moderately was in good esteem. And yet he, at this time, gave the most abundant proofs alike of his contempt of riches and of his humanity and good-nature. And at Rome, when he was created consul in name, but indeed received sovereign and dictatorial authority against Catiline and his conspirators, he attested the truth of Plato's prediction, that then the miseries of states would be at an end, when by a happy fortune supreme power, wisdom, and justice should be united in one.

It is said, to the reproach of Demosthenes, that his eloquence was mercenary; that he privately made orations for Phormion and Apollodorus, though adversaries in the same cause; that he was charged with moneys received from the king of Persia, and condemned for bribes from Harpalus. And should we grant that all those (and they are not few) who have made these statements against him have spoken what is untrue, yet that Demosthenes was not the character to look without desire on the presents offered him out of respect and gratitude by royal persons, and that one who lent money on maritime usury was likely to be thus indifferent, is what we cannot assert. But that Cicero refused, from the Sicilians when he was quaestor, from the king of Cappadocia when he was proconsul, and from his friends at Rome when he was in exile, many presents, though urged to receive them, has been said already.

Moreover, Demosthenes's banishment was infamous, upon conviction for bribery; Cicero's very honorable, for ridding his country of a set of villains. Therefore, when Demosthenes fled his country, no man regarded it; for Cicero's sake the senate changed their habit, and put on mourning, and would not be persuaded to make any act before Cicero's return was decreed. Cicero, however, passed his exile idly in Macedonia. But the very exile of Demosthenes made up a great part of the services he did for his country; for he went through the cities of Greece, and everywhere, as we have said, joined in the conflict on behalf of the Grecians, driving out the Macedonian ambassadors, and approving himself a much better citizen than Themistocles and Alcibiades did in the like fortune. And, after his return, he again devoted himself to the same public service, and continued firm to his opposition to Antipater and the Macedonians. Whereas Laelius reproached Cicero in the senate for sitting silent when Caesar, a beardless youth, asked leave to come forward, contrary to the law, as a candidate for the consulship; and Brutus, in his epistles, charges him with nursing and rearing a greater and more heavy tyranny than that they had removed.

Finally, Cicero's death excites our pity; for an old man to be miserably carried up and down by his servants, flying and hiding himself from that death which was, in the course of nature, so near at hand; and yet at last to be murdered. Demosthenes, though he seemed at first a little to supplicate, yet, by his preparing and keeping the poison by him, demands our admiration; and still more admirable was his using it. When the temple of the god no longer afforded him a sanctuary, he took refuge, as it were, at a mightier altar, freeing himself from arms and soldiers, and laughing to scorn the cruelty of Antipater.

Copyright © 2020 by ALICIA EDITIONS
Credits: CANVA, Wikimedia Commons
All rights reserved.
No part of this book may be reproduced in any form or by any electronic or mechanical means,
including information storage and retrieval systems, without written permission from the author,
except for the use of brief quotations in a book review.

Lightning Source UK Ltd.
Milton Keynes UK
UKHW012152260522
403581UK00002B/71